CONTEMPORARY HALAKHIC PROBLEMS

VOLUME IV

THE LIBRARY OF JEWISH LAW AND ETHICS
VOLUME XX
EDITED BY NORMAN LAMM

President and Jakob and Erna Michael professor of Jewish Philosophy
Yeshiva University, New York City

CONTEMPORARY HALAKHIC PROBLEMS

VOLUME IV

by

J. DAVID BLEICH

KTAV PUBLISHING HOUSE, INC.
YESHIVA UNIVERSITY PRESS
NEW YORK
1995

Library of Congress Cataloging-in-Publication Data

Bleich, J. David
Contemporary halakhic problems.

(The Library of Jewish law and ethics ; v. 20)
Includes bibliographical references and indexes.
1. Jewish law. 2. Judaism—20th century. I. Title. II Series
BM520.3.B5 296.1'8 77-3432
ISBN 0–88125–474–6

Manufactured in the United States of America
KTAV Publishing House, 900 Jefferson Street, Hoboken NJ, 07030

Contents

Editor's Foreword

The appearance of this fourth volume in J. David Bleich's series on "Contemporary Halakhic Problems" is a most welcome link in the chain of his thoughtful and challenging publications for the Library of Jewish Law and Ethics.

Our author's scholarly efforts and literary productivity are important for more than one reason. They not only enrich the literature on Halakhah in English, and not only make the treasures of Jewish law accessible to the English reader untrained in the intricacies of talmudic jurisprudence; they also make a statement that is theologically important: that this ancient legal system is capable of dealing with the most complex problems thrown up by the latest technologies and the most recent changes in social perspective, and that the Halakhah is therefore of the utmost significance to the spiritually sensitive Jew and to a Jewish community that has suddenly discovered that the continuity of the Jewish people is in mortal peril. Halakhah is, after all, but the legal distillation of the essence of Torah, and Torah and Israel are inextricably linked to each other. Any effort to sever that link is an affront to the dignity and, indeed, continuing vitality of both of them.

It is thus with the greatest pleasure that we present this newest volume by Rabbi Bleich, along with the hope that many more such volumes will continue to appear regularly in this series for the Library of Jewish Law and Ethics.

Norman Lamm
Editor

May 28, 1995

Preface

As was the case with the earlier volumes in this series, much of the material presented in this volume originally appeared in my "Survey of Recent Halakhic Periodical Literature" which is regularly featured in the columns of *Tradition.* Many of those items have been expanded and amplified for presentation in their present form. One section of this material was first published in the *Journal of Halacha and Contemporary Society.* Chapter four, which is devoted to a halakhic perspective regarding the penal authority of the secular state, appeared in the *Cardozo Law Review.* Portions of this work served as the subject matter of *shi'urim* and seminars conducted for students of the Benjamin N. Cardozo School of Law as well as of the Rabbi Isaac Elchanan Theological Seminary and its *Kollel le-Hora'ah*.

The format of this volume differs somewhat from that of previous volumes in this series. Earlier volumes were divided into two parts. One part was composed of chapters each of which contained a series of brief discussions of related issues. A second part was devoted to more extensive analyses of particular halakhic topics. The contents of the present volume are almost entirely of the latter nature.

This work is not intended to serve as a practical halakhic guide and, indeed, no attempt has been made to present definitive *psak halakhah.* It is devoted to an analysis of Halakhah and halakhic reasoning rather than to definitive statements of halakhic determinations. As such, it is directed primarily to those who have at least some background in the study of rabbinic literature but lack the requisite skills or the leisure to assimilate and analyze the maze of responsa pertaining to the topics treated in this volume. It is intended as an invitation to the reader to join in the noblest of Jewish activities and the supremest of joys—the study of Torah.

I wish to express my thanks to my brother-in-law, Rabbi Mordecai Ochs, for his painstaking reading of the manuscript; to my son, Rabbi Moshe Bleich, for drawing my attention to sources that otherwise would have eluded me and for his many valuable insights; to Dr. Joel Wolowelsky, Associate Editor of *Tradition*, both for his patience and for his many welcome suggestions; to Rabbi Jacob B. Mandelbaum of the Mendel Gottesman Library of Yeshiva University whose encyclopedic bibliographic knowledge has been of immeasurable aid; to Mr. Zalman Alpert, Mr. Zvi Erenyi, Mrs. Chaya Gordin and Mr. Tuvia Lasdun of the Mendel Gottesman Library for their constant helpfulness and assistance; to my student, Dr. Richard Weiss, for his research assistance; to Mrs. Racheline Habousha of the library of the Albert Einstein College of Medicine for her unfailing graciousness in expediting my many requests; to Mr. Joel Grantz of the Cardozo School of Law for his secretarial and editorial assistance and for his gracious help; to Mrs. Dina Stilerman and Mrs. Els Bendheim for proofreading the galleys; and especially to my students for their incisive and relentless questioning.

My thanks also to Dr. Norman Lamm for initiating the Library of Jewish Law and Ethics; to the publisher of this volume, Mr. Bernard Scharfstein for his unfailing indulgence and patience and his warm friendship; to Dr. Ya'akov Elman for making his technical and scholarly expertise available at all times; and to Dr. Richard White for his painstaking efforts, tirelessness and good humor in shepherding this complex manuscript through the various stages of publication.

Above all, I am grateful to the Almighty for my cherished collaborators—the members of my family. Our prayer to the Almighty is that we continue to be numbered among the *mashkimim le-divrei Torah* and, to paraphrase the words of the *hadran*, *ke-shem she-'azartanu le-sayyem sefer zeh, ken ta'azrenu le-hatḥil sefarim aḥerim u-le-sayyemam, lilmod u-le-lamed, lishmor ve-la'asot u-le-kayyem.*

Introduction

May it be Thy will, O Lord my God, that no mishap occur through me and that I not err in a matter of Halakhah . . . that I not declare the impure pure or the pure impure.

BERAKHOT 28b

The words cited above are the text of the prayer that R. Neḥunia ben ha-Kaneh was wont to utter upon entering the House of Study. Halakhah is an intellectual discipline but its pursuit is accompanied by awesome moral and religious responsibility. Halakhic pronouncements should bear a Surgeon General's warning that they may be dangerous to spiritual health and well-being. The onus of error is entirely analogous to that which in the realm of the physical accompanies the granting of a seal of approval or the issuance of a public warning of impending danger. An erroneous endorsement can easily lead to serious danger; an unwarranted interdiction can wreak havoc with human lives. R. Neḥunia ben ha-Kaneh well understood the awesome nature of every halakhic determination and the need for divine assistance in avoiding error. The prayer recorded in the Gemara is a poignant reminder for posterity that halakhic matters must be regarded with at least the same seriousness that attends the mundane. In its most fundamental sense *yir'at shamayim*, fear of Heaven, is the reflection of a conviction that halakhic error or laxity is as dangerous to the soul as other forms of error may be to the body.

In the absence of fear of Heaven, fulfillment of *miẓvot* is, in essence, a matter of cultural expression. Folk practices may be valued, but they are unlikely to become all-consuming. Chauvinism may dictate enthusiastic participation in ceremonies and rituals but will hardly command concern with minutiae and details. Fear of Heaven is the hallmark that serves to distinguish between cultural observance and religious observance; it is the factor that serves to separate those sectors of our community that recognize the centrality of Halakhah and its study from those that fail to accord Halakhah such primacy. For the latter, *miẓvot* are a matter of taste and preference and even of personal satisfaction; for the former, they are a matter of spiritual life and health. For the former, thirst for knowledge is never quenched.

It is that thirst that in recent years has elicited a plethora of publications, both in Hebrew and in the vernacular, devoted to matters of Halakhah. With the appearance of the fourth volume in this series it is perhaps time to examine the goals that works of this genre are designed to achieve and the effectiveness of the first three volumes in meeting those goals.

An author is often motivated as much by a desire to write for himself as by a desire to write for the reader. This is true not only in the sense of "More than the calf wishes to suckle, the cow desires to nurse" (*Pesaḥim* 112a) but also in an even more rudimentary sense. A colleague recently remarked, "We write in order to forget." To my ears, the comment initially seemed entirely inapt, if not nonsensical. But, upon reflection, the comment strikes me as an observation that serves to explain a phenomenon that has long puzzled me. I have often noticed that, after delivering a *shi'ur* (talmudic discourse), I am unable to concentrate with single-minded attention upon other matters. I tend to be unresponsive and distracted until the task of committing to writing any novellae developed in the course of the presentation has been completed. Once the material has been transcribed, the mind is again free to wander without fear that some insight may be forgotten and hence forever lost. In some strange way that perhaps a psychologist might be able to explain, fear of forgetting generates a tension that itself becomes an aide-mémoire. Experience teaches that, unfortunately, dissipation of the tension actually precipitates forgetfulness. The enduring nature of the written word serves to compensate for the fallibility of the human mind.

The same is assuredly true for the marshalling of sources dealing with any halakhic topic. References are culled, precedents discovered, analogies formulated and deductions made, but with the distinct danger that the process may not be recalled or even comprehensively replicated at some future time. At the very least, transcription serves to obviate the need for a time-consuming repetition of the entire process. Thus, the published volume becomes a reference work for the writer who becomes his own reader. Works such as this are designed primarily to identify sources and arguments and to make them accessible to one and all. The purpose of such works is to draw attention to particular problems, to isolate component issues and to indicate possible modes of resolution. Whatever else is accomplished in the process, although welcome, is secondary.

This much is certain: There is nothing in these volumes—or in others of this genre—that is innovative in the true sense of that term, just as there is nothing innovative in a treatise on physics. Both disciplines have as their subject matter a closed, immutable system of law—physical in the case of the latter, regulative in the case of the former. To be sure, the theoretical physicist may propose a previously unexpounded thesis in an attempt to explain the operation of the laws of nature; so also may a *rosh yeshivah* develop conceptual novellae in the course of an endeavor to explicate the meaning of the revealed law. In physics, a newly developed hypothesis may have a predictive value with regard to empirical phenomena; likewise, talmudic novellae may yield heretofore unarticulated halakhic propositions. But both in physics and in Halakhah the outgrowth is likely to be marginal to each of the systems viewed in its entirety. In each case the thesis must be tested against the totality of the system. Generally, contradiction by other aspects of the system is tantamount to demonstration of an inherent fallacy in the thesis.

Halakhah is a science in the sense that, in its pristine form, there is no room for subjectivity. That is not to say that there is no room for disagreement. Disagreement abounds in the natural sciences no less so than in Halakhah. But, in picking and choosing between contradictory and conflicting theses, the scientist acts on the basis of the canons of his discipline as understood by his quite fallible intellect, not on the basis of subjective predilections. The halakhic decisor faces the same constraints.

An anecdote that is perhaps apocryphal is related concerning one of the eminent rabbinic scholars of recent years, an individual renowned for his prodigious memory and encyclopedic knowledge. In the course of a discussion concerning a particular halakhic problem a student pointed out that a lenient view was to be found in a certain halakhic source. "To be sure, there is a lenient view," responded the scholar. "However, it is not necessarily compelling. One can usually find a lenient view if one searches determinedly. But one must be wary of ruling in accordance with such non-normative views. Indeed, if you knew the contents of as many responsa as do I and accepted each and every permissive view recorded in those responsa," he concluded, "you would in the end live as a *goy*," i.e., be entirely free of the yoke of commandments.

Leniencies and permissive rulings exist in abundance. The point is to seek neither the stringent nor the lenient, but the view that is most authoritative. Moreover, there usually is a view which has been accepted in practice by the majority of *poskim* as the accepted standard. Thereupon, such a ruling becomes normative and deviation cannot be considered other than by virtue of compelling reasons. It was the view of many of the most renowned personages in the annals of halakhic scholarship that the rulings accepted as authoritative by the community of Israel were accepted as such by virtue of the operation of divine providence.

Serious students of Halakhah trained in its methodology will regard the aforesaid as axiomatic and will but wonder why these points are being belabored. To the uninstructed—or better, the incompletely instructed—they are likely to be a source of puzzlement. In every age there are certain views that are "politically correct" and certain views that are "politically incorrect." In our age, men and women of good will, intelligence, of a liberal bent and unafraid of the modern world, are presumed to share a common *Weltanschauung*. That Halakhah is not always congruent with such views comes as something of a shock to some. It is not too surprising that, quite frequently, the reaction is to attack the messenger rather than the message. All too often there is a failure to recognize that a student of Halakhah—or of any intellectual discipline—is not autonomous in arriving at determinations drawn from a corpus of material accepted as authoritative. There are areas in which free will is simply not operational.

To be sure, not all minds think alike. As expressed long ago by the Sages, "Just as their countenances are not similar one to another, so are their intellects not similar one to another" (Palestinian Talmud, *Berakhot* 1:9). One person may regard an argument as compelling; another may not. One person may assign greater weight to a precedent or to the position of a given authority while another may assign lesser weight to the same precedent or position. Each may regard his assessment as crystal clear and regard the opposing view as ill-informed.

Halakhah is indeed an art as well as a science. Its *kunst* lies precisely in the ability to make judgment calls in evaluating citations, precedents, arguments, etc. It is not sufficient for a halakhic decisor to have a full command of relevant sources. If so, in theory at least, the decisor par excellence would be a computer rather than a person. The decisor must have a keen understanding of the underlying principles and postulates of Halakhah as well as of their applicable ramifications and must be capable of applying them with fidelity to matters placed before him. No amount of book learning can compensate for inadequacy in what may be termed the "artistic" component. The epithet "a donkey carrying books" is the derisive reference employed in rabbinic literature to describe such a person.[1]

This talent is partially innate and partially acquired. No one springs from the womb as an accomplished musician. Training and practice are

1. See, for example, *Ḥovot ha-Levavot*, *Sha'ar Avodat ha-Elokim*, chap. 4.

necessary prerequisites. Some teachers are certainly better pedagogues than others; some are certainly more proficient than others in transmitting subtlety in analysis, novelty in interpretation and sophistication in execution. But no amount of instruction and practice will make a musician of one lacking in musical talent. Any teacher of high school math will certify that a student who experiences little difficulty in solving problems presented in mathematical form but who scores significantly lower in analyzing verbal problems is the rule rather than the exception. Law school examinations typically take the form of hypotheticals and fact patterns designed to test, not simply knowledge of the law, but the ability to identify multifaceted issues as well as agility in applying legal theories to novel situations. Quite apart from breadth of knowledge, it is recognition of applicable categories and principles as well as depth of analysis with regard to substantive matters that distinguish the consummate halakhic scholar from the neophyte. When confronting conflicting positions and precedents, it is nuanced sophistication in applying canons of decision-making that is the hallmark of a proficient decisor.

Halakhah differs from other systems of law in that it does not permit policy considerations to adjudicate between competing theories or precedents. Nevertheless, in terms of public guidance, rabbinic authorities often do counsel, and correctly so, on the basis of what can best be described as "policy." Thus, the Gemara, *Ḥullin* 15a, reports that Rav accepted as normative a certain permissive tannaitic view concerning the permissibility of partkaing of food cooked on *Shabbat* in ignorance of the prohibited nature of the act and instructed his students accordingly, while in public discussions he promulgated the stricter view because of the presence of the ignorant masses.[2] Similarly, the Gemara, *Shabbat* 139a, reports that the inhabitants of a place known as Bashkar requested halakhic rulings concerning a number of different matters and received negative replies despite the fact that there were authoritative bases for permissive responses. One query regarded spreading a canopy over a bed on *Shabbat.* They were told, "We have investigated all ways of [erecting]

2. See also, *Tosafot*, *Baba Kamma* 99b, who similarly explain that Rav forbade an ignorant person to eat the meat of an animal that had been slaughtered by severance of the uppermost ring of the windpipe despite the fact that Rav espoused the permissive view that accepts such slaughter as proper. *Tosafot* assert that Rav counseled in accordance with the stringent view because he feared that the ignorant person would fail to appreciate the distinction between the uppermost ring and lower rings and consequently regard incision in the lower rings of the trachea as also being acceptable.

a canopy but we did not find any way in which it is permissible" despite the fact that an expedient was readily available. The reason given for the negative response was that the inhabitants of Bashkar "were not students of Torah." In effect, perfectly acceptable forms of activity on *Shabbat* were forbidden because the inhabitants of that city were poorly schooled in the laws of the Torah. Hence, they were likely to misapply a permissive ruling and incorrectly perceive other forbidden activities as halakhically sanctioned.[3]

Indeed, such considerations often led to formal rabbinic legislation designed to establish a fence around that which is biblically prohibited. The Mishnah, *Shabbat* 153a, indicates the manner in which a wayfarer who fails to reach his destination before the advent of *Shabbat* may safeguard his wallet and other valuables. Transporting an object a distance less than four cubits wholly within the public domain involves no infraction. Therefore, the Gemara, *Shabbat* 153b, in its discussion of the Mishnah, questions why the Mishnah does not advise a person to employ the simple expedient of transporting the valuables for a distance of less than four cubits, stopping or placing the object on the ground[4] and then repeating the process as many times as necessary until reaching a secure place. Citing the verse "Honor of God [requires] concealing a matter" (Proverbs 25:2), the Gemara declares that this information was purposely suppressed lest a person in such a situation transport the object over a distance greater than that which is, in fact, permitted. The Gemara further indicates that, in this instance, because of a fear of actual desecration of the Sabbath, the Sages promulgated a formal ordinance prohibiting the carrying of valuables in a public thoroughfare for a distance of less than four cubits when another expedient is available. In a similar vein, the Gemara, *Shabbat* 115a, reports that, upon becoming aware of the fact that his family was engaging in a certain practice in an improper manner, Rabbah informed members of his household that R. Yoḥanan had forbidden the practice entirely.[5]

In the case of the inhabitants of Bashkar no formal rabbinic ban was

3. Similarly, the Gemara, *Avodah Zarah* 59a, relates that R. Yoḥanan forbade the people of Gabla to eat certain vegetables preapred by gentiles despite the fact that the food in question was perfectly permissible. Again, the reason given is that the people of Gabla "were not students of Torah" and might be led to believe that other foods banned by rabbinic decree were permitted as well.

4. Some authorities advise the person to sit or to place the object on the ground; others deem stopping to be sufficient. See *Mishnah Berurah* 266:18.

5. See *Oraḥ Meisharim*, no. 9.

enacted, but the selfsame policy considerations dictated restrictive counsel. Concern for the wayward, desire to promote a lifestyle likely to foster enhanced religious observance and spiritual sensitivity, as well as promotion of physical and social welfare contribute to what in some circles is termed "*da'at Torah*," i.e., policy considerations reflected in, and dictated by, the corpus of Torah in its entirety. While Halakhah is normative and unchanging, matters of policy are undoubtedly situational and may vary with changing mores and perceptions.

Shakh, *Yoreh De'ah* 242, addenda, sec. 9, declares that when a decisor rules that something is forbidden, not because he is absolutely certain that such is the case, but because he is unable to decide between two conflicting views or because he regards the restrictive ruling as representing an accepted stringency beyond the normative Halakhah, he must so inform his interlocutor. Failure to do so may lead to confusion and, on occasion, to unacceptable leniencies in consequential ramifications stemming from a basically restrictive rule. Unfortunately or otherwise, it has become the practice in some highly erudite and respected rabbinic circles for halakhic authorities to issue pronouncements decrying certain practices without indicating that those statements are prompted by policy concerns rather than by immutable halakhic standards. This has given rise, in the eyes of some, to the entirely erroneous perception that Halakhah itself is policy-driven and hence, in the final analysis, subjective in nature.

There is a clear need to distinguish between matters of Halakhah and matters of policy. By the same token, it must be recognized that formulation of public policy with regard to such matters is properly within the province of masters of Halakhah. It is they who are most sensitive to the need to assure the integrity of Halakhah and it is they who are best able properly to understand and interpret the values and ideals that Halakhah is designed to foster.

In any such enterprise, issues must be presented within the framework of Halakhah as an autonomous discipline with its own sources, its own dialectic and its own values. The values and mores of other disciplines dare not be permitted to intrude. It is not sufficient that "politically correct" views of contemporary society not be accepted as dispositive; they must be given no deference.

The halakhic enterprise, of necessity, proceeds without reference or openness to, much less acceptance or rejection of, modernity. Modernity is irrelevant to the formulation of halakhic determinations. Torah is timeless and eternal. Modern insights may help us to understand and appreciate both principles and minutiae of Halakhah in ways heretofore unknown, but they do not at all effect particular determinations of Halakhah. Strides made in the modern age have facilitated observance of *miẓvot* with ease and comfort. Although modernity has opened new vistas it has, at the same time, created new problems. Modernity has also given rise to social as well as technological phenomena unknown in days gone by. Those problems and those phenomena must be appreciated by a halakhic decisor functioning in the modern age, but his decisions are made within a transcendental framework in which the term "modernity" has no cognitive meaning.

The social, political and economic upheavals of the past century resulted in displacement of entire Jewish communities. An entire way of life was uprooted. Adaptation to new habitats became a matter of physical and economic necessity. Acculturation to the mores of a new society was also widely perceived as a necessary means of retaining the religious identity and loyalty of a generation reared under changed conditions. The task of finding a way to accept the advantages proffered by a modern and open society without falling prey to alien ideological blandishments represented a formidable challenge. Unfortunately, during its period of nascent development, American Jewry did not rise to this challenge. For a variety of reasons that, given the circumstances of the time, are themselves quite understandable, the Jewish community did not develop either the leadership or the institutions necessary to cope with the multifaceted problems faced by the vast number of immigrants that flocked to these shores. As a result, the modest success that was achieved can only be regarded as wondrous.

Partially as a result of improved economic conditions, partially as a result of a process of communal maturation and partially as a result of an influx of immigrants to whom a traditional way of life was still a living memory, the spiritual health of the American Jewish community has taken a marked turn for the better during the post-World War II period. We have, however, suffered an irretrievable loss—not simply in terms of the number that have been lost through assimilation and disaffection—but also in terms of the quality of Jewish life that has been preserved. The decades of confrontation and compromise constitute a breach in the transmission of a positive value system from one generation to the next. The breach in the transmission of the heritage of Judaism, Heaven be praised, was far from total—but even a partial breach makes it necessary to scrutinize accepted mores through the crucible of authenticity. All *ba'alei teshuvah*, as it is now fashionable to term those who have found Judaism for the first time, are disadvantaged by virtue of not having had the benefit of the *mesorah* of Judaism in their formative years. They must not only learn new lessons, but unlearn old ones; they must not only assimilate new values, but shed false ones. All of us who were raised on these shores are "*ba'alei teshuvah*" in that we have been continually forced to overcome the pervasive and corrosive ideologies that insidiously made their way into our own camp. As a community, we have made great strides in "restoring the crown to its ancient [glory]," but the task is far from complete.

Our age has been phenomenally successful in rearing a generation of observant Jews. It has not had the same measure of success in transmitting the *yir'at shamayim* of past generations. As a result, there are in our community significant numbers who may be described as culturally observant Jews rather than as religiously observant Jews. Integral to the commitment for which we must strive is recognition and acceptance of the divine nature of the Halakhah in its entirety and its status as a self-contained value system. To those committed to modernity in all its guises, such notions are truly threatening. That threat must be met and countered. Denying its existence results only in arrested intellectual and spiritual development. These volumes were not intentionally designed to underscore the threat or to negate the premises upon which it is based. But if, for some, that has been the effect, that purpose alone would justify and ennoble the endeavor.

Indeed, matters of Halakhah must be presented with accuracy, clarity and comprehensiveness and dare not be tailored to predilections of the audience. However, no value is discrete and no teaching stands alone. All individual values are part of a system of values and all particular teachings are part of an all-inclusive corpus. In concentration upon details, the whole may not be adequately perceived just as, at times, the forest may not be seen because of the trees. Thus, almost paradoxically, the panoramic beauty of Torah may, at times, not be fully revealed when viewed through the prism of halakhic dialectic. The author of a work such as this seeks not simply to convey information but also to cultivate appreciation. For that reason the prayer of R. Neḥunia ben ha-Kaneh, in itself, does not suffice. To the words of that prayer I add a paraphrase of the words of the blessing recited each morning: May the words of Torah always be sweet to our mouths and to the mouths of all of Israel; may we and our children and our children's children, as well as the children of the entire people of Israel, ever be students of Torah for its own sake.

"Now these are the ordinances which you shall set before them." It should not enter your mind to say, "I shall teach them a section of Torah or a halakhah twice or thrice . . . but I shall not trouble myself to cause them to understand the reasons for the matter and its explanation. . . ."

RASHI, EXODUS 21:1

Chapter I

The *Bet Din:* An Institution Whose Time Has Returned

When a judge sits in judgment . . . the Holy One, blessed be He, leaves the highermost heavens and causes His Shekhinah to rest at the judge's side.

SHEMOT RABBAH 30:20

For whoever abjures Jewish judges and goes before gentile [judges] has first denied the Holy One, blessed be He, and thereafter denied the Torah.

TANḤUMA, MISHPATIM 3

I.

Contemporary Jewry has witnessed an incredible return to meticulousness in observance of the precepts of Judaism. Widespread laxity, often even among the knowledgeable, in observance of Sabbath laws, in many aspects of the dietary code, in the writing and fashioning of *tefillin,* in the *kashrut* of the four species, etc., has been replaced in ever-widening circles with concerted efforts to observe *mizvot* in an optimal manner and, to the extent possible, in accordance with the prescriptions of every recognized authority. This single-minded pursuit of stringency rather than leniency among the cognoscenti and the more pious has had a ripple effect that has served to raise standards of religiosity and observance across the entire spectrum of our community.

Yet, collectively and individually, the American Jewish community is guilty of continuous and ongoing violation of one of the six hundred and thirteen commandments. "Judges and court officers shall you place unto yourself in all your gates (Deuteronomy 16:17) is cited by numerous early authorities, including Rambam, *Sefer ha-Mizvot, mizvot aseh,* no. 176 and *Hilkhot Sanhedrin* 1:1; *Sefer Mizvot Gadol, esin,* no. 87; and *Sefer ha-Ḥinnukh,* no. 491, as establishing an obligation to institute ecclesiastic courts, or *Batei Din,* in every locale. Rambam, *Hilkhot Sanhedrin* 1:2, explicitly rules that the commandment is binding, not only in the Land of Israel, but in the Diaspora as well.[1] The sole distinction between the Land of Israel and the Diaspora with regard to the ambit of this commandment is that the obligation to establish *Batei Din* in each district is limited to the Land of Israel, while the obligation to establish *Batei Din* in each city is binding in the Diaspora as well. *Kesef Mishneh,* on the

1. There is no suggestion in Rambam's statement indicating that the commandment is no longer binding in our day. See *Kiryat Sefer, Hilkhot Sanhedrin,* chap. 5. See also *Revid ha-Zahav,* Exodus 22:7 and *Netivot ha-Mishpat* 1:1.

A somewhat different view is expressed by Ramban in his commentary on the Bible, Deuteronomy 16:18. Ramban asserts that the biblical command applies only to the appointment of judges who have been ordained, i.e., the recipients of the unbroken chain of *semikhah,* or ordination, originating in Moses' conferral of ordination upon the judges appointed by him in the wilderness. Subsequent to the abrogation of *semikhah* during the period of Roman persecution, rabbinic courts enjoy limited authority as the "agents" of the judges of antiquity. Their authority, asserts Ramban, is rooted in rabbinic edict. Since such courts lack authority in biblical law, their establishment cannot be mandated by biblical law and, accordingly, Ramban concludes, "we are not at all *biblically* obligated with regard to the commandment concerning appointment of judges" (emphasis added). The implication is that the obligation continues in our day by virtue of rabbinic decree as a concomitant of the rabbinic legislation establishing the authority of non-ordained judges. Rabbenu Yerucham, *Sefer Meisharim* 1:4, explicitly declares that, in the absence of ordained judges, the obligation to establish *Batei Din* is rabbinic in nature.

Ramban's assertion that appointment of judges is no longer biblically mandated is predicated upon his formulation of the antecedent premise that the "agency" of present-day rabbinic courts is rooted in rabbinic legislation. That view is also espoused by Ran, *Sanhedrin* 23a; Ramah, *Sanhedrin* 23a; Rashba, *Gittin* 88b; Ramban himself, *Sanhedrin* 23a; and *Tur Shulḥan Arukh, Ḥoshen Mishpat* 1:3. However, elsewhere, *Yevamot* 46b, s.v. *shemat minah,* Ramban concludes his comments with the remark that "it is possible" that the authority of non-ordained judges to act as "agents" of the ordained judges of an earlier era is biblical in nature. Cf. also the comments of Me'iri, *Bet ha-Beḥirah, Baba Kamma* 84b, also cited in *Shitah Mekubezet, ad locum,* to the effect that, absent such a rule, all biblical laws regarding jurisprudence would be abrogated and the world would be destroyed. If, even in our day, authority to sit in judgment continues to be rooted in biblical law, it then follows that establishment of *Batei Din* remains a biblical obligation. Cf., *Imrei Binah, Ḥoshen Mishpat,* chap. 1 and *Encyclopedia Talmudit,* III, 2nd ed. (Jerusalem, 5715), p. 162, note 366a.

basis of a statement in the Gemara, *Makkot* 7a, suggests that the Maimonidean text should read that the obligation incumbent in the Diaspora is to appoint judges in every district, but not in each city.[2]

Jewish law does indeed provide that in the event of a financial dispute each litigant may nominate one member of the *Bet Din* and that the two judges designated in this manner are empowered to choose the third member of the tribunal. That procedure is known as *zablo* (*zeh borer lo eḥad ve-zeh borer lo eḥad*—this litigant chooses one [judge] and that litigant chooses one [judge]). Since, subsequent to the destruction of the Temple, rabbinic courts are no longer authorized to impose penal sanctions, to what purpose is there an ongoing obligation to establish a standing court? The essential distinction between a communally established *Bet Din* and an *ad hoc* tribunal selected by the litigants is that an *ad hoc* court derives its authority from the consent of the litigants whereas an established *Bet Din* has the right to summon any person subject to its jurisdiction and to compel his appearance. The distinction is roughly parallel to that between an agreement to be bound by the decision of an arbitration panel and submission to the jurisdiction of a court. Establishment of a judiciary having the authority in Jewish law to assert jurisdiction and to enforce judgment constitutes the essence of the commandment.

European communities were organized on the basis of a *kehillah* system. In every town, village and hamlet the Jewish community designated individuals to administer communal institutions and to provide for the spiritual as well as the temporal needs of the inhabitants. A rabbinic scholar was designated to serve as chief rabbi of the city and was usually assisted by *dayyanim* who served as associate judges. Their primary responsibility was to rule on matters of religious law relating both to individual observance and to the community as a whole and to sit as a court to adjudicate any financial or interpersonal disputes that might arise. With such a court in place, a litigant could neither plead that he preferred to appear before the court of a neighboring city nor demand the right to designate a judge of his own choice. In many communities it was customary for all householders to affix their signatures to the formal *ketav rabbanut,* or rabbinic contract, presented to a newly appointed rabbi specifically designating him as the presiding judge of the local *Bet Din*. That practice was instituted in order to assure that no person might refuse to obey a summons issued by the communal rabbi on the plea that

2. For citation of sources regarding the role and function of regional *Batei Din* see *Encyclopedia Talmudit,* III, 151.

he did not recognize the rabbi's judicial authority. Thus was the commandment "Judges and court officers shall you place unto yourself" fulfilled.

Not so in America. The *kehillah* system has not been replicated in this country. Rabbis are engaged by individual congregations rather than by the community at large. Membership in a synagogue does not *ipso facto* imply binding acceptance of the authority of the synagogue's rabbi, no matter how qualified he may be, with regard to religious or jurisprudential matters that are personal in nature. The result is that no rabbi enjoys the authority to compel a litigant to appear before him and to accept his judicial authority. *Batei Din* established by rabbinic organizations or by a group of neighborhood rabbis, rather than by the community as a whole, enjoy no greater authority. To be sure, a plaintiff dare not have recourse to a secular court and a defendant may not simply ignore the summons of a *Bet Din,* but any litigant may insist upon his right not to appear before the court that has summoned him. Since, in our country, no *Bet Din* can compel appearance, we are in violation of the commandment "Judges and court officers shall you set unto yourself."

This charge is not novel, nor does it originate with this writer. It was leveled over forty years ago by no less a personage than the sainted Rabbi Yosef Eliyahu Henkin, of blessed memory:

> The positive commandment [concerning] appointment of judges is binding also in the Diaspora (at least in every district) even in our era. Even in a locale in which there are scholars, the community is not relieved [of its obligation] to appoint designated persons for that purpose.
>
> Come and let us protest concerning the many cities and large metropolises in America that have many Torah-observant individuals but, nevertheless, they do not appoint judges and decisors. . . .[3]

II.

Lamentably, the absence of formally established *Batei Din* in our country has given rise to the phenomenon of otherwise scrupulously observant Jews having recourse to civil courts for resolution of disputes involving other members of the Jewish community. Such action entails serious

3. Rabbi Yosef Eliyahu Henkin, "Madur ha-Halakhah," *Edut be-Yisra'el,* ed. Rabbi Asher Rand (New York, n.d.), p. 167.

violations of Jewish law.

R. Akiva Eger, in a gloss appended to *Ḥoshen Mishpat* 26:1, cites *Tashbaẓ,* II, no. 190, in declaring that acceptance of any monetary award of a secular court in excess of that which would have been awarded by a *Bet Din* in accordance with Jewish law constitutes an act of theft. The same authority rules that one who accepts such funds is disqualified under Jewish law from serving as a witness. Indeed, *Tashbaẓ* comments that "this matter is so simple that it need not be recorded."

More fundamental is the transgression involved in the very act of petitioning a civil court for redress. The standard translation of Exodus 21:1 is "And these are the ordinances (*mishpatim*) which you shall set before them," i.e., before the children of Israel. Rabbinic exegesis endows this passage with an entirely different meaning.

The Hebrew term "*mishpatim*" is a multivalent term and, depending upon the context, can connote either "ordinances" or "lawsuits." The Gemara, *Gittin* 88b, assigns the second meaning to this term in commenting "'And these are the lawsuits which you shall place before them'—but not before the courts of gentiles." The conventional translation of the biblical text renders the entire passage simply as an introduction to the lengthy list of jurisprudential ordinances that follow. Rabbinic tradition understands the passage as referring to litigation that may be brought on the basis of those statutes and as expressly commanding that such suits be brought before *them, viz.,* the judges designated for that purpose by Moses. The verse thus refers to the judges whose appointment is recorded in a preceding scriptural section, Exodus 18:13–26.[4]

The rationale underlying this prohibition is incorporated in *Shulḥan Arukh, Ḥoshen Mishpat* 26:1, in the words "And whosoever comes before [gentile courts] for judgment is a wicked person and it is as if he has blasphemed and lifted a hand against the Torah of our teacher Moses, may he rest in peace." Every student of Rashi's commentary on the Pentateuch is familiar with Rashi's depiction of such an individual as one who "profanes the Divine Name and ascribes honor to the name of idols." Halakhic sources recorded in *Ḥoshen Mishpat* 26:1 make it clear that the nature and provenance of the legal code administered by the gentile courts is entirely irrelevant. Recourse to such a forum is prohibited even if the law that is applied is in no way associated with an idolatrous cult and is forbidden even if the secular law applicable to the suit is identical to Jewish law in every respect. The essence of the transgression

4. Cf., R. Isaac Elchanan Spektor, *Be'er Yiẓḥak,* no. 10, sec. 3, s.v. *gam.*

lies in rejection of the law of Moses in favor of some other legal system; recourse to a gentile forum is tantamount to a declaration by the litigant that he is amenable to allowing an alien code of law to supersede the law of the Torah. Such conduct constitutes renunciation of the law of Moses. Little wonder then that, historically, in Jewish circles, suing a fellow Jew in a secular court has been regarded as ignominious in the extreme.

Both the nature and severity of the infraction are perhaps illuminated by amplifying a point that, in itself, may appear to be peripheral in nature. R. Chaim Pelaggi, *Ḥukkat Ḥayyim,* no. 1, observes that none of the authorities who name and enumerate the six hundred and thirteen commandments of the Torah include this prohibition in their reckoning of the negative commandments and questions the reason for its omission. It appears to this writer that that problem is entirely dispelled upon examination of the nature of the obligation reflected in the commandment to establish a judiciary.

The commandment "You shall not be afraid of the face of any man" (Deuteronomy 1:17) constitutes a charge to judges trying a case not to recuse themselves because they are in fear of the litigants. This exhortation is amplified in the *Sifrei, ad locum,* with the comment, "Lest you say, 'I am afraid of so and so lest he kill my son or lest he ignite my stack [of corn].'" The injunction cautioning the judge not to be influenced by the possible loss of his harvest is readily understandable. Administration of justice must be made to take precedence over pecuniary loss. The prohibition against withdrawal in face of mortal danger is less comprehensible. The general halakhic principle is that all prohibitions are set aside in face of danger to life. Consistent with that principle, it would follow that a judge who feels intimidated should be permitted to withdraw from the case in order to prevent danger to himself or to others. Some latter-day authorities do indeed believe that conclusion to be correct and offer rather tenuous interpretations of the comments of *Sifrei.*[5]

Nevertheless, it is evident that at least one early authority understood the comment of *Sifrei* literally and accepted the comment as definitive. Rabbenu Jonah Gerondi, *Sha'arei Teshuvah* 3:188, declares that ". . . one who sits in judgment should not fear that he may die [at the hands] of

5. See R. Jacob Reischer, *Teshuvot Shevut Ya'akov,* I, no. 143; R. Moses Schick, *Teshuvot Maharam Shik, Oraḥ Ḥayyim,* no. 303; *idem, Maharam Shik al Taryag Miẓvot,* no. 416; and R. Abraham I. Kook, *Mishpat Kohen,* no.143. Cf. sources cited in *Koveẓ ha-Poskim, Ḥoshen Mishpat* 12:1. See also this writer's comments regarding the views of those authorities, *Contemporary Halakhic Problems,* II (New York, 1983), pp. 134–138.

any man as it is written 'You shall not be afraid of the face of any man.'" Rabbenu Yonah's literal interpretation of *Sifrei* is supported by a narrative recorded by the Gemara, *Sanhedrin* 19a. A slave of King Yanai committed an act of homicide. Shimon ben Shetaḥ summoned Yanai to appear before the Sanhedrin as required by law. When Yanai demurred, Shimon ben Shetaḥ's fellow judges refused to support his demand that the trial proceed. They were obviously afraid of incurring the wrath of Yanai and of suffering punishment at his hands. Shimon ben Shetaḥ called upon God to punish his colleagues with the result that the angel Gabriel cast them to the ground and they died. A similar narrative is recorded by Josephus, *Antiquities* 14:9. King Herod was summoned to appear before the *Bet Din* on the charge that he had unjustly put people to death. When he appeared, attired in his royal robes and attended by armed warriors, the members of the Sanhedrin fell silent. Thereupon, Shammai chastised the judges of the Sanhedrin and predicted that they would fall by the sword.

Not only is a judge forbidden to decline to sit in judgment in a particular case on the plea that he may thereby endanger his life, but it would appear that a person is also obligated to assume mortal risk in order to assure that qualified judges will be available to administer justice in accordance with Torah law. The Gemara, *Sanhedrin* 13b, relates:

> . . . Rabbi Joshua said in the name of Rab: "May this man be remembered for good—his name is R. Judah ben Baba. Were it not for him the laws of fines would have been forgotten in Israel." Forgotten? But we could have learned them! Rather, the laws of fines would have been abrogated because on one occasion the wicked government decreed that whoever performed an act of ordination should be put to death and whoever was ordained should be put to death, the city in which the ordination took place should be destroyed, and the area within the boundaries within which one may travel on *Shabbat* should be uprooted. What did R. Judah ben Baba do? He went and sat between two great mountains [that lay] between two large cities between the Sabbath boundaries of Usha and Shefaram and there he ordained five sages. . . . As soon as their enemies discovered them [R. Judah ben Baba] said to them, "My sons, flee!" . . . It is said that the enemy did not move from its spot until they had driven three hundred spears into his body and made him like a sieve.

The narrative concerning R. Judah ben Baba demonstrates that martyrdom is required, or at least is permitted, for purposes of enabling the continued existence of a judiciary authorized to impose judgment in all areas of Jewish law. The admonition addressed to a judge warning him not to withdraw from a trial because of his fear of a litigant demonstrates that the judge must suffer martyrdom rather than allow the law to be abrogated by not being applied in a dispute that comes before him.

Why is this the case? Judaism requires martyrdom only with regard to *force majeure* demanding violation of one of the three cardinal transgressions: idolatry, homicide and certain forms of sexual licentiousness. Neither the negative commandment "You shall not be afraid of the face of any man" nor any positive obligation requiring a qualified scholar to sit in judgment seems to fall within any of these categories. Moreover, although some authorities disagree, Rambam, *Hilkhot Yesodei ha-Torah* 5:4, rules that, when under no normative obligation to do so, a person may not voluntarily accept martyrdom rather than transgress.

In order to explain this matter, the rationale underlying the severity of the prohibition concerning idolatry must be brought into focus. Rambam, *Hilkhot Sheḥitah* 4:11, rules that an animal slaughtered in the biblically prescribed manner by a gentile (*akum*) is forbidden as carrion. In support of that talmudic ruling, Rambam cites the verse "'and he shall call you and you will eat of his slaughter' (Exodus 34:15). Since [the Torah] admonishes lest you eat of his slaughter you are to infer that his slaughter is forbidden." The verse cited by Rambam occurs in the context of an admonition concerning idolatry. In light of Rambam's citation of a passage describing partaking of the meat of an idolatrous sacrifice, *Shakh, Yoreh De'ah* 2:2, understands Rambam's disqualification of a gentile as limited to a gentile who actually engages in idolatrous practices. That analysis of Rambam's position is substantiated by Rambam's immediately following ruling, *Hilkhot Sheḥitah* 4:12, in which he declares, "And [the Sages] erected a great fence in this matter [in declaring] that even the slaughter of a gentile who does not serve idols is carrion." Rambam thus indicates that the biblical disqualification is limited to idolatrous gentiles but is extended to all gentiles by virtue of rabbinic decree.

According to Rambam, the Torah does not exclude a gentile *qua* gentile from ritual slaughter, but rather excludes a gentile because he is an idolator. The exclusion of the gentile reflects the Torah's concern "lest you eat of his slaughter," i.e., of an animal that has been sacrificed to a pagan deity. Eating meat that an idol-worshipper has slaughtered for his personal needs is likely to lead to partaking also of flesh of an animal that he has sacrificed to an idol. Accordingly, it is only logical that the exclusion should apply with equal force to a Jewish idol-worshipper as well. The meat of any idolatrous offering is forbidden to a Jew regardless of whether the animal was sacrificed by a Jew or by a non-Jew. Hence, the Torah's concern prompting the disqualification of an idol-worshipper from service as a slaughterer serves to disqualify a Jewish idolator as well. Thus it is not at all surprising to find that Halakhah treats a Jewish idolator as a gentile in disqualifying him from serving as a slaughterer.

Remarkable, however, is Rambam's codification, *Hilkhot Sheḥitah* 4:14, of the rule that a desecrator of the Sabbath and a heretic are also treated as gentiles for this purpose. Were all gentiles, including those who do not engage in idolatrous practices, to be excluded, the exclusion of Sabbath desecrators and heretics would be entirely comprehensible. Such a classification would be predicated upon a recognition that renunciation of fundamental ideological commitments places a person outside the pale of the Jewish community and relegates him to the status of a gentile. Since, however, for the purpose of ritual slaughter, only an actual idolator is excluded, it is difficult to understand why a heretic or violator of Sabbath regulations who does not serve pagan deities should be equated with a gentile idolator.

Rambam's rulings become entirely cogent if it is recognized that the ignominy associated with idolatry is not based upon the act of idolatry *per se,* or upon acknowledgment of a pagan deity, but upon the fact that such an act entails renunciation of belief in the one God. Thus heresy is equated with idolatry because heresy reflects the essence of idolatry, *viz.,* renunciation of belief in the Deity. Public desecration of the Sabbath falls within the same category, not because of the particular severity of the transgression itself, but because desecration of the Sabbath was viewed by the Sages as renunciation of God's role as Creator. That, too, is tantamount to idolatry since the essence of idolatry involves the denial of God's unique nature, including God's role as sole Creator of the universe.

This analysis of the nature of the singular repugnance associated with idolatry and of the sanctions imposed against idolators is also reflected in Rambam's comments, *Hilkhot Teshuvah* 3:7. Rambam enumerates proponents of various erroneous doctrines and categorizes them as "*minin,*" or sectarians. Listed among these is one "who serves a star or constellation or something else so that it be an intermediary between him and the Master of the universe." That comment is problematic since Rambam, *Hilkhot Avodah Zarah* 2:1, declares that worship of any such body, even as a mere intermediary, constitutes idolatry which, ostensibly, constitutes a category distinct from that of "*minin.*" It appears, then, that in *Hilkhot Teshuvah* 3:7 Rambam seeks to underscore that fundamental ideological deviation and idolatry are essentially one and the same. Idolatry itself is treated with great severity, not because of the physical act involved in the transgression, but because of the false belief reflected in the act.[6]

If it is recognized that the stringency of the halakhic proscriptions associated with idolatry derives from the ideological deviation inherent in the act rather than from the act itself, it then follows that the obligation to accept martyrdom rather than transgress the prohibition against idolatry is not limited to acts of idolatry but extends to any act reflecting acceptance of heretical beliefs. That conclusion is clearly evident from the comments of R. Jacob Emden, *Migdal Oz, Even Boḥen* 1:35. R. Jacob Emden, citing *Teshuvot Radbaz,* rules that one must suffer martyrdom rather than deny the veracity of the Law of Moses. R. Jacob Emden adds that the same principle applies to denial of the Oral Law and the words of the Sages.

The obligation not to recuse oneself from serving as a judge even in face of danger as well as the obligation to endanger oneself in order to preserve the institution of *semikhah,* and through it a judiciary authorized to impose the laws of the Torah in their entirety, may then be understood as additional facets of the obligation to suffer martyrdom rather than renounce the Torah. Allowing the Law of Moses to be forgotten or to fall into disuse is the functional equivalent of its denial. Denial of Torah is a form of heresy which, in turn, is the essence of idolatry. Accordingly, the obligation to accept martyrdom in face of idolatry, *mutatis mutandis,* extends to situations in which the Torah itself is threatened, including situations in which enforcement of its judgments is threatened.[7]

The question raised by R. Chaim Pelaggi with regard to why the prohibition against recourse to secular courts is not enumerated among the negative commandments is thus readily resolved. Such action is categorized both as idolatrous and as tantamount to renunciation of the Law of Moses. In actuality, as has been shown, those two concepts are reflective of a common element. Fundamentally, idolatry is renunciation of God and

6. For further exposition of these theses see this writer's article "Be-Bi'ur Shitat ha-Rambam be-Sheḥitat Akum u-Mumar," *Bet Yiẓḥak,* no. 21 (5749), pp. 279–284.

7. For a discussion of an obligation to accept martyrdom rather than to issue an erroneous decision or to falsify a matter of Halakhah see *Contemporary Halakhic Problems,* II, 134–138.

His Torah. Hence recourse to non-Jewish courts, even when the law administered by such courts is not derived from idolatrous cults, does not involve a novel prohibition but constitutes a form of idolatry, i.e., the heresy of denying the applicability of the Law of Moses to adjudication of the matter in dispute. Thus, the prohibition against supplanting the Law of the Torah by another legal code is subsumed under the prohibition against idolatry and does not constitute an independent transgression.

III.

Establishment of communal *Batei Din* serves a purpose beyond prevention of recourse to gentile courts by assuring a forum endowed with authority to impose Torah law. In discussing the functions of the *Bet Din, Sefer ha-Ḥinnukh* declares, *inter alia,* that judges must be appointed so that "they may compel those who stray from the path of truth to return [to that path]; to command with regard to what it is proper to do; and to prevent disdainful matters. . . ." The *Bet Din* is charged, not merely with redressing grievances, but also with issuing declaratory judgments, providing injunctive relief and with using all the powers at its command to prevent transgression. By their very nature, such functions cannot be discharged other than by a body whose authority is recognized and accepted by the entire community.

The need for a *Bet Din* upon which such duties would be incumbent should not be minimized. Several brief personal anecdotes may serve to illustrate the need for the exercise of such functions and why it is impossible for such functions to be exercised under currently prevailing conditions.

The Gemara, *Pesaḥim* 108b, establishes an obligation to distribute parched corn and nuts to children on Passover eve so that the children remain awake and alert in order to ask questions. Nuts are readily available but parched corn is not.[8] Even if available, children today would probably find the taste of parched corn alien to the palate. Therefore it has been my practice to offer chocolates instead. A number of years ago, before *Pesaḥ,* I went to a grocery store and purchased a rather large box of chocolates for that purpose. The price was exorbitant, to put it mildly. The box was rectangular in shape, small in length and width, but standing almost a full foot high. At the *seder,* before recitation of the *mah nishtanah,* I brought the box of candy to the table. I carefully removed the cellophane

8. The *kelaiyot,* or parched corn, described in the Gemara are a form of grain and not among the *kitniyot* later prohibited in the Geonic period.

wrapper, lifted the cover and removed several pieces of chocolate. To my chagrin, I discovered that the box contained only one layer of chocolates. Underneath, the container was filled with styrofoam! I was shocked, not so much by the blatant dishonesty, but by the fact that it was carried out under the imprimatur of rabbinic certification reflecting a platinum standard of scrupulousness in observance of Passover restrictions.

Some time later, when I expressed a critical view of a rabbinic authority who would lend his name to so obvious a case of consumer fraud, a colleague shrugged off my censure with the remark: "If he would not have given the *hekhsher,* someone less scrupulous with regard to *kashrut* would have done so. We may be able to control *kashrut,* but there is simply no way that we can control business practices." That observation is probably correct. But it is correct only because we have no institutional method of censuring an improper grant of a *hekhsher,* much less a communal method of applying economic sanctions against purveyors who defraud their customers. Supervision of weights and measures is one of the prerogatives, nay duties, expressly assigned to a communal *Bet Din.*[9]

Shortly thereafter, a student solicited my help with regard to a family matter. His mother, a widow who had remarried, had recently been divorced. However, her husband refused to execute a religious divorce. The student asked for my help in dealing with the recalcitrant husband. I asked for the name of the synagogue frequented by the husband and discovered that the rabbi of the synagogue was an honored and respected colleague. Without delay, I telephoned the rabbi, described the problem and asked him to intervene either by having a word with the husband himself or by arranging an appointment for us to confront the gentleman together. His response was short and cut off any further conversation: "I don't get involved in such matters." It would have been superfluous to ask why he refuses to involve himself in such matters. There are four other synagogues and conventicles within a two-block radius of the synagogue in which he serves as rabbi. There was certainly reason to be apprehensive lest the recalcitrant husband respond to rabbinic pressure by abandoning his synagogue for another synagogue around the corner. Who would assure that the congregant would be made equally uncomfortable, not to speak of unwelcome, in a new venue? The rabbi was not prepared to publicize the matter among neighboring congregations lest he appear to be engaged in a personal vendetta.

---

9. See *Baba Batra* 89a; Rambam, *Hilkhot Geneivah* 8:20; and *Shulḥan Arukh, Ḥoshen Mishpat* 331:2.

A communal *Bet Din* accepted by all sectors of the community would have had no difficulty dealing with the situation. The rabbi would only have had to report to the *Bet Din* that the gentleman withdrew from his congregation because he sought to avoid moral pressure to perform a religious duty. Upon determining that such was indeed the case, the *Bet Din,* which could not be suspected of acting out of self-interest, would be in a position to insist that the recalcitrant congregant not be welcomed by any other congregation.

IV.

There is ample precedent for the establishment of a central *Bet Din* even in communities composed of disparate groups stemming from diverse backgrounds and with differing orientations. Jews flocked to the nascent *yishuv* in *Ereẓ Yisra'el* from various European communities, but in Jerusalem all combined in establishing a *Bet Din* that to this very day is universally held in the highest regard, the *Bet Din Ẓedek le-Khol Mik'halot ha-Ashkenazim*—the *Bet Din Ẓedek* of all Ashkenazic communities. Ideally, an American national *Bet Din* should be even more inclusive, a *Bet Din Ẓedek le-Khol Mik'halot Yisra'el.* That *Bet Din* would be empowered to designate local *Batei Din,* where appropriate, and to have its members "ride circuit" in areas in which it is not feasible, or not wise, to delegate authority.

Understandably, existing *kehillot* do not wish to relinquish autonomy and existing *Batei Din* may not wish to be dissolved. But establishment of such a national *Bet Din* need not constitute a threat to the prerogatives or power of any individual or group. Existing communities may continue to have recourse to their own rabbinic authorities in exactly the same manner as at present. Their authority depends upon voluntary acceptance of their jurisdiction. Halakhah recognizes the right of individuals to appear before any judges of their choice, so long as the parties are in agreement with regard to such appearance. The *Bet Din* established by a particular congregation or locale may have no difficulty imposing its authority upon its own members. However, even the most observant and most tightly knit community frequently experiences difficulty when a dispute arises between one of its adherents and a member of another community. Even those communities experience a very real need for a *Bet Din* enjoying "diversity jurisdiction" since frequently, each litigant seeks to prevail upon his adversary to accept the jurisdiction of the *Bet Din* of his own community. It is to be presumed that, at least initially, members of the national *Bet Din* would be drawn, to a large extent, from the membership of existing *Batei Din.*

Such a *Bet Din* cannot be established unless it is acceptable to all sectors of the community. Acceptance would require broad representation of each of those sectors. Its success would require that litigants feel compatibility with the *dayyanim* before whom they appear. Those goals are probably best attained by establishing a fairly large roster of *dayyanim* and permitting litigants to use a limited form of the *zablo* system, i.e., the system under which each litigant chooses one member of the tribunal. Litigants might be permitted to designate the members of the *Bet Din* that would hear their case but would be limited in being able to select a panel of *dayyanim* only from among the designated list of members of the national *Bet Din.*[10] Such a model would preserve the best aspects of both the voluntary, *ad hoc* system and the communal system. Universal acceptance of a national *Bet Din* as a communal entity would assure its binding judicial power and its status as a repository of religious and moral authority, while the ability of the litigants to exercise at least limited choice in naming the members of the tribunal that would hear their dispute would serve to satisfy the need for ethnic and cultural compatibility.

The American Jewish community has grown in maturity. It now possesses the spiritual and institutional resources needed to revitalize the *Bet Din* and to incorporate it as an integral aspect of Jewish life. Establishment of *Batei Din* can do much to enhance Jewish awareness, identity and commitment. The *Bet Din* is an institution which has been neglected for too long and whose time has returned.

---

10. This approach was suggested to me by the late Rabbi Jacob Kaminetsky, of blessed memory, in a somewhat different context. Some years ago, in urging adoption of the antenuptial agreement later published in *Or ha-Mizraḥ,* Tishri 5750 and in *Torah she-be-'al Peh,* vol. XXXI (5750), he recommended one modification of my draft. In order to avoid the procrastination that unfortunately develops in selecting the members of a *Bet Din* when the parties have recourse to *zablo,* and in order to establish a single *Bet Din* acceptable to all of the community, Rabbi Kaminetsky advised that the document provide a list of names and specify that each of the parties may select one of the *dayyanim* from among the named individuals.

Chapter II

The Appeal Process in the Jewish Legal System

Said the Holy One, blessed be He: "Know you that I sit with you and if you wrest judgment [it is] Me that you wrest."

MIDRASH SHOḤAR TOV, PSALM 82

A person had a lawsuit. He came to the judge and was exonerated. The person who was exonerated departed and said, "There is no one in the world who compares to that judge." After a time he had [another] lawsuit. He came to [the judge] and was found liable. He departed and said, "There is no judge who is a greater fool than he! They said to him, "Was [the judge] splendid yesterday and today a fool?" Therefore Scripture admonishes, "Do not curse the court" (Exodus 22:27).

SHEMOT RABBAH 31:8

I.

Establishment of a judiciary is rooted in the biblical command "Judges and court officers shall you appoint to yourself in all your gates" (Deuteronomy 16:18). The Jewish judicial system reflected the prescriptions of Jewish law and was comprised of tribunals composed of three judges that heard cases involving monetary disputes, courts consisting of twenty-three judges that were charged with judging persons accused of infractions punishable by death or stripes and a Great Sanhedrin comprised of seventy-one members that sat within the Temple precincts. Although the Great Sanhedrin enjoyed original jurisdiction with regard to certain particular matters, its most critical function was to resolve questions of law that were in doubt or the subject of dispute. Questions of that nature could be certified and brought before the Great Sanhedrin during the course of proceedings before a lower court or could be made the subject of a hearing entirely independent from any proceeding before a court of original jurisdiction.

Other than an interlocutory appeal of such nature to the Great Sanhedrin there is no explicit provision for appeal to a higher court on the basis of allegation of judicial error with regard to either matters of fact or of law. Although no formal provision for an appeals process is recorded in the various codes of Jewish law, a duly constituted rabbinical court of appeals does exist in the present-day State of Israel. The impetus for the establishment of a Supreme Rabbinical Court of Appeals in the State of Israel can be traced to two sources, one historical and the other political.

With the rise of Zionism and promulgation of the Balfour Declaration the *Ha-Mishpat ha-Ivri* Society was established in Moscow. Its stated agenda was to develop a corpus of law based upon Jewish law sources for integration into the legal system of a future secular Jewish state. In 1909–10 a judicial body known as *Mishpat ha-Shalom ha-Ivri* was established in Jaffa. The celebrated writer S.Y. Agnon served as the first secretary of that body. Later, tribunals were established in other cities in Palestine as well. Those tribunals had no official standing under either the Ottoman or British governments but functioned as arbitration panels.[1] Those bodies were composed of persons who, in general, lacked legal or rabbinic training and did not consider themselves bound by any particular system of law. Judgments were rendered on the basis of generally conceived "principles of justice, equity, ethics and public good."[2] Nevertheless, beginning in 1918, regulations were promulgated with regard to matters of procedure, evidence and the like. Lay arbitration is certainly not unprecedented in Jewish law.[3] However, the judicial system instituted by

1. For an account of the mode of operation of those tribunals see C. Daikan, *Toldot Mishpat ha-Shalom ha-Ivri* (Tel Aviv, 5724). See also Mordecai ben Hillel ha-Kohen, "Le-Toldot Mishpat ha-Shalom ha-Ivri," *Mishpat ha-Ivri: She'elotav le-Halakhah u-le-Ma'aseh* (Tel Aviv, 5685). For a critique of the ideological principles upon which those tribunals were based see J. Yonowitz, introduction to Simchah Assaf, *Ha-Onshim Aḥarei Ḥatimat ha-Talmud* (Jerusalem, 5683), pp. 5–6 and Simchah Assaf, *Batei Din ve-Sidreihem Aḥarei Ḥatimat ha-Talmud* (Jerusalem, 5788), pp. 6–9.

2. Cf., the language incorporated in the Foundations of Law Act adopted by the State of Israel in 1980. That act provides that, in the absence of legislation or precedent, legal issues must be resolved "in light of the principles of freedom, justice, equity and peace of the heritage of Israel." The influence of the framework governing the *Mishpat ha-Shalom ha-Ivri* seems readily apparent and, *mutatis mutandis,* is subject to the same critique.

3. See Rema, *Ḥoshen Mishpat* 8:1, and Louis Finkelstein, *Jewish Self-*

the *Mishpat ha-Shalom ha-Ivri* was innovative in its institution of a formal appellate forum.

There can be little doubt that, despite the limited scope and underutilization of the judicial system established by the *Mishpat ha-Shalom ha-Ivri,* the very establishment of a court of appeals within a system purporting to align itself with principles of Jewish law served to create or to reinforce a desire for an appellate system and to generate an aura of ideological acceptance. However, the proximate cause of the institution of a rabbinical court of appeals was governmental pressure in conjunction with the establishment of the Chief Rabbinate under the aegis of the Mandatory authority. On 15 Shevat 5681, in his opening address at the very first meeting of the committee appointed to convene a representative assembly for the purpose of electing a Chief Rabbinate, Mr. Norman Bentwich, Secretary of Justice in the Mandatory government and chairman of the meeting, emphasized that "one of the most important matters" to be addressed by the electoral body was the establishment of a rabbinical court of appeals.[4] At the time, the Mandatory authority was considering granting *Batei Din* autonomous jurisdiction with regard to matters of personal status upon the establishment of a Chief Rabbinate. Mr. Bentwich made it very clear that the British government "strongly insists upon the need for creation of an institution for appeals as a condition for enhancement of the jurisdiction of Jewish *Batei Din.*"[5]

That proposal met with immediate opposition. At a subsequent meeting held on 17 Shevat a document prepared by the "Office of the Rabbinate of Jaffa" was presented. The final paragraph of that document states, "There is no place for an appellate *Bet Din* according to the laws of the Torah. . . ."[6]

The meeting of the assembly charged with naming electors to designate the members of the proposed Chief Rabbinical Council met in Jerusalem on 14–16 Shevat 5721. The opening address was delivered by the British High Commissioner, Sir Herbert Samuel. In his charge, he exhorted the assemblage to consider the proposal of the preliminary committee for the establishment of a rabbinic court of appeals. He explicitly stated, "It is proposed that from among the [Chief Rabbinate] Council of eight there be formed a supreme religious court to which it will be possible to bring

Government in the Middle Ages (New York, 1924), pp. 356–359.

4. See *Ha-Tor,* vol. 1, no. 18 (3 Adar 1, 5681), p. 14.

5. *Loc. cit.*

6. *Ibid.,* p. 15.

an appeal from any *Bet Din* in *Ereẓ Yisra'el.* I support this proposal. . . ."[7] That proposal was reiterated by Mr. Bentwich in declaring that the Chief Rabbinate Council "would also be the officially recognized *Bet Din* of Jerusalem" and "if the proposal finds favor in your eyes, [the Chief Rabbinate Council] will establish a *Bet Din* for appeals. . . ."[8] Subsequently, a number of resolutions were presented for consideration by that assembly, including a resolution establishing a "*Bet Din* of appeals to be composed of six members of the Rabbinate Council under the chairmanship of one of its presidents,"[9] i.e., the Chief Rabbis would alternate as presidents of the court.[10] Although, at the assembly, both Sir Herbert Samuel and Norman Bentwich spoke of establishment of an appellate court as a "proposal," a certain Joseph Penigel, described as the secretary of the Office of the Rabbinate, asserted that the Mandatory authorities insisted upon establishment of such a body as "a necessary condition for enhancing the authority of the *Batei Din* and for granting legal effect to their decisions."[11] Apparently, that assembly did not formally act upon the resolution for the establishment of a rabbinic court of appeals.[12] Nevertheless, such a court was established by the Chief Rabbinate Council within a matter of months of its election.

The question of whether or not there exists a halakhic basis for a rabbinic court of appeals notwithstanding,[13] it is clear, as a matter of

7. *Ha-Tor,* vol. 1, no. 21–22 (24 Adar I, 5681), p. 3.

8. *Ibid.,* p. 4.

9. *Ibid.,* p. 5.

10. *Ibid.,* p. 15.

11. *Ibid.,* p. 14.

12. *Ibid.,* p. 24. See also R. Chaim Hirschensohn, *Malki ba-Kodesh,* I (St. Louis, 5679), 17, who states that "the nations will not agree under any circumstances" to recognize the authority of *Batei Din* in Palestine other than upon establishment of a court of appeals.

13. The modern-day discussions of a possible role for an appellate court focus upon establishment of such a body to hear appeals in matters of jurisprudence and family law. Indeed, insofar as statutory law is concerned, with the lapse in succession in the ordination of judges originating with Moses, *Batei Din* are no longer competent to impose penal sanctions. Nevertheless, during the medieval period, not only were such penalties imposed by Jewish courts, but frequently the right of judicial autonomy even in criminal matters was granted by the civil authorities. Simchah Assaf, *Batei ha-Din ve-Sidreihem,* p. 77, note 1, reports that in 1284 two Jews residing in Saragossa were convicted of murdering a relative and sentenced to excommunication and exile. Thereupon, the convicted criminals appealed the verdict to Pedro III of Aragon. The complainants argued

historical fact, that such judicial bodies did exist both during the medieval period and in modern times as well.[14] Whether the right to appeal is grounded in statutory law or was established in some jurisdictions on the basis of local communal *takkanot* or in response to governmental edicts is an entirely different matter.

There is some support for the position that Scripture itself provides for a system of appeals. The sixteenth century Italian exegete, R. Ovadiah Sforno, in his commentary on the Bible, presents an analysis of Exodus 18:21 indicating that the purpose of designating "rulers of thousands, rulers of hundreds, rulers of fifties and rulers of tens" was to establish a multi-layered system of appeals. According to Sforno's analysis, the "rulers of tens" had original jurisdiction. Successive appeals could be taken to higher levels and, ultimately, if the litigant remained unsatisfied, to Moses himself. Although, in terms of biblical exegesis, Sforno's analysis is not at all far-fetched, even if accepted, it does not establish a right of appeal as a matter of Halakhah. The officials appointed by Moses with jurisdiction over ten, fifty, one hundred and one thousand persons did not occupy offices designed to be preserved in perpetuity. Apparently, the appointments, and the particular offices themselves, were designed only to ease Moses' burden and, accordingly, were limited to the period of wandering in the wilderness. Hence, granted that these officials served as appellate judges, the right to lodge appeals before them may have been temporary in nature and limited to the generation of the wilderness.

The earliest record of the existence of an appellate court appears to be

---

that appeals were not recognized in Jewish law. Pedro, in turn, referred the matter to the head of the rabbinical court of Aragon for resolution of that issue and directed him to conduct a new hearing should he find that Jewish law provides for such a procedure. Assaf further reports that we do not have a record of the resolution of that case.

In actuality, while such information would be highly intriguing, resolution of the issue in that case would have little bearing upon the subject of this discussion. Authority for imposition of criminal sanctions in our day is the product of the extra-statutory *ad hoc* power of a *Bet Din* to preserve law and order. Accordingly, it would not be surprising to find that emergency measures are not subject to appeal, while decisions issued on the basis of the due process of ordinary judicial procedure are subject to appeal. On the other hand, it is possible, albeit unlikely, that local ordinances may have established a system of appeal limited to criminal matters precisely because the authority to impose such penalties is extra-statutory.

14. See Assaf, *Batei Din ve-Sidreihem,* pp. 74–85; Louis Finkelstein, *Jewish Self-Government in the Middle Ages,* pp. 359–360; Fritz Baer, *Die Juden in christlichen Spanien,* I (Berlin, 1936), 286; and Abraham A. Neuman, *The Jews of Spain* (Philadelphia, 1944), p. 118 and cf. p. 145.

that found among the enactments promulgated by a synod of Castilian communities convened in 1432. These enactments provided that any litigant had the right to appeal to the *Rab de la Corte,* i.e., the Chief Rabbi appointed by the King. The costs of the appeal were to be borne by the appellant if the latter did not prevail and he was required to take measures to assure that prompt payment of those expenses would be forthcoming. The appellant was also required to affirm that the appeal was based on belief in the justice of his cause rather than designed to serve as a means of evasion or procrastination.[15]

At roughly the same time, at least some communities of Aragon appointed judges to hear appeals. R. Isaac ben Sheshet refers by name to certain appellate judges, known as "*dayyanei ha-silukin*" who sat in Calatayud,[16] Hueska,[17] and Saragossa.[18] Simchah Assaf, a prominent Jewish law historian, asserts that it is unlikely that such an institution should have arisen during the period of decline of Iberian Jewry.[19] Consequently, he assumes that the written record reflects a practice of much older vintage.

Establishment of a formal system of appeals in Italy is found in an enactment promulgated by R. Moshe Zacutto in 1676 and accepted by an overwhelming majority of delegates to a synod of Italian Jewry. That ordinance provided that, unless the right to appeal was waived by the litigants at the time of submission of their dispute to the *Bet Din,* they were entitled to appeal to the "*Ba'alei Yeshivah*"[20] within eight days after issuance of a decision. The procedure does not seem to have provided for relitigation or presentation of additional allegations of fact or law by the litigants but provided that the "*Ba'alei Yeshivah*" summon the *dayyanim* who issued the ruling for an explanation of the grounds upon which it was based.[21]

Procedures governing appeals in the communities of Moravia are recorded by R. Menachem Mendel Krochmal, author of *Teshuvot Ẓemaḥ*

---

15. Assaf, *Batei Din ve-Sidreihem,* p. 75.

16. *Teshuvot Rivash,* nos. 227 and 381.

17. *Ibid.,* nos. 393 and 494.

18. *Ibid.,* nos. 506 and 388. The appellate judge is mentioned by name in the former responsum and in the latter responsum the place of residence of that individual is given as Saragossa. See Assaf, *Batei Din ve-Sidreihem,* p. 76.

19. Assaf, *Batei Din ve-Sidreihem,* p. 77.

20. See *Teshuvot Shemesh Ẓedakah, Ḥoshen Mishpat,* nos. 9, 13, 14, 19 and 24.

21. See Assaf, *Batei Din ve-Sidreihem,* pp. 78 and 133.

Ẓedek, in his *Takkanot ha-Medinah,* nos. 213–218. Appeals were permitted only in cases involving a value of ten "gold coins" or more and had to be lodged within forty-eight hours of issuance of the *Bet Din*'s decision. If he did not prevail, the appellant was held liable for losses and expenses sustained as a result of the appeal.

In some Polish communities a person found liable by the *Bet Din* was permitted to demand that the *Bet Din* be enlarged and a new hearing be scheduled. This practice was decried by *Ateret Ẓevi, Ḥoshen Mishpat,* no. 87.[22] Appellate procedures are also known to have existed in White Russia (Reisin). The protocols of the community of Petroviski of 1777 include a regulation promulgated with regard to appeals taken from decisions of the local *Bet Din.*[23] Appeals were permitted only with regard to decisions involving a sum of twenty-five rubles or more and only "in accordance with the ordinances of the land." Assaf notes with regret that there are no cognate sources that provide information with regard to the ordinances governing such appeals or with regard to the identity and composition of the appeals court.[24]

In more recent times, an appellate court was established in Bulgaria in 1900. With the establishment of the office of Chief Rabbi, provision was also made for the appointment of "two or more judges" who together with the Chief Rabbi would constitute a "*Bet Din ha-Gadol*" which would hear appeals of decisions issued by local *Batei Din.*[25] In a letter addressed to R. Chaim Hirschensohn,[26] R. Ya'akov Meir, who served first as *Ḥakham Bashi* and later as the first Sephardic Chief Rabbi of Palestine, reported that "there always were appellate courts in all the cities of Turkey" and at the same time asserted in a somewhat contradictory manner that a displeased litigant presented his appeal in writing to the

22. See *ibid.*, pp. 84–85.

23. Assaf, *ibid.*, p. 83, includes the appeals process of the *Va'ad ha-Medinah* of Lithuania in his enumeration of courts of appeal. It must however be noted that the recorded protocols of the *Va'ad ha-Medinah* refer solely to disputes regarding appointments to communal offices and fines imposed by the community. The reference is clearly to communal matters and involves matters of local ordinances and has no relationship to appeals regarding matters of ordinary financial litigation.

24. *Loc. cit.*

25. *Ibid.*, p. 85 and p. 140. See also *Teshuvot Ḥoshen ha-Efod, Ḥoshen Mishpat,* no. 42.

26. Published in R. Chaim Hirschensohn, *Malki ba-Kodesh,* IV (St. Louis, 5679–5682), 13–15. See also Assaf, *Batei Din ve-Sidreihem,* p. 77.

chief rabbi of the city who forwarded the appellant's petition together with the decision of the local *Bet Din* to Constantinople "and there there was a *Bet Din ha-Gadol* that investigated the decision and was empowered [either] to set aside the decision and issue another judgment or to confirm the judgment."[27] Rabbi Meir further reported that, when he served as Chief Rabbi of Salonika, he sought and received permission from the *Bet Din* in Constantinople to establish an appeals court in his own jurisdiction.[28] Rabbi Meir further claimed that there also existed an appeals process in Jerusalem and in many other Oriental communities.[29] Assaf relates that, when he expressed astonishment at the absence of any reference to such procedures in the responsa of Sephardic scholars, Rabbi Meir replied that instances of appeal were quite rare because of the distance and expense involved and that many people were unaware of the possibility of appeal.[30]

II.

Although, as earlier indicated, appellate courts as such were unknown in talmudic times and the relevant talmudic discussions neither speak of a formal appeals process nor spell out conditions upon which appeals are allowed, the Gemara does present an elaborate discussion of provisions for setting aside judgments on grounds of judicial error. The Mishnah, *Sanhedrin* 32a, declares that a decision of a *Bet Din* can be set aside on grounds of judicial error and the *Bet Din* must then issue a new decision. The Gemara, *Sanhedrin* 33a, cites an apparently contradictory statement found in the Mishnah, *Bekhorot* 28b, declaring that an erroneous judgment must be allowed to stand but that the judge is liable for any financial loss suffered as a result of his error and yet a further statement indicating that a qualified judge is granted immunity while the judgment is not disturbed. In the ensuing discussion various Amora'im resolve the contradiction by distinguishing situations in which the decision is reversed from situations in which the judgment is allowed to stand while the members of the *Bet Din* are either held liable for judicial malpractice or granted judicial immunity.[31] According to Rashi's analysis of that discussion,[32] Rav Nach-

27. *Malki ba-Kodesh,* IV, 14.

28. *Loc. cit.*

29. *Loc. cit.*

30. *Batei Din ve-Sidreihem,* p. 78, note 1.

31. For a survey of the applicable principles see *Encyclopedia Talmudit,* XX, 495–539. The normative *halakhot* are codified in *Shulḥan Arukh, Ḥoshen Mishpat,*

man declares that a decision of a *Bet Din* can be set aside by a *Bet Din* "greater in wisdom and number." It is evident that, in offering alternative resolutions of the contradiction, some of Rav Nachman's colleagues did not accept the notion of an appeal to a court "greater in wisdom and number" and considered only the possibility of a rehearing by the court of original jurisdiction with the result that a new verdict might be obtained only when the first *Bet Din* became convinced of its error. According to the analysis of that discussion advanced by *Yad Ramah* and Me'iri, *ad locum,* as well as by other authorities who interpret Rav Nachman's statement in an entirely different manner, there are no grounds for assuming that even Rav Nachman permits an appeal to a *Bet Din* "greater in wisdom and number."[33] Moreover, numerous authorities, including Rif, *Milḥamot ha-Shem* and Me'iri in their respective commentaries *ad locum,* regard Rav Nachman's position as having been rejected in the ensuing discussions and his opinion is not cited by either Rambam or *Shulḥan Arukh.*[34]

The Gemara, in one of the proffered resolutions of the contradiction that serves as the basis of the entire discussion, distinguishes between error in "black letter law" (*ta'ut be-devar mishnah*) and error in "judgment" (*ta'ut be-shikul ha-da'at*) defined as a judgment based upon reliance upon a minority or rejected opinion.[35] According to Rashi's analysis, both Rav Yosef, who presents an alternative resolution of the apparent contradiction between the Mishnah in *Sanhedrin* and the Mishnah in *Bekhorot,* and Rav Nachman recognize the ostensive cogency of a litigant's refusal to accept the judge's acknowledgment that a decision in his favor is based upon error on the plea that it is entirely possible that it is the reconsidered decision that is in error and that the original finding was

chap. 25.

32. See also sources cited in *Encyclopedia Talmudit,* vol. XX, p. 502, note 78.

33. See also sources cited by *Encyclopedia Talmudit, ibid.,* note 79. A related incident recorded in *Ketubot* 50b involving another statement by R. Nachman is also the subject of controversy in this regard; see *Tosafot, Ketubot* 50b and *Shitah Mekubeẓet, Baba Kamma* 12a, as well as sources cited in *Encyclopedia Talmudit, ibid.,* notes 78 and 79.

34. See *Encyclopedia Talmudit,* vol. XX, p. 513, note 213. Cf., R. Chaim Hirschensohn, *Malki ba-Kodesh,* II, 110, who writes, ". . . we do not need a clearer source for a supreme court of appeals than the words of Rav Nachman." Opponents of the concept of a court of appeals presumably recognized that a rejected opinion cannot serve as a "clear source" for any halakhic principle.

35. For further elucidation of this dichotomy see *Encyclopedia Talmudit,* XX, 498–501.

entirely correct. It may well be argued that such a plea is cogent not only with regard to an alleged error of "judgment," but also with regard to putative errors of "black letter law." Rav Yosef maintains that only an "expert" judge can force a reconsidered view upon an unwilling litigant; Rav Nachman asserts that only the opinion of a more erudite authority should prevail.[36] Nevertheless, *Tosafot* indicates that the discussion is limited to errors of "judgment" but that all concede that errors of "black letter law" may be reversed. *Tosafot,* however, does not spell out criteria of competence to reverse an already announced decision nor does *Tosafot* state whether admission of error on the part of the judge who issued the decision is necessary.

As codified by Rambam, *Hilkhot Sanhedrin* 6:6–9, it is only a plaintiff who, if he has some credible evidence, may demand that the defendant appear for a hearing before the Great Sanhedrin; a defendant does not enjoy that prerogative. Nevertheless, Rambam, *Hilkhot Sanhedrin* 6:6, rules that either litigant is entitled to demand a written decision setting forth the findings of the local court. The clear implication is that either the plaintiff or the defendant will then be entitled to lodge an appeal with the Great Sanhedrin based upon the written record. Rambam makes no reference to any mechanism for appeal other than to the Great Sanhedrin. It would therefore appear that when there is no possibility of appeal to the Great Sanhedrin, e.g., in a historical epoch in which that judicial body does not exist, there is no basis for a demand for a written decision upon which an appeal may be based. Nevertheless, Rema, *Ḥoshen Mishpat* 14:4, rules explicitly that, even in our day, the litigants are entitled to such a document.[37] Indeed, Rema indicates that such a document may be demanded only for an appearance before "a greater court."[38] It is thus

36. For a discussion of various conflicting interpretations of the disagreement between Rav Yosef and Rav Nachman, or the absence thereof, see *Encyclopedia Talmudit,* XX, 506–509.

37. Rema adds that a litigant is entitled to such a document only if the court compels appearance, but not if the parties voluntarily accept the jurisdiction of the *Bet Din.* Voluntary acceptance of the jurisdiction of the *Bet Din* is thus tantamount to acceptance of its final authority and renunciation of the right of appeal. *Teshuvot Noda bi-Yehudah, Mahadura Tinyana, Ḥoshen Mishpat,* no. 1, rules that in any situation in which the litigants are summoned to appear before the *Bet Din* their appearance is not to be regarded as voluntary acceptance of the authority of the *Bet Din.* Cf., however, R. Joseph Saul Nathanson, *Teshuvot Sho'el u-Meshiv, Mahadura Tinyana,* II, no, 84 and *Mahadura Revi'a'ah,* III, no. 101.

38. Rema indicates that the litigant is entitled to a written statement only of

evident that Rema recognized a right of appeal to "a greater court"[39] although he provides no guidance with regard to how a determination of the relative scholarly ranking of different courts is to be made or with regard to who is empowered to make such a determination.[40]

There are, however, a number of earlier sources that clearly indicate that Jewish law does not recognize a right of appeal. *Teshuvot ha-Rosh, klal* 85, no. 5, cited by *Bet Yosef, Ḥoshen Mishpat,* chapter 12, declares, ". . . subsequent to the decision of the judges that has already been rendered with regard to the orphan . . . the judgment that has been rendered with regard to the orphan stands. Why have you asked for another decision with regard to a case that has already been adjudicated? 'A *Bet Din* does not scrutinize [the actions] of another *Bet Din*' (*Baba Batra* 138b). Therefore . . . it is incorrect (*lo yitakhen*) to write another decision with regard to a case that has already been adjudicated by great and eminent men."[41] *Sema, Ḥoshen Mishpat* 19:2, and *Shakh, Ḥoshen Mishpat* 19:3, cite *Teshuvot ha-Rosh* as establishing the principle that a decision of a *Bet Din* cannot be overturned by another *Bet Din.*

Rema's position is particularly problematic. As has been noted, in

the claim and the decision itself, but not of the reasoning upon which it is based. In a parallel provision based on an incident described by the Gemara, *Baba Meẓi'a* 69a, *Shulḥan Arukh, Ḥoshen Mishpat* 14:4, rules that when a judge perceives that he is suspected of bias in favor of the prevailing party he should inform the losing party of the "reason" upon which the decision was based. In such a situation, and only in such a situation, does *Shulḥan Arukh* state that it is necessary to disclose the "reason." Moreover, as explicitly noted by Rema, such situations require only an oral disclosure rather than a written decision. Cf., however, *Teshuvot Ḥavot Ya'ir, hashmatot,* cited in *Pitḥei Teshuvah, Ḥoshen Mishpat* 14:10.

For a detailed treatment of the obligation to issue a reasoned decision or the absence thereof see Eliav Shochetman, "Ḥovat ha-Hanmakah ba-Mishpat ha-Ivri," *Shenaton ha-Mishpat ha-Ivri,* VI–VII (5739–5740), 319–397. See also R. Ovadiah Hedaya, *Teshuvot Yaskil Avdi,* II, *Ḥoshen Mishpat,* no. 2, sec. 8.

39. See R. Moses Feinstein, *Iggerot Mosheh, Ḥoshen Mishpat,* I, no. 76, who indicates that "in our day" there is no *Bet Din* that can be considered "a greater court."

40. *Arukh ha-Shulḥan, Ḥoshen Mishpat* 14:8, states that, although such a document may be requested by a litigant for submission to another *Bet Din,* "it appears to me" that the judges must write that they grant permission for review of their decision and that in the absence of such permission no other court may review their decision. That view, however, does not seem to be shared by any other authority.

41. Cf., *infra,* note 46.

Ḥoshen Mishpat 14:4 Rema rules that a litigant is entitled to a written verdict while in his commentary on *Tur Shulḥan Arukh, Darkei Mosheh, Ḥoshen Mishpat* 25:6, he records the view of *Teshuvot ha-Rosh* indicating that a second *Bet Din* cannot retry a case in which a decision has already been issued by a previous *Bet Din*. The latter position is also espoused by Rema in *Darkei Mosheh, Ḥoshen Mishpat* 20:2, in the citation of a similar ruling in the name of another work authored by Rosh, *Sefer Ḥazeh ha-Tenufah.*[42]

R. Ovadiah Hedaya, *Teshuvot Yaskil Avdi,* IV, *Ḥoshen Mishpat,* no. 2, distinguishes between a situation in which a *Bet Din* has issued a written decision that includes reasons and sources and a situation in which the reasons underlying a decision have not been committed to writing. When a record of the considerations leading to a decision is not available, declares *Yaskil Avdi,* the principle "a *Bet Din* does not scrutinize the actions of another *Bet Din*" is applied. However, when reasons and arguments are spelled out, the decision may be overturned. At first glance it appears paradoxical that the decisions of a *Bet Din* should be sacrosanct when issued autocratically with no attempt at justification but subject to reversal when a detailed explanation is provided. Nevertheless, *Yaskil Avdi* cogently reasons that when grounds for a verdict are spelled out and are found to be patently wrong it is obvious that the decision must be set aside, whereas when no reasons are given it is improper for a second *Bet Din* to reverse the decision because the second *Bet Din* cannot state definitively that error has been committed.[43]

It is, however, quite clear that the considerations upon which a decision is based are not routinely provided even in situations in which a written verdict is issued. R. Joseph Karo, *Teshuvot Avkat Rokhel,* no. 17, declares that explication of reasons and explanations is unnecessary.[44] Similarly,

---

42. See *Ḥazeh ha-Tenufah,* no. 40. *Ḥazeh ha-Tenufah* has been published as an appendix to R. Chaim Joseph David Azulai's *Teshuvot Ḥayyim Sha'al,* vol. II.

43. See also R. Ben-Zion Uziel, *Mishpetei Uzi'el, Mahadura Tinyana, Ḥoshen Mishpat,* no. 1, sec. 15. A similar position is advanced by Rabbi Y. ibn Zur, *Mishpat u-Ẓedekah be-Ya'akov,* II (Alexandria, 5663), no. 48. Cf., *Teshuvot Yaskil Avdi,* III, *Even ha-Ezer.* no. 2, *anaf* 1, secs. 4–6.

44. See *supra,* note 38. See, however, *Oraḥ Mishpat, Ḥoshen Mishpat* 14:4, who cites a comment of *Shelah, Parashat Mishpatim,* reporting that the latter had received a tradition from his father to the effect that even if there is no indication that he is suspected of a miscarriage of justice, the *dayyan* should disclose the reasons upon which his judgment is predicated in order to assuage and calm the mind of the losing party.

Rema, *Ḥoshen Mishpat* 14:4, rules that the document must recite only the claims and the final ruling but need not indicate the *Bet Din*'s reasoning and justification because, as explained by *Sema, Ḥoshen Mishpat* 14:26, if the decision is correct, any other court will reach the same decision since "there is [but] one Torah for all of us." *Sema, Ḥoshen Mishpat* 14:25, indicates that, if requested, the *Bet Din* must nevertheless make oral disclosure of its reasoning. However, if *Yaskil Avdi* is correct in his assumption that a judgment can be overturned only if the written decision incorporates reasons and explanations, it stands to reason that litigants should be entitled to a written decision containing such information as a matter of right. Rambam, *Hilkhot Sanhedrin* 6:6, states explicitly that litigants may demand a written verdict because they are entitled to say to the *Bet Din,* "Perhaps you have erred." Clearly, a demand for a written verdict is in contemplation of a reversal by another *Bet Din* and it is the right to such a reversal that justifies the demand. Consequently, a decision that cannot be used as the basis for an appeal is of no value to a litigant. Accordingly, if *Yaskil Avdi* is correct in his contention, the same consideration that compels issuance of a written decision should compel issuance of a reasoned decision.

R. Shimon ben Ẓemaḥ Duran, *Tashbaẓ,* III, no. 165, declares that a decision of a Bet Din can be reversed only if the original *Bet Din* acknowledges its error. Accordingly, if the members of the first *Bet Din* are not alive, the possibility of reversal does not exist.[45]

III.

Rabbinic scholars who deny that Jewish law recognizes a right of appeal adduce the dictum recorded in *Baba Batra* 138b, "a *Bet Din* does

45. See *infra,* note 49, as well as the accompanying text quoting *Baba Batra* 130b. The phrase "If I have a reason," strongly suggests that the written judgment stated nothing more than the award and did not include the reasoning upon which it was based. Despite the finding of error by other competent authorities, Rava insisted that the decision cannot be nullified unless he concedes error and hence there can be no possibility of reversal after his demise. At the same time, the phrase "a judge has nothing other than what his eyes behold" suggests that, if the decision has as yet not been executed or if any further action by a *Bet Din* is contemplated, a *Bet Din* that finds the decision to be in error is not obliged to enforce the judgment. The thrust of Rava's declaration is that, unless a *Bet Din* acknowledges and agrees that its decision may be vacated, other courts can take no action and hence must allow the situation to remain as presented without disturbing it in any way.

not scrutinize the actions of another *Bet Din,*" as the touchstone of their position.[46] That principle is adduced by Rambam in two separate contexts.

In *Hilkhot Edut* 6:4 Rambam writes:

> [If] a *Bet Din* has written "We were assembled as a tribunal and this instrument was authenticated before us" [the instrument] is authenticated even though [the *Bet Din*] has not made explicit in which of the five manners it has been authenticated for one does not say that a *Bet Din* may have erred. But it has been the practice of all *Batei Din* that we have observed and of whom we have heard to write the manner in which [the instrument] has been authenticated before them.

With regard to the particular matter of authentication of instruments, Rambam clearly rules that, as a matter of normative law, details need not be spelled out; explication would be purposeless because the action of the *Bet Din* in authenticating the instrument is not subject to review by any other body. Nevertheless, it has become an established practice to indicate the mode of authentication employed, presumably as a means of assuring confidence in the competence of the *Bet Din* and its fidelity to established rules of procedure.

In *Hilkhot Edut* 6:5, Rambam codifies the general rule:

> A *Bet Din* never examines [the actions] of another *Bet Din.* Rather, it assumes them to be proficient and not susceptible to error. Witnesses, however, are examined.

Rambam's language is somewhat ambiguous. It is unclear whether Rambam is simply stating that a *Bet Din* is entitled to give full faith and credit to the actions of another *Bet Din* on the presumption that all *Batei Din* are competent but, should a *Bet Din* choose to conduct its own independent investigation, it is entitled to do so, or whether Rambam's statement constitutes a declaration that the second *Bet Din* must rely upon the determination of the first *Bet Din* and is precluded from conducting

46. See, however, the responsum of R. David ibn Zimra, published in *Avkat Rokhel,* no. 21, as well as in *Teshuvot Mabit,* II, as an addendum to no. 172, in which that authority asserts that this principle was operative only in days of yore but "now that [judges] are not so proficient in law, we therefore scrutinize the actions of a *Bet Din.*" This is also the opinion of R. Chaim Pelaggi, *Teshuvot Semikhah le-Ḥayyim,* no. 9. See also, *idem, Teshuvot Ḥikekei Lev,* II, no. 17. That view is rejected by *Urim ve-Tumim, Urim* I, 19:3.

its own inquiry. Rephrased, the issue is whether there is no provision for an appeal for a rehearing before a second *Bet Din* as a matter of right but that an appeal for a rehearing may nevertheless be granted at the discretion of the second *Bet Din* or whether an appeal is entirely precluded. If the principle "a *Bet Din* does not scrutinize the actions of another *Bet Din*" does indeed serve to establish that such scrutiny is prohibited, the prohibition is presumably based upon a concern that the scrutiny itself, regardless of the outcome, would tarnish the prestige and standing of the first *Bet Din* (*ziluta de-bei dina*).

The principle "a *Bet Din* does not scrutinize the actions of another *Bet Din*" is formulated by the Gemara, *Baba Batra* 138b, in its analysis of a rule pertaining to the issuance of a certificate of *ḥaliẓah* and the like:

> Rava said, "*Ḥaliẓah* may not be performed unless the [*Bet Din*] knows [the widow and her brother-in-law]. Consequently, [the witnesses] may write a certificate of *ḥaliẓah* . . . even though they do not know [the parties].

That principle is enunciated in response to a query with regard to whether the prohibition against performing *ḥaliẓah* unless the parties are known and recognized by the *Bet Din* was instituted to protect against an "erring court," i.e., lest a second court permit the woman to remarry without determining that *ḥaliẓah* was indeed performed by the proper parties. In posing this question, the Gemara assumes that every *Bet Din* is obligated to conduct its own investigation into the identity of the parties and that the restriction placed upon the *Bet Din* performing the *ḥaliẓah* is a precautionary measure designed to protect against an "erring court" that does not properly discharge its duties by undertaking such an investigation. To this query the Gemara responds, "No, a *Bet Din* does not scrutinize the actions of another *Bet Din*."[47]

47. In the accompanying discussion, the Gemara states that witnesses may commit a certain matter to writing because "we do not suspect that a *Bet Din* will err" in acting upon the writing without additional testimony. The Gemara permits witnesses to a deathbed statement to record that the patient asserted on his deathbed that a certain person owed him a debt. The purpose of committing the assertion to writing is to preserve the information so that the heirs may press a claim. The claim, however, is unsubstantiated since the witnesses have no substantive evidence that serves to support the allegation. Nevertheless, the Gemara states that they may record the declaration made in their presence since the *Bet Din* will not err with regard to its nature and assume that the document is evidence of the veracity of the claim. Clearly, that statement simply reflects a

Rashbam, commenting on the concluding statement of the Gemara, observes:

> Therefore, they ordained that *ḥaliẓah* not be performed unless the identity of the parties is known for, if you say that *ḥaliẓah* may be performed even if the identity of the parties is not known, there would certainly be reason to be concerned lest a *Bet Din* act in error in permitting her remarriage without examination [i.e.], a second *Bet Din* might err in thinking that the first *Bet Din* properly identified the [parties] when they performed *ḥaliẓah* since a second *Bet Din* does not examine the actions of the first *Bet Din.*

Rashbam's comments serve only to establish that a *Bet Din* may extend full faith and credit to the actions of another *Bet Din* and hence it was necessary to promulgate an ordinance forbidding *ḥaliẓah* by unidentified parties. In effect, the Sages had to choose either to permit unidentified parties to perform *ḥaliẓah* and consequently to require subsequent substantiation of the relationship between the parties by a second *Bet Din* before permitting the widow to remarry or to prohibit *ḥaliẓah* without prior identification by the *Bet Din* before which *ḥaliẓah* is performed and thereby create a presumption of validity that might be relied upon by any subsequent *Bet Din.* In order to facilitate remarriage, the Sages ordained that the investigation be conducted by the first *Bet Din*. It is evident that in order to establish such a policy it was necessary to require an investigation by the *Bet Din* performing the *ḥaliẓah* but that it would not have been necessary to *forbid* a subsequent investigation by a *Bet Din* that felt prompted to confirm the validity of the prior *ḥaliẓah.*[48]

Nevertheless, as has been cited earlier, *Sema, Ḥoshen Mishpat* 19:2, declares that when a defendant has been exonerated, a second *Bet Din* is forbidden to hear the complaint of a plaintiff. The source of that position is the Mishnah, *Rosh ha-Shanah* 25a:

presumption of judicial competence and permits individuals to comport themselves in accordance with that general presumption but does not at all establish that specific allegations of error cannot be entertained.

48. R. Ovadiah Yosef, *Yabi'a Omer*, II, *Ḥoshen Mishpat,* no. 2, sec. 8, understands the principle "a *Bet Din* does not scrutinize the actions of another *Bet Din*" as negating a requirement for such scrutiny but not as forbidding discretionary scrutiny. The earlier cited statement of *Teshuvot ha-Rosh* and *Sema* he understands as serving to prohibit a rehearing of arguments by a second *Bet Din* but not as precluding examination of the decision for possible error.

> It occurred that two [witnesses] came and said, "We saw [the moon] in the morning in the east and in the evening in the west." R. Yoḥanan ben Nuri said, "They are false witnesses." When they came to Yavneh, Rabban Gamaliel accepted them. Also, two [witnesses] came and said, "We saw [the moon] in its proper time but on the following night it was not seen" and Rabban Gamaliel accepted them. R. Dosa ben Horkanos said, "They are false witnesses. How can people testify that a woman has given birth when the next day her abdomen is between her teeth?" R. Joshua said to him, "I accept your words." Rabban Gamaliel said to him, "I decree that you come to me with your staff and your money on the day on which *Yom Kippur* falls according to your reckoning." R. Akiva went and found [R. Joshua] in distress. [R. Akiva] said to him, "I can derive that everything Rabban Gamaliel has done is valid as it says, 'These are the appointed seasons of the Lord, holy convocations which you shall proclaim in their appointed seasons' (Leviticus 23:4), i.e., whether [they are proclaimed] at their proper times or other than at their proper time, I have no appointed seasons other than these." [R. Joshua] came to R. Dosa ben Horkanos. [R. Dosa ben Horkanos] said to him, "If we examine [the decisions of] the *Bet Din* of Rabban Gamaliel we must examine the decisions of every single *Bet Din* that has existed from the time of Moses until the present."

Both R. Akiva and R. Dosa ben Horkanos recognized the possibility of error on the part of Rabban Gamaliel. R. Akiva cited Scripture in support of the principle that, with regard to sanctification of the New Moon, even an erroneous decree of the *Bet Din* is endowed with validity. That principle, however, is limited to matters pertaining to the calendric system. R. Dosa ben Horkanos, on the other hand, justified Rabban Gamaliel's citation on the basis of a broad, universal principle establishing that the announced decision of a *Bet Din* is not subject to further scrutiny.

The problem, however, is why should an erroneous decision not be rescinded? Indeed, as evidenced by the Mishnah, *Sanhedrin* 32a, there does exist a contrary rule establishing that a decision based upon a patent error of law is to be set aside. The principle announced by R. Dosa ben Horkanos contradicts the rule established by the Mishnah, *Sanhedrin* 32a, unless each of these ostensibly conflicting principles is of limited application. If so, the question that must be resolved is when is a decision of a *Bet Din* final even though it is in error and when is it to be set aside?

Rabbenu Nissim, *Avodah Zarah* 7a, cites a statement of Ra'avad dealing, not with a matter requiring adjudication by a *Bet Din,* but with a non-adversarial matter involving a determination of religious law. Ra'avad declares that upon issuance of a negative ruling by a rabbinic decisor with regard to a foodstuff of questionable *kashrut* or the like "[the decisor][49] has rendered it an object of prohibition and it cannot subsequently be rendered permissible, and even if a second decisor declares it to be permitted it is not permitted."[50] Ra'avad declares this to be the case even if the second decisor is acknowledged to be a more erudite scholar than the first. In effect, Ra'avad declares the ruling of a competent decisor to be *res judicata* and not subject to review.[51] However, Ra'avad's position is limited to situations involving a legitimate matter of doubt or requiring adjudication between conflicting opinions or precedents. Ra'avad concedes that the decision must be overruled when it is based upon a patent error of law.

Ra'avad's view reflects an extreme application of the principle enunciated by R. Dosa ben Horkanos. In his dictum, R. Dosa ben Horkanos establishes the principle that a decision in a matter requiring a *Bet Din,* once issued, acquires standing and validity even if it is in error, at least until such time as it is reversed. Accordingly, the principle "a *Bet Din* does not scrutinize the actions of another *Bet Din*" may be understood as meaning simply that the second *Bet Din* is lacking in standing and authority to initiate such review with the result that the first decision remains in effect and, even if erroneous, is, as a matter of law, entirely valid.

But why is a *Bet Din* not empowered to review the action of another *Bet Din?* R. Dosa ben Horkanos declares that, if such review were to be

49. Cf., however, *Encyclopedia Talmudit,* vol. VIII, p. 507, note 304. The author of that note infers from the comments of *Teshuvot Radbaz,* I, no. 362, and *Teshuvot Rivash,* no. 379, that they understood that it is the petitioner who, in accepting the decision of the rabbinic scholar, has rendered the item an object of prohibition.

50. For further citations of Ra'avad's view see *Encyclopedia Talmudit,* vol. VIII, p. 507, note 301. Ra'avad's position is in accordance with that of both Ramban and Rashba. Rabbenu Nissim, however, maintains that the talmudic rule is based upon considerations of "the dignity of the first [decisor]" and a fear lest "the Torah appear as two *Torot.*" Consequently, Rabbenu Nissim opines that the earlier decision may be rescinded with the acquiescence of the first authority.

51. For a discussion of whether this principle applies even in situations in which the first decisor has issued a permissive ruling see *Teshuvot Radbaz,* I, no. 362; *Teshuvot Rivash,* no. 379; and *Sedei Ḥemed, Kelalim, Ma'arekhet ha-Ḥet,* sec. 77.

undertaken, consistency would require examination of the actions of every *Bet Din* going back to the time of Moses. The Mishnah does not say that such review is precluded or prohibited. The phraseology of the Mishnah indicates only that such review is unnecessary and superfluous. That principle, however, entails postulation of a logically antecedent principle to the effect that a decision, once issued, acquires validity at least until such time as it is set aside. Only when reviewed and overturned is the previous decision nullified retroactively.[52]

The conditions for review become apparent from the previously cited discussion of the Gemara, *Baba Batra* 130b:

> Rava said to R. Papa and to R. Huna the son of R. Joshua, "If a judgment of mine comes before you and you see a refutation, do not tear it up until you come before me. If I have a reason I will tell it to you; if not, I will reverse myself. After my death, do not tear it up but neither should you derive [any matter of law] from it. Do not tear it up since, had I been there, perhaps I would have told you the reason. Do not derive [any matter of law] from it because a judge has nothing other than what his eyes behold."[53]

52. This analysis will serve to reinforce the difficulty in explaining why a blessing is not pronounced by the *Bet Din* upon issuing a judgment. Despite the fact that the Gemara, *Ketubot* 106a, indicates that issuance of a judgment constitutes the fulfillment of the commandment "With justice shall you judge your fellow" (Deuteronomy 1:16), there is no source indicating that the members of the *Bet Din* must pronounce a blessing before announcing their decision. *Teshuvot ha-Rashba,* no. 18, states that the Sages did not ordain that a blessing be pronounced upon issuance of a decision by a *Bet Din* because of a fear that the litigants might not accept the decision. See also *Bi'ur ha-Gra, Oraḥ Ḥayyim* 8:1. *Teshuvot Ḥatam Sofer, Oraḥ Ḥayyim,* no. 54, maintains that the normative rule is that, contrary to the position of the Palestinian Talmud, a blessing may be pronounced only upon completion of the *miẓvah* and such completion, he maintains, does not occur until judgment is actually executed.

On the basis of the foregoing it might be argued that, if an erroneous decision is effective and valid, it should follow that issuance of the decision itself constitutes fulfillment of the commandment whether or not it is actually implemented by the litigants.

For an analysis of the difficulties inherent in this position as well as for an alternative thesis explaining why blessings were not ordained prior to performance of certain *miẓvot* see R. Baruch ha-Levi Epstein, *Tosefet Berakhah,* Deuteronomy 1:16.

53. Rashbam, in his commentary to *Baba Batra* 131a, indicates that the reversible error contemplated by R. Papa was one of judgment rather than the result of ignorance of a point of law. This is evident from Rashbam's use of the phrase

Clearly, this discussion envisions a review of an earlier announced decision. How did this situation differ from cases to which the general principle that a *Bet Din* does not review the decision of another *Bet Din* is applied? Undoubtedly, the answer is in the words "and you see a refutation," i.e., the general principle "a *Bet Din* does not scrutinize the actions of another *Bet Din*" serves to extend full faith and credit to the decisions of a qualified *Bet Din* on the basis of a presumption of competence and freedom from error. That principle is, in turn, but a derivative of the more general principle, "*lo maḥazakinan rei'uta,*" i.e., matters are presumed to be in good order unless there is reason to suspect otherwise.[54] That presumption is, however, rebuttable. Accordingly, when an irregularity is perceived, the decision becomes subject to review. Nevertheless, an erroneous decision, unless and until it is reversed, remains valid in the sense that a person who accepts funds on the basis of such a decision is, even in the eyes of Heaven, not guilty of theft or extortion.

Thus, the principle "a *Bet Din* does not scrutinize the actions of another *Bet Din*" must be qualified with the caveat "unless there is reason to suspect error or irregularity." Accordingly, a litigant cannot simply petition for a rehearing in the vague hope that he will prevail in a different forum. However, a litigant who advances a claim of identifiable judicial error is entitled to be heard even by a second *Bet Din* because he has identified a *rei'uta,* i.e., he has advanced a specific and cogent allegation of error, and thereby rebutted the presumption that the existing decision is error-free.

It is precisely this distinction that is formulated by *Teshuvot Ḥatam*

"for also with regard to a matter dependent upon reasoning a judge knows only that which his heart shows him." *Nimukei Yosef,* however, understands the error in question to be an error with regard to a clearly established point of law rather than an error in judgment, because, according to his opinion, a matter calling for the exercise of judgment not only cannot be reversed by another *Bet Din* but even the *Bet Din* that issued the decision is not empowered to rescind an already issued decision simply because it has changed its mind. In this, *Nimukei Yosef,* in effect, equates a decision predicated upon exercise of judgment with the rule applying to arbitration. A decision based upon arbitration rather than law, once issued, cannot be reversed or modified even by the original tribunal other than, of course, with the consent of both parties. It is for that reason that litigants cannot demand that the *Bet Din* reveal the considerations upon which an arbitration award is based. See *Koveẓ ha-Poskim,* I (New York, 5729), 295, s.v. *Be-Matteh Shimon.* Rashbam would apparently disagree with that point and maintain that, at least until judgment is executed, the original *Bet Din* retains jurisdiction and may reverse or amend its decision with regard to a matter of judgment no less so than with regard to a matter of law.

54. See, for example, *Beiẓah* 34a.

Sofer, VI, no. 50. The matter brought to the attention of *Ḥatam Sofer* involved a ruling of a communal rabbi recorded in the protocols of the community. The ruling stated that the oath of a certain individual was not to be accepted because he had been found guilty of a grave transgression. Subsequently, the rabbi died and another rabbinic figure, apparently the religious authority of another city, sought to set aside the disqualification or to reinvestigate its basis. In a short responsum, *Ḥatam Sofer* cites the Mishnah in *Rosh ha-Shanah* as establishing that a decision of a rabbinic court constitutes *res judicata* and points to the apparent contradiction of that principle inherent in the discussion recorded in *Baba Batra* 130b. *Ḥatam Sofer* resolves the contradiction by noting that the narrative recorded in *Baba Batra* refers to a decision incorporating an ostensive error. When error is apparent "a judge can act only in accordance with what his eyes behold." However, in the case brought to the attention of *Ḥatam Sofer* there existed only a memorandum of the ruling of the rabbinic authority without any indication of either the factual allegations or the halakhic considerations upon which it was based. *Ḥatam Sofer* stresses that, were error to be discovered, the deceased rabbi's ruling might indeed be set aside but that, in the absence of a record of the testimony or the halakhic provisions relied upon, the decision must be accepted at face value and is not subject to challenge.

Ḥatam Sofer notes that this principle is further reflected in the Mishnah, *Makkot* 7a, that declares, "Wherever two [witnesses] arise and declare, 'We testify that so-and-so was found guilty in such-and-such a court and that X and Y were the witnesses,' the [condemned] is to be executed." It is evident, declares *Ḥatam Sofer,* that testimony establishing that sentence has been pronounced results without further ado in the carrying out of the sentence of the *Bet Din* and, in the absence of specific evidence to the contrary, there is no basis to withhold imposition of punishment because of fear of either substantive or procedural error.

Similarly, R. Zevi Hirsch Kalisher, *M'oznayim le-Mishpat, Ḥoshen Mishpat* 19:2, asserts that a second *Bet Din* may hear a previously adjudicated dispute, but only if the *Bet Din* has found an error of law in the written decision of the first *Bet Din.*

This analysis is entirely consistent with a further statement of *Teshuvot ha-Rosh* in his previously cited responsum (*klal* 85, no. 5) to the effect that a second *Bet Din* may examine any ambiguity present in an already issued decision of an earlier *Bet Din* and the matter need not necessarily be referred back to the *Bet Din* of original jurisdiction because clarification of ambiguity represents a novel and as yet undecided issue. But the review must focus upon clarification of the ambiguity rather than upon adjudication of the issue *de nouveau.* In effect, the new proceedings are designed solely to clarify the intent of the earlier *Bet Din.*

Noteworthy is the fact that *Teshuvot ha-Rosh*'s citation of the dictum "a *Bet Din* does not scrutinize the actions of another *Bet Din*" occurs in the context of a discussion of a petition for a rehearing of the selfsame arguments presented to the *Bet Din* rather than in reference to an appeal on the basis of allegation of a particular error. This is apparent from Rosh's rhetorical query "Why have you asked for another decision with regard to a case that has already been adjudicated?" Thus, according to this analysis, Jewish law parallels other systems of law in providing for an appeal upon allegation of specific error but not simply for a rehearing of the original arguments and evidence before a different judicial body. It does, however, differ from other systems in permitting an appeal before any properly constituted tribunal rather than in formally providing for separate judicial bodies charged with the specific function of hearing appeals.

The distinction between a rehearing and an appeal is often obfuscated in discussions of the role of formal rabbinic courts of appeal that have appeared in recent times. The "appeals" permitted by the *Mishpat ha-Shalom* simply afforded a disgruntled litigant an opportunity for a rehearing. As earlier indicated, the quasi-judicial panels established by the *Mishpat ha-Shalom* did not apply a clearly defined corpus of law and hence their judgments are readily classified as arbitration awards. In Jewish law, as in other systems of law, arbitration decisions are generally not subject to appeal. Decisions of arbitrators cannot be appealed because they are inconsistent with provisions of law for the obvious reason that arbitrators are not bound to rule in accordance with the letter of the law. The procedures of the *Mishpat ha-Shalom* were innovative not only in establishing a formal appeals panel but in instituting a system of appeal with regard to decisions of arbitrators. Consistent with halakhic norms, the Chief Rabbinate, in instituting a Supreme Rabbinic Court of Appeals, provided for appeal only upon allegation of error and did not at all provide for a right of appeal when, in their original submission, the parties agree to *pesharah* or arbitration.

Recognition of a distinction between a rehearing and an appeal, despite occasional proclivity on the part of rabbinic writers for use of imprecise nomenclature, yields a clearer understanding of the comments of R. David

Pakiano, *Ḥoshen ha-Efod, Ḥoshen Mishpat,* no. 42. *Ḥoshen ha-Efod* reports that, with the institution of the office of crown rabbi in Bulgaria in 1900, a number of communal ordinances were promulgated including a provision for the appointment of "two or three" judges who together with the crown rabbi would constitute a "*Bet Din ha-Gadol.*" Thereupon, any litigant who was dissatisfied with the decision of a local *Bet Din* was permitted to relitigate before the "*Bet Din ha-Gadol.*" This procedure, *Ḥoshen ha-Efod* informs us, "is called 'appeal' in common parlance." The issue addressed by *Ḥoshen ha-Efod* involved a defendant who lost a case before the local court and demanded a hearing before the "*Bet Din ha-Gadol.*" The plaintiff who had prevailed before that tribunal argued that, since he had already appeared before a properly constituted court and his adversary had no new complaints or additional evidence, he should not be compelled to expend additional time and energy relitigating the case.

Ḥoshen ha-Efod responds that, in terms of the applicable rules of law, the demurring litigant is correct. Nevertheless, there are ample sources demonstrating that such matters may be varied on the basis of *takkanah* or communal legislation. Accordingly, since, in Bulgaria, communal ordinances made provision for such a procedure, the plaintiff may be compelled to relitigate his complaint. *Ḥoshen ha-Efod* adds that no objection can be made on the basis of inherent disrespect to members of the first tribunal, reasoning that, since all persons "know that this is a city ordinance there is no demeaning of the first *Bet Din* and from the beginning they entered with this awareness." Despite his use of the term "appeal" the procedure described by *Ḥoshen ha-Efod* is actually a rehearing. Accordingly, *Ḥoshen ha-Efod* should not be understood as asserting that appeals can be entertained only on the basis of *takkanah.* The issue of an appeal on the basis of allegation of judicial error is not at all addressed by that authority. His position with regard to the issue he does address, i.e., relitigation of the issues already resolved by an earlier court, is unexceptionable.

IV.

The authority of the Supreme Rabbinical Court of Appeals to sit as a court of appeals in accordance with the provisions of Jewish law was challenged in a number of proceedings before that body.[55] Although a court of appeals was instituted immediately upon establishment of the Chief Rabbinate Council, apparently its powers and procedures were not formally set forth by the Chief Rabbinate Council until the publication of its *Takkanot ha-Diyyun be-Batei ha-Din ha-Rabbaniyim* in 5703.[56] In a matter brought before the Supreme Rabbinical Court in 5702, the appellee apparently argued that the Court's authority was derived from, and therefore circumscribed by, the Rabbinical Courts Act. Accordingly, it was argued, the appellate power of the Supreme Rabbinical Court must be regarded as limited to appeals in cases heard by the rabbinical district courts on the basis of the authority vested in such judicial bodies by the law of the civil government. However, it was argued, in actions in which the parties were not bound to the jurisdiction of that body by virtue of the provisions of civil law but had recourse to rabbinic courts of their own volition, no appeal can be allowed. The argument seems to have been that the appellate powers of the Supreme Rabbinical Court are entirely a matter of civil law, without basis in Halakhah, and hence do not extend, even as a matter of civil law, to matters over which the law does not grant judicial authority to the rabbinical courts.[57] The Court rejected this argument

55. See also the comments of R. Israel Schepansky, *Ha-Takkanot be-Yisra'el* (Jerusalem, 5753), IV, 218, who writes concerning the establishment of a *Bet Din* for appeals that "it is difficult to find a source or reason for it in the works of the decisors."

56. The *Takkanot ha-Diyyun,* although not published until 5703, were apparently promulgated by the Chief Rabbinate Council on 2 Elul 5701 and became effective as of the beginning of 5702. See Shochetman, "Ḥovat ha-Hanmakah," p. 369.

57. Despite the fact that this argument was rejected in the decision of 5702, in a subsequent unpublished decision issued in 5716 the Supreme Rabbinical Court ruled that it had no authority to hear appeals in "non-adversarial" matters, i.e., in determining issues of Jewish religious law since such matters are not within the ambit of authority granted to the *Bet Din* by virtue of the civil law. The issue before the court involved the conversion of a minor child by its Jewish father in face of the announced opposition of its non-Jewish mother. The district court declared that it was not acting by virtue of the powers vested in a *Bet Din* to adjudicate disputes but was simply announcing a matter of religious law. The Supreme Rabbinical Court ruled that such matters are not subject to appeal. See Eliav Shochetman, *Seder ha-Din* (*Civil Practice in Jewish Law*) (Jerusalem, 5748), p. 450.

declaring:

> We have already made known many times that the *takkanah* [establishing] a *Bet Din* for appeals has been accepted without any reservation. Such was the practice introduced by our predecessors and we are not permitted to change [the practice] since all who appear for adjudication appear on that basis. This argument was presented before the [civil] court in Haifa and rejected; therefore we are obliged to accept all appeals even as a point of [civil] law.[58]

The Supreme Rabbinical Court herein advances two separate grounds for its appellate jurisdiction: 1) powers derived from *takkanah,* i.e., rabbinic legislation promulgated by the Chief Rabbinical Council[59]—a body that in the early years of its existence did not hesitate to assert legislative power as the designated rabbinical authority of the yishuv;[60] and 2) voluntary acceptance of its appellate authority by the parties to the litigation. In formulating the latter argument, the Supreme Rabbinical Court presumably reasons that such acceptance is implied by the appearance of the parties since the right of appeal is commonly known to be acknowledged by the rabbinic courts. That argument is, however, subject to challenge, or at least would have been subject to challenge in the first such appeal brought before the Supreme Rabbinical Court, on the grounds that a right of appeal in matters not governed by the Rabbinical Courts Act had as yet not been established. The weakness inherent in any argument based upon voluntary acceptance of such procedures by the litigants is that, at the time of their original submission to the authority of the *Bet Din,* either party might disavow any such acceptance and thereby deny his adversary the right of appeal.

In a subsequent decision handed down in 5734 the Supreme Rabbinical Court formulated the argument somewhat differently:

---

58. Unpublished decision, docket number 1/46/701, bearing the signatures of the members of the court including the Chief Rabbi, R. Isaac ha-Levi Herzog, cited by Shochetman, *Seder ha-Din,* p. 449.

59. In another unpublished decision, Rabbi Herzog describes the power of the Supreme Rabbinical Court of Appeals as grounded in communal legislation (*takkanot ha-kahal*). See Shochetman, *Seder ha-Din,* p. 450, note 32.

60. For a list of *takkanot* promulgated by the Chief Rabbinate Council see Menahem Elon, *Ha-Mishpat ha-Ivri* (Jerusalem, 5738), I, 667–676. See also Yitzchak Kister, *Torah she-be-'al Peh,* XII (5730), 49–57.

> In every decision there are two principles upon which the *Bet Din* for Appeals nullifies the decision of the district *Bet Din:* First, on the strength of the *Takkanot ha-Diyyun* and with that knowledge the parties litigate, [*viz.,*] that if there is an erroneous judgment the *Bet Din* of Appeals will examine the problem anew. . . . Secondly, since such was established by the *Takkanot ha-Diyyun,* it may be said that the [district] *Bet Din* ruled *ab initio* with that intention [i.e., that its judgment be given effect only if there is] no appeal to the Supreme Rabbinical Court.[61]

In this decision, the two grounds set forth in the 5702 decision are folded into a single argument in which the legislative authority relied upon is the explicit provisions of the *Takkanot ha-Diyyun* of 5703 rather than the earlier amorphous legislative action implied by the *ad hoc* establishment of the appellate court in 1921.[62] Implied acceptance of the authority of the appellate court, posited as an independent argument in 5702, is here incorporated in the first argument. The second argument advanced in the 5734 decision focuses upon the intent of the lower court rather than upon the intent of the litigants and, in effect, declares that, in light of the established right of appeal, all decisions of district *Batei Din* are conditional in nature.[63] The Supreme Rabbinic Court is herein relying

61. *Piskei Din shel Batei ha-Din ha-Rabbaniyim,* X, 180.

62. In another unpublished decision dated 5708, the Supreme Rabbinic Court, of which Rabbi Herzog was still a member, refused to hear an appeal from a decision of the *Edah ha-Ḥaredit* on the grounds that the *Takkanot ha-Diyyun* of 5703 apply only to cases heard by the *Batei Din* established by the State, although it is by no means obvious that such was the case. See Shochetman, p. 449, note 31 . No reference is made in that decision to an earlier *takkanah* of the Chief Rabbinate Council although, arguably, that *takkanah* might also be regarded as limited in scope. The matter is of course further complicated by the fact that the *Edah ha-Ḥaredit* does not acknowledge the authority of the Chief Rabbinate.

63. The difficulty presented by the second argument lies in the source of the appellate court's authority to issue a new verdict subsequent to hearing the appeal. If it is contended that the filing of an appeal has the effect, not simply of staying the decision of the trial court, but of rendering it entirely nugatory, it follows that the judgment of the appellate court does not serve to confirm or to rescind the judgment of the trial court but becomes the sole judicial decision in the case. The authority of the appellate court might then be regarded as predicated upon the original acceptance of the established judicial process on the part of the litigants in their original appearance, including the authority of the appellate court to issue its own decision. Alternatively, the appeals court might, in effect, constitute itself as a communally designated court of original jurisdiction that is

upon an unstated premise, *viz.,* that a *Bet Din* is halakhically empowered to issue a binding, conditional judgment of this nature, i.e., to issue a judgment that becomes final only upon acceptance by both parties as evidenced by failure to lodge an appeal within the prescribed time.

In a short and succinct published decision handed down on 9 Tevet 5705, the Supreme Rabbinical Court rejected a motion to dismiss an appeal on the grounds that, absent an explicit agreement at the time of submission to the authority of the trial court, there exists no right of appeal in Jewish law and declared:

> The *Bet Din ha-Gadol* finds that it does have the authority to judge this appeal since the matter of appeals has been accepted as a *takkanah* of the Sages,[64] whose binding effect is like the law of our holy Torah and all who enter into litigation enter with the intention [to accept an appeal].[65]

On the basis of the foregoing analysis, it may argued that the appellate power of the Supreme Rabbinical Court is firmly grounded in Halakhah. §135 of the *Takkanot ha-Diyyun* of 5753 provides that appeals may be heard upon allegations of: 1) halakhic error; 2) egregious error (*ta'ut ha-nir'et la-'ayin*) in judgment or in the establishment of facts; or 3) procedural defects having an effect on the results of the litigation.[66]

---

empowered to compel litigants to submit to its jurisdiction. This explanation does not, however, serve to resolve the problem since a court of original jurisdiction is forbidden to issue a decision without hearing the parties and examining witnesses who must personally appear before them. Accordingly, it is more likely that, in formulating this argument, the Supreme Rabbinical Court intended to assert that, in cases of appeal, the original judgment of the district *Batei Din* is rendered conditional subject to confirmation by the appellate court. That contention, however, serves to provide a basis only for confirmation or reversal by the appellate court, but not for modification of a judgment or reversal in part and confirmation in part. Such judgments are properly to be regarded as decisions of the appellate court rather than as decisions of the trial court. Hence the cogency of this argument in establishing the authority of the Supreme Rabbinical Court to act in such a manner remains unclear.

64. For a discussion of the halakhic scope of the authority of the Chief Rabbinate see R. Saul Israeli, *Shanah be-Shanah,* 5724, pp. 175–186, and I. Englard, *Ha-Praklit,* XXII (5726), 68–79. See also *Piskei Din Rabbaniyim,* X, 14 and Shochetman, "Ḥovat ha-Hanmakah, p. 370, note 168.

65. *Osef Piskei Din,* ed. Z. Warhaftig (Jerusalem, 5710), p. 71.

66. Identical language appears in §122 of the *Takkanot ha-Diyyun* of 5720. The original *Takkanot ha-Diyyun* of 5703 is silent with regards to grounds for

Procedural defects having a decisive effect upon the judgment of the *Bet Din* are indeed errors of Halakhah warranting reversal of the decision. Similarly, *Teshuvot Rivash,* no. 498 and *Shakh, Ḥoshen Mishpat* 25:9, rule that factual errors are to be equated with errors of law. Assuming that the phrase "error of judgment" (*ta'ut be-shikul ha-da'at*) is used in the sense of its talmudic meaning, i.e., in the sense of error of judgment in choosing between conflicting authority or precedent, that, too, may be tantamount to an error of law. *Tashbaẓ,* II, no. 272, rules that a ruling issued in reliance upon an opinion that is in conflict with the established judicial determination in a given locale is to be treated as an error with regard to a matter of law. That ruling, however, is disputed by *Shakh, Ḥoshen Mishpat* 25:10; *Urim ve-Tumim, Urim* 25:11; and *Netivot ha-Mishpat, Ḥiddushim* 25:11.

Thus, at least insofar as an appeal based upon an allegation of specific halakhic or factual error is concerned, the right of appeal would appear to be well-grounded in Halakhah and reliance upon *takkanah* or presumed acquiescence of the parties would be unnecessary. *Takkanah,* however, remains operative in another sense. When an error of law is alleged, the litigant is entitled to seek out any *Bet Din* of his choice in order to nullify the original decision. The *Takkanot ha-Diyyun* provide that appeals can be brought only before the Supreme Rabbinical Court. In effect, the establishment of a formal appeals court constitutes a *takkanah* depriving other courts of the right to hear the appeal.

It must also be noted that the earlier presented analysis does not reflect the position of all authorities. As cited earlier, *Tashbaẓ,* III, no. 165, maintains that the *Bet Din* having original jurisdiction must acknowledge its error in order to vacate the judgment. *Tashbaẓ* adduces the principle "a *Bet Din* does not scrutinize the actions of another *Bet Din*" in ruling that a decision of a *Bet Din* can be reversed on grounds of error only if the first *Bet Din* still exists and can be prevailed upon to concede its error. Similarly, Mahari Katz, cited in *Shitah Mekubeẓet, Baba Kamma* 12a, indicates that it was for this reason that, as recorded by the Gemara, *Ketubot* 50b, Rav Nachman admonished the judges of Nehardea to reverse themselves.[67] According to these authorities, reversal of a decision can be compelled only on the basis of *takkanah.* On the other hand, Rif and *Ba'al ha-Ma'or, Sanhedrin* 33a, Rosh, *Sanhedrin* 4:6 and *Yad Ramah, Sanhedrin* 33a, maintain that a scholar who is greater in wisdom and

appeal.

67. See also *Ḥazon Ish, Sanhedrin* 16:10.

stature may overturn a judgment on grounds of judicial error with regard to a matter of law even if the judge who issued the original verdict does not acknowledge his error. *Ḥazon Ish, Sanhedrin* 16:17, understands the position of *Tosafot, Ketubot* 50b, to be that a person appointed by the Exilarch as a judge over the entire country or province and to whom other judges are subservient enjoys that power. In the State of Israel, such status is certainly enjoyed by the Supreme Rabbinical Court.

Chapter III
Checks

A mortal examines his legal documents. If he finds that others owe him money, he produces his documents and collects from them; if he finds that he is liable to others, he suppresses the document and does not produce it. But with the Holy One, blessed be He, this is not so; when He finds that we are indebted to Him, He suppresses it . . . but, if He discovers something in our favor, He immediately produces it.
SHEMOT RABBAH 25:6

During the course of 5747, a sabbatical year, many technical questions, both old and new, with regard to observance of the laws of *shemittah* became topical issues. Somewhat tangentially, the status of checks in Jewish law also received renewed attention in the context of those discussions.[1] "Every creditor shall release that which he has lent unto his neighbor; he shall not exact from his friend and his brother" (Deuteronomy 15:2) serves as an injunction not to demand repayment of loans that remain outstanding during the course of the sabbatical year. An examination of the nature and function of a check is prompted by the question of whether a person who has received a check, but who has not cashed it prior to the close of the sabbatical year, may present the check for payment after *Rosh ha-Shanah* i.e., after expiration of the sabbatical year. Of course, as is the case with regard to all outstanding debts, the recipient of a check has the option of executing a *prozbol, viz.,* a device designed to permit the collection of debts after the expiration of the sabbatical year by means of a *pro forma* assignment of the debt to a rabbinic court. The identical question can thus be reformulated as a query as to whether it is necessary for the recipient of a check to execute a *prozbol* in order to be permitted to present the draft for payment after the sabbatical year has drawn to a close.

1. I am indebted to my son Moshe whose work in preparation of a paper on *prozbol* spurred my interest in this topic.

I. *Checks Presented as Gifts or as Payment for Merchandise*

Although, as will be shown, some scholars disagree, ostensibly there is no occasion to raise this question with regard to a check accepted in repayment of funds advanced as a loan. The underlying loan is cancelled by operation of the laws of *shemittah* and hence it is not permitted to present the check for payment. Rather, the question arises with regard to checks which are presented in the form of a gift, including, but not limited to, gifts on the occasion of a wedding, *bar mizvah,* or the like. The concern is that the issuance of a check may, in and of itself, constitute the generation of a debt; if so, cashing the check becomes tantamount to collecting a debt.

A similar question arises with regard to cashing a check that has been accepted as payment for merchandise. Ordinarily, the sabbatical year serves only as a release from repayment of loans or similar personal obligations. Obligations arising out of a commercial transaction are not cancelled unless the obligation has been converted to an ordinary personal debt. Issuance of a check, it may be contended, constitutes such a conversion, i.e., the commercial obligation is converted to an ordinary debt that is newly assumed by the obligee by virtue of issuance of the check. If this argument is accepted, a businessman would be constrained (in the absence of a *prozbol)* not to accept a check as payment for merchandise in the waning days of a sabbatical year unless he is confident that he will be able to present the check for collection prior to *Rosh ha-Shanah.* The same question in another guise arises with regard to wage earners or salaried employees who are paid by check. Payment of wages and salaries is ordinarily not forgiven by operation of the laws of *shemittah.* However, when wages are converted to ordinary debts, such obligations are extinguished upon the expiration of the *shemittah* year. The issuance of a check, it is argued, is tantamount to conversion of the existing obligation to a personal loan. If so, the employee would not be permitted to cash the check after *Rosh ha-Shanah* unless, of course, he had the foresight to execute a *prozbol* before *Rosh ha-Shanah.*

Rabbi Moshe Nachum Spira, author of a comprehensive two-volume work, *Mishnat Kesef* (Jerusalem, 5726 and 5733), devoted to a detailed analysis of laws pertaining to the release of debts at the close of the sabbatical year, has recently published *Dinei Shemittat Kesafim u-Prozbol,* a brief compendium of the operative regulations governing this area of

Halakhah. Appended to this publication, under the title *Kuntres Devar ha-Shemittah—Birurei Halakhah,* is a detailed discussion of the laws of *shemittah* as they bear upon the banking system. In the third chapter of his *Kuntres Devar ha-Shemittah,* Rabbi Spira asserts that all checks, including those given as gifts, must be cashed before *Rosh ha-Shanah* unless the payee has executed a *prozbol.* He bases this position upon the contention that every check, regardless of the purpose for which it is issued, constitutes a binding promissory note generating a personal debt.

As will be shown, Rabbi Spira's conclusions must be regarded as limited to checks issued and accepted with the presumption that the nature of the instrument is to be construed in accordance with Israeli law. Rabbi Spira's categorization of the nature and status of a check is incorrect insofar as the law in the United States as well as in most common law jurisdictions is concerned, and hence entirely different conclusions must be reached in applying the laws of *shemittah* with regard to gifts made in the United States in the form of a check. It must be noted that, in American law, checks and promissory notes are not identical instruments. A note is an undertaking by the maker to pay a specified sum. A check is an order to a third party, *viz.,* the bank, to deliver a specified sum to the person named in the instrument. It is indeed true that the law construes a check as a contract by means of which the drawer covenants with the payee that, upon presentation, the bank will pay the stipulated amount to the latter.[2] Nevertheless, common law provides that, to be a binding obligation on the drawer, the check must be supported by consideration. Absent consideration, the check is "a mere naked promise unenforceable in law."[3] In American law this provision is codified in U.C.C. §3–408. Thus, a check presented as a gift generates no legal obligation.[4] At least in the case of a check presented as a gift, a person may change his mind for any

2. See Henry J. Bailey, *Brady on Bank Checks* (Boston, 1979), p. 1–15.

3. See *Brady,* pp. 6–2 and 6–3. As early as 1865, in a decision rendered in *Jones* v. *Lock* (Eng. 1865) 14 W.R. 149, a British court found that the delivery of a check by the drawer to the payee is nothing more than a promise which cannot be enforced by the payee. In that case, a father, on returning from a journey, placed a check for £900 in the hands of his infant son and declared in the presence of the baby's mother and his nurse, "I give this to baby; it is for himself and I am going to put it away for him." He then placed the check in a locked safe and shortly thereafter died suddenly. The Court ruled that there was neither a gift to, nor a valid declaration of trust in favor of, the infant. See *Brady,* p. 6–33.

4. Nevertheless, lack of consideration is not a defense against a holder in due course of a check. See U.C.C. §3–408.

reason, or for no reason, and stop payment without incurring any penalty whatsoever. Checks issued in the form of a gift and checks issued in satisfaction of a debt constitute one and the same instrument. Although Jewish law, in general, recognizes no requirement of consideration in order to establish a binding obligation, it does require language of obligation in order to generate a gratuitous liability. The language of a check is not the language of a promissory note and declares no obligation; it merely directs payment by a third party. Nor can it be argued that, although defective insofar as intrinsic provisions of Jewish law are concerned, the issuance of a check nevertheless generates a binding obligation by virtue of *dina de-malkhuta* (the law of the land) or by virtue of custom and practice. Such an argument would be specious since, absent consideration, there exists no legal obligation.

Some confusion with regard to the halakhic status of a check arises by virtue of its similarity to two other instruments well-known in the annals of Jewish law. The earlier of these instruments probably originated in Spain during the Middle Ages. Known as a *mukaz,* an acronym of the words "*moẓi ketav zeh*" ("whosoever presents this writing"), signifying that the face amount is payable to the bearer, that instrument was, to all intents and purposes, a fully negotiable promissory note.[5] Unlike other forms of indebtedness, it could be assigned simply by delivery, whereas title to debts represented by other instruments could be assigned only by

5. In the absence of formal assignment of the debt by *kinyan* the theory on which a course of action could be sustained by the bearer who is not in a relation of privity with the maker is discussed by *Keẓot ha-Ḥoshen* 61:3. The instruments in question were regarded as the equivalent of a promissory note couched in the formula "I obligate myself to you and to all who come through you," which, in turn, has its source in a statement of R. Huna, *Baba Batra* 172a. Early authorities advanced three theories for the actionability of such instruments:

1) The efficacy is solely by virtue of rabbinic decree.
2) The bearer is, in effect, the agent of the obligee.
3) The indebtedness is deemed *ab initio* to have been to the bearer, i.e., the bearer is a third party beneficiary of the contract between the debtor and creditor. The contract does not fail for reason of indefiniteness (*bereirah*), argues *Keẓot ha-Ḥoshen,* because each and every human being might acquire the instrument in turn. Hence, since no one is necessarily excluded from being the beneficiary of the obligation, it is not regarded as lacking in determinacy or definitiveness. According to this theory, the actionability on the part of a bearer who was yet unborn at the time of the execution of the instrument would be problematic in light of the provision of Jewish law that stipulates that no obligation can be incurred in favor of an as yet nonexisting person. See also *Netivot ha-Mishpat* 61:3.

formal conveyance, e.g., written assignment.

During the medieval period another instrument having a strong resemblance to the modern bill of exchange came into use. The term by which that document is known is spelled variously as MMRI, MMRM or MMRN. MMRI is presumably a corruption of one of the other forms. Since vowels are omitted in written Hebrew, the vocalization may be either "*mamram,*" "*mamran,* "*mamrem,*" "*mamren,*" or even "*memorem.*" The etymology of the word is obscure. It has been suggested that the term is derived from the word "*membrana,*" the name given to the parchment on which a bond was commonly written. The term might also have been derived from the Latin phrase "*in memoriam,*" and hence it may parallel the term *shetar zekhirah* mentioned in *Tur Shulḥan Arukh, Ḥoshen Mishpat* 61:3. It has also been suggested that the term is really an abbreviation or an acronym. It is also possible that the term is derived from the Hebrew verb "*le-hamir*" meaning "to change."[6]

The *mamram* was in common use by the sixteenth century. The earliest reference to this document within the mainstream of rabbinic literature occurs in *Levush, Ḥoshen Mishpat* 48:1. A subsequent reference is found in *Sema, Ḥoshen Mishpat* 48:1.[7] Unlike other legal instruments, the *mamram* is a two-sided document. One side contains the signature of the debtor or the signatures of the witnesses; the amount of the debt and the date on which payment is due are recorded on the reverse side. There is no mention of consideration, the reason for execution of the note, the name of the creditor or the place of payment. As a result it may be transferred without written assignment or endorsement and hence, in its function, closely resembles a modern-day bill of exchange.

Later there developed an even more radical innovation, the blank or open *mamram.* This instrument contained only a signature. The amount of the debt and the due date were left blank when delivered by the debtor and were later filled in by the creditor himself. In usage such an instrument is readily comparable to a customer's delivery of a blank, signed check

6. See sources cited in "Mamram," *Encyclopedia Judaica* (Jerusalem, 1974), VI, 838–39, and Marcus Cohen, "Mamren," *Universal Jewish Encyclopedia* (New York, 1942), VII, 308; cf. Gotthard Deutsch, "Mamran," *The Jewish Encyclopedia,* VIII (New York, 1904), 278–79.

7. A much earlier reference to this instrument occurs in a work of R. Elchanan ben Isaac of Dampierre, *Tosafot Rabbenu Elḥanan, Avodah Zarah* 2a, s.v. *ve-lifro'a me-hen.* The comments of R. Elchanan reveal that the *mamram* was well-known in his day. However, *Tosafot Rabbenu Elḥanan* was not published until 1901 and hence is not cited in earlier rabbinic discussions.

to a merchant or supplier and leaving it to the latter to total the purchases and fill in the proper amount. It is quite possible that the open *mamram* was utilized in a similar manner in order to facilitate trade at public fairs which often took place over an extended period of time. However, from the comments of R. Joel Sirkes, *Teshuvot ha*-Baḥ, no. 32, it appears that the open *mamram* was really used in a manner analogous to operation of the open letter of credit of modern bankers. The person issuing the *mamram* was not the customer but a third party who lent his name and credit to the bearer. Although the maker was fully bound, the obligation would, in actuality, be satisfied by the true obligor whose name did not appear on the instrument. The maker was thus, in effect, an accommodation party and the service rendered was much like that of a commercial banker. *Shakh, Ḥoshen Mishpat* 48:2, declares that, unlike a usual *shetar* or promissory note, use of a *mamram* was not limited to a single transaction. Upon satisfaction of the debt there was no need for it to be destroyed; rather, it might be reissued and circulated anew. Thus, the *mamram* could be treated as a bank note and indeed the effect of the circulation of such instruments was to create a rudimentary banking system.[8]

The difference between a *mamram* and a check is obvious: it is precisely the difference between a personal bill of exchange or letter of credit and a check. The former are instruments which generate obligations. Checks ostensibly direct a bailee to transfer funds to a third party as designated by the bailor. However, in actuality and as a matter of law, the bank holds funds in checking accounts not as a bailee but as a borrower; the bank lends those funds to its own customers and generates profits thereby. Were the bank a bailee, such use would constitute unlawful conversion. Hence issuance of a check is simply an authorization of a third party to accept repayment of a loan on behalf of the creditor and an acknowledgment to the bank that it will be released thereby.

Israeli law governing contracts differs from American and common law, at least since amendment of the governing statute by the Israeli Knesset in 1973. Under present Israeli law, a contract need not be supported by consideration in order to be binding.[9] Moreover, Israeli law expressly

8. See George Horowitz, *The Spirit of Jewish Law* (New York, 1973), pp. 516–517.

9. See *Ḥok ha-Ḥozim,* (5733–1973), *Ḥelek Kelali.* Whether or not consideration was necessary prior to this amendment of the statute is a matter of some dispute. See Zev Zeltner, *Dinei Ḥozim shel Medinat Yisra'el* (Tel Aviv, 5734), I, 179; Daniel Friedman, "Torat ha-Temurah ba-Ḥakikah ha-Yisra'elit ha-Ḥadashah," *Iyyunei Mishpat,* III, 153ff; and Joel Sussman, *Dinei Shetarot* (Jerusalem, 5743),

categorizes a check as one of the various forms of a promissory note.[10] Thus, under Israeli law, a check is more than a directive to a third party to deliver funds. It serves concomitantly as an instrument generating an obligation. It then logically follows that, since consideration is unnecessary, even a check presented as a gift represents an actionable obligation in Israeli law. Since Halakhah similarly recognizes the validity of a unilateral obligation not supported by consideration, it may cogently be argued that a check drawn in Israel does indeed generate an obligation in Jewish law. Although the language of the instrument does not ostensibly employ terms of obligation, nevertheless, since usage and practice in Israeli commercial circles reflect Israeli law in treating a check as a promissory note, a check may be construed as a promissory note for purposes of Jewish law as well. Accordingly, it is reasonable to conclude that, in Israel, laws of *shemittah* apply to all uncashed checks, including checks presented by the drawer as a gift.[11]

The status of a check accepted as payment of wages or in return for merchandise is somewhat different insofar as the laws of *shemittah* are concerned. *Shemittah* does not ordinarily discharge obligations with regard to money owed as compensation for personal services or in exchange for merchandise. However, as noted earlier, such obligations are discharged if converted to an ordinary, personal debt. Rema, *Ḥoshen Mishpat* 67:14, records two opinions with regard to how such conversion is accomplished. The first opinion regards conversion as effected upon express stipulation of a date on which payment is to be due; the second opinion regards mere recording in a ledger of the total sum due and owing as conversion into an ordinary debt. Rabbi Spira, in his comprehensive work on the cancellation of debts by operation of the laws of *shemittah, Mishnat Kesef,* II, 67:14, *Panim Ḥadashot,* sec. 18, following R. Benjamin Silber, *Hilkhot Shevi'it,* II (Bnei Brak, 5726), 10:22, sec. 65, asserts that issuance of a check in payment of such obligations constitutes conversion according to all authorities.

---

p. 117.

10. *Pekudat ha-Shetarot (Nusaḥ Ḥadash)* §1.

11. An interesting ramification occurs in applying these principles to a case in which a check representing a gift is drawn on an American bank but presented in Israel. Israeli law appears to provide that the nature of the check is to be construed in accordance with the law of the locale in which the check is delivered. See *Pekudat ha-Shetarot (Nusaḥ Ḥadash)* §72(1).

II. *Checks Accepted in Repayment of Loans*

In sharp contradiction to this position, a number of authorities maintain that, even with regard to a personal loan, once a check has been issued the debt is not extinguished at the close of the sabbatical year even if the check has as yet not been presented for payment. Such a conclusion may be reached upon either of two arguments. The first argument was originally advanced with regard to the status of a check in conjunction with the prohibition against usury (*ribbit*) and may be formulated as follows: Acceptance of a loan in return for a promissory note requiring payment of a larger sum is clearly *ribbit.* However, discounting a promissory note issued by a third party does not constitute a violation of this prohibition even though the funds are not immediately collectible and the discount demanded reflects this fact. The funds advanced in return for the note are not construed as a loan to be satisfied with interest upon collection of the face amount on the date due, but as the purchase price of an object (*viz.,* an outstanding third-party debt) at its present value. The crucial distinction between such a transaction and a loan lies in the fact that a debt held by a creditor constitutes an object of value and may be transferred to another party by way of sale or assignment. Once the debt has been assigned, the successor has no recourse against the original creditor in the event that the debt is not satisfied unless, of course, pertinent facts have been withheld fraudulently from the assignee.[12] The very nature of a sale demands that attendant risks be borne by the purchaser. Were the assignee to have recourse against the assignor, the transaction, to all intents and purposes, would really be in the nature of a loan with the promissory note serving only as a form of collateral.

Quite obviously, discounting one's own promissory note does not avoid the prohibition against interest-taking. Execution of one's own note constitutes acceptance of a loan, not the initiation of a sale. Moreover, under such circumstances, the assignor, who is the maker, remains liable in case of default. Nevertheless, R. Raphael Joseph Hazan, *Ḥikrei Lev, Ḥoshen Mishpat,* II, no. 155, reports that he found it to be common practice for persons traveling on business to seek cash from business associates in the locale in which they found themselves. In return, the traveler issued a document directing his commercial agent to deliver a larger sum of money on a specified date. On first examination it would

12. See *Teshuvot Maharam Shik, Yoreh De'ah,* no. 161 and *Teshuvot Ketav Sofer, Yoreh De'ah,* no. 85.

appear that such a practice should be regarded as a prohibited form of interest-taking. Ostensibly, the agent is a bailee and his principal is, in fact, using his own bailed funds for repayment of an interest-bearing loan. Nevertheless, *Ḥikrei Lev* points out that, until such time as return of the funds are demanded by the principal, the commercial agents involved in these arrangements are vested with full authority to convert the funds entrusted to them to their own use. Hence, argues *Ḥikrei Lev,* the agent's status and liability are those of a debtor, not of a bailee. Thus, concludes *Ḥikrei Lev,* the instrument directing payment to the principal's assignee constitutes, in effect, the sale of a debt to a third party. Accordingly, *Ḥikrei Lev* justifies this practice provided that the nature of the transaction as the sale or assignment of a debt is expressly acknowledged, that a valid form of conveyance or assignment is employed and that, in case of default, the assignee is denied recourse against the maker of the instrument.

In a treatise on usury in Jewish law that has become a modern-day classic, R. Jacob Blau, *Berit Yehudah* 15:17, notes 38–39, argues that contemporary checks are identical in their halakhic status with the instruments described by *Ḥikrei Lev.* The bank does not hold funds as a "deposit" or bailment; rather, since it is authorized to lend those funds to its own customers, the bank stands as a debtor vis-à-vis its depositors. Hence, argues *Berit Yehudah,* delivery of a check is actually the assignment of a debt. *Berit Yehudah* pertinently adds that a check can be construed as an assignment of a debt only if the bank does in fact actually owe the depositor money, i.e., if there is a cash balance in the depositor's account. If, however, the check is drawn against overdraft privileges it can hardly be construed as an assignment of a debt since, in such a situation, the bank owes the depositor nothing. According to *Berit Yehudah,* a person with funds in his account may accept cash in return for a check drawn for a larger amount provided that the check is not postdated and hence is immediately payable. In his opinion, such a transaction is the assignment of a debt rather than instruction to an agent to repay a debt with bailed funds.

The implications of this position for the discharge of debts during the sabbatical year is obvious. Repayment of a loan with a check issued by a third party, it may be argued, serves to discharge the debt. Endorsement of the check to the creditor is tantamount to satisfying the obligation through the assignment of a third-party debt as full payment. Since the debt has been satisfied there is no longer an outstanding debt to be released by means of the sabbatical year. If the writing of the check is regarded as assignment of a debt due and owing the maker by the bank, the same result would obtain even when payment is in the form of a check issued by the debtor himself. Thus, since the debt has been satisfied by the very issuance of the check, it may be presented to the bank for payment even after the close of the sabbatical year. (This is, of course, true only if the bank in question is owned by non-Jews. Otherwise, absent a *prozbol* executed by the depositor-creditor or the successor in due course—i.e., the payee named in the check—the "debt" owed by the bank to its depositor is discharged at the close of the sabbatical year.)

However, the thesis developed by *Berit Yehudah* is predicated upon an erroneous premise. *Berit Yehudah* recognizes that, in order to be construed as a "sale" for purposes of Halakhah, the delivery of a check to the payee must be in the nature of an irrevocable assignment of the maker's claim against the bank for the amount of the check. Indeed, *Berit Yehudah* states that "the maker cannot void the check other than for limited cause." That statement is, however, simply incorrect. It is quite clear that the maker may issue a stop payment order which must be honored by the bank without inquiry into the reason prompting its issuance.[13] Any further recourse by the payee will be against the drawer of the check, not against the bank. It is clearly impossible to recover that which has been legally transferred to another. Thus the power to rescind is conclusive evidence of an unconsummated transfer.[14] Moreover, the bank's authority to pay a check is revoked by the death of the drawer although, generally, the bank

13. See U.C.C. §4–403 and *Brady,* pp. 20–2f.

14. This is true despite the fact that, when a check is issued in exchange for cash, merchandise or services, a bank that pays the check despite the issuance of a stop payment order will not suffer any liability. U.C.C. §4–407 states that in such circumstances "the payor bank shall be subrogated to the rights of any holder in due course on the item," i.e., since, even subsequent to the stop payment order, the payee has a valid claim against the drawer of the check, the bank is subrogated to the payer's right and can assert that right in defense of any suit brought by the drawer of the check against the bank. The concept of subrogation is analogous to the rule of *shi'buda de-Rabbi Natan* in Jewish law. Moreover, the bank in which the check is deposited, as a holder in due course, is not bound by a stop payment order issued by the drawer to his bank. The bank on which the check is drawn is also subrogated to the rights of the presenting bank and can defend itself against a suit by the drawer by claiming that it has, in effect, been assigned the rights of the presenting bank, which, as a holder in due course, is affected by the stop payment order. See White and Summers, U.C.C., 3rd ed., vol. I, 18–6.

may make such payment within ten days of the death of the drawer.[15] Again, were issuance of a check to be regarded as a consummated transfer of a debt owed by the bank, the demise of the drawer after such transfer should be entirely irrelevant. Accordingly, issuance of a check cannot be construed as a "sale" of a debt owed by the bank since a rescindable assignment certainly does not constitute a "sale."[16]

It appears to this writer that *Berit Yehudah*'s position is incorrect even with regard to checks drawn in Israel although, in Israeli law, issuance of a stop-payment order is, in most circumstances, a penal offense.[17] Israeli law regards the stopping of payment, followed by failure to pay the face amount of the check within ten days of demand, as presumptive evidence that the check was issued with the knowledge that it would not be honored.[18]

---

15. U.C.C. §4–405 provides that a bank's authority to pay a check is revoked by the death of the drawer, but that the bank is protected if it pays without knowledge of such death and that the bank may also pay for ten days following such death even with knowledge. Comment 2 to the Code section indicates that the provision for payment within a ten-day period following death of the drawer is designed to permit routine payment of checks without requiring holders to file claims in probate. Any person claiming an interest in the account, e.g, a creditor, may order the bank to stop payment and thereby prevent the bank from honoring the check even during the ten-day period.

16. This conclusion is in no way negated by the fact that it is generally illegal to stop payment on a check issued for consideration. Such an act is properly categorized as fraud rather than as theft. Cf., Michael Broyde, "The Practice of Law According to the Halacha," *Journal of Halacha and Contemporary Society,* no. 20 (Fall, 1990), p. 26, note 50.

17. *Ḥok ha-Onshim* (5737–1977) §432(c).

18. §224.5 of the Model Penal Code (1962) adopted by many American jurisdictions provides that a person who issues a check with the knowledge that it will not be honored by the drawer, e.g., a check drawn on a bank in which the issuer has no account, is guilty of a misdemeanor. Although some jurisdictions explicitly limit their enactments to situations involving fraud, the model statute is designed to encompass the issuance of bad checks even in situations in which nothing is obtained in return, as in the case of a gift, on the theory that, although the recipient has not been cheated, the check is nevertheless likely to be negotiated for cash, credit or property and thus will have an adverse effect on ordinary commerce. While there appears to be no case law dealing with such a contingency, it is not unlikely that a court would find issuance of a check with the clear intent to stop payment before the check is presented for collection to be a violation of this statute. Nevertheless, the statute certainly cannot be construed as prohibiting a person who issues a check in good faith from changing his mind and executing a stop-payment order or as establishing that execution of such an order constitutes presumptive evidence that the check was issued with the knowledge that it would not be honored.

The latter is a criminal offense punishable by a fine equal to four times the amount of the check or I£100,000, whichever is greater, or imprisonment for a period of one year.[19] The law, however, does not curb the maker's power to stop payment on a check and indeed expressly negates the bank's "obligation and authority" to render payment on a check subsequent to execution of a stop-payment order.[20] Hence it would appear that, even according to Israeli law, issuance of a check cannot be construed as the assignment of a debt.

Moreover, legally, a check or other draft does not of itself operate as an assignment of funds in the hands of the bank, as evidenced by the fact that the bank is not liable on the instrument until it accepts the check for payment.[21] The holder of a check cannot force the bank upon which it is drawn to honor the check and to issue the funds against which it is drawn. If, for any reason, the bank refuses to honor the check, the holder's only recourse is against the drawer or any prior endorsers. The bank may indeed be liable for wrongful dishonor if it fails to pay a proper order,[22] but the bank's liability for wrongful dishonor is to its own customer for breach of contract and not to the holder of the check which it declined to honor.[23]

Rabbi Spira, *Kuntres Devar ha-Shemittah,* chapter 3, also points out that should the drawer later issue a second check that is cashed before the first check is presented for collection, and thereby render the first check uncollectible for reason of insufficient funds, the payee of the first check has no claim whatsoever against the bank or against the payee of the second check. Were issuance of a check to be construed as assignment of a debt, it would preclude a second assignment of the same debt with the result that the second payee would acquire no rights whatsoever. Since issuance of the check does not preclude issuance of a second check on the very same funds, argues Rabbi Spira, delivery of a check to the payee can hardly be construed as a conveyance.

A second argument in support of the position that once a check has been issued the underlying debt is not extinguished at the close of the sabbatical year, even if the check has as yet not been presented for

19. *Ḥok ha-Onshim* §432(a). Subsequent to conversion of the *lira* to *shekel,* payment of the fine is in *shekalim* equal to I£100,000.

20. *Pekudat ha-Shetarot (Nusaḥ Ḥadash)* §75(1).

21. See *Brady,* p. 14–7 and pp. 18–21.

22. See U.C.C. §4–402.

23. See *Brady,* pp. 18–20ff.

payment, is advanced by R. Moshe Rosenthal, *Kerem Ẓion, Hilkhot Shevi'it* (Jerusalem, 5740) 20:1, *Giddulei Ẓion,* no. 1. The Gemara, *Gittin* 37a, declares that *shemittah* discharges uncollected debts, but debts which are "as if collected" (*ke-gavuy*) are not discharged. Hence a loan against a pledge of chattel is not discharged since, if the debtor were to default, the creditor would simply retain the pledge in satisfaction of the debt. Similarly, if a judgment of a court has been obtained commanding payment, the debt is regarded as if collected. The rationale underlying this provision is that, subsequent to the sabbatical year, the creditor is bound by the injunction "he shall not exact from his friend" (Deuteronomy 15:2) but remains free to collect his debt provided that it is not necessary to "exact" or demand payment, e.g., if he has the option of retaining the pledge or if the court has already demanded payment. R. Joseph Saul Nathanson, *Teshuvot Sho'el u-Meshiv, Mahadura Hamisha'ah,* no. 71, advances this consideration as one of an amalgam of reasons in ruling that a promissory note payable to the bearer may be used by an assignee to collect the debt even after the lapse of the sabbatical year. *Sho'el u-Meshiv* argues that only debts requiring a "demand" by the *creditor* are discharged; the assignee, however, is not the creditor and hence his "demand" is not deterred. Applying a similar line of reasoning, Rabbi Rosenthal argues that by issuing a check the debtor has discharged his responsibility to the creditor and the creditor need no longer "demand" payment of the debtor but of the bank. Rabbi Rosenthal does, however, concede that checks postdated and thereby made payable only after the close of the sabbatical year cannot be regarded "as collected." This position is also adopted by Rabbi Spira in his *Mishnat Kesef,* II, 67:14, *Panim Ḥadashot* 18:2–3, as well as in an appendix to that volume, "*Dinei Shemittat Kesafim u-Prozbol,*" chap. 2, sec. 6, and by R. Gavriel Zinner, *Nit'ei Gavri'el* (New York, 5747) 17:12, note 20.

This position is, however, rejected by R. Benjamin Silber, *Hilkhot Shevi'it* 10:22, note 73, who adopts an opposing view on the grounds that "the bank is the servant of the debtor; it stands at the service of the debtor." Similarly, Rabbi Spira, in his *Kuntres Devar ha-Shemittah,* chapter 3, reverses his earlier position and concurs in Rabbi Silber's ruling. Rabbi Spira cogently notes that, as long as the check is not presented for collection, the drawer of the check may withdraw his money from the bank. He also notes that, until the funds are actually delivered to the payee, the bank continues to make use of the funds for its own purposes. However, Rabbi Spira fails to note the most telling objection, *viz.,* that the check may be voided by means of a stop-payment order.[24] For each of these reasons the debt can hardly be considered "as collected."

III. *Bank Drafts and Cashiers' Checks*

Rabbi Silber distinguishes "bank drafts" from personal checks and regards only the former "as collected." Hence he rules that a debt satisfied by issuance of a bank check is not discharged by operation of the law of *shemittah,* even if the check is not presented for collection until after the close of the sabbatical year. Rabbi Silber regards debts satisfied by means of a bank draft "as collected" from the moment the draft is delivered, but does not view this to be the case with regard to personal checks. Rabbi Spira agrees that, insofar as the debtor is concerned, the debt may be regarded "as collected" if paid by means of a bank draft. However, he points out that a bank draft represents indebtedness incurred by the bank and hence, in the case of a bank owned by Jews, absent a *prozbol* executed by the payee, the bank's debt is itself cancelled and hence the check cannot be presented for payment.

The reason that these authorities regard a debt to be "as collected" when satisfied by means of a bank draft is somewhat obscure. Considerations similar to those cited with regard to personal checks apply to bank drafts as well, i.e., the bank may continue to use its funds until the draft is presented for collection, and may conceivably issue a second check upon the same funds, relying upon future deposits for coverage. Indeed, it is presumably for those reasons that Rabbi Spira requires the depositor to execute a *prozbol* in order to withdraw, or write checks upon, the funds on deposit with a bank owned by Jews. The selfsame considerations operate to render the debt "uncollected" insofar as the original debtor is concerned. R. Ovadiah Yosef, *Hilkhot Shemittat Kesafim u-Prozbol, Yalkut Yosef* (Jerusalem, 5747), p. 8, adopts the view that even bank checks are uncollectible after *shemittah* since the debt "is lacking in collection."

Nevertheless, the distinction drawn between bank checks and personal checks appears entirely correct for a completely different reason. Insofar as the debtor is concerned, the debt is not "as collected" but, in accordance with Jewish law, would be regarded as having been actually satisfied by

24. As noted earlier, even under Israeli law, which imposes criminal penalties for stopping payment of a check without justification, banks arc required to honor stop-payment orders without inquiry into the reason of issuance. See *Pekudat ha-Shetarot (Nusaḥ Ḥadash)* §75(1).

the creditor's acceptance of assignment of a third-party debt, i.e., the bank draft, as payment in full. Legally, a cashier's check, bank draft, or other direct bank obligation given in satisfaction of a debt discharges the debtor provided that the debtor is not a party to the bank obligation, i.e., the debtor has neither signed nor endorsed the instrument.[25] Failure of the creditor to execute a *prozbol* against the bank leaves him with no recourse against the debtor, both by reason of operation of the laws of *shemittah* and by virtue of the fact that failure to execute a *prozbol* against the maker of the instrument assigned to him constitutes negligence on his part. Hence, as recorded in *Shulḥan Arukh, Ḥoshen Mishpat* 67:38, he has no recourse against the assigning party.

It may be noted that certification of a check does have the effect of rendering the sum "as collected." As stated by the Court in *Marks* v. *Anchor Savings Bank:*

> It is established in law that the certification of a check transfers the funds represented thereby from the credit of the maker to that of the payee, and that, to all intents and purposes, the latter becomes a depositor of the drawee bank to the amount of the check, with the rights and duties of one in such a relation.[26]

Thus, subsequent to certification, the funds are acknowledged as held by the bank for the payee. It should, however, be noted that the payee acquires no rights against the certifying bank unless and until the check has been delivered[27] and, indeed, certification may be cancelled at the request of the drawer so long as the check remains in the possession of the drawer.[28] Hence, in order to avoid discharge of the debt by operation of the laws of *shemittah,* certification must be followed by delivery of the check to the creditor before the close of the sabbatical year.

It should also be noted that, not only may certification be secured by the drawer, but it is also an option available to any holder of a check. When the holder has the check certified, the drawer and all endorsers are discharged from liability, with the result that the holder may claim payment

25. See U.C.C. §3–802(1)(a) and *Brady,* p. 4–19.

26. *Marks* v. *Anchor Savings Bank* (1916) 252 Pa. 304, 97A. 399, 33B.L.J. 448. See also *Brady,* p. 10–10.

27. See *Brady,* p. 10–13, and *ibid.,* note 23.

28. See *Brady,* p. 10–20.

only from the bank.[29] The act of the holder in having the check certified is construed as release of the drawer not only from all liability on the check itself but also from the underlying debt for which the check had been given.[30] Consequently, it is clear that certification of a check by the holder renders the debt owed by the drawer "as collected" and not subject to cancellation by operation of the laws of *shemittah*. Of course, if the check is drawn upon a bank owned by Jews, a *prozbol* will be necessary in order to enable collection from the bank.

---

29. See U.C.C. §3–411(1) and N.I.L §188.

30. See *Brady*, p. 10–11.

Chapter IV

Jewish Law and the State's Authority to Punish Crime

A mortal prince rules over one province but does not rule over another province; even an emperor rules over dry land but does not rule over the sea. However, the Holy One, blessed be He, rules over sea and land.

PALESTINIAN TALMUD, BERAKHOT 9:1

Judaism regards its system of law as transnational and transgeographic in nature. All Jews, regardless of their place of domicile, are bound by the criminal and civil aspects of Jewish law no less than by those provisions of Jewish law that are entirely religious or ritual in nature.

Jewish law provides for the application of criminal sanctions only upon the testimony of two qualified eyewitnesses and a guilty verdict rendered by a court of competent jurisdiction composed of adherents to Judaism and established in conformity with the relevant provisions of the statutes governing judicial bodies. Prior admonition as well as a court composed of twenty-three "ordained" judges are necessary conditions for imposition of either capital or corporal punishment. The "ordination" required is a form of licensure originating in the designation of elders by Moses as recorded in Numbers 11:24. These elders, in turn, transmitted this authority to their successors. That authority was then passed on from generation to generation in an unbroken chain of transmission over a span of centuries until it was forcibly interrupted during the period of Roman oppression subsequent to the destruction of the Second Commonwealth. The result is that, at present, there are no individuals qualified to sit on such courts and hence, as a practical matter, Jewish penal law no longer regards existing rabbinic courts as competent to impose either capital or corporal punishment.

Capital punishment is regarded as having been abrogated for another reason as well. On the basis of a well-recognized principle of scriptural exegesis, the Gemara, *Sanhedrin* 52b, establishes that capital punishment can be imposed only when the biblically prescribed sacrificial rituals continue to be performed in the Temple in Jerusalem. Hence lapse of the sacrificial order necessarily led to abrogation of capital punishment.

Jewish law also posits severe strictures against delivering either the person or property of a Jew to a gentile. Thus, *Shulḥan Arukh, Ḥoshen Mishpat* 388:9, declares that the person and property of even a "wicked person" and a "transgressor" remain inviolate even if that individual is a source of "trouble" or "pain" to others. There is, however, an inherent ambiguity in this proscription. There may be reason to assume that the prohibition is limited to turning over a person or his property to the custody of an "oppressor" who inflicts bodily or financial harm in a manner that is malevolent or entirely extralegal. Indeed, the terminology employed by *Tur Shulḥan Arukh, Ḥoshen Mishpat* 388, in codifying this provision of Jewish law lends credence to such a restrictive interpretation since *Tur* incorporates the term "*anas*" or "oppressor" in recording the prohibition. Nevertheless, it may be the case that employment of this term does not serve to limit the scope of the prohibition but serves simply as illustration. Such a view finds support in the omission of the term "*anas*" in the subsequent codification of this provision in the *Shulḥan Arukh*. The latter interpretation would, in the absence of other considerations, have the effect of banning physical delivery of a Jew to non-Jewish authorities as well as prohibiting conveyance of information that might be used against him in either a criminal or civil action. In accordance with that interpretation, such actions would not be countenanced even in situations involving a clear violation of a criminal statute and would apply even when the accused is assured the protection of due process of law.

I. *The King's Justice*

The crucial theoretical issue in determining the correct interpretation of this provision of Jewish law is the formulation of a legal principle that might provide for recognition of the jurisdiction of non-Jewish judicial authorities. Clearly, causing judicially cognizable harm to another person constitutes a tort in virtually every legal system unless justification for such action is recognized by the system itself. It is equally clear that punishment meted out in accordance with the penal provisions of any given legal system is not regarded by that system as tortious in nature. Accordingly, the question that must be addressed is whether Jewish law is prepared to recognize the authority and jurisdiction of another system of law in such matters.

Quite distinct from the corpus of law that it regards as incumbent upon its adherents, Judaism concurrently posits a parallel legal code that it regards as binding upon all of humanity, *viz.,* the "Seven Commandments of the Sons of Noah" or the Noahide Code. Standards of evidence and rules of procedure that form an integral part of the Noahide Code are far less restrictive in nature than those adhered to by Jewish courts. Under the provisions of the Noahide Code, *inter alia,* testimony of a single witness is sufficient for conviction; no prior admonition is required; and the court may be composed of a single judge. In the Jewish Commonwealth, separate judiciaries were established: one exercised jurisdiction over the Jewish populace and administered Jewish law while the other sat in judgment upon non-Jewish nationals and rendered justice in accordance with the provisions of the Noahide Code.[1] The jurisdiction of non-Jewish courts and their authority to administer the Noahide Code was limited to gentiles.[2] Although the jurisdiction and authority of Noahide courts is not limited by either geographic area or historical epoch, Jewish law contains no explicit statutory provision that might serve to grant non-Jewish courts jurisdiction over Jewish malfeasors.

The earlier cited provisions regarding rules of evidence and matters of judicial procedure apply only to the imposition of penal sanctions by Jewish courts as provided by statute. The monarch, however, was empowered to ignore the judiciary and its unique form of due process in imposing extrastatutory punishment when he deemed it necessary to do so to preserve law and order. Thus, Rambam, *Hilkhot Rozeaḥ* 2:4, writes: "Each of these murderers and their like who are not subject to death by verdict of the *Bet Din,* if a king of Israel wishes to put them to death by virtue of the law of the monarchy and the perfection of the world, he has the right to do so." It is not immediately clear whether the authority to impose "the King's justice" is limited to Jewish monarchs or whether it is the prerogative of every sovereign ruler.

A literal reading of I Samuel 8:5 would seem to indicate that this power is shared by the kings of all nations. The elders of Israel demand of Samuel: "Appoint for us a king to judge us like all the nations," i.e., a

1. See Rambam, *Hilkhot Melakhim* 10:11.
2. See *Hilkhot Melakhim* 9:14.

monarch empowered to administer "the King's justice." In classic rabbinic sources, the phrase "to judge us" was certainly understood as having that connotation. Rabbenu Nissim Gerondi, *Derashot ha-Ran,* no. 11, seizes upon this phrase in explaining why the request for establishment of a monarchy aroused Samuel's ire. Appointment of a monarch to serve as the head of the Jewish commonwealth constitutes one of the 613 biblical commandments and its fulfillment is regarded as having become incumbent upon the populace upon entry into the Promised Land.[3] Rabbenu Nissim explains that a monarch is required for two purposes: 1) to serve as commander-in-chief of the army; and 2) to serve as chief magistrate in administering extra-statutory punishment when necessary to do so to preserve the social fabric. A request for appointment of a king could not, in and of itself, have been a matter for censure. Rabbenu Nissim asserts that Samuel became angry because the request was couched in a manner that gave voice to a perceived need for imposition of "the King's justice." A well-ordered, law-abiding society has no need for the imposition of emergency *ad hoc* measures by the monarch; the punishments provided by statute and their imposition in accordance with the rigorous standards of due process prescribed by Jewish law should suffice to protect societal concerns. The request presented to Samuel reflected a recognition by the petitioners that their society could not long endure on the basis of criminal procedure hobbled by a two-witness rule and a requirement for prior warning as well as a host of other impediments to actual imposition of penal sanctions. The anticipation by the petitioners of a breakdown of law and order, for which the sole remedy would have been imposition of "the King's justice," bespoke either an unacceptable lack of confidence in themselves or their peers or, even worse, a realistic assessment of moral degeneration.[4] Thus, explains Rabbenu Nissim, Samuel had ample cause for distress.[5]

Ostensibly, the phrase "like all the nations" indicates that this is a legitimate exercise of the royal prerogative among the nations of the

---

3. See Deuteronomy 17:15; *Sanhedrin* 20b; Rambam, *Hilkhot Melakhim* 1:1.

4. See R. Abraham Benjamin Sofer, *Ketav Sofer, Parashat Shoftim,* s.v. *od nireh li* and R. Yechiel Michal Epstein, *Arukh ha-Shulḥan he-'Atid, Hilkhot Melakhim* 71:6–7. The thesis herein presented incorporates elements elucidated by *Ketav Sofer* that are not explicitly formulated by *Derashot ha-Ran.*

5. Cf. *Sanhedrin* 20b which declares that the elders of the generation couched their petition in appropriate language as well as Rambam, *Hilkhot Melakhim* 1:2, who indicates that censure was occasioned by a disdain for the leadership of Samuel.

world. It may however be the case that employment of the phrase does not reflect a recognition of a normative, legal power vested in gentile sovereigns, but constitutes only a *de facto* statement of socio-political reality. In practice, in punishing evildoers, monarchs of antiquity certainly did not feel constrained by the limitations of the Noahide Code. Their customary practice may have been cited by the elders, not as an example of legitimate exercise of royal power, but simply as a paradigm for appointment of a monarch over the Jewish populace in whom such power would be legitimately vested. If administration of "the King's justice" is a power limited to the monarch of a Jewish state, that legal institution cannot serve as the legitimating basis for imposition of penal sanctions by a non-Jewish government.

II. *"The King's Justice" and Non-Jewish Sovereigns*

The question of whether or not Halakhah regards non-Jewish sovereign authorities as endowed with the authority to impose "the King's justice" appears to be a matter of controversy among medieval authorities. The Gemara records the well-known dictum of Rabbi Samuel, one of the Amora'im of the Talmud, who declared: "*Dina de-malkhuta dina*—The law of the land is the law."[6] Justification of that principle is far from obvious. Numerous theories have been advanced in an attempt to explain why civil ordinances having no basis either in Scripture or in the Oral Law should be binding in Halakhah, the system of law regarded by Jewish teaching as binding upon Jews. Noteworthy are the remarks of Rabbi Samuel ben Meir (Rashbam) in his commentary on the Gemara, *Baba Batra* 54b:

> All the taxes, levies and customs of the kings that are customarily promulgated in their kingdoms are the law because all the members of the kingdom accept upon themselves the laws of the King and his statutes and therefore it is absolute law.

Rashbam's comments are problematic. They might well be interpreted as limiting Samuel's dictum to monetary obligations such as payment of taxes and levies. On the surface, such an obligation might be explained on the basis of ordinary contract theory. Subjects who "accept upon themselves the laws of the King" voluntarily undertake to pay the taxes

6. *Gittin* 10b; *Baba Kamma* 113a; *Baba Batra* 54b; and *Nedarim* 28a.

imposed by the monarch. A contractual obligation to pay an already announced levy is certainly enforceable. However, contract law, as posited by Halakhah, does not recognize the enforceability of an unspecified, open-ended obligation, the extent of which is to be unilaterally determined by another party. Yet it is clear that a subject does not have the right to reject a tax newly imposed by the king on a claim that it was never previously accepted by him. Moreover, Halakhah declines to recognize the validity of virtually any contract unless recorded in a properly drafted instrument or entered into by means of a formal act of *kinyan*—for example, formal delivery of a kerchief or other artifact, which serves a function analogous to that of symbolic delivery of consideration in common law.[7] An oral undertaking not accompanied by a formal act of *kinyan* is regarded as "mere words" and may be renounced at will.

Rashbam's thesis becomes entirely cogent if the "acceptance" of which he speaks is understood, not as contractual acceptance of a monetary obligation, but as acceptance of the sovereignty of the monarch. If so, Rashbam's comments serve to establish the principle that an obligation of obedience flows directly from voluntary acceptance of the authority of the monarch. The Gemara, *Sanhedrin* 20b, posits the actions of the king portended in I Samuel 8:5 as legitimate perquisites of his office. Rashbam, then, in essence, does no more than spell out the prescribed manner in which a monarch is vested with those prerogatives. Unlike kings of a Jewish commonwealth who must be formally invested in office by the Great Sanhedrin and a prophet,[8] the authority of the monarch of a non-Jewish state is derived entirely from the consent of the governed, with such consent serving not only as a necessary condition, but also as the sufficient condition for exercise of royal powers. Accordingly, payment of taxes becomes a legitimate and legally binding obligation even in the absence of a specific undertaking with regard to such payment. The obligation is imposed by virtue of the authority of the sovereign, rather than freely assumed by the subject. It is only the sovereign's authority to act as sovereign that requires "acceptance" on the part of his subjects. Once such acceptance is forthcoming, no further legitimization is required for exercise of the prerogatives enumerated in I Samuel 8:5.

---

7. The kerchief does not however represent a symbolic *quid pro quo* in a manner analogous to the peppercorn but serves either to generate both firm intention and reliance, i.e., a meeting of the minds, or as evidence thereof. See R. Yecheskel Abramsky, *Dinei Mamonot,* 2d ed. (1969), pp. 9–13, who argues that the requirement of *kinyan* is not absolute.

8. See Rambam, *Hilkhot Melakhim* 1:3.

Of course, the premises implicitly assumed by such a theory include: (i) the existence of a biblically recognized institution of "monarchy" as a legal category;[9] (ii) extension of the halakhic institution of the monarchy to encompass non-Jewish sovereigns as well; and (iii) recognition of the authority of the non-Jewish sovereign as binding upon Jewish subjects as well as upon non-Jewish nationals. Since, according to Rashbam, a non-Jewish monarch is recognized as a "king" for purposes of Halakhah it may well be assumed that such a king enjoys all the perquisites of monarchy including the right to impose penal sanctions in administering "the King's justice."

This thesis is echoed in Rambam, *Hilkhot Gezeilah ve-Aveidah* 5:18. The preceding sections of chapter five are devoted to a full explication of Samuel's dictum "*Dina de-malkhuta dina.*" In the concluding section of that chapter Rambam writes:

> All of these matters are stated concerning a king whose coin circulates in those lands, for the inhabitants of that land have agreed upon him and rely that he is their master and they are his servants. But if his coin does not circulate he is [in the category] of a robber who uses force and like a group of armed bandits whose laws are not law. Similarly, such a king and all his servants are robbers in every respect.

Rambam clearly regards the halakhic status and authority of the king to be contingent upon the consent of the governed which, in turn, may be ascertained by a determination of whether or not his coin is accepted *de facto* as legal tender. The right of coinage is not only a jealously safeguarded monarchial prerogative but constitutes a hallmark, indeed, the litmus test, of sovereignty. Acceptance of the king's currency bespeaks tacit acceptance of his authority and reliance upon his protection and rule. Thus, it is only a king who rules by virtue of the acceptance or acquiescence of his subjects who may legitimately exercise the royal prerogatives enumerated in I Samuel 8.

Rashbam and Rambam should be regarded as advancing an identical theory of *dina de-malkhuta dina* despite the fact that Rambam speaks of acceptance of the king's authority while Rashbam focuses upon acceptance

9. The monarch's power need not be unlimited, nor must such power be vested in an individual rather than in a legislative or executive body. See Ramban, addenda to Rambam's *Sefer ha-Miẓvot,* no. 17, who, in a different context, defines a monarch as "a king, a judge or whoever exercises jurisdiction over the populace."

of "the king's laws and statutes." Rashbam should not be understood as predicating the binding authority of the laws and ordinances of the kingdom upon explicit acceptance of each law individually. Rather, he should be understood as asserting that investiture of an individual in royal office *ipso facto* constitutes conferral of lawmaking authority. Hence "acceptance" of the king as monarch is tantamount to acceptance of his laws. The notion that acceptance of a monarch is at one and the same time the acceptance of his legislative authority is explicitly formulated by Ramban, in his commentray on *Yevamot* 46a, who equates the two concepts in stating, "since they accept his sovereignty and they accept his edicts."

It is quite evident that both Rambam and Rashbam regard *dina de-malkhuta dina* to be binding by virtue of the fact that promulgation of "the law of the kingdom" is a legitimate exercise of royal authority by the sovereign. Since the principle *dina de-malkhuta dina* is enunciated with regard to the laws of gentile nations it is clear that, for both Rambam and Rashbam, a non-Jewish ruler must enjoy the halakhic status of a monarch.[10] Since even a gentile monarch is entitled to exercise the prerogatives enumerated in I Samuel it may well be argued that such a monarch may legitimately punish disobedience of his decrees.[11]

That conclusion is reflected in the comments of Ritva, recorded in *Shitah Mekubeẓet, Baba Meẓi'a* 83b, who declares that a gentile king may apprehend and execute thieves and that, accordingly, a Jew is permitted to turn over thieves to the king's officers. The talmudic discussion that serves as the basis for Ritva's comment is of seminal importance:

R. Eleazar, son of R. Shimon, met an officer who was engaged in

---

10. See also Ramban, Rashba and Ritva, *Baba Batra* 55a; *Shitah Mekubeẓet, Baba Kamma* 97b, s.v. *katav ha-Ramah;* Me'iri, *Baba Kamma* 113a and 113b; R. Joseph Karo, *Teshuvot Avkat Rokhel,* no. 47; and R. Moses di Trani, *Kiryat Sefer, Hilkhot Gezeilah,* chap. 5

11. There are, of course, other theories of *dina de-malkhuta dina* that not only fail to provide a basis for penal authority but also seem to negate the view that non-Jewish sovereigns enjoy the prerogatives enumerated in I Samuel 8. For example, Rabbenu Nissim, in his commentary on *Nedarim* 28a, declares that the principle of *dina de-malkhuta dina* is limited to a gentile ruler "because the land is his and he can say to [his Jewish subjects], 'If you do not fulfill my commands I will banish you from the land.'" According to Rabbenu Nissim's analysis, *dina de-malkhuta dina* serves only to establish the monarch's right to collect feudal dues or to collect "rent" in the form of taxes levied upon those granted a right of domicile. See also R. Dov Berish Weidenfeld, *Teshuvot Dovev Meisharim,* III, no. 89 and R. Shlomoh Zalman Auerbach, *Ma'adanei Ereẓ,* no. 20, sec. 12.

> arresting thieves. [R. Eleazar] said to him, "How can you detect them. . .? Perhaps you take the innocent and leave behind the wicked." [The officer said,] "And what shall I do? It is the king's command." [R. Eleazar] said to him, "Come, I will teach you what to do. Go into a tavern at the fourth hour of the day. If you see a man drinking wine, holding a cup in his hand and dozing, ask who he is. If he is a scholar, he has risen early to pursue his studies; if he is a laborer, he has risen early to do his work; if his work is at night, he may have been rolling thin metal. If he is none of these, he is a thief; arrest him." A report was heard in the royal court. They said, "Let the reader of the letter become the messenger." R. Eleazar, son of R. Shimon, was brought and he proceeded to apprehend thieves. R. Joshua, son of Karḥah, sent word to him, "Vinegar, son of wine! How long will you deliver the people of our God for slaughter?" [R. Eleazar] sent the reply, "I eradicate thorns from the vineyard." [R. Joshua] responded, "Let the owner of the vineyard come and eradicate his thorns." One day a laundryman met [R. Eleazar and] called him "Vinegar, son of wine." Said [R. Eleazar] to himself, "Since he is so insolent, he is certainly a wicked man." He exclaimed, "Seize him! Seize him!"[12]

Ritva questions how it was possible for Rabbi Eleazar ben Shimon to pass judgment without testimony of witnesses or prior warning and how it was possible for him to do so in a historical epoch in which the Sanhedrin no longer existed. Ritva explains that Rabbi Eleazar ben Shimon was the agent of the king and that the king may rightfully execute evildoers even in the absence of prior admonition and without the benefit of the testimony of two eyewitnesses.[13] Ritva further points to the extrajudicial execution of the Amalekite proselyte by King David, recorded in II Samuel 1:15, as an example of punishment on the basis of administration of "the King's justice." Thus Ritva explicitly states that, according to Rabbi Eleazar ben Shimon, even non-Jewish monarchs are authorized to administer extrastatutory punishment in accordance with "the King's justice."

Nevertheless, examination of the talmudic discussion reveals that the

---

12. *Baba Meẓi'a* 83b.

13. See R. Benjamin Rabinowitz-Teumim, *Ha-Torah ve-ha-Medinah,* IV, 80, who notes that R. Eleazar ben Shimon acted in an official capacity and, even according to Ritva, only a person specifically delegated by the monarch to perform such functions may deliver a criminal into the hands of civil authorities.

matter is the subject of significant controversy. Rabbi Joshua ben Karḥah remonstrated with Rabbi Eleazar ben Shimon in exclaiming "How long will you deliver the people of our God for slaughter?"[14] Moreover, the discussion concludes with a report that, when Rabbi Ishmael ben Yosi acted in a similar manner, the prophet Elijah appeared to him and voiced the identical complaint. When Rabbi Ishmael offered the same defense, "What shall I do? It is the king's command," Elijah responded, "Your father fled to Asia, you flee to Laodicea!"[15] Since the opposing position of Rabbi Joshua ben Karḥah is endorsed by none other than the prophet Elijah there is strong reason to assume that Rabbi Eleazar ben Shimon's position is to be rejected as a normative legal position.

There is, however, a parallel narrative involving Elijah that may shed light upon this exchange as well. The Palestinian Talmud, *Terumot* 8:4, reports that a fugitive, a certain Ula bar Kushav, took refuge in Lod. The civil authorities surrounded the city and demanded that he be surrendered to them, threatening that the entire populace would be annihilated if the townspeople failed to acquiesce. Rabbi Shimon ben Lakish convinced the fugitive to allow himself to be turned over to the authorities. The Palestinian Talmud records that the prophet Elijah had been wont to reveal himself to Rabbi Shimon ben Lakish on a regular basis but that subsequent to that event he failed to do so. Rabbi Shimon ben Lakish fasted repeatedly until Elijah again revealed himself. However, Elijah remonstrated that he was being forced to appear to an individual who had delivered a Jew to gentile authorities. Rabbi Shimon ben Lakish defended his actions, arguing that they were entirely in accordance with Jewish law. To this Elijah retorted, "Is this then the law of the pious?" The incident recounted in the Palestinian Talmud similarly involved deliverance of a fugitive to the hands of civil authorities for punishment in accordance with the law of the land, albeit in a situation in which the surrender of the individual in question was demanded by the authorities upon pain of death of all concerned, including the fugitive. Elijah did not protest that such action is not sanctioned by Jewish law. Rather, he argued that, although entirely legitimate, such action does not behoove the pious. Similarly, the controversy between Rabbi Eleazar ben Shimon and Rabbi Joshua ben Karḥah may be understood, not as regarding a matter of normative law, but as pertaining to proper formulation of "the law of the pious." Both agree that the king is empowered to execute those who flout

14. *Loc. cit.*
15. *Loc. cit.*

his laws. Rabbi Joshua ben Karḥah, however, maintains that a pious person should not act in such a manner, while Rabbi Eleazar ben Shimon maintains that, on the contrary, since the individual is clearly a wicked person, even "piety" demands that he be surrendered for punishment as a means of "eradicating the thorns from the vineyard."

Support for this analysis of the exchange between Rabbi Eleazar ben Shimon and Rabbi Joshua ben Karḥah may be found in the commentary of Ritva as recorded in his own novellae on that talmudic discussion. In stating the normative rule, Ritva offers the following comment: "Nevertheless, in a situation in which the king, in accordance with the laws of the kingdom, may not act in such a manner, his officer is similarly not permitted [to do so]; and if the king orders him to do so he must suffer death and not transgress."[16] The novel legal principle enunciated by Ritva is that the monarch may not act in an arbitrary and capricious manner, but must himself conform to the laws promulgated in his kingdom. Concomitantly, illicit orders of the monarch must be resisted, even if such resistance entails martyrdom.

Ritva does, however, affirm that punishment may be imposed by the monarch when such punishment is in conformity with the laws of the kingdom. Ritva's conclusion in this regard is remarkable in light of the fact that the prophet Elijah endorsed the view of Rabbi Joshua ben Karḥah who maintains that a monarch may not legitimately impose "the King's justice" even under such circumstances. If so, whether the king's action is in accordance with the "laws of the kingdom" or is entirely capricious should be entirely irrelevant. Ritva's comments are cogent only if Rabbi Joshua ben Karḥah's position, and Elijah's endorsement of that view, are regarded as based upon considerations of pious conduct rather than upon normative halakhic principles. Understood in that manner, Ritva asserts that, strictly as a matter of law, the king may order execution only in accordance with the laws of the land, but should he order execution in violation of established law one must suffer martyrdom rather than carry out an illicit directive. It nevertheless remains an act of piety to disregard the king's command to execute punishment in circumstances in which Jewish law does not provide for punishment to be imposed even though such punishment is in accordance with the law of the land.

Nevertheless, Ritva's caveat remains problematic. If the authority of a gentile sovereign to impose "the King's justice" is derived from I Samuel 8, it is difficult to fathom why his actions are legitimate only if they are

16. *Shitah Mekubeẓet, Baba Meẓi'a* 83b. See also Ritva, *Baba Batra* 55a.

predicated upon "the laws of the kingdom."[17] As has been shown earlier, acceptance of the authority of a monarch is not limited to contractual acceptance of already established legal norms. Indeed, acceptance of capital punishment cannot be made a matter of contractual stipulation. Accordingly, acceptance can only mean acceptance of the authority of the king. Pursuant to such acceptance on the part of his subjects, exercise by the monarch of the prerogatives recorded in I Samuel 8 becomes legitimate. There is no explicit statement in I Samuel requiring that the monarch act in accordance with a formally promulgated code of law rather than in accordance with his perception, on a case-by-case basis, of the need for punishment as a deterrent to antisocial behavior.

This limitation upon the king's power, denying him the right to punish transgressors other than in accordance with a formally promulgated code of law, can be explained on the basis of the position of Rabbi Shimon ben Ẓemaḥ Duran (*Tashbaẓ*).[18] While Ritva's statement is limited to criminal matters, *Tashbaẓ* makes a much broader assertion in declaring:

> The king may not enact new laws other than those already enacted . . . for the laws of the monarchy are known to all and are already set down. Just as we have laws of the kingdom as declared by Samuel to Israel. . . similarly other nations have laws known to the kings and it is with regard to [those laws] that [the Sages] declared *dina de-malkhuta dina*. . . .[19]

Rashba similarly states:

> Just as we have laws of the kingdom as declared by Samuel to Israel similarly gentile kingdoms possess known laws and it is with regard to such laws that the Sages declared that their laws are valid; but the laws on the basis of which the courts judge are not the law of the kingdom, rather the courts judge unto themselves on the basis of what they find in the works of [earlier] judges. . . .[20]

17. Cf. the descussion of a similar problem in other sources by Dayan I. Grunfeld, *The Jewish Law of Inheritance* (Oak Park, 1987), pp. 29–33.

18. *Teshuvot Tashbaẓ,* I, no. 158. See also *Teshuvot ha-Rashba,* III, no. 29.

19. *Tashbaẓ,* I, no. 158. A similar view is expressed by Ramban, *Baba Batra* 55a.

20. *Teshuvot ha-Rashba,* III, no. 29; see also *Bet Yosef, Tur Shulḥan Arukh, Ḥoshen Mishpat* 26 (end).

Thus Rashba explicitly excludes "judge-made law" from the ambit of *dina de-malkhuta dina.*

These authorities apparently understand the phrase "like all the nations" that occurs in I Samuel 8:5 as indicating that the peoples of antiquity shared a common corpus of law firmly established and known to all. That corpus of law bestowed certain powers upon the monarch, but not necessarily those powers announced by Samuel as the prerogatives of the rulers of the Jewish commonwealth. Nevertheless, according to both Rashba and *Tashbaẓ,* gentile kings are limited to enforcement of statutes incorporated in that corpus of law just as Jewish kings could not exceed the authority vested in them by virtue of Samuel's declaration.

Ritva seems to adhere to this position in part and to deviate in part. Ritva presumably did not understand the phrase "like all the nations" as limiting the power of gentile kings to enforcement of the specific provisions of already enacted legislation handed down from antiquity; rather, he understood the phrase as curtailing a monarch's authority to criminalize an act *post factum* and restricting his penal authority to enforcement of the provisions of a previously announced system of law. According to Ritva, this is the salient point of the reference to the practice of the monarchs of "all the nations" whose penal system merited endorsement and legitimization. The effect of incorporation of that phrase in the canon of Scripture is to deny non-Jewish monarchs the authority to act in an arbitrary or capricious manner. Thus Samuel's pronouncement serves to limit the authority of gentile sovereigns in a manner somewhat analogous, but not entirely parallel, to the manner in which the power of Jewish monarchs was limited. The power of Jewish kings was limited to the exercise of the prerogatives specifically delineated by Samuel whereas non-Jewish kings were denied absolute dictatorial power on an *ad hoc* basis but were charged only with ruling and meting out justice in accordance with a formal system of law, the content of which was left to their discretion.

Support for this analysis of Ritva's position that the talmudic controversy is limited to "the law of the pious," but that all agree that non-Jewish sovereigns may legitimately administer "the King's justice," is found in another medieval source. Rashba explicitly states that the controversy between Rabbi Eleazar ben Shimon and Rabbi Joshua ben Karḥah is solely with regard to how the pious should comport themselves but that, as a matter of law, both agree that it is permissible to assist the king in apprehending criminals.[21] Rashba writes:

> R. Eleazar ben Shimon apprehended thieves at the king's command and punished them as did R. Ishmael ben Yosi even though R. Joshua ben Karḥah called him "Vinegar, son of wine" . . . as did Elijah of R. Ishmael ben Yosi. Nevertheless, we should not deem them to be totally in error with regard to explicit legal provisions. Rather, because of their piety, they should have refrained from administering punishment not mandated by the Torah. That they were called "Vinegar, son of wine" was because they did not conduct themselves with piety as did their fathers. . . . For anyone who is appointed by the king for this purpose may judge and act according to the sovereign decrees, for the king preserves the land by means of such judgments.[22]

However, the position that even a non-Jewish sovereign may legitimately impose "the King's justice" is contradicted by Rambam, *Hilkhot Roẓeaḥ* 2:4, in his statement that "each of these murderers and their like who are not subject to death by verdict of the *Bet Din,* if a king of Israel wishes to put them to death by royal decree for the benefit of society he has the right to do so." In ascribing such authority only to "a king of Israel," Rambam appears to reject explicitly the notion that a gentile monarch is authorized to impose "the King's justice" and implies that even non-Jewish subjects must be judged solely in accordance with the provisions of the Noahide Code.[23] Rambam's position is all the more remarkable in light of the fact that, as noted earlier, in another section of his *Mishneh Torah, Hilkhot Gezeilah ve-Aveidah* 5:18, Rambam limits the application of the principle of *dina de-malkhuta dina* to the edicts of a monarch whose

21. See *Bet Yosef, Tur Shulḥan Arukh, Ḥoshen Mishpat* 388.

22. This analysis of the position espoused by Ritva and Rashba is reflected in a responsum of R. Moses Schick, *Teshuvot Maharam Shik, Ḥoshen Mishpat,* no. 50. The case involved a woman suspected of poisoning her husband. The question posed to Maharam Schick was whether or not she should be turned over to civil authorities in order to stand trial. After citing both Ritva and Rashba, Maharam Schick concludes that "sages of Israel" should not become actively involved, but should maintain a passive stance in the matter. Reflected in that position is the view that, although such acts would not be illicit, piety demands that "sages of Israel" not deliver the culprit for possible execution.

23. Cf. *Teshuvot Maharam Shik, Ḥoshen Mishpat,* no. 50. For a discussion of Maharam Schick's interpretation of Rambam, see this writer's "Hasgarat Poshe'a Yehudi she-Baraḥ le-Ereẓ Yisra'el," *Or ha-Mizraḥ,* Nisan-Tammuz 5747, p. 254.

sovereignty has been accepted by the populace. In doing so, Rambam implies that the authority of *dina de-malkhuta dina* is based upon the legitimate exercise of royal power, the monarchial prerogatives recorded in I Samuel 8. If so, Rambam's position is self-contradictory. If Rambam does indeed predicate *dina de-malkhuta dina* upon I Samuel 8, he must necessarily regard non-Jewish monarchs as vested with the prerogatives conferred by Scripture upon incumbents in royal office. If so, then, *mutatis mutandis,* a gentile king must also be vested with the authority to impose "the King's justice."

Rambam's position may be understood on the basis of a responsum authored by Rabbi Moses Sofer, *Teshuvot Ḥatam Sofer, Likkutim,* no. 14. The primary question addressed by *Ḥatam Sofer* in that responsum is whether a non-Jewish judge may accept a bribe. His response is that, although the biblical injunction "Thou shalt not take a bribe"[24] is addressed to Jews and not to Noahides, nevertheless, a Noahide is commanded to render a true and just verdict and hence he dare not accept a bribe for purposes of subverting justice.[25] A judge who knowingly renders an unjust judgment, opines *Ḥatam Sofer,* is guilty of a capital crime under the Noahide Code. Accordingly, he rules that a Jew who presents a bribe to a non-Jewish judge, not only wrongs his adversary, but is also guilty of "placing a stumbling-block before the blind" in causing the judge to issue an unjust decision. *Ḥatam Sofer* then proceeds to distinguish between civil actions and criminal proceedings. Since bribery of a gentile is forbidden only if the bribe is designed to assure a favorable judgment without regard to the merits of the case, a gift designed to assure only impartial deliberation and expeditious disposition of the case is not prohibited.[26] Accordingly, rules *Ḥatam Sofer,* a bribe designed to assure acquittal in a criminal proceeding cannot be forbidden since

---

24. Deuteronomy 16:19.

25. For further discussion of bribery under the Noahide Code see Ramban, *Commentary on the Bible,* Genesis 34:13; R. Joseph Saul Nathanson, *Teshuvot Sho'el u-Meshiv, Mahadura Kamma,* I, no. 230; *Encyclopedia Talmudit,* vol. III, p. 355, note 256; R. Bernard Chavel, *Peirush Ramban al ha-Torah,* I, 192, s.v. *u-be-Yerushalmi;* R. Jonathan Eibeschutz, *Urim ve-Tumim* 9:1; R. Joshua Leib Diskin, *Teshuvot Maharil Diskin,* II, *Kuntres Aḥaron,* no. 5, sec. 223.

26. In contradistinction to the law governing Noahide judges, a Jew may not accept a gift from a litigant even if it is only of trivial value, even if any attempt to influence the verdict is expressly disavowed, and even if gifts of equal value are presented by both parties. See Rambam, *Hilkhot Sanhedrin* 23:1 and 23:5.

> certainly there is no way that a Jew may [halakhically] incur the death penalty by operation of their laws [since they impose the death penalty] without witnesses, prior admonition and a court composed of twenty-three qualified Jewish judges and, accordingly, such execution is always contrary to the law of the Torah.[27]

Ḥatam Sofer's rejection of the authority of non-Jewish courts to impose the death penalty upon Jewish defendants would appear to apply with equal force to corporal punishment as well as to incarceration.[28]

Elsewhere, however, *Ḥatam Sofer* appears to espouse an entirely different view. In another responsum, *Teshuvot Ḥatam Sofer, Oraḥ Ḥayyim,* no. 208, that authority poses a fundamental question. Granting that enumeration of specific prospective actions in I Samuel 8 constitutes conferral of authority upon the monarch to engage in such practices, an examination of those verses reveals that they refer entirely to property rights and matters of personal service; no mention whatsoever is made of either corporal or capital punishment. Where, then, is the source of authority for even a Jewish king to impose such sanctions other than in accordance with statute?

Ḥatam Sofer finds a source for the exercise of such power in Ramban's comments on Leviticus 27:29, "*Kol ḥerem asher yeḥeram min ha-adam lo yipadeh, mot yamut.*" The standard translation of the verse, "None devoted, that may be devoted of men, shall be ransomed; he shall surely be put to death," renders its meaning utterly incomprehensible. Little wonder, then, that medieval rabbinic exegetes and commentaries struggled to arrive at a proper interpretation of the verse. Ramban understands the term "*ḥerem*" as used in this context as connoting societal proscription of certain acts upon pain of death. Understood in this manner, the verse, by inference, serves to confer legislative power upon society for the purpose of achieving socially desirable goals and also to confer penal authority to enforce such decrees. According to Ramban, the verse must be understood as an elliptical reference to the violation of a *ḥerem* pronounced by society and serves to forbid substitution of a financial penalty for capital punishment incurred in violation of a communal edict. The verse then should be rendered as "No [violation] of a *ḥerem,* pronounced as a *ḥerem* by man, shall be ransomed; he [the violator of the *ḥerem*] shall surely be put to death." The biblical narrative, I Samuel 14:24–45, recounting the

27. *Teshuvot Ḥatam Sofer, Likkutim,* no. 14.

28. See *Taz, Yoreh De'ah* 157:8.

actions of Jonathan and his incurrence of capital liability is explained by Ramban as predicated upon this scriptural provision. In eating honey Jonathan violated the communal edict pronounced by King Saul against partaking of food on the day of battle against the Philistines; hence Jonathan was subject to the death penalty. The verse "So the people rescued Jonathan, that he died not" (I Samuel 14:45) is understood by Ramban as meaning that the community retroactively nullified its edict and, pursuant to that nullification, Jonathan was exonerated. Such edicts may be promulgated, asserts *Ḥatam Sofer,* either by the community as a whole or by the sovereign as the executive authority of the community. It is quite apparently *Ḥatam Sofer*'s opinion that such authority is vested only in the Jewish community and hence only in a Jewish monarch. To be sure, the Jewish community in any country, utilizing its power of *ḥerem,* could promulgate an edict making *lèse majesté* against the gentile sovereign a culpable offense as a violation of Jewish law. However, no such edict was ever promulgated. Accordingly, only the sovereign of a Jewish state may legitimately impose penal sanctions upon violators of his decrees.

Nevertheless, *Ḥatam Sofer* finds alternative grounds for asserting that non-Jewish monarchs may legitimately impose extra-statutory punishment. That authority, as well as authority for the principle of *dina de-malkhuta dina, Ḥatam Sofer* regards as being based, not upon I Samuel 8, but upon Song of Songs 8:12. The verse "My vineyard, which is mine, is before me; you, O Solomon shall have the thousand, and those that keep the fruit thereof two hundred" is cited by the Gemara, *Shevu'ot* 35b, in support of a statement to the effect that a king who causes the death of one-sixth of the world's population is not subject to punishment. The authors of *Tosafot, ad locum,* understand that verse as granting Solomon dispensation to cause the death of two hundred individuals to conquer and preserve the thousand. "Those that keep the fruit" may sacrifice two hundred so that Solomon shall "have the thousand." The king is granted authority to go to war for reasons of state even though casualties necessarily result, provided that casualties are limited to a ratio no greater than two hundred in twelve hundred, leaving a remainder of one thousand (a casualty ratio no greater than one-sixth). That dispensation, argues *Ḥatam Sofer,* is not limited to casualties incurred as a result of warfare but extends as well to infliction of loss of life among the king's own subjects in the course of actions designed to benefit the nation or to enhance the grandeur and honor of the sovereign.[29] The king, as "keeper of the fruit," may compromise the lives and welfare of some of his subjects to preserve the integrity of his "vineyard." *Tosafot*'s statement indicating that the king is empowered to sacrifice lives for national purposes is understood by *Ḥatam Sofer* as not limiting such authority to casualties incurred in the course of war but as empowering the king to execute citizens for any legitimate purpose involving "preservation of the vineyard," with warfare simply serving as a paradigm. *Ḥatam Sofer* draws a further inference in stating that the verse "and those that keep the fruit thereof two hundred" serves to establish not only the right of the monarch to take the lives of subjects in order to safeguard the State, but also authorizes him to take lesser measures, including expropriation of property, to provide for the needs of society. Accordingly, concludes *Ḥatam Sofer, dina de-malkhuta dina,* as a principle of jurisprudence expressive of the State's authority to disturb the rights of its citizens to lawful enjoyment of property, is predicated upon Song of Songs 8:12.

In presenting the novel thesis that Song of Songs 8:12 serves as validation of the principle *dina de-malkhuta dina, Ḥatam Sofer* underscores the point that gentile monarchs are also vested with the power to impose penal sanctions upon miscreants. *Dina de-malkhuta dina,* as a normative principle of Jewish law, applies to the laws of non-Jewish states. If it is derived from Song of Songs 8:12 it follows that the verse must be regarded as delineating the authority of all monarchs, gentile as well as Jew. Accordingly, penal authority derived from that verse must also be vested in non-Jewish monarchs. There emerges, however, a contradiction between the position recorded in *Teshuvot Ḥatam Sofer, Oraḥ Ḥayyim,* no. 208, and his statement in *Teshuvot Ḥatam Sofer, Likkutim,* no. 14,denying the authority of a gentile king to impose capital punishment upon his Jewish subjects. Resolution of that problem requires a careful reading of the language employed in the latter responsum. *Ḥatam Sofer* declares such execution to be "*she-lo me-din Torah,*" literally, that is "not *from* the law of the Torah"; he does not employ language categorizing capital punishment as imposed by civil authorities to be in violation of, or contradictory to, the law of the Torah. It would seem that in his careful choice of nomenclature, *Ḥatam Sofer* seeks to draw attention to the fundamental distinction between capital punishment as imposed by the *Bet Din* and capital punishment imposed by the king: the latter is viewed as entirely discretionary whereas

29. See also *Teshuvot Ḥatam Sofer, Ḥoshen Mishpat,* no. 44, which reiterates the same principle.

the former is mandatory. In his enumeration of the 613 commandments recorded in Scripture, Rambam, *Sefer ha-Miẓvot, miẓvot aseh,* nos. 226–229, declares that implementation of capital punishment by the *Bet Din,* when required by law, constitutes fulfillment of a mandatory biblical commandment. In fact, the *Bet Din* was required to impose four different forms of capital punishment in punishment of various transgressions of biblical law and Rambam posits a separate commandment mandating administration of each of those four modes of execution. When the requirements of law pertaining to evidence and judicial procedure have been satisfied, the *Bet Din* has no choice but to pronounce its verdict and to impose the appropriate punishment; the *Bet Din* does not enjoy discretion to suspend the sentence or to impose a lesser punishment. Not so with regard to "the King's justice." The king's power is *ad hoc* in nature and is intended to be exercised only in accordance with the needs of the hour. Hence the king may ignore the infraction, grant a pardon, commute or suspend a sentence. Thus, imposition of capital punishment by the king is categorized by *Ḥatam Sofer* as "not from the law of the Torah" in the sense that, since it is discretionary in nature, it is not mandated by Torah law. Since gentile courts may impose the death penalty upon Jews or incarcerate criminals only by virtue of their power to impose "the King's justice" and since, according to Jewish law, imposition of such sanctions by the sovereign cannot be mandatory, *Ḥatam Sofer* finds no impropriety in any attempt to avoid imposition of such a penalty.

Acceptance of *Ḥatam Sofer*'s thesis provides a basis for resolving the apparent contradiction in Rambam's codification. As earlier noted, I Samuel 8:5 does not contain any reference to either capital or corporal punishment. Rambam may well agree with *Ḥatam Sofer* in regarding that power as being derived from Leviticus 27:29. In any event, since it is not derived from I Samuel it is not among the royal prerogatives enjoyed by "all the nations that surround us" and hence Rambam, *Hilkhot Roẓeaḥ* 2:4, maintains that such power is limited to the ruler of a Jewish commonwealth. In adopting that view Rambam is nevertheless at variance with *Ḥatam Sofer* in maintaining that gentile kings are not authorized to impose capital punishment in administrating "the King's justice." Presumably, Rambam understood the talmudic declaration exonerating a king who causes the death of one-sixth of the population as limited to casualties inflicted in the course of licitly undertaken warfare. Such a position is entirely compatible with a literal reading of *Tosafot*'s analysis of that dictum.

Accordingly, Rambam may be understood as maintaining that *dina de-malkhuta dina* is a derivative of royal authority conferred upon all monarchs on the basis of I Samuel and as maintaining that any sovereign "accepted" by the populace may exercise that authority. However, maintains Rambam, since penal sanctions are not enumerated in I Samuel, the sovereign has no authority to impose such sanctions other than in accordance with the statutory provisions of the Noahide Code. It therefore follows that, according to Rambam, it is forbidden to deliver a Jew to civil authorities for punishment; rather, the normative law, according to Rambam, is in accordance with the pronouncement of Rabbi Joshua ben Karḥah: "Let the owner of the vineyard come and eradicate his thorns."[30]

According to this analysis, Rambam regards Rabbi Joshua ben Karḥah as asserting a normative halakhic position rather than as asserting a standard of pious conduct as has earlier been shown is evidently the position of Ritva and Rashba. There then emerges somewhat of a problem with regard to the nature of the controversy between Rabbi Joshua ben Karḥah and Rabbi Eleazar ben Shimon. If it is accepted that Rabbi Eleazar ben Shimon bases his position upon Song of Songs 8:12, as is the view of *Ḥatam Sofer,* it is extremely unlikely that Rabbi Joshua ben Karḥah would reject the halakhic principle derived from that verse without making it clear that the exegetical basis of the principle is in dispute. It is similarly unlikely that Rabbi Eleazar ben Shimon regards the authority of a monarch derived from that verse to be limited to infliction of casualties in the course of warfare, as may well be assumed on the basis of the comments of *Tosafot,* since that, too, should have been made clear in the words of the talmudic protagonists themselves.[31]

It should also be pointed out that Ritva's analysis of the controversy between Rabbi Joshua ben Karḥah and Rabbi Eleazar ben Shimon is rejected by a number of early authorities and hence, even ignoring the difficulties with regard to that controversy posed by *Ḥatam Sofer*'s thesis, an alternate analysis of that controversy must be sought that will accommodate the position of the early authorities who do not accept Ritva's

30. *Baba Meẓi'a* 83b.

31. If, as is the position of both Ritva and Rashba, both R. Joshua ben Karḥah and R. Eleazar ben Shimon agree that the king enjoys the power to execute evildoers, there is no reason for them to present any further explanation of their conflicting views regarding the standard to be applied to the pious. That is the case even if such authority is derived from Song of Songs rather than I Samuel 8, as is the view of *Ḥatam Sofer.* Presumably, the exegetical reference was omitted since it was well known and not at all a matter of controversy.

justification of Rabbi Joshua ben Karḥah's action. Ritva's contention that the monarchial prerogatives specified in I Samuel may be exercised by gentile rulers is clearly disputed by *Tosafot, Sanhedrin* 20b, in their comments upon another talmudic discussion. *Tosafot* are understandably troubled by the divine censure of the conduct of King Ahab as is recorded in I Kings 21. Nabot refused to sell his vineyard to Ahab and, consequently, Ahab had him put to death and seized the vineyard. However, if I Samuel serves as a declaration of royal prerogatives, Ahab acted in an entirely licit manner in expropriating Nabot's land and, since Nabot was culpable in not acceding to the king's demand, Ahab's action in punishing Nabot did not at all warrant censure. *Tosafot* resolve the problem by declaring that the royal prerogatives described in I Samuel may legitimately be exercised only by a king who rules "over all of Israel and Judea by virtue of divine appointment." Since Ahab neither ruled over "all of Israel and Judea" nor ruled by virtue of divine appointment, he had no right to exercise the powers delineated in I Samuel. Since, according to *Tosafot,* even a Jewish king who does not rule by virtue of divine right as announced by a prophet or whose sovereignty is limited to only a portion of the Jewish populace enjoys none of the halakhic prerogatives of a monarch, it follows *a fortiori* that such powers are not recognized by Jewish law as being vested in a gentile king whose reign cannot be described as satisfying those two necessary conditions. Thus, unlike Ritva, *Tosafot* certainly regard I Samuel as inapplicable to a non-Jewish sovereign.[32]

Accordingly, it may be suggested that Rabbi Eleazar ben Shimon's dictum "I am eradicating thorns from the vineyard"[33] can be understood in a manner other than as reliance upon the prerogatives associated with royal office.

Rema, *Ḥoshen Mishpat* 388:12 and 425:1, rules that, in an age of collective punishment, a person who engages in counterfeiting or the like may be turned over to civil authorities for punishment. As justification for that ruling, Rema cites the law of the "pursuer" (*rodef*), the provision of Jewish law that not merely permits, but mandates, that a bystander come to the rescue of a putative victim whose life is threatened and that, if there is no other way of preserving the life of the intended victim, rescue be effected by taking the life of the aggressor.[34] In the talmudic

32. See R. Abraham Kahana-Shapiro, *Teshuvot Dvar Avraham,* I, no. 1, note appended to *anaf* 2.

33. *Baba Meẓi'a* 83b.

34. This rule is codified by Rambam, *Hilkhot Roẓeaḥ* 2:4.

narrative that serves as the focus of the dispute between Rabbi Eleazar ben Shimon and Rabbi Joshua ben Karḥah, the criminals sought by the king were not only breaking the law but were, in actuality, jeopardizing the lives of innocent parties. Rabbi Eleazar ben Shimon came upon an official of the king who was apprehending individuals and delivering them for execution without at all endeavoring to distinguish between the innocent and the guilty.[35] Indeed, Rabbi Eleazar ben Shimon demonstrates that the thieves were avoiding detention because "they hide themselves as animals who secrete themselves by day" and hence only the innocent were being apprehended. The officer's response was "What shall I do? It is the command of the king!" The officer clearly recognized that his actions were unjust but pleaded *force majeure.* In all probability, the king was well aware of the fact that arrests were being made indiscriminately but pursued such a policy because of a desire to instill fear in the hearts of thieves in an effort to cause them to desist from their nefarious conduct. Execution of the innocent was designed either to create a feeling of apprehension in those who were indeed criminals and had reason to fear that they too would be apprehended or to secure the cooperation of the citizenry, who as a result of the institution of that policy had reason to fear for their own lives, and bring pressure to bear upon the thieves to desist from their criminal activities. In any event, it is clear that the king was, in fact, executing the innocent because of the acts of some few malfeasors among the populace. It is, of course, possible that the king genuinely desired that only the guilty be apprehended but that the officer acted with misplaced zeal because he feared that were he to fail to report success in bringing the guilty to justice his own life would be forfeit. Either way, *de facto,* innocent persons were being put to death because of the activities of thieves. Thus, thieves were "pursuers" of the innocent no less so than the counterfeiters described by Rema on whose account the authorities were prepared to engage in collective punishment. Since the thieves refused to abandon their criminal activities, they were branded as "pursuers" by Rabbi Eleazar ben Shimon who declared that "I am eradicating thorns from the vineyard." The import of that statement may be taken to mean that the criminals were a threat to the innocent just as thorns are a threat to the grapes that would otherwise flourish in the vineyard. If so, Rabbi Eleazar ben Shimon was not merely defending his activities as not being in violation of Jewish law, as must be understood as having been the case according to Ritva's interpretation, but was

35. *Baba Meẓi'a* 83b.

declaring his actions to be obligatory. In branding the thieves as "thorns" Rabbi Eleazar ben Shimon colorfully depicts them as persons engaged in destruction of the entire "vineyard" with the result that it was incumbent upon him to eliminate them to preserve innocent persons endangered by their activities.

If this analysis of the position of Rabbi Eleazar ben Shimon is correct, Rabbi Joshua ben Karḥah's response, "Let the owner of the vineyard come and destroy his thorns," becomes problematic. The retort does not seem to involve a denial of the facts of the case. If the facts were as described, Rabbi Eleazar ben Shimon's halakhic analysis is beyond cavil.

The controversy between Rabbi Eleazar ben Shimon and Rabbi Joshua ben Karḥah may well reflect disagreement regarding the level of certainty of impending loss of life that is required to trigger the law of pursuit. Even if Rabbi Joshua ben Karḥah did not himself appreciate the fact that the thieves were in actuality "pursuers" as well, once he heard Rabbi Eleazar ben Shimon declare "I am destroying thorns in the vineyard" Rabbi Joshua ben Karḥah's retort "Let the Master of the vineyard come and eradicate his thorns" is entirely inappropriate. Rabbi Joshua ben Karḥah acquiesces in the assignment of the appellation "thorns" to the evildoers. If so, to refrain from taking action against them would constitute a violation of the biblical command "And you shall cut off her hand, your eye shall not have pity" (Deuteronomy 25:12).[36]

The Gemara, *Sanhedrin* 72a, employing biblical exegesis, develops the principle that a burglar must also be presumed to be intent upon taking the life of the householder whose home he enters. It is to be presumed that if the householder discovers the intruder he will instinctively resist with all means at his disposal in order to preserve hearth and home. The burglar, in turn, recognizes the likelihood that lethal force will be used against him and hence it must be presumed that, if discovered by the householder in the course of breaking into his home, the burglar, fearing for his own life, will endeavor to strike first. Since the burglar is not only engaged in felonious activity but is also responsible for creating the danger to the householder, he is adjudged a "pursuer." The Gemara declares that an exception to this rule occurs in the case of a father engaged in burglarizing his son's home. In that case, the talmudic presumption is that a father will not attempt to kill his own son and, since this is known to the son as well, the son, if he should kill his burglarizing

36. Rambam, *Hilkhot Roẓeaḥ* 1:7, records the law of the "pursuer" as being predicated upon this verse.

father, cannot seek exoneration by pleading that he was entitled to invoke the law of pursuit. In other cases, however, there exists a legal presumption that the burglar is a "pursuer." In their commentaries upon that discussion both Rashi and *Tosafot* indicate that, in the absence of a presumption of law, the "pursuer" may not be killed unless murderous intent on his part is known with certainty; the "law of the pursuer" cannot be invoked on the basis of mere suspicion or in a case of doubt.[37]

A contemporary authority, the late Rabbi Moses Feinstein, *Iggerot Mosheh, Ḥoshen Mishpat,* II, no. 69, sec. 2, declares that the law of pursuit applies only in situations in which the murderous intent of the aggressor is known on the basis of an assessment "approaching certainty." However, a leading authority of the previous generation, Rabbi Chaim Ozer Grodzinski, *Teshuvot Aḥi'ezer,* I, no. 123, sec. 2, adopts a somewhat looser standard. In discussing the propriety of a therapeutic abortion which, according to some, may be performed only when the life of the mother is threatened by the fetus as "pursuer," *Aḥi'ezer* is prepared to rely upon the "assessment" of medical practitioners but does not indicate that their prognosis must be couched in terms indicating that, absent intervention, the likelihood that the mother will die "approaches certainty." The most elastic standard is apparently that of Rabbi Elijah of Vilna, *Bi'ur ha-Gra, Ḥoshen Mishpat* 388:74, who understands Rema as permitting summary execution of counterfeiters even when the danger to the community is not known with certainty but is only "feared" (*ḥeshasha*). In support of this view, *Bi'ur ha-Gra* comments that the principle is derived from the biblical provisions concerning a burglar and indicates that he regards the danger to the life of the householder in such a situation to be less than certain.

It may be the case that Ritva, in explaining the conduct of Rabbi Eleazar ben Shimon as based upon implementation of "the King's justice," declined to explain the matter on the basis of the "law of the pursuer" because he did not regard it as being clear that the king would continue to apprehend and execute the innocent together with the guilty. Particularly with the king's appointment of Rabbi Eleazar ben Shimon as the official charged with bringing evildoers to justice pursuant to his becoming impressed with that scholar's wisdom and sagacity, there may well have been reason to assume that the king's wrath was assuaged and that he would no longer pursue the matter so assiduously or that Rabbi Eleazar ben Shimon would be in a position to dissuade the king from imposing

37. See also R. Isaac Schorr, *Teshuvot Koaḥ Shor,* no. 20, s.v. *gedolah me-zu.*

punishment indiscriminately upon the innocent as well as upon the guilty.

Tosafot and Rambam, however, certainly understood the talmudic narrative as reflecting a conviction on the part of all concerned that such practices would continue. Nevertheless, it may be postulated that Rabbi Eleazar ben Shimon did not know with certainty, or even in a manner "approaching certainty," that this would occur. The essence of the controversy between Rabbi Eleazar ben Shimon and Rabbi Joshua ben Karḥah may then have been with regard to whether or not the "law of the pursuer" may be invoked when the danger to the victim cannot be established with certainty or in a manner "approaching certainty." Accordingly, Rabbi Joshua ben Karḥah maintained that the "law of the pursuer" is applicable only in cases of virtual certainty while Rabbi Eleazar ben Shimon maintained that a significantly lesser degree of certainty is sufficient.

III. *Natural Law and the Penal Authority of the State*

Yet another theory explaining the principle *dina de-malkhuta dina* is advanced by Rashi in his commentary on *Gittin* 9b. The Mishnah declares that all civil instruments executed by non-Jewish courts are valid for purposes of Jewish law even though the attesting witnesses are gentiles. Included in that category are deeds to real property that serve to give legal effect to the transfer and which, ostensively, must be signed by competent Jewish witnesses to do so. Bills of divorce similarly executed are explicitly declared by the Mishnah to be invalid, presumably because of the absence of qualified attesting witnesses. Rashi endeavors to resolve the problem by indicating that, although gentiles are not subject to the provisions of biblical law concerning divorce, they are bound by the Noahide Code which includes a commandment concerning "*dinin.*" Rambam, *Hilkhot Melakhim* 9:14, defines *dinin* as an obligation to enforce the other provisions of the Noahide Code by appointing judges and other law enforcement officials while Ramban, *Commentary on the Bible,* Genesis 34:13, defines "*dinin*" as commanding the establishment of an ordered system of jurisprudence for the governance of financial, commercial and interpersonal relationships.

Rashi's comments are remarkable because the Gemara itself, *Gittin* 10b, provides a different explanation for the validity of instruments drafted by gentile courts as posited by the Mishnah. The Gemara explains simply that the rule stipulated in the Mishnah is predicated upon the principle *dina de-malkhuta dina.* Accordingly, such instruments are regarded as valid in Jewish law because they are recognized as valid by "the law of the kingdom." Rashi's comment must then be understood, not simply as justification of the provision recorded in the Mishnah, but as an explication of the talmudic analysis of that position. Thus, in offering this comment, Rashi formulates a novel theory in justification of the principle *dina de-malkhuta dina.*

Rashi's thesis is compatible with Ramban's definition of *dinin* as understood by Rabbi Naphtali Zevi Judah Berlin, *Ha'amek She'elah, She'ilta* 2, sec. 3. Although Ramban clearly states that the commandment regarding *dinin* serves to mandate establishment of a fully developed system of jurisprudence, he is silent with regard to the nature of the contents of that corpus of law. Rema, *Teshuvot Rema,* no. 10, and Rabbi Moses Sofer, *Teshuvot Ḥatam Sofer, Likkutim,* no. 14, assert that gentiles govern their affairs by means of the applicable provisions of Jewish law as they pertain to civil matters and are not at liberty to reject or modify those provisions. According to this analysis of Ramban's position, *dinin* is simply the incorporation by reference into the Noahide Code of the jurisprudence of the Sinaitic Code. Rabbi Naphtali Zevi Judah Berlin expresses an opposing view in asserting that, according to Ramban, the Noahide Code is silent with regard to specific provisions of law pertaining to matters of jurisprudence. The commandment mandates only that laws be propagated to preserve the social order; the content of those laws is left to be determined in accordance with the need and discretion of each society.[38] According to that thesis, Rashi may be understood as declaring that *dina de-malkhuta dina* represents the exercise of the legislative authority sanctioned by the commandment concerning *dinin.* Hence, according to Rashi, the ultimate authority that renders "the law of the kingdom" binding upon the populace is the commandment concerning *dinin.*

However, one problem remains with regard to this analysis of Rashi's comment. Jews are bound by the 613 precepts of the Sinaitic Code rather than by the Noahide Code. Accordingly, the commandment concerning *dinin* is not part of the corpus of law binding upon Jews. Hence any novel aspect of law predicated upon the principle of *dinin* should apply only to non-Jews but not to Jews. Moreover, although *dinin* may confer authority upon gentiles to enact legislation as they see fit, as is the opinion of Rabbi Naphtali Zevi Judah Berlin, the jurisprudential aspects of Jewish law are established by biblical statute and are not subject to

---

38. This is also the position of R. Iser Zalman Meltzer, *Even he-Azel, Hilkhot Malveh ve-Loveh* 27:1.

modification by society. Jews certainly do not have the right, for example, to abrogate the biblical obligation requiring an employer to pay a day-laborer's hire immediately and to permit a 30-day grace period for payment. Similarly, Jews cannot vary the provisions governing qualifications of attesting witnesses. Rashi's comment might adequately serve to explain why instruments drafted by gentile courts may be recognized and enforced among Noahides but completely fails to address the question of why they may properly be accepted and enforced by a *Bet Din* against a Jewish litigant.

Rashi's comment may be understood on the basis of a remarkable provision recorded by Rambam in the final section of his *Mishneh Torah*. Subsequent to a detailed codification of the provisions of the Noahide Code in general and of *dinin* in particular as well as of the provisions of law pertaining to the resident alien domiciled in the Jewish commonwealth who formally agrees to be bound by the Noahide Code, Rambam, *Hilkhot Melakhim* 10:11, writes:

> The *Bet Din* of Israel is obligated to establish judges for these resident aliens to judge them in accordance with these laws in order that the world not be destroyed. If the *Bet Din* sees fit to appoint judges from among them, they may do so; and if they see fit to appoint Jewish judges for them, they may do so.

However, Rambam himself, in an earlier ruling, *Hilkhot Melakhim* 9:14, states that establishment of a judiciary for this purpose is an obligation incumbent upon gentiles. In keeping with the fact that *dinin* is a commandment addressed to Noahides rather than to Jews, there seems to be no basis in talmudic sources for positing the establishment of a Noahide judiciary as an obligation binding upon Jews as well as upon non-Jews. The Noahide Code requires gentiles to manage their own affairs without establishing a concomitant obligation in Jewish law requiring Jews to fill any lacunae resulting from nonfeasance on the part of Noahides. Rambam's justification of this ruling, "so that the world not be destroyed," is not culled from any prior rabbinic source and is not rooted in any particular commandment. It would appear that the obligation recorded by Rambam is not predicated upon any dogmatic precept but is entirely the product of reason; the mandate is in the nature of what may be termed an obligation of natural law. Society cannot exist long in a state of anarchy. Preservation of society—and of the world—is mandated by reason; hence reason dictates that the *Bet Din* must guarantee preservation of law and order by establishing a judicial system to administer the provisions of the Noahide Code.

Rashi's comment may be explained on the basis of a similar consideration. Although gentiles are explicitly commanded with regard to *dinin,* the need to establish a system of jurisprudence is dictated by reason as well. Even if the Noahide Code were to be silent concerning such matters, reason dictates that laws governing matters of jurisprudence be established and enforced. Normative principles discovered by reason are binding upon Jews and gentiles alike. Accordingly, it may be postulated that Rashi concludes that Jews living in societies in which they lack legal autonomy are bound to obey the law of the host country. Although, as a commandment, *dinin* is addressed only to Noahides, reason requires that Jews be bound by legislation authorized by that commandment.[39]

Rashi's comments elsewhere serve to indicate that reason further mandates that evildoers be punished in as severe a manner as necessary to deter others. The Gemara, *Niddah* 61a, records the following narrative:

> It was rumored concerning certain Galileans that they killed a person. They came to Rabbi Tarfon and said to him, "Sir, hide us!" [Rabbi Tarfon] replied, "What shall I do? If I do not hide you, you will be seen. Should I hide you? The Sages have said that rumors, even though they may not be accepted, nevertheless, should not be dismissed. Go and hide yourselves."

Tosafot comment that Rabbi Tarfon was concerned that the rumors might be true, the fugitives may indeed have committed an act of murder, and that, if so, Rabbi Tarfon's own life would be "forfeit to the king" as punishment for having harbored fugitives. Rashi, however, comments simply, "perhaps you have committed murder and it is forbidden to save you" without at all suggesting that Rabbi Tarfon was motivated by fear of punishment at the hands of the civil authorities. On the contrary, Rashi indicates that Rabbi Tarfon's concern was founded upon the illicit nature of the contemplated act of concealment rather than fear of retribution.[40]

---

39. For a fuller discussion of reflections of natural law theory in rabbinic sources as well as of the positions of Rambam and Rashi see this writer's "Judaism and Natural Law," *Jewish Law Annual,* VII (1988), 5–42.

40. This is certainly how Rashi was understood by Rosh, *Niddah* 61a. But cf., R. Jacob Ettlinger, *Arukh la-Ner, Niddah* 61a, who understands Rashi's comment as referring to applicable secular law.

Rashi clearly assumes that, in terms of Jewish law, harboring a guilty fugitive constitutes an illicit act even though the guilty person is a fugitive from the justice of the civil state. That position is cogent only if it is antecedently granted that the prosecuting authorities may legitimately impose penal sanctions upon evildoers. Hence Rashi may readily be numbered among the authorities who maintain that a non-Jewish sovereign may legitimately impose penal sanctions in accordance with "the King's justice."[41]

Nevertheless, one point requires clarification. Punishment of malfeasors may be a royal prerogative. That, however, does not establish an obligation to assist the king in exercising that prerogative. Surely this is true of the other royal prerogatives enunciated in I Samuel 8 and is equally true if the authority of the sovereign is derived from Song of Songs 8:12. Scripture merely grants licence to the monarch to expropriate property, to exact personal services or to endanger the lives of the populace and also to punish those who disobey his edicts. However, Scripture does not require him to impose such punishment or demand that others assist him in doing so. By the same token, although the king may administer punishment on an *ad hoc* basis, there is no apparent statutory provision indicating that a person may not conceal an individual sought by the king. Rashi, then, must be understood as positing an obligation not to do so based solely upon the dictates of reason. Reason demands that a murderer be brought to justice and punished. Reason similarly demands that punishment be carried out only in accordance with legal procedures and only by duly constituted authorities because the alternative would similarly lead to a breakdown of the social order. Just as reason forbids a person to take the law into his own hands, it also mandates that there be no interference with the administration of justice by properly constituted authorities. Hence Rashi concludes that it is forbidden to shield a murderer and that Rabbi Tarfon could not allow himself to be in the position of doing so. A similar position attributed to Rashba is cited by Rabbi Joseph Karo in his commentary on *Tur Shulḥan Arukh, Bet Yosef, Ḥoshen Mishpat* 388. *Bet Yosef* quotes that authority as declaring "for if everything is left to stand on the law of the Torah, as when the Sanhedrin imposes judgment, the world would be desolate." Rashba's comment is expressed in the context of a justification of the imposition of penal sanctions by civil authorities

41. For justification of imposition of penal sanctions by secular authorities with consent of the governed on the basis of a theory of inherent powers of society, see R. Joseph Dov Cohen, *Ha-Torah ve-ha-Medinah,* I, 20–26.

upon Jewish nationals and similarly reflects the position that such authority is derived on the basis of reason alone.[42]

42. A similar theory is propounded by the 19th-century rabbinic scholar, R. Zevi Hirsch Chajes (*Maharaẓ Ḥayes*), in *Torat Nevi'im,* chap. 7, published in *Kol Sifrei Maharaẓ Ḥayes,* I, 48. *Maharaẓ Ḥayes* observes that disobedience of law leads to anarchy, but instead of asserting that there exists a natural law basis for enforcement of a criminal code, he argues that the sovereign is empowered to punish transgressors by virtue of the "law of the pursuer." For a discussion of the difficulties inherent in *Maharaẓ Ḥayes'* position see this writer's discussion in *Or ha-Mizraḥ,* Nisan-Tammuz 5747, pp. 268–269.

Chapter V
Sabbath Questions

The emperor said to R. Joshua ben Ḥanania, "Why is the aroma of Sabbath food so fragrant?" He replied, "We have a seasoning called Shabbat *which we pour into [the food] and the aroma becomes fragrant." "Give me some of it," said the emperor. R. Joshua said, "It is efficacious to those who observe the Sabbath, but is of no benefit to those who do not observe the Sabbath."*

SHABBAT 119a

Extending Sabbath Invitations to the Non-Observant

One of the happier developments of recent decades is the return to religious observance on the part of countless individuals. Young people, perceiving a spiritual vacuum in their lives, have come to appreciate the purpose and richness of meaning to be found in a life devoted to *shmirat ha-miẓvot.* Their quest has been guided by a cadre of teachers and outreach professionals and a network of committed laymen drawn from all sectors of the Orthodox community. This newly awakened interest has spawned a plethora of publications designed to meet the thirst for knowledge manifested by the newly observant. This phenomenon is also reflected in problems addressed in contemporary halakhic literature.[1]

Congregational rabbis and Talmud Torah teachers have long found themselves in an uncomfortable position. On the one hand, it is often their professional duty to organize and to encourage attendance at Synagogue services as well as participation in educational and social events held on *Shabbat.* On the other hand, they are fully aware that many of

1. Two volumes devoted to the particular and unique problems encountered by *ba'alei teshuvah* (or better, returnees to Jewish observance) and their mentors are to be highly recommended: R. Moshe Newman and R. Mordecai Becher, *Avotot Ahavah* (Jerusalem, 5752); and R. Moshe Weinberger, *Jewish Outreach: Halakhic Perspectives* (Hoboken, 5750).

the invitees will travel to and from these events by means of prohibited forms of transportation. In recent years, with the proliferation of organizations and programs devoted to introducing uncommitted and unobservant Jews to the richness of the Jewish heritage, the problem has become even more vexing. To a large extent, success of such programs, and with such success the hope of effecting a transformation in the lives of the persons reached in this manner, depends upon exposure to a *Shabbat* atmosphere. But again, for some individuals, encouragement to participate in such programs is tantamount to an invitation to engage in forbidden modes of travel.

The ramifications of the halakhic issues posed by this dilemma may well vary with the nuances of particular situations. Unfortunately, a comprehensive survey of the underlying halakhic considerations and their application in varying circumstances has, as yet, not been forthcoming. Nevertheless, a number of brief discussions of various scenarios as well as statements in the form of general guidelines have appeared.

An early discussion of one of the many guises of the problem is presented by R. Moses Feinstein, *Iggerot Mosheh, Oraḥ Ḥayyim,* I, no. 98. For pedagogic reasons, a synagogue apparently wished to institute a youth *minyan.* However, by virtue of the fact that the youngsters lived at some distance from the synagogue it was certain that they would travel by car. In a brief and somewhat cryptic statement Rabbi Feinstein declares that it is "obvious and clear" that institution of a youth *minyan* under such circumstances is forbidden. Presumably feeling that any further discussion would be superfluous, *Iggerot Mosheh* adds simply that "training" with regard to prayer assuredly does not take precedence over "training" with regard to Sabbath observance. The clear implication is that children should be taught to remain at home rather than to violate Sabbath prohibitions even for the purpose of participating in synagogue services. Rabbi Feinstein adds that, in such cases, establishing a youth *minyan* would be tantamount to an overt directive to participate in synagogue services even if such participation entails desecration of *Shabbat.* Hence the very establishment of a youth *minyan* under such circumstances seems to convey an incorrect lesson and to inculcate a false system of values. Rabbi Feinstein emphasizes that these considerations pertain even if the children are below the age of *bar miẓvah.* Although it can hardly be anticipated that pre-*bar miẓvah* children will themselves drive to the synagogue, the cogency of Rabbi Feinstein's comment is not diminished by its contextual superfluousness.

Rabbi Feinstein does not at all enter into a discussion of whether anyone other than a father bears a formal responsibility for the "training" (*ḥinnukh*) of a child or whether there is an obligation to admonish a minor to desist from a prohibited activity. His response is simply that the innovation, albeit well-intentioned, is counterproductive. The inadvertent but inescapable effect of such activities is to confirm children in their non-observance of the Sabbath and to teach them that Sabbath observance is of lesser importance than communal prayer. That is a far more serious matter than responsibility for individual acts of omission or commission on the part of minors. Transmission of a false value system is assuredly prohibited to all.

In the immediately following responsum, *Iggerot Mosheh, Oraḥ Ḥayyim,* I, no. 99, a responsum actually authored some two years prior to the preceding responsum, Rabbi Feinstein offers somewhat broader guidance. The question posed to him is whether it is permissible to invite people to attend synagogue services when it is known that they will travel by automobile in order to do so. He responds by ruling that it is forbidden to extend such invitations to people living at a distance from which it is impossible to come by foot on the grounds that the invitation constitutes a forbidden act of "placing a stumbling block before the blind" that is prohibited on the basis of Leviticus 19:14. He further advances a novel thesis in declaring that an invitation of such nature entails an additional transgression in the form of "enticement" (*meisit*). Deuteronomy 13:7–12 establishes successful enticement to commit an act of idolatry as a capital transgression. Citing the statement of the Gemara, *Sanhedrin* 29a, declaring the serpent that tempted Eve to partake of the fruit of the Tree of Knowledge as having had the status of an "enticer," Rabbi Feinstein argues that enticement to commit any infraction constitutes a distinct sin, although only enticement to idolatry constitutes a capital transgression.[2]

Iggerot Mosheh further rules that the prohibition against "placing a stumbling block" applies even if travel by foot is not impossible but "it is known" that the invitees will nevertheless travel by automobile for the sake of convenience. However, he asserts that in such cases the prohibition

2. *Iggerot Mosheh*'s assertion that the prohibition against "enticement" is not limited to idolatry is not found in earlier sources and is directly contradicted by R. Meir Dan Plocki, *Klei Ḥemdah, Parashat Re'eh,* sec. 4. The serpent's declaration, "You shall be as God, knowing good and evil" (Genesis 3:5), constituted enticement to deny a fundamental principle of faith. Denial of fundamental principles of faith constitutes heresy which, in turn, is tantamount to idolatry in other areas of Jewish law as well, as shown in this writer's "Be-Bi'ur Shitat ha-Rambam be-Sheḥitat Akum u-Mumar," *Bet Yiẓḥak,* XX (1989), 279–284.

against "enticement" is not applicable.

Iggerot Mosheh further discusses the even more usual situation in which explicit language of invitation is not employed but an announcement with regard to services is made for the benefit of those residing within walking distance although "it is known" that others who live beyond walking distance will also respond. Rabbi Feinstein declares that, in such circumstances, the prohibition against "enticement" does not apply but expresses doubt with regard to the applicability of the prohibition against "placing a stumbling block before the blind." Unfortunately, he does not spell out the reasons or considerations pro or con that give rise to his uncertainty. He further declares that, insofar as children and students who are offered inducements for attending services are concerned, it must be explicitly announced that prizes or rewards will be available only to those who come on foot.

The matter is revisited a third time by Rabbi Feinstein in *Iggerot Mosheh, Oraḥ Ḥayyim,* IV, no. 71. In that responsum, Rabbi Feinstein writes that a teacher "did well" in not encouraging students to attend synagogue services on *Shabbat* since "there is reason to suspect" that they would engage in prohibited travel on *Shabbat* in order to do so.

In the latter responsum, Rabbi Feinstein also addresses another related question. The teacher's duties included informing students of the date of a program or celebration to be held on *Shabbat* and preparing them to take part in that program, i.e., coaching them in preparing parts for a play or the like. An obvious analogous problem arises with a much higher degree of frequency with regard to *bar mizvah* teachers who must determine the date of the *bar mizvah* and teach the student the *haftorah.*

Rabbi Feinstein responds by noting that, should the teacher decline to perform those duties, another instructor would surely be found for that purpose. That, he claims, removes the act from the ambit of the biblical prohibition against "placing a stumbling block before the blind." Nevertheless, a rabbinic prohibition remains in place even under such circumstances. However, concludes Rabbi Feinstein, since 1) the instruction does not take place immediately prior to the *Shabbat* on which the program is to be held and 2) it is not certain that the children will travel by automobile, "it is possible" that the teacher need not sacrifice his or her position by refusing to perform such duties.

Again, *Iggerot Mosheh* fails to cite precedents or to explain his reasoning. The distinction that *Iggerot Mosheh* draws in stating that no biblical prohibition against "placing a stumbling block" pertains in situations in which that act will readily be performed by another is a matter of significant controversy. As a paradigm of "placing a stumbling block before the blind" the Gemara, *Avodah Zarah* 6a, offers the example of a person extending a cup of wine to a Nazirite and declares that a biblical transgression is incurred only if the Nazirite and the person extending the cup of wine to him are standing on opposite banks of a river, i.e., only if it would be impossible for the Nazirite to reach the wine without the assistance of the other person. If, however, both are on the same side of the river, no biblical transgression is incurred since the Nazirite, if he chose to do so, could reach the wine without assistance. But what of a case in which physical assistance is required but other individuals are available who are ready and willing to offer such assistance? *Tosafot, Ḥaggigah* 13a, indicates that, if a non-Jew is available to offer the necessary assistance in commission of a transgression, a Jew rendering the same assistance is not in violation of a biblical prohibition. *Mishneh le-Melekh, Hilkhot Malveh ve-Loveh* 4:2, distinguishes between situations in which a non-Jew, who bears no culpability for "placing a stumbling block," is available to render such assistance, and situations in which only a fellow Jew is available for such aid. *Mishneh le-Melekh* reasons that, in a situation in which the transgression can be performed only with the forbidden cooperation of a Jew, the individual who renders such assistance is culpable. Since all Jews are equally bound not to render assistance, no Jew can claim that the transgression would have been committed even in the absence of forbidden assistance. Accordingly, the person who actually provides such aid is guilty of "placing a stumbling block before the blind."

A number of authorities, including R. Abraham Samuel Benjamin Sofer, who authored a classic and comprehensive responsum devoted to the ramifications of this prohibition, *Teshuvot Ketav Sofer, Yoreh De'ah,* no. 83, take issue with *Mishneh le-Melekh*. Nevertheless, many writers, including *Sedei Ḥemed, Ma'arekhet ha-Vav, klal* 26, sec. 9, and R. Ya'akov Kanievski, *Kehillat Ya'akov, Likkutim,* II, no. 6, declare that the weight of authority supports the position of *Mishneh le-Melekh.*[3] Since in the case discussed by *Iggerot Mosheh* it must be presumed that only Jewish teachers were available to provide the required services, those authorities would maintain that the availability of other teachers has no impact upon the applicability of the prohibition against "placing a stumbling block before the blind."

---

3. For additional sources see R. Isaac Elijah ha-Kohen Adler, *Lifnei Iver* (Ofakim, 5749), chap. 3, sec. 5.

Inviting or encouraging forbidden forms of travel constitutes "placing a stumbling block" even though such travel could readily have been undertaken without an express invitation. Causing a transgression by presenting a forbidden substance to a person who had no prior intention of committing a transgression, although he was fully capable of doing so without assistance were he to have desired to do so, constitutes a violation of the biblical prohibition.[4] Moreover, it seems to this writer that the very act of extending an invitation whose acceptance entails commission of a sin constitutes "harmful advice" that is independently prohibited as a form of "placing a stumbling block before the blind."

A quite similar question is frequently posed with regard to inviting guests to one's home on *Shabbat*. Many individuals involved in outreach endeavors directed toward persons who have not had the benefit of a traditional Jewish upbringing and designed to motivate them to adopt a Jewish lifestyle have found that invitations to a *Shabbat* or *Yom Tov* meal often leave a profound impression and contribute greatly to developing an ongoing personal relationship. They have also found such invitations to be a most effective way of providing a meaningful experience in Jewish living. However, not infrequently, the invited guests choose to avail themselves of forbidden forms of transportation. R. Moshe Sternbuch, *Teshuvot ve-Hanhagot,* I, no. 358, reports that he was consulted by a newly-observant young man regarding the propriety of inviting his parents to *Shabbat* meals in the hopeful anticipation that their enjoyment of *Shabbat* would, over a period of time, lead them to become observant. His concern was that it might be improper for him to do so because of the fact that they customarily travel to and from his home by automobile.

Rabbi Sternbuch responded with a short but novel analysis of the prohibition "nor shall you place a stumbling block before the blind" (Leviticus 19:14). Rabbinic tradition as recorded in *Mekhilta, ad locum,* teaches that this verse serves as a prohibition against counseling a person in a manner that does not serve that individual's best interests and, as stated by the Gemara, *Pesaḥim* 22b, as a prohibition forbidding a person to assist another in the commission of a transgression. Rabbi Sternbuch asserts that this interpretation does not yield an absolute prohibition with regard to facilitating a transgression. In light of the phraseology employed in this verse, Rabbi Sternbuch argues that the prohibition applies only in situations in which an act is designed to cause damage or harm in the

4. See, however, *Sedei Ḥemed, Ma'arekhet ha-Vav, klal* 26, sec. 7 and cf., *Lifnei Iver,* chap. 4, sec. 4.

form of a transgression but that any act intended to yield an ultimate benefit is, by definition, not a "stumbling block." The intention to benefit, argues Rabbi Sternbuch, is, in effect, exculpatory. Rabbi Sternbuch compares this prohibition to the prohibition against "wounding" which does not apply in the case of a physician who performs a surgical procedure designed to promote health and well-being. Accordingly, concludes Rabbi Sternbuch, an invitation designed to advance the spiritual well-being of the parents cannot be categorized as a "stumbling block" and hence is not forbidden.

Rabbi Sternbuch's thesis is appealing but, at least as formulated by him, it is not supported by the sources that serve to define the prohibition. His comparison of "placing a stumbling block" in order to achieve a goal that is beneficial and laudatory to therapeutic "wounding" is entirely inapt. Causing a person to transgress is regarded by the *Mekhilta* as explicitly forbidden by this commandment; causing the transgression is defined as a *malum per se.* Therapeutic "wounding" is permitted, not because of the benevolent intent of the physician, but because therapeutic wounding is, by definition, not a battery. Rambam, *Hilkhot Ḥovel u-Mazik* 5:1, carefully states that one who wounds "in the manner of an aggressor" (or, according to a variant reading, "in a humiliating manner") is guilty of a biblical infraction. A surgeon performing his professional duties does not commit an act fitting that description.

There is, however, a long list of sources that discuss the question of whether it is permissible to cause a person to "stumble" and commit a comparatively minor transgression in order to preserve him from a more severe transgression as well as the related question of whether it is permissible to cause a person to commit a single transgression if doing so will effectively preclude him from committing a multiple number of transgressions. Those discussions focus upon the net effect of action over inaction rather than upon benevolent intent.

The *Shabbat* invitation question might be recast in precisely those terms: May a person be invited to desecrate the Sabbath in order to preserve him from multiple acts of desecration in the future? *Avnei Nezer, Yoreh De'ah,* no. 126, permits the sale of improperly slaughtered animals to a habitual sinner because the net effect is to prevent the more numerous transgressions incurred in eating meat of a nonkosher species. Similar reasoning is tentatively employed by R. Akiva Eger in a gloss on *Yoreh De'ah* 181:6 in resolving a related question and in contemporary times by R. Shlomoh Zalman Auerbach, *Minḥat Shlomoh,* no. 35, sec. 1, and is advanced as a consideration by R. Moses Feinstein, *Iggerot Mosheh, Yoreh De'ah,* I, no. 72. *Tiferet Shmu'el,* in his commentary on Rosh, *Baba Meẓi'a* 5:3, comments that "perhaps" it is permitted for a borrower to accept funds under conditions in which payment of a premium for use of the funds is prohibited as usury by rabbinical decree if, in doing so, he denies the lender the opportunity to use the same funds for an interest-bearing loan that is biblically proscribed. A similar view is suggested by *Maḥaẓit ha-Shekel, Oraḥ Ḥayyim* 163:2.

On the other hand, R. Chaim Joseph David Azulai, *Birkei Yosef, Ḥoshen Mishpat* 9:3, rules that it is forbidden for a litigant to present a gift to a judge in order to dissuade him from unjustly favoring the opposing party. Acceptance of a bribe is forbidden even if the gift is designed to prevent a prohibited miscarriage of justice and its presentation even under such circumstances, rules *Birkei Yosef,* constitutes a forbidden form of "placing a stumbling block." R. Eliezer Waldenberg, *Ẓiẓ Eli'ezer,* XV, no. 19, notes that R. Akiva Eger and *Maḥaẓit ha-Shekel* make their points only tentatively and also cites equivocal language with regard to the applicability of the rabbinic prohibition against "assisting transgressors" even when the "assistance" is designed to prevent a biblical infraction.[5] It should also be noted that even the permissive views regard such acts as permissible only in situations in which it is a certainty, or a near certainty, that more serious transgressions will be avoided. That is assuredly not the case when invitations are extended as part of a process of encouraging adoption of an observant lifestyle but without any assurance of success.

Nevertheless, there are a number of other factors delineating the parameters of the prohibition concerning "placing a stumbling block" that impact upon each of the earlier posed questions:

1. *Sedei Ḥemed, Ma'arekhet ha-Vav, klal* 26, sec. 32, cites a number of authorities who declare that "placing a stumbling block" serves to prohibit only conduct requiring a physical act and, consequently, mere oral assistance or encouragement to transgress is not included in the prohibition. *Mikhtam le-David, Yoreh De'ah,* no. 33, invokes the dictum excluding transgressors from agency, "The words of the master and the words of the student, whose words does one obey?" as establishing as well that there can be no culpability for verbal encouragement of transgression since the transgressor must always be presumed to be following his own inclination.

Nevertheless, Rambam, *Hilkhot Terumot* 6:3, declares that there is

5. See also the discussion presented in *Lifnei Iver,* chap. 20.

culpability in the eyes of heaven for causing or assisting in sin in any manner "even through mere speech." Similarly, Rambam, *Hilkhot Ḥovel u-Mazik* 5:13, followed by *Shulḥan Arukh, Ḥoshen Mishpat* 380:2, states that a person who directs another to commit a tort "is an accomplice in the sin and is a wicked person for he caused a blind person to stumble and has strengthened the hands of evildoers." It cannot be maintained that, by definition, "placing a stumbling block" involves a physical act since the *Mekhilta, Kedoshim* 2:14, explicitly includes offering harmful advice as a biblical violation of the prohibition.[6] Indeed, as noted earlier, it would seem that encouraging or inviting a person to commit a transgression constitutes "placing a stumbling block" before the blind for two reasons: 1) it facilitates transgression; and 2) *ipso facto* it constitutes harmful advice.

2. In most of the cases in which these questions arise, the invitation to attend programs or synagogue services need not absolutely involve forbidden travel. Quite often, the destination is within walking distance even though the distance makes walking inconvenient; at times, if one wishes to do so, it is possible to secure accommodations for *Shabbat* within walking distance. May one create a situation in which it is not absolutely necessary for a person to transgress, although it is likely that he may do so? In effect, the question is, since the transgression can be avoided if desired, does such an invitation constitute a stumbling block?

The Mishnah, *Shevi'it* 5:6, enumerates specific agricultural implements which may not be sold during the course of the Sabbatical year but excludes a number of other implements and concludes with the explanatory statement: "This is the principle: everything whose use is designed for a transgression is forbidden; [everything whose use is designed] for a transgression and for a permitted activity is permitted." Similarly, a subsequent Mishnah, *Shevi'it* 5:8, records that Bet Hillel permits the sale of a plow animal to a person suspected of ongoing violations of the prohibition concerning agricultural activity during the Sabbatical year "because he can slaughter it." Ritva, *Avodah Zarah* 15b, understands the Mishnah as positing the rule that even in situations involving a biblical transgression, i.e., the purchaser could not have committed the transgression but for the assistance of the seller, such sale is permitted because an object that can be used for a legitimate purpose is, by definition, not a stumbling block. If so, since the invitation to services and the like could be acted upon without transgression, extending an invitation under such circumstances

6. Cf., *Lifnei Iver,* chap. 7, sec. 1.

would appear to be permissible according to Ritva.

There are, however, at least two authorities, *Tosafot Anshei Shem* and *Mishnah Rishonah,* who, in their respective commentaries on *Shevi'it,* interpret the permissive ruling of the Mishnah regarding the sale of utensils that can be used for both permissible and forbidden purposes as limited to situations in which such utensils are also available from other sources. Availability from other sources transforms the situation to one comparable to individuals standing "on the same bank of the river" in which the prohibition against abetting a transgressor is only rabbinic in nature. Nevertheless, a host of authorities, including *Teshuvot Ḥatam Sofer, Yoreh De'ah,* no. 19; *Teshuvot Pnei Yehoshu'a, Yoreh De'ah,* no. 3; R. Isaac Elchanan Spektor, *Ein Yiẓḥak,* I, *Oraḥ Ḥayyim,* no. 13; as well as *Iggerot Mosheh, Yoreh De'ah,* I, no. 72 and *Oraḥ Ḥayyim,* II, no. 62, in effect follow the position of Ritva in permitting assistance of a nature that can be utilized either in a legitimate or a forbidden manner.[7]

There is one other aspect of the ruling of the Mishnah in *Shevi'it* that is germane, *viz.,* the definition of an implement "used for both permitted and forbidden purposes." Must the implement be used by the majority of people for permissible purposes, or is it sufficient if even a minority uses the implement for permitted purposes? With regard to the parallel rule governing the sale of a farm animal, Ramban, Ran and Rashbam, in their respective commentaries on *Baba Batra* 92b, appear to be of the opinion that there must be at least an equal chance that the purchaser will use the animal for a permissible purpose, i.e., he will slaughter it for meat rather than use it for plowing his fields. On the other hand, Rashi, *Avodah Zarah* 15a, and *Tosafot, Avodah Zarah* 15a and 15b, permit the sale of the animal even if the majority of customers purchase such animals for a forbidden purpose.

Among later authorities, R. Chaim Sofer, *Teshuvot Maḥaneh Ḥayyim,* I, no. 47 and *Teshuvot Zivḥei Ẓedek,* II, no. 18, rule that a sale of this nature is permissible only if the majority of purchasers utilize the object sold for permitted purposes.[8] However, it seems that *Taz, Yoreh De'ah* 151:1, permits such a sale even if only a minority of customers use the purchased object for a legitimate purpose.[9] This is also the position of *Teshuvot Imrei Yosher,* II, no. 115. R. Eliezer Waldenberg, *Ẓiẓ Eli'ezer,*

---

7. Cf., *Teshuvot Imrei Yosher,* II, no. 115, and *Ḥazon Ish, Shevi'it* 12:9.

8. Cf., also, R. Abraham I. Kook, *Shabbat ha-Areẓ* 7:5 as well as sources cited in *Lifnei Iver,* no. 13, sec. 3 and *ibid., Birurim ve-Ḥakirot,* no. 1, sec. 8.

9. See *Lifnei Iver,* no. 13, sec. 3, p. 75.

IV, no. 5, chap. 4, citing *Teshuvot Ḥatam Sofer, Yoreh De'ah,* no. 19, rules that the sale is rendered permissible on the basis of the mere possibility that the object sold will be used for a legitimate purpose. This also seems to be the position of R. Yechiel Ya'akov Weinberg, *Seridei Esh,* II, no. 19.

It would appear, however, that none of these authorities would sanction the sale of an implement that can be used for a legitimate purpose if it is known with certainty that the purchaser will use it in a forbidden manner. R. Shlomoh Kluger, *Tuv Ta'am va-Da'at, Mahadura Telita'ah,* II, no. 50, forbids the sale of a razor to a person who is known to shave with a razor even though the implement can be used in a permissible manner to cut hair growing on the head since it is certain that he will also shave with it. A similar view is espoused by R. Moshe Mordecai Epstein, *Levushei Mordekhai, Mahadura Tinyana, Oraḥ Ḥayyim,* no. 48.

Nevertheless, *Iggerot Mosheh, Yoreh De'ah,* no. 72, finds grounds to permit the sale even under such circumstances. *Iggerot Mosheh* argues that a person who violates agricultural proscriptions and who buys agricultural implements that can be used for permitted purposes will almost certainly use them for forbidden purposes as well. Yet, the Mishnah permits such sale. *Iggerot Mosheh* reasons that this is permitted since the sale is designed for a permitted purpose and hence does not constitute a '"stumbling block;" any forbidden use is the result of the purchaser causing himself to stumble. *Iggerot Mosheh* points out that, if this line of reasoning is not accepted, it would be forbidden to sell pots and pans to Sabbath desecrators since they will certainly use those utensils for cooking on the Sabbath. This position is reiterated in *Iggerot Mosheh, Oraḥ Ḥayyim,* II, no. 62, although in the latter responsum it is expressed with a measure of hesitation (*ein hetter zeh barur*). According to those authorities who understand the ruling enunciated by the Mishnah in *Shevi'it* as referring only to situations in which similar implements may be acquired from other sources, there is no basis for deducing such a principle with regard to the biblical prohibition. Moreover, the ruling of the Mishnah in *Shevi'it* may be limited to situations in which it is possible that the implement may be utilized solely for a purpose that is entirely legitimate.[10]

3. It is also possible, and indeed likely, that, even if acceptance of the invitation necessarily entails forbidden travel, the invitation will not be accepted, in which case no transgression of *Shabbat* prohibitions will occur. However, that contingency does not serve to render the invitation

10. Cf., *Lifnei Iver, Birurim ve-Ḥakirot,* no. 1, sec. 8.

permissible since, as pointed out by *Teshuvot Maḥaneh Ḥayyim,* I, no. 46, the sale of implements designed solely for agricultural use is forbidden even though it is entirely possible that they will not be put to any use. Nevertheless, language employed by *Toldot Yiẓḥak* in his commentary on the Palestinian Talmud, *Shevi'it* 5:3, indicates that "placing a stumbling block," by definition, is limited to situations in which the transgression is certain to occur because an act "cannot be called placement of a stumbling block unless the unfortunate effect is known at the time that it is placed before him. But if it is doubtful whether [the victim] will perform the unfortunate act and it is within his power not to do so, this is not presenting him with a stumbling block; rather it is called causing himself to stumble." A similar view is expressed by R. Aharon Kotler, *Mishnat Rabbi Aharon,* I, no. 3. Those authorities apparently understand that, in prohibiting the sale of agricultural implements to a person suspected of violating regulations pertaining to the Sabbatical year, the Mishnah is addressing situations in which actual prohibited use of those tools is virtually a foregone conclusion. According to those authorities, extending an invitation that, if accepted, is likely to result in forbidden travel would be permissible in situations in which it is not at all certain that the invitation will be accepted.

In a letter addressed to the administration of Yeshivat Ohr Sameach in Jerusalem, R. Shlomoh Zalman Auerbach writes:

> It is permissible to invite even a person who lives at a distance from the place of prayer and to offer him a place to sleep close to that place in a manner such that he will not need to desecrate the Sabbath. Even if he does not accept the offer, there is no obligation to tell him to refrain from coming because of that, nor is it necessary to admonish him that it is forbidden to travel by automobile.[11]

Rabbi Auerbach presumably maintains that the offer of a place of lodging obviates the prohibition against "placing a stumbling block" even if there is little likelihood that it will be accepted and is in agreement with the authorities who maintain that the prohibition is limited to situations in which a transgression will necessarily result. According to Rabbi Auerbach, such an offer once made need not be withdrawn even if it becomes clear that it will indeed lead to transgression; since the offer does not

11. A less literal translation of this letter is published in *Jewish Outreach,* p. 80.

constitute a stumbling block, it is the invitee who causes himself to stumble in insisting upon transgressing.

Withdrawing the offer or admonishing the invitee regarding the infraction might nevertheless be required as a form of *tokhaḥah* or admonition in fulfillment of the command "you shall admonish your fellow" (Leviticus 19:17). Rabbi Auerbach presumably maintains that, because of the prevalent lack of awareness of the nature and severity of the infraction, it is permitted and indeed preferable to refrain from admonishing the transgressor until such time as a receptive relationship is established. In that manner the prospects for success and acceptance of admonition and instruction will be enhanced.[12]

Use of Mircrowave Ovens on Shabbat

Microwaves are waves generated by electromagnetic radiation and include frequencies between 100 million and 300,000 hertz (cycles per minute) and hence are located in the spectrum between ultra-high-frequency television and the far infrared. They are known as "microwaves" because they are between 30 centimeters and one millimeter in length. Microwaves pass through some objects, e.g.. pottery and paper, without effect, much in the same way that light waves pass through transparent substances. Substances such as metal reflect microwaves in a manner analogous to that of a mirror reflecting light. Other substances, primarily liquids, absorb the microwaves which then vibrate the molecules of the substance they have penetrated with the result that heat is produced.

Microwave ovens are box-like appliances that produce microwave radiation than can be harnessed for purposes of cooking. Microwave radiation cooks by means of vibrating liquid molecules within the food placed in the oven. Since the walls of the microwave oven and the food containers are made of substances that do not absorb microwaves they are unaffected by the cooking process and remain cold other than for a minimal amount of heat that may be transferred secondarily through contact with the heated food or that may be radiated by the food. Microwave cooking differs fundamentally from other forms of cooking in that conventional cooking is accomplished by means of transference of heat from an external source to the foodstuff, whereas microwave cooking involves no external source of heat whatsoever; rather, the heat is produced internally within

12. For an examination of sources discussing the *mizvah* of *tokhaḥah* see *Lifnei Iver,* part 4 and *Jewish Outreach,* pp. 1–30.

the food as a result of friction caused by vibration of molecules.

The question that has been raised with increasing frequency in recent years in the wake of increased use of microwave ovens is whether or not utilization of this medium in preparation of food constitutes "cooking" in the halakhic sense of the term. The question is usually framed as a query with regard to whether such an act is intrinsically forbidden on *Shabbat* as one of the thirty-nine forbidden forms of labor. The identical question may be raised with regard to whether microwave cooking of milk and meat in combination is forbidden. Although, by virtue of rabbinic decree, milk and meat that have been mixed together in any manner may not be eaten, the ban against the act of cooking milk with meat as well as the prohibition against deriving any benefit from the cooked dish is limited to the halakhically defined notion of cooking. Upon reinstitution of sacrifices one may anticipate a similar question will be posed with regard to whether or not it is permissible to roast the paschal sacrifice in a microwave oven.[13]

For purposes of Sabbath strictures, the Gemara, *Shabbat* 39a, declares that it is entirely permissible to use the heat of the sun for cooking. A dispute exists between R. Yosi and the Sages with regard to whether a

---

13. Other areas of Halakhah contingent upon a technical definition of cooking include the broiling of liver or meat without previous soaking and salting, baking of *maẓah,* the blessing to be recited over baked bread, boiling water for purposes of *kashering* utensils, cooking wine so that it may be touched by a non-Jew, the biblical prohibition against consumption of uncooked blood, cooking of already cooked food on *Shabbat* which does not constitute a biblical prohibition and others. See *Pri Megadim, Oraḥ Ḥayyim, Mishbeẓot Zahav* 318:1; *Minḥat Ḥinnukh,* no. 7; and Prof. Ze'ev Low, *Teḥumin,* VIII (5747), pp. 1–33. The applicability of the prohibition against eating food cooked by a gentile to food prepared in a microwave oven is discussed by Prof. Ze'ev Low, *Moriah,* Shevat 5750, pp. 98–104.

The availability of frozen bread and *ḥallah* dough for baking in a microwave oven renders the question of whether bread baked in such fashion requires recitation of *ha-moẓi* and *birkat ha-mazon* as well as the suitability of use of such bread for Sabbath and *Yom Tov* meals a topical issue. *Shulḥan Arukh* 168:16 rules that the blessing for cake is pronounced over bread baked by the heat of the sun. *Tur Shulḥan Arukh,* however, declares that if the dough is fashioned into a proper loaf the blessing for bread is to be recited. *Bi'ur ha-Gra* rules in accordance with the view of *Shulḥan Arukh.* However, *Mishnah Berurah* 165:92 advises that one should be careful not to eat a quantity of such bread sufficient "to cause satiation" (*kedei sevi'ah)* other than with other bread upon which the requisite blessing has been pronounced. It would appear that, *mutatis mutandis,* the selfsame considerations and opinions apply to bread baked in a microwave oven.

secondary form (*toladah*) of solar heat may be used for cooking purposes on *Shabbat,* e.g., whether food may be roasted in a material that has been heated by the sun's rays. The normative ruling is that such cooking is forbidden by rabbinic decree lest confusion arise between use of materials that have been heated by the sun's rays and use of materials that have been heated in a similar manner by fire. No such decree was promulgated to forbid use of solar heat directly because it was assumed that the distinction between utilization of the heat of the sun and application of heat produced by fire was readily apparent and that permitting the practice of cooking in the heat of the sun to continue unabated would not lead to forbidden forms of cooking.

Rashi, in his commentary on *Shabbat* 39a, explains that utilization of the heat of the sun for cooking on *Shabbat* is permitted "because such is not the manner of cooking." R. Moses Feinstein, *Iggerot Mosheh, Oraḥ Ḥayyim,* III, no. 52, points out that, although use of direct solar heat may not constitute a usual form of cooking, there is nevertheless nothing unusual about the use of derivative forms of solar heat for cooking purposes. Thus, use of boiling water for cooking is entirely usual. The nature and quality of such cooking is the same regardless of whether the water has been boiled over a fire or has been brought to a boil by exposure to the sun.[14] Yet, boiling in the thermal "waters of Tiberias" is permitted by biblical law, because the original source of heat is the sun rather than fire. Such cooking, argues *Iggerot Mosheh,* cannot be regarded as unusual.[15] Moreover, it should be noted that, although forbidden acts are not biblically proscribed when they are performed in an unusual manner, they are forbidden by virtue of rabbinic decree. Why then, queries *Eglei Tal, Melekhet Ofeh,* sec. 44, is cooking in the sun's rays not similarly forbidden by rabbinic decree?

Iggerot Mosheh explains that Rashi must be understood as focusing, not upon the unusual nature of the act of cooking *per se,* but upon the fact that such cooking, because of the source of heat involved, is not comparable to the "cooking" that was undertaken in the course of construction of the Tabernacle in the wilderness, i.e., the boiling of dyes used in preparation of the various materials that entered into the construction

14. Cf., however, R. Ezekiel Landau, *Ẓlaḥ, Pesaḥim* 74a, and *idem, Noda bi-Yehudah, Mahadura Tinyana, Yoreh De'ah,* no. 43.

15. In rebutting this view, Prof. Low cites the description of baking in the heat of the sun recorded in the Gemara, *Pesaḥim* 37a. There is, however, nothing in that text to indicate whether that mode of cooking was common or unusual.

of the Tabernacle. It is, of course, the various forms of labor utilized in constructing the Tabernacle that serve as the paradigm for acts forbidden on the Sabbath. Ordinary fuel, rather than the heat of the sun, was used for purposes of "cooking" materials used in the construction of the Tabernacle and hence, for that reason alone, solar cooking is not forbidden on *Shabbat.* Rashi's comment to the effect that this is not the usual form of cooking must be understood as necessary in order to explain why cooking by means of the heat of the sun is not regarded as a derivative (*toladah*) form of cooking since it is at least comparable to the method of cooking employed in the construction of the Tabernacle. The proscribed forms of labor include many activities that, although they were themselves not employed in the Tabernacle, are sufficiently similar in nature to be included in the prohibited categories of labor. In order to obviate that question, Rashi indicates that use of solar heat for cooking is uncommon; hence such cooking is not regarded as even derivatively similar to the type of cooking associated with the construction of the Tabernacle. Accordingly, cooking by use of any form of heat derived from the sun, rather than from fire, is not excluded because such forms of cooking are unusual; rather, cooking by means of such heat is excluded because, since such sources of heat are derivatives of solar heat, those forms of heat are not encompassed within the paradigmatic form of cooking that serves as the basis of the prohibition.

Basing himself on this analysis, *Iggerot Mosheh* concludes that any form of cooking that is entirely usual and common must be regarded as a derivative of the proscribed cooking employed in the construction of the Tabernacle, regardless of the source or nature of the heat used in the cooking process. Accordingly, *Iggerot Mosheh* rules that use of a microwave oven for cooking on *Shabbat* constitutes a transgression of a biblical commandment.

R. Benjamin Silber, *Oz Nidberu,* I, no, 34, notes that if Rashi's comment is to be understood in this manner, it would follow that, if use of solar heat in cooking should at any time come into vogue as a common practice, such cooking would have to be regarded as prohibited by biblical law. This, he argues, is already the case in Israel where solar heaters are commonly used for heating tap water. Accordingly, if Rashi's comment is to be understood in this manner, such heating constitutes a form of "cooking." R. Joshua Neuwirth, *Shemirat Shabbat ke-Hilkhatah,* 2nd edition (Jerusalem, 5739), chapter 1, note 127, presents a similar objection in the name of R. Shlomoh Zalman Auerbach. *Magen Avraham, Oraḥ*

Ḥayyim 301:57, compares drying clothes in the sun to cooking by means of solar rays and rules that drying clothes in the sun on *Shabbat* similarly involves no biblical transgression. Rabbi Auerbach cogently notes that drying clothes in the sun is certainly a common and usual practice. If so, the clear implication of *Magen Avraham*'s remark is that even conventional use of solar heat for cooking does not render the act biblically forbidden.[16]

Iggerot Mosheh's analysis of Rashi's view leaves a serious question unresolved. As recorded in Exodus 12:9, the paschal sacrifice must be roasted and cooking the sacrifice in water is explicitly forbidden. The Gemara, *Pesaḥim* 41a, declares that cooking the paschal sacrifice in the thermal "waters of Tiberias" does not constitute a transgression of the negative commandment prohibiting cooking in water. *Eglei Tal, Melekhet Ofeh,* sec. 44, notes the obvious difficulty. If cooking by means of the heat of the sun is merely an uncommon or unusual mode of cooking it must nevertheless be categorized as being intrinsically a form of cooking. Unlike the rule with regard to Sabbath prohibitions, unusual forms of cooking are included in the prohibition regarding preparation of the paschal offering.[17] If so, cooking the paschal sacrifice in the "waters of Tiberias" should constitute a transgression of the prohibition against cooking the sacrificial animal. *Eglei Tal* explains that, in terming solar cooking an "unusual" form of cooking, Rashi intends to indicate that cooking by means of solar heat is intrinsically different from conventional cooking, i.e., for halakhic purposes, solar heat and heat of a fire are regarded as qualitatively different. Hence, preparation of food by means of solar heat does not constitute "cooking," not because it is not analogous to the cooking performed in the construction of the Tabernacle, but because, by definition, it is not "cooking." There can be no question that, according to *Eglei Tal,* microwave cooking is similarly, by definition, not to be regarded as cooking; microwaves are even less similar in nature to a

16. Prof. Low similarly cites *Magen Avraham* in refutation of the position espoused by *Iggerot Mosheh.*

17. See, however, R. Elchanan Wasserman, *Kovez̧ Shi'urim, Ketubot* 60a, who asserts that unusual acts are not only outside the ambit of Sabbath prohibitions but are also excluded from other biblical prohibitions. Thus, he argues, there is no biblical prohibition against cooking the paschal offering by means of solar heat. The same is true with regard to heat derived from the sun: Just as cooking in the "waters of Tiberias" on *Shabbat* is not biblically forbidden since the heat is derived from an unusual source so is cooking the paschal sacrifice in the "waters of Tiberias" excluded from the biblical prohibition. Cf., R. Benjamin Silber, *Oz Nidberu,* I, no. 34.

flame than are solar rays.[18]

R. Benjamin Silber, *Oz Nidberu,* I, no. 34, understands Rashi's comment, not as addressing the question of why cooking in the heat of the sun is not forbidden by biblical law, but as addressing the question of why such cooking was not proscribed by rabbinic decree. In resolving that question, Rashi comments that, since cooking directly in the rays of the sun is uncommon, such cooking is not likely to be confused with forbidden forms of cooking and hence the Sages found no reason to prohibit use of solar heat in cooking on the Sabbath.[19] If Rashi's comment is understood in that vein, there is no basis for regarding microwave cooking on *Shabbat* as halakhically forbidden.

Moreover, even if *Iggerot Mosheh*'s understanding of Rashi is accepted as correct, it seems to this writer that his conclusion to the effect that cooking in a microwave oven on *Shabbat* is a transgression of a biblical prohibition does not necessarily follow. Whether or not use of solar heat is sufficiently similar to the mode of cooking employed in the construction of the Tabernacle to constitute an analogous form of cooking may well be a matter of debate. However, the basic premise, *viz.,* that only those modes of cooking are forbidden that are similar in nature to the type of cooking employed in the construction of the Tabernacle is unexceptionable. The cooking employed in the making of dyes involved the transfer of heat from one body to another, i.e., from the flame to the dyes. Thus, transfer of heat seems to be a necessary condition of "cooking" as an activity prohibited on *Shabbat*. Indeed, it is certainly arguable that this element is a *sine qua non* of the definition of cooking as a halakhic concept for all areas of Jewish law. Heat generated by microwaves involves no transfer of heat whatsoever; rather, it is *sui generis* to the foodstuff itself. If so, not only would microwave cooking be excluded from the biblical prohibition against cooking on *Shabbat,* but boiling the paschal sacrifice in water heated by microwaves would not constitute a violation of the prohibition against cooking the sacrifice.

It further appears to this writer that microwave cooking on *Shabbat* does not constitute a forbidden form of cooking even by virtue of rabbinic edict. The Sages forbade only cooking by means of a medium heated by

---

18. See also R. Gedaliah Rabinowitz, *Torah she-be-'al Peh,* XXIV (5743), who attempts to explain the "unusual" nature of solar cooking in another manner.

19. A similar analysis of Rashi's comment is presented by Prof. Low, *ibid.,* p. 31. See also Prof. Low's analysis of Rashi presented in a later article published in *Torah she-be-'al Peh,* XXXIV (5753), 102–104.

the sun's rays, e.g., water or cloth; they did not forbid cooking in the sun's rays directly. The underlying rationale is that the observer will not be aware that the heat of the water or of the cloth was derived from the sun and may err in assuming that all forms of cooking, other than cooking directly over a fire, are permitted on *Shabbat*. The same observer will readily recognize that the sun is not fire and that, although cooking in the sun is permitted, cooking over a flame is not. Microwaves should certainly be treated no more stringently than sun rays and indeed microwaves are far less comparable to fire than the sun. Thus, although cooking in water that has been heated in a microwave oven may well be included in the rabbinic transgression, cooking directly by means of microwaves themselves is entirely analogous to cooking in the heat of the sun.[20]

R. Israel Rosen, *Shanah be-Shanah,* 5743, draws attention to an entirely different consideration in arguing that microwave cooking may constitute a biblically prohibited form of cooking on the Sabbath. R. Shlomoh Zalman Auerbach, *Kovez̦ Ma'amarim be-Inyanei Ḥashmal be-Shabbat* (Jerusalem, 5738), p. 85, note 3, makes an interesting observation with regard to use of a heating element[21] for purposes of boiling water on *Shabbat*. Rabbi Auerbach argues that since the heat is generated by means of an electric current rather than by a flame it must be regarded as being a derivative of the "sun" and hence cooking in such a manner is forbidden only by virtue of rabbinic decree. Accordingly, Rabbi Auerbach advised that hospitals, for example, use such a method for boiling water on *Shabbat* when hot water is necessary in the treatment of seriously ill patients, e.g., for purposes of sterilizing instruments or the like. Rabbi Auerbach reports that *Ḥazon Ish* disagreed and maintained that since

20. Prof. Low, *Teḥumin,* VIII, 31, argues that microwave cooking is to be regarded as included in the rabbinic edict forbidding cooking in heat derived from the sun because it takes place within an oven and a microwave oven is readily confused with an ordinary oven. That argument may have merit with regard to promulgation of a new decree but is irrelevant to delineation of existing rabbinic legislation. It is certainly permissible to cook food enclosed within a box provided that the heat utilized for this purpose is exclusively solar heat. A box or oven using microwaves as the source of heat is no different.

21. For the sake of accuracy it should be noted that Rabbi Auerbach speaks of an "electric fork whose edges are distant and a circuit is created by means of the water." This categorization seems to be imprecise since 1) there is no commercially available heating device that relies upon the water to complete the electric circuit and 2) such a method seems to be highly inefficient and impractical for use in boiling water. The theory propounded by Rabbi Auerbach seems equally cogent when applied to an ordinary immersion-heating element.

electric current "generally" produces a flame it must be regarded as an "embryonic" fire and, asserted *Ḥazon Ish,* an "embryonic" flame is no less a fire than is a "derivative" of a flame. One can readily understand that Rabbi Auerbach finds this comparison farfetched, to say the least.

Rabbi Rosen purports to find a source for *Ḥazon Ish*'s position in the comments of R. Menachem ha-Me'iri, *Shabbat* 38b. Me'iri rules that an egg may not be cooked in lime (*sid*) on *Shabbat.* It is readily understood that one may not cook in lime that has been heated by fire. Me'iri, however, asserts that it is also forbidden to cook in lime that has been heated and that has become cold because, even if it has cooled, "the heat coming from the power of fire has not departed from it; rather, it becomes concentrated at the time [the fire] is extinguished." Me'iri, presumably, is describing a procedure in which the lime becomes hot as a result of a chemical reaction set into motion by means of mixing the lime with water.[22] However, as Rabbi Rosen quite correctly notes, remarkable as Me'iri's position is, heat released by lime is readily distinguishable from heat generated by an electric current: Lime—on the basis of Me'iri's own description—at one point absorbs the heat of a fire and hence the fire may be regarded as latent in the lime; electric current used to heat a coil is not the stored heat of a fire and never produces a flame. Nevertheless, Rabbi Rosen tentatively argues that, since microwaves are generated by electricity, the use of microwave ovens should be regarded as biblically forbidden according to the position of *Ḥazon Ish.* This argument is only tentative for, as Rabbi Rosen himself notes, the electric current does not heat the food cooked in microwave ovens; the current merely produces microwaves. The microwaves, in turn, generate heat in the foodstuff. It is difficult to perceive the microwaves—removed and separate as they are from the electrical current and themselves entirely incapable of generating a flame—as constituting an "embryonic" flame.

A quite similar discussion of Me'iri's view and its application to microwave cooking is presented by Prof. Ze'ev Low. Prof. Low, *Teḥumin,* VIII, (5747), 26, reports that microwave ovens commonly contain "a burning wire that emits electrons." Accordingly, basing himself upon the comment of Me'iri, he advances the argument that the heat produced by the effect of the microwaves should then be considered a derivative of fire. Prof. Low dismisses that argument on the basis of a number of considerations. Chief among those considerations is the fact that the microwaves are separate and distinct from both the wire and the food.

22. See *Teshuvot Lev Ḥayyim,* III, no. 74.

Since, unlike lime, the microwaves themselves are not heated at any point, they cannot be regarded as a receptacle or conduit of heat.[23]

However, distinguishing microwave cooking from prohibited forms of "cooking" does not necessarily mean that no other form of prohibited activities are associated with use of a microwave oven for purposes of cooking. One of the thirty-nine forms of labor prohibited on the Sabbath is "banging with a hammer" (*makeh be-patish*), i.e., completing a manufacturing process. The Palestinian Talmud, *Shabbat* 7:2, maintains that this category of prohibited activity is applicable to the preparation of food as well. Although there is some controversy with regard to this matter, many authorities, including Rema, *Oraḥ Ḥayyim* 318:4; Levush, *Oraḥ Ḥayyim* 318:4; *Pri Megadim, Eshel Avraham, Oraḥ Ḥayyim* 318:16; and *Teshuvot Maharsham,* I, no. 164, rule that cooking of food on *Shabbat* involves this infraction. *Nishmat Adam, Hilkhot Shabbat* 20:5, asserts that the prohibition is attendant upon food that cannot be eaten without cooking. In disagreement with this position, *Tehillah le-David, Oraḥ Ḥayyim* 314:4 and *Bi'ur Halakhah, Oraḥ Ḥayyim* 314:4, maintain that the Babylonian Talmud rejects the view expressed in the Palestinian Talmud and maintains that this category of forbidden labor does not include the preparation of foodstuffs on the Sabbath. *Iggerot Mosheh, Oraḥ Ḥayyim,* III, no. 52, regards the controversy as unresolved.

Quite apart from the prohibition against "cooking" food on *Shabbat,* any act resulting in the heating of a wire or coil is obviously forbidden. Moreover, *Ḥazon Ish, Oraḥ Ḥayyim* 50:9, maintains that the completion of any electrical circuit on *Shabbat* constitutes a proscribed act of "building" (*boneh*).[24] Somewhat similarly, R. Isaac Schmelkes, *Teshuvot Bet Yiẓḥak, Yoreh De'ah, Hashmatot,* no. 31, and R. Chaim Ozer Grodzinski, *Ha-Darom,* no. 32 (Tishri 5731), reprinted in his *Teshuvot Aḥi'ezer,* IV (Bnei Brak, 5746), no. 6, maintain that generating a flow of current is rabbinically forbidden as a form of "causing to be born" (*molid*), i.e., the generation of a new entity similar in nature to the generation of a flame which is forbidden by rabbinic decree even on *Yom Tov* when cooking is permitted. Although, theoretically, a microwave oven could be constructed in a manner such that there is a constant flow of electricity even when it is not in use, in practice, the electrical circuit is completed by the closing

23. See also Prof. Low, *Torah she-be-'al Peh,* pp. 99–100.

24. Cf., R. Shlomoh Zalman Auerbach, *Koveẓ Ma'amarim be-Inyanei Ḥashmal be-Shabbat* (Jerusalem, 5735), *Milu'im,* no. 1, reprinted in *idem, Minḥat Shlomoh,* no. 11.

of the door of the microwave oven.[25] Furthermore, as has been noted earlier, the microwaves themselves are emitted by "a burning wire that emits electrons." Thus closing the door of the microwave oven also serves to cause the microwave-producing wire to become heated. Accordingly, even if the microwave oven is turned on before *Shabbat,* closing the door of the oven—as it is presently designed—constitutes an act forbidden on the Sabbath. Since this arrangement has been adopted not only for reasons of economy and practicality, but for considerations of safety as well, construction of an oven designed to produce microwaves even when the door is open would be highly inadvisable.

Yet another barrier exists with regard to the use of most currently manufactured microwave ovens for purposes of cooking on *Shabbat.* Unlike food baked or broiled by means of external sources of heat, food cooked by means of microwaves does not brown on the surface. In order to give food cooked in microwave ovens the taste and appearance of conventionally cooked food, many manufacturers have added an electrical element for the specific purpose of browning food cooked in microwave ovens. Since cooking on *Shabbat* by means of an electrical element is forbidden, use of an oven containing a browning element on *Shabbat* is obviously also forbidden.

For all of these considerations including the unequivocally negative view of the late Rabbi Moses Feinstein, use of microwave ovens on *Shabbat* remains a matter of theoretical speculation rather than practical application.

Cosmetic Powder On Shabbat

The use of most cosmetics, including, but not limited to, lipstick, rouge, mascara, eyeshadow, as well as cleansing and moisturizing creams, on the Sabbath is forbidden. The application of cosmetics prepared in stick or pressed block form involves a biblically proscribed act of *memaḥek,* or "scraping." Included in the prohibition is not only the reduction of a solid substance to a powder, but also removing the roughness from the surface of a material by means of grinding, polishing, rubbing or smoothing. A second prohibition, which applies to liquid makeup no less than to cosmetics prepared in a solid state is *ẓove'a* or "dyeing." All manner of dyeing, painting and coloring is forbidden on the Sabbath.

25. Cf., the footnote appended by the editor of *Teḥumin* to Prof. Low's article, *ibid.,* p. 24, note 5.

There is, however, some controversy with regard to the circumstances under which the act of coloring or painting constitutes a biblical infraction and the circumstances under which such an act constitutes a rabbinic infraction. Rambam, *Hilkhot Shabbat* 9:13, maintains that only the application of a pigment or coloring agent which causes a "permanent" change in the color of the object to which it is applied constitutes a biblically proscribed act. According to Rambam, the use of a coloring agent in circumstances in which the color produced is not durable (*eino mitkayyem)* is not biblically proscribed but is forbidden by rabbinic decree.[26]

A coloring agent which adheres for even a minimal period of time is generally regarded as being in the category of *eino mitkayyem. Sefer Miẓvot Gadol* and *Sefer Yere'im* disagree with Rambam and maintain that, when there is intent to paint or color a substance or object, the act is forbidden by virtue of biblical law even if the intention is only for a temporary or transitory pigmentation. Hence, according to all authorities, application of liquid as well as solid-state cosmetics on *Shabbat* constitutes a forbidden form of "dyeing;" the sole dispute is whether the prohibition is biblical or rabbinic in nature.[27] Thus, *Ḥayyei Adam, Hilkhot Shabbat* 24:2, states that a woman "who paints her face or hands" incurs a rabbinic transgression according to Rambam even though the "paint" is a substance lacking in durability (*davar she-eino mitkayyem),* while according to *Sefer Miẓvot Gadol* the infraction is biblical "since such is the wont of women (*kivan she-darkan bekakh*).[28] However, *Mishnah Berurah* 303:79 rules that the "painting" or "dyeing" involved in the application of cosmetics is rabbinic in nature by virtue of an entirely different consideration, i.e., *Mishnah Berurah* rules that the painting of the human skin on *Shabbat*

26. The precise definition of *mitkayyem* (lit: "permanent" or "enduring") with respect to Sabbath laws is the subject of some doubt among latter-day authorities. *Mishnah Berurah, Sha'ar ha-Ẓiyun* 303:68, questions whether the term is to be understood literally, i.e., as connoting permanent pigmentation, or whether adherence of the coloring substance for the period "of the Sabbath day" renders the color "*mitkayyem.*" In another context, *Bi'ur Halakhah* 340:4 suggests that only an effect which is quasi-permanent or intended to endure for an extended period of time is to be regarded as *mitkayyem. Minḥat Ḥinnukh,* no. 32, sec. 15, regards adherence for even a brief period (*zman mah*) as *mitkayyem.* See also, R. Abraham Chaim Noe, *Keẓot ha-Shulḥan, Badei ha-Shulḥan* 146:20; and R. Abraham Blumenkrantz, *Le-Torah ve-Hora'ah: Sefer Zikkaron* (New York, 5749), pp. 203–205.

27. Cf., however, Me'iri, *Shabbat* 95a, and other lesser known early-day authorities cited by R. Abraham Blumenkrantz, *Le-Torah ve-Hora'ah,* p. 205.

28. For alternative explanations see R. Abraham Blumenkrantz, *loc. cit.*

involves a rabbinic, rather than a biblical, transgression even if the coloration is designed to be "permanent'' in nature.[29]

In an early responsum, *Iggerot Mosheh, Oraḥ Ḥayyim,* I, no. 114, Rabbi Moses Feinstein explicitly affirms the prohibition against the use of lipstick on *Shabbat* whether in a solid or in a liquid (i.e., lip gloss) form. Rabbi Feinstein, however, adds a further comment: "But to cast (*lizrok*) white powder on the face which does not remain at all (*she-eino mitkayyem klal*) does not involve a prohibition of 'dyeing.'" It has been generally assumed that Rabbi Feinstein's ruling reflects no major halakhic *novellum,* but was predicated upon the entirely empirical presumption that talcum powder, when "cast upon the face," does not adhere to the skin but instead tends to fall off. A similar ruling was much earlier recorded by R. Abraham Chaim Noe in his halakhic compendium, *Keẓot ha-Shulḥan,* VIII, *Badei ha-Shulḥan* 146:20.

This is certainly the sense in which Rabbi Feinstein's ruling was construed by the *Debrecziner Rav,* R. Moshe Stern, *Teshuvot Be'er Mosheh,* VI, no. 123. The *Debrecziner Rav* permits the use of white powder on *Shabbat* but forbids the use of colored powder. While signifying his agreement with Rabbi Feinstein's ruling regarding the use of white powder on *Shabbat,* the *Debrecziner Rav* takes sharp issue with R. Ephraim Padawer, *Piskei Hilkhot Shabbat,* I (New York, 5735), 7:5, who quotes Rabbi Feinstein as permitting the use of colored powder as well. The *Debrecziner Rav* protests, "In truth, *Iggerot Mosheh* explicitly permits only white powder. . . I do not know on what basis the author wrote in his name the opposite of his words which are explicit in his work (*Iggerot Mosheh, Oraḥ Ḥayyim,* I, no. 114)."

The practical effect of this ruling is rather dubious since it does not seem to be the case that women customarily utilize talcum powder or white face powder as a cosmetic other than in conjunction with other cosmetic agents which do adhere to the skin. Although the practical application of this halakhic ruling is not enhanced thereby, it appears to this writer that the consideration that women do *not* customarily use talcum powder as a coloring agent in and of itself renders the practice permissible. *Mishnah Berurah* 303:79 and 320:58 points out that the prohibition against "dyeing" is applicable only with regard to a substance which is customarily used for dyeing or coloring purposes. Thus, there is no restriction against handling foodstuffs, such as cherries and the like,

29. See also R. Mordecai Brisk, *Teshuvot Maharam Brisk,* no. 23; cf., however, *Minḥat Ḥinnukh,* no. 32, sec. 15.

which stain the skin. Similarly, *Mishnah Berurah* 303:79 rules that a male may apply colored substances to his face since it is not the custom for men to use such substances for purposes of coloring or staining. Thus, there is no question that talcum powder may be applied to the body of a child on the Sabbath and, arguably, such powder may be used by women as well on the grounds that it is not the usual practice to use talcum powder as a coloring agent. In a like manner, R. Yechezkel Posen, *Sefer Kiẓur Hilkhot Shabbat* 21:4, writes: "Nevertheless, it may be permitted [to a woman] to apply that powder (face powder) to her face in order [to absorb] sweat if the color of the powder is the same as the color of the skin . . . since her intention is not for coloring."

The language of his earlier responsum notwithstanding, Rabbi Feinstein, in a brief item appearing in *Le-Torah ve-Hora'ah,* no. 7 (Elul 5737), p. 28, declares that his earlier ruling applies with equal force to "colored powder" as well. Were the ruling understood as applying only to colored powder possessing the selfsame property ascribed to the "white powder" discussed in *Iggerot Mosheh,* i.e., colored powder "which does not remain at all," the permissive conclusion could readily be explained. The prohibition against dyeing applies only in situations in which the coloring agent adheres to the surface upon which it is applied. Accordingly, the application of colored powder "which does not remain at all," but which falls off without adhering to the skin, would appear to be entirely permissible. This conclusion would also appear to be consistent with the ruling of *Keẓot ha-Shulḥan.* Although, in formulating his ruling, *Keẓot ha-Shulḥan* sanctions only the use of "powder" and explicitly forbids the use of a colored base, he permits the use of powder on *Shabbat* on the grounds that "it is dry and does not adhere firmly (*ve-einah mitdabbeket dibbuk gamur*) to the skin of the face." It would follow that colored powder of a similar nature would also be permissible. The permissive rulings of Rabbi Feinstein and *Keẓot ha-Shulḥan* are also endorsed by R. Ovadiah Yosef, *Yabi'a Omer,* VI, *Oraḥ Ḥayyim,* no. 38 and *Yeḥaveh Da'at,* IV, no. 28.[30] Nevertheless, two extraneous questions would be in order: one, empirical; the second, pragmatic. 1) Is such a powder commercially available? 2) What cosmetic purpose would be served by use of such a powder?

Further clarification of Rabbi Feinstein's position is contained in a letter reproduced and translated in the October-November, 1984 issue of *Jewish Woman's Outlook.* Rabbi Feinstein states that upon "testing and investigation" it appears that blanket permission cannot be given for the

30. See also R. Abraham Blumenkrantz, *Le-Torah ve-Hora'ah,* pp. 206–207.

use of even "white powder" since most powders sold as cosmetics contain an oil base which causes powder to adhere to the skin. A similar distinction is drawn by Rabbi Yosef. Rabbi Feinstein reports, however, that there are indeed some cosmetic powders which do not remain on the skin and, hence, use of those powders is permissible He cautions, however, that "without experience in assessing a matter of this nature it is difficult to make a determination."

The item which appears in *Jewish Woman's Outlook* includes an addendum enumerating specific cosmetic powders which purportedly conformed to the criteria specified by Rabbi Feinstein, *viz.,* cosmetic powders which do not adhere to the skin. Hence, consistent with Rabbi Feinstein's ruling, the use of those cosmetics on the Sabbath is permitted. Those products were tested by Rabbi David Weinberger, who was then a member of the *kollel* of the Rabbinical Seminary of America and who is a highly competent scholar in his own right. Rabbi Weinberger cautions that "no base or water be applied to the face" prior to the application of the powder. Quite obviously, such application would have the effect of causing the powder to adhere to the skin. *Keẓot ha-Shulḥan, Badei ha-Shulḥan* 146:20, notes that, for the same reason, powder may not be applied on *Shabbat* even if the cosmetic base has been applied prior to the Sabbath.

Attempts to confirm the findings reported in *Jewish Woman's Outlook* were unsuccessful. Five of the cosmetic powders approved for Sabbath use were selected at random and applied to the surface of the skin. In each case the color remained clearly visible for periods varying between 60 and 90 minutes. Ordinary talcum powder was found to be recognizable for 45 minutes subsequent to application. An attempt was made to remove those products by brushing and rubbing the skin lightly. No appreciable difference was found in the effort required to remove the approved substances as distinct from the effort required to remove non-approved substances. To be sure, since such tests do not lend themselves to precise quantification, the assessment of the results is largely subjective. Nevertheless, it would appear to this writer that those substances are encompassed within the category of *davar she-eino mitkayyem,* i.e., substances which adhere but which do not adhere for an extended period of time, and hence the use of such substances is proscribed *de minimis* by virtue of rabbinic decree.

It should be noted that *Iggerot Mosheh*'s permissive ruling regarding the use of talcum powder has been challenged by at least one prominent authority. R. Joshua Neuwirth, *Shemirat Shabbat ke-Hilkhatah,* I (Jerusalem, 5739) 14:58, note 158, quotes the noted Jerusalem scholar, R. Shlomoh Zalman Auerbach, as forbidding even the use of talcum powder on the Sabbath "for whenever there is intention to color even for a short period of time on what basis [are there grounds] to permit [the practice]?" Rabbi Auerbach's ruling is predicated upon two empirical presumptions, both of which are entirely cogent: (1) Talcum powder, when applied to the face, is designed to modify skin color. (2) Talcum powder *does* adhere to the face for at least a minimal period of time.

R. Israel Abraham Landau, *Teshuvot Bet Yisra'el* (Brooklyn, 5736), no. 56, forbids the use of talcum powder on different grounds. The Palestinian Talmud, *Shabbat* 7:2, declares that application of a substance designed to enhance the white color of the face constitutes a forbidden form of *melaben,* i.e., "whitening" or cleaning. However, R. Yeshayah Kaufman, writing in a publication of the *kollel* of New Square, *Zera Emet,* Iyar 5744, points out that *Amudei Yerushalayim, ad locum,* records a variant reading of the text of the Palestinian Talmud which completely changes the meaning of that statement. Moreover, accepting the published version of the text, R. Mordecai Brisk, *Teshuvot Maharam Brisk,* II, no. 98, sec. 20, shows that this position is rejected by the Babylonian Talmud.

Teshuvot Maharam Brisk, I, no. 23, accepts the premise that application of talcum powder is designed to effect some change in facial color but nevertheless permits its use on *Shabbat. Maharam Brisk* bases his ruling upon a determination that the cosmetic "painting" or coloring of human skin is prohibited only by virtue of rabbinic decree and that use of a *davar she-eino mitkayyem* is similarly forbidden only by virtue of rabbinic decree. He further adduces authorities who maintain that, although deepening or enhancing an already existing color on *Shabbat* is forbidden, such an act is not forbidden by biblical law but is proscribed only by rabbinic edict. The application of white powder to the skin is designed to enhance or highlight the natural color of the skin. Since it enhances an already existing color but does not change the basic color, such an act, argues *Maharam Brisk,* is only rabbinically enjoined even if its effect would be permanent. Hence, application of talcum powder on *Shabbat* would be forbidden only upon a configuration of three rabbinic decrees: (1) a prohibition against coloring by means of a *davar she-eino mitkayyem;* (2) a prohibition against painting or coloring human skin; and (3) a prohibition against enhancing an already existing color. Although *Maharam Brisk* concedes that acts involving a configuration of two rabbinic edicts are indeed proscribed, he asserts that rabbinic legislation does not forbid acts involving the configuration of three rabbinic decrees.[31] *Maharam Brisk* forbids the application of colored powder on *Shabbat* since such use would involve a configuration of only two rabbinic prohibitions.

Although the consideration is not applicable to the ordinary use of cosmetics, there may be grounds for permitting the use of cosmetic agents designed to hide a disfiguring birthmark or skin blemish when the cosmetic is applied by a non-Jew. *Tosafot, Shabbat* 50b, declares that a condition which causes a person embarrassment of a magnitude such that the individual is ashamed to appear in public constitutes a form of grave pain. Thus, the psychological anguish which may result from not being able to engage in normal social intercourse is halakhically regarded as a form of severe pain. A person experiencing such pain is, arguably, in the category of a patient afflicted by a "sickness of the entire body" on whose behalf a non-Jew may be directed to perform an otherwise forbidden act as recorded in *Shulḥan Arukh, Oraḥ Ḥayyim* 328:17. Indeed, were the remedy to involve an act forbidden only by virtue of rabbinic edict, the act might be performed even by a Jew provided that it is performed in an unusual manner, e.g., by use of the left hand. However, as stated by *Mishnah Berurah* 328:54 and 328:57, only rabbinically proscribed acts may be performed in an unusual manner under such circumstances. Therefore, since cosmetics generally utilized for such purposes require use of substances involving the biblical prohibition of *memaḥek,* they may be applied only by a non-Jew. A liquid substance which does not involve the prohibition of *memaḥek* is, minimally, a *davar she-eino mitkayyem,* the use of which, for some authorities, as indicated earlier, entails a biblical prohibition of "dyeing" and, if designed to adhere for a significant period of time, the use of such a substance constitutes a biblical transgression according to other authorities as well. In light of those considerations, a substance designed to cover a disfiguring blemish should be applied only by a non-Jew.

Cholent

Cooking is enumerated among the thirty-nine activities specifically forbidden on the Sabbath. The prohibition against cooking precludes not only placing uncooked food over a fire but also replacing partially cooked food on the stove. Rema, *Oraḥ Ḥayyim* 253:2 and *Shulḥan Arukh, Oraḥ*

31. Cf. *Pri Megadim,* introduction to *Oraḥ Ḥayyim, Hanhagat ha-Sho'el ve-ha-Nish'al,* I, sec. 14.

Ḥayyim 318:4, rule that food which has not been thoroughly cooked may not be replaced on the stove even though the food is already readily edible. Use of a *blech* or metal covering which is placed over the flame serves only to eliminate the rabbinic ban which prohibits returning even already thoroughly cooked food to the stove and allowing incompletely cooked food to remain on the stove during the Sabbath. Although no act of cooking is involved, these practices are forbidden by rabbinic decree lest one be prompted to "stir the embers" in order to increase the intensity of the heat. This rabbinic prohibition is suspended when the flame is covered on the principle that covering the flame manifests absence of concern for maximization of heat. However, use of such metal covering in no way mitigates the biblical prohibition attendant upon replacing food which is less than thoroughly cooked upon a stove. *Shulḥan Arukh, Oraḥ Ḥayyim* 254:4, rules that, when return of a pot to the stove is forbidden, the replacement of a lid upon a pot on the stove is forbidden as well. Placing a lid on a pot serves to contain the heat which, in turn, causes the cooking process to proceed more rapidly. Hence placing or replacing a lid upon a pot constitutes an act of cooking.

Since cooking on the Sabbath is forbidden, it has long been the practice among Jews to prepare a stew-like dish, known as *cholent,* containing various ingredients which is placed upon the stove on Friday and allowed to remain overnight on a low flame. The food is then removed in time for the midday meal on the Sabbath. Ingredients vary in accordance with ethnic and culinary preferences. Popular varieties of *cholent* contain meat, potatoes, beans and barley in various combinations and proportions. Among Oriental Jews it is customary to use rice as the staple ingredient. During the medieval period this culinary dish was known as *ḥamin* or "hot food." It is now usually referred to by Western Jews as "*cholent*" which some linguists maintain is derived from the French *chaud,* meaning "hot," or *chaleur,* meaning "heat." It has been conjectured that the term may be a contraction of the French words *chaud* and *lent,* meaning hot and slow, to form a word connoting "slow heat." A less likely suggestion is that the term *cholent* originated as a contraction of the German or Yiddish words *shul ende,* meaning "end of synagogue services," the hour at which the Sabbath-day meal is customarily eaten. Although the meaning of the term may be obscure, the practice of eating *cholent* is ubiquitous and, for many, is closely associated with enjoyment of the Sabbath day. For that reason recent discussions of a halakhic problem posed in the preparation of this dish have aroused wide interest.

In Israel, due to the almost prohibitive cost of beef, it is common to use fowl in the preparation of the *cholent.* The long and slow cooking process has the effect of making the relatively soft chicken bones quite edible and tasty. Of late, there has been some debate among rabbinic scholars in Israel with regard to whether or not it is permissible to remove some of the *cholent* prepared in this manner on Friday evening and thereafter replace the pot on the stove or, for that matter, whether the lid of the pot may be raised and replaced. This question is addressed by Rabbi Moses Feinstein, *Iggerot Mosheh, Oraḥ Ḥayyim,* IV, no. 76. A conflicting view is expressed by Rabbi Shlomoh Zalman Auerbach in the Ḥeshvan 5742 issue of *Moriah* and by Rabbi Abraham Isaac Hoffman in the Shevat-Adar 5742 issue of *Ha-Pardes*.

Rabbi Feinstein rules that the prohibition against cooking does not extend to bones since bones are not deemed to be a foodstuff. He maintains that there exists no prohibition against cooking bones even by a person intent upon consuming them subsequent to cooking because whether or not an item is deemed a foodstuff is determined by general practice rather than by subjective inclination. A contrary view was earlier expressed by R. Joshua Neuwirth in the second edition of his highly regarded compendium of Sabbath laws, *Shemirat Shabbat ke-Hilkhatah,* I (Jerusalem, 5739) 1:18, in the name of Rabbi Shlomoh Zalman Auerbach.

In his contribution to *Moriah* Rabbi Auerbach explains the basis of his negative ruling. Rabbi Auerbach reports that, contrary to the assumption of Rabbi Feinstein, both meat and bones are commonly consumed by persons eating this type of *cholent.* Hence, concludes Rabbi Auerbach, even though bones are not included in the prohibition against partaking of carrion or of milk and meat which have been cooked together, nevertheless, in a locale in which bones are customarily eaten, they must be deemed a foodstuff which may not be cooked on the Sabbath. In a subsequent responsum addressed to Rabbi Auerbach, *Iggerot Mosheh, Oraḥ Ḥayyim,* IV, no. 77, Rabbi Feinstein expresses incredulity at the report that it is common practice in Israel to eat the chicken bones found in the *cholent*. Nevertheless, he readily concedes both that the halakhah as formulated by Rabbi Auerbach is correct under the circumstances described by the latter and that Rabbi Auerbach is more familiar than he with the eating habits of Israelis.

In point of fact, a similar problem may well exist in other countries as well. Rabbi Feinstein notes that the entire question of replacing a *cholent* pot on Friday evening did not arise in earlier times. In Europe, until recent times, it was customary to place the *cholent* not upon the stove, but within an oven which was subsequently sealed in order to preserve the heat. The *cholent* was therefore not removed on Friday evening in order to eat some portion of that dish in the course of the evening meal both because of the inconvenience involved and because the loss of escaped heat would interfere with proper cooking of the *cholent.* Thus the practice of removing a portion of the *cholent* on Friday evening is of fairly recent origin. It is entirely likely that the *cholent* may not yet be fully cooked at the time of its removal on Friday evening, particularly if it has been placed on the stove late in the day on Friday. Under such circumstances, it is not permitted to return the *cholent* to the stove.

Rabbi Hoffman argues that this practice is forbidden under virtually all circumstances. He notes that, even when the other ingredients are otherwise fully cooked, the flavor of the meat is enhanced by continued cooking in the juices of the bones throughout the night. Hence, argues Rabbi Hoffman, return of the pot to the stove so long as the taste of the *cholent* continues to improve through further cooking is encompassed within the biblical prohibition as indicated by *Mishnah Berurah* 318:91. Accordingly, Rabbi Hoffman advises that the *cholent* not be removed from the stove prior to the noon meal on *Shabbat.* The factual assumption underlying this line of reasoning is subject to question and, in all likelihood, will vary from one *cholent* recipe to another.

Chapter VI

Returning from Missions of Mercy on the Sabbath

On account of what merit did Judah receive kingship? On account of the merit of having rescued [Reuben] from death.

MEKHILTA, BESHALAḤ 14

In recent years there has been a marked increase in the number of observant young men and women entering medicine as a profession. Committed, as they are, to rendering the best medical care of which they are capable and to meticulous observance of the commandments, at times they find themselves confronted with conflicts between professional and religious commitments and their personal needs. With increasing frequency rabbinic decisors are called upon by observant health care professionals to offer guidance in resolving problems of this nature. Providing for the proper care of patients in a manner consistent with Sabbath regulations as well as with the physician's physical and spiritual need for Sabbath repose is a source of particular concern.

It is a fundamental and well-known principle of Jewish law that halakhic strictures regarding observance of *Shabbat* and *Yom Tov* may not interfere with the treatment of a dangerously ill patient. Thus there is no question whatsoever that a physician is required to attend a patient who becomes ill on *Shabbat* or *Yom Tov* even if his visit requires travel entailing acts which in other circumstances would be biblically proscribed. However, otherwise prohibited acts are permitted only for the benefit of the patient but not for the convenience of the doctor. Thus, once the treatment of the patient has been completed, further restricted activities cannot be sanctioned. A physician called to the hospital or to the patient's home on *Shabbat,* while quite prepared to fulfill his responsibilities toward his patient on the *Shabbat,* no less than on a weekday, is understandably distressed at the prospect of being deprived of Sabbath rest and enjoyment of the company of his family even after his professional services are no longer needed. Accordingly, doctors frequently inquire whether there exist grounds for permitting them to make the return journey in order to spend the balance of the day with their families in a Sabbath atmosphere.[1] Similar queries have been addressed to rabbinic authorities by various local chapters of Hatzolah, a network of volunteers who provide ambulance service and emergency medical assistance in the New York metropolitan area. Indeed, a number of published responsa addressing this topic were solicited because Hatzolah groups found it necessary to establish communal policy with regard to this issue. Useful surveys of rabbinic sources pertaining to this question have been authored by R. Menachem Waldman, *Teḥumin,* III (5742), 38–48, and R. Mordecai Halperin, *Assia,* IV (5743), 60–71. The practices of Hatzolah are also the subject of a responsum authored by R. Yom Tov Schwarz, *Teshuvot Adnei Neḥoshet* (New York, 5750), no. 72.

I. *Talmudic Sources*

There are, to be sure, talmudic sources indicating that at least some infractions of Jewish law are permitted in order to enable individuals engaged in life-saving missions to return to their homes on *Shabbat.* Ordinarily, on the Sabbath a person may stroll no more than 2,000 cubits beyond an inhabited area. Travel beyond that distance is forbidden even within another inhabited area. A significant exception is made for persons who have completed a mission of mercy. The Mishnah, *Rosh ha-Shanah* 23b, declares, ". . . even a midwife who comes to assist in birthing and one who comes to deliver from fire, from soldiers, from the river or from a ruin are as the inhabitants of the city and have [the privilege of walking] two thousand cubits in every direction." The identical rule is extended by the Mishnah, *Eruvin* 44b, to encompass a person who embarks upon a mission of mercy but whose services prove to be unnecessary: "One who has exited [beyond the ordinarily permitted area of two thousand cubits]

1. Situations in which there is a reason to presume that the physician's services or the ambulance will be required by another patient present an entirely different question. See R. Yisra'el Aryeh Zalmanowitz, *No'am,* IV (5721), 175–178; and R. Joshua Neuwirth, *Shemirat Shabbat ke-Hilkhatah,* I (Jerusalem, 5739) 40:69. See also *ibid.,* 40:67 and 40:71. However, in an age of ubiquitous telephone and radio communications it is generally not necessary to return immediately in anticipation of such need. See R. Isaac Liebes, *Halakhah u-Refu'ah,* III (5743), 73, reprinted in his *Teshuvot Bet Avi,* IV, *Oraḥ Ḥayyim,* no. 16.

and they said to him, 'The matter has already been completed,' has [the privilege of walking] two thousand cubits in every direction . . . for all who depart in order to deliver from danger [are permitted to] return to their place."

The latter formulation, however, contains an inherent discrepancy. The Mishnah accords the rescuer a right of Sabbath travel identical to that enjoyed by the individuals whom he seeks to rescue, *viz.,* the right to travel by foot within a radius of 2,000 cubits of the perimeter of the city in which he finds himself. The Mishnah then concludes with an explanatory phrase indicating that such individuals may return to their point of departure. The implication of the latter statement is that they may journey even more than 2,000 cubits if it is necessary for them to do so in order to return to their homes.[2] The Gemara offers two resolutions of this apparent contradiction, each of which is predicated upon the thesis that the Mishnah records two separate and distinct rules. R. Judah explains in the name of Rav that the individuals in question are granted the right to travel only a distance of 2,000 cubits. However, if their homes are within that distance, individuals who come to the defense of fellow Jews during periods of unrest are permitted to carry their weapons with them when returning to their homes. Thus the regulation formulated in the final clause of the Mishnah refers only to rescuers involved in warding off attackers but not to individuals whose mission does not require the use of arms. The Gemara reports that this dispensation was granted in the wake of a specific historical occurrence. Originally, upon completion of their mission, people who in the course of a mission of rescue were compelled to bear arms on the Sabbath were wont to leave their weapons in the house nearest the city wall. On one occasion, individuals returning from such a mission were recognized and pursued by the enemy. Finding themselves endangered, they entered the house in which the arms had been deposited in order to retrieve their weapons. The enemy pursued them into the house with the result that the rescuers "trampled one another and killed among themselves more than the enemy killed." At that time the Sages ordained that on future occasions of a like nature the rescuers should carry their weapons with them until reaching the safety of their homes. R. Nachman bar Yitzchak (according to the text and commentary of Rabbenu Chananel)

2. *Tosafot Yom Tov, Eruvin* 4:3, suggests that, according to R. Judah, the term "their place" in the phrase "[are permitted to] return to their place" should be understood as meaning the "place" permitted by the Sages, *viz.,* a radius of 2,000 cubits.

maintains that the 2,000-cubit limit applies in most cases of life-saving activity, including rescue from an enemy, provided that the enemy has been totally routed. The rule permitting the would-be deliverers to return to their places of origin, declares R. Nachman bar Yitzchak, pertains only to situations in which the enemy has gained the upper hand and is designed to afford retreating rescuers a measure of protection from marauding soldiers. Thus, with the exception of bearing arms in a situation fraught with potential danger, the sole dispensation explicitly granted to those engaged in missions of mercy is the right to travel by foot within a radius of 2,000 cubits upon completion of their mission.

II. *Hittiru Sofan Mishum Teḥillatan*

However, Rashba, *Beiẓah* 11b, and *Tosafot, Eruvin* 44b and *Rosh ha-Shanah* 23b, add an additional point of elucidation that is absent in other sources and which has the effect of placing the matter in a somewhat different halakhic perspective. Both authorities adduce the halakhic principle "they permitted the end for the sake of the beginning (*hittiru sofan mishum teḥillatan*)." This formula reflects the fact that in order to encourage certain activities the Sages found it necessary to sanction subsequent actions as well even though those subsequent actions are ordinarily proscribed. Thus, the Gemara, *Beiẓah* 11b, records that it is permitted to spread the hides of an animal on the ground in order that they be softened by being trampled upon by passersby, to replace shutters upon portable market stalls and for a priest serving in the Temple to replace a bandage removed prior to his participation in the sacrificial ritual. Each of those actions is ordinarily forbidden on *Shabbat* and *Yom Tov* by virtue of rabbinic decree but is permitted in order to encourage the slaughter of fresh meat, to make food readily available for the holiday repasts and to induce the priests to perform their assigned duties. Justification for the suspension of those prohibitions is couched in the formula "[with regard to] three matters did they permit the end because of the beginning." Rashba, in his commentary on *Beiẓah* 11b and as cited by *Shitah Mekubeẓet, ad locum,* remarks that dispensation to move about within a 2,000-cubit radius of the city was similarly granted to persons engaged in life-saving activities in order to encourage them to embark upon missions of mercy. Absent such dispensation, they would have been restricted to an area of four cubits from wherever they might find themselves upon completion of their tasks. According to Rashba, an exception was made for persons engaged in the preservation of life because the prospect of being faced by inconvenience upon completion of their mission might result in a lack of resolve or in procrastination in embarking upon a life-saving endeavor. The author of *Shitah Mekubeẓet,* citing his teacher, apparently maintains that this dispensation does not constitute the suspension of a rabbinic prohibition as an inducement to engage in life-saving activity but represents an integral, equitable adjustment of rabbinic enactments governing Sabbath travel adopted in the guise of assigning to the rescuers the selfsame domicile as the rescued.

Nevertheless, even according to Rashba, there are no apparent grounds for permitting infractions of biblical law in the course of a return journey. The dispensation with regard to travel on the Sabbath granted to those embarking upon a mission of rescue is the product of rabbinic legislation. Ramban, *Eruvin* 43a, takes note of the principle that there is no rabbinic authority to sanction overt violation of biblical prohibitions and explicitly remarks that the dispensation granted by the Sages with regard to travel on the Sabbath is limited to infractions which are only rabbinic in nature. Although he does not cite the comments of Ramban, R. Joseph Babad, *Minḥat Ḥinnukh,* no. 24, s.v. *ve-hinneh mevu'ar,* notes that, although walking a distance greater than 2,000 cubits is proscribed by virtue of rabbinic edict, many early authorities maintain that traversing a distance of more than three parasangs (twelve *mil*) is forbidden by biblical law. Hence, rules *Minḥat Ḥinnukh,* one who has already travelled more than three parasangs even in order to save lives must remain within four cubits of wherever he finds himself. Since each act of moving more than four cubits beyond a distance of three parasangs constitutes a violation of biblical law, concludes *Minḥat Ḥinnukh,* such action is not subject to rabbinic dispensation.[3] The identical principle applies to all matters

3. Although the basic principle is not the subject of dispute, R. Menachem Waldman, *Teḥumin,* III (5742), 47, points out that its application must be modified somewhat according to the position espoused by Ramban, *Eruvin* 43a. In his initial discussion Ramban assumes that, although no biblical infraction is involved in a Sabbath journey of less than three parasangs, nevertheless, beyond that distance every step constitutes an additional transgression. (Cf., however *Minḥat Ḥinnukh,* no. 24, s.v. *ve-hinneh mevu'ar,* who maintains that even one who has travelled more than three parasangs is entitled to move about within an area of four cubits.) Ramban, however, concludes that a culpable transgression is incurred only upon traversing another distance of three parasangs. (See also *Or Sameaḥ, Hilkhot Shabbat* 27:1.) It would then follow that persons who have travelled even further than three parasangs on a mission of rescue would be permitted to traverse an additional distance of 2,000 cubits.

which are permitted on the basis of *hittiru sofan mishum teḥillatan* as is clearly indicated by *Shitah Mekubeẓet, Beiẓah* 11b; Baḥ, *Oraḥ Ḥayyim* 49, s.v. *ha-shoḥet; Magen Avraham, Oraḥ Ḥayyim* 497:18; *Nishmat Adam* 91:1; and R. Zevi Pesach Frank, *Teshuvot Har Ẓevi, Oraḥ Ḥayyim,* II, no. 10. Thus, since the Sages are without power to sanction overt abrogation of biblical law, in every case in which the principle *hittiru sofan mishum teḥillatan* is invoked only rabbinic prohibitions are suspended in order to encourage the desired result.

Moreover, it is not clear that even a rabbinic prohibition, e.g., permitting a non-Jew to operate a motor vehicle, may be violated in undertaking the return journey. On the contrary, individuals who engage in life-saving missions are treated as residents of the locale in which they find themselves and even for purposes of returning to their place of domicile they are granted the right of travel within a radius of 2,000 cubits, but not beyond, because travel over a greater distance would entail violation of a rabbinic edict. Particularly according to the authorities who fail to cite the principle of *hittiru sofan mishum teḥillatan* as grounds for the dispensation with regard to strolling within a radius of 2,000 cubits, this regulation should be regarded as integral to the rabbinic edict governing delimitation of the area which may be traversed on the Sabbath rather than a license to ignore rabbinic prohibitions. As earlier noted, dispensation to carry weapons on the return trip is rooted in a concern for the safety of the travellers and certainly cannot serve as a paradigm for the suspension of other prohibitions, even of those that are rabbinic in nature.

Nevertheless, the comments of *Tosafot, Eruvin* 44b, and a literal reading of Rashba, *Beiẓah* 11b, convey the impression that those authorities regard violations of even biblical prohibitions as permitted to these individuals on their homeward journey on the basis of *hittiru sofan mishum teḥillatan.* As noted earlier, the Gemara, *Eruvin* 45a, does permit at least limited violation of biblical prohibitions in the course of the return journey. R. Judah in the name of Rav permits the carrying of weapons on the return journey within a distance of 2,000 cubits; R. Nachman bar Yitzchak permits the bearing of arms during the course of a return journey of even an unlimited distance in a situation in which the enemy has obtained the upper hand. Rabbenu Yehonatan, in his commentary on *Rif, ad locum,* observes that no qualification is posited by the Gemara with regard to the halakhic classification of the area in which the arms may be transported. Hence, under the circumstances described, the weapons may be transported even through a public thoroughfare despite the fact that such an act ordinarily constitutes a transgression of a biblical prohibition. However, the grounds for such dispensation are ostensibly that the individuals described are themselves endangered and, accordingly, permission to transport weapons is predicated upon a concern for the preservation of their lives. Hence those provisions of Halakhah cannot serve as a paradigm for permitting violation of biblical prohibitions on the return trip by rescuers who are themselves in no danger. This analysis of the discussion in *Eruvin* is clearly enunciated by *Shitah Mekubeẓet, Beiẓah* 11b.

However, *Tosafot, Eruvin* 44b, speak of the dispensation regarding the carrying of arms on the return journey as an instance of invocation of the principle of *hittiru sofan mishum teḥillatan.*[4] A literal reading of Rashba, *Beiẓah* 11b (rather than as understood by *Shitah Mekubeẓet*), yields a similar impression. If this analysis of the position of *Tosafot* and Rashba is correct, it would appear that, according to those authorities, all persons engaging in life-saving activities may ignore even biblical proscriptions on their return journey. This is indeed the position of R. Moses Sofer, *Teshuvot Ḥatam Sofer, Oraḥ Ḥayyim,* no. 203, *Ḥoshen Mishpat,* no. 194, and VI, no. 99 and apparently also of R. Jacob Emden, *She'ilat Ya'aveẓ,* I, no. 132, s.v. *u-de-kashya.* In *Ḥoshen Mishpat,* no. 194, *Ḥatam Sofer* implies that a physician called on *Shabbat* to the bedside of a gravely ill patient may disregard biblical prohibitions if it is necessary for him to do so in order to return to his home. Responding to the argument that the Sages do not have the power to sanction overt suspension of biblical law, *Ḥatam Sofer,* VI, no. 99, s.v. *de-ika,* responds that authority to do so is limited to infractions of Sabbath laws which may be suspended solely to encourage life-saving activity. The Gemara, *Yoma* 85b, apparently understanding the word "*ve-shameru*" which occurs in Exodus 31:16 as connoting "The children of Israel shall *preserve* the Sabbath," formulates the dictum "Better to violate one Sabbath in order to observe many Sabbaths" as justification for the violation of Sabbath restrictions for the sake of preserving life. *Ḥatam Sofer* argues that the same rationale may be employed in the context of *hittiru sofan mishum teḥillatan* in order to assure that "many Sabbaths" be observed.[5]

---

4. *Teshuvot Adnei Neḥoshet,* no. 72, sec. 2, suggest a minor emendation in the caption of *Tosafot* with the effect that *Tosafot*'s statement is limited to travel within 2,000 cubits. See also *Teshuvot Adnei Neḥoshet,* no. 72, sec. 5.

5. In the context of ignoring Sabbath restrictions *Ḥatam Sofer*'s explanation must be understood as meaning that it is necessary to permit such acts in order to encourage life-saving activity so that those whose lives are saved may "observe many Sabbaths." Cf., R. Eliezer Waldenberg, *Ẓiẓ Eli'ezer,* XI, no. 39, sec. 6,

However, not all rabbinic decisors agree that rabbinic prohibitions may be ignored in order to complete the return journey on *Shabbat.* The inference that *Tosafot* and Rashba sanction violations of biblical law for the purpose of a return journey by all engaged in life-preserving activity is rebutted by R. Zevi Pesach Frank, *Teshuvot Har Ẓevi, Oraḥ Ḥayyim,* II, no. 10. Rabbi Frank notes that such dispensation is explicitly recorded only with regard to those who travel to defend against armed attack but not with regard to a midwife or one who engages in saving a potential drowning victim.[6] Rabbi Frank apparently maintains that, at least according to *Tosafot* and Rashba, placing oneself in a situation of danger which then requires violation of biblical proscriptions in order to save one's life is prohibited only by virtue of rabbinic decree.[7] According to

who apparently misses the thrust of *Ḥatam Sofer*'s point. See also *Kiryat Sefer, Hilkhot Shabbat* 2:23.

6. Similar objections are advanced by R. Shlomoh Zalman Auerbach, *Moriah,* Sivan-Tammuz 5731, p. 29, reprinted in *idem, Minḥat Shlomoh,* no. 7, sec. 3, s.v. *ulam.* Moreover, Rabbi Auerbach argues that *Ḥatam Sofer* does not, in fact, sanction such infractions of biblical prohibitions by a physician. *Ḥatam Sofer*'s comments are made in the context of a case in which a Jewish doctor was called upon to visit non-Jewish patients on *Shabbat.* Rabbi Auerbach argues that such a situation is comparable to the case of individuals who are engaged in delivering their brethren from soldiers since failure to attend a gentile might lead to retribution against Jews. The status of a physician engaged in the treatment of a Jewish patient, argues Rabbi Auerbach, is entirely dissimilar. In the latter instance the doctor's status is comparable to that of a midwife who is not permitted to travel beyond 2,000 cubits. This writer, however, fails to understand how this analysis of *Ḥatam Sofer*'s position resolves the problems attendant thereupon since those rescuing their brethren from attack are permitted to carry their weapons only because of possible danger to themselves and are permitted to travel more than 2,000 cubits only "when the hand of the gentiles is strong"—situations which surely do not pertain in the case of a physician attending a non-Jewish patient. It should also be noted that in the case of a Jewish physician attending a non-Jewish patient *Ḥatam Sofer* concludes that since failure to treat the patient would invite retaliation against all Jews, and certainly against the doctor personally, the physician is, in effect, acting for reasons of self-preservation. Since no inducement need be offered in order to encourage a person to save his own life the principle of *hittiru sofan mishum teḥillatan* does not apply and hence, concludes *Ḥatam Sofer,* in such situations no prohibitions are suspended in order to enable the physician to return to his home on *Shabbat.*

7. Cf., R. Benjamin Silber, *Mekor Halakhah al Massekhet Shabbat,* II, no. 35, s.v. *ve-ha-nireh,* who maintains that, when undertaken on *Shabbat,* such a course of action is biblically prohibited. Cf., also, *Yeshu'ot Ya'akov, Oraḥ Ḥayyim* 331:5; and R. Isaac Liebes, *Halakhah u-Refu'ah,* III, 81, reprinted in *Teshuvot Bet Avi,* IV, *Oraḥ Ḥayyim,* no. 16.

Rabbi Frank, it is that decree, and that decree alone, which, by application of the principle *hittiru sofan mishum teḥillatan,* is suspended on behalf of individuals who have been engaged in life-saving activities.[8] Thus the rescuers are permitted to embark on their return journey by virtue of rabbinic dispensation. Having done so, they find themselves in danger and, accordingly, may transport weapons in order to protect themselves. The sole infraction consists of having placed themselves in danger in the first instance. That infraction, which is rabbinic in nature, is permitted on the basis of *hittiru sofan mishum teḥillatan.*

Rabbi Frank contends that *Tosafot* and Rashba invoke the concept of *hittiru sofan mishum teḥillatan* in permitting biblical infractions only in the case of those who render aid in defending against marauding soldiers, i.e., when the rescuers are themselves subject to danger during the course of the return journey, but not in the case of a midwife or one who rescues from drowning, i.e., individuals who are themselves not endangered in their attempt to save others. However, an examination of the words of Rashba in his commentary on *Beiẓah* 11b[9] reveals that this contention is contradicted by Rashba himself since Rashba explicitly states that the midwife is permitted to return to her locale on the basis of the principle *hittiru sofan mishum teḥillatan*. Rashba's comment is indeed problematic since, as noted by *Shitah Mekubeẓet,* it appears to contradict the ruling of the Mishnah which permits a midwife to travel only a distance of 2,000 cubits but does not extend *carte blanche* for unlimited travel in the course of the return voyage. Nevertheless, insofar as an analysis of Rashba's comments is concerned, there is no reason to assume that the midwife is herself endangered in any way and there is certainly no hint of such a contention in the words of Rashba. Assuming that Rashba agrees that travel over a distance greater than three parasangs is biblically forbidden, it must be concluded that Rashba maintains that even biblical prohibitions are suspended in order to protect against possible future laxity or laziness.[10]

Ḥatam Sofer's position was, in effect, rejected at a much earlier time

8. Cf., R. Abraham Avidan, *Darkei Ḥesed* (Jerusalem, 5738) 10:3, note 3, pp. 136–138.

9. As understood by *Shitah Mekubeẓet,* Rashba does not at all refer to suspension of biblical prohibitions. Rabbi Frank, however, cites and analyses the comments of Rashba as they appear in the commentary of Rashba without the interpretation of *Shitah Mekubeẓet.*

10. Cf., R. Moses Feinstein, *Teḥumin,* I (5740), reprinted in *Iggerot Mosheh, Oraḥ Ḥayyim,* IV, no. 80, who reaches the same conclusion regarding Rashba's position but on the basis of somewhat different reasoning.

by R. Shlomoh Kluger, *Teshuvot u-Vaḥarta ba-Ḥayyim,* no. 99. Rabbi Kluger forbade a person travelling on the Sabbath for the purpose of summoning medical assistance to return on the Sabbath in a situation in which the return journey would have involved a distance greater than three parasangs and hence, according to many authorities, entailed a biblical infraction. *Ḥatam Sofer*'s position is also disputed by R. Shalom Mordecai Schwadron in his *Hagahot Maharsham, Rosh ha-Shanah* 22b, and in his *Orḥot Ḥayyim* 597:11.[11] Similar rulings limiting the application of *hittiru sofan mishum teḥillatan* to infractions of rabbinic law are recorded by R. Shlomoh Zalman Auerbach, *Moriah,* Sivan-Tammuz, 5731, pp. 29–30, reprinted in his *Minḥat Shlomoh,* no. 7, and no. 8;[12] R. Eliezer Waldenberg, *Ẓiẓ Eli'ezer,* VIII, no. 15, chap. 7, sec. 12 and chap. 13, sec. 8, and XI, nos. 39 and 40; R. Joshua Neuwirth, *Shemirat Shabbat ke-Hilkhatah* (Jerusalem, 5739) 40:69–71; R. Isaac Liebes, *Halakhah u-Refu'ah,* III (5743), reprinted in his *Teshuvot Bet Avi,* IV, *Oraḥ Ḥayyim,* no. 16; and Dr. Abraham S. Abraham, *Nishmat Avraham, Oraḥ Ḥayyim* 329:9, note 7.[13]

III. *Rambam's Position*

Rambam's codification of the regulations formulated in *Eruvin* 45a is fraught with difficulties. Rambam, *Hilkhot Shabbat* 27:17, records the general rule that those who have embarked upon a life-saving mission may journey a distance of 2,000 cubits upon completion of their mission but concludes that "if the hand of the gentiles is strong and they are afraid to remain in the place where they effected the rescue they may return to their own location on the Sabbath with their arms." This ruling certainly seems to reflect the opinion of R. Nachman bar Yitzchak. However, elsewhere, Rambam appears to record an entirely contradictory ruling. In an earlier reference to the identical situation involving individuals who have come to defend their brethren against armed attack, Rambam, *Hilkhot Shabbat* 2:23, rules that "when they have delivered their brethren they are permitted to return to their own location with their weapons on

11. *Ḥatam Sofer*'s position is also rejected by *Teshuvot Adnei Neḥoshet,* no. 72, sec. 5.

12. The latter responsum originally appeared in *Sefer ha-Zikkaron le-Maran ha-Grash Kotler Zaẓal,* ed. R. Joseph Bucksbaum (Jerusalem, 5743), pp. 123–131.

13. Cf. also, R. Yisra'el Aryeh Zalmanowitz, *No'am,* IV, 175–178; and *Teshuvot Dvar Yehoshu'a,* III, *Yoreh De'ah,* no. 69.

the Sabbath *in order not to cause them to be remiss in the future* (*she-lo le-hakhshilan le-'atid lavo*)." Similar apparently contradictory rulings, obviously based upon Rambam's statements, are recorded in *Shulḥan Arukh, Oraḥ Ḥayyim* 329:9 and 407:3. It follows that, if the rationale recorded in *Hilkhot Shabbat* 2:23 is regarded as normative, all persons engaged in missions of mercy may violate biblical prohibitions when it is necessary to do so in order to complete their return journey "*she-lo lehakhshilan le-'atid lavo,*" i.e., so that they not be lax or procrastinate on future occasions when the lives of others are endangered.

Since there is no talmudic source for the statement recorded by Rambam in *Hilkhot Shabbat* 2:23 and, moreover, since that statement is contradicted both by the discussion in *Eruvin* 45a and by Rambam's own ruling in *Hilkhot Shabbat* 27:17, most commentators on Rambam's ruling maintain that Rambam intended to express only a general rule in 2:23 to be modified and made precise in 27:17. This analysis of Rambam's position is espoused by *Maggid Mishneh; Merkevet ha-Mishneh; Ma'aseh Rokeaḥ; Yad Eitan, Sefer ha-Likkutim, Shabbat* 2:23; *Eliyahu Rabbah* 407:6; R. Shlomoh Kluger, *Teshuvot u-Vaḥarta ba-Ḥayyim,* no. 99; and R. Eliezer Waldenberg, *Ẓiẓ Eli'ezer,* XI, no. 39, sec. 7. Although Rambam's employment of the phrase "*she-lo le-hakhshilam le-'atid lavo*" is not really explained in an adequate manner by these sources,[14] they understand Rambam as agreeing that, save for persons defending against armed aggressors, individuals engaged in delivering others from danger may not violate biblical restrictions in order to return to their homes.[15]

---

14. Similarly, the attempt of R. Menachem Waldman, *Teḥumin,* III (5742), 43–44, to explain Rambam's invocation of this principle appears to this writer to be less than convincing. R. Isaac Liebes, *Halakhah u-Refu'ah,* III, 71–73, reprinted in his *Teshuvot Bet Avi,* IV, *Oraḥ Ḥayyim,* no. 16, understands Rambam's invocation of the principle "*she-lo le-hakhshilan le-'atid lavo*" in *Hilkhot Shabbat* 2:23 as limited to explanation of the dispensation to travel within a radius of 2,000 cubits. Understood in that sense the connotation is identical with the principle "*hittiru sofan mishum teḥillatan*" that is invoked by *Tosafot.* A similar analysis was earlier advanced by *Sheyarei Knesset ha-Gedolah, Oraḥ Ḥayyim* 407:2. Cf., *Teshuvot Dvar Yehoshu'a,* III, no. 69, sec. 1. Cf. also *Teshuvot Adnei Neḥoshet,* no. 72, secs. 3–4.

15. See R. Isaac ha-Levi Herzog, *Ha-Torah ve-ha-Medinah,* V–VI, 26–27, reprinted in his *Teshuvot Heikhal Yiẓḥak, Oraḥ Ḥayyim,* no. 32, who maintains that Rambam rules according to Rav but understands Rav as permiting the carrying of weapons on the return journey regardless of its distance and regardless of whether or not Jews are victorious in the encounter. Yet, as pointed out by Rabbi Waldman, *Teḥumin,* III, 43, this is contradicted by Rambam himself as is Rabbi Herzog's explanation of why Rambam adduces the principle *she-lo le-*

The need to sanction transgression of biblical law for the specific purpose of preventing individuals from being remiss on future occasions is posited by the Gemara in an entirely different context. Sabbath laws must be disregarded in order to enable the *Bet Din* to sanctify the new moon on the proper day. Accordingly, witnesses who sight the new moon must immediately proceed to the *Bet Din,* even though this involves violating the Sabbath in order to testify to this event for purposes of enabling the *Bet Din* to sanctify that day as *Rosh Ḥodesh.* The Mishnah, *Rosh ha-Shanah* 21b, reports, "It happened once that more than forty pairs [of witnesses] were on their way and R. Akiva detained them in Lod. Rabban Gamaliel thereupon sent to him saying, 'If you prevent the multitude [from coming to give evidence] you will cause them to stumble in the time to come (*atah makhshilan le-'atid lavo*).'"[16] As noted by R. Jacob Emden, *She'ilat Ya'aveẓ,* I, no. 132, and by *Teshuvot Ḥatam Sofer, Oraḥ Ḥayyim,* no. 203, the rationale "you will cause them to stumble in the time to come" is apparently sufficient justification to warrant suspension of even biblical prohibitions. Witnesses to the appearance of the new moon customarily carried staffs and took food with them on their journey for appearance before the *Bet Din* and, presumably, transported those items even through public thoroughfares (*reshut ha-rabbim*). Moreover, the journey from Lod to the *Bet Din* (which at the time sat either in Jerusalem or Yavneh)[17] presumably spanned a distance of more than

---

hakhshilan le-'atid lavo. Rabbi Herzog, however, concedes that this is permissible only when the return journey is dangerous if attempted without arms and hence his position with regard to how a physician may comport himself on the return journey should not be equated with that of *Ḥatam Sofer;* cf., R. Menachem Waldman, *Sefer Assia,* IV (5743), 71. Cf., also R. Yissakhar ha-Levi Levine, *Ha-Torah ve-ha-Medinah,* VII-VIII, 257–260. Rabbi Mordecai Halperin, *Assia,* IV, 63–69, understands Rambam as permitting violation of even biblical prohibitions *she-lo le-hakhshilan le-'atid lavo* but does not adequately explain why the Gemara's discussion in *Eruvin* does not take cognizance of that consideration.

16. *She'ilat Ya'aveẓ,* I, nos. 131 and 132, are devoted to showing that this incident took place on *Shabbat* and that the concern was for possible improper desecration of the Sabbath rather than merely a concern for needless imposition upon the time of the *Bet Din.* This is also the view of *Teshuvot Ḥatam Sofer, Oraḥ Ḥayyim,* no. 203. Cf., *Turei Even, Rosh ha-Shanah* 25b, who asserts that the incident took place on a weekday. See, however, the discussion recorded in the Palestinian Talmud, *Megillah* 2:7, which clearly indicates that the event described took place on a *Shabbat.*

17. See *She'ilat Ya'aveẓ,* I, no. 132, s.v. *mah she-katavta* and R. Menachem Waldman, *Sefer Assia,* IV, 70–71.

three parasangs.[18] Rabban Gamaliel's statement, however, appears to be limited to the situation described in the Mishnah rather than a paradigm governing other cases as well. Since any act necessary for sanctification of the new moon is permitted on the Sabbath, and since the new moon was as yet not sanctified, all the witnesses were indeed engaged in the actual process of sanctification. Moreover, it may be contended that Sabbath restrictions are suspended not only for the immediate sanctification of the new moon on that Sabbath day but also, if necessary, to ensure the sanctification of any future new moon as well.[19] Hence, since there existed a genuine concern that on some future occasion the Court might find itself without witnesses, permitting travel on the Sabbath by all witnesses does actually serve to make possible the sanctification of some future new moon.[20]

IV. *Suspension of Biblical Prohibitions*

Among contemporary decisors, the late Rabbi Moses Feinstein is the sole authority who permits violation of biblical prohibitions in the course

18. See, however, R. Jacob Ettlinger, *Arukh la-Ner, Rosh ha-Shanah* 21b; and R. Shalom Mordecai Schwadron, *Hagahot Maharsham, Rosh ha-Shanah* 23a; and *idem, Orḥot Ḥayyim* 497:11, who maintain that the witnesses were permitted to ignore only rabbinic prohibitions.

19. See *Teshuvot Ḥatam Sofer, Oraḥ Ḥayyim,* no. 203 and *Ḥoshen Mishpat,* no. 194; cf. *She'ilat Ya'avez,* I, no. 232.

20. R. Shlomoh Kluger, *Teshuvot u-Vaḥarta ba-Ḥayyim,* no. 99, further argues that there is, in fact, no reason to fear future laxity or procrastination with regard to actions necessary to preserve life. Individuals may be unwilling to suffer undue inconvenience in the fulfillment of a *mizvah,* and hence the Sages perceived a need to grant certain dispensations *she-lo lehakhshilan le-'atid lavo,* but would not necessarily have regarded similar dispensations as imperative in order to assure that lives would not be endangered. R. Shlomoh Kluger finds support for this position in the words of the Mishnah, *Rosh ha-Shanah* 23b, which permits witnesses testifying to the sighting of the new moon to move about within a radius of 2,000 cubits and continues with the statement, "Not only these but also a midwife who comes to assist in birthing . . . have [the privilege of walking] two thousand cubits in every direction." The implication of that statement is that it is more radical to allow travel within an area of 2,000 cubits to persons engaged in life-saving activities than it is to grant that privilege to witnesses engaged in fulfillment of a *mizvah.* Thus there is no reason to assume that a dispensation granted to witnesses for reason of *she-lo le-hakhshilan le-'atid lavo* is similarly granted to persons engaged in missions of rescue. See also R. Shlomoh Zalman Auerbach, *Minḥat Shlomoh,* no. 8.

of a return journey.[21] Rabbi Feinstein's views are recorded in contributions to *Teḥumin,* I (5740), reprinted in *Iggerot Mosheh, Oraḥ Ḥayyim,* IV, no. 80, and briefly noted in his contribution to *Halakhah u-Refu'ah,* III (5743).[22] Although he understands *Tosafot* and Rashba as sanctioning even the violation of biblical prohibitions on the basis of *hittiru sofan mishum teḥillatan,* Rabbi Feinstein recognizes that the Mishnah permits a midwife who has completed her ministrations to travel a distance of only 2,000 cubits even in order to return to her home. He proceeds to argue that such a limitation applies only to individuals who recognize that their life-saving mission, by virtue of its very nature, may be prolonged beyond the Sabbath. Such individuals, he argues, prior to setting out on their mission of rescue fully comprehend that they may not be able to return to their homes during the course of *Shabbat.* Since they have, in fact, embarked upon their mission, it is clear that such individuals are not deterred by the prospect of being discomfited by virtue of being away from their homes and families for the duration of the entire Sabbath. Nor, since they have correctly ignored considerations of personal comfort, is it to be presumed that such considerations will deter them in the future. Therefore, no special dispensation need be granted them in the event that they complete their tasks at an early hour. Others, such as a physician whose ministrations are usually not unduly prolonged, do not anticipate a delay which would prevent them from returning to the comfort of their homes for the balance of the Sabbath. Hence refusing to allow them to return to their homes because of Sabbath restrictions would have the effect of causing them to procrastinate or even categorically to refuse to undertake missions of mercy on the Sabbath. Individuals whose activities fall within this category, argues *Iggerot Mosheh,* may ignore Sabbath restrictions in order to return home on the basis of the principle *hittiru sofan mishum teḥillatan.*

Iggerot Mosheh similarly endeavors to show that R. Nachman bar Yitzchak's dictum permitting the carrying of weapons on the return journey when the enemy prevails, while forbidding such action when Jews prevail, is not predicated upon considerations of danger to the rescuers but upon the selfsame distinction with regard to application of the principle of

---

21. *Teshuvot Dvar Yehoshu'a,* III, *Yoreh De'ah,* no. 69, argues in support of *Ḥatam Sofer*'s position but declines to rule in accordance with that view and accordingly permits only violation of rabbinic prohibitions *she-lo le-hakhshilan le-'atid lavo.*

22. The latter item is reprinted in *Or ha-Shabbat,* no. 2 (5745).

hittiru sofan mishum teḥillatan. In direct contradiction to the understanding of all previous commentators, *Iggerot Mosheh* interprets R. Nachman bar Yitzchak's statement as permitting those rendering aid to return home only when "the hand of Israel is strong" but not when "the hand of gentiles is strong." This distinction, contends Rabbi Feinstein, is in conformity with his general thesis. He defines "the hand of Israel is strong" as meaning, not that the Jews are victorious, but as a description of a situation in which Jews are generally secure and protected by the government and hence the incident posing a threat to Jewish lives is an isolated occurrence and without governmental sanction. Under such circumstances, argues *Iggerot Mosheh,* those offering assistance to their beleaguered brethren have every reason to assume that the attackers will not dare to engage in a prolonged operation. Accordingly, those rendering assistance believe that the encounter will be brief in duration and that they will yet be able to return to their homes on the Sabbath. Rabbi Feinstein defines "the hand of gentiles is strong" as referring, not to a victory by the enemy, but to a situation in which Jews are generally insecure and cannot rely upon protection by the government. In such circumstances attackers have no fear of intervention by civil or military authorities and hence they perceive no need for haste in carrying out their act of aggression. Accordingly, since the rescuers have no reason to assume that the confrontation will be brief, they are not permitted to return to their homes even if the engagement is terminated quickly.

Quite apart from the absence of any clear talmudic evidence compelling the distinction drawn by Rabbi Feinstein, it is not at all obvious that the activities of those persons specifically restricted by the Mishnah to travel of no more than 2,000 cubits are of a nature requiring service over a prolonged period of time. The Mishnah enumerates "the midwife who comes to assist in birthing and one who comes to deliver from fire, from soldiers, from the river or from a ruin." Although a midwife is certainly aware of the fact that labor may be prolonged, in many cases labor is relatively swift. The midwife may well be willing to accept the *possibility* of not being able to return home on the Sabbath but not the *certainty* of not being able to do so. Moreover, it is only in unlikely situations that "rescue from fire" requires service over a prolonged period of time while rescue "from the river," i.e., from drowning, is virtually always swift.

R. Shlomoh Zalman Auerbach, *Minḥat Shlomoh,* no. 8, takes sharp issue with the position of *Iggerot Mosheh* and points out that even witnesses to the sighting of the new moon are forbidden to return to their homes if the return journey entails a trip of more than 2,000 cubits. There is no evidence, he argues, that people will be deterred from undertaking a mission of rescue because they are unwilling to accept the inconvenience of being away from home and separated from their families for the rest of *Shabbat.*[23]

As noted earlier, R. Zevi Pesach Frank maintains that individuals engaged in life-saving activities, upon completion of their mission, are permitted to travel by foot within a radius of 2,000 cubits because such travel involves no abrogation of any rabbinic enactment. Rather, in ordaining a limit of 2,000 cubits the Sages provided that such individuals be deemed to have been domiciled from the commencement of the Sabbath in the locale in which they find themselves upon completion of their mission and are accorded the same travel privileges as inhabitants of that area. The concept of *hittiru sofan mishum teḥillatan,* as formulated by *Tosafot* and Rashba, is regarded by Rabbi Frank as limited to permitting such individuals to place themselves in a position of endangerment during the return journey with the result that violation of biblical prohibitions becomes necessary in order to avoid threats to their own lives. Thus, according to Rabbi Frank, there is no basis for permitting infraction of other rabbinic prohibitions on the basis of *hittiru sofan mishum teḥillatan.*[24] Accordingly, Rabbi Frank rules that, while a physician may certainly walk a distance of 2,000 cubits beyond the inhabited area in which he finds himself, he may not direct or permit a non-Jew to drive him home in a motor vehicle. Most authorities, however, understand the principle of *hittiru sofan mishum teḥillatan* as rendering nugatory all rabbinic prohibitions under such circumstances, including the prohibition against directing a non-Jew to perform acts forbidden to a Jew.[25]

---

23. See, however, the concluding section of this discussion.

24. See, however, *Rosh, Beiẓah* 1:18, and *Teshuvot Ḥavot Ya'ir,* no. 112, who apparently maintain that other rabbinic prohibitions are also suspended by virtue of the priniciple *hittiru sofan mishum teḥillatan.* See also *Teshuvot Dvar Yehoshu'a,* III, *Yoreh De'ah,* no. 69, secs. 5 and 6.

25. The earliest source permitting a physician to be transported home on *Shabbat* by a non-Jew is *Teshuvot Ḥatam Sofer, Ḥoshen Mishpat,* no. 194. [As noted earlier, *Teshuvot Ḥatam Sofer, Oraḥ Ḥayyim* no. 203, and VI, no. 99, sanctions even violation of biblical prohibitions under such circumstances.] R. Shlomoh Zalman Auerbach, *Minḥat Shlomoh,* no. 8, voices qualms similar to those expressed by *Har Ẓevi* with regard to this permissive ruling. Although he declines to dispute *Ḥatam Sofer*'s ruling "since the elder has already issued a ruling" he suggests that *Ḥatam Sofer*'s leniency is limited to a physician who lacks accommodations for the remainder of the Sabbath whereas "a physician who can

V. *Professionals as Distinct From Volunteers*

Nevertheless, it appears to this writer that there is another consideration which, if applicable, effectively cancels this dispensation, in at least some circumstances, insofar as physicians are concerned. *Shulḥan Arukh, Oraḥ Ḥayyim* 526:6, rules that, on the second day of a festival, it is permissible to escort the deceased to a cemetery located even more than 2,000 cubits beyond the city and permits such persons to return to their homes on *Yom Tov* as well. Those individuals are permitted to travel distances even greater than 2,000 cubits on their return journey lest they be remiss on future occasions and decline to participate in funerals on *Yom Tov.*[26] *Bi'ur Halakhah, ad locum,* expresses reservations with regard to whether paid members of the *ḥevra kaddisha* enjoy a similar dispensation. He reasons that dispensation from rabbinic proscriptions is granted solely in order to assure that such services will be performed on future occasions. Such encouragement is required in order to assure that volunteers will not be deterred by resultant inconvenience. Individuals who are motivated by a desire to receive a fee for services rendered, he reasons, will not be deterred and hence do not require further inducement.[27] It would appear

---

remain with dignity in the hospital or the like but prefers to be in his own home, perhaps, even according to *Ḥatam Sofer,* it is forbidden [for him to be driven home] even by a gentile."

26. Although those enumerated in the Mishnah, *Rosh ha-Shanah* 23b, are permitted to travel only 2,000 cubits, persons participating in burials of a deceased on the second day of the festival may return to their homes even if the journey involves a greater distance. The source of this ruling is Ramban, *Torat ha-Adam, Kitvei Ramban,* ed. R. Bernard Chavel (Jerusalem, 5724), II, 114. Although expressing hesitation, Ramban cites another case of *attah makhshilan le-'atid lavo* in which an entirely different prohibition is suspended. The Gemara, *Yoma* 77b, reports that R. Joseph permitted the inhabitants of Bei Tarbu to traverse a stream on *Yom Kippur* in order to attend a discourse but denied them permission to do so on their return. Abaye protested and permitted them to pass through the stream on their return as well "lest you cause them to stumble in the time to come," i.e., lest they abstain from attending discourses in the future because of the inconvenience of being required to wait until the end of *Yom Kippur* in order to return home. Ramban reasons that since the observance of the second day of the festival is rabbinic in nature any prohibition is suspended *she-lo le-hakhshilan le-'atid lavo.*

27. A similar distinction with regard to salaried policemen is made by R. Isaac ha-Levi Herzog, *ha-Torah ve-ha-Medinah,* V–VI, 27, reprinted in his *Teshuvot Heikhal Yiẓḥak, Oraḥ Ḥayyim,* no. 32, and with regard to soldiers acting pursuant to military orders by Rabbi Halperin, *Sefer Assia,* IV, 66. Cf., however, R. Abraham Avidan, *Darkei Ḥesed* 10:3, note 3, s.v. *ve-nireh le-hokhiaḥ* (pp.

that the same reasoning applies in the case of a doctor who charges a fee for his services even if he renders a bill for total treatment *(havla'ah)* rather than a specific charge for care rendered on *Shabbat* or *Yom Tov.*[28] This consideration would also appear to apply to a salaried physician who is contractually obligated to respond to a request for treatment.[29] However, in this writer's opinion, it does not apply to a resident or hospital physician who is not remunerated on a fee per visit basis and who finds himself in a situation in which a decision to visit the patient is left to his discretion or professional judgment. In such situations the concern that the doctor's judgment may be clouded by concern for personal inconvenience is certainly cogent and hence, even according to *Bi'ur Halakhah,* he would be permitted to be driven home by a non-Jew. *Bi'ur Halakhah*'s caveat certainly does not apply to members of Hatzolah who serve on a volunteer basis.

Moreover, it may be argued that, at least under some circumstances, there are grounds for permitting volunteers who participate in the life-saving activities of Hatzolah themselves to drive home on *Shabbat* upon completion of their rescue efforts.[30] There is, to be sure, a significant corpus of opinion that stands in contradiction to the position of *Ḥatam*

138–139), who demonstrates on the basis of Rambam, *Hilkhot Melakhim* 6:13, that the principle of *hittiru sofan mishum teḥillatan* applies to soldiers engaged in battle.

28. For sources that discuss the propriety of accepting a fee for medical services rendered on *Shabbat* see *Shemirat Shabbat ke-Hilkhatah* 28:67, note 147 and 40:14, note 42; *Nishmat Avraham, Oraḥ Ḥayyim,* 306:8, note 1; *Ẓiẓ Eli'ezer,* XIII, no. 15, chap. 13; and *Iggerot Mosheh, Oraḥ Ḥayyim,* IV, no. 79.

29. Accordingly, a physician or nurse on duty during part of *Shabbat* would certainly not be permitted to have a non-Jew drive him or her home upon completion of his or her shift; cf., however, Abraham S. Abraham, *Nishmat Avraham, Oraḥ Ḥayyim* 229:9, note 7. When such a person's shift begins on *Shabbat,* he or she is certainly required to complete any forbidden travel prior to the commencement of *Shabbat.* See *Teshuvot Ḥatam Sofer, Yoreh De'ah,* no. 338, s.v. *gam; Iggerot Mosheh, Oraḥ Ḥayyim,* I, no. 131; *Shemirat Shabbat ke-Hilkhatah* 32:34; and R. Isaac Liebes, *Halakhah u-Refu'ah,* III, 83, reprinted in *Teshuvot Bet Avi,* IV, *Oraḥ Ḥayyim,* no. 16; cf., however, *Nishmat Avraham, loc. cit.,* and *Shemirat Shabbat ke-Hilkhatah* 40:23, notes 64 and 65.

30. Experience has amply demonstrated the unfeasibility of engaging a non-Jewish driver. The alacrity of persons available for such employment does not match that of volunteers, with the result that the precious moments lost in tarrying while the driver readies himself can spell the difference between success and failure of the life-saving mission. Cf., R. Moses Feinstein, *Halakhah u-Refu'ah,* III (5743), 53 and *Or ha-Shabbat,* no. 2 (5745), p. 7.

Sofer. However, the ambit of that disagreement may not be as broad as it appears to be upon first impression.

Rabban Gamaliel permitted all persons who had sighted the new moon to travel to the *Bet Din* since he deemed that necessary in order to assure that witnesses would always be available for sanctification of the new moon. R. Akiva did not dispute the basic point; he simply did not deem it cogent to assume that witnesses might be remiss on future occasions. Similarly, all authorities agree that individuals involved in missions of rescue may transport their weapons with them on their return journey, even though such a course of action involves acts which are biblically proscribed. The dispute is whether the principle *hittiru sofan mishum teḥillatan* as formulated by *Tosafot* and Rashba is limited to situations involving an element of danger to the rescuers or whether it constitutes *carte blanche* for them to do whatever is necessary in order to enable them to return home. According to *Ḥatam Sofer,* the discussion in *Eruvin* 45a indicates that the Sages perceived a need to induce persons to engage in missions of mercy and issued a general edict with regard to that matter; according to those who disagree, rescue of persons in danger required no such inducement whereas witnesses to the sighting of the new moon did need encouragement in order to be motivated to undertake a journey for the purpose of appearing before the *Bet Din.*

The issue, then, is whether there exists a blanket dictum regarding *she-lo le-hakhshilan le-'atid lavo.* It may however be argued that, at a time and place where it is demonstrably known that inability to return home has resulted in loss of life because would-be rescuers decline to undertake such missions, any action deemed imperative to encourage preservation of life may be sanctioned. Such dispensation would not be rooted in the discussion in *Eruvin* 45a but in empirical reality regarding what is necessary in order to save lives. Nor are there grounds for maintaining that a formal rabbinic decree is required in such circumstances. Rabban Gamaliel's original declaration to R. Akiva, which reflects a similar principle, certainly has the flavor of a pronouncement issued as an *ad hoc* assessment of the situation rather than of a formal decree although, presumably, its redaction in the Mishnah effectively raised it to the status of a rabbinic edict.

Parallel instances in which presently unnecessary infractions are permitted in order to assure that lives will not be lost at some future time are not unknown in the annals of Halakhah. Thus *Taz, Oraḥ Ḥayyim* 328:5, takes issue with Rema and permits the total disregard of Sabbath restrictions on behalf of a seriously ill person even though no harm would be done to the patient if the same act were to be performed by a non-Jew or in an unusual manner *(shinnuy)*. *Taz* advances two considerations in rejecting Rema's ruling: (1) An onlooker might conclude that intervention by a Jew or intervention in a usual manner is forbidden with the result that, on a future occasion, he may seek to minimize the infraction in circumstances in which delay might indeed be deleterious to the patient. (2) The non-Jew may not be alacritous in providing immediate and proper assistance.[31]

Those who disagree with *Taz* do so because they do not believe that his fear in this regard is cogent, not because they reject the underlying principle. A similar principle is established by R. Joshua Leib Diskin, *Teshuvot Maharil Diskin,* no. 41. The Gemara, *Sanhedrin* 26a, records that R. Yanai permitted the planting of crops in the Sabbatical year because of a need to pay taxes levied upon the produce. *Tosafot* explains that failure to pay the required levy would have endangered Jewish lives. Maharil Diskin notes that R. Yanai granted blanket dispensation to till the soil, apparently to the wealthy who had other resources which might have been applied to payment of taxes no less so than to the poor who had no other means of payment available to them. Maharil Diskin reasons that, had the wealthy not worked their fields, the poor would have been embarrassed to do so.[32] Therefore, in order to assure that the poor would not

31. *Teshuvot Adnei Neḥoshet,* no. 72, secs. 6–11, asserts that even *Taz* would agree that, in situations such as those confronting Hatzolah, a non-Jewish driver should be engaged even for purposes of driving the ambulance to the hospital. *Taz* himself suggests that error on the part of an onlooker can be avoided by means of a public announcement that the services of a non-Jew have been utilized only because the non-Jew was immediately available. In the case of Hatzolah, it may also be publicized that a non-Jewish driver is engaged for *Shabbat* in order to obviate the need for persons rendering assistance to remain away from their homes and families for the duration of *Shabbat.* He further contends that *Taz* would agree that a professional driver, particularly a paramedic, who is compensated for his services, will indeed perform his duties promptly and efficiently. Moreover, *Mishnah Berurah* 318:10 rules that, in the absence of a clear danger or an expert opinion confirming that there exists a threat to life, the service of a non-Jew should be utilized, as is the position of Rema, if it is possible to do so without compromising treatment of the patient.

32. See also R. Moshe Sternbuch, *Mo'adim u-Zemanim,* II, no. 140, who explains in a similair vein R. Israel Salanter's ruling regarding eating on *Yom Kippur* during the cholera epidemic that occured in Vilna in 1848. Rabbi Salanter demanded that the entire populace refrain from fasting. It might well be assumed that, since it was presumed that fasting was dangerous for those who might become afflicted by the illness or that weakness enhanced susceptibility to the

be endangered, it was necessary to command the wealthy to plant crops as well.[33]

It may be readily conceded that neither of these sources establishes that people will not engage in life-saving activity on *Shabbat* unless they are permitted to return to the comfort of their own homes. It may also be granted that in times gone by such a consideration would not have been a deterrent. But the human condition is hardly immutable. It has been reported that in some areas Hatzolah has not been able to enlist sufficient numbers of volunteers willing to participate on *Shabbat* and *Yom Tov* because wives and families have objected to being deprived of the presence of husbands and fathers for virtually the entire *Shabbat* and *Yom Tov*. The result, it is claimed, is that lives have indeed been lost. Without passing moral and halakhic judgment upon persons who manifest a skewed priority of values, it may be argued, as noted, that under such circumstances all agree that such volunteers may be permitted to drive home if they

disease, Rabbi Salanter considered every person exposed to the disease to be at least posssibly at risk were he to fast. See R. Yechiel Ya'akov Weinberg, *Seridei Esh*, IV, 289 and R. Benjamin Rabinowitz-Teumim, *No'am*, V (5722), 283. See also sources cited by Hillel Goldberg, *Between Berlin and Slobodka: Jewish Transition Figures from Eastern Europe* (Hoboken, 1989), p. 163, note 28. Rabbi Sternbuch, however, opines that Rabbi Salanter feared that if some individuals would fast others would also claim that they were not in danger and that, as a result, lives would be lost. According to Rabbi Sternbuch, Rabbi Salanter therefore commanded that even the perfectly healthy eat on *Yom Kippur* so that the sick would do so as well. It should be noted that, at the time, R. Betzalel ha-Kohen together with the other members of the Vilna *Bet Din* issued a public statement vehemently opposing Rabbi Salanter's ruling. The Vilna *Bet Din* insisted that a decision regarding the permissibility of eating on *Yom Kippur* be made on a case-by-case basis in accordance with the physical condition of each individual.

33. It would thus appear that, whenever there exists a formal rabbinic edict sanctioning violation of a halakhic norm that is predicated upon consideration of a contingency that may result in loss of life, no person may claim that he will remain unaffected and hence need not commit the infraction. Thus, when there exists a formal dispensation in the form of *hittiru sofan mishum teḥillatan*, e.g., permission to return with weapons within 2,000 cubits, a person may not ostentatiously refuse to avail himself of that dispensation since others following his example may also hesitate to do so but then proceed to refrain altogether from engaging in missions of rescue. Similarly, persons who have sighted the new moon may not refrain from travelling to the *Bet Din* on *Shabbat* although they know that other witnesses have made the journey lest their example be followed even when no other witnesses are available. Cf., however, Rabbi Mordecai Halperin, *Sefer Assia*, IV, 65–66.

would otherwise not volunteer for duty on *Shabbat. Ḥatam Sofer*'s basic point, *viz.,* that the principle "Better to violate one Sabbath in order to observe many Sabbaths" is sufficiently strong to warrant any infraction which will result in preservation of life. Granting the position of those who disagree with *Ḥatam Sofer* and maintain that there is no blanket rabbinic legislation governing the return journey, and indeed even of those who maintain that the rule recorded in the Mishnah with regard to returning from a mission of rescue is not at all predicated upon the principle *hittiru sofan mishum teḥillatan,* the matter nevertheless remains an issue regarding which rabbinical authorities may rule on an *ad hoc* basis.

Chapter VII

Observance of *Shabbat* by a Prospective Proselyte and by a *Ger she-Mal ve-Lo Taval*

When a would-be proselyte seeks to convert, one should stretch out a hand to him to bring him under the wings of the Shekhinah.

VA-YIKRA RABBAH 2:8

In recent years the concern of the Jewish community has been focused upon problems associated with conversion of non-Jews to Judaism. The problems that have gripped the attention of world Jewry almost exclusively involve persons who seek conversion for purposes of marriage and whose commitment to observance of commandments is quite frequently minimal or non-existent. Regardless of the auspices under which such conversions are performed their validity even *post factum* is a matter of serious doubt and disagreement among rabbinic authorities.[1] The policies of some rabbinic practitioners, Orthodox as well as non-Orthodox, notwithstanding, Halakhah certainly does not endorse conversions undertaken for ulterior motives such as facilitating marriage to a Jewish spouse.

In most historical epochs, *gerei ẓedek,* observant proselytes who convert to Judaism because of deep and sincere theological conviction have been few and far between. For unknown reasons, or better, for reasons that are shrouded in divine mystery, in recent years, the number of converts who are completely and utterly sincere has grown appreciably. Converts whose sincerity has been demonstrated beyond cavil are of course welcomed without reservation. Frequently, this genre of candidates for conversion does, however, present significant technical problems for rabbinic consideration, but, happily, they present problems that spring from religious zeal rather than the opposite. Judaism places certain restrictions upon the

1. See *Contemporary Halakhic Problems,* I, 270–296.

mizvot that a non-Jew is permitted to perform. Understandably, would-be converts whose sincerity is beyond question wish to be fully observant even prior to conversion and are extremely troubled by any limitation placed upon their religious observance.

Such would-be converts experience the most keenly felt disability in the area of Sabbath observance. The Gemara, *Sanhedrin* 58b, declares that a non-Jew is forbidden to observe *Shabbat.* Over the course of the last two centuries there have been a significant number of endeavors on the part of rabbinic scholars to devise ways and means to enable such would-be converts to accomplish that which is apparently impossible, *viz.,* both to observe and not observe *Shabbat* at one and the same time. The impetus for a number of those investigations is associated with an even more unusual situation, namely, the prohibition concerning Sabbath observance as it impacts upon a person who has begun, but who has not completed, the conversion process—a person who has already been circumcised but who has as yet not undergone immersion in a *mikveh*.

I. *Historical Background*

In the history of rabbinic scholarship, there have been occasions upon which questions have been posed that, seemingly, are unlikely to arise on future occasions with any degree of frequency but that nevertheless have sparked controversies that reverberate in the annals of Halakhah. On rare occasions, some facet of a seemingly circumscribed problem generates wide-ranging discussion and receives the type of detailed attention that results in illumination of theretofore scantily plumbed areas of Jewish law.

One such event occurred in Jerusalem in 5608 (1848) on a Tuesday, the 23rd of Adar II, 5608. A certain gentile, a Moroccan émigré, underwent circumcision for purposes of conversion in the presence of the Ashkenazic *Bet Din* of Jerusalem. The incision did not heal as quickly as might have been anticipated and, as a result, the prospective convert was unable to complete the conversion process by immersing himself in a *mikveh* prior to the ensuing *Shabbat.* The gentleman in question was meticulously observant of all aspects of Jewish law and, indeed, had been observant for some time prior to commencement of the conversion proceedings. It is reported that despite the absence of any doubt that, on *Shabbat,* a non-Jew may attend to the needs of a Jew who is ill, the would-be convert refused to permit a gentile to kindle a fire in his home on that

Shabbat.[2]

The Chief Rabbi of the Ashkenazic community at the time of this incident was the renowned R. Shmuel Salant. Rabbi Salant had, however, journeyed to Europe on a fund-raising mission on behalf of the nascent *yishuv.* Substituting for him as the principal rabbinic authority of the community was one of the members of his *Bet Din,* R. Asher Lemel. Late on the *Shabbat* afternoon in question, it was reported to R. Asher Lemel that the sick convert was languishing in cold and damp quarters but refused to allow a gentile to kindle a fire on his behalf. R. Asher Lemel immediately responded that, in his opinion, not only was the would-be convert himself permitted to engage in labor on *Shabbat* but, moreover, in light of the prohibition posited by the Gemara, *Sanhedrin* 58b, forbidding a non-Jew to observe the Sabbath, he was obliged to do so since he had not yet completed the conversion process by immersing himself in a *mikveh.*[3] After *minḥah* prayers, the individuals to whom R.

2. It seems to this writer that even a Jew might properly have directed a gentile to perform such services on behalf of this individual despite the fact that, in actuality, his status was that of a non-Jew. The prohibition against allowing a non-Jew to perform forbidden acts on *Shabbat* is limited to acts performed on behalf of a Jew. Accordingly, a gentile may be requested to perform such acts on behalf of himself or on behalf of a fellow gentile provided that the acts are performed with materials that do not belong to a Jew. See Ramban, *Commentary on the Bible,* Exodus 12:16, as well as *Shulḥan Arukh* and Rema, *Oraḥ Ḥayyim* 307:21. Accordingly, a Jew might have requested a gentile to perform such services on behalf of the would-be convert even if he were to have been perfectly healthy.

R. Abraham Menachem Steinberg, *Teshuvot Maḥazeh Avraham,* I, no. 54, tentatively permits a Jew to direct a non-Jew to minister to the needs of a dangerously ill circumcised but unimmersed convert on the ground that the principle "Better to desecrate a single Sabbath in order to observe many Sabbaths" may be relied upon in vitiation of a rabbinic prohibition. [See, however, R. Meir Arak, *Teshuvot Imrei Yosher,* II, no. 130, who states, albeit somewhat equivocally, that the principle is normative in all cases of otherwise certain loss of life and serves to permit violation even of biblical prohibitions. Cf., however, *Teshuvot Ḥelkat Yo'av,* II, no. 8. See also R. Eliezer Waldenberg, *Ẓiẓ Eli'ezer,* X, no. 25, chap. 2, and R. Mordecai ha-Kohen Deutsch, *Birkat Kohen* (Jerusalem, 5749), no. 20.] In light of the rule that a gentile may be directed to perform proscribed acts on behalf of another gentile, appeal to the principle "Better to desecrate a single Sabbath in order to observe many Sabbaths" seems to be entirely superfluous.

3. Cf. the discussion of R. Aryeh Leib Grossnass, *Teshuvot Lev Aryeh,* I, no. 33. Without citing any of the sources discusssing this topic, Rabbi Grossnass argues that, the controversy regarding whether a prospective convert may be taught Torah notwithstanding, the prospective convert may certainly be instructed

Asher Lemel had announced his opinion sought out the convert and informed him of R. Asher Lemel's ruling. The convert, who apparently had been scrupulous in observing *Shabbat* restrictions for a number of years prior to his conversion, complied with that directive, but tears filled his eyes at being compelled to violate the Sabbath. In compliance with R. Asher Lemel's directive he wrote several letters on a piece of paper or, according to another version of this story, he signed his name in the vernacular.

On the morrow, a furor erupted in the city. The Sephardic as well as the Ashkenazic scholars of the city contended that requiring a candidate for conversion who had already been circumcised and who had accepted the yoke of the commandments to desecrate the Sabbath was entirely without precedent. Upon his return to Jerusalem, R. Shmuel Salant sided with those scholars. R. Asher Lemel felt compelled to author a lengthy exposition in defense of his controversial ruling. That material was later published in *Shomer Ẓion ha-Ne'eman,* a prestigious rabbinic journal edited by R. Jacob Ettlinger.

Now, close to one hundred and fifty years later, the Kollel Institute of Greater Detroit has performed a valuable service in collecting and reprinting the articles and responsa spawned by this intriguing controversy. The collected material, which appears in a memorial volume titled *Yad Shlomoh* (New York, 5747), includes the responsum of R. Asher Lemel, reprinted from *Shomer Ẓion ha-Ne'eman,* nos. 154–158 (Altona, 5613); the rebuttal of R. Jacob Ettlinger, published in the same journal, no. 158, as well as in his *Teshuvot Binyan Ẓion,* no. 91; the opinion of R. Shmuel Salant, as recorded by R. Yechiel Michal Tucatzinsky and published in R. Aryeh Leib Frumkin, *Toledot Ḥakhmei Yerushalayim,* IV, addenda to vol. III, p. 67; the responsum of R. Jehoseph Schwartz, *Teshuvot Divrei Yosef,* no. 24; and the responsum of the Sephardic scholar and rabbinic authority of Tiberias, R. Jacob Chai Zerichan, *Ha-Me'asef,* vol. VIII, no. 1.[4]

---

with regard to the halakhic obligations and restrictions that will devolve upon him immediately upon conversion since ignorance of such matters would lead to inadvertent transgression. Similarly, suggests Rabbi Grossnass, he may observe the Sabbath prior to conversion in order to habituate himself to conduct appropriate for the Sabbath. That argument, however, has no bearing upon the issue at hand. Indeed, a non-Jew may, in general, refrain from prohibited activities on *Shabbat* and a prospective convert should be encouraged to do so precisely for the reason advanced by Rabbi Grossnass. The issue is whether he is required to perform an isolated act of "labor" and thereby negate his observance of *Shabbat* as a day of rest in its entirety.

4. In addition to the reports in the rabbinic literature, an account of R. Shmuel

II. *Authorities Who Prohibit Sabbath Observance*

R. Asher Lemel composed an extensive treatise to bolster a position that, *prima facia,* is unassailable. The ruling of the Gemara, *Sanhedrin* 58b, forbidding a non-Jew to observe the Sabbath is unchallenged. Equally incontrovertible is the fact that the Gemara, *Yevamot* 46b, posits circumcision and immersion as the *sine qua non* of conversion. Ergo, a candidate for conversion who has as yet not immersed himself in a *mikveh* remains a non-Jew and, as such, is forbidden to observe the Sabbath.

Furthermore, the conclusion that candidates for conversion retain their status as non-Jews until they have undergone immersion is confirmed by the Gemara, *Yevamot* 46a and *Avodah Zarah* 59a. The Gemara relates that R. Ḥiyya bar Abba visited a certain city and became aware of a number of cases in which Jewish women had been impregnated by "converts who were circumcised but who had not immersed." He reported this situation to R. Yoḥanan who directed him to announce publicly that those children were not of legitimate Jewish parentage.[5] In that context the Gemara expressly declares with regard to the status of such a proselyte, "since he has not undergone immersion he is a gentile." Similarly the Gemara, *Berakhot* 47b, states that such a convert cannot be counted in the quorum of those required for the blessing of *zimun* in conjunction with recitation of Grace after Meals. Moreover, the Gemara, *Yevamot* 47b, indicates that a convert acquires capacity to contract a valid marriage only upon immersion. It may readily be deduced that, were a candidate for conversion to enter into a marriage subsequent to circumcision but

---

Salant's role in this incident appears in Jacob Rimon and Joseph Zundel Wasserman, *Rabbi Shmu'el be-Doro* (Tel Aviv, 5721), p. 136. The statement in that source that R. Shmuel Salant addressed this issue in "fifteen responsa of which seven were published in *Ha-Me'asef*" is factually incorrect.

5. R. Yoḥanan maintained that the issue of a gentile father and a Jewish mother is a *mamzer*. The normative rule, however, is that such progeny are both Jewish and legitimate. Nevertheless, R. Dov Berish Weidenfeld, *Teshuvot Dovev Meisharim,* I, no. 7, advances the rather surprising view that, although the child of a gentile father and a Jewish mother is Jewish, the child of a circumcised but unimmersed father is a gentile. He reasons that the son of a gentile father is Jewish because Halakhah fails to recognize a paternal relationship between the biological father and son and, accordingly, for halakhic purposes, the child has only one parent, *viz.,* its mother. *Dovev Meisharim* argues that circumcision is sufficient to endow the biological father with the legal capacity to establish a halakhically recognized paternal relationship and hence the child acquires the status of its father, i.e., the child is a gentile. That position is vigorously rebutted by R. Meshullem Roth, *Teshuvot Kol Mevaser,* I, no. 23.

prior to immersion, a bill of divorce would not be required to dissolve the union.

The sole area of Halakhah in which, at least according to some authorities, such a convert does not have the status of a gentile is with regard to the permissibility of wine that he has touched.[6] Such wine is forbidden because of a fear that the gentile may have rendered the wine unfit for use by a Jew by virtue of having used it in the performance of an idolatrous act. *Tosafot* and Rosh, *Avodah Zarah* 67b, argue that since the convert has already accepted the "yoke of the commandments" there is no basis to fear that he may have intended to perform an idolatrous libation and hence there is no reason for the Sages to have included wine touched by such an individual in their edict prohibiting wine of gentiles. Nevertheless, Rabbenu Nissim, *ad locum,* disagrees. Pointing out that even the convert's acceptance of the yoke of the commandments is intended as acceptance of such obligations only as of the time of completion of the conversion process, Rabbenu Nissim contends that the Sages had ample reason to include a person of such status in their edict. The ruling of Rabbenu Nissim is accepted and followed by *Shulḥan Arukh, Yoreh De'ah* 124:2, while Rema, as understood by *Shakh, Yoreh De'ah* 124:4, rules in accordance with the permissive view of *Tosafot* and Rosh.[7]

III. *The Permissive View*

There is, however, one early source that appears to contradict this

6. See, however, R. Zevi Pesach Frank, *Mikra'ei Kodesh,* I, 12, who cites evidence adduced by R. Isaac ha-Levi Herzog to the effect that such an individual may offer not only an *olah,* which may be offered by a gentile, but other sacrifices as well.

7. R. Judah Shaviv, in a contribution to *Barka'i,* no. 4 (Spring, 5747), avers that the permissibility of Sabbath observance on the part of a person in this status is contingent upon the conflicting views regarding the permissibility of the wine touched by him since that controversy is, in turn, predicated upon diverse assessments of the nature of the convert's acceptance of the "yoke of the commandments" at the time of circumcision. The editor of that journal, R. Saul Israeli, rebuts that contention by correctly pointing out that the authorities who permit such wine do so because a person who has begun the conversion procedure and commits himself to subsequent immersion and acceptance of the "yoke of the commandments" has *ipso facto* renounced idolatry and hence prohibitions predicated upon suspicion of idolatrous practices do not extend to him. There is nothing in that position that yields the inference that circumcision alone entails immediate assumption of an obligation regarding any commandment or that it allows for voluntary assumption of the obligation of Sabbath observance.

conclusion, at least insofar as observance of *Shabbat* is concerned. *Midrash Rabbah,* Deuteronomy 1:18, states:

> Said R. Yosi the son of Ḥanina: A gentile who observes the Sabbath prior to accepting circumcision upon himself is liable to the death penalty. Why? Because he was not commanded concerning it. And what causes you to say that a gentile who observes the Sabbath is liable to the death penalty? Said R. Ḥiyya the son of Abba in the name of R. Yoḥanan: In the practice of the world [if] a king and a courtesan sit and converse with one another, one who comes and interposes himself between them, is he not liable to the death penalty? So is the Sabbath between Israel and the Holy One, blessed be He, as it is said "between Me and between the children of Israel (Exodus 31:13)." Therefore, a gentile who comes and interposes himself between them prior to accepting circumcision upon himself is liable to the death penalty. The Sages said: Moses said before the Holy One, blessed be He, "Sovereign of the universe! Since gentiles have not been commanded with regard to the Sabbath, if they observe it, will you be gracious unto them?" Said the Holy One, blessed be He, "Of this you are afraid? By your life! Even if they observe all of the commandments of the Torah I will cast them before you."

The clear inference of the phrase "prior to accepting circumcision upon himself" would indicate that the prohibition against observance of *Shabbat* is suspended not only subsequent to circumcision, even though immersion has not occurred, but even upon mere "acceptance" of circumcision, i.e., upon resolute determination to convert to Judaism.

R. Jehoseph Schwartz bases his opposition to the ruling of R. Asher Lemel upon these midrashic comments. Moreover, contends Rabbi Schwartz, were the convert to have been forbidden to refrain from "labor" on the Sabbath day, he should not have been directed to write on *Shabbat* but should have been instructed to perform some other act of labor. Rabbi Schwartz advances the novel view that a gentile who performs no forms of "labor" on the Sabbath other than writing is in violation of his obligation to desist from observing the Sabbath as a day of rest. The Gemara, *Sanhedrin* 58b, derives this prohibition from the verse "day and night shall not cease" (Genesis 8:22) which in talmudic exegesis is rendered "day and night they shall not rest."[8] Noting the context in which the

8. For reasons that elude this writer, R. Moses Schick, *Teshuvot Maharam*

verse appears, Rabbi Schwartz understands the talmudic statement as requiring gentiles to engage in acts contributing to "settlement of the world" every day of the week, i.e., acts relating to agriculture or manufacture that are productive in nature.[9] In his opinion, acts such as writing, erasing, or even dyeing, do not satisfy that requirement. Thus, according to Rabbi Schwartz, forcing the convert to write on the Sabbath was both unnecessary and, if necessary, of no avail.

In response to the argument based upon the midrashic statement, R. Asher Lemel notes that, apart from the general principle that normative halakhic rulings are not to be derived from aggadic statements, the words of the Midrash are explicitly contradicted by talmudic statements. The prohibition formulated by the Midrash is predicated entirely upon the unique relationship that exists between God, Israel and the Sabbath. However, the Gemara, *Sanhedrin* 58b, clearly prohibits a non-Jew from observing *any* day of the week as a day of rest. Moreover, he argues, mere "acceptance" of circumcision does not turn a gentile into a Jew. Hence, logically, such an individual should continue to be categorized as an interloper "between Me and the children of Israel." Accordingly, argues R. Asher Lemel, the term "acceptance," as employed by the Midrash in this context, must be understood as connoting, not merely acceptance of circumcision, but as the carrying out of that acceptance, i.e., actual circumcision followed also by immersion in a *mikveh.*

Curiously, R. Asher Lemel does not cite the position of *Tosafot Yeshanim, Yevamot* 48b, which is identical to that of *Midrash Rabbah. Tosafot Yeshanim* declares that a gentile who has firmly resolved to convert to Judaism may observe *Shabbat* with impunity. Although this view is rejected by virtually all later authorities, it is apparently accepted by *Teshuvot Ereẓ Tovah,* no. 2, sec. 3.

An immediate response was published by R. Jacob Ettlinger in *Shomer*

Shik, Oraḥ Ḥayyim, no. 145, contends that a literal reading of the verse which begins "all the days of the earth" would indicate that the reference is to natural phenomena rather than to human activity and, accordingly, the concluding phrase should be understood as meaning that day and night shall not cease all the days of the earth. However, comments Maharam Schick, if that were the meaning of the verse, the verse should properly read *lo yishbetu.* Since, however, the verse reads *lo yishbotu,* Maharam Schick argues that the phrase must be understood as referring to people rather than days even though people are not previously mentioned in the verse, and, accordingly, the verse must be rendered "they shall not cease [from labor]."

9. This analysis follows Rashi's interpretation of the talmudic discussion and is an interpretation and refinement of that position. See *infra,* note 19.

Ẓion ha-Ne'eman, no. 158. Rabbi Ettlinger, who was also the editor of that journal, candidly concedes that R. Asher Lemel's ruling was "apparently" based upon "foundations of law and truth." Nevertheless, upon further investigation, he discovered that it was never the wont of rabbinic authorities involved in the conversion of proselytes to insist that the candidates for conversion not observe *Shabbat* prior to immersion.[10] Accordingly, he seeks to uncover a source for that practice. He also points out that the Gemara, *Shabbat* 132a, describes observance of the Sabbath as a "covenant" and comments that, logically, it would be inappropriate for one who has entered the "covenant" of circumcision to be required to abnegate another "covenant," i.e., the Sabbath.

R. Jacob Ettlinger finds support for the accepted practice in the words of *Tosafot, Keritut* 9a. *Tosafot* describe the nature of circumcision as practiced by our ancestors prior to the Exodus from Egypt and remark that they circumcised themselves for the purpose of "entering into the covenant and in order to become separated from other peoples." Through this act of "separation" from other peoples, opines R. Ettlinger, the convert acquires an intermediate status between that of gentile and Jew. The accepted practice is thus apparently based upon a presumption that the prohibition against observance of a day of rest is limited only to gentiles, but not to a candidate for conversion who has undergone circumcision and who has thereby placed himself in this intermediate state between gentile and Jew.

IV. *Authorities Who Maintain That Sabbath Observance Is Obligatory*

R. Shmuel Salant similarly postulates an intermediate status between that of Jew and gentile and bases that position upon a comment of Rashba, *Yevamot* 71a. The Gemara notes that, according to R. Akiva, a convert who is circumcised but who has not completed the conversion process by undergoing immersion may not partake of the paschal sacrifice, but only because of an exclusionary pleonasm in the verse restricting participation

10. R. Asher Lemel's position is echoed in a letter by R. David Schifman of Tiberias to R. Eliyahu Chazan, the chief rabbi of Alexandria, that appears in the latter's *Ta'alumot Lev,* III (Alexandria, 5663), no. 19. Although the responsum, written in ungrammatical rabbinic Hebrew, is somewhat unclear, the author seems to urge the *Bet Din* of Alexandria to insist that such candidates for conversion perform acts of "labor" on *Shabbat* and encourages Rabbi Chazan in that regard in stating that "this will be a matter of glory to [you] in Alexandria."

in the consumption of the paschal sacrifice. Rashba tentatively objects that no specific exclusion should be required since such an individual remains a non-Jew, but immediately counters with the remark that a pleonasm is required since "although he has not completed his conversion, nevertheless, he has already begun and entered somewhat into the Jewish religion (*nikhnas keẓat be-dat yehudit*)." Rabbi Salant further writes, albeit without any specific evidence, that, upon completion of the conversion process by means of immersion in a *mikveh,* the convert is regarded as having acquired the status of a Jew retroactively from the time of circumcision. He may, of course, abjure the conversion at any time until its completion. The availability of the option of renouncing conversion prior to immersion led Rabbi Salant to a remarkable conclusion: Violation of one of the Sabbath restrictions during this period is tantamount to renunciation of the conversion procedure and serves to negate the act of circumcision with the result that a would-be convert who fails to observe the Sabbath subsequent to conversion cannot be regarded as a Jew even if he subsequently undergoes immersion.[11] Presumably, such an individual retains the option of beginning the process anew by "letting blood of the covenant."

Rashba's comment did not go unnoticed by R. Asher Lemel. He cites Rashba's statement but regards it as merely an analysis of the provisions of Jewish law that would have been applicable in the absence of a verse designed to exclude the unimmersed convert from partaking of the paschal offering. The effect of that exclusion, argues R. Asher Lemel, is to establish that the status of such a convert is identical to that of a non-Jew in every respect. This is presumably the position of *Tosafot, Yevamot* 46b, who raise the same question as posed by Rashba and declare that the biblical phrase in question serves to establish the principle that there cannot be conversion other than through both circumcision and immersion. R. Asher Lemel cogently argues that Rashba's comment can readily be understood

11. R. Joseph Rosen, *Ẓofnat Pa'aneaḥ, Mahadura Tinyana, Hilkhot Yesodei ha-Torah* 5:5 (p. 43a), independently advances the thesis that, upon immersion, the convert acquires the status of a Jew retroactively from the time of circumcision. *Ẓofnat Pa'aneaḥ,* however, makes no statement with regard to whether or not violation of Sabbath restrictions constitutes renunciation of the conversion procedure. If, according to *Ẓofnat Pa'aneaḥ,* such an act does not serve to nullify the conversion, that act would retroactively constitute an act of Sabbath desecration on the part of a Jew and would clearly be forbidden. *Ẓofnat Pa'aneaḥ*'s novel view is cited and discussed by R. Isaac ha-Levi Herzog, *Heikhal Yiẓḥak,* I, no. 17, and R. Meir ha-Levi Steinberg, *Likkutei Me'ir* (London, 5730), no. 20.

in a similar vein and, accordingly, there is no reason to posit a controversy between these early authorities.

R. Jacob Ettlinger notes that members of the generation of the Exodus acquired status as Jews by means of circumcision and immersion, i.e., circumcision before their departure from Egypt and immersion immediately prior to the giving of the Torah at Sinai. Hence, at the time of the offering of the first paschal sacrifice on the eve of the Exodus from Egypt, their status was that of circumcised converts who had as yet not undergone immersion. Yet the Gemara, *Shabbat* 87b, declares that the commandment concerning Sabbath observance was given at Marah, before revelation at Sinai. Indeed, a literal reading of the sequence of events described in Exodus 16:22–30 indicates that our ancestors were commanded to observe the Sabbath prior to experiencing revelation at Mount Sinai.[12] Accordingly, argues Rabbi Ettlinger, it may be deduced that the commandment concerning Sabbath observance is binding upon all who enjoy a similar status, i.e., upon converts who have undergone circumcision but who have as yet not undergone immersion. Thus, according to R. Jacob Ettlinger, such individuals are not only permitted to observe the Sabbath but are required to do so. Indeed, he argues, if not for a specific exclusion of the circumcised but unimmersed convert, such an individual would be required to participate in the paschal offering as well, since his status is identical to that of those who offered the first paschal sacrifice.[13]

Avnei Nezer, Yoreh De'ah, no. 351, also compares the status of an unimmersed convert to that of our ancestors at the time of the giving of the commandment concerning *Shabbat* at Marah[14] but notes that, although *Tosafot, Yevamot* 46b, and Rashba, *Yevamot* 71a, disagree regarding an extraneous matter, both employ language implying that circumcision imposes no obligations upon a candidate for conversion. *Avnei Nezer* leaves unresolved the question of whether a circumcised but unimmersed convert

12. It should be noted that Rabbi Schwartz remarks parenthetically that, prior to receiving the Torah at Sinai, our ancestors refrained only from the activity expressly proscribed in Exodus 16–29, *viz.,* collecting manna on the Sabbath, but did not refrain from other restricted activities. In a somewhat similar vein, *Ḥatam Sofer, Shabbat* 87b, cites an earlier authority who maintains that, although commanded at Marah, Sabbath restrictions became binding only at Sinai.

13. Cf., *Avnei Nezer, Yoreh De'ah,* no 351, sec. 4.

14. See also R. Meir Dan Plocki, *Klei Ḥemdah al ha-Torah, Parashat Niẓavim,* no. 1, sec. 3, as well as the comments of R. Shema'yah Steinberg appended to R. Abraham Menachem Steinberg's *Teshuvot Maḥazeh Avraham,* I, addenda, no. 54.

is bound by Sabbath restrictions.[15]

R. Jacob Chai Zerichan rebuts R. Jacob Ettlinger's arguments in asserting that prior to the giving of the Torah at Sinai "conversion" was effected by means of circumcision alone. In support of that position he argues that even the circumcision referred to by *Tosafot, Keritut* 9a, is not identical with circumcision as commanded at Sinai. *Tosafot, Yevamot* 71b, indicates that Abraham and his progeny were commanded only to sever the foreskin. Removal of the pupis, i.e., the membrane under the foreskin (*peri'ah*), was commanded for the first time at Mount Sinai and hence, even though it is now an integral part of circumcision, *peri'ah* was not previously practiced. Nevertheless, *Tosafot, Keritut* 9a, describes circumcision as practiced in Egypt as serving to "separate" Jews from other peoples. This must be, argues R. Zerichan, because, prior to Sinai, severance of the foreskin was itself sufficient to accomplish "conversion."

V. *Sabbath Observance by the Patriarchs*

Prior to the controversy surrounding the Jerusalem convert, the ambit of the prohibition against Sabbath observance on the part of a non-Jew was the subject of considerable discussion in an entirely different context. The Gemara, *Yoma* 28b, declares that Abraham observed all the commandments, including rabbinic decrees, despite the fact that the commandments had as yet not been revealed. Thus, Abraham observed the Sabbath. Since our ancestors are depicted by the Gemara, *Keritut* 9a, as having been "converted" to Judaism at the time of revelation at Sinai, Abraham and his progeny enjoyed the status of Noahides. As such, they were ostensibly bound by the injunction forbidding gentiles to observe *Shabbat.* How, then, was it possible for Abraham to observe the Torah in its entirety?[16]

Some latter-day authorities, including *Parashat Derakhim, Derush* 1, and R. Joseph Engel, *Bet ha-Oẓar, Ma'arekhet Alef, klal* 1, marshal a variety of sources in support of the position that the Patriarchs, although

15. R. Betzalel Stern, *Teshuvot Be-Ẓel ha-Ḥokhmah,* 1, no. 52, sec. 4, assumes as a matter of course that a convert becomes obligated with regard to Sabbath observance only upon immersion in a *mikveh. Be-Ẓel ha-Ḥokhmah* fails to mention any of the earlier discussions of this question.

16. Cf., the novel view of R. Zevi Hirsh Chajes, *Torat Nevi'im,* chap. 11, to the effect that the commandments directed to the Sons of Noah are binding only subsequent to revelation at Sinai but that, prior to that event, they were observed only as salutary customs.

not formally bound by the Sinaitic covenant, nevertheless enjoyed the status of full-fledged Jews for all other purposes.[17] If so, the problem is immediately resolved. However, even those authorities cite midrashic sources that serve to render the issue a matter of doubt or controversy.

Resolution of the problem of Sabbath observance on the part of the Patriarchs has engaged the attention of numerous scholars over the centuries. Renewed discussion of that topic followed in the wake of the Jerusalem controversy. The resolutions of the problem that emerge from those discussions, a number of which will be noted presently, tend to escape between the horns of the dilemma by positing modes of conduct that constitute "labor" insofar as non-Jews are concerned but that nevertheless do not constitute violation of Sabbath restrictions for Jews. R. Jacob Ettlinger, *Teshuvot Binyan Ẓion,* no. 126, points to a statement of the *Tosefta* in a different context in order to show that such a possibility must indeed exist. The Tosefta, *Makhshirin* 1:7, states that an abandoned child found in a city in which the Jewish and non-Jewish populations are exactly equal must conduct himself in accordance with the stringencies applicable both to Jews and to gentiles. The implication, contends *Binyan Ẓion,* is that it is possible simultaneously to follow the stringencies of both a Jew and a gentile with regard to Sabbath observance.[18] If such a thesis is accepted, the entire controversy could be skirted by giving the circumcised but unimmersed convert the option of engaging in an act of that nature. The same option might also be offered to a prospective convert who feels uncomfortable engaging in conduct that profanes the Sabbath.

17. The *Brisker Rav,* R. Yiẓḥak Ze'ev ha-Levi Soloveichik, citing Ramban, *Commentary on the Bible,* Leviticus 24:10, argues that, since the days of Abraham, our ancestors enjoyed the status of Jews and hence, for them, Sabbath observance was not a "novel" religious observance. Nevertheless, prior to revelation at Sinai, they were not bound by the commandments. See *Ḥiddushei Maran ha-Griz ha-Levi al Tanakh ve-Aggada,* published in *Batei ha-Leviyim* (Jerusalem, 5746), no. 13, p. 7.

18. Cf., however, *Minḥat Ḥinnukh,* no. 32, *Kuntres Mosekh ha-Shabbat,* who observes that, according to Rambam's analysis of this prohibition, one who refrains from labor on *Shabbat* because of fear of possible transgression can hardly be categorized as having devised a new religious observance. *Teshuvot Maharam Shik, Oraḥ Ḥayyim,* no. 154, without citing *Binyan Ẓion,* observes that "doubtful" fulfillment of a positive commandment takes precedence over "doubtful" violation of a negative commandment. He also reiterates the thesis advanced in an earlier responsum, *Oraḥ Ḥayyim,* no. 142, to the effect that matters of "doubt" are permitted to Noahides.

1. *Me'iri*

The comments of Me'iri, *Sanhedrin* 58b, are valuable not only for the intriguing insight presented therein but also for the manner in which they illuminate this issue and suggest a resolution of an entirely different order. Me'iri addresses the underlying rationale of the talmudic ban prohibiting gentiles from engaging in the performance of two specific *mizvot, viz.,* observance of *Shabbat* and study of Torah. The prohibition against establishing a day of rest, asserts Me'iri, is predicated upon a concern that, in doing so, the non-Jew "would appear as if he is one of our nation and others will learn from him." Similarly, comments Me'iri, if a gentile engages in the study of Torah "he deserves to be punished because people will think he is one of ours for they will see that he is knowledgeable and, following him, they will come to err." Proficiency in Torah and observance of *Shabbat* are the unique hallmarks of a Jew. According to Me'iri, the fundamental concern underlying this prohibition is that Jews will mistakenly assume that a non-Jew who becomes proficient in Torah or who observes *Shabbat* is a coreligionist and hence they may seek to emulate his conduct in other areas as well. Since such a person does not conduct himself as a Jew with regard to other matters, those who would pattern their own conduct upon his might easily become enmeshed in activities prohibited to Jews. According to Me'iri, these prohibitions reflect a concern that is germane only in an epoch in which there exist Jews who might be misled. Prior to Sinai, there simply were no Jews to be misled. Moreover, no one could conceivably be misled by a person such as Abraham who observed the Torah in its entirety. Hence, Abraham would have had no cogent reason to refrain from either Torah study or Sabbath observance.

It is certainly arguable, although less convincingly so, that this concern does not pertain in the case of a circumcised but unimmersed convert. Although Me'iri is silent with regard to Sabbath observance, he adopts an even more radical position with regard to Torah study in declaring that a non-Jew, even if he does not contemplate conversion, may engage in Torah study for the purpose of fulfilling the "fundamental commandments" of Judaism. Quite apparently, Me'iri feels that no one will be led astray by such an individual and that such anomalous situations are not encompassed within the formal prohibition. The same would appear to be the case with regard to circumcised but unimmersed converts. Regrettably, since the commentary of Me'iri was published only in recent years,[19]

19. Me'iri was born in 1249 in Perpignan and died there in 1306. His talmudic

Me'iri is not cited by the many scholars who have discussed this issue. It is nevertheless clear that many early authorities understand these prohibitions in a manner that is at variance with Me'iri's interpretation.[20]

---

commentary, *Bet ha-Beḥirah* was published on individual tractates on the basis of various manuscripts limited to those tractates. The first volume to appear was *Bet ha-Beḥirah* on *Megillah* (Amsterdam, 5529). Me'iri's commentary on all tractates of the Talmud has been available only since the discovery of the Parma manuscript in the 1920's. *Bet ha-Beḥirah* on *Sanhedrin* was edited and published by Abraham Sofer, Frankfurt am Main, 5690.

20. According to Rambam, *Hilkhot Melakhim* 10:9, establishment of a day of rest is forbidden because it constitutes the institution of a novel religious observance. Indeed, according to Rambam, the prohibition is not limited to Sabbath observance but serves as a paradigm prohibiting a gentile from devising his own rituals. Thus, Rambam writes, "[We] do not allow him to create a ritual (*le-ḥaddesh dat*) of his own accord."

Yad Ramah, Sanhedrin 58b, comments that, according to Rambam, a non-Jew is forbidden to observe *Shabbat* only when that day is observed as a day of rest out of a sense of religious obligation, either because the non-Jew believes that he is commanded by God to observe *Shabbat* or because he observes the day of rest as a devotee of a pagan cult. It would appear that, according to *Yad Ramah,* a non-Jew who recognizes that he has no obligation regarding *Shabbat* but who wishes nevertheless to observe the Sabbath out of a sense of monotheistic religious fervor incurs no transgression.

R. Meir Dan Plocki, in his discussion of Noahide law, *Ḥemdat Yisra'el* (Pietrkow 5687), *Kuntres Ner Mizvah,* p. 227, comments that observance of a ritual is forbidden only (i) if the gentile asserts that he is divinely commanded to do so, or (ii) if he does so in service of a pagan deity. *Ḥemdat Yisra'el* attributes this position to *Yad Ramah.* It nevertheless appears to this writer that a novel ritual observance devised by the non-Jew is indeed forbidden to him even though he acknowledges that it is not of divine origin and that a close reading of the text in question indicates that *Yad Ramah* does not intend to state that such is permitted to him.

Nevertheless, as evidenced by Rambam's ruling, *Hilkhot Melakhim* 10:10, a non-Jew who recogonizes that he is under no obligation to observe the commandments of the Torah may nevertheless do so in order to receive reward. If observance of *Shabbat* and of other commandments are entirely parallel in nature, as Rambam implies, it should follow that voluntary observance of *Shabbat* by a non-Jew with full recognition that such obligation is not incumbent upon him should be permitted. Cf., *Ḥemdat Yisra'el, loc. cit.,* s.v. *u-le-fi zeh.* It must, however, be noted that this conclusion does not emerge in any of the latter-day discussions of this prohibition. *Ḥemdat Yisra'el* does however note that, according to *Yad Ramah*'s understanding of Rambam, observance of a day of rest for entirely secular and mundane purposes, even on a regular basis, is entirely permissible. Moreover, Radbaz, *Hilkhot Melakhim* 10:9, appears to be of the opinion that, according to Rambam, intentional observance of a day of rest is forbidden to a non-Jew under any circumstances. According to Radbaz, establishment of an

2. *R. Meir Dan Plocki*

R. Meir Dan Plocki, *Ḥemdat Yisra'el* (Pietrkow, 5687), *Kuntres Ner Miẓvah,* p. 227, addressing himself to the question of Abraham's observance of the commandments, posits a limitation upon the ambit of the prohibition against Sabbath observance on the part of a non-Jew that would also render the prohibition inoperative insofar as a circumcised convert is concerned. *Shabbat* constitutes not only a commemoration of God's creation of the universe but also of his ongoing providential guardianship. The people of Israel enjoy a unique relationship with God in that He exercises a direct and individual form of providence over them. In contradistinction, divine guardianship of non-Jews is less direct and is channeled through the stellar constellations or forces of nature. This distinction is paraphrased in the talmudic dictum, *Shabbat* 156a and *Nedarim* 32a, "Israel is not governed by the constellations (*Ein mazal le-Yisra'el*)." Jews, who are under the guardianship of God Himself, are commanded to emulate Him by resting on the seventh day. Non-Jews, whose destiny is regulated by the constellations, must pattern their conduct upon that of the stars, i.e., they dare not desist from labor on any day of the week just as the celestial bodies have not ceased from their divinely ordained tasks since the moment of their creation. Thus the comment of the Midrash describing a non-Jew who observes *Shabbat* as an interloper interjecting himself into the unique relationship between God and Israel is equally applicable to a situation in which a non-Jew observes any day of the week as a day of rest. In observing any day as a day of rest, the non-Jew, in effect, announces that he does not emulate the celestial bodies because he is not dependent upon them as the conduits of providence but

---

observed day of rest is forbidden even if the observance is undertaken for health, economic or pragmatic reasons. If so, Sabbath observance is not entirely parallel to observance of other commandments insofar as this prohibition is concerned since Rambam certainly permits observance of other commandments on a voluntary basis for purposes of accumulating merit and earning reward. Cf., *Ḥemdat Yisra'el, loc. cit.*

Rashi maintains that the nature of this prohibition is not at all theological or "religious" in nature but reflects the telos of creation. According to Rashi's interpretation, just as celestial bodies proceed continuously in their orbits and just as day and night unceasingly succeed one another, so also must non-Jews fulfill their destined role in the created universe on a continual basis. Accordingly, they are forbidden to desist from productive labor over a full twenty-four hour period. Nevertheless, Radbaz, *loc. cit.,* opines that even according to Rashi, a non-Jew is culpable only if he intentionally ordains a given day as a day of rest, but that mere inadvertent or unwitting failure to perform an act of "labor" engenders no guilt.

enjoys the unmediated guardianship of God as do the people of Israel.

Sabbath observance posed no problem for Abraham, asserts *Ḥemdat Yisra'el,* because he was commanded by God, "Exit from your stargazing! Israel is not governed by the constellations" (*Shabbat* 156a and *Nedarim* 32a). Upon renouncing idolatry, Abraham became the recipient of God's direct providential guardianship and, as such, became entitled to emulate Him in observing *Shabbat* as well. *Ḥemdat Yisra'el* applies the same thesis in elucidating the problematic position of Rashi, *Yevamot* 48b, who maintains that a resident alien (*ger toshav*) is obliged to observe *Shabbat.*[21] The *ger toshav,* in accepting the Seven Commandments of the Sons of Noah, has renounced idolatry and, asserts *Ḥemdat Yisra'el,* thereby acquires a status similar to that of Abraham. It may certainly be argued that a circumcised convert who has accepted the "yoke of the commandments" is similarly no longer bound by the constraint against Sabbath observance on the part of gentiles.[22]

---

21. Subsequent commentators found Rashi's position puzzling and were at a loss to find a talmudic source substantiating that view. It may be the case that, according to Rashi, the obligation is derived from "acceptance" of the status of *ger toshav.* If so, it may well be argued that a circumcised convert who has accepted the "yoke of the commandments" is similarly bound to observe *Shabbat* by virtue of his "acceptance" of the "yoke of the commandments" which certainly includes acceptance of the obligations assumed by a *ger toshav.* [In a similar vein, *Sefer Ḥasidim,* no. 690, declares that a candidate for conversion "who has accepted the yoke of the commandments" may not be given non-kosher food to eat.] Thus, according to Rashi, a circumcised convert would not only be permitted to observe *Shabbat* but would be obligated to do so. However, since Rashi's reasoning is elusive, that conclusion cannot be stated with certainty. Indeed, Rabbenu Nissim, *Avodah Zarah* 67b, declares that the status of an unimmersed convert is inferior to that of a *ger toshav* because the former's acceptance of the "yoke of the commandments" is intended to be binding only upon subsequent immersion. Moreover, the institution of *ger toshav* as a formal halakhic construct has lapsed with the destruction of the Temple; see *Arakhin* 29a, and Rambam, *Hilkhot Avodah Zarah* 10:6, *Hilkhot Shabbat* 20:14 and *Hilkhot Issurei Bi'ah* 14:8. Accordingly, a convert who accepts the "yoke of the commandments" cannot *ipso facto* be assumed to have acquired the status of a *ger toshav.* Cf., however, *Teshuvot Radbaz,* III, no. 479, who, in a different context, equates the status of an unimmersed convert with that of a *ger toshav.* For attempts by contemporary scholars to reconcile Rashi's position with the talmudic prohibition against Sabbath observance by non-Jews see R. Jacob Kaminetsky, "Be-Inyan Ger Toshav," *Sefer ha-Zikkaron le-Zekher Moreinu ve-Rabbeinu ha-Ga'on R. Rafa'el Barukh Sorotzkin,* ed. R. Abraham Shoshanah (n.d.), pp. 198–200, and R. Moshe Sternbuch, *Edut,* no. 6 (Adar II, 5749), p. 30.

22. This point is also amplified in this writer's article, "Sabbath—Prism of

3. *Ḥatam Sofer*

An ingenious solution to the problem of how the Patriarchs licitly observed the Sabbath is recorded in the name of *Ḥatam Sofer* by his disciple, R. Moses Schick, *Teshuvot Maharam Shik, Oraḥ Ḥayyim,* no. 145.[23] As evidenced by the ruling of *Shulḥan Arukh, Oraḥ Ḥayyim* 13:1, a garment to which *ẓiẓit* have been improperly attached may not be worn in a public thoroughfare (*reshut ha-rabbim)* on *Shabbat,* not only because of the abrogation of the commandment concerning *ẓiẓit,* but also because wearing a garment of that nature constitutes "carrying" on *Shabbat. Ẓiẓit* are attached to a garment solely for purposes of fulfilling a religious obligation; when that obligation is fulfilled they become an integral part of the garment. However, when the *ẓiẓit* fail to satisfy the stipulated requirements, the *miẓvah* is not fulfilled and, since they serve no purpose, the *ẓiẓit* do not become an integral part of the garment but instead constitute a "burden."

Ḥatam Sofer argues that the Patriarchs needed only to don a garment to which *ẓiẓit* had been attached and, so attired, walk from a private domain into a public thoroughfare. From a perspective that regards the Patriarchs as Jews intent upon fulfilling the commandment of *ẓiẓit,* no infraction was incurred. For Jews, *ẓiẓit* become an integral part of the garment to which they are attached and garments are not deemed a "burden." However, if the Patriarchs are regarded as Noahides who are under no obligation to affix *ẓiẓit* to their garments, those appendages do not become an integral part of the garment and, accordingly, constitute a "burden." Hence, argues *Ḥatam Sofer,* as Noahides, the act of transporting *ẓiẓit* affixed to a garment from a private domain into a public thoroughfare served to nullify their observance of *Shabbat.*

Ḥatam Sofer's solution appears to this writer to be problematic. His reasoning is based upon the assumption that *ẓiẓit* do not constitute a burden only because their presence is an absolute requirement. It may well be argued that *ẓiẓit* become an integral part of a garment not only when necessary to discharge an absolute obligation (*ḥiyyuv*) with regard to a commandment but even when they serve as voluntary fulfillment (*kiyyum*) of a nonobligatory commandment. As reflected in the plain meaning of Rambam's ruling, *Hilkhot Melakhim* 10:10, and even more

Emunah," Jewish Observer, June, 1970, pp. 19–24.

23. A similar solution is presented by *Teshuvot Ḥeshek Shlomoh* (Warsaw, 5648), addenda, p. 151.

explicitly in one of his responsa,[24] non-Jews may fulfill *miẓvot* on a voluntary basis for purposes of receiving reward.[25] *Ẓiẓit* affixed to a garment and worn by a non-Jew for the purpose of fulfilling a *miẓvah* should logically be regarded as an integral part of the garment since they serve a purpose and their permanent attachment is clearly desired by the wearer. Their status should not be inferior to that of decorations permanently affixed to a garment for aesthetic purposes. Such embellishments are deemed to be an integral part of the garment and not a "burden."

R. Jacob Chai Zerichan develops a novel thesis on the basis of which he dismisses the solution offered by *Ḥatam Sofer*. Of the thirty-nine forbidden categories of "labor" on *Shabbat*, thirty-eight are derived from the verse "you shall do no work" (Exodus 20:10). The thirty-ninth, transfer of an object from a private domain to a public thoroughfare or transport of an object over a distance of four cubits in a public thoroughfare, is not derived from that verse but is the subject of a tradition received by Moses at Sinai (*halakhah le-Mosheh mi-Sinai*). Based upon Rambam's ruling, *Hilkhot Melakhim* 9:10, it has become a well-established principle that such traditions are directed solely to Jews, but are inapplicable and of no effect insofar as Noahides are concerned.[26] Accordingly, argues Rabbi Zerichan, since "labor" is only that which is defined as such by Scripture, carrying a "burden" in a prohibited area does not constitute a form of "labor" insofar as non-Jews are concerned. Hence performing an act of this nature would not negate the "rest" which is forbidden to non-Jews over a twenty-four hour period.[27]

---

24. *Teshuvot ha-Rambam,* ed. Alfred Freimann (Jerusalem, 5694), no. 124.

25. Cf., however, R. Moses Feinstein, *Iggerot Mosheh, Yoreh De'ah,* I, no. 3 and *Yoreh De'ah,* II, no. 7. For a fuller discussion of this point see *Contemporary Halakhic Problems,* I, 317–323.

26. Cf., however, *infra,* note 29 and accompanying text.

27. See also *Pirḥei Nisan* included by R. Yitzchak Reitbard in his *Kehillat Yizḥak al ha-Torah* (Vilna, 5660), *Parashat Toldot. Pirḥei Nisan,* discussing the problem of Sabbath observance by the Patriarchs, advances a somewhat modified form of this solution. He assumes that the status of the Patriarchs was "doubtful," i.e., that it was not clear whether their status was that of Jews or that of Noahides. Accordingly, he indicates that they had the option of wearing a garment with *ẓiẓit* and making the express stipulation that if their status be that of Jews they don the garment with the intention of fulfilling the commandment, but that if their status be that of Noahides they have no intention to fulfill the commandment.

That discussion suggests an expedient that may readily be utilized by a prospective convert who is discomfited by the prospect of overt violation of Sabbath restrictions. Clearly, when the *ẓiẓit* are not worn for the purpose of fulfilling a

4. *R. Pinchas ha-Levi Horowitz*

The earliest reference to the desire of a would-be convert to observe all the tenets of Judaism, including *Shabbat,* and to the attendant problem, is probably that recorded by R. Akiva Eger in the index (apparently compiled by R. Akiva Eger himself) to his responsa collection. The indexed responsum, no. 121, deals with an entirely different problem related to a particular case of conversion. However, in a concluding note inserted in the index to that responsum, R. Akiva Eger states his desire to point out by way of *obiter dictum* his dissatisfaction with regard to a practice that was apparently not uncommon in his day. He refers disparagingly to householders who maintained in their employ non-Jewish maids who contemplated conversion and conducted themselves as Jews in every regard. R. Akiva Eger censures those householders on the grounds that in countenancing Sabbath observance by their servants they encourage transgression. Accordingly, he counsels that the women in question be restrained from conducting themselves in such a manner and that they be counseled either to undergo immersion for the purpose of conversion or to perform some act of "labor" on *Shabbat.*

Subsequently, R. Akiva Eger had occasion to qualify and defend his exhortation. In a short item included in a series of addenda appended to later editions of his responsa collection, R. Akiva Eger, addendum to responsum no. 121, reports that "a long time" after his original note was published there appeared in print the work of R. Pinchas ha-Levi Horowitz on the Pentateuch, *Panim Yafot.* In a comment on *Parashat Noaḥ,* that scholar remarks that the "day" which a non-Jew is forbidden to observe as a day of rest is not a "day" of the Jewish calendar which begins in the evening and ends the following evening but consists of a twenty-four hour period beginning and ending at daybreak as indicated by the order of the words of the verse "day and night shall not cease" (Genesis 8:22). *Panim Yafot* elaborates upon this thesis in explaining that the "day" of the pre-Sinaitic era referred to in early sections of the Bible is consistently a day beginning with daybreak and concluding with the ensuing night. The identical thesis is reiterated by R. Pinchas ha-Levi Horowitz in his talmudic commentary, *Ha-Makneh, Kiddushin* 37b. Accordingly, the talmudic rendition of the verse "day and night they shall not rest" should similarly be understood as positing a prohibition against observance of a

---

miẓvah they constitute a "burden." Accordingly, a non-Jew who desires to observe *Shabbat* might avail himself of the expedient of stipulating categorically that he dons the garment with *ẓiẓit* with the express intention of not fulfilling the *miẓvah.* Thus, for him, the *ẓiẓit* would constitute a burden.

twenty-four hour period of rest beginning with daybreak. Since Sabbath restrictions commence on Sabbath eve and continue until the next evening, a non-Jew who performs an act of "labor" during daylight hours on Friday and also on Saturday after nightfall has refrained from desecration of the Sabbath without violating the admonition not to rest for the span of an entire "day." If this thesis is accepted, observes R. Akiva Eger, it follows that his earlier admonition regarding Sabbath observance by non-Jewish maids was misplaced.

R. Akiva Eger, however, rejects *Panim Yafot*'s definition of a "day" for purposes of this prohibition on the basis of a comment of *Tosafot, Sanhedrin* 59a. *Tosafot* remark that, subsequent to receiving the Torah at Mount Sinai, Jews are not bound by the prohibition against refraining from labor for the period of a full day only because they were subsequently explicitly commanded to the contrary. *Panim Yafot* himself cites *Tosafot*'s comment in his own discussion and points out that, if his position is correct, there is no inherent contradiction between a commandment to observe the Sabbath from Friday evening until Saturday night and a prohibition against refraining from work during a twenty-four hour period beginning and ending at daybreak. *Tosafot,* who posit a contradiction, must then have regarded the "day" on which rest is forbidden as coextensive with the "day" on which the Sabbath is to be observed. *Panim Yafot* dismisses that objection with the observation that since, technically, *Yom Kippur* may fall on a Friday or a Sunday, situations may well arise in which a Jew is commanded to abstain from all labor for a consecutive forty-eight hour period. Therefore, argues *Panim Yafot, Tosafot* regard the commandments concerning *Shabbat* and *Yom Kippur* as abrogating the prohibition against resting from labor for an entire day.

R. Akiva Eger refutes that argument in a rather ingenious way. In a talmudic controversy between himself and R. Yochanan, Resh Lakish maintains that any act that goes unpunished because the infraction involves a measure or quantity below the limit for which punishment is stipulated (*ḥaẓi shi'ur*) is biblically permissible and forbidden only by virtue of rabbinic edict. Indeed, *Mishneh le-Melekh, Hilkhot Shabbat* 18:1, asserts that, insofar as Sabbath restrictions are concerned, Resh Lakish's position is undisputed.[28] If so, notes R. Akiva Eger, it is entirely possible to observe both *Shabbat* and *Yom Kippur* and yet not rest for an entire twenty-four hour period. If *Yom Kippur* occurs on Sunday it is possible,

28. See also *Teshuvot Ḥakham Ẓevi,* no. 86; *Teshuvot Torat Ḥesed, Oraḥ Ḥayyim,* no. 44; and *Pri Megadim,* introduction to *Hilkhot Shabbat.*

for example, to harvest half of the proscribed quantity of produce on the Sabbath and again to harvest half of the proscribed quantity on Saturday night after the conclusion of *Shabbat,* i.e., on *Yom Kippur* eve. Since the "labor" is not completed on either *Shabbat* or *Yom Kippur* there is no biblical violation of the sanctity of either day whereas, insofar as the prohibition "day and night they shall not work" is concerned, an act of labor has been performed in its entirety on a single "day," i.e., within the span of a twenty-four hour period measured from daybreak to daybreak. The result, argues R. Akiva Eger, is that observance of both *Shabbat* and *Yom Kippur* on consecutive days is possible without "resting" on a single "day" as the latter term is defined for purposes of the prohibition of enjoyment of a complete "day" of rest. Since *Tosafot* does posit a contradiction, argues R. Akiva Eger, *Tosafot* must reject *Panim Yafot*'s thesis regarding the definition of a "day" in the pre-Sinaitic era.[29]

29. A thesis identical to that of *Panim Yafot* is also cited in the name of an anonymous rabbi by *Ḥeker Halakhah,* no. 15 and rebutted by the latter authority. R. Joseph Saul Nathanson, *Yad Sha'ul, Yoreh De'ah* 293:4 (pp. 72b-73a), similarly cites this thesis but rebuts it on the basis of the fact that a verse describing an event prior to the Exodus is cited by the Gemara, *Rosh ha-Shanah* 20b, in establishing that festivals commence in the evenings. R. Jacob Chai Zerichan dismisses that argument on the contention that the verse in question is designed to establish post-Sinaitic regulations. *Teshuvot Torat Ḥesed,* no. 25, advances a similar objection based upon a statement of the Palestinian Talmud, *Ḥalah* 2:1, that impliedly regards the commencement of the day prior to revelation at Sinai as occurring in the same manner as in the post-Sinaitic era. Similarly, *Teshuvot Binyan Ẓion,* no. 126, cites *Ḥullin* 83a in pointing out that the day is regarded as commencing with nightfall on the basis of verses describing creation. Although those arguments may be cogent with regard to the determination of other issues, it seems to this writer that they are not applicable to the particular question of the delineation of the twenty-four hour period during which "rest'' is forbidden to a Noahide. That issue does not necessarily involve the general question of when a day was regarded as having begun prior to Sinai; it involves only the explication of the meaning of the phrase "day and night shall not cease." In that context, although perhaps in no other, "day" precedes "night" in the Scriptural phrase and thereby indicates that the twenty-four hour period commences with daybreak. *Binyan Ẓion,* however, dismisses the argument that the phrase "day and night shall not cease" establishes a different definition of the day for purposes of the prohibition concerning observance of a day of rest by a Noahide. See also the rebuttal of that argument by R. Joseph Patzanovski, *Pardes Yosef, Parashat Noaḥ,* sec. 22.

It may also be argued that *Panim Yafot*'s thesis is not necessarily contradicted by *Tosafot* since *Tosafot* may maintain that, although the pre-Sinaitic commandment is binding upon Jews, its parameters are determined by general post-Sinaitic canons. Cf. R. Shimon Moshe Diskin, *Mas'et ha-Melekh, Ḥullin* 100b. Neverthe-

5. *R. Jacob Ettlinger and Minḥat Ḥinnukh*

R. Jacob Ettlinger, *Teshuvot Binyan Ẓion,* no. 126, points out that a facile solution to this problem may be found in the fact that Jews are culpable for Sabbath violation only if a specified measure of "labor" is performed. Rambam, *Hilkhot Melakhim* 9:10, declares that minimum quantities (*shi'urim*) with regard to violation of biblical commandments are stipulated only with regard to commandments directed to Jews. The Gemara, *Sukkah* 6a, indicates that the concept of a minimum quantity is rooted in a *halakhah le-Mosheh mi-Sinai,* an oral tradition transmitted to Moses at Sinai. According to Rambam, those traditions were transmitted only to Jews, but not to non-Jews, with the result that there is no concept of a minimum quantity with regard to any rule of law addressed to Noahides.[30] Accordingly, a non-Jew might harvest less than the forbidden quantity of produce (*ḥaẓi shi'ur*) and thereby have refrained from "rest" as that concept applies to non-Jews since even minimal labor constitutes labor for Noahides, but nevertheless not have breached the sanctity of the Sabbath as that concept is defined for Jews. *Binyan Ẓion* offers this suggestion only according to the talmudic opinion that regards *ḥaẓi shi'ur* as not only excluded from punishment but as entirely permitted.

A similar line of reasoning is presented by *Minḥat Ḥinnukh,* no. 32, toward the end of his *Kuntres Mosekh ha-Shabbat. Minḥat Ḥinnukh* adds that, granted that an act involving less than the culpable measure or quantity is biblically forbidden even with regard to Sabbath prohibitions, nevertheless, a gentile who performs an act of that nature in order not to transgress the biblical commandment prohibiting rest for an entire day would not be in violation of Sabbath regulations. Those who maintain that even acts involving minimal quantities are biblically forbidden regard such actions as forbidden because of the fact that, when additional quantities are added, the aggregate constitutes a biblical prohibition. Thus, for example, it is forbidden to write a single letter because subsequent writing of a second letter results in culpability. Since there could be no culpability without the writing of the first letter, it follows that the writing of the first letter must also have been biblically forbidden. *Minḥat Ḥinnukh* argues that this reasoning is cogent only in a situation in which the first

less, as noted above, in this case, it is not the post-Sinaitic definition of "day" that may serve to determine the issue but the meaning of the phrase "day and night shall not cease" which is not necessarily related to the definition of "day" in other contexts.

30. Rambam's position is however disputed by *Tosafot, Ḥullin* 33a. See also *Sedei Ḥemed, Kelalim, Erekh Gimel,* sec. 46.

act may potentially be combined with a second in a manner that would lead to culpability. However, an individual who desires to observe the Sabbath but who performs an act involving less than the culpable quantity in order not to be guilty of a transgression will assuredly not repeat the act in a manner that will render him culpable for transgression of the Sabbath. Hence, argues *Minḥat Ḥinnukh,* since there will never be an aggregate quantity for which the individual would be culpable, an act involving a lesser quantity is not biblically proscribed.

6. *R. Jacob Ettlinger's Second Approach*

An entirely different solution is advanced in the same responsum by *Binyan Ẓion,* no. 126. As noted earlier, *shi'urim* were transmitted to Moses at Mount Sinai. Prohibitions addressed to Noahides at an earlier time were not predicated upon particular *shi'urim.* Since, as Rambam maintains, those prohibitions were not modified at Sinai they remain in effect precisely as they were originally instituted. Similarly, argues *Binyan Ẓion,* since the thirty-nine categories of forbidden labor were formulated only at Sinai, the concept of "rest" forbidden to Noahides at an earlier time could not have been defined in terms of "rest" from those thirty-nine categories of labor. The definition of "work" or "labor" must have been a colloquial one, i.e., any activity requiring exertion or travail. The concept of "labor" as delineated by the thirty-nine categories of labor prohibited to Jews on *Shabbat* is entirely divorced from the colloquial meaning of that term. Thus, transporting a needle in a public thoroughfare or striking a match is a form of "labor" forbidden on *Shabbat,* whereas carrying a heavy burden in a private domain is not at all a form of "labor" that is forbidden on the Sabbath. However, argues *Binyan Ẓion,* since the Noahide prohibition against "resting" for an entire day is to be defined colloquially, a non-Jew who transports a needle in a public thoroughfare, but refrains from all other forms of labor, remains in violation of the Noahide prohibition against "resting." Conversely, a non-Jew who carries a heavy burden in a private domain has not "rested" on the Sabbath even though, for a Jew, such an act does not constitute an act of "labor." Accordingly, a non-Jew who engages in an activity of that nature, i.e., carrying a heavy burden in a private domain, has observed the Sabbath without violating the admonition "day and night they shall not rest."

7. *Pardes Yosef*

R. Joseph Patzanovski, *Pardes Yosef, Parashat Noaḥ,* sec. 22, offers an additional solution to this problem on the basis of the statement of the Gemara, *Shabbat* 75b, indicating that an individual who transports an object from which it is forbidden to derive any benefit is not culpable. Accordingly, *Pardes Yosef* argues that the Patriarchs simply had to transport some object from which it is forbidden to derive benefit, e.g., an item utilized for purposes of idol worship. If the Patriarchs enjoyed the status of Jews, no violation of Sabbath restrictions was incurred. Non-Jews, however, are permitted to derive benefit from such objects. Since he may derive benefit from such objects, a non-Jew who transports such an object on *Shabbat* has not "rested" from labor. Accordingly, if the Patriarchs are to be regarded as Noahides, transportation of such objects by them would have constituted an act of labor and would have sufficed to bring them into compliance with the command "day and night they shall not rest."

It would seem that this solution is viable only if it is assumed that the status of the Patriarchs was "doubtful" but that it would not serve to solve the problem of a non-Jew who clearly enjoys the status of a Noahide but wishes to observe the Sabbath. Since such a person *may* derive benefit from such an object if he so chooses, it stands to reason that, objectively, the item must be regarded to be a burden.[31] Nevertheless, it may serve to meet the psychological needs of a prospective convert who may be concerned with practice or habituation in the observance of *mizvot* rather than with technical halakhic considerations.

8. *R. Jacob Chai Zerichan*

R. Jacob Chai Zerichan assumes as axiomatic that a non-Jew who refrains from labor without the intent to observe the day as a day of rest, but simply out of laziness or because of a desire for relaxation without intending to celebrate the day as a day of religious observance, is not in violation of the biblical prohibition.[32] Accordingly, he advises that a non-Jew may refrain from violation of Sabbath prohibitions simply upon the mental determination that he refrains from activity prohibited to Jews,

31. *Teshuvot Maharam Shik, Oraḥ Ḥayyim,* no. 245, employs a similar line of reasoning in dismissing the notion that the Patriarchs observed *Shabbat* as Jews while desecrating it as Noahides by separating food forbidden to Noahides (*viz., mefarkeset*), but not to Jews, from other food in a manner forbidden on *Shabbat* (*borer*). *Maharam Shik* cogently argues that, since such food was objectively forbidden to the Patriarchs, they could not have sorted such food in this manner while observing *Shabbat* as Jews.

32. Cf., the opinion of Radbaz cited *supra,* note 17.

not for purposes of religious observance, but solely because he has no desire to perform such actions. Rabbi Zerichan's solution is problematic, to say the least. The non-Jew who conducts himself in this manner is obviously motivated by religious considerations and would candidly concede that it is such motivations which prompt him to seek ways and means of refraining from acts of labor on the Sabbath. It is precisely a religious consideration that causes such a non-Jew to observe *Shabbat* as a day of rest and relaxation. Under such circumstances it appears quite doubtful that a mere mental resolution to observe the day as a day of rest and relaxation is sufficient to negate the religious connotations of rest on the seventh day of the week.

9. *Maharam Schick*

R. Moses Schick, *Teshuvot Maharam Shik, Oraḥ Ḥayyim,* no. 145, advances a solution to this problem based upon the position advanced by *Magen Avraham, Oraḥ Ḥayyim* 448:4. *Magen Avraham* maintains that, although there is no halakhic concept of agency with regard to acts performed by a gentile on behalf of a Jew or, vice versa, nevertheless agency does exist as a halakhic construct with regard to acts performed by a gentile at the behest of another gentile. Maharam Shik contends that, since (at least according to Rashi) the prohibition "day and night they shall not rest'' requires the performance of some constructive act designed to promote the development of a settled and developed universe,[33] such an act need not be performed personally but may be performed by an agent. The concern, contends Maharam Shik, is not the physical act *per se* but its teleological effect. Accordingly, argues Maharam Shik, the obligation can be discharged by employment of an agent to perform an act having the requisite effect. Accordingly, the Patriarchs might have availed themselves of the expedient of directing a gentile to perform such an act on their behalf. As Noahides, they would have been credited with performing an act of labor as a result of an act performed on their behalf by their designated agent; as Jews, designation of a non-Jew as an agent would have been of no effect and hence the agent's act would have been of no significance for the principal. Hence, as Jews, the act of the putative agent would not have constituted a violation of Sabbath restrictions on the part of the principal.[34]

33. See *supra,* note 19.

34. See also additional solutions advanced by *Teshuvot Maharam Shik, Oraḥ Ḥayyim,* no. 145, and R. Joseph Engel, *Bet ha-Oẓar, Ma'arekhet Alef,* sec. 14. Numerous other attempts to resolve this problem can best be described as homiletical endeavors falling short of the standards of halakhic dialectic.

Chapter VIII

Fetal Tissue Research: Jewish Tradition and Public Policy

A mortal heals the bitter with that which is sweet, but the Holy One, blessed be He, heals the bitter with that which is bitter.

TANḤUMA, BESHALAḤ 24

The results of preliminary scientific research in medical centers throughout the world indicate a strong possibility that further investigation will yield a cure for one or more of a variety of medical conditions, including diabetes and Parkinson's disease. Further research will require experimentation upon abortuses and the treatment, if perfected, will entail transplantation of fetal tissue.

Public funding of such research has become a matter of controversy in the United States. A significant moral issue is posed by the fact that both research and treatment depend upon the use of fetal cadavers obtained through induced non-therapeutic abortions. Opponents of public funding argue that governmental support implies endorsement of all aspects of the research protocol and hence constitutes collusion in the abortion itself.[1] It is also contended that the prospect of utilization of the abortus for a life-saving purpose may influence the decision of a woman who is vacillating with regard to a decision to terminate her pregnancy.[2] Both

1. See James Bopp and James T. Burtchaell, "Human Fetal Tissue Transplantation Research Panel: Statement of Dissent," *Report of the Human Fetal Tissue Transplantation Research Panel,* December, 1988, I, 63ff.

2. See Kathleen Nolan, "*Genug ist Genug:* A Fetus is Not a Kidney," *Hastings Center Report,* December, 1988, p. 16, and James Bopp and T. Burtchaell, "Statement of Dissent," pp. 52–63. The recommendations included in the report of the Human Fetal Tissue Transplantation Research Panel candidly concede that knowledge of the possibility for using fetal tissue in research and transplantation might constitute motivation, reason or incentive for a pregnant woman to have an abortion; see *Report of the Human Fetal Tissue Transplantation Research*

considerations are likely to result in a net increase in the number of abortions performed.

Analysis of the propriety of fetal tissue research from the perspective of Jewish law involves a number of rather complex questions. In addition to the aforementioned concerns, issues such as whether or not there is an obligation to accord the fetus burial, whether benefit may be derived from a fetal cadaver and how such concerns are to be balanced against possible preservation of life must be examined.

Most significantly, in formulating advice for purposes of influencing public policy in a non-Jewish society, these questions must be examined from the vantage point of the Noahide Code in which greater or lesser weight is assigned to each of these considerations than is the case in Jewish law as applied to Jews.

In this endeavor the author will delineate the halakhic considerations reflected in his minority report as a member of a consultative body of the National Institutes of Health, an agency of the U.S. government, that was empaneled for the purpose of making policy recommendations with regard to the morality of fetal tissue research.

I. *The Status of the Fetus*

One of the few explicit talmudic references to the status of a fetus occurs in *Sanhedrin* 91b. The Gemara records:

> Said Antoninus to Rabbi [Judah the Prince], "When is the soul placed in man; at the time of conception or at the time of creation (i.e., when the fetus assumes human form as evidenced by the development of flesh, sinews and bones)?" [Rabbi] said to him, "From the time of creation." [Antoninus] responded, "Is it possible for a piece of meat to stand three days without salt without becoming putrid? Rather, from the time of conception." Said Rabbi: "This matter Antoninus taught me and Scripture supports him for it is written, 'And your decree has preserved my spirit'[3] (Job 10:12)."

Panel, I, 4.

3. I.e., my soul. Support from this verse bolstering Antoninus' position is based upon the use of the term "*pekidah*" or "decree" in the phrase "and Your decree—*u-fekudatkha.*" The term employed by the Gemara for conception is also "*pekidah*" or "decree." Rashi explains the use of this nomenclature by stating that the literal reference is to the moment the angel turns his attention to the "*tipah*" (i.e., the fertilized ovum) and brings it before God for a decree

A first and plausible reading of this exchange yields the impression that the subject of dispute between Antoninus and R. Judah is the precise time at which ensoulment takes place. Both R. Judah and Antoninus agree from the very outset that ensoulment takes place no later than the stage of gestation at which the developing embryo acquires a distinct human form; the dispute is only with regard to whether that phenomenon occurs even earlier, at the time of conception. R. Judah ultimately concedes that Antoninus is correct and that ensoulment takes place at the moment of conception. Nevertheless, a significant controversy exists among early post-talmudic rabbinic scholars with regard to whether or not feticide, even in the final stages of gestation, constitutes a form of homicide.[4] Moreover, the narrative involving the exchange between Antoninus and R. Judah is completely ignored in the post-talmudic discussions of that question. Clearly, those authorities regarded this narrative as irrelevant to a determination of the status of the fetus insofar as the prohibition against feticide is concerned. Indeed, closer examination of the text reveals that it does not even follow from the debate between Antoninus and R. Judah that the fetal soul is endowed with immortality. Elsewhere, *Sanhedrin* 110b, the Gemara records that various Amora'im, in disagreement with one another, assert that immortality is acquired at the time of conception, upon circumcision or at the time that the child begins to talk. Thereupon, the Gemara adduces a tannaitic dictum that serves to establish that immortality is acquired only upon recitation of "Amen" by the child.[5] None of the commentaries finds any discrepancy between that discussion and the view reflected in the exchange between Antoninus and R. Judah.

It is of interest to note that these differing issues are eloquently illustrated in Plato's discussion of the immortality of the soul. Plato's *Phaedo* is devoted to the formulation of a series of elegant proofs demonstrating the immortality of the human soul. However, no attempt is made to demonstrate that the soul exists; rather, the existence of the soul is taken for granted. Given his understanding of the meaning of the term, this is not at all an unwarranted presumption on the part of Plato. Certainly, the existence of a soul as a discrete ontological entity requires demonstrative proof and indeed such a categorization of the soul follows from the proof of its

concerning its fate as described in the Gemara, *Niddah* 16b.

4. For a discussion of those sources see *Contemporary Halakhic Problems,* I, 326–339.

5. With regard to resurrection of *nefalim,* see *Ketubot* 111a and *Avnei Nezer, Yoreh De'ah,* no. 472, sec. 7.

immortality. The proposition assumed by Plato without proof is entirely different. What is assumed is simply the existence of both an animating force and a rational faculty.[6] There is certainly no gainsaying the fact that man is a vital organism and that he is endowed with reason. Those verities are self-evident and require no dialectical demonstration. The duality of spirit and flesh, the independent ontological status of the soul and its immortality are entirely different issues. Since at least the time of Aristotle, philosophers and theologians, both non-Jewish and Jewish, have carefully coined diverse terms designed to distinguish between the animal soul and the rational soul. Antoninus and R. Judah must be understood as disagreeing with regard to when the animal soul, or the animating faculty, comes into existence.[7] The rational faculty may or may not be an ontological entity unto itself; as an independent ontological entity it may or may not be immortal. Those are the points Plato seeks to demonstrate in the *Phaedo*. Judaism also posits those truths with regard to the soul, but does so quite independently of the exchange between Antoninus and Rabbi Judah.

Consequently, it becomes apparent that ensoulment is a matter of philosophical, rather than halakhic, interest. Similarly, "personhood" is not a category of halakhic discourse. To be sure, there are statements in the writings of early rabbinic authorities to the effect that a fetus is not to be categorized as a *nefesh.*[8] However, the concept of a "*nefesh*" is not to be equated with the connotative meaning of the term "person." A *treifah,* i.e., a person suffering the loss or perforation of one of a list of specifically defined vital organs[9] is not a *nefesh;* but a *treifah* is certainly a person. Leviticus 24:17 provides that one who smites a *nefesh* shall be put to death. Talmudic exegesis of that verse as recorded in the Gemara, *Sanhedrin*

---

6. Indeed, in the *Phaedrus* 246a, Plato defines the soul as "that which moves itself" and in Book X of the *Laws* 892b-896d he not only speaks of the soul as the name that language gives to "the motion which can move itself" but also states that all motions of the body are caused by prior movements of the soul. Hence, for Plato, the presence of motion in the body is tantamount to a demonstration of the existence of the soul.

7. See, for example, the concluding comments of R. Jonathan Eibeschutz, *Binah le-'Ittim, Hilkhot Yom Tov* 1:23, who states that the "'spiritual soul' comes to man at the moment of birth." In light of the concluding statements of the discussion in *Sanhedrin* 110b it must be assumed that this soul is not endowed with immortality until a later time.

8. See Rashi, *Sanhedrin* 72b, s.v. *yaẓa rosho.*

9. Cf., however, Rambam, *Hilkhot Roẓeaḥ* 2:9.

78a, yields a dispute with regard to capital culpability of one who hastens the death of a person who has already sustained a mortal wound at the hands of a previous aggressor. The disagreement is with regard to whether the phrase "*kol nefesh*" should be rendered as "a complete *nefesh*" or as "any *nefesh*" in the sense of even a minimal *nefesh.* Nevertheless, all are in agreement that there is no capital culpability for the killing of a *treifah.* Quite obviously, *a treifah* is not a *nefesh* and hence if a *treifah* is the victim of homicide the perpetrator is not guilty of a capital crime; yet for virtually all other aspects of Jewish law a *treifah* must certainly be regarded as a person. In an analogous manner, as already noted, a person who murders an individual who has already sustained a mortal wound is not executed because the victim is not a "complete *nefesh*"; yet there is no question that, so long as vital signs remain present, the victim remains a "complete person" for all other matters of law. As is the case with regard to many words and phrases employed in any legal system, the word "*nefesh*" is a technical term endowed with a narrow and precisely defined halakhic meaning that is not readily translatable into non-technical terms employed in common parlance.

Judaism teaches that human life is sacred from the moment of generation of genoplasm in the gonads until decomposition of the body after death. At every stage along this continuum human tissue must be treated with dignity and respect. Not surprisingly, the manifestations of honor due the body and its components vary in a manner appropriate to the various stages of its development and degeneration. Similarly, sanctions imposed for infractions of the duties of honor and respect to be accorded the human organism in its various states are not uniform in nature. The question of the propriety of fetal tissue research centers upon the duties and obligations owed to the fetal cadaver. Those duties are the subject of significant discussion and controversy in the annals of rabbinic literature.

II. *Burial of the Fetus*

There is ample textual evidence demonstrating that burial of a *nefel,* a term that includes an abortus, a stillborn baby and a non-viable neonate, was the common practice among Jews in antiquity. For example, the Gemara, *Ketubot* 20b, speaks of places regarded as ritually impure by virtue of the fact that "women bury their *nefalim*" at such sites. *Sifrei,* Deuteronomy 19:14, declares that it is not permissible for a person to sell his gravesite in an ancestral burial ground.[10] *Sifrei* indicates that the prohibition becomes effective only upon actual use of the plot as a burial site but that interment of a *nefel* does not constitute dedication of the site as a burial ground for purposes of rendering this prohibition operative.[11] Nevertheless, on the basis of these sources alone, it is not possible to determine whether burial of a *nefel* is merely a customary practice or a normative halakhic requirement.[12]

One early authority, *Hagahot Maimuniyot,* in his commentary on Rambam's *Hilkhot Milah* 1:10, declares explicitly that insofar as *nefalim* are concerned "there is no *mizvah* to inter them." In support of that position he cites the narrative recorded in the Tosefta, *Oholot* 16:6, and cited by the Gemara, *Pesaḥim* 9a and *Avodah Zarah* 42a, regarding a maidservant who cast her *nefel* into a pit and a *kohen* who subsequently came to see whether it had reached a stage of gestational development that would make the regulations governing childbirth applicable to the mother and to determine the sex of the child for those purposes. Similarly *Or Zaru'a, Hilkhot Avelut,* no. 422, rules that burial of an abortus does not constitute a *mizvah.*[13]

An opposing view is adopted by *Magen Avraham, Oraḥ Ḥayyim* 526:20. Rebutting the argument formulated by *Hagahot Maimuniyot, Magen Avraham* asserts that placing a *nefel* in a "pit" as described by the Tosefta was, in fact, a form of burial. His principal argument in support of his own position is based upon a comment of *Sifra,* Leviticus 21:2, adducing an exegetical basis for prohibiting a *kohen* from defiling himself in conjunction with the burial of a child who is a *nefel.* The implication, argues *Magen Avraham,* is that a *nefel* requires burial. Moreover, argues *Magen Avraham,* it may be inferred from the comments of the Gemara, *Niddah* 57a, that it is forbidden to leave a *nefel* unburied overnight.[14]

---

10. Cf., *Baba Batra* 100b and *Shulḥan Arukh, Ḥoshen Mishpat* 217:7.

11. See R. Naphtali Zevi Judah Berlin, *Emek ha-Neẓiv, ad locum.*

12. Cf., however, R. Joseph Saul Nathanson, letter of approbation to publication of *Sifrei,* Lemberg, 5626. The Palestinian Talmud, *Shabbat* 18:3, reports that the placenta was commonly buried in the ground. However, burial of the placenta is not depicted as a halakhic requirement but as a "pledge," i.e., a symbolic acknowledgement that every person will eventually be buried, as manifested in the burial of the placenta immediately following birth.

13. See also R. David ibn Zimra, *Teshuvot ha-Radbaz,* I, no. 512.

14. The grounds for this inference are far from unequivocal; see *Teshuvot Noda bi-Yehudah, Mahadura Kamma, Oraḥ Ḥayyim,* no.16. Cf., however, *Maḥaẓit ha-Shekel* in his comments on *Magen Avraham, ad locum,* and *Binah le-'Ittim,*

The comments of *Magen Avraham* serve as the focal point for subsequent discussions of this question in rabbinic literature. Some decisors cite his comments with approbation; others engage in concerted efforts to refute his arguments. R. Jonathan Eibeschutz, *Binah le-'Ittim, Hilkhot Yom Tov* 1:23, maintains that the ruling established by *Sifra* prohibiting a *kohen* to defile himself in conjunction with the burial of a *nefel* does not at all imply an obligation to inter a *nefel.* On the contrary, asserts R. Jonathan Eibeschutz, it is precisely because there is no obligation to inter either an abortus or a non-viable neonate that a *kohen* may not come into contact with a *nefel.* Thus, according to R. Jonathan Eibeschutz, this comment of *Sifra* serves to establish that a *nefel* does not require burial.[15] R. Jacob Ettlinger, *Teshuvot Binyan Ẓion,* no. 113, points out that, as recorded in *Shulḥan Arukh, Yoreh De'ah* 373:5, some authorities maintain that the *kohen*'s obligation to defile himself through contact with the corpse of a close relative is not limited to defilement in the course of fulfilling his obligation with regard to the burial of the deceased. Hence, absent specific scriptural exclusion, he might well be obligated to defile himself by coming into contact with the *nefel* even if there is no obligation with regard to its interment. In rebuttal, R. Chaim Eleazar Shapiro, *Teshuvot Minḥat Elazar,* no. 52, argues that although, according to these authorities, the *kohen*'s license to defile himself through contact with the corpse is not limited to the necessities of burial, it is nevertheless a function of his obligation to bury a deceased relative. Or, to express the point in somewhat different language, in situations in which an obligation to bury the deceased pertains, defilement is a mandatory requirement and, accordingly, the prohibition against defilement is suspended entirely; when no such obligation exists, the prohibition remains in force. Both *Binyan Ẓion* and R. Jonathan Eibeschutz also cite the Mishnah, *Oholot* 16:5, as reflecting the fact that permanent interment was not provided on behalf of *nefalim.*[16]

Mishkenot Ya'akov, Oraḥ Ḥayyim 526:5, refutes *Magen Avraham*'s argument in another manner. A newborn that dies within the first thirty

---

Hilkhot Yom Tov 1:23.

15. *Binah le-'Ittim*'s analysis of *Sifrei* is rejected by *Teshuvot Zera Emet,* II, no. 138 and *Teshuvot Minḥat Elazar,* I, no. 52. Both argue that, had the Torah wished to exclude *nefalim* from the *mizvah* of interment, the exclusion would have been directly formulated in the context of that commandment rather than in this indirect and hence equivocal manner.

16. R. Jacob Ettlinger's view that there is no obligation to inter a *nefel* by virtue of the biblical commandment regarding burial of the dead is reiterated in *Teshuvot Binyan Ẓion,* no. 119.

days following parturition is regarded as a "doubtful" *nefel,* i.e., although death may ostensibly have been caused by illness or accident, the baby may actually have succumbed, or have been destined to succumb, because of a congenital or gestational defect. If the latter was indeed the case, the neonate was never a viable infant and hence would be categorized as a *nefel.* Nevertheless, burial is required in such instances of doubt because of the possibility that death resulted from post-parturitional causes. Accordingly, since burial *is* required, albeit for reason of doubt, it might be presumed that a father who is a *kohen* is also commanded to defile himself in conjunction with the burial of a neonate. Accordingly, an exegetical source is required to establish that a *kohen* may not defile himself in situations in which burial is mandated only by virtue of doubt. Hence, even though a known *nefel* does not require burial, explicit exclusion of a *nefel* from the requirement that a *kohen* must defile himself in the burial of close relatives must be understood as necessary only for application in situations in which it is not known with certainty that the deceased neonate is a *nefel.* R. Yehudah Asad, *Teshuvot Yehudah Ya'aleh,* no. 361, and R. Ezekiel Landau, *Teshuvot Noda bi-Yehudah, Mahadura Kamma, Oraḥ Ḥayyim,* no. 16, similarly rule that even those authorities who maintain that a *nefel* does not require burial[17] would concede that a child who has been carried to term but who dies within thirty days of birth requires burial by reason of its doubtful status.[18] This is also the position

17. This is indeed *Noda bi-Yehudah*'s own view as expressed in *Teshuvot Noda bi-Yehudah, Mahadura Kamma, Yoreh De'ah,* no. 90; see, however, *infra,* sec. III.

18. The position of *Ḥatam Sofer* with regard to the burial of a child who dies within thirty days of birth is somewhat obscure. In *Teshuvot Ḥatam Sofer, Oraḥ Ḥayyim,* no. 144, he appears to espouse the view that burial of such an infant is required as a matter of doubt. Elsewhere, *Ḥatam Sofer al ha-Torah, She'elot u-Teshuvot,* no. 3 (reprinted in *Likkutei Teshuvot Ḥatam Sofer* [London, 5725], no. 35), *Ḥatam Sofer* rules that burial of a child carried to term but who dies within thirty days of birth is required as a matter of biblical law, not because of doubt but as a matter of halakhic certainty. In that responsum, *Ḥatam Sofer* expresses the view that the fact that the majority of fully developed neonates are viable is sufficient to establish that the child in question is not regarded by Halakhah as a *nefel* even though it died in early infancy. Death of the fully developed neonate is to be attributed to causes other than lack of gestational development. Citing *Tosafot, Ḥullin* 12a, *Ḥatam Sofer* declares that all talmudic references to the fact that a child who dies within thirty days of birth is a "possible" or "doubtful" *nefel* reflect rabbinic stringencies and do not contradict the principle that, for purposes of biblical law, the child is regarded as viable. Since, for purposes of biblical law, the child is not regarded as a *nefel, Ḥatam*

espoused by the interlocutor cited in *Teshuvot Binyan Ẓion,* no. 113. *Binyan Ẓion* himself, however, appears to reject this view and to maintain that, as a matter of normative law as distinct from custom, even a child who dies within thirty days of birth does not require burial.[19]

Binyan Ẓion further cites a statement found in Tractate *Semaḥot* and subsequently quoted by Rosh, *Mo'ed Katan* 3:88, and codified by Rambam, *Hilkhot Avel* 1:6–8, declaring that a *nefel* requires no attention whatsoever (*ein mit'askin imo le-khol davar*) as further evidence that a *nefel* does not require burial. However, *Teshuvot Minḥat Elazar,* 1, no. 42, cogently notes that, as a halakhic principle, the phrase "*ein mit'askin imo le-khol davar*" does not encompass burial. Rambam, *Hilkhot Avel* 1:11, and *Shulḥan Arukh, Yoreh De'ah* 345:1, employ the identical phrase with regard to a suicide. Yet, *Shakh, Yoreh De'ah* 345:1, citing early authorities, carefully notes that the reference is to rending garments and observance of the rites of mourning, but not to dressing the body in shrouds and interment in the ground which *are* required even in the case of a suicide. Similarly, concludes *Minḥat Elazar,* the phrase, as applied to a *nefel,* should be understood as excluding only the obligations to rend garments and to observe the rules of mourning. A careful reading of *Shulḥan Arukh, Yoreh De'ah* 343:8 and *Shakh, Yoreh De'ah* 343:6, indicates that those authorities are of this opinion as well.

Quite apart from textual citations demonstrating the absence of such a requirement, R. Jonathan Eibeschutz finds no cogent reason for requiring interment of a *nefel.* The Gemara, *Sanhedrin* 46b, posits two possible

Sofer forbids exhumation of the body for any purpose, including removal of its foreskin.

19. *Teshuvot Noda bi-Yehudah, Yoreh De'ah, Mahadura Kamma,* no. 90, similarly makes the point that there is no requirement to bury a *nefel* because the consideration of "honor" is not applicable. Cf., however, *Teshuvot Noda bi-Yehudah, Yoreh De'ah, Mahadura Kamma,* no. 164, which states with reference to a child that died within a week of birth that disinterment of the partially decomposed body is prohibited because of the prohibition concerning *nivul ha-met* since "the defilement also affects the living who see that man is destined to similar defilement." In light of both that explanatory comment and *Noda bi-Yehudah*'s failure to require burial of a *nefel* in order to prevent *nivul* it may be argued that *Noda bi-Yehudah* prohibits only disinterment and viewing of a decomposing *nefel* but would not prohibit dissection of a *nefel.* Cf., however, R. Yitzchak Arieli, *Torah she-be-'al Peh,* VI (5724), 50, who does not draw this distinction. *Noda bi-Yehudah*'s ruling regarding disinterment of a *nefel* is contradicted by *Teshuvot Knesset Yeḥezkel,* no. 44. See also *Be'er Heitev, Yoreh De'ah* 263:3 and *Pitḥei Teshuvah, Yoreh De'ah* 263:11.

considerations for obligatory burial of a corpse: (1) burial in the ground serves to expiate the sins of the deceased (*kapparah*); (2) burial serves to obviate the shame and humiliation of the family which would be attendant upon decomposition of the unburied corpse (*bizyona*). Neither of these considerations, asserts R. Jonathan Eibeschutz, applies in the case of a *nefel.* Expiation of sin in the case of a minor child who has died, argues this authority, is in reality expiation of the sins of the parents. Such expiation is absent in the case of a *nefel,* argues R. Jonathan Eibeschutz, "since the heart of the father or mother is not at all pained, as is known," i.e., the emotional anguish suffered by parents upon the loss of a fetus or of a prematurely born child is not comparable to that suffered upon the loss of a child with whom a parental relationship has been established through a process of bonding. Nor, asserts R. Jonathan Eibeschutz, is a comparable sense of shame or humiliation attendant upon non-burial of a fetus.

R. Moses Sofer, *Teshuvot Ḥatam Sofer, Oraḥ Ḥayyim,* no. 144, in endorsing the view that a *nefel* requires some form of burial, readily concedes that the purpose of interring a *nefel* cannot be expiation of sin but nevertheless asserts that burial is required for purposes of avoiding shame and humiliation. *Ḥatam Sofer* maintains, however, that the requirements attendant upon burial of a *nefel* are not identical in every respect with those of other interments. Burial for purposes of *kapparah,* asserts *Ḥatam Sofer,* must be underground; however, *bizyona,* he argues, may be avoided by casting the corpse into a pit. Accordingly, rules *Ḥatam Sofer,* unlike other obligations of burial, a *nefel* may simply be cast into the ground but need not be covered with earth. *Ḥatam Sofer* asserts that it is the latter form of interment that is described by the Mishnah, *Oholot* 16:5, and by the previously cited Tosefta in referring to utilization of a "pit" in association with the interment of *nefalim.*[20]

R. Yekuti'el Yehudah Teitelbaum, *Teshuvot Avnei Ẓedek, Yoreh De'ah,* no. 145, regards the dispute among his predecessors with regard to whether

20. *Ḥatam Sofer* explains that, in forbidding a *kohen* to come into contact with a child born as *a nefel, Sifra* establishes the principle that defilement by a father who is a *kohen* is limited to situations in which interment is mandated for purposes of *kapparah.* A further ramification of this thesis is reflected in *Ḥatam Sofer*'s ruling that a *kohen* may not defile himself through contact with a relative who has expressed a desire not to be buried and who has thereby renounced the *kapparah* attendant upon interment even though such a person must nevertheless be buried because of considerations of *bizyona.* Cf., *Contemporary Halakhic Problems,* I, 125–126.

or not the obligation of burial extends to *nefalim* as entirely academic in nature. In its discussion of burial, the Gemara, *Sanhedrin* 46b, prior to establishing that interment of the dead constitutes a *miẓvah,* depicts burial as required *de minimis* by virtue of custom. From ancient times until the present, it has certainly been the custom among Jews to bury *nefalim.* Since this is the established practice, concludes *Avnei Ẓedek,* failure to accord any particular *nefel* this dignity would redound to the humiliation of both the *nefel* and its family since it would be assumed that the corpse has been neglected because of some stigma associated with its birth. Avoidance of such humiliation is regarded by the Gemara as mandated at least by virtue of *minhag* or custom.

Interment of a *nefel* may, however, be required for reasons entirely extraneous to the *miẓvah* of burying the dead. In another responsum, R. Jacob Ettlinger, *Teshuvot Binyan Ẓion,* no. 119, asserts that burial of a *nefel* is required, not by reason of the *miẓvah* concerning interment of the deceased, but lest a *kohen* inadvertently become defiled by virtue of finding himself under the same roof as a *nefel.* The Mishnah, *Shekalim* 1:1 and *Mo'ed Katan* 2a, requires that a grave or burial site be clearly marked. Citing a number of scriptural sources, the Gemara, *Mo'ed Katan* 5a, indicates that this requirement is normative in nature and is predicated upon a need to prevent defilement of *kohanim.* Accordingly, concludes *Binyan Ẓion,* since a *nefel* causes such defilement, as is evident from the discussion of the Gemara, *Ḥullin* 89b, the corpse of a *nefel* must be buried in order to prevent inadvertent defilement of *kohanim. Binyan Ẓion* notes, however, that if this concern is indeed the sole consideration in requiring burial of a *nefel,* burial need not necessarily be carried out on the very day of the fetus' death. Similarly, interment in the ground would not necessarily be required. Simply depositing the *nefel* above ground in a site known to be off limits to *kohanim,* i.e., a cemetery or mausoleum, would be sufficient for this purpose.

Another consideration that may result in an obligation to inter a *nefel* arises from the fact that it is forbidden to derive any benefit from the human cadaver. As will be shown in the following section, if it is established that it is forbidden to derive benefit from a fetal cadaver, that prohibition would, in and of itself, serve as the basis of a requirement for the burial of a fetal cadaver. An obligation of burial is attendant upon all objects from which it is forbidden to derive benefit (with the exception of those objects which require burning, e.g., *ḥameẓ* on *Pesaḥ*). The requirement for burial is predicated upon a concern that, if not disposed of by burial, some benefit may unwittingly be derived from some such objects.

The minimum gestational age at which a fetus requires interment is not spelled out by any of these authorities. Within the first forty days of conception the nascent embryo is described by the Gemara, *Yevamot* 69b, as "mere water" and hence certainly does not require burial. R. Shalom Mordecai Schwadron, *Teshuvot Maharsham,* IV, no. 146, rules that a three-month fetus does not require burial but fails to state at what age burial is required.[21] R. Joseph Saul Nathanson, in a note included in his letter of approbation upon the publication of the Lemberg 5626 edition of the *Sifrei,* rules that a fetus that has reached a gestational age "of five or six months" requires burial provided that it is "complete in its limbs."[22]

III. *Issur Hana'ah*

Although R. Ezekiel Landau, *Teshuvot Noda bi-Yehudah, Mahadura Kamma, Yoreh De'ah,* no. 90, is among the authorities who maintain that the *mizvah* of interring the deceased does not apply to a *nefel,* he nevertheless agrees that burial is required for an entirely different reason. In a short and rather cryptic statement, *Noda bi-Yehudah* enunciates the position that the ambit of the prohibition against deriving benefit from a corpse extends to a fetal cadaver as well. Accordingly, *Noda bi-Yehudah* rules that burial is required in order to prevent possible infraction of that prohibition.[23] The selfsame provision applies to all objects from which no benefit may be derived.[24]

The prohibition against deriving benefit from a *nefel* is established by R. Jonathan Eibeschutz, *Binah le-'Ittim, Hilkhot Yom Tov* 1:23, in the course of his response to an extraordinary and sorrowful question that was addressed to him. A woman suffered a miscarriage that yielded a grotesquely deformed fetus. The family suffered dire poverty and is described as being "without bread." It occurred to the husband that if he were to travel among "the towns and villages" of the countryside he might display the fetus to the public in the hope that viewers would

21. Cf., however, R. Yekutiel Yehudah Grunwald, *Kol Bo al Avelut,* II, 66.

22. The comments of this authority are also cited in *Ḥayyim u-Berakhah le-Mishmeret Shalom, ot kuf,* sec. 13.

23. This is also the position of R. Jacob Emden, *She'ilat Ya'avez,* I, no. 141, s.v. *ve-teda.*

24. For a discussion of the sources and nature of that requirement see R. Chaim Chizkiyahu Medini, *Sedei Ḥemed, Kelalim, Ma'arekhet ha-Alef,* sec. 306.

reward him with "one or two" copper coins. The interlocutor sought advice with regard to whether it would be permissible for him to support his family by means of what may aptly be categorized as something akin to the side-shows of itinerant circuses of a later age—but, in this case, by means of an exhibition involving the display of a fetal corpse. R. Jonathan Eibeschutz replied that quite apart from the fact that a fetal corpse requires burial, at least by virtue of custom, the proposed enterprise could not be sanctioned because it is forbidden to derive benefit from any human corpse, including the corpse of a fetus.

Approximately a century later, a related but quite different query was addressed to *Binyan Ẓion*. That incident involved the miscarriage of a normal, fully-developed fetus. A Jewish doctor wished to preserve the fetus in whiskey in a glass jar for the purpose of scientific study "as is the wont of physicians." *Binyan Ẓion,* no. 119, cites the earlier responsum of *Noda bi-Yehudah* in which the latter rules unequivocally that no benefit may be derived from a fetal cadaver.[25] *Binyan Ẓion,* however, questions

25. Remarkably, *Binyan Ẓion* does not speak of examination of the fetal cadaver for purposes of deriving scientific information as constituting a form of prohibited benefit. Instead, he confines his discussion to the prohibition against retaining in one's possession an object from which it is forbidden to derive benefit lest some benefit be derived unwittingly. In responsa examining the permissibility of post-mortem examinations in general, both *Ḥatam Sofer, Yoreh De'ah,* no. 336, and *Maharam Shik, Yoreh De'ah,* no. 344, declare that acquiring medical information by means of such procedures constitutes a forbidden benefit. In support of that position *Maharam Shik* cites the ruling found in the Mishnah, *Nedarim* 48a, to the effect that a person who, by means of a vow, generates a prohibition against benefiting from a fellow townsman is forbidden to use scrolls or books that constitute property owned by the community. Quite apparently, the knowledge gleaned from such books is regarded as a "benefit" forbidden to such an individual. This argument is rebutted by R. Yitzchak Arieli, *Torah she-be-'al Peh,* VI (5724), who argues, *inter alia,* that examination of a cadaver for scientific purposes constitutes an "unusual" form of benefit and hence is not forbidden under such circumstances. That position is based upon *Teshuvot Radbaz,* III, no. 548. A permissive view is also espoused by R. Chaim Sofer, *Teshuvot Maḥaneh Ḥayyim,* II, no. 60. The tenor of *Binyan Ẓion's* discussion tends to support this permissive view; see R. Yehudah Leib Graubart, *Ḥavalim be-Ne'imim,* III, no. 64. However, R. Akiva Eger, *Gilyon ha-Shas, Avodah Zarah* 12b, declares that even "unusual" forms of benefit may not be derived from a corpse since the prohibition is not couched as a prohibition against "eating." That principle is codified by Rambam, *Hilkhot Ma'akhalot Asurot* 14:10, with regard to *basar be-ḥalav* and *kila'ei ha-kerem.* Conflicting views regarding the permissibility of deriving "unusual" forms of benefit from a corpse are recorded by R. Mordecai Winkler, *Teshuvot Levushei Mordekhai,* III, *Oraḥ Ḥayyim,* no. 29. See also *infra,* p. 228.

that assertion. The prohibition against deriving benefit from a cadaver is formulated by the Gemara, *Sanhedrin* 47b, on the basis of a *gezeirah shaveh,* a hermeneutic principle applied to the occurrence of an identical term in different contexts. An identical term is used in describing the ritual of the *eglah arufah,* breaking the neck of a heifer in expiation of an unsolved homicide, as prescribed in Deuteronomy 21:4, and in the description of the burial of a human corpse, as recorded in Numbers 20:1, in conjunction with the burial of Miriam. The use of an identical term in both instances is understood by the Gemara as signaling the transposition of the already established prohibition against deriving benefit from the heifer to a prohibition against deriving benefit from a human corpse. *Binyan Ẓion* argues that, since the prohibition is derived from a description of interment, it is forbidden to derive benefit only from a corpse that must be buried in fulfillment of the *miẓvah* of burying the dead. Indeed, *Mishneh le-Melekh, Hilkhot Avel* 14:21, cites Ramban in support of the position that it is permitted to derive benefit from a non-Jewish cadaver for precisely this reason, *viz.,* the locus of the prohibition against deriving benefit indicates that it is a concomitant of the *miẓvah* of burial. Since there is no biblical requirement commanding the interment of a non-Jewish corpse, reasons *Mishneh le-Melekh,* there is no prohibition against deriving benefit from such a corpse. Similarly, if the *miẓvah* of burying the dead does not include burial of a *nefel*—as *Binyan Ẓion* indeed maintains—it then "perhaps" follows, argues *Binyan Ẓion,* that there is no prohibition against deriving benefit from the corpse of a *nefel. Binyan Ẓion* nevertheless refused to grant permission for the contemplated external embalming and preservation of the *nefel* because, as noted earlier, he maintained that burial of a *nefel* is mandated, not as a *miẓvah per se,* but in order to prevent priestly defilement.

R. Moses Sofer, *Teshuvot Ḥatam Sofer, Oraḥ Ḥayyim,* no. 144, tentatively advances an argument identical to that formulated by *Binyan Ẓion* in refutation of R. Jonathan Eibeschutz' contention that there is a prohibition against deriving benefit from a fetal cadaver, but proceeds to refute that argument. *Ḥatam Sofer* contends that the derivation of the prohibition against benefiting from a corpse is not predicated upon the phrase describing the burial of Miriam but from the corresponding phrase describing her death. Accordingly, *Ḥatam Sofer* asserts that the prohibition against deriving benefit from a corpse is not at all contingent upon an obligation of burial.[26] Hence, maintains *Ḥatam Sofer,* it is forbidden to derive benefit

---

26. Nevertheless, *Teshuvot Ḥatam Sofer, Yoreh De'ah,* no. 336, citing *Mishneh*

from a *nefel* even though there is no commandment mandating its burial. Nevertheless, *Ḥatam Sofer* maintains that burial of a *nefel* is required, not in fulfillment of the commandment "for you shall surely bury him on that day" (Deuteronomy 21:23), but because all *issurei hana'ah,* i.e., objects from which benefit may not be derived, require burial lest some forbidden benefit inadvertently be derived therefrom. It is for this reason, opines *Ḥatam Sofer,* that the Samaritans accorded fetuses temporary burial in their homes as described by the Gemara, *Niddah* 56b.[27]

IV. *Issur Hana'ah and Non-Jewish Cadavers*

Certainly, if the prohibition against deriving benefit from a cadaver does not apply to the cadaver of a non-Jew, there can be no such prohibition with regard to the fetus of a non-Jewish mother.

Although there are brief references to this question in earlier sources, the first detailed attempt to analyze this issue and elucidate the views of various early authorities appears in *Mishneh le-Melekh, Hilkhot Avel* 14:21, as one of the issues considered in addressing the propriety of commercial traffic in mummies. The mummies are described as coming from locales which "no Jewish foot has traversed." The most significant source by far is adduced by *Mishneh le-Melekh* in a final comment and described as having come to his attention only subsequent to the completion of his lengthy exposition. That source is a succinct statement of the Palestinian Talmud, *Shabbat* 10:5. The Palestinian Talmud indicates that it is universally held that removal of *issurei hana'ah,* including a corpse, from a private to a public domain on the Sabbath constitutes a culpable offense because removal of the corpse is always an act necessary for its own sake (*ẓerikhah le-gufah*), i.e., in order to be rid of the object from which it is forbidden to derive benefit. The Palestinian Talmud then proceeds to indicate that removal of the corpse of a gentile is not *ipso facto* a culpable offense. The distinction, reasons *Mishneh le-Melekh,* lies in the fact that there exists no prohibition against deriving benefit from a non-Jewish cadaver. Since there is no prohibition against deriving benefit

---

le-Melekh, Hilkhot Avel 14:21, espouses the view that no *issur hana'ah* is associated with a gentile cadaver. However, he makes no attempt to explain the rationale underlying this position. Cf., however, *infra,* and p. 186.

27. See also R. Jacob Emden, *She'ilat Ya'aveẓ,* I, no. 40, s.v. *ve-teda,* who declares in a somewhat cryptic statement that no benefit may be derived from a fetal cadaver. In a parenthetical comment he also declares that a *nefel* requires burial but fails to provide further elucidation of the nature of that obligation.

from the corpse of a gentile, the removal of a gentile corpse is not necessarily undertaken for a purpose intrinsic to such removal and hence is not a culpable offense in any and all circumstances.

The basis for the distinction between Jewish and non-Jewish cadavers is assumed by *Mishneh le-Melekh* to be the previously cited derivation of the *issur hana'ah* attendant upon a corpse. As noted earlier, that derivation is predicated upon the scriptural description of the death and burial of Miriam.[28] Accordingly, concludes *Mishneh le-Melekh,* "it is possible" that the *issur hana'ah* is limited to corpses similar to that of Miriam, i.e., corpses of Jews only.[29]

Although the source is not cited by *Mishneh le-Melekh,* further evidence that there is no prohibition attendant upon deriving benefit from a non-Jewish cadaver can be found in a narrative related by the Gemara, *Bekhorot* 45a. The students of R. Ishmael sought to confirm the number of "organs" found in the human body. In order to do so they boiled the body of a harlot who had been condemned to capital punishment by the civil authorities and counted two hundred and fifty-two "organs." *Teshuvot Ḥatam Sofer, Yoreh De'ah,* no. 336, notes the obvious problem presented in this narrative by the fact that, ostensibly, scientific information was acquired by utilization of a source from which benefit may not legitimately be derived.[30] *Ḥatam Sofer* resolves the problem by commenting that the subject of this experiment was undoubtedly a non-Jewess from whose corpse it is not forbidden to derive benefit.[31]

Mishneh le-Melekh readily concedes that his permissive view with regard to deriving benefit from gentile cadavers is not universally accepted. Although Rambam and *Tur Shulḥan Arukh* both record the prohibition attendant upon deriving benefit from a corpse, neither of these codifiers indicates in any way that the reference is limited to the corpse of a

28. This thesis was earlier formulated by Ramban, *Ketubot* 60a, and *Radbaz, Hilkhot Avel* 14:21.

29. Cf., however, *supra,* note 26.

30. See *supra,* note 25.

31. Actually, *Ḥatam Sofer* seems to have had a talmudic text which read "maidservant" rather than "harlot." He nevertheless states that the reference must be to an "Amalekite maidservant," i.e., a gentile, or possibly to a woman having the status of a Canaanite slave. Assuming that there is no *issur hana'ah* associated with the corpse of a non-Jew, there remains some question with regard to whether this exclusion from that prohibition extends to Canaanite slaves as well; see *Tosafot, Baba Kamma* 10a, and *Mishneh le-Melekh, loc. cit.*

Jew.[32] Even more explicit is the ruling of *Shulḥan Arukh, Yoreh De'ah* 349:1, declaring that no benefit may be derived from the shrouds of "either a gentile or a Jew."[33] It is clear that the prohibition is not limited to shrouds but that the identical restriction applies to the corpse itself.[34] Similarly, *Shitah Mekubeẓet, Ketubot* 60a, cites a statement attributed to Re'ah indicating that "there is no difference between a gentile and a Jew" in this regard. On the other hand, Ramban, *Ketubot* 60a, advances an opposing view in remarking, "I know of no prohibition with regard to a non-Jew since we derive [the prohibition] from Miriam." *Mishneh le-Melekh,* however, notes that in other places Ramban's comments, if not expressly contradictory, are at least equivocal as are the comments of *Teshuvot ha-Rashba,* 1, nos. 364 and 365.[35] Other authorities cited by *Mishneh le-Melekh* who espouse the view that it is not forbidden to derive benefit from the corpse of a non-Jew include *Sefer Yere'im,* no. 310, and *Tosafot, Baba Kamma* 10a.[36]

---

32. See Radbaz, *Hilkhot Avel* 14:21.

33. As is well known, the author of the *Shulḥan Arukh,* R. Joseph Caro, was also the author of *Kesef Mishneh,* a classic commentary on Rambam's *Mishneh Torah.* Curiously, this authority, in his *Kesef Mishneh, Hilkhot Arakhin ve-Ḥaramin* 5:17, seems to assume that no *issur hana'ah* is attendant upon the corpse of a non-Jew. Cf., however, *Mishneh le-Melekh*'s attempt at reinterpretation of the comments of *Kesef Mishneh.*

34. *Mishneh le-Melekh* also cites the interpretation of King David's demand, "Deliver my wife, Michal, whom I betrothed to me for a hundred foreskins of the Philistines" (II Samuel 3:14), recorded in the Gemara, *Sanhedrin* 19b. According to the Gemara's analysis, Saul regarded the marriage to be a nullity *ab initio* because he deemed the foreskins delivered to the bride as consideration to be worthless. David, on the other hand, regarded them as objects of at least minimal value since they could be fed to dogs or cats. Since *issurei hana'ah* cannot be used as consideration for the purpose of contracting a marriage, the implication is that there was no transgression associated with any benefit that might have been derived from the foreskins of the Philistines. *Mishneh le-Melekh* notes, however, that it is possible that the foreskins were severed from the Philistines before they were put to death and hence no prohibition against deriving benefit would have been attendant upon them. Cf., R. Chaim Sofer, *Teshuvot Maḥaneh Ḥayyim, Yoreh De'ah,* II, no. 60, who maintains that no *issur hana'ah* is attendant upon the corpses of prisoners captured in battle. Cf. also, R. Azriel Hildesheimer, *Teshuvot R. Ezri'el, Even ha-Ezer,* no. 30, who avers that no *issur hana'ah* is attendant upon the foreskin of a cadaver, but fails to set forth any substantive demonstration of that thesis.

35. Elsewhere, in his commentary on *Ketubot* 60a, Rashba espouses the position of *Tosafot.* Cf., *Bedek ha-Bayit, Yoreh De'ah* 349.

36. For discussions of this question by latter-day authorities see *Teshuvot*

V. *Rescue of Human Life*

The cataloguing of violations and possible violations of Jewish law incurred in fetal tissue research would constitute little more than an academic excursus were it to be shown that the undertaking falls within the category of *pikuaḥ nefesh,* i.e., preservation of life.[37] Indeed, with the exception of the three cardinal sins, *viz.,* idolatry, homicide and certain sexual offenses, all prohibitions are suspended for purposes of preserving life.

Nevertheless, it would appear that scientific research, even of a nature that might yield a life-saving therapy, is not encompassed within the category of life-saving activity for which suspension of halakhic restrictions is sanctioned. The source upon which such an assessment is predicated is the classic responsum of R. Ezekiel Landau, *Teshuvot Noda bi-Yehudah, Mahadura Tinyana, Yoreh De'ah,* no. 210, concerning the propriety of post-mortem pathological examinations. *Noda bi-Yehudah* states definitively that the suspension of a halakhic prohibition is sanctioned only for the benefit of an already endangered patient or, to use the phrase later coined by R. Moses Sofer, *Teshuvot Ḥatam Sofer, Yoreh De'ah,* no. 336, a *ḥoleh le-faneinu* (lit: "a patient before us"). The concept of a *ḥoleh le-faneinu* is, roughly speaking, the halakhic analogue of the term "present" in the legal concept of a "clear and present danger." Prohibitions may, and indeed must, be ignored for purposes of rescuing an endangered life, but halakhic strictures are not suspended in anticipation of a hypothetical eventuality. *Noda bi-Yehudah* demonstrates the cogency of this position by means of a *reductio ad absurdum.* If halakhic restrictions may be suspended in anticipation of some vaguely possible future benefit to a person as yet not endangered, no prohibition would be meaningful. Compounding medications and manufacture of medical instruments on *Shabbat*

---

ha-Radbaz, III, no. 979; *Teshuvot Maharam Shik, Yoreh De'ah,* no. 349; R. Jacob Emden, *She'ilat Ya'aveẓ,* I, no. 41; R. Meir Shapiro, *Teshuvot Or ha-Me'ir,* no. 74; as well as sources cited by *Pitḥei Teshuvah, Yoreh De'ah* 349:1 and *Sedei Ḥemed, Kelalim, Ma'arekhet ha-Mem,* no. 103.

Pitḥei Teshuvah also cites *Teshuvot Even Shoham,* no. 30, who maintains that although the *issur hana'ah* pertaining to a Jewish corpse is biblical in nature, the prohibition regarding a non-Jewish corpse is of rabbinic origin; cf., *Sedei Ḥemed, loc. cit.,* s.v. *ve-katav.* See also R. Jacob Emden, *She'ilat Ya'aveẓ,* I, no. 41.

37. See R. Isaac Liebes, *Teshuvot Bet Avi,* III, no. 132, who, without citing considerations of *pikuaḥ nefesh,* relies upon the position of *Magen Avraham* in permitting the autopsy of a *nefel* in the hope of discovering a means of enabling the mother to carry subsequent fetuses to term.

could conceivably lead to the saving of lives in an unanticipated emergency. Moreover, cooking on the Sabbath, for example, would be justified on the grounds that perhaps some person might take sick and require cooked food. Children, in particular, are prone to various illnesses that are potentially life-threatening and hot water or cooked food might well be required in treating them. There is virtually no act which might not, in some presently unanticipated way, contribute to the preservation of life.[38] In order to justify violation of a halakhic stricture there must be a discernible connection between the contemplated act and elimination of an existing danger. Accordingly, *Noda bi-Yehudah* rules that an autopsy may not be performed in the vague hope that some potentially life-saving knowledge may be gained serendipitously in the process of a post-mortem examination.

However, *Noda bi-Yehudah* carefully notes that were the surgeon to have under his care another patient awaiting surgery for the same condition that afflicted the deceased, and were the surgeon to require an autopsy in order to discern the proper site at which to incise the abdomen or in order to minimize the surgical trauma, the autopsy would be perfectly permissible. The condition which must be satisfied is the cogent anticipation of obtaining otherwise unknown and unobtainable information which, in turn, may lead to life-saving therapeutic treatment. Hence, it might appear that most forms of basic research fail to fall within those parameters since such research is not designed to cure any particular patient presently afflicted by disease. Such a conclusion, however, is not entirely accurate. Although the existence of a presently afflicted patient is an obvious instance in which suspension of halakhic strictures is warranted, it is by no means the only example. It is entirely possible that prophylactic measures involving violations of Jewish law may be necessary in times of epidemic in order to prevent the spread of contagious disease. In such situations, the individuals requiring protection are as yet entirely healthy. Yet, *Ḥazon Ish* had no difficulty in sanctioning such prophylactic measures even in instances in which the epidemic is, as yet, an immediate threat only in a neighboring town.[39] The reasoning appears to be quite clear: Although there is no "*patient* before us" there is indeed a "*danger* before us" even though the danger is geographically removed.

A further amplification of this principle is reflected in the ruling of the late Chief Rabbi of Israel, Rabbi Iser Yehudah Unterman, regarding

38. See also *Ḥazon Ish, Kovez̧ Iggerot,* I, no. 207.

39. See *Ḥazon Ish, Oholot,* no. 22, sec. 32.

organ banks in time of war[40] and in his ruling regarding preparation and transport of ammunition in time of danger.[41] Indeed the selfsame principle is involved in setting up military field hospitals on the Sabbath. Army units preparing for battle customarily take with them material and equipment to be used in setting up field hospitals. The Chief Rabbinate was asked whether such preparations may be carried out, despite the halakhic infractions involved, in light of the fact that at the time at which those actions are undertaken no casualties have yet occurred and, indeed, no shot has as yet been fired. The Chief Rabbinate had no qualms in sanctioning such procedures. The reasoning is self-evident: Military conflicts inevitably yield casualties. Although there is no "patient before us" and despite the fact that, prior to commencement of hostilities, there is not even a "danger before us," the very determination to engage in battle constitutes a clearly identifiable "*cause* of danger" which is present here and now.

Another extension of this principle is found in responsa discussing provisions required for meeting public health needs on *Shabbat.* In many outlying settlements in Israel there is but a single qualified health-care provider in residence, usually a nurse. Not infrequently, an emergency occurs on *Shabbat* and, in order to monitor the patient's condition and administer interim medical care, the nurse must accompany the patient in the vehicle transporting the patient to the nearest hospital. During her absence there is no trained professional qualified to provide emergency care should any other inhabitant become afflicted by illness or suffer an accident. May the nurse ignore *Shabbat* prohibitions in order to return to her post? At first glance, the situation would seem analogous to *Noda bi-Yehudah*'s hypothetical situation involving, for example, a mother's concern that her child might become ill. Nevertheless, a number of rabbinic authorities distinguish between these differing situations on the basis of statistical probabilities. The likelihood that a child in any specific family will become afflicted with a life-threatening illness on any given *Shabbat* is extremely remote. Hence the mother's preparation for that eventuality cannot be categorized as an act of *pikuaḥ nefesh.* However, when past

40. See *Torah she-be-'al Peh,* XI (5729), 14, reprinted in *No'am,* XIII (5730), 4.

41. See *Ha-Torah ve-ha-Medinah,* V, 29. Cf., also, *idem, Shevet me-Yehudah* (Jerusalem, 5715), p. 49. See also *No'am,* V (5722), 283, for R. Benjamin Rabinowitz-Teumim's analysis of R. Israel Salanter's well-known ruling directing the entire population of Vilna to refrain from fasting on *Yom Kippur* during the 5621 cholera epidemic in that city. Cf., however, R. Moshe Sternbuch, *Mo'adim u-Zemanim,* II, no. 140, and *supra,* p. 142, note 32.

experience points to a significant likelihood that one person in a large population of individuals will be stricken in such a manner, a number of rabbinic decisors have ruled that the statistical probability of the occurrence of such an event is sufficient to warrant the nurse's return to her post. In effect, present awareness of the statistical probability of impending danger renders the danger itself present in nature.[42]

Application of these criteria to at least some forms of fetal tissue research yields a similar conclusion. Actuarial figures demonstrate beyond cavil that longevity anticipation of diabetics is significantly diminished. There is significant medical evidence indicating that the same is true of patients afflicted by Parkinson's disease.[43] Accordingly, the eradication of those maladies must be regarded as a matter of *pikuaḥ nefesh.* If, as is probably the case, the benefits of fetal tissue research will be realized within a time-span that would provide treatment for patients already afflicted with these conditions, the requirement of *ḥoleh le-faneinu,* even in its literal sense, would be satisfied. Even if this is not the case, the statistical certainty of presently healthy persons succumbing to the complications of those diseases would serve to warrant suspension of possibly applicable strictures of Jewish law in order to perfect a cure.

One caveat is, however, in order. Just as antibiotics may not be manufactured on *Shabbat* on the nebulous claim that they may be required for some unanticipated emergency that might occur on that day, so also proscribed acts having no direct bearing upon the cure or welfare of an already ill person may not be performed in the vague hope that, serendipitously, some benefit may result. The issue requiring further analysis is the delineation of precise criteria to be employed in distinguishing between procedures that may be instituted even in face of halakhic strictures in order to preserve life and procedures that may not be instituted even under such circumstances. Particular experimental procedures involving infractions of Halakhah may then either be sanctioned, or not be sanctioned, depending upon whether actual demonstrated efficacy is required in order to sanction such procedures or whether a cogent scientific basis for as-

42. See R. Yisra'el Aryeh Zalmanowitz, *No'am,* IV (5721), 175–178; and R. Joshua Neuwirth, *Shemirat Shabbat ke-Hilkhatah,* I (Jerusalem, 5139) 40:71. See also *ibid.,* 40:67 and 40:69. Cf., R. Isaac Liebes, *Halakhah u-Refu'ah,* III (5743), 73, reprinted in *idem, Teshuvot Bet Avi,* IV, *Oraḥ Ḥayyim,* no. 16.

43. See Fletcher McDowell and Jesse Cederbaum, "The Extrapyramidal System and Disorders of Movement," *Baker's Clinical Neurology,* ed. Robert Joynt (Philadelphia, 1988), p. 32; and J. Kurtzke, *Neurology,* vol. 38, no. 10 (October, 1988), pp. 1558–61.

suming that the protocol may lead to therapeutic success is itself sufficient for this purpose.

Analysis of this question requires a detailed examination of the Mishnah, *Yoma* 83a, which discusses a remedy used in antiquity in the treatment of rabies and of the talmudic commentaries thereupon. Resolution of this significant question is important not only for purposes of determining the propriety of fetal tissue research but also for determining the propriety of undertaking other experimental procedures in violation of *Shabbat* restrictions and the like. It is also crucial in determining whether a patient is under obligation to seek a particular therapy. This issue, which is essentially extraneous to the present endeavor and has ramifications far beyond the issue at hand, merits independent examination and will be addressed in the following chapter.

VI. *Abortion For Preservation of Human Life*

The foregoing notwithstanding, not every prohibition may be ignored for purposes of preserving life. Some time ago, the media presented a sensationalized report of a woman who sought to conceive a child in contemplation of undergoing an abortion in order to harvest neural tissue for the purpose of a transplant in an effort to cure her father of Parkinson's disease. Destruction of a fetus for the purpose of saving the life of the mother has received a great deal of attention in rabbinic literature.[44] The Mishnah, *Oholot* 7:6, declares that when "hard travail" of labor endangers the life of the mother an embryotomy may be performed in order to save her life. So long as the head of the child or a major portion of its body has not emerged from the uterus, the life of the unborn fetus may be sacrificed in order to preserve that of the mother. However, in codifying the principle enunciated in the Mishnah, Rambam, *Hilkhot Roẓeaḥ* 1:9, is not content to state simply that the life of the fetus is subordinate to that of the mother but adds a further explanation. He describes the child as being, in effect, an aggressor engaged in "pursuing" the life of the mother. Rambam's incorporation of this rationale in his *Mishneh Torah* has given rise to considerable discussion and analysis and is the primary source for the view of numerous authorities who maintain that Jewish law forbids even therapeutic abortion in non-life-threatening situations. By invoking the "law of pursuit" Rambam indicates that the life of the fetus is forfeit

44. For a survey of this literature see *Contemporary Halakhic Problems,* I, 347–354.

only because it is, in some sense, an aggressor. When the fetus is not the proximate cause of the threat to the life of the mother, this rationale does not apply. Similarly, the law of pursuit can be invoked to eliminate the "pursuer" only when failure to intervene will render loss of the victim's life a virtual certainty.[45] Rambam's comment serves to establish that feticide is a form of homicide, albeit a form of homicide that does not entail capital punishment. Rambam's position is the source which led the Chief Rabbinate of Israel, in the course of public debate of abortion legislation, to declare the performance of an abortion to be an act of murder.[46] There are, to be sure, authorities who regard the halakhic strictures against feticide as based upon other prohibitions; according to those authorities, an abortion may be performed in order to preserve the life of the mother in all instances of *pikuaḥ nefesh,* even in situations in which the fetus is not a "pursuer."[47] Indeed, some authorities permit therapeutic abortion for considerations of maternal health as distinct from maternal life.[48]

However, this is the case only with regard to Jewish law as it applies to Jews. Judaism also posits a series of obligations binding upon non-Jews, *viz.,* the "Seven Commandments of the Sons of Noah," sometimes known as the Noahide Code. Feticide is an even more serious offense in the Noahide Code than it is in Jewish law as applied to Jews. The prohibition against feticide as applied to non-Jews is derived from Genesis 9:6 which in talmudic exegesis is rendered as "He who sheds the life of a man within a man, his blood shall be shed." "Who is 'a man within a man?'" queries the Gemara, *Sanhedrin* 57b. The immediately ensuing response, "This is a fetus within its mother's innards," serves to establish, not only that feticide is forbidden to non-Jews, but that it constitutes a capital crime in the Noahide Code.

Thus, it would appear that, in the Noahide Code, no distinction is made

45. See Rashi, *Sanhedrin* 72a, s.v. *hakhi garsinan,* and Rashi, *Pesaḥim* 2b, s.v. *hakhi ka-amar; Teshuvot Koaḥ Shor,* no. 20; and *Iggerot Mosheh, Ḥoshen Mishpat,* II, no. 69, sec. 2, s.v. *ve-la-khen.* Cf., *Teshuvot Aḥi'ezer,* I, no. 23, sec. 2. See also *Tiferet Yisra'el, Oholot, Bo'az* 7:10. Cf., however, *Bi'ur ha-Gra, Ḥoshen Mishpat* 388:74 and this writer's article in *Or ha-Mizraḥ,* Nisan-Tammuz, 5747, pp. 260–261.

46. *JTA Daily News Bulletin,* December 7, 1974. This is also the position of many other contemporary rabbinic authorities, including the late Rabbi Moses Feinstein, *Iggerot Mosheh, Ḥoshen Mishpat,* nos. 69 and 71.

47. See *Contemporary Halakhic Problems,* I, 347–354.

48. See *Contemporary Halakhic Problems,* I, 354–356.

between the status of a fetus and that of a neonate. An apparent ramification of ascription of an identical halakhic status to both a fetus and an infant is a significant disparity between Jewish law and Noahide law with regard to measures to be taken when pregnancy or parturition would entail loss of the mother's life. As has been shown, in Jewish law, the fetus is regarded as "a pursuer" whose life is subordinate to that of the mother. However, the previously cited Mishnah, *Oholot* 7:6, concludes with the statement that once the forehead or the major portion of the body has entered the birth canal "one does not set aside one life for another." Once the child is regarded as having been born, the two lives are regarded as equal and one can not be sacrificed in order to preserve the other. The implication is that, prior to birth, the fetus is not a "life" (*nefesh*) in the full sense of that term and hence is subordinate to the life of the mother in status and value. The fact that Jewish law does not impose the death penalty for the crime of feticide serves to underscore that the fetus is not a "*nefesh*" in the full legal sense of the term. However, under Noahide law, feticide is a capital offense. Hence, it would seem that, for a non-Jew, the fetus is indeed a "*nefesh.*" If so, insofar as Noahides are concerned, the fetus, even in its gestational state, is as much the moral and legal equal of the mother as is the child whose head has emerged in the birth canal. Accordingly, it should follow that a non-Jew may not terminate a pregnancy even in situations in which failure to do so would inevitably result in maternal death.[49] Despite the weight of this argument, *Tosafot, Sanhedrin* 59a, without formulating the grounds for their reservation, express doubt with regard to whether the Noahide prohibition against feticide applies in situations in which failure to terminate pregnancy will result in the loss of the life of the mother.[50] The normative rule is

49. For a discussion of the principles governing situations in which failure to intervene will result in the loss of both mother and child see *Contemporary Halakhic Problems,* I, 356–361.

50. Although *Tosafot* fail to elucidate the nature of the doubt expressed, two sides of the question may be formulated on the basis of a number of different theses:

1. The question may hinge on the nature of the prohibition against feticide as formulated in the Noahide Code. If, in extending the death penalty to the killing of the fetus in the Noahide Code, the Torah intends to indicate that insofar as Noahides are concerned fetal life is to be considered on a par with other human life, then it follows that a Noahide may not sacrifice a fetal life in order to rescue the mother. The law of pursuit cannot be invoked if, under the Noahide Code, the fetus is considered to be a "*nefesh*" just as the law of pursuit does not apply in Jewish law after the emergence

of the fetal head in the birth canal at which juncture the fetus is deemed a "*nefesh*" according to the Sinaitic code. On the other hand, the Torah may not deem the fetus to be a "*nefesh*" even with regard to Noahides, but nevertheless have ordained feticide as a capital crime under the Noahide Code as a transgression totally unrelated to the concept of taking human life. If the Noahide prohibition is extraneous to the exhortation against homicide, it follows that the life of the mother would take precedence over that of the fetus. Since feticide is not encompassed within the prohibition against homicide, the prohibition against feticide, no less than other prohibitions, may be set aside in order to preserve human life.

2. Homicide constitutes one of the exceptions to the general rule that prohibitions of law are suspended for purposes of preserving human life. The rationale is expressed by the Gemara, *Sanhedrin* 74a, as reflecting the principle "Why do you deem your blood to be sweeter than the blood of your fellow?" Although feticide is a capital offense in the Noahide Code, it remains the case that it is a lesser offense under the Sinaitic covenant. Since, under Jewish law as applied to Jews, feticide is not a capital crime, it may be deduced that fetal life is intrinsically not equal in worth to maternal life. On the contrary, the life of the mother is "sweeter" than the life of the fetus, as is manifest in the comparable provisions of the Sinaitic Code. If so, the life of the fetus may be sacrificed in order to preserve the life of the mother even though it is regarded as a *nefesh* in the Noahide Code.
3. Assuming that, even in the Noahide Code, the taking of a fetal life is not entirely comparable to murder, it is clear that a Noahide would be permitted to commit this infraction in order to save his own life. The Gemara, *Sanhedrin* 74b, states that a Noahide may commit any transgression, including idolatry, at least in private, in order to save his own life. Nevertheless, *Minḥat Ḥinnukh,* no. 296, asserts that a Noahide may not transgress any provision of the Noahide Code in order to preserve the life of his fellow since he is not bound by the biblical commandment "Nor shall you stand idly by the blood of your fellow" (Leviticus 19:16). *Teshuvot Koaḥ Shor,* no. 20, p. 33a, espouses an opposing view and asserts that a Noahide may transgress any commandment, including the three cardinal sins, in order to save the life of his fellow. The doubt expressed by *Tosafot* may reflect these two opposing views.
4. *Minḥat Ḥinnukh,* no. 296, opines that the license granted a Noahide to transgress prohibitions of the Noahide Code in order to preserve his own life, as indicated by the Gemara, *Sanhedrin* 74b, is limited to situations in which the Noahide is presented with a choice between transgression and martyrdom but does not include situations in which there exists no *force majeure,* e.g., situations involving life-threatening illness. A similar distinction is made by Rambam, *Hilkhot Yesodei ha-Torah* 5:4 and 5:6, with regard to transgression of the three cardinal sins. A person is required to sacrifice his life rather than transgress one of those commandments regardless of whether the threat to his life is in the form of *force majeure* or illness. Nevertheless, in instances in which the individual has acted incor-

cogently formulated by R. Isaac Schorr, *Teshuvot Koaḥ Shor,* no. 20, p. 32, who concludes that, at best, the matter remains in doubt and hence active intervention to extinguish the life of the fetus cannot be sanctioned.

---

rectly and has transgressed in order to save his life, Rambam draws a distinction *post factum* between *force majeure* and therapeutic violation. Rambam rules that, although his action is not sanctionable, the individual in question is not subject to capital punishment if his act was compelled by *force majeure.* However, if the individual transgressed in order to save his life in the absence of external coercive force he is fully culpable and is to be punished in accordance with his act.

5. Assuming that, under the Noahide Code, a fetus is not a *nefesh,* and assuming that in the Noahide Code the prohibition against feticide is not suspended for the purpose of saving human life, the issue of whether the taking of a fetal life is warranted when the fetus is an aggressor remains an open question. *Teshuvot Ben Yehudah,* no. 21, and *Sedei Ḥemed, Kelalim, Ma'arekhet ha-Gimel,* no. 44, maintain that the law of pursuit is not operative in the Noahide Code. However, *Minḥat Ḥinnukh,* no. 296, and *Teshuvot Koaḥ Shor,* no. 20, p. 32b, maintain that the law of pursuit extends to Noahides as well. This position seems to be reflected in the language of Rambam, *Hilkhot Melakhim* 9:4. See also R. Chaim Soloveichik, *Ḥiddushei Rabbeinu Ḥayyim ha-Levi al ha-Rambam, Hilkhot Roẓeaḥ* 1:9. See also *Teshuvot Bet Yiẓḥak, Yoreh De'ah,* II, no. 162, sec. 4; and R. Meir Dan Plocki, *Ḥemdat Yisra'el* (New York, 5725), p. 178. These conflicting views may be reflected in the doubt expressed by *Tosafot,* i.e., *Tosafot* may subscribe to a view identical to that of Rambam, *viz.,* that the fetus may be sacrificed in order to save the live of the mother only by operation of the law of pursuit, but be in doubt with regard to whether the law of pursuit is incorporated in the Noahide Code.

6. *Koaḥ Shor* notes that the Gemara, *Sanhedrin* 74b, states that a Noahide may commit any transgression including idolatry in order to preserve his own life and contends that the extension of this provision to encompass homicide as well is the subject of the doubt expressed by *Tosafot.* R. Samuel Yaffe-Ashkenazi, *Yefeh To'ar* (Furth, 5452), *Bereishit* 44:5, argues that this dispensation extends to murder as well. However, *Mishneh le-Melekh, Hilkhot Melakhim* 10:2, states explicitly that the taking of another's life in order to save one's own is forbidden even to Noahides since with regard to homicide this injunction is not derived from the commandment to "sanctify the Name" but is based upon the *a priori* principle, "Why do you deem your blood to be sweeter than that of your fellow?" See also R. Meir Simchah ha-Kohen of Dvinsk, *Or Sameaḥ, Hilkhot Yesodei ha-Torah* 5:6. See also *Pitḥei Teshuvah, Yoreh De'ah* 155:4, who discusses the question of whether or not the principle "and you shall live by them" applies to Noahides. See also *Minḥat Ḥinnukh,* no. 286 and *Parashat Derakhim, Derush* 2. The grandson of the author of *Koaḥ Shor* raises this point in a note appended to this responsum, p. 35a, but fails to cite *Mishneh le-Melekh.*

Since human life may be sacrificed only when there is firm and unequivocal authority for doing so, *Koaḥ Shor* rules that the life of a fetus must remain inviolate.[51]

Thus, insofar as application of the relevant halakhic principles is concerned, a non-Jew could not be permitted to perform an abortion even for the purpose of saving another life. Utilization of fetal tissue for purposes of preserving life in no way exculpates the abortion performed as a means of acquiring the tissue.

VII. *Benefiting From Unethical Research*

Nevertheless, regardless of the unethical nature of the abortion itself, once it has been performed there need be no compunction with regard to utilization of the abortus in a manner otherwise consistent with applicable provisions of Jewish law. It is readily conceded by all that organs derived from a homicide may be used for any purpose for which organs obtained from the corpse of a person who has died of natural causes may be used and that such use in no way entails complicity in the act of homicide.[52] *Mutatis mutandis,* the same conclusion must be drawn with regard to use of fetal tissue obtained by means of an abortion. Although performance of an abortion is a grievous offense, Jewish law does not posit a "Miranda principle" or an exclusionary rule that would, *post factum,* preclude use of illicitly procured tissue for an otherwise sanctioned purpose.[53]

It has been argued that research upon fetal tissue derived from an induced abortion implies moral acquiescence or complicity with the antecedent abortion.[54] Similar moral concern has been raised with regard to application of research data derived from the barbarous activities of Nazi physicians during World War II.[55] A number of scientists and staff

51. See also *Contemporary Halakhic Problems,* I, 369. Cf., R. Aryeh Leib Grossnass, *Ha-Pardes,* Shevat 5732, and *idem, Lev Aryeh,* II, no. 32, who suggests that the "doubt" expressed by *Tosafot* is limited to the destruction of the fetus of a Jewish mother in order to save her life, but does not extend to the abortion of a non-Jewish fetus. This view is not supported by convincing argument or by earlier sources.

52. Cf., James Bopp and James T. Burtchaell, "Statement of Dissent," p. 68, note 99.

53. See this writer's article in *Or ha-Mizraḥ,* Nisan-Tammuz 5748, pp. 297f.

54. See James Bopp and James T. Burtchaell, "Statement of Dissent," pp. 63ff.

55. See *infra,* chap. 10.

members of the Environmental Protection Agency vociferously protested a research program based upon the findings of German experiments with phosgene gas on prisoners of war. The German experiments involved exposure of fifty-two prisoners to the gas in order to test a possible antidote and led to the death of four prisoners.[56] As a result, the chief of the Environmental Protection Agency barred inclusion in his agency's report of any data acquired from the German research. The moral misgivings expressed by these researchers were that "to use such data debases us all as a society, gives such experiments legitimacy, and implicitly encourages others, perhaps in less exacting societies, to perform unethical human 'experiments.'"[57] Shortly thereafter, Dr. Robert Pozos, the director of the hypothermia research laboratory of the University of Minnesota announced his intention to republish, along with his own analysis, a Nazi study in which concentration camp inmates were subjected to extreme cold in order to show that study's possible application to his own research on ways to save persons swept into icy seas.[58] Reaction to this announcement was swift. Dr. Daniel Callahan, director of the Hastings Institute, emphatically declared, "We should under no circumstances use the information. It was gained in an immoral way." Abraham H. Foxman, national director of the Anti-Defamation League of B'nai B'rith, concurred in stating, "I think it goes to legitimizing the evil done. I think the findings are tainted by horror and misery."[59] This issue was the subject of a conference sponsored by the Center for Biomedical Ethics of the University of Minnesota in May, 1989.[60]

As will be explained at length in chapter ten of this volume, there is, however, no principle of Jewish law or ethics that would preclude use of information gleaned as a result of unethical research.[61] By the same

56. *New York Times,* March 23, 1988, p. A1.

57. *Ibid.,* p. A17. See also *BioLaw, Updates and Special Sections,* vol. 2, no. 13 (April, 1988), p. U:873.

58. *New York Times,* May 12, 1988, p. A9.

59. *Loc. cit.*

60. See *New York Times,* May 21, 1989, p. A34 and *JTA Community News Reporter,* May 26, 1989.

61. Articles authored by R. Abraham Meir Israel of Vienna and R. Tibor Stern of Miami Beach prohibiting medical use of the fruits of Nazi research appear in the Tishri 5750 issue of *Ha-Pardes.* Those contributions, while emotionally heart-rending, are nevertheless halakhically irrelevant. The arguments presented are as follows:

1. The experiments conducted by the Nazis were diabolical in nature and

token, the absence of an exclusionary principle means that there is no moral barrier preventing the research scientist or the manufacturer of pharmaceutical products from utilizing fetal tissue procured by means of induced abortion for purposes that are otherwise moral, provided that such utilization of fetal tissue does not involve collusion in, or encourage-

---

were not undertaken for purposes of scientific investigation. As a result they yielded no reliable information.

2. It is forbidden to derive benefit from a cadaver.
3. Halakhah, as recorded in Rambam, *Hilkhot Yesodei ha-Torah* 5:6, prohibits therapeutic measures involving idol worship, certain forms of sexual licentiousness and homicide.
4. The Gemara, *Sanhedrin* 45b, declares that a stone, gallows, sword or other object used for purposes of execution must be buried. Accordingly, *Sefer Ḥasidim,* no. 1,113, rules that no benefit may be derived from a sword found with slain Jews and that it must be interred. On the basis of the above-cited talmudic statement, *She'ilat Ya'aveẓ,* II, no. 158, ruled that it is forbidden to fashion a slaughterer's knife from an executioner's sword. Similarly, R. Meshullem Roth, *Kol Mevaser,* I, no. 58, forbade a *ḥazan* to fashion a *gartel* (belt worn during prayer) from a noose preserved on Mount Zion as a relic of the Holocaust.
5. R. Judah he-Hasid, in his ethical will, addenda, sec. 6, reiterates the prohibition against deriving benefit from an object used to commit murder and adds that such use entails a grave danger to the user and to his entire household.

Applied to the question at hand these arguments constitute a non-sequitur. Questions concerning the reliability and medical value of studies performed in concentration camps are clearly a matter for scientific determination and entirely outside the purview of rabbinic scholars. There is certainly no halakhic or theological reason why such research could not have yielded scientifically valid data. Whether in actuality this was or was not the case is a matter for scientists to determine.

The prohibition against deriving benefit from a cadaver or from an object used to accomplish an act of homicide is suspended in cases of *pikuaḥ nefesh.* More significantly, the arguments fail to distinguish between use of the cadaver itself or of the actual murder weapon for therapeutic purposes and use of mere information gleaned either before or after death. Even those authorities who forbid visual examination of a corpse for purposes of scientific study as constituting a forbidden form of benefit recognize that such information, once obtained, may be used for beneficial purposes since it is the derivation of knowledge from the corpse that constitutes a forbidden benefit not its subsequent application.

Most egregious is the citation of the prohibition against homicide even in a therapeutic context. The sources cited serve only to support the proposition that the three cardinal transgressions may not be breached even for purposes of saving a life. Those sources most certainly do not establish a prohibition *post factum* against utilizing even tissue or organs of a homicide victim for purposes of preserving a life.

ment of, the abortion itself.

VIII. *Federal Funding*

However, it cannot be gainsaid that, in point of fact, fetal tissue research programs require procurement of significant numbers of fetuses that are the product of non-therapeutic abortions. Federal sponsorship of fetal tissue research involving fetuses obtained in this manner adds an entirely new dimension with regard to the question of the propriety of such research.

Generation of the potential for preservation of life through the intermediacy of abortion must perforce diminish the odium associated with that procedure. As an instrument for good, the act of abortion will not be perceived as an unmitigated evil. A torn, tormented and guilt-ridden young woman struggling with the moral dilemma associated with a resolution of the question of whether "to abort or not to abort" will now have forced upon her one additional consideration to be added to the potpourri of social, economic and moral forces pushing and tugging in opposite directions. Moreover, involvement of prestigious institutions and respected members of the scientific community coupled with implied governmental approval, as evidenced by the NIH funding of research in which utilization of the aborted fetus is crucial, combine to endow the abortion procedure with an aura of moral acceptability. Surely, in at least some instances, those factors will tip the decision-maker's scales against preservation of the fetus.[62]

---

62. It is certainly not uncommon for women generally disposed against abortion to decide to terminate an unwanted pregnancy. Such women are reported to experience a significant degree of cognitive dissonance. See Michael B. Bracken, Lorraine V. Klerman and Mary Ann Bracken, "Abortion, Adoption, or Motherhood: An Empirical Study of Decision-Making During Pregnancy," *American Journal of Obstetrics and Gynecology,* vol. 130, no. 3 (February, 1978), pp. 256–257; and Michael B. Bracken, "The Stability of the Decision to Seek Induced Abortion," *Research on the Fetus,* HEW Publication No. (OS) 76–128, p. 16–15. Thus it is not surprising that conflict during decision-making is reported as being quite prevalent. *Ibid.,* p. 16–16. The percentage of women who undergo at least one change of decision with regard to abortion is reported to be approximately one third. *Ibid.,* pp. 16–2 and 16–16. Given the vacillation which is known to exist, any relevant factor may become decisive in the decision-making procedure. Although, in the absence of statistical data, it is impossible to predict the percentage of women to whom beneficial aspects of participation in fetal tissue transplantation projects may become the factor in the absence of which a final determination to abort would not occur, it is certain that for at least some women this will be the

It must be emphasized that these objections would not necessarily obtain in a situation involving organ tissue obtained from a homicide victim. Homicide is recognized by all, and commonly by the perpetrator himself, as a heinous offense and as a crime against society. From the societal perspective, homicide is aberrant behavior. Homicide is a crime and the murderer, if apprehended, will be prosecuted to the fullest extent of the law. Utilization of the body of the victim for scientific purposes could not conceivably be construed as an endorsement of the antecedent homicide. Nor could such utilization, or the contemplation of such utilization, possibly lead to an increase in the incidence of homicide. Abortion, on the other hand, is regarded in some sectors of our society as innocuous and condoned as a morally neutral act. Establishment of a government program involving procurement of abortuses will assuredly be construed as a governmental seal of moral approval. Such approval could not reasonably be imputed to aberrant, socially condemned acts of homicide. Moreover, the sheer number of abortions required to sustain such research programs serves to magnify the immoral nature of the offense. We are confronted, not by isolated, individual acts of immorality in which the product of the act can be isolated from the act itself, but with programs and policies predicated upon the assumption that abortions are performed as a matter of course and are performed in inordinately large numbers.

Recognition that governmental funding will inevitably result in an increase in the number of abortions performed gives rise to a significant issue with regard to the legitimacy of such sponsorship. The question is directly analogous to that of whether a person may rescue a life knowing full well that the life of a fellow human being will be extinguished through the resultant act of another malevolent individual. Questions of that nature have been addressed in halakhic literature over a period of centuries and, most recently, were the subject of a number of responsa authored during the period of the Holocaust. Numerous sources indicate that, although a person may seek to avoid potential danger even if, as a result, the selfsame danger will befall another individual, nevertheless, once the danger is actually experienced he may not seek to escape from it if, as a result, another person will be even indirectly endangered.[63]

The question with regard to federal funding of fetal research is further

---

case.

63. See *Teshuvot Maharibal,* II, no. 40; *Shakh, Ḥoshen Mishpat* 163:18; *Teshuvot Noda bi-Yehudah, Mahadura Tinyana, Yoreh De'ah,* no. 74; and R. Zevi Hirsch Meisels, *Teshuvot Mekadshei ha-Shem,* I (Chicago, 5715), *Sha'ar Maḥmadim,* sec. 1.

complicated by virtue of the moral responsibility devolving upon Noahides to prevent acts of feticide. In defining the commandment of "*dinin,*" the last of the Seven Commandments of the Noahide Code, Rambam, *Hilkhot Melakhim* 9:14, states that the essence of the commandment is to establish courts for the purpose of punishing those who transgress the first six of the seven commandments "and to admonish the populace." Admonition, exhortation and prior restraint are intrinsic to fulfillment of this commandment. Since Noahides are not normatively bound to engage in acts of rescue by virtue of the commandment "Nor shall you stand idly by the blood of your fellow" (Leviticus 19:16) the principle of *pikuaḥ nefesh* does not function as a countervailing consideration. Thus it follows that any action or policy that would lead to an increment in the number of abortions performed is antithetical to the obligation to "admonish the populace" which, according to Rambam, is normatively binding upon all non-Jews.

Chapter IX

Experimental Procedures: The Concept of *Refu'ah Bedukah*

The Lord has brought drugs out of the earth; with them the physician heals a wound and with them the apothecary compounds medicaments.
BEREISHIT RABBAH 10:6

Judaism teaches that the value of human life is supreme and takes precedence over virtually all other considerations. This attitude is most eloquently summed up in a talmudic passage, *Sanhedrin* 37a, regarding the creation of Adam: "Therefore only a single human being was created in the world, to teach that if any person has caused a single soul of Israel to perish, Scripture regards him as if he had caused an entire world to perish; and if any human being saves a single soul of Israel, Scripture regards him as if he had saved an entire world." Human life is not a good to be preserved as a condition of other values but an absolute, basic and precious good in its own right. The obligation to preserve life is commensurately all-encompassing.

The halakhic provision that all prohibitions, save the three cardinal transgressions, are set aside for purposes of saving a life is a firmly established principle of Jewish law. Equally firm is the principle that such prohibitions are to be ignored even if the danger is only doubtful in nature. Moreover, the effectiveness of the act designed to preserve an endangered life need not be guaranteed; the mere possibility that it will succeed in preserving a life is sufficient to require that it be carried out even though, in other circumstances, it would be a prohibited act. However, determination that an illness or affliction is life-threatening in nature or that it serves to decrease longevity anticipation does not necessarily render nugatory halakhic proscriptions for the sake of any and all putative therapy. Assuredly, halakhic restrictions are suspended in the quest for a cure, or enhancement of longevity, even if success is not guaranteed. Nevertheless, there must be some reason to believe that a cause and effect relationship exists between the otherwise proscribed act and the desired effect. In the absence of a therapy known to be efficacious in the treatment of his condition, a patient may understandably grasp at untried and untested remedies in the vague hope that they may prove to be of some benefit. Although such a pursuit is never mandatory[1] it is not forbidden, provided that utilization of the putative therapy involves no infraction of Jewish law.

The question that requires careful analysis is the nature of the evidence required to establish the efficacy of the proposed therapy in order that it may be legitimately employed even in face of halakhic prohibitions. Of particular concern is the status of procedures that are essentially experimental in nature as well as of scientific research designed to discover a cure for afflicted individuals whom Halakhah would define as belonging to the category of *ḥoleh le-faneinu.*[2] It is quite clear that halakhic strictures are suspended in the treatment of a patient with a life-threatening malady even if there is no certainty that the otherwise forbidden act will either achieve a cure or eliminate the danger. No therapy is accompanied by a guarantee of efficacy. Quite to the contrary, every therapy carries with it its own risks and dangers. In the words of Ramban, "With regard to cures, there is naught but danger; what heals one kills another."[3] Moreover, Halakhah unequivocally specifies that its strictures are suspended even in situations in which success in preserving human life is only doubtful. The mere possibility of eliminating a threat to life suffices to set aside restrictions of religious law.

Nevertheless, even "doubt" must be defined. Arguably, there must be a threshold level of anticipation of success below which the contemplated therapy cannot be deemed to be of even "doubtful" potential. A fervent hope that a cure may be obtained serendipitously cannot seriously be regarded as encompassed within the zone of doubt of which Halakhah takes cognizance. It is precisely the notion of cognizable doubt that Halakhah strives to elucidate in establishing the dichotomous categories that have come to be known as *refu'ah bedukah* and *refu'ah she-einah bedukah.* Not surprisingly, the precise delineation of these mutually exclusive categories is a matter of significant controversy among early halakhic author-

1. See R. Jacob Emden, *Mor u-Keẓi'ah, Oraḥ Ḥayyim* 328.

2. For a delineation of that concept, see *supra,* chap. 8, pp. 188–192.

3. *Torat ha-Adam,* published in *Kitvei Ramban,* ed. R. Bernard Chavel (Jerusalem, 5724), II, 43.

ities.

The locus of this principle is a statement of the Mishnah, *Yoma* 83a: "One who has been bitten by a mad dog should not be fed of the lobe of its liver. But R. Mattia ben Ḥeresh permits [this practice]." The practice of prescribing the liver of the attacking dog, apparently in roasted form, as a prophylactic measure against contracting rabies seems to have been fairly widespread among physicians of antiquity[4] and appears to have survived in at least some primitive societies until comparatively recent times.[5] R. Mattia ben Ḥeresh seems to have maintained that, since consumption of liver was an accepted treatment for the bite of a mad dog and apparently was commonly recommended by physicians, the prohibition against eating the flesh of unclean animals may be disregarded. Although the therapeutic or prophylactic efficacy of this remedy could not be demonstrated, to say the least, the victim was, nevertheless, permitted to eat the liver of the dog because the liver was regarded as possibly, albeit doubtfully, efficacious.[6] It is the position of the Sages, whose opinion is normative,[7] that requires elucidation. An examination of the talmudic commentaries of early authorities yields three diverse modes of understanding the controversy between the Sages and R. Mattia ben Ḥeresh. The divergent analyses of this controversy will lead to differing conclusions with regard to the propriety of modern-day experimental procedures entailing infractions of Jewish law.

1. R. Menahem ha-Me'iri, *Bet ha-Beḥirah, Yoma* 82a, comments that R. Mattia ben Ḥeresh permitted consumption of the liver "because he thought it to be therapeutic" while the Sages forbade the practice "because it is not a cure" even though it was categorized as such by the masses. Me'iri apparently maintains that the dispute recorded in the Mishnah was entirely factual: R. Mattia ben Ḥeresh accepted the prevalent use of the liver as demonstrating at least the possibility of therapeutic benefit while the Sages were convinced that the liver was devoid of any therapeutic value.[8] According to Me'iri's analysis, the ruling of the Sages serves to

4. See sources cited by Julius Preuss, *Biblical and Talmudic Medicine,* trans. Fred Rosner (New York, 1978), p. 196, note 90.

5. *Ibid.,* note 91.

6. Preuss regards use of the liver of the rabid dog as a form of antitoxin treatment; see *Biblical and Talmudic Medicine,* p. 196.

7. See Rambam, *Commentary on the Mishnah, loc. cit.;* and Me'iri, *Bet ha-Beḥirah, Yoma* 82a.

8. A similar analysis is independently advanced by Maharam ben Habib, *Tosafot Yom ha-Kippurim, Yoma* 83a.

exclude only therapies that are known to be of no avail. Thus, according to Me'iri, use of what in contemporary times would be categorized as a quack remedy could not be sanctioned when such use entails a violation of Jewish law; nevertheless, use of another therapy of doubtful efficacy would be acceptable simply on the basis of its acceptance as a folk remedy.

2. According to the Ibn Tibbon version of the *Commentary on the Mishnah, Yoma* 83a, Rambam declares:

> The law with regard to this is not in accordance with R. Mattia ben Ḥeresh who permits feeding a person the liver of a dog that bites because this does not benefit other than by way of a *segulah.* But the Sages declare that one may not transgress the commandments other than in conjunction with a therapy, i.e., with regard to things which cure in accordance with nature. That is, a true matter derived by reason or[9] experience that approaches truth. But to treat by means of things that cure by virtue of their *segulah* is forbidden because their power is weak, not [known] by virtue of reason and its [demonstrated efficacy on the basis of] experience is far-fetched; its advocacy by one who is in error is weak.

The Kapaḥ (Kafih) version of the same text reads:

> But the Sages declare that one may not transgress the law other than in conjunction with therapy that is a clear matter mandated by reason or[10] simple experience but not for treatment by means of *segulot* because they are weak in nature, not mandated by reason and its [demonstrated efficacy on the basis of] experience is far-fetched but is [nevertheless] advocated by its advocate.

Both versions stress reason and experience as the crucial criteria distinguishing between these two categories. Although the text is somewhat ambiguous, the terms "reason" and "experience" are presumably used disjunctively.[11] Rambam thus, in effect, defines *safek pikuaḥ nefesh* insofar

9. The *vav* appearing in the text is ambiguous. It may serve as a *vav ha-ḥibbur* and mean "and" or as a *vav ha-pirud* meaning "or." I believe that it is correctly rendered "or"; see *infra,* note 11.

10. See *supra,* note 9.

11. Rambam, *Guide of the Perplexed,* Book III, chap. 37, certainly accepts the

as therapy is concerned as connoting, not any conceivable remedy or any remedy not demonstrated as being devoid of value, but a remedy whose possible efficacy has been cogently demonstrated on the basis of reason or experience. Absent rational or experimental support, the putative remedy is not regarded as even "doubtfully" efficacious.

The term "*teva*" or "nature" that appears in the Ibn Tibbon version in contradistinction to "*segulah*" reveals that the crucial factor sought by reason, and which serves to distinguish ordinary medical remedies from *segulot,* is a causal connection rooted in the laws of nature as opposed to putative effects that can be explained only in some non-natural or metaphysical manner.[12] Rambam does not, however, dismiss consumption of

medical efficacy of therapy "that has been verified by experiment, although it cannot be explained by analogy." Included in that category are wearing the egg of a certain species of locust, a fox's tooth and a nail from the gallows of an impaled convict, each of which was worn as a putative remedy for a specific disorder. Those therapies are specifically permitted according to the normative opinion of R. Meir recorded in the Mishnah, *Shabbat* 67a. Rambam, in the *Guide,* explains that "the ways of the Amorite" are forbidden "because they are not arrived at by reason, but are similar to the performances of witchcraft, which are necessarily connected with the influences of the stars," but that the earlier enumerated therapies are permitted nevertheless because "these things have been considered in those days as facts established by experiment." On the basis of Rambam's remarks both in his *Commentary on the Mishnah* in *Yoma* and in the *Guide,* it might be argued that Rambam assumes that whenever medical efficacy is confirmed by experience it must be presumed that the therapy is in accordance with the natural order even though the nature of the causal relationship between the medicament and the cure is not understood. This analysis of Rambam's position cannot be accepted for a number of reasons: 1) Other medieval authorities clearly recognized that the items enumerated by the Mishnah in *Shabbat* had no natural therapeutic properties; see, for example, *Teshuvot ha-Rashba,* I, no. 411. 2) Rambam, in the Guide, comments: "They served as cures, in the same means as the hanging of the peony over a person subject to epileptic fits, or the application of a dog's excrement to the swellings of the throat, and of the vapors of vinegar and marcasite to the smelling of tumors." The clear implication is that the enumerated remedies were recognized as non-natural *segulot.* 3) Most significant is Rambam's explicit categorization in his *Commentary on the Mishnah, Shabbat* 67a, of the practices referred to by the Mishnah as remedies advocated by "*ba'alei ha-segulot.*" Moreover, and perhaps most significantly, when there is cogent scientific reason to believe that a proposed therapy will even possibly be effective it must be assumed that such therapy constitutes *safek pikuaḥ nefesh* even though the hypothesis lacks experimental confirmation; see *infra,* note 22 and accompanying text. See also *Teshuvot ha-Radbaz le-Leshonot ha-Rambam,* no. 63 (1,436), and R. Isaac Joseph Nunez-Vaes, *Siaḥ Yiẓḥak, Yoma* 83a.

12. See the comments of *Teshuvot Shemesh Ẓedakah,* no. 29, s.v. *hineh.*

the liver of a rabid dog as totally without purpose; he merely regards any possible benefit as being rooted in something other than the natural properties of the liver. For purposes of *safek pikuaḥ nefesh,* halakhic prohibitions are suspended only in the pursuit of benefits comprehended by reason, i.e., benefits flowing from cause and effect relationships manifest in the natural universe.[13]

---

13. There does not appear to be any reason to assume that Rambam adopts a thoroughly rationalist position and denies the possibility of a cure that cannot be explained in terms of the laws of nature. Codifying the statement of the Mishnah, *Shabbat* 61a, as amplified in the Gemara, *Shabbat* 61a and 61b, Rambam, *Hilkhot Shabbat* 19:14, rules that one may enter a public thoroughfare on the Sabbath wearing an amulet provided that the presumptive therapeutic efficacy of the amulet has been established by means of it having already cured three persons or having been made by an individual who has cured three other persons by means of his amulets. Rambam in no way demurs from accepting the curative efficacy of the amulets in question. Elsewhere, Rambam, *Hilkhot Avodat Kokhavim* 11:11, in ruling that it is permissible to utter an incantation over a snake bite, declares utterance of the incantation to be of absolutely no therapeutic benefit but rules that it is permissible nevertheless because, since it was commonly believed to be effective, omission of the incantation might cause agitation or anguish (*tiruf ha-da'at*) that could enhance the danger to the victim. Rambam makes no similar comment with regard to amulets. If the wearing of amulets is similarly permitted only because of *tiruf ha-da'at,* it is difficult to explain the distinction that is drawn between an amulet of demonstrated efficacy and an untried amulet. It is a bit far-fetched to assume that *tiruf ha-da'at* is attendant only upon the withholding of an amulet of demonstrated efficacy. Moreover, the very concept of an amulet of demonstrated benefit (*mumḥeh*) indicates that the amulet was regarded as efficacious. However, in the *Guide for the Perplexed,* Book 1, chap. 61, Rambam writes:

> You must beware of sharing the error of those who write amulets. Whatever you hear of them or read in their works, especially in reference to the names which they form by combination, is utterly senseless; they call these combinations *shemot* [names] and believe their pronunciation demands sanctification and purification and that by using them they are able to work miracles. Rational persons ought not to listen to such men nor in any way believe their assertions.

These comments negating the efficacy of amulets seem to contradict the clear ruling of the Mishnah, *Shabbat* 60a. Indeed, Shem Tob, in his commentary on the *Guide, ad locum,* indicates that Rambam intended to negate error that might arise on the basis of that mishnaic comment. However, Shem Tob seems to be unaware of Rambam's own seemingly contradictory comments in the *Mishneh Torah, Hilkhot Shabbat* 19:14. See also the comments of Jacob I. Dienstag, *Talpiyot,* vol. IV, no. 1–2 (Tammuz 5709), p. 261. Rambam's negative comment in *Hilkhot Mezuzah* 5:4, cited below, although somewhat ambiguous, seems to refer to treatment of *mezuzot* as amulets rather than to amulets themselves and is interpreted in that matter in the Hyamson translation of the passage.

This contradiction might perhaps be resolved by positing that Rambam accepted the ruling of the Sages regarding entering a public thoroughfare on *Shabbat* while wearing the objects described in the Mishnah, *Shabbat* 60a, even though he regarded them as devoid of any therapeutic efficacy. Rambam might have assumed that the Sages ruled in this manner because, since the masses accepted their efficacy, albeit erroneously, such items acquired the status of articles of clothing or of ornaments simply by virtue of being customarily worn as a cure or prophylaxis. See Rashi, *Shabbat* 60a. Alternatively, Rambam may have regarded the practice as being permitted because, in light of the fact that the items in question "are not carried in the usual manner," no transgression of a biblical prohibition is involved. See *Teshuvot ha-Radbaz, le-Leshonot ha-Rambam,* V, nos. 63 (1,436) and 153 (1,526); and the comments of the interlocutor as reported in *Teshuvot Shemesh Ẓedakah,* no. 29. Since no biblical prohibition is entailed, and since the masses were desirous of wearing amulets because of their misplaced beliefs regarding therapeutic properties ascribed to such amulets, the Sages did not choose to disturb the practice with a rabbinic interdiction against wearing them on the Sabbath.

Those explanations, however, are entirely unlikely. However, another resolution of Rambam's conflicting comments does suggest itself. In context, Rambam's comments in the *Guide* occur in the course of a discussion of the various names of God and indicate that only the tetragrammaton is the *nomen proprium* of the Deity, while all other appellations are simply reflective of divine attributes indicating the relationship of certain actions to Him but are in no way reflective of the divine essence. Moreover, Rambam insists that all divine attributes are negative in nature and are designed to negate the possibility of certain actions or qualities but tell us nothing of the nature of the Deity in a positive sense. Rambam's critical comments concerning amulets may, then, have been directed only against writers of amulets containing various divine names or various combinations of divine names and their ascription of supernatural properties to those names. Indeed, amulets written during the medieval period were of that nature. Since Rambam denies that those divine names define the essence of the Deity, he categorically rejects the efficacy of amulets employing such names. Those names neither reflect the essential nature of the Deity nor do they reflect His qualities or attributes in any positive sense. Thus they cannot conceivably be endowed with any mystic power. It is noteworthy that in *Hilkhot Mezuzah* 5:4 Rambam decries the practice of inscribing on the inside of the *mezuzah* "the names of angels, holy names, a biblical verse or seals . . . as if it were an amulet for their own benefit as has occurred to their foolish minds that this is something that yields benefit with regard to the vanities of the world." The amulets described in the Talmud, to which he refers in *Hilkhot Shabbat,* may well have been of an entirely different nature. Their nature is, of course, unknown to us. But those amulets, when demonstrated to have been efficacious, were accepted by Rambam and their curative power acknowledged by him.

It must be noted that *Bi'ur ha-Gra, Yoreh De'ah* 179:13, asserts that Rambam denies the efficacy of amulets and declares that Rambam was misled by his

The question that remains to be resolved is whether, according to Rambam, violation of halakhic restrictions is permitted only in conjunction with the use of remedies whose curative properties are understood by reason or whether similar license exists with regard to therapies whose efficacy has been demonstrated experimentally but which are not scientifically explainable. Or, to put the matter somewhat differently, does Rambam understand all *segulot,* i.e., all non-natural remedies, as forbidden if their use necessitates violation of halakhic restrictions, or does he understand the Mishnah as excluding only *segulot* of unconfirmed efficacy but placing no similar restriction upon administration of tried and tested *segulot* whose value has been confirmed by experience?

Maharam ben Habib, *Tosafot Yom ha-Kippurim, Yoma* 83a, seems to be of the opinion that transgression of biblical prohibitions can never be sanctioned in conjunction with a *segulah.* This is also the manner in which Rambam was understood by *Admat Kodesh,* I, *Yoreh De'ah,* no. 6, and by *Teshuvot Pri ha-Areẓ,* III, no. 3.[14] Those authorities asked if a non-kosher chicken might be fed to a person who was suffering from some form of mental illness. The cure is described as a *segulah.* We are, however, informed that it was well-known that the lives of many people were saved by means of this therapy. Although those authorities permit use of the remedy in question, they indicate that Rambam would have forbidden the use of even a tried and tested *segulah* under such circumstances but that according to other authorities any known therapy, even a *segulah,* may be utilized in cases of danger. R. Chaim Joseph David Azulai, *Birkei Yosef, Oraḥ Ḥayyim* 301:6, applies the same analysis to the propriety of writing an amulet on *Shabbat,* apparently even when the success of the procedure is not in doubt.[15] Similarly, R. Shlomoh Kluger, both in his *Teshuvot Tuv Ta'am va-Da'at, Mahadura Kamma,* no. 239, and in his *Teshuvot u-Vaḥarta ba-Ḥayyim,* no. 87, forbids desecration of

philosophical speculations. If the foregoing analysis of Rambam's ruling in *Hilkhot Shabbat* is correct and Rambam did acknowledge the therapeutic powers of the amulets described in the Mishnah, *Bi'ur ha-Gra*'s criticism of Rambam must be understood as directed toward Rambam's invective against amulets composed of divine names. Such criticism would then be based upon *Bi'ur ha-Gra*'s own conviction of the efficacy of such amulets, and hence of his certainty that the amulets to which the Talmud refers were of such nature, rather than Rambam's putative rejection of explicit talmudic arrestation of their validity.

14. See also *Teshuvot Shemesh Ẓedakah,* no. 29.

15. See also R. Chaim Joseph David Azulai, *Teshuvot Ḥayyim Sha'al,* II, no. 38, sec. 81.

the Sabbath in order to secure the prayer of a saint even if it were to be known with certainty that the prayer will effect a cure.[16]

R. Chaim Sofer, *Teshuvot Maḥaneh Ḥayyim, Yoreh De'ah,* II, no. 60, explains that availing oneself of the ministrations of a physician is permitted only because of specific dispensation granted by the verse "and he shall cause him to be thoroughly healed" (Exodus 21:20). Permission to utilize medical remedies entails an obligation to use them in the preservation of life and the obligation to preserve life, in turn, serves to obviate strictures of religious law. However, the obligation arising out of that verse, asserts *Maḥaneh Ḥayyim,* is limited to use of natural remedies; no similar obligation exists with regard to the use of non-natural, occult or metaphysical powers in effecting a cure. Infractions of Jewish law are permitted for purposes of preserving life only because such measures are demanded by Halakhah. Accordingly, *Maḥaneh Ḥayyim* maintains that, according to Rambam, even *segulot* of demonstrated efficacy may not be used despite danger to life if such use involves an infraction of a halakhic prohibition.

Proof to the contrary cannot be adduced from the fact that the Sages permitted entering a public thoroughfare on *Shabbat* while wearing the objects described in the Mishnah, *Shabbat* 60a, since such items acquire the status of articles of clothing or of ornaments by virtue of being customarily worn as a cure or prophylaxis;[17] or, alternatively, the practice was permitted because, in light of the fact that the items in question are not "carried" in the usual manner, no transgression of a biblical prohibition is involved.[18]

Nevertheless, the language employed by Rambam in his *Commentary*

---

16. See also R. Avraham David of Buchach, *Eshel Avraham, Oraḥ Ḥayyim* 328:2. Cf., *Minḥat Shabbat,* no. 84, sec. 29, and *Shiyurei Minḥah,* sec. 6, as well as R. Eliezer Waldenberg, *Ẓiẓ Eli'ezer,* IV, no. 4, sec. 17, who cite a responsum of R. Shalom Mordecai Schwadron forbidding a Jew to write the text of a telegram on *Shabbat* in order that it be sent to a *ẓaddik* so that he might pray on behalf of a patient. However, it would appear that that authority would have permitted the sending of a telegram were it known with certainty that the *ẓaddik*'s prayer would be effective. It is not clear whether, in some instances, Maharsham would have, in effect, ruled in accordance with the authorities who disagree with Rambam or whether he understood Rambam as permitting infractions of halakhic prohibitions in situations in which the efficacy of the *segulah* has been established on the basis of experience.

17. See Rashi, *Shabbat* 60a.

18. *Teshuvot ha-Radbaz le-Leshonot ha-Rambam,* nos. 63 (1,436) and 153 (1,526); and the interlocutor in *Teshuvot Shemesh Ẓedakah,* no. 29.

on the Mishnah, Yoma 83a, clearly supports the opposite view.[19] Rambam's reference to "experience" would be entirely superfluous if "reason" is the sole criterion permitting suspension of halakhic prohibitions. However, if "reason" and "experience" are disjunctive terms, use of the dual terms is crucial and readily understood. If this is indeed Rambam's intention, his comments must be understood as designed to distinguish between "experience that approaches truth" (Ibn Tibbon) or "simple experience"[20] (Kapaḥ) and experience that is "far-fetched" (*raḥok*), i.e., between experience that is demonstratively compelling and experience that is inconclusive."[21] The result then is that, according to Rambam, *segulot* or inexplicable remedies are to be regarded in the same way as natural remedies insofar as violation of halakhic restrictions is concerned only when their efficacy has been firmly established. This analysis of Rambam's position is supported by *Tiferet Yisra'el, Yoma* 6:32, who cites Rambam's comments with regard to cure by means of a *segulah* in the face of halakhic strictures

19. Although he does not cite Rambam, R. Ya'ir Chaim Bacharach, *Teshuvot Ḥavot Ya'ir,* no. 105, appears to permit the use of a *segulah* of demonstrated therapeutic value. *Ḥavot Ya'ir* forbade swallowing lice in an attempt to cure jaundice, but only because the remedy was untried and untested. That remedy seems to have been regarded as a *segulah* rather than a conventional remedy since it was stipulated that the lice must be taken from the patient's head. See *Ẓiẓ Eli'ezer,* VIII, no. 15, chap. 8, sec. 5.

20. The term "simple experience" (*ha-nisayon ha-pashut*) is presumably used in the sense of "common experience."

21. Although he does not predicate his position upon this comment of Rambam, *Mizbeaḥ Adamah,* I, *Yoreh De'ah,* no. 6, distinguishes between the degree of experience required for use of a *segulah* under such circumstances and the experience required for use of other remedies. *Mizbeaḥ Adamah* requires that the curative power of a *segulah* be demonstrated in three cases whereas, with regard to other forms of therapy, he accepts one cure as sufficient. *Hagahot Maimuniyot, Hilkhot Ma'akhalot Asurot* 14:2, permits therapeutic use of forbidden food provided that it is a known cure, and adds the comment that "perhaps testing for a cure does not require extensive testing as is the case with regard to an amulet." The situations discussed by *Mizbeaḥ Adamah* involved feeding a mentally-ill patient a chicken that died of natural causes as a cure for his malady, whereas the incident discussed by *Hagahot Maimuniyot* involved feeding an epileptic an unclean flying creature. A lesser degree of experience is required, opines *Mizbeaḥ Adamah,* because, as already noted by *Hagahot Maimuniyot,* unlike a *segulah,* the unclean creature cures by virtue of the "strength" or "power" of its physical properties whereas an amulet, for example, cures only by virtue of the "power of a *mazal.*" See *infra,* note 22. The assumption that, were there some cogent reason to assume that consumption of such creatures is medically effective, no prior experience would be required is compatible with that position.

and concludes, "Therefore, any [such remedy] whose cure is not certain is forbidden."[22] The threshold level of possible efficacy, and hence of *safek pikuaḥ nefesh,* is satisfied if the putative therapeutic property of the medicament in question is perceived by reason or if it has been established on the basis of experience. Since even *safek pikuaḥ nefesh* is sufficient to warrant disregard of halakhic constraints, it is not necessary that reason or experience establish therapeutic efficacy beyond cavil; it is sufficient that reason or experience point to probable, or even possible, benefit. Nevertheless, in the absence of experiential evidence of past success or cogent reason to assume therapeutic value, utilization of the contemplated remedy does not rise to the level of "doubtful" *pikuaḥ nefesh.* However, when therapeutic value has been demonstrated on the basis of experience, remedies in the nature of a *segulah* are treated no differently than established medical cures.[23]

It would thus appear to be the case that, according to Rambam, any

22. See R. Menachem Mendel Schneerson, *Teshuvot Ẓemaḥ Ẓedek, Oraḥ Ḥayyim,* no. 38, who declares that "it is possible" that Rambam would concede that a tested *segulah* might be used under such circumstances.

23. Presumably, "experience" should be defined as success in three instances that can be attributed to the *segulah* even though the *segulah* in question may have failed to cure other patients. Rambam, *Hilkhot Shabbat* 19:14, rules that three cures serve to establish the curative powers of an amulet. This is clearly the position adopted by *Mizbeaḥ Adamah,* I, *Yoreh De'ah,* no. 6; cf., *supra,* note 21. It is quite possible that *Tosafot* espouse a position similar to that of Rambam but require that the therapeutic power of a *segulah* be known with "certainty" in any situation in which its use involves violation of a halakhic prohibition. The Talmud declares that Elijah and Phineas were one and the same person. *Tosafot, Baba Meẓi'a* 114b, questions the permissibility of Elijah's conduct in resuscitating the son of the widow of Zarephath. Since Phineas was a priest, he was forbidden to defile himself through tactile contact with a corpse. How, then, was he permitted to revive the dead child? *Tosafot* answer that since Elijah was certain of the success of his endeavor, violation of the priestly code was permissible. *Tosafot*'s comment is puzzling since the general principle is that halakhic strictures are suspended even on the mere chance that the procedure may succeed in saving a life. R. Abraham Jacob Neumark, *Eshel Avraham* (Tel Aviv, 5708), *Pinot Genosar,* no. 23, cites Rambam's discussion of remedies in the nature of a *segulah* and, asserting that according to Rambam a *segulah* may be employed in face of halakhic strictures only if its curative powers are known with certainty, explains that Elijah's use of prophetic powers was also a "non-natural" therapy and hence was justified only because of his certainty of success. See also R. Iser Yehudah Unterman, *Ha-Torah ve-ha-Medinah,* IV, 25f., and *idem, Shevet me-Yehudah,* I, *Sha'ar Rishon,* chap. 7. For other interpretations of *Tosafot*'s thesis see *Contemporary Halakhic Problems,* I, 389–391.

remedy whose benefit has been demonstrated by means of experimental evidence may be utilized in face of danger to life even if use of the remedy entails violation of halakhic restrictions. Favorable experimental results are certainly a form of "experience" serving to establish therapeutic efficacy. Indeed the term used by Rambam is "*nisayon*" which has the connotation of both "experience" and "experiment." Moreover, even if clinical experiments have not yet been carried out, a researcher seeking to administer a drug on the basis of a reasoned scientific hypothesis would be justified in doing so. Although a "hit or miss" attempt undertaken on the outside chance that some benefit may be derived would not justify violation of halakhic restrictions, a remedy proposed even tentatively on the basis of known scientific considerations would constitute a remedy "derived by reason."

3. Rashi, in his commentary on *Yoma* 83a, adopts a position strikingly different from that of both Me'iri and Rambam. Rashi explains the position of the Sages forbidding feeding a portion of the dog's liver to the victim by stating, "Even though physicians are wont to use this therapy it is not a *refu'ah gemurah* to [warrant] permitting him [violation of the] prohibition regarding an unclean animal for that [purpose]." Rashi further explains that R. Mattia ben Ḥeresh disagrees because he regards the remedy to be a *refu'ah gemurah.* Completely absent in Rashi's comments is any hint of a distinction between natural versus metaphysical remedies or of a distinction between a cogently understood remedy and one which is not comprehended by reason. Nor does Rashi assume that the Sages were convinced of the futility of the remedy. Instead, Rashi introduces the notion of known or demonstrated efficacy. It must be assumed that the term "*refu'ah gemurah*" is synonymous with the term "*refu'ah bedukah*" employed by latter-day scholars. As such, the term connotes a tried and tested remedy as opposed to an experimental remedy. If so, Rashi distinguishes between the "doubt" of an unknown remedy and other forms of doubt. Although halakhic prohibitions are ignored even in cases of doubtful danger and even if it is doubtful that a known remedy may help a particular patient, a therapy whose efficacy is untried and untested does not rise to the threshold level of "doubt."[24] Put somewhat differently, the commandment "and he shall cause him to be thoroughly healed" (Exodus 21:20) imposes an obligation to utilize only what is known to possess therapeutic power, but not to engage in random activity or even to initiate research in

24. See *Teshuvot ha-Radbaz le-Leshonot ha-Rambam,* no. 153 (1,526).

the hope that a cure may be achieved.[25] Since there is no obligation to avail oneself of such measures, their use in face of halakhic prohibitions is not permitted.[26] If this analysis is correct, Rashi's interpretation of the controversy yields only limited license for setting aside halakhic restrictions in pursuit of a cure. According to Rashi, such prohibitions may be ignored only when therapeutic efficacy has actually been demonstrated in at least some cases.[27]

Rashi's position seems to be reflected in the comments of other early authorities as well. R. Meir of Rothenberg, *Teshuvot Maharam ben Barukh* (Prague, 5368), no. 160, and *Hagahot Maimuniyot, Hilkhot Ma'akhalot Asurot* 14:2, permit an epileptic to eat a forbidden food as a cure for his disease only if it is a *refu'ah yedu'ah.* The term "*refu'ah yedu'ah*" or "known remedy" appears to be used in much the same manner as the term "*refu'ah gemurah*" is employed by Rashi. Maharam Rothenberg's view is cited as normative by *Issur ve-Heter, klal* 59.[28] Even more

25. Cf. *Mor u-Keẓi'ah, Oraḥ Ḥayyim* 328. In this discussion *Mor u-Keẓi'ah* does not refer to the Mishnah in *Yoma* or refer to the suspension of halakhic restrictions for life-saving purposes. *Mor u-Keẓi'ah* posits the category of *refu'ah she-einah bedukah* in delineating therapies a patient cannot be compelled to accept and regards virtually all cures for internal maladies "which even the physician does not know and recognize with clarity but rather by estimation only and which he attempts [to cure] by medicaments with regard to which he himself is in doubt" to be included in that category. Although he regards abjuration of such remedies to be commendable even on weekdays, *Mor u-Keẓi'ah* apparently regards necessary violation of Shabbat restrictions and the like in conjunction with administration of such remedies to be permitted on behalf of a patient who relies upon the physician's advice. Presumably, then, *Mor u-Keẓi'ah* would accept either the analysis of Me'iri or of Rambam in explaining the controversy between Rambam and R. Mattia ben Ḥeresh.

26. See *Teshuvot Kol Ben Levi,* no. 2.

27. The attempt by R. Eliezer Waldenberg, *Ẓiẓ Eli'ezer,* VIII, no. 15, chap. 8, sec. 2, to identify Rashi's position with that of Rambam and to interpret Rashi as excluding only remedies in the nature of a *segulah* falls short of the mark and is contradicted by all the authorities cited in the text who require a *refu'ah yedu'ah.* A similar attempt to identify Rashi's position with that of Rambam was earlier undertaken by *Teshuvot Shemesh Ẓedakah,* no. 29. *Shemesh Ẓedakah* understands the term "*yedu'ah*" as excluding *segulot* whose medicinal properties are not understood. At the other extreme, the interlocutor cited in *Teshuvot Shemesh Ẓedakah,* no. 29, endeavors to harmonize the views of Rambam and Rashi by arguing that both concede that therapeutic efficacy must be known with certainty and that Rambam's comments merely indicate that the efficacy of a *segulah* can never be known with certainty.

28. *Taz, Yoreh De'ah* 84:34, cites an identical ruling by Maharshal, apparently

significantly, Rema, *Yoreh De'ah* 155: 3, citing *Issur ve-Heter,* rules that forbidden foods may be fed to a sick person only if the cure is "known" (*yedu'ah*) or upon the direction of an expert (*mumḥeh*). *Bi'ur ha-Gra, Yoreh De'ah* 155:23, cites the ruling of the Mishnah in *Yoma* as the source for the requirement of a *refu'ah yedu'ah. Magen Avraham, Oraḥ Ḥayyim* 328:1, cites Rema's ruling as normative. *Pri Megadim, Eshel Avraham, Oraḥ Ḥayyim* 328:1, takes issue with *Magen Avraham* in expressing amazement that an unknown remedy should be forbidden since it is an accepted principle that halakhic prohibitions are suspended even in cases of *safek pikuaḥ nefesh.*[29] Nevertheless, the ruling of Rema and of *Magen Avraham* is accepted by *Shulḥan Arukh ha-Rav, Oraḥ Ḥayyim* 328:2; *Ḥayyei Adam* 68:2; and *Mishnah Berurah* 328:5. Those authorities, following the ruling of Maharam of Rothenberg, are seemingly in agreement with Rashi's view that, even insofar as medicaments are concerned, not every putative remedy can be dignified as a *safek.*[30] Only remedies commonly known to be effective or those whose efficacy is established on the basis of an expert can be considered to be of even doubtful benefit.[31] *Tosafot Yom ha-Kippurim,* rejecting the positions of both Ma-

---

based upon the same source. See also *Hagahot Maimuniyot, Hilkhot Ma'akhalot Asurot* 14:2.

29. *Pri Megadim* advances the opinion that Rema's comments are limited to foods forbidden only by virtue of rabbinic decree and apply to feeding such foods to a patient suffering from a non-life-threatening malady on whose behalf rabbinic restrictions are suspended. However, this does not appear to be the import of Rema's ruling and this interpretation is not supported by other latter-day authorities. The attempt of R. Eliezer Waldenberg, *Ẓiẓ Eli'ezer,* VIII, no. 15, chap. 8, sec. 4, to explain that Rema requires an expert only when the proposed remedy is in the nature of a *segulah* is similarly unacceptable.

30. Cf., the comments of R. Moshe Rosen, *Nezer ha-Kodesh, Yoma* 83a. *Nezer ha-Kodesh* cites a comment of Ran, *Yoma* 82b, in which Ran analyses another statement of Rashi as indicating that Rashi maintains that the principle of "majority" (*rov*) applies even to matters of *pikuaḥ nefesh.* Accordingly, *Nezer ha-Kodesh* opines that, according to Rashi, a forbidden foodstuff may be used as a medicament only if it is found to be effective in the majority of cases. *Nezer ha-Kodesh* concedes, of course, that the normative rule is not in accordance with this putative view. Hence, if that analysis of Rashi's position is correct, the view of the latter-day authorities cited in the text remains unexplained.

31. It seems clear that, according to Rashi, it must be known that the proposed remedy has successfully cured the particular malady for which it is now being prescribed. This is clearly stated in a note by the son of the author appended to *Teshuvot Shemesh Ẓedakah,* no. 29. If Rema, in his reference to a *refu'ah yedu'ah,* intends to codify Rashi's opinion, the phrase must be understood as connoting a remedy known to be efficacious in curing the particular illness being treated.

haram of Rothenberg and Rashi, rules that therapies of doubtful efficacy may be used even when such use entails violation of halakhic prohibitions.[32] That position follows Rambam's analysis of the Mishnah in *Yoma.*[33]

Of course, since, according to Rashi and those who adopt his position, transgression of halakhic prohibitions cannot be sanctioned in the absence of empirical evidence of efficacy and empirical evidence of efficacy is impossible without transgression, the result is a Catch-22 situation. Efficacy may, however, be established on the basis of treatment of non-Jews who are not bound by dietary restrictions and the like. Moreover, since Halakhah posits no exclusionary rule, once efficacy has been established by means of illicit use, subsequent use of the remedy is entirely appropriate and legitimate. Thus, even according to Rashi, once therapeutic benefit has been conclusively established, halakhic restrictions are suspended in order to effect a cure.

It may then be concluded that, according to Rambam, halakhic restrictions may be ignored in administering an experimental therapy or carrying out any scientific research designed to benefit a *ḥoleh le-faneinu* provided that the research pursued is grounded upon cogent scientific reasoning indicating probable or possible success. According to Me'iri, it may perhaps be the case that any proposed remedy may be pursued, provided that it has not been demonstrated to be ineffective. However, for Rashi, such research cannot be sanctioned unless therapeutic efficacy has already been established in some manner. Once efficacy of the treatment has been established, further research designed to refine the treatment for purposes of maximizing success or reducing risk would appear to be warranted even according to Rashi.

Cf., however, R. Iser Yehudah Unterman, *Ha-Torah ve-ha-Medinah,* V, 25, who inexplicably asserts that Rema's reference is to a remedy known to be effective, not necessarily in the treatment of the malady in question, but to anything that "is known to be a cure for *any illness whatsoever*" (emphasis in the original).

32. Cf., however, *Sedei Ḥemed, Asifat Dinim, Ma'arekhet Yom ha-Kippurim,* no. 3, sec. 24, s.v. *u-lekhorah.*

33. *Petaḥ ha-Dvir, Oraḥ Ḥayyim* 328:2, asserts that this is also the position of *Tur Shulḥan Arukh;* cf., however, *Sedei Ḥemed, ibid.,* s.v. *ve-ra'iti.* See also *Teshuvot ha-Rashba ha-Meyuḥasot le-Ramban,* no. 271; *Teshuvot Shemesh Ẓedakah, Yoreh De'ah,* no. 29; *Knesset ha-Gedolah, Yoreh De'ah* 84:114; *Orḥot Ḥayyim* 328:3; and *Sedei Ḥemed, ibid.,* s.v. *u-be-She'elot u-Teshuvot Besamim Rosh* and *ibid.,* s. v. *ve-hineh.*

Chapter X

Utilization of Scientific Data Obtained Through Immoral Experimentation

One may heal with all things except with the wood of a tree devoted to idolatry.

PESAḤIM 25a

Of late much attention has been focused upon use of scientific data compiled by German scientists during the Holocaust. That information was obtained as the result of cruel and inhumane, not to speak of immoral, experiments conducted upon inmates of concentration camps and prisoners of war. Controversy first erupted some time ago when the Environmental Protection Agency engaged in an attempt to perfect an antidote to phosgene, a poison gas. During World War II the Nazis engaged in a similar endeavor in the course of which they conducted experiments upon prisoners of war. A number of those prisoners died from the effects of the poisonous gas. Some staff scientists of the EPA were adamantly opposed to making use of the information gleaned by the Germans as a result of those experiments and, ultimately, material associated with the Nazi undertaking was excluded from the report prepared by the agency. Subsequently, and perhaps more significantly, the Hypothermia Research Laboratory of the University of Minnesota investigated procedures utilized in the rescue of persons accidentally swept into icy water. Among the most brutal of Nazi crimes were experiments involving hypothermia in humans performed at the Dachau concentration camp. Ostensibly, those studies were designed to establish the most effective treatment for victims of immersion hypothermia, particularly German airmen shot down over the cold waters of the North Sea. Some three hundred persons, mostly Jews, were placed in near-freezing water for varied periods of time and then warmed by different techniques. Approximately one third of the victims died.[1] In this case as well, information derived from experiments upon inmates of concentration camps was deemed to be significant.[2] For obvious reasons, those experiments could not be duplicated.[3]

Opposition to use of data gleaned from Nazi research was voiced by Dr. Henry Beecher in an article published in the June 16, 1966 issue of the *New England Journal of Medicine.*[4] Dr. Beecher formulates what

---

1. Robert L. Berger, "Nazi Science—The Dachau Hypothermia Experiments," *New England Journal of Medicine,* May 17, 1990, pp. 1435–1440, reports that the experiments were conducted on 280 to 300 victims (p. 1436) and that at least 80 to 90 victims died (p. 1437). A detailed evaluation of the hypothermia experiments was presented by Leo Alexander, "The Treatment of Shock from Prolonged Exposure to Cold, Especially in Water," Combined Intelligence Objectives Subcommittee, Item No. 24, File No. XXVl–37, Office of the Publication Board, Department of Commerce, Washington, D.C., Report No. 250, July, 1945, pp. 1–228. However, he subsequently reversed his position and concluded that the results were not dependable. See Leo Alexander, "Medical Science Under Dictatorship," *New England Journal of Medicine,* July 14, 1949, p. 43.

2. At least forty-five research articles published after the war, most of which are in the field of hypothermia, draw on Nazi data. See Kristine Moe, "Should the Nazi Research Data Be Cited?" *Hastings Center Report,* December, 1984, p. 5.

3. Another major research effort focused on the introduction of a pectin-based preparation, Polygal, to prevent blood clotting. It was hoped that prophylactic use of Polygal tablets would reduce bleeding from wounds sustained in combat or during surgical procedures. Combat wounds were simulated by the amputation of the extremities of camp prisoners without anesthesia or by shooting the prisoners though the neck, chest or spleen. The number of lives lost in those experiments is not reported. See Berger, "Nazi Science," p. 1439, and Alexander, "Medical Science Under Dictatorship," p. 42. Another series of high-altitude experiments on humans resulted in 70 to 80 deaths. See Berger, "Nazi Science," p. 1439. Other experiments were designed to test the efficacy of vaccines and drugs against typhus and to achieve heteroplastic transplantation of limbs. See Alexander, "Medical Science under Dictatorship," p. 43. Data yielded by those unsuccessful inhuman experiments appear to be of no significance to ongoing scientific research. These and other immoral experiments are described in some detail by Telford Taylor in the opening statement of the prosecution, *Trials of War Criminals Before the Nuremberg Military Tribunals Under Control Council Law 10,* vol. 1 (Washington, D.C.: Superintendent of Documents, U.S. Government Printing Office, 1950); Military Tribunal Case 1, *United States v. Karl Brandt et al.,* October 1946–April 1949, pp. 27–74, reprinted in *The Nazi Doctors and the Nuremberg Code: Human Rights in Human Experimentation,* ed. George J. Annas and Michael A. Grodin (New York and Oxford, 1992), pp. 67–93.

4. Henry K. Beecher, "Ethics and Clinical Research," *New England Journal of Medicine,* June 16, 1966, pp. 1354–1360.

may be categorized as a "Miranda argument" in asserting that illicitly obtained information dare not be recognized and admitted as evidence in the conduct of scientific investigations. This exclusionary principle would require that such information be totally and completely ignored on the grounds that use of immorally obtained data is itself immoral. More recently, use of such data has been decried by ethicists such as Dr. Daniel Callahan, director of the Hastings Center, and by Abraham Foxman, national director of the Anti-Defamation League of B'nai B'rith.[5] The issue has also been addressed by a number of rabbinic writers.[6]

Perhaps the most fundamental argument against use of information obtained by the Nazis is not ethical in nature, but scientific, i.e., that the data are unreliable. The methodology employed by those scientists, it is argued, was sloppy, the experiments poorly designed, the research shoddy and the reports incomplete, inconsistent, unreliable and probably freely fabricated.[7] That is a matter to be resolved by scientists, not by ethicists

5. See *New York Times,* May 12, 1988, p. A28. See also, William E. Seidelman, "Mengele Medicus," *Millbank Quarterly,* vol. 66, no. 2 (1988), pp. 221–239.

6. See R. Abraham Meir Israel, "Terufot shel Meḥkarei ha-Naẓim Yemaḥ Shemam," *Ha-Pardes,* Tishrei 5750, pp. 11–13; and R. Tibor Stern, "Issur Hana'ah me-Harugei Malkhut," *Ha-Pardes,* Tishri 5750, pp. 13–14. See *supra,* p. 198, note 61.

7. See A. Mitscherlich and F. Mielke, *Doctors of Infamy: The Story of the Nazi Medical Crimes,* trans. by H. Norden (New York, 1949); Harmut Hanauske-Abel, "From Nazi Holocaust to Nuclear Holocaust: A Lesson to Learn," *Lancet* (August 2, 1986), p. 271; and Berger, "Nazi Science," pp. 1439–1440. Most notably, Berger describes the medical officer who supervised the hypothermia high-altitude and blood-clotting experiments, Dr. Sigmund Rascher, as unqualified and depicts him as an opportunist seeking to establish qualifications for a university appointment. Berger cites a document introduced at the Nuremburg trials in which Professor Karl Gebhardt, a general in the SS and Himmler's personal physician, is reported to have told Rascher with regard to his experiments on hypothermia through exposure to cold air that "the report was unscientific; if a student of the second term dared submit a treatise of the kind [Gebhardt] would throw him out." Berger further cites a statement authored by a German general found among the papers of Leo Alexander, a psychiatrist and consultant to the American Chief of Counsel for War Crimes, that asserts:

> In an attempt to please Himmler by proving that the growth of the Aryan population could be accelerated through an extension of the childbearing age, Rascher made it known that his wife had given birth to their children in quick succession after turning 48 years old. During her fourth "pregnancy," Mrs. Rascher was arrested for attempting to kidnap an infant. The ensuing investigation disclosed that the other three Rascher children had not been born to Mrs. Rascher but had been bought or abducted.

or rabbinic decisors. There is, however, no gainsaying the fact that some respected researchers do indeed believe that such data can prove to be of value in their own work.[8] Whether those scientists are correct or incorrect is irrelevant to a discussion of either the ethical or halakhic issues involved; they are fully entitled to their convictions. In formulating the relevant questions of Jewish law, the possibility of deriving potential benefit must be taken as a given.

Moreover, although the German experiments are not only the most widely known but also involved the most heinous examples of unconscionable scientific research, they are by no means the sole examples of immoral experimentation. There have been numerous instances involving human research in the United States in which human rights were flagrantly disregarded.[9] No rule, either of science or logic, postulates that moral repugnance necessitates scientific unreliability. Other instances of immoral

Himmler felt betrayed and had his protégé arrested in April 1944. Berger further reports that, besides complicity in the kidnapping, Dr. Rascher was accused of financial irregularities, the murder of a German assistant and scientific fraud. Dr. and Mrs. Rascher were subsequently executed at one time, presumably on Himmler's orders.

8. Robert Pozos, a physiologist specializing in hypothermia, asserts that data derived from the Dachau experiments can advance contemporary research and save lives. See Robert Pozos, "Can Scientists Use Information Derived from Concentration Camps?" in Conference on the Meaning of the Holocaust for Bioethics, Minneapolis, May 17–19, 1989: Transcript of the official recording, pp. 1–17. Similarly, John S. Hayward of the University of Victoria in British Columbia has used Nazi cooling curves to determine how long cold-water survival suits will protect people at near-fatal temperatures. See Moe, "Should the Nazi Research Data Be Cited?" p. 5.

At one time Leo Alexander regarded the Nazi hypothermia experiments as having been conducted in a reliable manner. See Alexander, "The Treatment of Shock from Prolonged Exposure to Cold, Especially in Water." However, he subsequently reversed his position and concluded that the results were not dependable. See Alexander, "Medical Science Under Dictatorship," p. 43.

9. The Tuskegee, Alabama study involving 412 poor black sharecroppers suffering from syphilis is probably the best known and most notorious case. Physicians observed the ravages of the disease, including blindness, paralysis, dementia and early death without disclosing the diagnosis. Even after penicillin proved to be an effective treatment for syphilis the patients were left both untreated and uninformed. Other examples include the Willowbrook hepatitis study in which retarded children were deliberately given the hepatitis virus, and placebo-controlled studies of the treatment of streptococcal pharyngitis which predictably led to many avoidable cases of rheumatic fever. See Beecher, "Ethics and Clinical Research," pp. 1354–60.

experimentation might yield data regarded as valuable beyond cavil. Accordingly, the question of utilization of immorally obtained data cannot be brushed aside as entirely speculative. An obvious example may be found in the area of presently ongoing fetal tissue research involving use of fetuses obtained as a result of non-therapeutic abortions.

A number of arguments auguring against use of data derived from Nazi experimentation have appeared in articles published in rabbinic journals. The most sweeping criticism of utilization of this information is based upon an appeal to a well known and fundamental principle of Jewish law: "Everything may be utilized for healing, save for idolatry, some forms of sexual licentiousness and homicide" (*Pesaḥim* 28a). It is alleged that it is this principle that is employed by Rambam in his *Commentary on the Mishnah, Pesaḥim* 66a, in explaining the basis of the approbation expressed by the Sages for certain actions on the part of King Hezekiah. The Gemara reports that Hezekiah suppressed a certain medical work and that his conduct found favor in the eyes of the Sages. Rambam, together with other classical commentators on the Talmud, is troubled by the Sages' endorsement of what appears to have been a singularly irrational act. Medical works are indispensable aids in effecting cures and preserving life. One would have anticipated that the Sages would have advocated the broadest possible dissemination of medical knowledge rather than its suppression. One explanation offered by Rambam in resolution of this perplexity is that the work in question advocated modes of therapy "which the Torah does not permit to be used for healing." Rambam's reference is either to practices that are themselves idolatrous in nature, or more likely, to the "ways of the Amorites" and kindred practices prohibited because of their association with idolatry and encompassed within the ambit of the prohibition "and you shall not walk in their statutes" (Leviticus 18:3). Nevertheless, in context, Rambam's comments must be understood as restricted to a ban against performance of an illicit act for therapeutic purposes, not as banning subsequent utilization of information gleaned from the performance of such an illicit act.

This distinction comes sharply into focus in the formulation of two entirely disparate hypothetical questions that might have been posed to a rabbinic decisor during the period of the Holocaust by a physician seeking to conduct himself according to the dictates of Halakhah. In both hypothetical situations the physician has been ordered by the commandant of a concentration camp to perform certain bioethical experiments and has been warned that non-compliance will result in his own death.

In the first scenario, the physician informs the rabbi, "My experiment requires the bodies of males having blue eyes, blond hair and being at least six feet tall. If I agree to engage in this research, cadavers will be obtained in the course of future selections. Rather than being sent to labor camps, males possessing these physical characteristics will be marked for extermination so that their bodies may be made available for experimentation." A responsible rabbinic decisor would be hard put to find grounds upon which to sanction cooperation on the part of the physician. Non-cooperation on the part of the physician would prevent the experiments from being carried out and effectively thwart any scheme to select for death six feet tall, blue-eyed, blond males. Hence, the physician's acquiescence would involve complicity in the murder of persons whose lives would otherwise be spared. Judaism teaches that a person is obligated to suffer martyrdom rather than cause the death of another, even if his action is only an indirect cause of the illicit taking of a human life. This is so even if a specific number of persons will be put to death in any event and the issue is only selection of particular individuals.

The second scenario involves a situation in which the physician informs the rabbi, "I have been asked to conduct scientific research using the bodies of persons executed by the Nazis. I will select the cadavers appropriate for my work from among the victims already put to death. The Germans conducting the selection know nothing of my requirements and will make their determinations on grounds entirely extraneous to the need for cadavers appropriate for my experiment." The latter situation is readily distinguishable from the former in that the physician is not at all implicated in causing the death of an innocent person. His involvement is limited to the use of the corpse after death has already occurred. Assuredly, the execution of innocent victims is immoral and reprehensible. But, although the physician could learn nothing of scientific value without the antecedent taking of human life in a wanton and diabolical manner, that heinous act is already a *fait accompli* at the time of the physician's involvement. Accordingly, since the physician is not saving his own life at the cost of the life of another, the physician can do as he is ordered. Since there exists a clear threat to the life of the physician, lesser prohibitions concerning the violation of the corpse are suspended for purposes of *pikuaḥ nefesh.*

Interestingly, it is precisely this distinction that is illuminated by Rambam's comments explaining Hezekiah's suppression of the medical work referred to by the Mishnah in *Pesaḥim* on the grounds that it recommended illicit therapeutic measures. Rambam distinguishes between the motives of the author of that medical work and the use to which it was put by its readers. The anonymous author, Rambam tells us, composed the work "by way of knowledge of the nature of reality," i.e., as a work of theoretical science rather than for purposes of clinical implementation and, declares Rambam, "this is permissible." "Moreover," continues Rambam, "it should be clear to you that there are matters which God prevented [us] from carrying out but which it is permitted to study and to understand." Although, for example, performance of an act of idolatry is forbidden even for life-saving therapeutic purposes, it is nevertheless permitted to investigate and study the curative properties of the act in order to apply them in a licit manner. Hezekiah intervened only when it became apparent that the medical work in question was being utilized clinically for purposes that could not be sanctioned. Similarly, while lives may not be sacrificed in order to achieve a cure or to preserve life, that principle does not serve to bar investigation of the manner in which the homicide was committed or to forbid an anatomical examination of the organs of the victim in order to discover potentially life-saving information.

Another objection to utilization of such data has been raised on the basis of a consideration advanced in the eighteenth century by R. Jacob Emden, *She'ilat Ya'aveẓ,* II, no. 158, and amplified by the late R. Meshullem Roth, *Teshuvot Kol Mevaser* I, no. 58. Located in an institution in Jerusalem on Mount Zion is a museum containing artifacts relating to the Holocaust. It was the institution's practice to conduct an annual memorial service in commemoration of the atrocities committed during the course of World War II. For many years it was the practice of the *ḥazan,* the officiant leading the service, to gird himself with one of the artifacts on display, *viz.,* a hangman's noose that had been used to execute Jewish victims. The organizers of this event deemed it appropriate to utilize this tool of execution for a sacred purpose in memorializing the victims of those atrocities and hence the practice arose for the *ḥazan* to use that piece of rope as a *gartel* (belt) while leading the prayer service. Apparently, after the practice had been established and confirmed over a period of time, objections were raised regarding the propriety of the practice and Rabbi Roth was approached and asked to render a halakhic ruling.

Rabbi Roth found a precedent in a somewhat different question discussed by R. Jacob Emden in his *She'ilat Ya'aveẓ.* The matter presented to R. Jacob Emden involved a situation in which an individual had acquired a sword previously used by an executioner in dispatching his victims. That person wished to fashion the sword into a knife to be utilized for the ritual slaughter of kosher animals. *She'ilat Ya'avez* rules that such use is not sanctioned by Jewish law. The Mishnah, *Sanhedrin* 45b, declares, "The stone with which [the condemned] was stoned, the stake on which he was hanged, the sword with which he was beheaded, and the cloth with which he was strangled, are all buried with him." Jewish law requires that the various artifacts used by the *Bet Din* in administering the respective forms of capital punishment be disposed of by means of interment. Both Rashi, *ad locum,* and Rabbenu Peretz, cited by *Yad Ramah, Sanhedrin* 45b, indicate that the requirement for burial is established on the basis of a scriptural pleonasm. *She'ilat Ya'avez* asserts that the requirement for burial is not limited to items used in the execution of transgressors, but extends also to any object employed in causing death. *She'ilat Ya'avez* asserts that no benefit may be derived from the sword that had been used as a tool of execution. Accordingly, he rules that such a sword may not be used as a slaughtering knife and must be buried.[10] Rabbi Roth cites that discussion in similarly ruling that no benefit may be derived from the hangman's noose and that it should be disposed of by means of burial.

It is, however, not entirely clear that the stipulations posited by the Mishnah in *Sanhedrin* support the conclusions of *She'ilat Ya'avez* and *Kol Mevaser*. In clarifying this provision of Jewish law, Rambam, *Hilkhot Rozeah* 15:9, states that burial of the artifacts used to put the condemned transgressor to death is mandated "so that he will not be remembered for evil and people not say, 'This is the stake upon which so and so was hung.'" According to Rambam, burial of such articles is designed to prevent ignominy to the deceased. A similar explanation is advanced by the Gemara, *Sanhedrin* 54b, with regard to the rationale underlying the requirement for execution of an animal utilized as a participant in an act of bestiality. As noted by *Lehem Mishneh, ad locum,* Rambam, in advancing this rationale, is not citing a statement of the Gemara or of any earlier rabbinic source explicitly advanced in elucidation of this particular provi-

10. Much earlier, R. Judah he-Hasid, *Sefer Hasidim,* no. 1,113, ruled that an executioner's knife found in a grave in which martyrs had been buried must be returned to its burial site. See also *Azharot Nosafot,* sec. 6, appended to the Jerusalem, 5717 edition of *Sefer Hasidim* on the basis of the Munich manuscript. In the latter comment *Sefer Hasidim* declares that one who derives benefit from a sword with which a Jew has been put to death causes "grave danger to himself and to his entire family" and advises that the sword be interred together with the victim.

sion of Jewish law. Moreover, it is not Rambam's general practice to incorporate the rationale reflected in specific *mizvot* in his codification of the pertinent provisions of Jewish law. The fact that Rambam does so in this case suggests that there are halakhic ramifications that are attendant upon the rationale and hence the rationale forms an integral part of the ruling. Rambam, as well as *Yad Ramah,* who also posits the identical rationale for these halakhic provisions, may well have been of the opinion that these artifacts are not at all *asur be-hana'ah,* i.e., that these artifacts are not to be numbered among those objects from which it is forbidden to derive benefit. Indeed, *She'ilat Ya'avez* himself cites a latter-day authority who apparently maintained that there is no *issur hana'ah* associated with such artifacts. Although, to be sure, objects from which benefit may not be derived require burial in order to eliminate the possibility of violation of the *issur hana'ah,* conversely, the fact that an object requires burial does not *ipso facto* indicate that it is *asur be-hana'ah.* A corpse requires burial by virtue of the explicit biblical command "you shall surely bury him the same day" (Deuteronomy 21:23). Yet the prohibition against deriving benefit from a cadaver is deduced by the Gemara, *Avodah Zarah* 29b, from an entirely different source. Rambam may well have incorporated the rationale underlying the requirement for burial of the implements of capital punishment in order to demonstrate that the requirement for burial is not the product of an *issur hana'ah.*[11]

However, even if it is to be granted that an *issur hana'ah* is attendant upon implements of execution as well as upon any artifact utilized in putting a Jew to death, such a provision of Halakhah is not at all germane with regard to the question under consideration. Any prohibition of this

---

11. Moreover, it may be cogently argued that, according to Rambam, the requirement for burial of the implement of execution "so that he will not be remembered for evil" is limited to artifacts used in the execution of persons guilty of capital transgressions. Such individuals are put to death for having performed ignominious deeds and anything that focuses attention upon the nature of their death does no honor to their memory. The death of a victim of wanton persecution or ordinary homicide is in no way ignominious. Quite to the contrary, *Teshuvot Ḥatam Sofer, Yoreh De'ah,* no. 333, describes such a person as a "*kadosh*—a holy one." Certainly, one finds no explicit reference in rabbinic literature of a need to suppress publicization of the nature of such a death.

It may be noted that "the stake upon which he was hanged" refers to the hanging of the body of the executed transgressor subsequent to administration of one of the forms of capital punishment. The prohibition against deriving benefit from the "stake" clearly applies only in the context of capital punishment administered by the *Bet Din.*

nature applies solely to benefit derived from the actual implement of execution or homicide but to nothing else.[12] For example, unlike the *issur hana'ah* associated with objects of pagan worship, money derived from the sale of such items is not *asur be-hana'ah.* By the same token, while it may be forbidden to utilize such objects for purposes of deriving scientific information, nevertheless, if information is obtained in violation of this prohibition, the information does not itself become *asur be-hana'ah;* hence such information, once obtained, may be utilized for any beneficial purpose.[13]

Yet another argument against use of data derived from Nazi experimentation is based upon a general *issur hana'ah* concerning derivation of benefit from a cadaver and may be rebutted in the selfsame manner. In a discussion of the propriety of post-mortem dissections, R. Moses Sofer, *Teshuvot Ḥatam Sofer, Yoreh De'ah,* no. 336, and R. Moses Schick, *Teshuvot Maharam Shik, Yoreh De'ah,* no. 344, rule that anatomical studies may not be performed upon a cadaver because of the *issur hana'ah* attendant upon a corpse. These authorities role that *histaklut,* mere examination or gazing upon the body for purposes of acquiring information is a prohibited form of benefit.[14] This contention, first formulated by *Ḥatam Sofer,* has been the focus of much discussion in subsequent rabbinic literature. In particular, R. Chaim Sofer, *Teshuvot Maḥaneh Ḥayyim,* III, no. 60, rules that mere examination or *histaklut* does not entail a violation of the *issur*

12. R. Abraham Meir Israel, *Teshuvot va-Ya'an Avraham, Yoreh De'ah,* no. 66, reports that he was asked whether it was permissible to fashion *mezuzah* cases from metal pipes through which gas was channeled in the murder of Jews in the concentration camps. Rabbi Israel cites the statement of the Gemara regarding implements used in carrying out the death penalty as well as the rulings of *Sefer Ḥasidim* and *She'ilat Ya'aveẓ* regarding the executioner's sword and rules that the pipes in question are *asur be-hana'ah* and require burial. Those sources, however, do not support his conclusion. The gas used in execution of hapless victims may indeed be compared to the executioner's sword; the pipe through which the gas is channeled, however, is merely a container for the gas and is not the proximate cause of the victim's death.

13. Benefit is prohibited only when the object that is *asur be-hana'ah* is the proximate cause of the benefit. Accordingly, an indirectly desired future benefit is always permissible. See Rashba, *Sukkah* 31b.

14. Cf. R. Meir Schapiro, *Teshuvot Or ha-Me'ir*, no. 74, sec. 4, who apparently did not recognize this to be the thrust of *Hatam Sofer*'s concern and hence advances the consideration cited *supra*, note 13, in refutation of *Ḥatam Sofer*'s position.

hana'ah.[15]

R. Yitzchak Arieli, *Torah she-be-'al Peh,* vol. VI (5724), argues that although acquisition of knowledge may be a "benefit," insofar as a corpse is concerned, acquisition of knowledge is *she-lo kederekh hana'ah,* i.e., such benefit constitutes an "unusual" form of benefit that is not subsumed under the *issur hana'ah* associated with a cadaver. That argument, however, is based upon a disputed premise. Although a 16th-century authority, R. David ibn Zimra, *Teshuvot Radbaz,* III, no. 547, did permit "unusual" forms of benefit to be derived from a corpse, both *Mishneh le-Melekh, Hilkhot Avel* 14:21, and R. Akiva Eger, *Gilyon ha-Shas, Avodah Zarah* 12b, adopt a contrary view. The latter two authorities observe that "unusual" forms of benefit are excluded only from those *issurei hana'ah* with regard to which the prohibition is couched in scriptural terminology proscribing "eating." Although, in such contexts, reference to "eating" does not limit the prohibition exclusively to gastronomical activity, it does serve to establish a paradigm in prohibiting only those activities that are analogous to "eating," i.e., activities from which pleasure or benefit is derived in an ordinary and usual manner. With regard to prohibitions in which no such scriptural paradigm exists, the prohibition against "benefit" includes even pleasure or benefit derived in an unusual manner. Thus, no benefit whatsoever may be derived from milk and meat that have been cooked together or from the growth of mixed species of grain and grapes that have been commingled in planting. In each of those cases, the prohibition is not expressed as an admonition against "eating" and hence even unusual forms of benefit are proscribed. R. Akiva Eger, noting that the prohibition against deriving benefit from a corpse is also not couched in such phraseology, declares that it is forbidden to derive even unusual forms of benefit from a corpse.

The basic issue, of course, is whether, for purposes of Halakhah, mere examination or *histaklut* constitutes a form of benefit. In support of that position *Maharam Shik* cites a statement of the Mishnah, *Nedarim* 48a. A person who, by means of a vow, generates a prohibition against deriving

15. R. Mordecai Winkler, *Teshuvot Levushei Mordekhai, Mahadura Telita'ah, Oraḥ Ḥayyim,* no. 29, regards *histaklut* as a forbidden form of benefit but nevertheless cites the comments of Ran, *Nedarim* 39b, in permitting mere visual examination of a cadaver for purposes of acquiring information necessary for the treatment of a sick person on the grounds that treatment of the patient constitutes a *miẓvah. Levushei Mordekhai* rules that benefit derived passively, i.e., without an overt action, for purposes of fulfilling a *miẓvah,* is not prohibited. See also R. Yehudah Leib Graubart, *Teshuvot Ḥavalim ba-Ne'emim,* III, no. 64.

benefit from his fellow townsmen is forbidden to benefit from property owned by the "town" since such property is regarded as held collectively by the inhabitants of the town. The Mishnah explicitly enumerates "*sefarim,*" i.e., Torah scrolls and scrolls of the Prophets and Hagiographa, among the items of property owned by the townspeople collectively from which, under such circumstances, benefit may not be derived. Obviously, the benefit derived from "*sefarim*" is the knowledge and information that is obtained as a result of reading the scrolls. Accordingly, it is evident from this source that discovery of previously unknown facts or acquiring new insights and understanding constitutes a "benefit" that may not be derived from an object that is *asur behana'ah.*

It should, however, be noted that *Bet Yosef, Yoreh De'ah* 224, cites the ruling of Rashba who permits use of *sefarim* under such circumstances, presumably because his text of the Mishnah did not include the word "*sefarim.*" If that crucial word is absent in the Mishnah there is, of course, no textual evidence establishing the proposition that acquisition of information constitutes a form of *hana'ah* of which Halakhah takes cognizance and, accordingly, there exists no talmudic evidence supporting a prohibition against mere visual examination of a cadaver for scientific purposes.

The principle established by the accepted text of the Mishnah as it appears in all published editions seems to stand in contradiction to another accepted principle of Jewish law. It is categorically forbidden to derive mundane "benefit" from property belonging to *hekdesh,* i.e., property that has been consecrated for use in maintenance and upkeep of the Temple. Benefit derived in violation of this prohibition constitutes the transgression of *me'ilah* and carries a statutory punishment. In this context, a clear definition of benefits excluded from such punishment is forthcoming. The Gemara, *Pesaḥim* 26a, declares, "Sound, sight and smell do not constitute *me'ilah (kol, mareh va-reaḥ ein ba-hen mishum me'ilah).*" In context, the Gemara is defining and limiting the concept of *hana'ah,* or benefit. Although other forms of sensual pleasure do constitute *hana'ah,* benefit derived by means of "sight" does not rise to the level of a prohibited "benefit." The principle is made explicit with regard to the prohibition concerning *me'ilah* but, logically, it is equally applicable to all categories of *issurei hana'ah.*

This, however, does not necessarily mean that such forms of *hana'ah* are entirely innocuous and hence permissible. The talmudic statement "*ein ba-hen mishum me'ilah*" serves only to establish that enjoyment of such benefit does not constitute a punishable infraction. Despite the fact that no punishable offense is engendered as a result of deriving benefit from "sound, sight or smell," the act may yet remain prohibited, albeit unpunishable. Indeed, the Gemara, *Pesaḥim* 26a, declares explicitly that derivation of such benefit is an infraction of Jewish law. That prohibition is recorded by Rambam, *Hilkhot Me'ilah* 5:16. Nevertheless, *Tosafot, Shabbat* 21a, cites a statement of the Gemara, *Sukkah* 53a, to the effect that a woman is permitted to sort kernels of wheat by the light illuminating festivities attendant upon the drawing of water on *Sukkot* (*simḥat bet ha-sho'evah*). Illumination was provided by means of fuel purchased with consecrated funds devoted to defraying the cost of that celebration. The woman's activity is entirely secular and mundane. Although an alternate interpretation is suggested, *Tosafot* cite a comment of the Palestinian Talmud indicating that the woman's activity is entirely permissible, i.e, that there is no prohibition whatsoever against deriving a benefit by means of "sight" from that which is otherwise *asur be-hana'ah.*[16] However, even according to *Tosafot,* the Babylonian Talmud appears to prohibit benefit in the form of "sound, sight or smell."[17]

The prohibition concerning "sight, sound and smell" is not limited to benefit derived from consecrated property (*hekdesh*) but extends to other forms of *issurei hana'ah* as well.[18] The issue with regard to forbidden forms of smell arises with regard to the prohibition against deriving benefit from *ḥameẓ* on *Pesaḥ*. On *Pesaḥ,* may a Jew, knowingly and willingly, inhale the pleasant aroma of freshly baked bread? On the basis of a statement found in a gloss appended to *Issur ve-Heter he-Arukh* 39:33, it is clear that such pleasure is forbidden to a Jew on *Pesaḥ*. A similar ruling is recorded by *Shulḥan Arukh ha-Rav, Oraḥ Ḥayyim* 443:3, and *Ma'adanei Shmu'el* 113:2. Similarly, with regard to sight, *Shulḥan Arukh, Yoreh De'ah* 142:15, rules that it is forbidden to enjoy the aesthetic pleasure derived from gazing upon an object of beauty if the *objet d'art* is associated with idolatrous practices. Accordingly, it would follow that the prohibition against deriving benefit from a corpse would serve to

16. Cf., *Tosafot, Pesaḥim* 26a, s.v. *me'ilah* and *Pnei Yehoshu'a, Shabbat* 21a. See also R. Ovadiah Yosef, *Yabi'a Omer,* III, *Yoreh De'ah,* no. 20.

17. See the discussion of R. Joseph Cohen in his *Harerei be-Sadeh,* annotations on R. Zevi Pesach Frank, *Har Ẓevi, Oraḥ Ḥayyim,* I, no. 183.

18. See, however, *Teshuvot Kol Eliyahu,* II, *Oraḥ Ḥayyim,* no. 23, who asserts that, according to Rambam, the prohibition is indeed limited to benefit derived from consecrated property. Cf., the differing opinions regarding Rambam's position cited by *Yabi'a Omer,* VI, *Oraḥ Ḥayyim,* no. 34, sec. 3.

prohibit even benefit derived solely from visual examination.[19]

Nevertheless, the controversy concerning a prohibition attendant upon visual examination of a cadaver is not germane to the issue of utilization of scientific data yielded by immoral experimentation. Accepting the position of *Ḥatam Sofer* that it is forbidden to examine a corpse for purposes of acquiring medical knowledge, one nevertheless searches responsa literature in vain for a ruling to the effect that a person who has attended medical school and has illicitly studied anatomy is subsequently forbidden to earn a livelihood by utilizing that knowledge and skill as a surgeon. The sole question is whether a medical student may examine a corpse in order to study the anatomy of the human body. Although that issue is a matter of controversy, no rabbinic authority has ruled that such knowledge, once acquired, cannot be utilized for a beneficial purpose. The original derivation of the information may indeed constitute a forbidden benefit; yet, once such information has been assimilated, the prohibition has *ipso facto* been irreversibly violated regardless of whether or not such information is subsequently put to practical use. Subsequent benefit generated by utilization of that knowledge is not proscribed.

It has been said that the history of medicine is strewn with the products of immoral experimentation. Nevertheless, prior to the discussions concerning Nazi experimentation, no ethicist has sought to ban the benefit derived from research conducted in violation of moral norms. According to *Ḥatam Sofer,* any medical information obtained at autopsy is the product of an illicit act. Yet, no rabbinic authority has banned the use of such information once it has been obtained.

Quite to the contrary, there are other talmudic sources that seem to confirm the permissibility of utilization of information obtained in an illicit manner. The Gemara, *Bekhorot* 45a, recounts that the students of R. Ishmael obtained the body of a harlot who had been executed by civil authorities and boiled the cadaver in order to determine the number of organs in the human body. Similarly, the Gemara, *Niddah* 24b, relates that Abba Sha'ul said of himself that at an earlier period in his life he was professionally involved in the burial of the dead and that it was his

19. Although the distinction is not made explicitly by *Maḥaneh Ḥayyim* in his discussion of this issue, that authority may have intended to distinguish between "sight" (*mar'eh*) in the sense of illumination and "sight" as a means of acquiring information. *Maḥaneh Ḥayyim* apparently regards illumination enabling a person to see properly as a form of proscribed sensual benefit, whereas *histaklut,* or visual examination, yielding intellectual benefit that is non-sensual in nature, he regards as permissible.

wont to scrutinize the bones of the deceased. As a result of his examinations he discovered that "The bones of one who drinks undiluted wine are burned; those of one who drinks properly diluted wine are black (or dry, according to the second explanation of Rashi). The bones of one whose drinking exceeds his eating are burned; [those of one] whose eating exceeds his drinking are black (or dry); [those of one who eats and drinks] properly are [moist with] oil." Elsewhere, the Gemara, *Nazir* 52a, addresses a question pertaining to ritual defilement that hinges upon whether a number of spinal vertebrae come from a single cadaver or from the corpses of a multiple number of individuals. The Gemara relates that a container full of bones was brought to the synagogue. Thereupon a certain Theodos the Physician entered the synagogue accompanied by "all the physicians." Upon examining the bones they declared that the vertebrae did not come from a single spinal column. R. Mordecai Winkler, *Teshuvot Levushei Mordekhai, Mahadura Telita'ah, Oraḥ Ḥayyim,* no. 29, cites this narrative and questions how it was possible for Theodos and his colleagues to make such a determination unless they had previously studied the shape and configuration of vertebrae in other cadavers. These sources serve to establish one of two halakhic principles: either (1) there exists no prohibition against deriving benefit from the corpse of a non-Jew, as *Ḥatam Sofer* does in fact deduce on the basis of *Bekhorot* 45a; or (2) mere examination of a cadaver does not constitute a forbidden form of *hana'ah.*

There is yet another source that is unequivocal. The Gemara, *Niddah* 32b, records a narrative concerning Cleopatra, queen of Alexandria. The subject of the underlying discussion is the question of the precise stage of gestation at which a fetus may be regarded as already having been "formed" and whether there is any distinction between a male and a female fetus in this regard. The Gemara reports that Cleopatra condemned a number of pregnant maidservants to be put to death on the forty-first day of gestation and examined their bodies subsequent to execution. She reported that both male and female fetuses were already "formed." The Gemara recognized that Cleopatra could have arranged for insemination of these slaves exactly forty days prior to execution but questions how she could have been certain that the women in question were not already pregnant at the time that she had them inseminated. If they were already pregnant there would, of course, be no proof that a fetus acquires a "form" by the fortieth day of gestation. The Gemara replies that Cleopatra administered an abortifacient to each of these women in order to destroy any already existing fetus. She was thereby assured that they were no longer pregnant and was thus enabled to determine the precise stage of gestation by controlling the time of insemination. It must be assumed that destruction of those fetuses was illicit. Nevertheless, the Gemara did not hesitate to utilize the data derived from this immoral experiment in order to establish a scientific fact. Even those talmudic Sages who are recorded as having rejected Cleopatra's evidence did so because they distrusted her ability to control conception, not because of any moral qualms they may have felt with regard to acting upon information illicitly derived.

It should be emphasized that, even if the evidence explicitly permitting utilization of information obtained by immoral means might be rebutted, such use must nevertheless be regarded as legitimate for purposes of *pikuaḥ nefesh* unless there is clear and convincing evidence to the contrary. Any and all measures must be utilized for purposes of preserving life unless there exists clear evidence predicated upon talmudic sources indicating that some measure must be abjured. This does not mean that one cannot empathize with those who decry the use of data derived from Nazi experimentation. Such reactions are intuitive and emotional; indeed, such intuitions and emotional reactions are entirely salutary. Nevertheless, the postulates of Halakhah are by no means always identical with intuitive reactions.

The Gemara, *Sanhedrin* 17a, declares that no person is qualified to serve as a member of a Sanhedrin unless he is capable of advancing one hundred and fifty reasons in favor of freeing a rodent from ritual impurity. It is nevertheless quite clear that the Torah has rendered a rodent impure. Accordingly, any argument advanced to the contrary must be incorrect. If so, queries *Tosafot,* why should a candidate for judicial office be required to be proficient in advancing arguments predicated upon "vain sharpness" (*ḥarifut shel hevel*). R. Baruch ha-Levi Epstein, *Tosefet Berakhah, Parashat Shemini,* answers *Tosafot*'s question by remarking that one of the requirements for sitting on a Sanhedrin is a recognition that, at times, Halakhah is counterintuitive. Only a person who can cogently argue even for the purification of a rodent can appreciate the fact that biblical provisions are sometimes contrary to the inclination of the human intellect. One who cannot do so perceives no conflict whatsoever. The ability to suspend one's own subjective judgment is a necessary condition and prerequisite for service as a judge and as a rabbinic decisor.

It may well be true that, in terms of human sensibilities, the atrocities of the Nazis should be so abhorrent that, left to our own inclinations, we should not consider using such data for even the most exemplary purposes. Nevertheless, Halakhah teaches that, difficult though it may be, when confronted with a matter of *pikuaḥ nefesh,* those inclinations must be transcended because "my Father in Heaven has so decreed."[20]

These comments notwithstanding, the recently enunciated policy of the *New England Journal of Medicine* against publication of articles based upon unethical research, regardless of scientific merit, is, subject to some reservations, a position deserving of commendation.[21] It is evident from the editorial comments announcing that decision that the unethical nature of research whose product the *Journal* feels constrained to reject lies in either 1) failure to obtain meaningful informed consent; 2) use of a placebo group in a clinical trial when there is already good reason to believe that the treated group will fare better; or 3) exposure of consenting subjects to appreciable risks without the possibility of commensurate benefits.

The same editorial eloquently presents the reasons for not publishing the fruits of unethical research. Publication is probably the primary goal motivating scientists to engage in medical research. It is unquestionably a highly significant consideration since publication is surely "an important part of the reward system in medical research." Accordingly, investigators would not undertake unethical studies if it were known in advance that the results simply will not be published. Conversely, publication would reinforce such behavior and lead to further unethical research. Use of data derived from unethical experimentation, it is argued, involves prospective complicity in sending the wrong message to future scientists.

Paradoxically, it is precisely because the Nazi experimentation—or the

20. It is instructive to note that studies concerning the effects of malnutrition and starvation were performed by Jewish physicians in the Warsaw ghetto and the results were smuggled out of the ghetto at considerable risk. See Leon Tushnet, *The Uses of Adversity* (New York, 1966), a work devoted to the description of that endeavor. See also Myron Winick, ed., *Hunger Disease* (New York, 1979). Although those studies involved no complicity of the Jewish doctors in the nefarious schemes of the Nazis, they do reflect an entirely correct recognition that it is not improper to derive and utilize beneficial information that would have been unavailable save for immoral acts.

21. See Marcia Angell, "The Nazi Hypothermia Experiment and Unethical Experiments Today," *New England Journal of Medicine,* May 17, 1990, pp. 1462–1464. See also *idem,* "Editorial Responsibility: Protecting Human Rights by Restricting Publication of Unethical Research," *The Nazi Doctors and the Nuremberg Code,* pp. 276–285.

notorious Tuskegee syphilis studies[22]—were so bestial that citation of data yielded by those studies will not serve as an impetus for the repetition of those horrendous practices. Nor is refusal to cite those results likely to serve as a deterrent to a diabolically inclined madman. As the *Journal* insightfully notes, "the unethical research of today reflects thoughtlessness more than callousness." To paraphrase a Yiddish aphorism: A lock upon the door of prestigious journals is designed to deter the basically honest researcher; for the basically dishonest or morally corrupt, no lock is effective. It is precisely because of the fact that "if small lapses were permitted we would become inured to them and this would lead to larger violations" that, in this context, we need to be more concerned with small lapses than with larger violations. Moreover, "small lapses" are usually designed only to assure speed and to promote efficiency. If a study is rejected for publication because of ethical insensitivity to "small" matters the study may be repeated by the same investigator or by others using ethically irreproachable methods. Studies involving gross improprieties, by their very nature, cannot be replicated.

Nevertheless, there may well be circumstances in which refusal to publish will not yield the desired effect or in which delay necessitated by repetition of the study may jeopardize lives. Such circumstances generate a true moral conflict. Fortunately, there are options available that make it possible to escape from between the horns of this dilemma. Publication is not incompatible with concomitant censure and sanctions by appropriate professional and scientific organizations.[23] Editorial disclaimer and repudiation of the breeches of ethical propriety involved in the research are both obvious forms of peer sanction as well as strong disincentives to future lapses. Since enhancement of scientific reputation as well as ego gratification are a function of frequency of citation in scientific and medical literature it should become the accepted norm for ethically tainted studies to be cited without attribution of authorship.[24]

22. See *supra,* note 9.

23. Professor Arthur Caplan, at the time a bioethicist at the University of Minnesota and presently at the University of Pennsylvania, has taken the position that Nazi data can be used so long as the purpose is an important one and the data are presented with a clear moral denunciation of the methods utilized in obtaining the information presented. See Mills, "Use of Nazi Data," p. 51.

24. It must, of course, be recognized that if publication is to be accompanied by editorial censure and, in addition, the prospect of recognition in the form of future citation is closed it is unlikely that any researcher would consent to publication of his name in association with an ethically unacceptable study.

Indeed, he would probably seek to withdraw his submission from publication and this proposal would become self-defeating insofar as saving of human life is concerned. That, too, may be remedied. Attendant legal problems notwithstanding, once it has been determined that a study submitted for publication is based, in whole or in part, upon procedures that society cannot condone, in this writer's opinion, considerations of *pikuaḥ nefesh* would render it entirely ethical to publish such a study anonymously without the consent of the author or authors. If such a policy is found to be ethically sound and pragmatically effective the obvious legal obstacles to implementation can be overcome by equally obvious legal devices. Thus, medical and scientific journals might publish a brief notice that all submissions will be subjected to peer review for determination of ethical propriety and, with such review serving as consideration, require that, as a condition of submission, the author waive both the right of withdrawal and the right of attribution in the event that the reviewers determine that an ethical impropriety has occurred.

Chapter XI

In Vitro Fertilization: Maternal Identity and Conversion

Indeed, the world was created only for procreation as it is said, "He created it not a waste, He formed it to be inhabited" (Isaiah 45:18).

GITTIN 41b

The question of maternal identity in situations involving a host mother as well as the issue of maternal identity in instances of in vitro fertilization have been addressed in earlier volumes of this series.[1] In vitro techniques are employed when it is not possible for a woman to become pregnant by natural means because of her inability to produce viable ova, because of a blockage of the fallopian tubes, because the husband suffers from an inability to produce a sufficient number of sperm or because pregnancy has not occurred in utero for other, sometimes unknown, physiological reasons. When normal ovulation does occur an ovum or, more commonly, a multiple number of ova are removed from the ovaries. The ova are then fertilized in a petri dish by sperm ejaculated by the husband and, after undergoing a number of cell divisions, the developing zygote is inserted into the uterus of the woman from whom the ovum was removed. If, however, the woman cannot produce viable ova an ovum, or a multiple number of ova, may be donated by a relative or stranger, fertilized by means of an in vitro procedure and inserted into the uterus of the otherwise infertile woman and carried to term. When the fertility problem arises from the woman's inability to sustain a pregnancy for the full period of gestation the fertilized zygote may be implanted in the uterus of another woman, i.e., a host mother, who will carry the fetus to term. In each of these cases there is some question with regard to whether the genetic mother or the gestational mother is regarded as the child's mother for matters in which such a relationship is significant in Jewish law, e.g., consanguinity, inheritance, laws of mourning, etc.

1. See *Contemporary Halakhic Problems,* I, 106–109 and II, 91–93.

Although there is a minority view that regards the donor mother as the sole mother of a child born of in vitro fertilization,[2] the consensus of rabbinic opinion is that a maternal-filial relationship is generated between the gestational mother and the child, despite the absence of any genetic relationship, by virtue of parturition alone.[3] Whether or not the genetic mother, i.e., the woman who produced the ovum from which the child was conceived, is also a mother from the vantage point of Jewish law is a more complex question. The question of whether the baby may, in effect, have two halakhic mothers must be regarded as yet open.[4]

I. *Absence of a Maternal Relationship*

R. Eliezer Waldenberg, *Ẓiẓ Eli'ezer,* XV, no. 45,[5] has advanced the novel view that, in the eyes of Halakhah, a child born of in vitro fertilization has neither a father nor a mother even if the biological mother and the gestational mother are one and the same, as is the case in the majority of instances in which in vitro procedures are employed.[6] Rabbi Walden-

2. See R. Shlomoh Goren, *Ha-Ẓofeh,* 7 Adar I 5744. See also R. Joshua Feigenbaum, *Sha'arei Torah,* vol. IV, no. 4; Prof. Ze'ev Low, *Emek Halakhah,* II (Jerusalem, 5749), 163–172; Dr. Itamar Warhaftig, *Teḥumin,* V (5744), 268–269; and R. Ezra Bick, *Teḥumin,* VII (5746), 266–270.

3. In addition to the sources cited herein see R. Moshe Hershler, *Halakhah u-Refu'ah,* I, (Jerusalem, 5740), 316–320; R. Menasheh Grossbart, *Sha'arei Torah, Sha'ar Menasheh,* XV (5684), no. 3; R. Zevi Hirsch Friedling, *Ha-Be'er,* VI (5691), no. 3; and R. Betzalel Ze'ev Safran, *Ha-Be'er,* VII (5692), no. 2, reprinted in *Teshuvot ha-Rabaz* (Jerusalem, 5722), *Teshuvot mi-Ben ha-Meḥaber,* no. 5.

4. See, for example, R. Moshe Sternbuch, *Be-Shevilei ha-Refu'ah,* no. 8 (Kislev 5747), p. 33 and *Contemporary Halakhic Problems,* I, 108. This possibility will be discussed in a later section of this chapter.

5. This responsum originally appeared in *Assia,* vol. IX, no. 1 (Tammuz 5742) and is reprinted in *Sefer Assia* (5746), V, 84–93. Cf., the comments of R. Avigdor Nebenzahl, *Assia,* vol. IX, no. 2 (Tishri 5743), reprinted in *Sefer Assia,* V, 92–93.

6. Curiously, in a later responsum discussing host mothers, *Ẓiẓ Eli'ezer*, XIX, no. 40, Rabbi Waldenberg cites and reaffirms his earlier statements and then proceeds to set forth a seemingly contradictory position. In this responsum Rabbi Waldenberg cites *Teshuvot Even Yekarah*, III, no. 29, who rules that the recipient of transplanted reproductive organs is to be regarded as the halakhic mother of all subsequently born children. *Even Yekarah* cogently reasons that the reproductive organs become an integral part of the body of the recipient in a manner analogous to the status of a grafted branch with regard to *orlah* as discussed by the Gemara, *Sotah* 43b. Rabbi Waldenberg then proceeds to argue, rather incon-

berg's arguments, which are not based upon cited precedents or analogy to other halakhic provisions, are three in number: 1) Fertilization in the course of an in vitro procedure occurs in an "unnatural" manner through the intermediacy of a "third power" extraneous to the father or mother, i.e., the petri dish. 2) Conception occurs in a manner "that has no relationship to genealogy." 3) In natural reproduction the ovum remains "attached" to the body and is fertilized therein. Maternal identity is consequent solely upon fertilization that occurs while the ovum is yet attached to the mother's body. Thus, upon "severance" and removal of the ovum from the mother's body any genealogical relationship between the ovum and the mother is destroyed.

To this writer, those arguments appear to be without substance. In response to the first argument it must be stated that the petri dish is not a "third power" and in no way contributes biologically or chemically to the fertilization process. It is simply a convenient receptacle designed to provide a hospitable environment in which fertilization may occur.[7] Rabbi Waldenberg's second argument, if indeed he intended to present it as an independent argument, is entirely conclusory. In order to demonstrate that no maternal relationship exists some evidence or argument must be presented that would serve to demonstrate that genealogical relationships are generated solely in utero. Rabbi Waldenberg provides no such demonstration. Whatever cogency the third argument may have is lost if it is recognized that parturition, in and of itself, establishes a maternal relationship.

In the early days of in vitro fertilization a position similar to that

---

gruously, that, "*a fortiori,*" the fertilized ovum becomes an integral part of the host mother's body.

7. It is indeed true that culture media are required in order to enable cell division to occur. The specific components of the medium used for this purpose vary widely from one in vitro center to another but usually include human blood serum or, in some places, fetal calf serum to which antibiotics and other chemical products are added. Frequently, but not always, the serum is derived from the patient's own blood. Nevertheless, there is no reason to assume that nutrients utilized to support metabolism constitute a "third power" effecting parental relationships. It is not inconceivable that medicine may find a way to introduce artificial nutrition intravenously into the fetus in utero in order to compensate for certain natural deficiencies. Indeed, in utero blood transfer is already employed as a means of overcoming certain incompatibilities between fetal and maternal blood. No rabbinic decisor has suggested that introduction of blood or nutrients from a source other than the bloodstream of the mother casts doubt upon the maternal-filial relationship.

advanced by Rabbi Waldenberg was presented by R. Judah Gershuni in the Tishri 5739 issue of *Or ha-Mizraḥ.*[8] Rabbi Gershuni's argument is based upon a statement of *Divrei Malki'el,* IV, no. 107. There is a significant disagreement among rabbinic authorities with regard to whether a paternal relationship may occur as a result of artificial insemination or whether such a relationship can arise only as the result of a sexual act.[9] *Divrei Malki'el* expresses tentative support for the latter position but does so on the basis of the novel view that "once the semen has been emitted and has warmth only because of the ministration of the physician and his skill with the pipette or due to the heat of the bath" a baby born as a result of that process is not regarded as the son of the donor. Although *Divrei Malki'el* stands virtually alone in developing this argument[10] and

8. This article is reprinted in Rabbi Gershuni's *Kol Ẓofayikh* (Jerusalem, 5740), pp. 361–367.

9. The primary source affirming a paternal relationship is *Hagahot Semak,* cited by *Mishneh le-Melekh, Hilkhot Ishut* 15:4; *Baḥ, Yoreh De'ah* 195; and *Bet Shmu'el, Even ha-Ezer* 1:10. A similar view is expressed by *Ḥelkat Meḥokek, Even ha-Ezer* 1:8; *Teshuvot Tashbaẓ,* III, no. 263; *Turei Even, Ḥaggigah* 15a; *Bnei Ahuvah, Hilkhot Ishut* 15; *Arukh la-Ner, Yevamot* 10a; *Mishneh le-Melekh, Hilkhot Issurei Bi'ah* 17:13; *She'ilat Ya'aveẓ,* II, no. 97; *Maharam Shik al Taryag Miẓvot,* no. 1; *Teshuvot Divrei Malkiel,* II, no.107; R. Shlomoh Zalman Auerbach, *No'am,* I (5717),155; R. Israel Ze'ev Mintzberg, *No'am,* I, 129; R. Joshua Baumol, *Teshuvot Emek Halakhah,* I, no. 68; R. Avigdor Nebenzahl, *Sefer Assia,* V, 92–93; and R. Ovadiah Yosef, quoted by Moshe Drori, *Teḥumin,* I (5740), 287, and Abraham S. Abraham, *Nishmat Avraham, Even ha-Ezer* 1:5, sec. 3. An opposing view is expressed by *Taz, Even ha-Ezer* 1:8; *Birkei Yosef, Even ha-Ezer* 1:14; R. Ovadiah Hedaya, *No'am,* I, 130–137; R. Moshe Aryeh Leib Shapiro, *No'am,* I, 138–142; and R. Ben Zion Uziel, *Mishpetei Uzi'el, Even ha-Ezer,* no. 19, reprinted in *Piskei Uzi'el* (Jerusalem, 5737), pp. 282–283. *Teshuvot Ḥelkat Ya'akov,* I, no. 24, regards the issue as a matter of doubt.

10. In his previously cited article in *Be-Shevilei ha-Refu'ah,* p. 30, R. Moshe Sternbuch presents an argument quite similar to that advanced by *Divrei Malki'el* in rejecting a paternal relationship between the donor of the semen and the child born of subsequent in vitro fertilization even when the zygote is implanted in the donor's wife. Rabbi Sternbuch argues that "the act of conception takes place in the sterile petri dish itself which acts to commence conception, to unite both of them (i.e., the ovum and the sperm) as in the womb. This is not in the manner of conception since another power is combined therein, that is, the petri dish."

The effect of denying paternal identity, asserts Rabbi Sternbuch, is to prohibit in vitro fertilization entirely. Rabbinic authorities who permit ejaculation of semen by the husband for purposes of artificial insemination sanction that procedure only because it leads to procreation. However, if in vitro fertilization does not result in a father-child relationship it does not serve to fulfill the commandment to "be fruitful and multiply" and hence ejaculation of semen for purposes of in vitro procedures is not permissible. See sources cited *supra,* note 8. With regard to artificial insemination, some authorities, including *Arukh la-Ner, Yevamot* 10a, and *Maharam Shik al Taryag Mizvot,* no. 1, maintain that, although the child is considered the son of the donor, the donor does not fulfill the precept of procreation because no sexual act is involved. Rabbi Gershuni, although he too denies that artificial insemination results in a paternal-filial relationship, nevertheless regards the procedure as permissible for a married couple. Rabbi Gershuni argues that although artificial insemination does not serve to fulfill the commandment to "be fruitful and multiply," nevertheless, since the procedure results in procreation of the human species, it serves to fulfill the prophetic mandate "He created [the universe] not to be a waste, He formed it to be populated" (Isaiah 45:18) and hence ejaculation of semen for that purpose is not for naught.

For a vaguely similar reason Rabbi Sternbuch, p. 29, opines that destruction of an embryo fertilized outside of a woman's body is not prohibited. He states that ". . . . the prohibition against abortion is in the woman's uterus, for the [embryo] has the potential to develop and become complete in her womb and it is destroyed. But here, outside the womb, an additional operation is required to implant [the embryo] in the woman's uterus and without this it will . . . of its own not reach completion. . . ." Rabbi Sternbuch cites no sources in support of that distinction. A similar view is advanced, without elaboration or citation of sources, by R. Chaim David Halevy, *Assia,* vol. XII, no. 3–4 (Kislev 5750). One source that might be cited in support of such a conclusion is *Teshuvot Ḥakham Ẓevi,* no. 93. Citing *Sanhedrin* 57b, *Ḥakham Ẓevi* rules that destruction of a *golem* does not constitute an act of homicide and is not prohibited because its gestation is not in the form of a "man within a man," as evidenced by the fact that the Gemara, *Sanhedrin* 65b, reports that Rabbi Zeira commanded a person created by utilization of *Sefer Yeẓirah* to return to dust. That statement, however, cannot be taken as definitive since *Ḥakham Ẓevi* concludes that a *golem* lacks status as a Jew or as a human being for other purposes as well. See also R. Joseph Rosen, *Teshuvot Ẓofnat Pa'aneaḥ* (Jerusalem, 5728), II, no. 7. Genesis 9:6 is cited by the Gemara and rendered "Whosoever sheds the blood of a man within a man his blood shall be shed" in establishing feticide as a capital transgression in the Noahide Code. Accordingly, there would be strong grounds to assume that a Noahide does not incur capital punishment for destruction of an embryo fertilized in vitro, but not for support of the position that a person born of in vitro fertilization may be destroyed with impunity or even for the position that there is no halakhic consideration forbidding a Jew to destroy a developing embryo outside the human body. Moreover, Ramban, cited by Ran, *Yoma* 82a, and Rosh, *Yoma* 8:13, maintains that Sabbath restrictions and the like are suspended for the purpose of preserving the life of a fetus. Those comments clearly reflect the view that there is an obligation to preserve fetal life. Thus, there are no obvious grounds for assuming that nascent human life may be destroyed with impunity simply because it is not sheltered in its natural habitat, i.e., its development takes place outside the mother's womb. R. Samuel ha-Levi Woszner, *Teshuvot Shevet ha-Levi,* V, no. 47, expresses the opinion that Sabbath restrictions are not suspended for the preservation of a zygote that has as yet not been implanted in the gestational mother on the grounds that the vast majority of such zygotes are not viable but himself concludes that a child born of artificial insemination is indeed the child of the donor, Rabbi Gershuni observes that a fertilized zygote sustained in a petri dish by means of "artificial nutrition and blood serum" should not be regarded by Jewish law as the child of either parent. The earlier presented rebuttal of Rabbi Waldenberg's argument applies with equal force to that advanced by Rabbi Gershuni. Moreover, any cogency the argument may have with regard to establishment of a paternal relationship notwithstanding, if parturition, in and of itself, serves to establish a maternal relationship, the sources of antecedent nutrition of the fetus are totally irrelevant.

II. *Parturition as a Determinant*

The view that the maternal relationship is predicated upon parturition is based upon the statement of the Gemara, *Yevamot* 97b, to the effect that a fraternal relationship exists between male twins born to a woman who converts to Judaism during the course of her pregnancy. Since a proselyte is regarded as a "newly born child" and all halakhic relationships with existing blood relatives are severed upon conversion, the relationship of the child to its mother, and through her to its twin sibling, cannot be regarded as having arisen at the moment of conception.[11] From the vantage

adds the cautionary note that the empirical situation, and hence the halakhic ruling, may change with advances in the development of reproductive knowledge and techniques. The clear implication of his position is that destruction of such nascent life cannot be countenanced. R. Mordecai Eliyahu, *Teḥumin,* XI (5750), states unequivocally that surplus ova may not be destroyed. For a further discussion of the propriety of destroying fertilized ova see this writer's article, "Ethical Concerns in Artificial Procreation: A Jewish Perspective," *Publications de l'Academie du Royaume du Maroc,* vol. X: *Problèmes d'Éthique Engendrés par les Nouvelles Maîtrises de la Procréation Humaine* (Agadir, 1986), pp. 143–145.

There are, however, strong reasons to assume that there is no prohibition against the destruction of a nonviable fetus, as is stated by Rabbi Sternbuch, *loc. cit.* See Abraham S. Abraham, *Nishmat Avraham, Ḥoshen Mishpat* 425:1, sec. 19, and R. Zalman Nechemiah Goldberg, *Teḥumin,* V, 250. Nevertheless, such a conclusion is contrary to the view expressed by R. Eleazar Fleckles, *Teshuvah me-Ahavah,* no. 53, with regard to a nonviable neonate. See also *Teshuvot Radbaz,* II, no. 695.

11. R. Chaim Soloveitchik is reported to have resolved an entirely different issue by declaring that this statement is limited to the case of a woman who converts to Judaism within the first forty days of gestation. See R. Elchanan Wasserman, *Kovez̤ He'arot,* no. 73, sec. 12, and *infra,* note 31. According to Reb Chaim's interpretation of this source, no further conclusion can be drawn

point of Halakhah, the situation of a pregnant convert is analogous to that of a woman who receives an ovum into her uterus that has been fertilized outside of her body. Upon conversion, all relationships with relatives, including her own fetus, are severed. Accordingly, the status of her fetus at the moment of conversion is precisely identical to that of a fetus that is abruptly thrust into her uterus, i.e., a fetus that has not been conceived within her body.[12] Clearly then, since a maternal relationship is recognized by Jewish law in the case of a pregnant convert, it must be the process of parturition that, at least in such instances, establishes the maternal relationship.[13] If so, it follows that the site in which fertilization occurs or

---

with regard to determination of maternal identity. However, Reb Chaim's understanding of the limited application of the Gemara's statement is not reflected in the compilations of any of the codifiers of Jewish law, in the responsa literature or in the talmudic commentaries.

12. In a note appended to the articles published in *Teḥumin,* the editor, Dr. Itamar Warhaftig, expresses the opinion that, logically, the biological mother, i.e., the donor of the ovum, should be considered to be the mother of a child born of in vitro fertilization. Without offering demonstrative proof, he assumes that any sources indicating that parturition establishes a maternal relationship serve to establish only that parturition gives rise to a maternal relationship vis-à-vis a biological child or vis-à-vis a child with regard to whom Halakhah abrogates the biological relationship, *viz.,* a convert. He entirely fails to consider the possibility of dual maternal relationships. See also R. Ezra Bick, *Teḥumin,* VII, 267–268.

Dr. Warhaftig does however point to what he considers to be a halakhic anomaly. Biblical law provides financial compensation to be paid to the father in cases of fetal death resulting from battery of the mother. Rambam, *Hilkhot Ḥovel u-Mazik* 4:2, rules that, in the event that the father has died before the miscarriage occurs, compensation is to be paid to the mother. Although all authorities agree that compensation is to be paid to the mother in the case of the miscarriage of a pregnant convert or in the case of the wife of a convert who is deceased, Rambam's position is novel in a situation in which the Jewish husband has died leaving heirs. *Kesef Mishneh, ad locum,* explains that in describing this untoward event Scripture employs the phrase "and her children emerge" thereby indicating a possessive relationship vested in the mother. That source, however, does not at all serve to establish a halakhic relationship for other areas of Jewish law. Compensation for loss of fetal life is rooted in a property interest established by Scripture solely for that purpose. Establishment of that property interest is not necessarily predicated upon a familial relationship recognized for other purposes of law. Moreover, as Rabbi Goldberg points out, miscarriage of the fetus is tantamount to parturition and hence miscarriage itself serves to establish a maternal relationship. Cf., also, *infra,* note 12.

13. It would be reasonable to assume that delivery of a viable fetus by means of a cesarean section similarly serves to establish a maternal relationship since

the provenance of the ovum is irrelevant;[14] parturition, in and of itself,

such delivery is equated with normal birth for other purposes of Jewish law. See R. Abraham Kilav's response to Prof. Ze'ev Low, *Emek Halakhah,* II, 173. Indeed, *Tosafot, Niddah* 44a, declare that, if a pregnant woman predeceases her fully-developed fetus, the fetus inherits its mother's estate and causes it to pass to the fetus' paternal relatives. The fetus inherits, according to *Tosafot,* because upon the mother's death its vitality is no longer derived from the mother. Clearly, there could be no inheritance in the absence of a filial relationship. That relationship, then, is established, not by parturition *per se,* but upon termination of gestation regardless of how that event occurs. Cf., R. Zalman Nechemiah Goldberg, *Teḥumin,* V, 252, note 4. However, contrary to the presumption of R. Ezra Bick, *Teḥumin,* VII, 269, there is no basis upon which to assume that termination of gestation at a stage at which the fetus is as yet not viable is tantamount to parturition; assuredly, this could not be the case when the embryo is as yet "mere water." Accordingly, removal of an as yet non-viable embryo and subsequent artificial gestation in an incubator or the like in a manner similar to that portrayed by Aldous Huxley in his *Brave New World* might well result in a situation in which the child has no mother for purposes of halakhic provisions predicated upon the existence of a maternal relationship. Cf., however, Prof. Ze'ev Low, *Emek Halakhah,* II, 164–165, and R. Abraham Kilav, *Emek Halakhah,* II, 173. Rabbi Kilav asserts that, under such conditions, a halakhically recognized maternal relationship exists between the child and its genetic mother but offers no evidence in support of that view. Rabbi Kilav rejects the existence of a maternal relationship with the donor of the ovum in usual circumstances because the birth mother or the gestational mother is regarded as the mother for halakhic purposes and, he asserts, a child cannot have two mothers. He, however, offers no concrete support for those views. As will be shown in a later section, the possibility that a child may well have two mothers for purposes of Halakhah cannot be summarily dismissed. By the same token, if Halakhah does not recognize a maternal relationship based solely upon contribution of the ovum, a fetus nurtured in an incubator may well have no mother in the eyes of Halakhah. Cf., R. Ezra Bick, *Teḥumin,* VII, 270.

14. Cf., however, R. Zalman Nechemiah Goldberg, *Teḥumin,* V, 253–255, who tentatively suggests that the Gemara, in postulating such a fraternal relationship, may be doing so only according to the view that maintains that the fetus is an integral part of the mother's body (*ubar yerekh imo*). See, for example, *Avnei Milu'im, Even ha-Ezer* 4:3 and 13:4; and *Bet Ya'akov, Ketubot* 11a, who maintain that although the Gemara, *Yevamot* 78a, speaks of the fetus as itself a convert, that description is accurate only according to the talmudic position that maintains that the fetus is not an integral part of the mother's body. If so, argues R. Goldberg, parturition may establish a maternal relationship only if the fetus is in reality an integral part of her body, i.e., if the fetus is biologically her own, but not in situations in which the fetus is conceived outside of her body and subsequently implanted in her uterus. Nevertheless, there is considerable discussion with regard to whether Rambam maintains *ubar yerekh imo* or *ubar lav yerekh imo* (see *Leḥem Mishneh, Hilkhot Avadim* 7:5 and later sources cited *infra,* note

establishes a mother-child relationship.[15] This principle is also reflected

---

46) despite the fact that in *Hilkhot Issurei Bi'ah* 14:14 Rambam clearly rules that a fraternal relationship does indeed exist. Hence it may be assumed that the principle that parturition establishes a maternal relationship is not a product of that dispute. Cf., R. Joshua Ben-Meir, *Assia,* vol. XI, no. 1 (Nisan 5746), pp. 28–29 and 39.

15. R. Zalman Nechemiah Goldberg, *Teḥumin,* V, 255–256, endeavors to show that the statement of the Gemara, *Yevamot* 97b, regarding the fraternal relationship between fetal converts is not dispositive according to the novel position of one latter-day authority regarding another matter of personal status. R. Jacob of Lissa, in a responsum published in *Teshuvot Ḥemdat Shlomoh, Even ha-Ezer,* no. 2, opines that a child born to a Jewish mother but fathered by a gentile requires conversion despite the fact that the Gemara, *Bekhorot* 47a, declares that if such a child is the firstborn child of its Jewish mother it requires redemption of the first-born. Since converts do not require redemption, postulation of a requirement for redemption would seem to contradict the thesis advanced by R. Jacob of Lissa. R. Jacob of Lissa responds by stating that, prior to conversion, the child of a Jewish mother and a non-Jewish father is a gentile by virtue of his status as the son of a non-Jewish father and, as a gentile, the child does not require redemption. R. Jacob of Lissa further states that, as the non-Jewish issue of a gentile father, the child can have no Jewish relatives. However, asserts R. Jacob of Lissa, conversion has the effect of severing all prior relationships, including the paternal one. At that point, a maternal relationship is automatically and retroactively established. As the firstborn of a Jewish mother the child requires redemption. If so, argues Rabbi Goldberg, it is conceivable that, according to R. Jacob of Lissa, parturition establishes a maternal relationship only in situations in which the fetus undergoes conversion during the course of pregnancy and hence has no already existing filial relationship, but that under different circumstances a preexisting maternal relationship established genetically or on the basis of gestation precludes any other maternal relationship, just as a non-Jewish paternal relationship precludes the genesis of a Jewish maternal relationship. However, Rabbi Goldberg's argument is not compelling. Even according to R. Jacob of Lissa, it is only the child's status as a gentile that precludes the genesis of a parental Jewish relationship; there is no evidence whatsoever that an already existing paternal or maternal relationship prevents the existence of a second relationship of a like nature. Rabbi Bick, both in *Teḥumin,* VII, 268, and in his later article, "Ovum donation: A Rabbinic Conceptual Model of Maternity," *Tradition,* vol. XXVIII, no. 1 (Fall, 1993), argues that the Gemara, *Ḥullin* 70a, explicitly denies that birth alone is the determinant of maternity. The Gemara queries:

> What is the law [regarding the sanctity of a first-born animal] if the two wombs were affixed and [the fetus] went out of one and entered the other? Its own womb is exempted [from future status of a first-born, as this was its firstborn], the one not its own is not exempted, or perhaps the one not its own is also exempted.

If any proof is to be brought from this text it must be in support of the

in the observation of *Tosafot, Ketubot* 11a, to the effect that the fetus of a pregnant woman who undergoes conversion is itself a convert but nevertheless inherits its mother's estate.[16] Quite obviously the child can be an heir only if a maternal-filial relationship has been established and in the case of a pregnant proselyte that relationship can come into being only by virtue of parturition.[17]

---

proposition that maternal identity is established by birth. The issue left unresolved by the Gemara is then whether a fetus can be "born" twice by emerging from two different uteri and thereby precluding any future firstborn to the second mother as well. The phrase "its own womb," upon which Rabbi Bick dwells, connotes nothing more than the notion that parturition is a phenomenon of halakhic significance only as the culmination of gestation in utero.

This source is discussed in a somewhat peripheral vein by R. Zalman Nechemiah Goldberg in his contribution to *Teḥumin,* V, 253. Rabbi Goldberg certainly does not find that it contradicts the thesis that motherhood is determined at parturition. In point of fact, no halakhic writer has cited this text as a source for the definition of maternal identity. They have not done so for the good reason that status as "*peter reḥem,*" i.e., a fetus that "opens a womb," has no bearing on maternal identity. No one has suggested that a neonate—even one which has no mother, if such is halakhically possible—subsequently inserted into the uterus of a woman acquires a mother simply by emerging from the birth canal of its host. One must assume that it is birth in the mode of disengagement from the physiological systems of the host, or at least as the result of labor, that is a determinant of a maternal identity. The question posed by the discussion in *Ḥullin* is whether "*peter reḥem*" is to be defined in the same manner or whether mere opening of the womb by a fetus suffices to exempt future fruit of that womb from the status of a "*peter reḥem.*" The term "its own womb" employed by the Gemara and the transmuted term "its own child" found in Rambam connote nothing more than a gestational fact and have no import whatsoever for the determination of halakhic motherhood.

16. It is clear that the fetus of a pregnant proselyte undergoes conversion simultaneously with the mother as indicated by the statement of the Gemara, *Yevamot* 78a, questioniong the absence of a requirement for separate immersion of the child. The Gemara establishes that the mother's body does not constitute an interposition or barrier (*ḥaẓiẓah*) between the waters of the *mikveh* and the child because "that is its natural growth." This is the normative halakhic position as reflected in the comments of *Dagul me-Revavah, Yoreh De'ah* 268:6.

17. Rabbi Bick assumes that a child can have but one mother and suggests that when motherhood is established at conception (or, it may be added, at an early stage of gestation), the existence of such a relationship serves to bar any second maternal relationship. Accordingly, he argues that only in the case of a pregnant convert does parturition establish a maternal relationship since it has not been preempted by a previously existing relationship.

The response to that argument is quite simple. Having conceded that birth is, at least in some circumstances, a determinant of motherhood, it becomes necessary

It might, however, be argued that although this source amply demonstrates that generation of the ovum is not the definitive criterion of the existence of a maternal relationship, nevertheless, it may be gestation rather than parturition that constitutes the factor serving to establish such a relationship. The convert would then be considered to be the mother of the child on the basis of having nurtured the fetus in her womb during the post-conversion period of gestation. This would lead to the conclusion that a naturally conceived fetus that is subsequently transferred from the womb of one woman to that of another would have two mothers for purposes of Halakhah. There are, however, aggadic sources that speak of the intrauterine transfer of Dinah from the womb of Rachel to Leah and of Joseph from Leah to Rachel.[18] Subsequent scriptural references to

---

to prove: a) that a child cannot have two halakhic mothers; and b) that conception (or gestation) is indeed itself a determinant of maternity; and c) that it preempts any subsequent maternal relationship. *Yevamot* 97b establishes parturition as a determinant of maternal relationship. The contention that this relationship is established with the birth mother only if it is not preempted by a biological mother is an additional proposition. Methodologically, that proposition cannot be entertained unless supported by proof. Such proof is entirely lacking.

Rabbi Bick further argues that the maternal relationship may well be established at the time of birth, but only between the child and the woman who is the source of the ovum from which the child develops. I would rephrase that position in somewhat different terms and express it in the proposition that birth is the cause (*sibah*) of the maternal relationship but that the biological relationship is a condition precedent (*tenai*). The response to that argument is: 1) The burden of demonstrating the existence of such a condition has not been fulfilled, particularly if a baby may have two (or more) halakhic mothers. 2) Were it indeed the case that generation of the ovum is a condition of maternal identity, I fail to understand how birth can establish a maternal relationship between a mother and her proselyte child. It must be clearly recognized that Halakhah takes no direct cognizance of genetics as a significant factor in and of itself. There is no evidence that what Rabbi Bick calls "historical facts" are at all of halakhic relevance. There is no support of which I am aware for the notion that "genetic continuity" is, halakhically speaking, a *sine qua non* of parenthood. Consequently, since conversion nullifies any preexistent relationship, if it be insisted that continuity of identity between the donor (or gestational mother) and the birth mother is a necessary condition of halakhic motherhood, the inescapable conclusion would be that the child born to a pregnant convert has no (halakhic) mother.

18. The conflicting halakhic inferences drawn by various writers from the aggadic statement to the effect that Dinah was originally conceived by Rachel and subsequently transferred to the womb of Leah, are cited and discussed in detail in *Contemporary Halakhic Problems,* II, 92–93. See also R. Shlomoh Goren, *Ha-Ẓofeh,* 7 Adar I, 5744.

This aggadic source was first cited by R. Menasheh Grossbart some seventy

Dinah as the daughter of Leah and of Joseph as the son of Rachel ostensibly indicate that each child had but a single mother. If so, it must be parturition, rather than gestation, that establishes the maternal relationship.[19] Of course, aggadic sources are not dispositive with regard to matters of Halakhah and, accordingly, the matter cannot be regarded as entirely resolved.

III. *Gestation as a Determinant*

In an article published in *Teḥumin,* vol. V (5744), R. Zalman Nechemiah Goldberg cites one significant source in support of the position that gestation establishes a maternal relationship even prior to parturition and, accordingly, that source would support the conclusion that a woman who carries a fetus in her womb for any portion of the gestational period—at least during the last two trimesters of pregnancy—is regarded as the baby's mother for purposes of Halakhah.[20]

The Gemara, *Ḥullin* 113b, declares that the biblical prohibition against cooking and eating commingled milk and meat is not attendant upon meat cooked with the milk removed from an animal that has been slaughtered. Milk derived from a slaughtered animal is excluded from the prohibition because, according to talmudic exegesis of the verse "you shall not cook a kid in the milk of its mother" (Exodus 23:19; Exodus 34:26; Deuteronomy 14:21), the biblical prohibition applies only to the milk of an animal "that has the capacity to become a mother" (*re'uyah lehiyot em*). Obviously, a dead animal can no longer bear a child and hence lacks

years ago in a contribution to *Sha'arei Torah, Sha'ar Menasheh,* vol. XV (5684), no. 3, and subsequently discussed by R. Joshua Feigenbaum, *Sha'arei Torah,* vol. XV, no. 4; R. Zevi Hirsch Friedling, *Ha-Be'er,* vol. VI (5691), no. 3; and R. Betzalel Ze'ev Safran, as reported by his son in *Ha-Be'er,* vol. VII (5692), no 2. This source is also cited and discussed by R. Moshe Hershler, *Halakhah u-Refu'ah,* I (Jerusalem, 5740), 319–320, by R. Abraham Isaac ha-Levi Kilav, *Teḥumin,* V, 267, as well as by *Ẓiẓ Eli'ezer,* XIX, no. 40, and others.

19. Cf., R. Moshe Soloveichik, *Or ha-Mizraḥ,* Tishri-Tevet 5741, p. 125 and R. Abraham Kilav, *Teḥumin,* V, 267.

Cf., also, the comments of R. Isaac Berger, *Seridim,* no. 4 (5743), who assumes that either parturition or "pregnancy" may serve to establish a maternal relationship. Accordingly, he concludes that the donor of the ovum has no maternal relationship to the child. However, neither his sources nor his analysis serve to demonstrate that it is "pregnancy," i.e., gestation, rather than contribution of the ovum that serves to establish this relationship.

20. *Teḥumin,* V, 249.

the capacity to become a mother.

In his notes on *Shulḥan Arukh, Yoreh De'ah* 87:6, R. Akiva Eger queries whether the milk of a live animal that is a *treifah* is similarly excluded from the prohibition. The talmudic principle is that a *treifah* (i.e., an animal that suffers from one of a number of specified anatomical defects either congenitally or as the result of trauma causing loss or perforation of the organ) cannot conceive and carry a fetus to term. Hence, comments R. Akiva Eger, since a *treifah* cannot become a mother, it might be assumed that the milk of a *treifah* is excluded from the prohibition against cooking or consuming commingled milk and meat. Nevertheless, R. Akiva Eger cites a statement of the Gemara, *Sanhedrin* 69a, to the effect that a male who has sired a fetus is to be termed a "father" immediately upon expiration of the first trimester of pregnancy. If the male parent of a fetus is a "father" it would stand to reason that the female parent is similarly to be regarded as a "mother." As applied to the question before him, R. Akiva Eger remarks that the talmudic reference to a parental relationship vis-à-vis a fetus may be limited to a relationship with a viable fetus and hence, since the fetus of a *treifah* is not viable, there may well be no halakhic relationship between the fetus of a *treifah* and its gestational mother. Nevertheless, it would appear that, in the case of a viable fetus, such a relationship does indeed exist. Thus R. Akiva Eger's comment serves to establish that the gestational mother is a mother in the eyes of Jewish law. However, insofar as a child born of in vitro fertilization is concerned, since the Gemara recognizes a paternal relationship only subsequent to the expiration of the first trimester and R. Akiva Eger equates inception of the maternal relationship with that of the paternal relationship, R. Akiva Eger's comments do not serve to establish the existence of a halakhically recognized relationship with the genetic mother. By virtue of the nature of in vitro fertilization, the physiological relationship between the donor of the unfertilized ovum and the fetus is severed long before the end of the first trimester of pregnancy.

Rabbi Goldberg points out that R. Akiva Eger's position is contradicted by at least one authority. R. Joseph Engel, *Bet ha-Oẓar, erekh av,* argues that, although the sire of a fetus is a "father," nevertheless the female carrying the fetus in her womb is not recognized as a "mother" in the eyes of Jewish law until the moment of parturition. The Gemara, *Megillah* 13a, notes the redundancy inherent in the phrases "for she did not have a father or a mother" and "upon the death of her father and her mother" (Esther 2:7) and indicates that the second phrase is designed to convey additional information to the effect that Esther did not have a father or mother for even a single day. The Gemara comments that Esther's father died as soon as her mother conceived and that her mother perished upon her birth. The Gemara carefully spells out that Esther is described as never having had a father because her father died following conception before he could properly be termed a "father," i.e., before the end of the first trimester of pregnancy, and that she is described as never having had a mother despite the fact that her mother survived until the end of the gestational period. Esther is described as not having a mother because her mother died in childbirth. Hence this talmudic passage clearly indicates that a woman may properly be termed a "mother" only upon parturition. Presumably, the distinction between the male and female parent is based upon the fact that the male's role in reproduction ceases upon fertilization of the ovum and, accordingly, he is termed a "father" as soon as the fetus has reached a significant stage of development, whereas the female's role remains incomplete until the moment of birth.[21] Why R. Akiva Eger ignored the discussion in *Megillah* is unclear.[22] He may have regarded that discussion as aggadic in nature and hence as not being a proper source for derivation of a halakhic principle.

It should also be noted that the comments of Maharal of Prague in his explication of this verse in his commentary on the Book of Esther[23] suggest that he understood the Gemara's statement as being predicated upon the position that a fetus is an integral part of the mother (*ubar yerekh imo*). It then follows that during gestation mother and fetus constitute an undivided entity; accordingly, the maternal progenitor cannot become a "mother" until a physiological separation occurs, i.e., parturition.[24] If,

21. See R. Yitzchak Ya'akov Rabinowitz, *Zekher Yiẓḥak,* I, no. 4.

22. See Maharal of Prague, *Or Ḥadash,* s.v. *va-yehi omen.* Indeed, even if no compelling evidence can be adduced demonstrating recognition of dual maternal relationships, the possibility of dual relationships cannot be excluded unless there is evidence to that effect.

23. *Loc cit;* see also R. Meir Dan Plocki, *Klei Ḥemdah, Parashat Toldot,* sec. 1.

24. Maharal of Prague, *Or Ḥadash,* s.v. *va-yehi omen,* explicitly states "and at the time that she became [Esther's] mother, *at the time she was born* (emphasis added), for at the time of conception she could not yet be termed a mother since the fetus did not separate [itself] from her." Those words are cited by R. Joseph Engel, *Bet ha-Oẓar, erekh av,* in declaring that his view is identical with that of Maharal. Not only do these authorities declare that parturition is a determinant of motherhood, they also declare that any earlier maternal relationship is an impossibility. That declaration effectively precludes the possibility of a child

however, the opposing view is adopted and the fetus is not regarded as an integral part of the mother (*ubar lav yerekh imo*) there is no reason to assume, according to Maharal, that the maternal relationship is established any differently from the paternal relationship with the result that according to that view the maternal-filial relationship is established at a much earlier stage of gestation.

IV. *Dual Maternal Relationships*

Although, as discussed earlier, there is strong evidence supporting the position that parturition serves to determine maternal relationship, those sources serve only to establish that parturition establishes a maternal-child relationship but do not preclude the possibility that Halakhah may recognize two or more maternal relationships,[25] i.e., a relationship arising from

---

having two halakhic mothers. See, however, *supra,* note 21.

25. Cf., *supra,* note 4. *Tosafot, Sotah* 42b, maintain that it is physically possible for two sperm to penetrate a single ovum. It would undoubtedly be technically much more difficult—but hardly logically or biologically impossible—for genetic material in the form of different chromosomes to be drawn from the ova of two different women. The result would be a child who draws maternal genes from two different women, i.e., a child having two biological mothers.

The present discussion, however, concerns halakhic rather than biological motherhood. There are indeed legal systems that, for limited purposes, recognize dual sets of legal parents. Unlike Roman law that recognized adoption as extinguishing all legal consequences of the natural relationship and consequently permitted consanguineous marriages between adopted children and their natural parents or siblings, Western society does not regard the natural relationship as having been completely destroyed in the legal sense. Nevertheless, some American jurisdictions prohibit marriages between individuals whose sole relationship with one another is the product of adoption. Such marital relationships are regarded as legaly incestuous for sound psychological and social reasons. See Margaret Mead, "Anomalies in American Post-Divorce Relationships," *Divorce and After,* Paul Bohannan, ed. (New York, 1970), pp. 104–108; and J. Areen, *Cases and Materials on Family Law* (New York, 1992), p. 10. In effect, in such jurisdictions, the law recognizes the existence of two sets of parents for at least some legal purposes. [See Uniform Marriage Act (U.M.A.) §207 (1979). A number of states have prohibited both adopted sibling marriage and incest. Some states apparently prohibit marriage only between adopting parents and their adopted children but not between adoptive siblings or with relatives of the adopting parents. In the absence of language explicitly referring to adoptive relationships, courts in a number of states have refused to construe incest statutes as including adopted children. For a survey of those decisions and of relevant statutes see Walter J. Wadlington, III, "The Adopted Child and Intrafamily Marriage Prohibitions," *Virginia Law Review,* vol. XLIX, no. 3 (April, 1963), pp. 478–491. In at least

parturition and an additional relationship or relationships arising from gestation or provision of a gamete.[26]

The possibility of "doubtful" dual maternal relationships is raised in one recent discussion of this issue, albeit on the basis of entirely different considerations. A talmudic discussion regarding a similar quandary in the area of agricultural law is cited by Professor Ze'ev Low, *Emek Halakhah,* II (Jerusalem, 5749), 165–169, as reflecting the principle to be employed in resolving the issue of maternal identity. It is forbidden to consume newly harvested grain crops until the *omer* has been offered in the Temple on the second day of Passover. That offering renders permissible not only already harvested grain but also grain in the field that has taken root but which has, as yet, not fully matured. Any crop planted subsequent to the offering of the *omer* does not become permissible for use as food until the following Passover. The Gemara, *Menaḥot* 69b, posits a situation in which a stalk of grain is planted and has reached a stage of development equal to a third of its ultimate growth (i.e., the stage at which the produce has reached a state of maturity at which it is recognized, for halakhic purposes, as a grain product); having reached this stage of development, the stalk is removed from the ground before the *omer* is offered and replanted after the offering of the *omer* whereupon it continues to mature and ultimately reaches its normal state of growth. The question posed by the Gemara is whether the *omer* renders the entire plant permissible since the primary growth of the stalk occurred before the time of offering of the *omer* or whether, because of its enhanced growth subsequent to the

---

one state, marriage between adopted siblings has been declared unlawful by a County Court despite the absence of a specific statutory exclusion on the grounds that adopted siblings are the functional equivalent of natural siblings for the purpose of the incest statute. See *In re MEW and MLB,* 3 Fam. L. Rep. (BNA) 2601 (Pa. Ct.C.P., Allegheny Cty, 1977). In sharp contrast, a Colorado statute enacting restrictions against adopted sibling marriages was declared unconstitutional by the Colorado Superior Court in *Israel* v. *Allen,* 577 P.2d 762 (Colo. 1978). For a reasoned critique of that decision see George I. Katz, "Adopted Sibling Marriage in Colorado: *Israel* v. *Allen,*" *University of Colorado Law Review,* vol. LI, no. 1 (Fall, 1979), pp. 135–151.]

26. Even the statement recorded in *Megillah* 13a serves to establish only that the maternal relationship comes into being at the *time* of parturition but not that such a relationship is limited to the birth mother. It should be remembered that the paternal relationship arises upon termination of the first trimester of pregnancy. No "paternal" act is performed at that time; it is simply the moment at which the relationship is halakhically recognized. Similarly, parturition may be the moment at which all maternal relationships are recognized, including a maternal-filial relationship based upon contribution of the ovum from which the fetus developed.

offering of the *omer,* the produce may not be eaten. The Gemara identifies a similar problem with regard to *orlah,* the fruit of a tree that is forbidden during the first three-year period after planting. The problem involves a situation in which a young sapling already bearing fruit is grafted onto a mature tree and that fruit subsequently greatly increases in size. The question is whether the newly grown portion of the fruit produced by the grafted sapling is to be regarded as the product of the mature tree and hence permissible or whether, since the identity of the fruit has been established as *orlah* prior to grafting, the newly grown portion of the fruit is also infused with that identity. A third problem occurs with regard to *kilayim,* produce that is forbidden because of mingling in the planting of diverse species. The situation discussed by the Gemara involves a vegetable that has been planted in a vineyard; the vines are then uprooted and the vegetable continues to grow after the vine has been removed. Both the vegetable and the grapes become forbidden upon mingling of the species in planting. The question is whether the additional growth of the vegetable subsequent to removal of the grape vine is permissible since that portion of the vegetable was never commingled with grapes or whether the identity of the vegetable was established as forbidden produce upon its planting in the vineyard and hence all subsequent growth acquires the same identity.

A number of talmudic commentators make it clear that they regard the issue in each of these related cases, not as involving a question concerning the admixture of a small quantity of a forbidden foodstuff with a much larger quantity of a permitted foodstuff, as might perhaps be presumed, but as a question of determination of identity in cases in which there is continued growth and development. Is the identity of a stalk of grain determined with finality as soon as it is halakhically recognized as grain? If so, then, having acquired identity and status as grain before the offering of the *omer*, it retains the identity of "pre-omeric" (and hence presently permissible) grain even if a significant portion of its growth occurs after the offering of the *omer,* much in the same manner that we regard a person who gains a considerable amount of weight to be the same person after the weight-gain as before or in the manner that we regard an infant who grows to adulthood as retaining the same identity he possessed as a child. Or do we regard the portion of the grain added as a result of accretion or incremental growth of the grain as having an independent identity since that growth occurs subsequent to a second "post-omeric" (and hence as yet forbidden) planting? Has the identity of the fruit of the sapling been irreversibly determined upon its first appearance so that it predetermines the identity of the even much greater portion of the fruit that develops after grafting with the result that the entire fruit is forbidden *orlah* or does the added portion of the fruit that grows after grafting have its own identity as a permitted fruit? A vegetable planted in a vineyard acquires identity as a forbidden planting of diverse species. But does that identity infuse even the portion of the vegetable that comes into being after the grapevine is removed or does the newly developing portion of the vegetable acquire an identity of its own, *viz.,* an identity as a vegetable that has not been compromised by diverse planting in a vineyard? These questions are left unresolved by the Gemara with the result that, in any given case, the stringencies of both possible resolutions of the issue must be applied, i.e., the grain is forbidden because of the possibility that the previously-acquired status does not control the enhanced growth of the grain, but the fruit of the grafted sapling and the increased growth of the vegetable are forbidden because the earlier acquired identity may indeed control the identity of that which is a natural outgrowth of the old.

If this analysis of these talmudic questions is accepted as correct, argues Prof. Low, the question of maternal identity of progeny born as the result of in vitro fertilization of a donated ovum may be regarded as analogous. Maternal identity is established in the first instance by production of the gamete. The question is whether that determination is also dispositive with regard to the identity of the fetus whose later physical development is attributable to the gestational host or whether the identity of the developing fetus is derived from its nurturer, *viz.,* the host mother, in which case the child could be regarded as having two mothers just as, for example, a single grain of wheat may be, in part, "pre-omeric" and, in part, "post-omeric." Since the Gemara leaves the basic issue unresolved and, accordingly, rules that the stringencies of both possible identities must be applied, a child born of in vitro fertilization, on the basis of this analogy, would to all intents and purposes be regarded as having two mothers.

However, the analogy does not resolve the issue in its entirety. Presented in this manner it assumes as axiomatic that, in the first instance, motherhood is genetically determined but that the original relationship can perhaps be nullified by establishment of a subsequent maternal relationship. The thrust of the analogy is to establish that the earlier relationship is not extinguished. The crux of the question, however, is whether Halakhah at all recognizes a maternal relationship based upon donation of an ovum, i.e., a relationship based solely upon genetic considerations. That is an issue with regard to which there may well be no evidence in rabbinic sources.[27] Only after it is established that there exists halakhic cognizance of a maternal relationship based upon donation of an ovum can the question of possible subsequent nullification or supersedure be addressed. Nevertheless, the analogy does serve a valuable purpose. The thrust of this analogy, if it is properly understood, is to demonstrate that Halakhah may recognize two maternal relationships with the effect that the possibility of a maternal relationship based upon a genetic relationship cannot be regarded as excluded simply because there is evidence that Halakhah recognizes a different maternal relationship based upon parturition or gestation. The analogy to agricultural laws does not, however, serve to provide affirmative evidence demonstrating that Halakhah recognizes a maternal relationship based upon genetic considerations.[28]

Although some scholars are reported as questioning the aptness of any analogy based upon determination of species or status with regard to agricultural law, Prof. Low concludes that the analogy cannot be dismissed out of hand and that, accordingly, at least for purposes of halakhic stringency, the child must be regarded as having two mothers. This writer would concur in that conclusion even in the absence of any analogy to agricultural law.[29] The halakhic (as distinct from aggadic)[30] evidence

27. R. Joshua Ben-Meir, in a critical review of earlier published material concerning this issue that appears in *Assia,* vol. XI, no. 1 (Nisan 5746), cites a comment of Rashi, *Yevamot* 98a, in support of the view that maternal identity is determined at conception. Rashi comments simply that recognition of consanguineous maternal relationships in the case of a pregnant proselyte and her fetus is evidence that the fetus does not enjoy the status of a "newly born child" bereft of any halakhically recognized blood relatives, as is the case with other converts. Although Rabbi Ben-Meir expresses astonishment that other discussants have not cited Rashi's comment in their discussion of this issue, this writer finds Rashi's comment to be entirely irrelevant to the matter under discussion. Rashi states only that the fetus of a proselyte is not a "newly born child." He does not declare or imply that the relationship is established at conception—much less so at the time of the sexual act—rather than at parturition. See *Assia,* pp. 36–37 and 40.

28. Cf., R. Abraham Kilav, *Emek Halakhah,* II, 174, who fails to distinguish these points as separate issues, possibly because he declines to recognize the possibility of dual maternal relationships.

29. In point of fact, there may be evidence pointing to similar principles specifically with regard to determination of identity and status of animal species as well. It is clear that identity in terms of classification as a member of a particular species is determined at the beginning of life. Thus, a mature non-kosher

animal is intrinsically non-kosher rather than merely the *yoẓeh,* or derivative, of the newly-born animal from which it developed. Accordingly, if the animal is eaten as food, the culpability incurred is that associated with partaking of food that is intrinsically non-kosher rather than for violation of the less stringent prohibition associated with derivatives of non-kosher species, e.g., the brine of non-kosher species or, for most authorities, the milk of a non-kosher animal.

Moreover, there is evidence that identification in terms of a particular forbidden status is determined at the earliest stage of existence to the exclusion of other prohibitions that might be generated by other causative factors. It is a general principle that, in ordinary circumstances, a prohibition cannot be superimposed upon an already existing prohibition (*ein issur ḥal al issur*) of equal severity. One example discussed by the Gemara, *Ḥullin* 90a, is the nature of the prohibition against partaking of the sciatic nerve of the progeny of a sacrificial animal. If not for a specific exception to the general principle, the prohibition regarding eating the sciatic nerve would not apply to the offspring of sacrificial animals. Rashi, *ad locum,* explains: "For from the moment that it comes into being it is sanctified, but the nerve is, as yet, not generated for one observes that the creation of the embryo precedes the generation of the nerve." The embryo undergoes repeated cell divisions and at some point in the early stages of gestation there is a differentiation with regard to the characteristics of cells destined to become diverse organs and tissues. The nerve cells, and indeed the matter of which they are composed, do not exist at conception or in the earliest stages of gestation. The cells of the nascent sciatic nerve are new, not only to the nerve in the sense that cells possessing such characteristics do not exist at a previous stage, but to the embryo itself in the sense that they are newly generated from nutrients derived from the mother's bloodstream. Thus, when those cells come into being, they are generated as being simultaneously both cells of a sanctified animal and cells of a sciatic nerve. Yet, for purposes of Halakhah, their identity as an integral part of a sacrificial animal is regarded as prior to their identity as a sciatic nerve. It follows then, that the earlier identity and status of the animal determines the identity and status of newly formed cells despite the interposition of a new casual factor that would otherwise govern status and identity, i.e., appearance of the distinctive characteristics of the sciatic nerve.

Here, then, according to Rashi's analysis, is an example of an instance in which the identity of an organism is determined with finality by the earliest causal factor and in which that organism's identity serves to control the organism throughout its life despite the fact that, absent the earlier acquisition of identity and status, the identity of later growths or developing appendages would be determined by other factors. Indeed, while with regard to plant identification and agricultural law the issue is regarded by the Gemara as unresolved and hence, in practice, this principle is applied only as a matter of "doubt" and stringency, with regard to animal species it appears to be the normative rule. This in no way contradicts the earlier conclusion that parturition serves to establish maternal identity. It means only that Halakhah may recognize two mothers, *viz.,* a birth mother and a "generative" mother.

However, *Tosafot,* as well as several other early commentaries on that talmudic discussion, speak of the sciatic nerve and other fetal tissues as coming into

supporting parturition as determining motherhood does not serve to preclude the possibility of a dual maternal relationship. Hence the possibility of such a relationship cannot be ignored unless evidence of its non-existence is adduced.

This point notwithstanding, it seems to this writer that the analogy to the provisions of agricultural law fails entirely with regard to in vitro fertilization if the statement of the Gemara, *Yevamot* 69b, categorizing an embryo within the first forty days of gestation as "mere water" is to be understood literally. If the fetus is entirely lacking in status and identity during this period it would stand to reason that no maternal relationship can be established during that period. It is only logical that an entity that has no identity cannot be the subject of a relationship, or better, it stands to reason that that which is "mere water" knows no mother. On the other hand, if, as many authorities maintain, categorization of an embryo in the early stages of development as "mere water" is limited in application and, for example, does not serve to prohibit destruction of the embryo during that period,[31] the analogy is quite apt.

Moreover, an entirely different analogy may be offered in demonstrating that, at least for some authorities, the child born of in vitro fertilization should be regarded as having two mothers. The Gemara, *Ḥullin* 79a, in discussing the classification of the offspring born as a result of the interbreeding of different species, records one opinion which maintains that the identity of the male partner is to be completely disregarded in determining the species of the offspring. According to this view, since it is the mother who nurtures and sustains the embryo, it is the female parent alone who determines the species of the offspring. It is thus the identity of the mother which is transferred to members of an inter-species.

There is, however, a conflicting opinion which asserts that "the father's

---

existence simultaneously and explain the priority of other prohibitions over that pertaining to the sciatic nerve on the basis of the fact that in early stages of development the sciatic nerve lacks the distinctive features associated with that structure. Since none of those authorities offers an explicit reason for diverging from Rashi's analysis, it is not possible to ascertain the precise nature of their disagreement with Rashi. It is, however, entirely possible that the controversy is precisely with regard to this point, i.e., that they reject the notion that identity and status of animal structures are determined from the earliest moment of existence in a manner that unalterably determines the identity of later accretions as well.

30. See *supra,* note 17.

31. For a discussion of the status of the fetus during this period see *Contemporary Halakhic Problems,* I, 339–347.

seed is to be considered" (*ḥosheshin le-zera ha-av*). Presumably, according to this view, "the father's seed is to be considered" because the father plays a dynamic role in the birth of the offspring. In an analogous manner, a similar line of reasoning may be applied in determining the maternity of a child born of a fertilized ovum implanted in the womb of a host mother. It is the host mother who nurtures the embryo and sustains gestation. However, the role of the genetic mother in the determination of identity is a dynamic one and analogous to that of "the seed of the father." It may therefore be argued according to those who assert with reference to the classification of hybrids that "the seed of the father is to be considered" that, in the case of a donated ovum, the maternal relationship between the child and the donor mother is to be "considered" no less than "the seed of the father." Of course, the result of consideration of that principle in situations involving implantation of an already fertilized ovum would be to establish, not a paternal relationship, but rather a second maternal relationship between the child and the donor of the ovum.

V. *A Non-Jewish Ovum Donor*

Yet another complication arises in cases of in vitro fertilization in which the donor of the ovum is a gentile. Ova produced by another woman and donated to the childless couple are utilized in situations in which the infertile woman does not ovulate, or does not produce viable ova, but her uterus is capable of receiving a fertilized ovum and carrying it to term. In such situations the couple may seek a gentile donor, fertilize her ovum with the sperm of the infertile woman's husband by means of an in vitro procedure and implant the zygote in the wife's uterus. If parturition is accepted as the sole criterion to be employed in determining maternal identity it might be assumed that, since the child has a Jewish mother, the child is also Jewish. However, if the donor mother also enjoys a maternal relationship with the child and the child, in effect, has two mothers, the resulting status of the child of two mothers, one a Jewess and the other a non-Jewess, is far from clear. Moreover, there is reason to conclude that some early authorities would maintain that a child whose genetic mother is non-Jewish requires conversion even if the child is regarded by Halakhah as the child of a Jewish mother. There may even be reason to infer that this conclusion is compelled by statements of the Gemara itself.

This rather anomalous conclusion is based upon the position formulated by Ramban in his commentary on *Yevamot* 47b. Ramban maintains that a male child born to a woman who has converted to Judaism during pregnancy requires circumcision for purposes of conversion. Ramban acknowledges that immersion of the mother in a *mikveh* for the purpose of conversion constitutes immersion of the fetus as well but that, in the case of a male, circumcision is required in order to complete the conversion process. However, as noted earlier, the Gemara, *Yevamot* 97b, declares that, should the same woman give birth to twins, a fraternal relationship exists between the children. If so, Ramban's position is problematic. If, as he maintains, the conversion is as yet incomplete, how can a fraternal relationship arise? Upon completion of the conversion process, each of the children is deemed to be "a newly born child" and, in the eyes of Jewish law, lacks any familial relationship with previously born relatives even if they, too, become converts to Judaism.[32]

Addressing himself to the problem presented by Ramban's position, Rabbi Moshe Sternbuch, *Be-Shevilei ha-Refu'ah,* no. 8 (Kislev 5747), resolves the difficulty by suggesting that the maternal relationship—and consequently any other maternal blood relationship—is indeed established at the time of parturition and therefore the baby is not "a newly born child" bereft of blood relatives. Nevertheless, since the child's genotype is non-Jewish, the child requires conversion in order to eliminate "impurity" associated with the gentile state. Similarly, a child born of in vitro fertilization would be deemed the child of the Jewish birth mother but would yet require conversion because of its non-Jewish genetic origin.[33]

Rabbi Sternbuch's discussion is unclear with regard to one point, i.e., the problem that he addresses exists even if Ramban's position with regard to circumcision is not accepted.[34] The Gemara, *Yevamot* 78a, clearly states that immersion of the mother for purposes of conversion constitutes immersion of the fetus. Implicit in that statement is the proposition that the fetus requires conversion. Yet, as noted earlier, the Gemara, *Yevamot* 97b, declares that if the pregnant proselyte gives birth to twins they are regarded as maternal siblings. If the fetus is a proselyte lacking

32. R. Chaim's thesis that a fraternal relationship exists only if the mother converted during the first forty days of pregnancy was advanced as a resolution of this difficulty inherent in Ramban's position; see *supra,* note 10.

33. An identical thesis is advanced by Rabbi Kilav, *Teḥumin,* V, 263, in resolution of a different problem.

34. The same point may be made with regard to Reb Chaim's assertion cited *supra,* note 10. Reb Chaim is quoted as having raised the problem only in conjunction with Ramban's position.

blood relatives, including a mother, how can it later acquire a brother at the time of parturition? To be sure, absent Ramban's position maintaining that conversion is not complete until circumcision is performed, the problem might be resolved by postulating that, since parturition gives rise to a maternal-filial relationship, parturition subsequent to conversion also serves to generate a maternal relationship even though the fetus is a proselyte. However, that solution gives rise to a further problem: If parturition generates a maternal relationship, why does it not also serve to establish the status of the neonate as a Jew? If so, antecedent conversion of the fetus in utero, as posited by the Gemara, *Yevamot* 78a, would be superfluous. This problem is resolved if it is understood that conversion is required in all instances in which the maternal genetic origin of the child is non-Jewish in nature. If so, that conclusion follows directly from the discussion of the Gemara itself rather than from Ramban's analysis thereof.

Rabbi Sternbuch points to an interesting historical parallel in illustrating his thesis. Our ancestors became "converts" to Judaism at the time of revelation on Mount Sinai and, indeed, many of the principles concerning conversion are derived from biblical passages concerning that event. Nevertheless, asserts Rabbi Sternbuch, prohibitions concerning incest were fully binding upon our ancestors at that time and encompassed blood relatives who themselves became "converts" contemporaneously. In accordance with the talmudic dictum "A proselyte who converts is comparable to a newly born child" (*Yevamot* 22a and *Bekhorot* 47a) the recipients of the Torah at Mount Sinai should, ostensibly, have been regarded as "newly born children" lacking blood relatives. Rabbi Sternbuch suggests that the status as Jews enjoyed by our ancestors at Mount Sinai was assured by virtue of the fact that they were the progeny of Abraham the Patriarch and that "conversion" at Sinai was necessary only in order to remove the "impurity" associated with the gentile state and concludes that conversion required solely for the purpose of eliminating such impurity does not give rise to status as "newly born children" that would, in turn, serve to render consanguineous relationships permissible.

In point of fact, Rabbi Sternbuch's assertion that our ancestors did not have the status of "newly born children" at Mount Sinai is a matter of some dispute. Rabbi Sternbuch's position echoes that of Maharal of Prague, *Gur Aryeh, Parashat Va-Yigash* (Genesis 46:8), cited by the author of *Shev Shem'atata* in section 9 of his introduction to that work. Maharal of Prague is of the opinion that, unlike subsequent proselytes, the recipients of the Torah at Mount Sinai did not acquire status as "newly born children" and, accordingly, they were forbidden to marry close relatives. However, Maharal offers a rationale entirely different from that advanced by Rabbi Sternbuch in explaining why those who became Jews at Mount Sinai were not deemed to be "newly born children." Acceptance of the commandments at Sinai is described by the Gemara, *Shabbat* 88a, as having been coerced. Status as "newly born children," asserts Maharal, is acquired only when acceptance of commandments is voluntary. Nevertheless, R. Meir Simchah of Dvinsk, *Meshekh Ḥokhmah, Parashat Va-Etḥanan* (Deuteronomy 5:27), espouses an opposing view in declaring that previously existing consanguineous relationships were not terminated at Sinai as evidenced by the fact that all participants were directed, "Return to your tents" (Deuteronomy 5:27), i.e., they were granted permission to resume conjugal relations prohibited in the preparatory period before receiving the Torah at Mount Sinai. Indeed, *Meshekh Ḥokhmah* points to that directive as the biblical source of the talmudic dictum "A proselyte who converts is comparable to a newly born child."[35]

The thesis advanced by Rabbi Sternbuch in postulating two types of conversion is remarkably similar to that expounded by R. Naphtali Trop in his *Shi'urei ha-Granat, Ketubot* 11a,[36] save that Reb Naphtali's comments are expressed in the positive rather than in the negative.[37] Rabbi Sternbuch's analysis of the principle "A proselyte who converts is comparable to a newly born child" and his conclusion that it is inapplicable to the recipients of the Torah at Mount Sinai are also identical to those of Reb Naphtali. In resolving a number of problems involving the difficulty associated with Ramban's position, Reb Naphtali explains that there are two forms of conversion: 1) conversion for the purpose of becoming a Jew, i.e., a member of the community of Israel; and 2) conversion for the purpose of acquiring sanctification as an Israelite (*kedushat Yisra'el*). Reb Naphtali suggests that one who enjoys the status of a member of the Jewish community is under obligation to undergo conversion in order to

35. See R. Zalman Nehemiah Goldberg, *Teḥumin,* V, 255, note 5.

36. Three versions of Reb Naphtali's *shi'urim* as recorded and transcribed by his students have been published: 1) *Shi'urei ha-Granat* (Jerusalem, 5715); 2) *Sefer Duda'ei Mosheh: Shi'urei ha-Granat he-Ḥadashim,* 2nd edition (Bnei Brak, 5745), edited by R. Moshe David Dryan; 3) *Ḥiddushei ha-Granat ha-Shalem* (Jerusalem: Oraita, 5749).

37. Cf., *Zekher Yiẓḥak,* I, no. 4, who expresses a similar concept in speaking of conversion, not for purposes of becoming a Jew, but in order to remove "disqualification as a gentile" *(psul akum).*

acquire the "sanctity of an Israelite." Presumably, the implication of that position is that obligations pertaining to fulfillment of commandments are contingent upon acquiring the "sanctity of an Israelite." Thus he asserts that even those authorities who maintain that the child of a Jewess whose father is a non-Jew requires conversion agree that conversion of such a child for purposes of membership in the Jewish community is unnecessary since membership in the Jewish community is transmitted by virtue of matrilineal succession. According to those authorities, Reb Naphtali asserts, conversion is necessary solely for the purpose of acquiring "sanctity of an Israelite" which is acquired automatically upon birth only if both parents are Jews. Similarly, maintains Reb Naphtali, even according to Ramban, a child born to a proselyte who was pregnant at the time of her conversion acquires status as a member of the community of Israel by virtue of having been born to a Jewish mother and, accordingly, a maternal-filial relationship is also established by virtue of parturition for all genealogical purposes. Conversion, according to Ramban, asserts Reb Naphtali, is necessary only for the purpose of acquiring the "sanctity of an Israelite."[38] Reb Naphtali similarly asserts that conversion at the time of revelation at Mount Sinai was solely for the purpose of acquiring the "sanctity of an Israelite" and, accordingly, prohibitions with regard to sexual relations with blood relatives remained in effect.

On the basis of the thesis developed by R. Naphtali Trop it would follow that a fetus transplanted from a gentile woman to a Jewess would require conversion for purposes of *kedushat Yisra'el.* It would appear to be the case that such conversion might be performed even during pregnancy by means of immersion of the pregnant mother in a *mikveh* as is the case with regard to the fetus of a pregnant non-Jewess who converts to Judaism.[39] According to this thesis, the same would be true of a fetus conceived from an ovum donated by a gentile donor.[40]

---

38. This material first appeared in *Ha-Metivta,* Ḥeshvan 5703.

39. The sole question is whether such conversion is biblically valid or whether the status is that of a "rabbinic" conversion. R. Akiva Eger, *Ketubot* 11a, maintains that biblical conversion of a fetus is possible only when the conversion is simultaneously performed on behalf of the mother. Cf., however, *infra,* note 42.

40. Acceptance of this thesis in explanation of the requirement for conversion of the fetus of a pregnant proselyte may have a significant practical halakhic ramification with regard to in vitro fertilization. The authorities who permit ejaculation of semen by the husband for purposes of artificial insemination do so only because, in their opinion, the procedure serves to fulfill the commandment to "be fruitful and multiply." Cf., *supra,* notes 8 and 9. Hence emission of semen

In a contribution to *Teḥumin,* vol. V, devoted to a discussion of the status of a child born as the result of in vitro procedures, Rabbi Abraham Kilav accepts the basic principle that a maternal relationship is established by virtue of parturition. Nevertheless, Rabbi Kilav denies that parturition serves to establish such a relationship in situations in which the ovum was donated by a non-Jewish woman.[41] The fact that a fetus carried by a proselyte at the time of her conversion itself requires conversion leads to the conclusion that a fetus born of in vitro fertilization of an ovum donated by a gentile also requires conversion. Yet, maintains Rabbi Kilav, a maternal relationship exists in the case of the pregnant proselyte but not in the ease of an implanted ovum of gentile origin. In the former case, conversion takes place during pregnancy and at the time of birth the child is already Jewish. In the case of in vitro fertilization, the gestational mother is Jewish and no conversion of the fetus takes place during pregnancy. Since conversion of the fetus does not occur prior to parturition, argues Rabbi Kilav, no relationship to the mother is established by parturition. Rabbi Goldberg, on the other hand, maintains that, although the child requires conversion, parturition nevertheless serves to establish a maternal relationship even in such circumstances.

The conclusion reached by Rabbi Goldberg seems to be compelled according to the position of Ramban. Ramban maintains that conversion

for the insemination of a gentile woman could not be sanctioned for the simple reason that, since Jewish law does not recognize a paternal relationship between a Jewish father and his non-Jewish progeny, ejaculation does not lead to fulfillment of the obligation to "be fruitful and multiply." If a fetus that develops from an ovum donated by a non-Jewish woman requires conversion despite the fact that the gestational mother is Jewish, the ostensive halakhic implication is that there is no paternal relationship between the child and its biological father and hence ejaculation of semen by the husband for utilization for the purpose of in vitro fertilization could not be sanctioned in such situations. If, however, identity as a member of the community of Israel as well as a maternal-filial relationship is established on the basis of the gestational mother's identity as a Jewess, the birth of such a child may serve to fulfill the commandment to "be fruitful and multiply" as well. Accordingly, if a paternal relationship is recognized in usual cases of artificial insemination, Jewish law would recognize a paternal-filial relationship between the Jewish donor of the semen and the child of a Jewish gestational mother for all other aspects of Jewish law even though the ovum was donated by a non-Jewess. On the other hand, if there is no maternal relationship between the Jewish gestational and birth mother and the child born of an ovum donated by a non-Jewish woman, ejaculation for purposes of fertilizing such an ovum cannot be sanctioned.

41. *Teḥumin,* V, 263–264.

of a male fetus is not complete until circumcision is performed after birth. Nevertheless, as has been noted earlier, the existence of a maternal relationship between a proselyte and the children converted with her as fetuses during pregnancy is clear. According to Ramban, that relationship exists despite the fact that circumcision for the purpose of conversion did not occur.[42] Hence, the same relationship should exist even if the conversion process has not commenced, e.g., a non-Jewish fetus is implanted in the womb of a Jewish mother, or, according to *Dagul me-Revavah, Yoreh De'ah* 268:6, if the *Bet Din* was unaware of the pregnancy at the time of the mother's conversion. Similarly, if R. Naphtali Trop's thesis is accepted, the identical conclusion may be reached even without reliance upon Ramban's position. According to that thesis, membership in the community of Israel is established on the basis of parturition while conversion is necessary for purposes of *kedushat Yisra'el.* Hence, in the case of the implantation of an ovum donated by a non-Jewish woman, parturition would serve to establish membership in the community of Israel and would simultaneously serve to establish a maternal relationship with the birth mother while conversion would be required for purposes of *kedushat Yisra'el.*[43]

Rabbi Goldberg adds one caveat that is apparently not accepted by either Rabbi Sternbuch or Rabbi Kilav. Rabbi Goldberg asserts that, according to those who maintain that the fetus is an integral part of the mother's body (*ubar yerekh imo*), a fetus implanted in the womb of a Jewess does not require conversion in situations in which the donor of

42. Rabbi Kilav apparently maintains that in the case of a pregnant proselyte conversion of the fetus is accomplished, according to Ramban, by immersion of the mother and Ramban intends only to indicate that failure to perform circumcision prior to immersion does not serve as a barrier to conversion. See *Teḥumin,* V, 264.

43. R. Akiva Eger maintains that conversion of the fetus is valid in biblical law only if conversion is simultaneously performed on behalf of the mother and, accordingly, only under such circumstances can there be a maternal-filial relationship. See *supra,* note 38. If R. Akiva Eger does not accept Reb Naphtali's thesis, conversion of the fetus or neonate conceived from a gentile ovum would not result in a maternal-filial relationship with the gestational mother. Insofar as biblical law is concerned, the child remains a non-Jew even if conversion takes place during pregnancy. Were a biblically valid conversion to occur subsequent to parturition it would clearly result in status as a "newly born child" and serve to sever any possible maternal relationship. Nor is there evidence that rabbinic law established a maternal-filial relationship in cases of in vitro fertilization or embryo transplants. See R. Joshua Ben-Meir, *Assia,* vol. XI, no. 1, pp. 30–33 and 40.

the ovum is a non-Jewess. Rabbi Goldberg argues that, upon implantation, the fetus becomes part of the mother and, hence, part of a Jewish body with the result that conversion of the fetus becomes unnecessary. In making this point without further discussion, Rabbi Goldberg seems to ignore the possibility that, if non-Jewish identity is established prior to implantation in the uterus of a Jewish woman, transformation into a limb of the gestational mother may not *ipso facto* result in negation of previously acquired identity as a gentile.

Prof. Low reports an intriguing opinion with regard to a hypothetical question involving a Jewish woman who becomes pregnant as the result of in vitro fertilization utilizing an ovum donated by a non-Jewish woman and who wishes to accomplish conversion of the fetus prior to its birth by undergoing immersion in a *mikveh* during the course of her pregnancy. Prof. Low cites an oral opinion expressed by R. Shlomoh Zalman Auerbach to the effect that "for [the purpose of conversion] the immersion of the host mother is of no effect" insofar as the fetus is concerned but fails to report the grounds supporting that conclusion. A communication from Rabbi Avigdor Nebenzahl is also cited by Prof. Low in which Rabbi Nebenzahl expresses a similar view even with regard to a situation in which an already fertilized ovum is removed from the non-Jewish natural mother and subsequently reinserted into her own uterus. Rabbi Nebenzahl apparently maintains that, in such circumstances, immersion of the mother is not efficacious on behalf of the fetus. The more usual case, of course, is a situation in which the donor of the ovum is a gentile woman and the Jewish gestational mother would prefer to immerse the child in utero rather than delay the immersion of the neonate until medically advisable.

In each of these cases it is difficult to comprehend why the mother's immersion should not *ipso facto* be deemed immersion of the fetus. The Gemara, *Yevamot* 78a, certainly recognized the efficacy of fetal conversion in the case of natural pregnancy. In the course of that discussion the Gemara questions why the mother's body should not be deemed a barrier between the fetus and the water of the *mikveh* since, because of the interposition of the mother, the fetus does not at all come into contact with the water. The response of the Gemara is, "A fetus is different. That is the way it grows (*hainu reviteih*)." The import of that response is that, whether or not the fetus is regarded as an "organ of its mother," i.e., as an integral part of her body, the mother's body is not a foreign entity separating the fetus from the water. Since attachment to the uterine wall is normal, natural and essential to the fetus, the mother's body does not constitute an interposition (*ḥaẓiẓah*) for purposes of immersion.

As a ramification of the laws of interposition, the talmudic ruling permitting conversion of the fetus in utero would appear to be entirely unrelated to the principles that serve to determine maternal identity. It is certainly arguable that immersion of the pregnant woman may serve to effect a valid conversion even if she is not the genetic mother and even if the fetus is subsequently transferred to the uterus of another woman prior to term. Although there is no report to that effect, one may speculate that those who are quoted as adopting an opposing view consider the Gemara's statement regarding interposition to be limited to natural pregnancy.[44] That, too, is difficult to comprehend since, assuredly a skin graft or, hypothetically, a graft of an entire limb that has become a functioning part of the recipient's body does not constitute an interposition invalidating immersion in a *mikveh.* This would be true even if the skin graft covered the entire surface area of the body. The fact that the mother's body will ultimately become separated from the fetus at birth while the graft is destined to remain in place throughout the recipient's life should not serve to negate the underlying rationale expressed in the dictum "That is the way it grows," i.e., since pregnancy by its nature is transitory the ultimate separation of the fetus from its mother should not interfere with the non-interposing status of the mother's body.

VI. *Implantation Within the First Forty Days*

R. Aaron Soloveichik is quoted by his son, R. Moshe Soloveichik, *Or ha-Mizraḥ,* Tishri-Tevet 5741, p. 127, as being of the opinion that, although the status of the fetus of a pregnant woman who converts to Judaism is that of a convert, nevertheless, the status of a fetus of a proselyte who converts within the first forty days of pregnancy is not that of a convert but is that of a child born to a Jewish mother. That position is based upon the statement of the Gemara, *Yevamot* 69b, categorizing a fetus during the first forty days following conception as "mere water." Hence, it is argued, at the time that it acquires the status of a fetus, i.e., following the expiration of the first forty days of gestation, it is the fetus of a Jewish

44. Rabbi Kilav, *Emek Halakhah,* II, 174, suggests that, to be valid for the fetus, the immersion must be efficacious for some other purpose, e.g., conversion of the mother. It is, however, difficult to comprehend the reason for such a requirement since, if the mother's body is not an interposition, the fetus should be regarded as if it has come into direct contact with the water of the *mikveh.*

mother.[45] If so, it would logically follow that, *mutatis mutandis,* a host mother in whom the developing zygote has been implanted immediately after fertilization should be regarded as the halakhic mother of the child, not necessarily because the host mother is the birth mother, but because at the time of implantation the fetus has as yet not acquired identity with the result that at the stage of development that it can acquire identity it acquires identity in relationship to the gestational mother. Since, at least at present, implantation of the fertilized ovum in the uterus of the gestational mother takes place in the very early stages of cell division, the effect of this position is to eliminate the need for conversion in all cases involving non-Jewish donors.

This line of reasoning is best understood if it is assumed that the prohibition against feticide does not apply during this early period of gestation because the fetus is "mere water." However, if, as is the opinion of many authorities, the prohibition against feticide applies even during this early stage of pregnancy[46] because, although the fetus may be "mere water" with regard to other matters of Halakhah, it is nevertheless regarded as a nascent life from the moment of conception, that conclusion may serve to establish the principle that the developing fetus is a "person" in its own right and hence may, even at that early stage of development, enjoy a status independent of that of its gestational mother.

Moreover, if, as is the position of many authorities, including Rabad, *Hilkhot Avadim* 7:5, Rabbenu Nissim, *Ḥullin* 8a, R. Akiva Eger, *Ketubot* 11a, and others, a fetus is not an integral part of the mother's body (*ubar lav yerekh imo*)[47] it is not clear that the child becomes a Jew other than through conversion, (i.e., the conversion of the mother which serves concomitantly as conversion of the child as well) even though the mother's conversion occurs within the first forty days of gestation. To be sure, even according to the authorities who maintain that a fetus is not regarded as an integral part of the mother's body, a child conceived by a Jewish

45. R. Aaron Soloveichik's view seems to reflect that of his grandfather, R. Chaim Soloveitchik, as reported by R. Elchanan Wasserman, *Koveẓ He'arot,* no. 73, sec. 12; see *supra,* note 10.

46. For a discussion of that issue see *Contemporary Halakhic Problems,* I, 339–347.

47. Cf., however, *Tosafot, Baba Kamma* 47a, *Ḥullin* 58a and *Sanhedrin* 60b; *Taz, Yoreh De'ah* 89:5; *Shakh, Yoreh De'ah* 89:8; and *Leḥem Mishneh, Hilkhot Avadim* 7:5. See also *Sedei Ḥemed, Kuntres ha-Kelalim, Ma'arekhet ha-'Ayin,* no. 62; *Melo ha-Ro'im,* "Ubar Yerekh Imo," secs. 6–8; and *Kesef Nivḥar,* no. 132, sec. 9.

mother is Jewish by virtue of the fact that it springs from the ovum of a Jewess. Even though the ovum itself is "mere water," the developed fetus is nevertheless the product of a Jewish maternal forebear. However, halakhically speaking, the embryo within the uterus of a woman who converts to Judaism is regarded as *sui generis*. Accordingly, if the fetus is not regarded as an integral part of the mother there is no apparent reason why the embryo should automatically acquire her status.[48]

In his article published in *Teḥumin,* Rabbi Kilav explicitly rejects any distinction between situations involving implantation of a developing embryo during the first forty days following conception and implantation

48. Dr. Abraham S. Abraham, author of *Nishmat Avraham,* graciously acceded to my request to contact Rabbi Auerbach for clarification of his position. In a communication dated 22 Shevat 5751, Dr. Abraham writes that Rabbi Auerbach expressed doubt with regard to the efficacy of conversion of the fetus during pregnancy "because perhaps she is not its mother and she has no jurisdiction over it" (my translation). Rabbi Auerbach's hesitation is apparently born of reservations with regard to the conditions necessary for the conversion of gentiles during their minority. It may be inferred from the comments of Rashi, *Ketubot* 11a, that the application of the child's father or, in his absence, of the mother is necessary in order to effect a valid conversion of a minor. Some authorities maintain that a minor may present himself for conversion while other authorities maintain that the *Bet Din* may act on its own initiative. See sources cited in *Encyclopedia Talmudit,* VI, 445. An obvious problem arises in situations in which a child is surrendered for adoption but the natural parents do not know that the child is to be adopted by a Jewish couple and certainly do not formally consent to conversion. A number of contemporary decisors have expressed the view that all authorities agree that when the gentile parents have abandoned their interest in the child, parental application or permission is not required. See, for example, R. Meir ha-Levi Steinberg, *Likkutei Me'ir* (London, 5730), pp. 68–69. If this concern is the sole impediment to conversion during pregnancy it would appear that it may be obviated by obtaining permission from the donor mother for conversion.

Parenthetically, Rabbi Auerbach seems to have no question with regard to the efficacy of conversion if performed after birth, presumably because parturition establishes a maternal relationship between the child and the birth mother. If, however, the child has two mothers it is not clear that the rights and prerogatives of the donor mother become extinguished (unless, of course, Reb Naphtali's thesis to the effect that conversion is required only for purposes of *kedushat Yisra'el* is accepted). If, on the other hand, parturition and only parturition establishes a maternal-filial relationship, the fetus has no mother before parturition and there is scant reason to assume that a minor "orphan" cannot be converted. Moreover, according to R. Akiva Eger, the selfsame problem may remain after birth as well since, according to R. Akiva Eger, parturition may not establish a maternal-filial relationship in such cases; see *supra,* note 42.

during later periods of gestation.[49] The Gemara, *Kiddushin* 69a, posits a situation in which a Jewess may give birth to a child whose status is that of a slave. The Sages, whose opinion in this regard is accepted as normative, declare that a master may emancipate a female slave who is pregnant without simultaneously emancipating the fetus. The master thereby reserves the fetus to himself as a slave subsequent to birth. There is no hint in the Gemara or in the subsequent codifications of this halakhic provision that such a reservation is ineffective if the female slave is less than forty days pregnant. Hence it cannot be assumed that because the nascent embryo is described as "mere water" it lacks independent status and identity. Similarly, R. Ezekiel Landau, *Dagul me-Revavah, Yoreh De'ah* 268:6, in discussing a related situation, fails to distinguish between the various stages of pregnancy. *Dagul me-Revavah* expresses doubt with regard to the efficacy of the mother's conversion vis-à-vis her child in situations in which the pregnancy was not made known to the members of the *Bet Din* at the time of her immersion in a *mikveh,* but does not indicate that failure to disclose this information is immaterial if conversion takes place within the first forty days of pregnancy. In his contribution to *Be-Shevilei ha-Refu'ah,* no. 8, Rabbi Sternbuch similarly maintains that conversion of the fetus is required even if the mother becomes a convert within the first forty days of gestation.

VII. *A Jewish Donor and a Non-Jewish Gestational Mother*

As yet, there has not appeared a detailed discussion of the status of a child born to a non-Jewish gestational mother by means of in vitro fertilization of an ovum donated by a Jewish woman. On the basis of the foregoing discussion it may be assumed that the child would require conversion in order to be recognized as a Jew. That conclusion would be the necessary result of acceptance of parturition as the determining factor with regard to a maternal-child relationship. Even if the possibility of a dual maternal relationship is recognized, conversion would appear to be required at the very minimum for the purpose of acquiring *kedushat Yisra'el* because of the existence of a non-Jewish genealogical relationship. That conclusion would follow *a fortiori* from the requirement for conversion of the fetus of a proselyte who converts while pregnant and for the conversion of a non-Jewish fetus implanted in a Jewish gestational mother.

49. *Teḥumin,* V, 262.

It is also entirely conceivable that a dual maternal relationship would result in a status of "half-Jew, half-gentile" analogous to the status of "half-slave, half-freeman," posited by the Gemara in other contexts. If so, the "half-gentile" would require the usual form of conversion. However, Rabbi Kilav, in a cryptic statement, expresses the opinion that in such circumstances the child is a Jew.[50] That view is consistent with his position that in the converse situation of a non-Jewish ovum donor the child is a gentile and that parturition determines only maternal identity but not religious status.

At issue is not simply the status of such a child. Determination of that question has obvious and serious implications with regard to the issue of ovum donations by Jewish women on behalf of non-Jewish infertile couples. Obviously, such donations cannot be sanctioned if they result in situations in which a Jewish child, or a child who is "half-Jew, half-gentile," is reared as a gentile and allowed to become "assimilated among the nations." On the other hand, if the child's status is that of a non-Jew, the permissibility of such a donation is far from clear since, apart from technical halakhic considerations, the procedure is contrary to ideological norms of Judaism. In the case of idol-worshippers, the Gemara, *Avodah Zarah* 26a, censures various forms of assistance in the propagation of pagan children because the mother "gives birth to a child for idolatry." Permission for such assistance is granted only when withholding of necessary services would result in enmity toward Jews.

Indeed, even donation of an ovum to a Jewish infertile couple in situations in which the child will not be provided with a Jewish education and reared in an observant home is fraught with both halakhic and ideological difficulties that are beyond the scope of this discussion. Moreover, if a maternal-filial relationship between the donor and the child is recognized by Halakhah, suppression of the identity of the genetic mother would be forbidden because of the potential for an incestuous marriage at some future time,[51] not to speak of the general odium associated in Jewish

50. *Teḥumin,* V, 267.

51. The statement of the Gemara, *Yevamot* 37b, forbidding a man from establishing multiple families whose identities are not known to one another serves as the basis for a ban upon any suppression of information that might prevent an incestuous relationship. See, for example, R. Moses Feinstein, *Iggerot Mosheh, Yoreh De'ah,* I, no. 162, regarding a similar application of that principle in cases of adoption. See also, R. Shlomoh Goren, *Ha-Ẓofeh,* 7 Adar I (5744).

teaching with interference with, and distortion of, normal familial relationships.

VIII. *Animal Gestation of a Human Embryo*

The possibility of dual maternal relationships may acquire particular significance when, and if, implantation of a human fetus in a member of an animal species becomes an empirical possibility. Gestational development would then occur in the uterus of the animal which would serve as a sort of living incubator. Although, at present, the possibility seems extremely remote, recent developments in science and technology amply demonstrate that the science fiction of today may become the reality of tomorrow. Development of immuno-suppressive drugs has made zenografts a distinct possibility and, although some may find such a procedure repugnant, those developments may conceivably lead to use of animals for gestational purposes. In such an eventuality the crucial question will be whether the product of such gestation is to be accorded status as a human being.

It is evident from the discussion of the Gemara, *Niddah* 23b, that identity as the member of a particular species is determined, not by distinguishing physical characteristics, but by birth. Thus, an animal-like creature born to a human is regarded as a human being. The Gemara clearly recognized the theoretical possibility of a converse situation, *viz.*, of a human-like creature being born to an animal. If born to a member of a kosher species the Gemara questions whether or not the offspring may be slaughtered for food since, although it possesses a "hoof," it does not have the characteristic split hoof of a kosher species. From the very formulation of the question it is manifestly evident that the Gemara did not regard a creature of this nature as enjoying the status of a human being.

Thus, if parturition is regarded as the sole determining criterion in all matters of personal status to the exclusion of genetic considerations, the Gemara's discussion may one day become entirely germane to the determination of the status of a human zygote implanted in an animal uterus. If, on the other hand, the possibility of dual maternal relationships is accepted, such offspring may acquire the identity of the genetic mother as well as that of the gestational mother.

IX. *Conclusions*

In the opinion of this writer, the preponderance of evidence adduced from rabbinic sources demonstrates that parturition, in and of itself, serves to establish a maternal relationship. Nevertheless, the possibility that Jewish law may recognize a second maternal relationship based upon donation of an ovum cannot be excluded and indeed there is some evidence indicating that such an additional relationship is recognized. It is also possible that an additional non-genetic and non-parturitional relationship, or even multiple relationships of that nature, may be established on the basis of gestation. Thus, for purposes of Jewish law, the relationship arising from parturition must be regarded as firmly established whereas genetic and gestational relationships must be regarded as doubtful (*safek*). The primary effect, but by no means the sole implication, of recognition of this "doubtful" relationship is to prohibit marriage between genetic siblings and other genetic relatives.

A child born of an in vitro procedure in which the ovum was donated by a non-Jewish woman requires conversion. Although the grounds are not entirely clear, some authorities maintain that, in such cases, immersion for purposes of conversion must be performed after birth and cannot be accomplished on behalf of the child by immersion of the mother during pregnancy. Whether or not there exists a maternal relationship between the Jewish birth mother and the child converted after birth is a matter of some dispute.

This endeavor addresses only issues of maternal identity and conversion in situations in which a child has been born as the result of in vitro fertilization. A comprehensive analysis of the various issues that must be addressed in discussing the permissibility of utilization of in vitro procedures or ovum donations in order to overcome problems associated with infertility is beyond the scope of this undertaking. Those issues represent matters of grave halakhic and moral significance requiring informed halakhic guidance.

Chapter XII

May Tissue Donations Be Compelled?

Whoever preserves a single soul of Israel, Scripture regards him as though he had preserved an entire world.

SANHEDRIN 37a

I. *The Obligation to Rescue*

In late 1990 it was determined that a Jewish teenager, Meir Shor, of Queens, N.Y., was suffering from leukemia. His physicians advised that the only treatment likely to save his life was a bone marrow transplant. A campaign to identify a suitable donor was immediately instituted by the National Jewish Children's Leukemia Foundation. Six months later, after some three thousand people were tested, a perfect match was found. However, the potential donor declined to provide the necessary marrow on the plea that he was unable to absent himself from work in order to make himself available for the transplant procedure. Since the federally funded testing program assures donor confidentially and anonymity it proved to be impossible even to communicate with the potential donor in an attempt to persuade him to reconsider.[1]

To be sure, unless a potential donor can be identified and located, all other questions are moot. Nevertheless, this case serves to focus attention upon a complex ethical issue. Assuming that the potential donor could be located but that he remained adamant in his refusal, would such refusal be justified and, if not, could he be compelled to serve as a donor of a life-saving transplant?

At least one virtually identical case has been considered by an American court. In 1978, David Shimp, a resident of Pittsburgh, Pennsylvania, initially undertook to donate bone marrow to his terminally ill cousin,

1. See *JTA Community News Reporter,* vol. 31, no. 40 (Oct. 4, 1991), p. 1, col. 2.

Robert McFall, but later reneged on his agreement. Mr. McFall initiated proceedings in Allegheny County Court to compel his cousin to donate bone marrow but did not prevail.[2] Indeed, the Court's ruling was virtually inescapable since common law does not require a person to render life-saving assistance to another unless the person of whom the demand is made has in some manner assumed a duty of care. Good Samaritan statutes providing a penalty for failure to intervene exist only in Vermont[3] and Minnesota[4] and even in those jurisdictions the statutes cannot fairly be read as mandating invasion of a person's body without his consent.

Judaism, on the contrary, posits a clear and unequivocal obligation to preserve the life of another. The attitude reflected in that requirement is most eloquently captured in a talmudic passage regarding the creation of Adam: "Therefore, only a single human being was created in the world, to teach that if any person has caused a single soul of Israel to perish, Scripture regards him as if he had caused an entire world to perish; and if any human being saves a single soul in Israel, Scripture regards him as if he had saved an entire world" (*Sanhedrin* 37a). The normative obligation to save the life of an endangered person is formulated by the Gemara, *Sanhedrin* 73a, on the basis of two separate biblical texts. The first is the scriptural exhortation with regard to restoration of lost property, "and you shall return it to him" (Deuteronomy 22:2). On the basis of a pleonasm in the Hebrew text, the Gemara declares that this verse establishes an obligation to restore a fellow man's body as well as his property. A second source is the command "nor shall you stand idly by the blood of your fellow" (Leviticus 19:16). As indicated by the Gemara, *Sanhedrin* 73a, the latter obligation mandates not only the rendering of personal assistance, as is the case with regard to the positive obligation applicable to restoration of lost property, but, by virtue of inclusion in the negative commandment, the obligation is expanded to encompass commitment of financial resources for the sake of preserving the life of a fellow man.[5]

2. *McFall* v. *Shimp,* 10 Pa. D. & C.3d 90 (1978).

3. Vermont, *Annotated Statutes,* Title 12, §579 (1973). The Vermont statute provides for a fine of not more than $100 for willful violation.

4. Minnesota, *Annotated Statutes,* §604.05 (1992). Violation constitutes a "petty misdemeanor." Under §609.02(4a) of the Minnesota *Statutes* a petty misdemeanor is punishable by a fine of not more than $200.

5. For sources elucidating the specific application of these obligations to medical intervention see this writer's "The Obligation to Heal in the Judaic Tradition: A Comparative Analysis," *Jewish Bioethics* (New York, 1981), ed. Fred Rosner and J. David Bleich, pp. 1–55; and J. David Bleich, *Judaism and*

Although an individual is obligated to intervene in order to preserve the life of another, the existence of an obligation to do so when such intervention entails self-endangerment is fraught with controversy. The Palestinian Talmud, *Terumot* 8:4, reports that Rav Ami was abducted and faced imminent execution. A debate ensued with regard to whether or not an attempt should be made to use force in an attempt to secure his release. Rav Yonatan rejected the proposal declaring, "Let the corpse be wrapped in its shroud." Resh Lakish, however, insisted upon embarking upon an attempt at rescue and announced, "Either I will kill or I shall be killed."[6] R. Joseph Karo, both in his commentary on the Mishneh Torah, *Kesef Mishneh, Hilkhot Rozeaḥ* 1:14, and in his commentary on *Tur Shulḥan Arukh, Bet Yosef, Ḥoshen Mishpat* 425, citing *Hagahot Maimuniyot,* rules that one must place one's own life in jeopardy in order to preserve the life of another. That ruling is apparently in accordance with the opinion of Resh Lakish.[7] In his *Kesef Mishneh,* R. Joseph Karo explains the rationale underlying this position, *viz.,* that it is predicated upon the premise that if there is to be no intervention the victim will surely die, whereas the threat to the life of the rescuer is merely "doubtful." Consequently, the certainty of rescuing one life must be accorded precedence over the doubtful loss of another.[8] Nevertheless, as *Sema* comments

Healing (New York, 1981), pp. 1–10.

6. This interpretation is reflected in the comments of *Pnei Mosheh, ad locum,* and is in accordance with the plain meaning of the text. Cf., however, R. Ovadiah Yosef, *Dinei Yisra'el,* VII (5737), 28, who suggests that Resh Lakish was merely expressing the foolhardiness of single-handed intervention and intended to indicate that he would organize a large party to assist him in that endeavor. Earlier, R. Chaim Heller, *Sefer ha-Mizvot* (Jerusalem, 5706), p. 175, in a strained interpretation of the terminology employed by the Palestinian Talmud, explained Resh Lakish's comment as expressing a plan to ransom Rav Ami.

7. See also the citation of *Berakhot* 33a by *Torah Temimah,* Leviticus 19:16, as a source for this ruling. Cf., however, R. Ovadiah Yosef, *Dinei Yisra'el,* VII, 41, and R. Pinchas Baruch Toledano, *Barka'i,* no. 3 (Fall, 5746), p. 28, note 3.

8. Hence, even according to this view, there is no obligation for a rescuer to expose himself to risk unless the likelihood of preserving a life is virtually a certainty; in situations in which the likelihood of success is less certain a potential rescuer need not intervene even if the probability of saving the life of another is significantly greater than the likelihood of losing his own life. See *Agudat Ezov, Derushim,* p. 38b; *Teshuvot Amudei Or,* no. 96, p. 80a; R. Meir Dan Plocki, *Klei Ḥemdah, Parashat Ki Tezei;* R. Chaim Heller, *Sefer ha-Mizvot,* p. 175; R. Yitzchak Ya'akov Weisz, *Teshuvot Minḥat Yizḥak,* VI, no. 103; R. Ovadiah Yosef, *Dinei Yisra'el,* VII, 29; R. Moshe Hershler, *Halakhah u-Refu'ah,* II (Jerusalem, 5741), 125; and R. Meir Yosef Slutz, *Halakhah u-Refu'ah,* III (Jerusalem, 5743), 161–163.

ad locum, it is noteworthy that R. Joseph Karo did not incorporate this ruling in his *Shulḥan Arukh* and that no such ruling appears in the compendia of earlier authorities. That position is, however, espoused by R. Ya'ir Chaim Bacharach, *Teshuvot Ḥavot Ya'ir,* no. 146, and R. Chaim David Abulafia, *Teshuvot Nishmat Ḥayyim, Derushim,* p. 11a.

A contrary position is espoused by a long line of rabbinic decisors beginning with the thirteenth-century authority, R. Jonah Gerondi, *Issur ve-Heter* 59:38. That view is, however, most frequently cited in the name of the sixteenth-century authority, R. David ibn Zimra, *Teshuvot Radbaz,* III, no. 1052.[9] Radbaz alludes to the principle enunciated by the Gemara, *Baba Meẓi'a* 62a, in R. Akiva's dictum "Your life takes preference over the life of your fellow" and declares that avoidance of even "one's own doubtful [danger] takes precedence over the certainty of one's fellow."[10] That position is endorsed by numerous authorities, including *Eliyahu Rabbah, Oraḥ Ḥayyim* 329:8; *Knesset ha-Gedolah, Ḥoshen Mishpat* 425:18; *Pri Megadim, Mishbeẓot Zahav, Oraḥ Ḥayyim* 328:7; *Agudat Ezov,* cited by *Pitḥei Teshuvah, Ḥoshen Mishpat* 426:2; *Shulḥan Arukh ha-Rav,* II, *Oraḥ Ḥayyim* 329:8 and V, *Hilkhot Nizkei Guf va-Nefesh,* sec. 7; *Teshuvot Maharam Shik, Yoreh De'ah,* no. 155; and *Arukh ha-Shulḥan, Ḥoshen Mishpat 426:4.*[11] *Arukh ha-Shulḥan* adds an appropriate

Cf., however, *Teshuvot Ḥavot Ya'ir,* no. 146, who adopts an opposing view. See also Baḥ, *Shulḥan Arukh, Ḥoshen Mishpat* 426:2.

9. For a further discussion of self-endangerment as a limiting factor see this writer's "AIDS: A Jewish Perspective," *Tradition,* vol. XXVI, no. 3 (Spring, 1992), pp. 69–74.

10. Cf., however, the apparently contradictory comments of *Teshuvot Radbaz,* V, no. 1,582. R. Ovadiah Yosef, *Yeḥaveh Da'at,* III, no. 84, reprinted in *Halakhah u-Refu'ah,* III, 61–63, endeavors to explain Radbaz' earlier responsum as not requiring self-endangerment only when there is at least an equal chance of losing one's own life. See also R. Ovadiah Yosef, *Dinei Yisra'el,* VII, 27–28, 30 and 41; *Maharam Shik al Taryag Miẓvot,* no. 238; and Abraham S. Abraham, *Nishmat Avraham,* I, *Oraḥ Ḥayyim* 329:6. That explanation of Radbaz' position is apparently based upon the comments of R. Chaim Heller, *Sefer ha-Miẓvot,* p. 175. A similar analysis is presented by R. Moshe Hershler, *Halakhah u-Refu'ah,* II, 123–124; R. Eliezer Waldenberg, *Ẓiẓ Eli'ezer,* X, no. 25, chap. 28; and R. Samuel ha-Levi Woszner, *Halakhah u-Refu'ah,* IV (Jerusalem, 5745), 139–140. That interpretation, however, is not supported by the text of Radbaz' earlier responsum and assuredly is not to be attributed to the numerous later authorities who rule that self-endangerment is not required.

11. See also *Ha'amek She'elah, She'ilta* 147:4; *Teshuvot Amudei Or,* no. 96, sec. 3; and *Minḥat Ḥinnukh,* no. 237. Cf., *Ḥiddushei Ḥatam Sofer, Ketubot* 61b, s.v. *m'ai ta'am;,* and *Teshuvot Imrei Binah, Oraḥ Ḥayyim,* no. 13, sec. 5.

cautionary note indicating that the proper course of action in any given situation depends upon the attendant circumstances and that all factors must be carefully weighed lest one be overly protective of oneself with the resultant loss of the life of another.[12] It is likely that the ruling of these authorities reflects a decision to accept the opinion of Rav Yonatan in his dispute with Resh Lakish. Alternatively, it may be based upon their assessment of Resh Lakish's conduct as reflective of an act of piety rather than as compelled by a halakhic norm.[13] It is also possible that those authorities understood the discussion found in the Babylonian Talmud, *Sanhedrin* 73a,[14] or one or more of several other discussions in the Babylonian Talmud,[15] as being in disagreement with the position of Rav

12. The comments of R. Iser Yehudah Unterman, *Shevet me-Yehudah* (Jerusalem, 5715), *sha'ar rishon,* chap. 9, p. 23, although they do not constitute a definitive halakhic norm, are nevertheless instructive. Rabbi Unterman suggests that, in making a decision, the potential rescuer should ask himself if he would incur the identical danger in order to rescue a cherished possession. If yes, he should cherish the life of his fellow equally and accept the danger.

13. See *Teshuvot Yad Eliyahu,* no. 43, p. 48b; *Ha'amek She'elah, She'ilta* 147:4; *Ẓiẓ Eli'ezer,* IX, no. 45, sec. 5; and R. Ovadiah Yosef, *Dinei Yisra'el,* VII, 23–28. This analysis is inconsistent with the position of Radbaz, who describes a person who acts in such a manner as a "pious fool"; see *infra,* note 20. *Teshuvot Yad Eliyahu* offers an alternative interpretation of Resh Lakish's conduct in stating that self-endangerment is permitted in order to rescue the life of a great scholar. See *Sefer Ḥasidim* (Jerusalem, 5720), no. 698; R. Jacob Emden, *Migdal Oz, Even Boḥen* 1:78 and 1:85; and *Ẓiẓ Eli'ezer,* X, no. 25, secs. 9–11.

14. *Ha'amek She'elah, She'iltot de-Rav Aḥa'i Ga'on* 457:4, asserts that the Babylonian Talmud, *Nedarim* 80b, disagrees with the Palestinian Talmud and hence it is the position of the Babylonian Talmud that is accepted by the majority of rabbinic decisors. For a survey of conflicting discussions regarding the proper understanding of *Nedarim* 80b see R. Ovadiah Yosef, *Dinei Yisra'el,* VII, 32–36.

Teshuvot Yad Eliyahu, no. 43, p. 48b, and *Agudat Ezov, Derushim,* p. 3b, opine that, according to the interpretation of *She'iltot de-Rav Aḥa'i Ga'on,* the Babylonian Talmud, *Niddah* 61a, disagrees with the Palestinian Talmud. Their argument is rebutted by R. Chaim Heller, *Sefer ha-Miẓvot,* p. 175. It should also be noted that *Ha'amek She'elah, She'ilta* 129:4, finds support for the position of the Palestinian Talmud in that discussion. See also R. Eliezer Waldenberg, *Ẓiẓ Eli'ezer,* IX, no. 45, sec. 5. Cf., however, *Teshuvot Bet Ya'akov,* no. 107 and R. Ovadiah Yosef, *Dinei Yisra'el,* VII, 28.

Discussion of other statements found in the Babylonian Talmud that may serve to establish existence of a dispute between the two Talmuds are presented by *Teshuvot Yad Eliyahu,* no. 43; R. Chaim Heller, *Sefer ha-Miẓvot,* p. 175; and R. Ovadiah Yosef, *Dinei Yisra'el,* VII, 36–38.

15. See *Arukh la-Ner, Sanhedrin* 73a; *Agudat Ezov* cited in *Pitḥei Teshuvah, Ḥoshen Mishpat* 426:2; *Arukh ha-Shulḥan, Ḥoshen Mishpat* 426:4; R. Chaim

Yonatan that is recorded in the Palestinian Talmud.

R. Meir Simchah of Dvinsk, *Or Sameaḥ, Hilkhot Roẓeaḥ* 7:8, adduces support for this position from phraseology employed by Rambam in codifying the rule regarding exile in a city of refuge. The Mishnah, *Makkot* 11b, states that a person who has inadvertently committed an act of homicide for which he is required to go into exile may not leave the city of refuge under any circumstances. Rambam follows the statement recorded in the Mishnah in ruling that the exile may not depart from the city of refuge even if "all of Israel are needful of his succor" and, moreover, "if he leaves he surrenders himself to death." The latter phrase does not occur in the Mishnah and *Or Sameaḥ* suggests that it was added by Rambam in order to establish the underlying rationale, i.e., the reason that the exiled manslaughterer is not required to disregard the rules regarding exile in order to preserve the lives of others (as he would be required to do with regard to other provisions of law) is that he is not obligated to endanger himself to save others from certain death.[16]

The same author, in his novellae on the Pentateuch, *Meshekh Ḥokhmah,* Exodus 4:19, finds an intriguing allusion to this principle in the verse "Go, return to Egypt for the people who sought your life have died." Since God explicitly commanded Moses to return to Egypt, all other considerations would appear to be immaterial. Why, then, does Scripture expressly tell us that Moses was informed that the danger had passed? *Meshekh Ḥokhmah* comments that God's command to Moses was inherently no different from any other commandment of the Torah and, despite the fact that Moses' mission was designed to rescue the lives of the children of Israel, Moses was under no obligation to risk his own life in fulfilling a divine command. Hence Moses might legitimately have declined to undertake the mission of rescue.[17] Only divine assurance that the

Heller, *Sefer ha-Miẓvot,* p. 195; and R. Ovadiah Yosef, *Dinei Yisra'el,* VII, 31–32.

16. Cf., however, R. Shlomoh Yosef Zevin, *Le-Or ha-Halakhah* (Tel Aviv, 5717), pp. 15–16, who cogently argues that this proof is not conclusive. See also, *Klei Ḥemdah, Parashat Pinḥas,* who sharply disagrees with *Or Sameaḥ.* See also R. Ovadiah Yosef, *Dinei Yisra'el,* VII, 26, who analyzes other talmudic statements cited by *Or Sameaḥ.*

17. Similarly, when God directed Samuel to anoint David as king, Samuel responded, "How can I go? If Saul hears he will kill me" (I Samuel 16:2). In both instances, self-endangerment serves not simply as exemption from performance of a statutory commandment but even as grounds for avoidance of an *ad hoc* command. See R. Yitzchak of Vilna, *Bet Yiẓḥak* (Jerusalem, 5733), *Parashat Bo.*

danger no longer existed made it impossible for him to decline on a plea of self-endangerment.[18]

II. *Transplants*

R. David ibn Zimra, *Teshuvot ha-Radbaz,* III, no. 627, addresses another, and perhaps even more intriguing, question as well. A certain feudal potentate demanded that a Jew permit him to amputate "an organ upon which life is not dependent" and warned that if that individual refused to acquiesce to the amputation the life of another person would be forfeit. Radbaz was asked whether there exists an obligation to sacrifice a limb in order to rescue the life of one's fellow. Radbaz astutely divides the question into two separate issues: 1) Is there an obligation to endanger oneself in order to preserve the life of another? and 2) assuming that the amputation itself poses no danger to the rescuer, is a person required to sacrifice a limb in order to save the life of another?

To the latter question Radbaz responds that the Torah, "whose ways are ways of pleasantness" (Proverbs 3:17), could not possibly demand the sacrifice of a limb even for such a noble purpose.[19] Nevertheless, a person who is willing voluntarily to make such a sacrifice without endangering his own life acts in accordance with the highest traits of piety and merits approbation. If, however, the procedure involves self-endangerment, Radbaz dismisses the act as that of a "pious fool."[20]

---

18. The comments presented in *Or Sameaḥ* and *Meshekh Ḥokhmah* serve to establish that self-endangerment is not required even if the entire community of Israel, rather than a single individual, is endangered. Cf., however, R. Abraham I. Kook, *Mishpat Kohen,* nos. 142–144; *Klei Ḥemdah, Parashat Pinḥas;* R. Isaac ha-Levi Herzog, *Teshuvot Heikhal Yiẓḥak, Oraḥ Ḥayyim,* no. 34; R. Ovadiah Yosef, *Dinei Yisra'el,* VII, 38–40; and R. Pinchas Baruch Toledano, *Barka'i,* III, 32.

19. Radbaz' interlocutor informed him that he had "found it written" that sacrifice of a limb is obligatory in order to save the life of another person. That view is espoused by R. Menachem Recanati, *Piskei Recanati,* no. 470, and is cited by R. Yehudah Ashkenazi of Tiktin, *Be'er Heiteiv, Yoreh De'ah* (Amsterdam, 5529), 157:13, who declares that "some say" that it is indeed obligatory to sacrifice a limb in order to preserve the life of another person; cf., *Naḥal Eitan, Hilkhot Ishut* 21:11. See also *Hagahot Mordekhai, Sanhedrin,* sec. 718, who states that a person may cut off the limb of another in order to save his own life.

20. The term "pious fool" would appear to denote a person who is foolhardy in his pursuit of pious deeds and assignment of this appellation certainly implies that such acts should not be encouraged. However, in context, the term does appear to connote that the act performed by the individual is forbidden. Although

the verse "and your brother shall live with you" (Leviticus 25:36) is cited by R. Akiva, *Baba Meẓi'a* 62a, as establishing that one dare not give preference to the life of another over one's own life, that discussion serves only to prohibit the sacrifice of one's own life on behalf of another but not to prohibit acceptance of a measure of danger in order to save the life of another. To be sure, as explicitly stated by *Teshuvot Radbaz,* III, no. 1,052, the principle expressed in the dictum formulated by the Gemara, *Sanhedrin 74a,* "Why do you think that your blood is sweeter than the blood of your fellow?" is valid in the converse as well, *viz.,* "Why do you think that the blood of your fellow is sweeter than your own blood?" However, application of that principle would require passive nonintervention only when the danger to one's own life is greater or equal to the danger to the person in need of rescue. In a situation in which the danger to the endangered person is significantly greater than the danger to the rescuer that consideration does not appear to be applicable. Hence, although the Torah does not demand self-endangerment even under such circumstances, the act of rescue, when posing a hazard to the rescuer, should be regarded as discretionary, albeit foolhardy, rather than as prohibited.

Nevertheless, *Ẓiẓ Eli'ezer,* IX, no. 45, sec. 13, cites Radbaz' use of the term "pious fool" in ruling that self-endangerment is forbidden even for the purpose of preserving the life of another. That position is reiterated in *Ẓiẓ Eli'ezer,* X, no. 25, chap. 7, secs. 5 and 12 and no. 25, chap. 28. See also R. Chaim David Halevi, *Sefer Assia,* IV (5743), 256–257, and R. Shemayah Dikhovski, *Ne'ot Deshe,* II, 155–156. An identical view is also espoused by R. Moshe Hershler, *Halakhah u-Refu'ah,* II, 123. However, in the course of resolving the contradiction between *Teshuvot Radbaz,* III, no. 1,052 and *Teshuvot Radbaz,* V, no. 1,582 (see *supra,* note 10), Rabbi Hershler limits the prohibition to situations in which the potential danger to the rescuer is equal to, or greater than, the danger to the person to be rescued since he regards Radbaz as requiring intervention when the danger to the victim is disproportionate to that of the intervenor. *Ẓiẓ Eli'ezer*'s discussion is rather confusing since he also resolves the contradiction in a manner similar to the resolution presented by Rabbi Hershler (see *supra,* note 10), but in his definitive rulings does not seem to apply the principle that arises therefrom. Most striking is his ruling in *Ẓiẓ Eli'ezer,* XIII, no. 101, to the effect that blood donations cannot be compelled because of the attendant danger. See *infra,* note 28. As will be shown shortly, *Ẓiẓ Eli'ezer*'s rulings with regard to kidney transplants are also inconsistent with this principle. Moreover, *Ẓiẓ Eli'ezer,* IX, no. 45, sec. 5, himself states that Resh Lakish's self-endangerment did not reflect a controversy with Rav Yonatan but represented an act of piety. That statement is inconsistent with the view that self-endangerment is prohibited.

A number of authorities explicitly declare that, under such circumstances, self-endangerment is discretionary but permissible. *Teshuvot Minḥat Yiẓḥak,* VI, no. 103, declares that the controversy between *Hagahot Maimuniyot* and Radbaz is limited to whether or not there is an obligation of rescue when there is a hazard to the rescuer but that all agree that "it is permissible if he so desires." *Minḥat Yiẓḥak,* however, qualifies that statement with the caveat that self-endangerment is permitted only if such self-endangerment will "with certainty" lead to the rescue of the victim. See *supra,* note 8. R. Moses Feinstein, *Iggerot*

Mosheh, Yoreh De'ah, II, no. 174, *anaf* 4, explicitly permits a person to risk his own life in order to save the life of another provided that he does not expose himself to "certain death." Similarly, R. Samuel ha-Levi Woszner, *Teshuvot Shevet ha-Levi,* V, no. 119, reprinted in *Halakhah u-Refu'ah,* IV, 139–142, finds no transgression in endangering oneself in order to preserve the life of another provided that the probability of survival is more than fifty percent. R. Moshe Dov Welner, *Ha-Torah ve-ha-Medinah,* VII-VIII (5715–5719), 311, also regards self-endangerment for purposes of rescuing another person to be permissible. See also Jacob Levy, *No'am,* XIV (5731), 319.

The hazards involved in donation of a kidney are not insignificant. See *infra,* note 109. Accordingly, the propriety of transplantation of a kidney from a living donor is directly related to the resolution of the issue of whether or not a person may risk his own life in order to preserve the life of another. Despite his earlier cited comments in resolving the contradiction found in Radbaz' responsa, in *Ẓiẓ Eli'ezer,* IX, no. 45, sec. 13 and *Ẓiẓ Eli'ezer,* X, no. 25, chap. 7, secs. 5 and 12, Rabbi Waldenberg asserts that, pursuant to the opinion of Radbaz, such donations are prohibited. Although in *Ẓiẓ Eli'ezer,* IX, no. 45, sec. 13, Rabbi Waldenberg concludes that such transplants cannot be sanctioned unless it is medically determined that "the matter does not entail possible danger to the life of the donor," in *Ẓiẓ Eli'ezer,* X, no. 25, chap. 7, he incongruously cites his earlier discussion of this topic and rules that such transplants may be permitted "where the danger is not certain and medical science states that it is reasonable [to assume that as a result both will remain alive." That conclusion is inconsistent not only with his earlier ruling but also with his discussions in the same chapter. R. Pinchas Baruch Toledano, *Barka'i,* III, 26 and 32, similarly understands Radbaz as prohibiting self-endangerment and rules that donation of a kidney by a living person is forbidden. R. Saul Israeli, *Barka'i,* III, 35, notes 1 and 2, takes no definitive stand with regard to whether self-endangerment constitutes a transgression but opines that Radbaz' negative view regarding self-endangerment is limited to situations involving a significant immediate danger. He also suggests that Radbaz' comments are limited to the danger experienced in the loss of an external organ that would render the donor a cripple. However, neither qualification of Radbaz' position is supported either by the text of the responsum or by an analysis of the underlying position.

The earlier cited authorities who permit self-endangerment for the purpose of preserving the life of another would certainly sanction transplantation of a kidney from a live donor. Such procedures are also permitted, at least under usual conditions, by R. Ovadiah Yosef, *Dinei Yisra'el,* VII, 41–43; *idem, Yeḥaveh Da'at,* III, no. 84 and *Halakhah u-Refu'ah,* III, 61–63; R. Shlomoh Zalman Auerbach, as cited by *Nishmat Avraham,* II, *Yoreh De'ah* 157:4 (sec. 2), s.v. *akh katav li;* R. Moshe Hershler, *Halakhah u-Refu'ah,* II, 124; R. Saul Israeli, *Barka'i,* III, p. 35, note 1 (cf., however, *idem,* p. 36, note 2); R. Moshe Meiselman, *Halakhah u-Refu'ah,* II, 119–125; R. Chaim David Halevi, *Sefer Assia,* IV, 257; and *Ne'ot Deshe,* II, 156.

It is certainly clear that Radbaz himself not only permitted amputation of a limb in order to preserve the life of another but also lauded such a sacrifice as an act of inordinate piety and voiced such approbation despite his observation that

Although Radbaz emphatically declares that the Torah would not demand the sacrifice of a limb because "its ways are ways of pleasantness" that statement is essentially conclusory and does not really serve to explain the basis upon which exemption from such a requirement is based. It is, however, not at all difficult to fill in the lacuna in Radbaz' reasoning. The obligation to preserve the life of one's fellow, while mandating both personal intervention and expenditure of financial resources, is not all-encompassing. In general, the fulfillment of a positive commandment requires the expenditure of no more than one fifth of one's net worth. However, the obligation not to violate a negative commandment is much more onerous. A person is obligated to spend his entire fortune rather than transgress a negative commandment. The commandment to preserve life is not expressed solely in positive terms, but is repeated in negative language—"nor shall you stand idly by the blood of your fellow." Transgression of that commandment, however, is through passive nonperformance rather than by means of an overt, forbidden act. Since no overt act of transgression is involved in failing to rescue an endangered person, is the expenditure of twenty percent of one's financial resources sufficient, or, since the commandment is couched in negative terms, does the fulfillment require expenditure even of one's entire fortune? There is significant dispute among rabbinic scholars with regard to the resolution of that question.[21]

Formulation of a monetary maximum in limiting obligations for fulfillment of a *miẓvah* serves to establish limits with regard to nonpecuniary matters as well. Although it is a truism that many matters of importance in human life cannot be acquired in exchange for money and hence do

---

loss of blood resulting from perforation of an earlobe has been known to result in loss of life. Radbaz explicitly maintained that even the relatively high risk associated with amputation of a limb, particularly in his day, did not rise to the threshold of risk acceptable only to a "pious fool." The comment of *Ẓiẓ Eli'ezer,* IX, chap. 45, sec. 11, stating that, "since the multitude has trodden thereupon," the surgical amputation of a limb does not rise to the halakhically significant threshold of danger is both empirically incorrect and contradicted by Radbaz' comments concerning perforation of an earlobe. See Jacob Levy, *No'am,* XIV, 322. Accordingly, contrary to the comments of *Ẓiẓ Eli'ezer* and others, prohibition of a kidney transplant from a living donor cannot be sustained even according to their understanding of Radbaz. Cf., *Ne'ot Deshe,* II, 156.

21. See sources cited in *Ḥiddushei R. Akiva Eger, Yoreh De'ah* 157:1 and *Pitḥei Teshuvah, Yoreh De'ah* 157:4. See also R. Shalom Mordecai Schwadron, *Teshuvot Maharsham,* V, no. 54; *Teshuvot Shevet ha-Levi,* V, no. 174; and *Nishmat Avraham,* III, *Ḥoshen Mishpat* 426:1.

not carry a price tag, it is certainly possible to express a hypothetical value for such matters in monetary terms. A burden that cannot possibly be avoided upon payment of a fee can nevertheless be evaluated monetarily in terms of how much one would be willing to expend in order to avoid the burden, were that to be an available option. A burden may be evaluated in terms of how much a person would be willing to spend in order to escape this onus. If the sum equals more than one fifth of a person's financial resources he need not assume that burden in order to fulfill a *mizvah.* If it may be assumed that people in general would willingly expend a fifth of their net worth in order to avoid such a particular burden, the burden in question need not be assumed in order to fulfill a *mizvah.* Thus, *Teshuvot Ḥelkat Yo'av,* I, *Dinei Ones,* sec. 7, rules that a person need not expose himself to the risk of illness in order to discharge a religious obligation. Although *Tosafot, Pesaḥim* 28b and *Yevamot* 70a, fails to offer an explicit explanation, it is presumably this consideration[22] that constitutes the basis of *Tosafot*'s ruling that a person need not submit to a surgical procedure in order to become physically capable of fulfilling a *mizvah.*[23] Normal people, endowed with a balanced set of values, would cheerfully part with much more than one fifth of their possessions in order to avoid surgery or the threat of significant illness.[24]

There are also burdens that a person would cheerfully surrender his entire fortune in order to avoid. A person would do so if he deemed the burden to be more onerous than the loss of all his earthly possessions. Such a burden need not be assumed even in order to save a human life since no authority requires the expenditure of more than one's entire fortune even for that noble purpose. Radbaz presumably assumes that a reasonable person would place a higher value upon a limb or an organ than upon material wealth and hence would willingly expend his entire fortune in order to preserve a limb or organ of the body.[25] Consequently,

22. Cf., however, *Teshuvot Pri Yizḥak,* I, no. 32.

23. Cf., however, Me'iri, *Yevamot* 72a.

24. For a further discussion of the absence of an obligation to expose oneself to illness in the performance of a *mizvah* see sources cited by R. Ya'akov Weingold, *Halakhah u-Refu'ah,* IV, 339–362, and *Nishmat Avraham,* III, *Ḥoshen Mishpat* 420:4 (sec. 3). See also R. Moshe Sternbuch, *Halakhah u-Refu'ah,* IV, 147. Cf., however, R. Chaim Pinchas Scheinberg, *ibid.,* pp. 125–138.

25. See *Iggerot Mosheh, Yoreh De'ah,* II, no. 174, *anaf* 4, and R. Moshe Meiselman, *Halakhah u-Refu'ah,* II, 116–118.

In a similar vein R. Jacob Emden, *Migdal Or, Even Boḥen* 1:83, declares that a person is not obligated to accept "severe and bitter pain" in order to preserve

Radbaz rules that a person need not sacrifice a limb in order to prevent the execution of a fellow Jew. However, although not mandated, expenditure of more than that which is normatively required, when such is feasible, does constitute an act of piety. Accordingly, Radbaz remarks that a person who is prepared to sacrifice a limb in order to save the life of another is deserving of highest approbation.

The essential factor serving to distinguish limbs and organs from wealth is that material resources can be replenished while body organs cannot be regenerated. The reason that a person is prepared to surrender his entire fortune rather than sacrifice a limb is that the lost limb can never be replaced. That rationale is certainly absent in the case of replenishable body tissues such as blood and bone marrow. Certainly, the phenomenon of some people selling blood for extremely modest sums is rather common. The discomfort of blood donation is generally limited to the prick of the needle. Aspiration of bone marrow is performed under anesthesia in order to eliminate pain. The donor is kept in the hospital for one or two days for observation. Occasional infection is readily treated with antibiotics. Usually, the only side effect is soreness in the area of the pelvis from which the bone marrow is aspirated. Donations of both blood and bone marrow are not at all burdensome because, generally, both are present in the body at levels in excess of need and, moreover, when removed in medically acceptable quantities, are replenished within a rather short period of time. In bone marrow donations the quantity removed is between three and five percent of the donor's total bone marrow and is restored within two or three weeks. Accordingly, it would seem that Halakhah would compel donations of such tissue in life-threatening situations, just

---

the life of another. It is readily understood that excruciating pain constitutes a greater burden than loss of one's fortune. In *Even Boḥen* 1:13, R. Jacob Emden offers a similar analysis of the remarkable statement of the Gemara, *Sanhedrin* 75a, declaring that a woman should not engage in sexually provocative activity in order to save a person from death because of the "dishonor of her family." R. Jacob Emden explains that the degradation and embarrassment engendered by such conduct is more onerous than loss of an entire fortune. See also *Iggerot Mosheh, Yoreh De'ah,* III, no. 179 and *Teshuvot Minḥat Yiẓḥak,* V, no. 8. Cf., however, R. Ovadiah Yosef, *Dinei Yisra'el,* VII, 24, who expresses difficulty in understanding R. Jacob Emden's comments in light of the many sources indicating that a person must suffer discomfort and even pain in order to save the life of another. If R. Jacob Emden's position is understood to be in accord with the foregoing comment the difficulties are resolved: R. Jacob Emden refers only to pain the burden of which is at least equal to the burden of losing one's entire fortune while the sources cited by Rabbi Yosef refer to a much lower level of pain.

as it mandates dedication of financial resources for the purpose of saving a life. Since the burden of such donations is *de minimis* it falls far short of a burden equal to twenty percent of one's net wealth and hence would be mandated according to all authorities, provided, of course, that the procedure does not endanger the life of the donor.[26]

To be sure, although there is no reported case of fatality as a result of bone marrow donation, the removal of bone marrow is not entirely without risk. The risk to the donor is, however, limited to the hazard of general anesthesia.[27] Nevertheless, it may be argued that the risks of general anesthesia in an otherwise normal and healthy person do not rise to the threshold of risk of which Halakhah takes cognizance.[28]

There is an obvious tension between the pertinent talmudic dicta bearing upon actions which pose a hazard to life or health. The Gemara, *Shabbat* 32b, declares, "A man should not place himself in a place of danger." Yet elsewhere, (*Shabbat* 129b and *Niddah* 31a as well as other places), the Gemara cites the verse "The Lord preserves the simple" (Psalms 116:6) as granting sanction to man to place his trust in divine providence and to ignore possible danger. The Gemara itself dispels what would

26. Cf., R. Moshe Meiselman, *Halakhah u-Refu'ah,* II, 118, who concludes that donation of blood and skin is obligatory. Similarly, R. Samuel ha-Levi Woszner, *Teshuvot Shevet ha-Levi,* V, no. 119, reprinted in *Halakhah u-Refu'ah,* IV, 139–142, apparently regards ordinary blood donations as mandatory. See, however, *infra,* note 28.

27. Until now, medical studies conducted in conjunction with bone marrow procedures have failed to uncover a linkage between donation of bone marrow and an increased incidence of either mortality or morbidity. In the unlikely event that further studies yield data pointing to the existence of such a causal connection the issues herein discussed will require reexamination.

28. Cf., *Ẓiẓ Eli'ezer,* XIII, no. 101, sec. 6, who rules that even donation of blood cannot be regarded as compulsory because of the attendant danger. A similar view is advanced by R. Moshe Dov Welner, *Ha-Torah ve-ha-Medinah,* VII-VIII, 311. An identical ruling, but without accompanying explanation, is reported in the name of the *Brisker Rav,* R. Yiẓḥak Ze'ev Soloveitchik, by R. Avigdor Nebenzahl in a letter to the editor, *Assia,* vol. 14, no. 1–2 (Elul 5754), p. 208. Rabbi Waldenberg, *Halakhah u-Refu'ah,* IV, 143, advances an additional, albeit fanciful, reason for his refusal to regard blood donations as mandatory. Citing the verse "For the life of the flesh is in the blood" (Leviticus 17:11), Rabbi Waldenberg argues that requiring the donation of more than a minimal amount of blood (the quantity of a *revi'it*) is tantamount to requiring a person to surrender his life. Apart from the obvious objections that might be raised, that position is difficult to maintain in view of the fact that the Talmud regards bloodletting as therapeutic and beneficial in preserving health. Cf., *Iggerot Mosheh, Ḥoshen Mishpat,* II, no. 103.

otherwise be an obvious contradiction by stating that certain actions which contain an element of danger are permitted since "the multitude has trodden thereupon."

The concept embodied in this dictum is not difficult to fathom. Willfully to commit a daredevil act while relying upon God's mercy in order to be preserved from misfortune is an act of hubris. It is sheer audacity for man to call upon God to preserve him from calamity which man can himself avoid. Therefore, one may not place oneself in a position of recognized danger even if one deems oneself to be a worthy and deserving beneficiary of divine guardianship. Nevertheless, it is universally recognized that life is fraught with danger. Crossing the street, riding in an automobile, or even in a horse-drawn carriage for that matter, all involve a statistically significant danger. It is, of course, inconceivable that such ordinary activities be denied to man. Such actions are indeed permissible since "the multitude has trodden thereupon," i.e., since the attendant dangers are accepted with equanimity by society at large. Since society is quite willing to accept the element of risk involved, any individual is granted dispensation to rely upon God who "preserves the simple." Under such circumstances the person who ignores the risk is not deemed to be presumptuous in demanding an inordinate degree of divine protection; on the contrary, he acts in the manner of the "simple" who pose no questions. An act which is not ostentatious, which does not flaunt societally accepted norms of behavior and does not draw attention to itself, is not regarded by Halakhah as an unseemly demand for divine protection. The risk involved may be assumed with impunity, even for purely discretionary purposes, if the individual desires to do so.

The current mortality risk of general anesthesia for all patients is generally estimated as being in the neighborhood of 1 in 10,000.[29] Although precise data seem to be unavailable, there is strong reason to believe that mortality attributable to anesthesia in healthy young adults is far lower, particularly

29. See Alan F. Ross and John H. Tinker, "Anesthetic Risk," *Anesthesia,* 3rd edition (New York, 1990), ed. Robert Miller, I, 721. Of course, mortality attributed to anesthesia was not always so low. A 1944 study reported an incidence of anesthetic death of 1:1,000. Among later studies, a 1961 study reported the incidence of death resulting primarily from anesthesia at 1:536, while a 1960 report set the mortality rate at an astonishing 1:232. A highly regarded multi-institutional survey conducted in 1954 reported a mortality rate of 1:2,680. *Ibid.,* pp. 721–722. The high risk of general anesthesia in times past may account, at least in part, for the view of some contemporary authorities who are reported to have ruled that bone marrow donations cannot be compelled. These rulings, and the reasons upon which they are based, are unfortunately not available in writing.

when the patient is anesthetized for only a brief period.[30] That risk is commonly assumed in undergoing elective surgery and is accepted even for purposes of cosmetic surgery. It seems to this writer that in our society that hazard is either disregarded or accepted with equanimity. Since "the multitude has trodden thereupon" it is a hazard which is to be ignored for purposes of halakhic consideration.[31]

III. *Pediatric Donations in American and Israeli Case Law*

The permissibility of tissue donations by a minor, even with his or her consent, presents a far more complex problem. The legal ramifications of the problem are illuminated by a ruling of an Illinois court in July, 1990. A twelve-year old boy, Jean-Pierre Bosze, was diagnosed as suffering from leukemia and failed to respond to available therapy. His physicians predicted that he would die unless he underwent a successful bone marrow transplant. A number of family members were tested but were found to be incompatible as bone marrow donors. The boy's father, Tamas Bosze, had been named in a successful paternity suit by a woman to whom he was not married. Subsequently, Jean-Pierre's mother, Nancy Curran, gave birth to fraternal twins fathered by another man. Jean-Pierre's father requested Nancy Curran to permit the twins, who were three years old at the time, to be tested in order to determine possible compatibility for a bone marrow transplant. Since the twins and Jean-Pierre were half-siblings, tissue compatibility was a distinct possibility. Nancy Curran refused to accede to this request. Thereupon, Mr. Bosze filed suit in Cook County Circuit Court to compel her to permit the test to be performed. On July 18, 1990 his suit was dismissed.[32] In her decision, Judge Monica Reynolds declared that "to subject a healthy child to bodily intrusions" would "seriously impinge and forsake the constitutional rights of the child and

30. Two studies conducted in the early 1970's indicate a marked decrease in prospective mortality in patients who were either healthy or had mild systemic disease. However, the death rate reported in those studies represents overall prospective mortality, rather than deaths from anesthesia exclusively. See *Anesthesia,* pp. 723–724.

31. Other facets of the obligation to donate blood and bone marrow are discussed by this writer in an article published in *Ha-Pardes,* Ḥeshvan 5752, pp. 11–14.

32. *New York Times,* July 19, 1990, p. A17, col. 2.

render him a victim."[33] That decision was confirmed by the Supreme Court of Illinois on September 28, 1990.[34] Jean-Pierre died while a motion for the Illinois supreme Court to reconsider its decision was pending.[35]

Although the *Bosze* decision represents the culmination and synthesis of a series of decisions handed down by American courts regarding pediatric organ donations, the legal doctrine announced therein is the subject of a somewhat checkered judicial history. The crucial issue is whether or not parents themselves enjoy legal capacity to make such decisions on behalf of their children. The earliest consideration of the issue arose indirectly in *Bonner* v. *Moran*[36] in conjunction with an action for assault and battery brought by a minor who had consented to the removal of a "tube of flesh" to be utilized as a skin graft on behalf of a severely burned cousin who had become a helpless cripple. The results were unsatisfactory and the child, who was fifteen years of age at the time, was hospitalized for close to two months. The child then brought an action for damages resulting from assault and battery. The trial court instructed the jury that if they believed that the child was capable of appreciating, and did indeed appreciate, the nature and consequences of the surgical procedure and had consented to the operation, they must deny him damages. Damages were denied and an appeal was brought. The issue before the U.S. Court of Appeals for the District of Columbia was whether those instructions were correct as a matter of law or whether the consent that is required is consent of the parents. The Court of Appeals found that, with certain limited exceptions, consent of the parents is required and accordingly ordered a new trial to determine whether or not there had been such consent by subsequent ratification.[37] The sole issue

33. *New York Times,* July 30, 1990, p. A8, col. 1.

34. 141 Ill.2d 473, 566 N.E.2d 1319; *New York Times,* September 29, 1990, p. A11, col. 1.

35. *New York Times,* November 20, 1990, p. 89, col. 1.

36. 126 F.2d 121,75 U.S. Ap. D.C. 156(1941).

37. Mature minors have at various times been found to have capacity to consent to at least some procedures. In all such cases the minor has been seventeen years old or older. See *Bakker* v. *Welsh,* 144 Mich. 632, 108 N.W. 94 (1906) (17 years); *Gulf & Ship Island Railroad Co.* v. *Sullivan,* 155 Miss. 1, 119 So. 501 (1928) (seventeen years); *Bishop* v. *Shurly,* 237 Mich. 76, 211 N.W. 75 (1926) (nineteen years); *Lacey* v. *Laird,* 166 Ohio St. 12, 139 N.E.2d 25 (1956) (eighteen years). The general rule is that capacity exists when the minor has the ability of the average person to weigh the risks and benefits of the procedure to which he

addressed by the court was whether parental consent is needed or whether the consent of a mature child is sufficient to prevent the invasion from creating liability.[38] The clear implication of that decision is that consent of the parents would certainly be sufficient and might be relied upon even in situations in which the procedure is of no therapeutic benefit to the minor. Parental authority to consent to a tissue donation of such nature was not at all questioned by the court.

Parental consent for donation of a kidney to a sibling by a minor was subsequently addressed in three separate unreported Massachusetts cases.[39] In two of those cases, the minors were fourteen years of age; in the third, the child was nineteen. In each case the court found that the parents had the legal authority to authorize the donation.

The underlying legal doctrine is enunciated in *Strunk* v. *Strunk*[40] and in *Hart* v. *Brown.*[41] In 1816, in *Ex parte Whitebread,*[42] a British court held that a court of equity has the power to make financial provisions for a needy brother from the estate of an incompetent. Later, in *In re Earl of Carysfort,*[43] the Lord Chancellor permitted the payment of an annuity out of the income of the estate of the lunatic earl to the latter's aged and infirm personal servant on the finding that, although no supporting evidence was advanced, the court was "satisfied that the Earl of Carysfort would have approved if he had been capable of acting himself."[44] That rule has been recognized in this country since 1844 when in *In re Willoughby*[45] a New York court ruled that a chancellor has the power to deal with the estate of an incompetent in the same manner as the incompetent would have acted were the incompetent in possession of his faculties. This rule has been extended to cover not only property matters but also the personal

---

consents. See *Prossor and Keiton on the Law of Torts,* 5th ed. (St. Paul, 1984), p. 115.

38. Consent of a person on whom an otherwise actionable invasion is inflicted is not effective in eliminating liability if that person lacks capacity to consent, e.g., because of infancy. See *Prossor and Keiton on the Law of Torts,* p. 114.

39. *Masden* v. *Harrison,* No. 68651, Eq. Mass. Sub. Jud. Ct. (June 12, 1957); *Hershey* v. *Harrison,* No. 68666, Eq. Mass Sub. Jud. Ct. (August 20, 1957); *Foster* v. *Harrison,* No. 68674, Eq. Mass. Sup. Jud. Ct. (November 20, 1957).

40. 445 S.W.2d 145; 35 A.L.P.3d 683 (1969).

41. 29 Conn. Supp. 368; 289 A.2d 386 (1972).

42. [1816]2 Mer. 99, 35 Eng. Rep. 875 (Ch).

43. [1846] Craig & Ph. 76, 41, Eng. Rep. 418.

44. Annot. 24 A. L. R. 3d 863 (1969).

45. 11 Paige Ch. 257 (N.Y. Ch. 1844).

affairs of an incompetent.[46] The right of a court of equity to act for an incompetent has been termed the "doctrine of substituted judgment" and has been recognized as covering all matters pertaining to the well-being of legally incapacitated persons. Substituted judgment requires the guardian of an incompetent person to examine the incompetent's life history to ascertain that person's previously held interests, attitudes and values and to act in accordance with the motives and considerations that would have moved the incompetent.[47]

In *Strunk,* the lower court, in permitting the transplanting of a kidney from a mentally incompetent brother, did not rely upon the doctrine of substituted judgment but found that the procedure "would not only be beneficial to Tommy but also beneficial to Jerry because Jerry was greatly dependent upon Tommy, emotionally and psychologically, and that his well-being would be jeopardized more severely by the loss of his brother than by the removal of a kidney."[48] Although in a 4 to 3 decision affirming that judgment the Kentucky appellate court, in its concluding statement, referred to the circuit court's finding that "the operative procedures in this instance are to the best interest of Jerry Strunk,"[49] that decision, unlike the decision of the circuit court, dwells primarily and at some length upon the doctrine of substituted judgment.

Writing for the minority, Judge Steinfeld candidly acknowledged that his "sympathies and emotions are torn between a compassion to aid an ailing young man and a duty to fully protect unfortunate members of society"[50] and that he was particularly conflicted by his "indelible recollection of a government which, to the everlasting shame of its citizens, embarked on a program of genocide and experimentation with human bodies."[51] Despite, or perhaps because of, that conflict, the minority

46. See 27 *American Jurisprudence* 2d 592, Equity §69.

47. See, for example, *City Bank* v. *McGowan,* 323 U.S. 594, 599 (1944).

48. *Id.* at 146.

49. *Id.* at 149.

50. *Id.*

51. *Id.* In response to similar concerns expressed by a guardian *ad litem,* Judge Day, in a minority opinion in *In re Guardianship of Pescinski,* 67 Wis.2d 4, 226 N.W. 2d 180 (1975), wrote: "I fail to see the analogy—this is not an experiment conducted by mad doctors but a well-known and accepted surgical procedure necessitated in this case to save the life of the incompetent's sister. Such a transplant would be authorized not by a group of doctors operating behind a barbed wire stockade but only after a full hearing in an American court of law." *Id.* at 183.

insisted upon applying a best interest standard and declared that no other standard was authorized by statute. In applying a best interest standard the minority found that a kidney donation by a person lacking legal capacity to consent cannot be authorized unless it is conclusively demonstrated that it would be of significant benefit to the incompetent donor. In the words of Judge Steinfeld: "The evidence here does not rise to that pinnacle. To hold that committees, guardians or courts have such awesome power even in the persuasive case before us, could establish legal precedent, the dire result of which we cannot fathom. Regretfully, I must say no."[52]

Hart v. *Brown* involved an action for a declaratory judgment permitting an isograft kidney transplant from a seven-year old girl to her identical twin. As was the case in the appellate court's decision in *Strunk,* the court relied heavily upon the doctrine of substituted judgment but simultaneously seemed to suggest that the transplant could be justified by application of a best interest standard as well. The court relied upon medical testimony, perhaps overly optimistic in nature, to the effect that "the only real risk" to the donor would arise in the case of trauma to the one remaining recovering kidney "but testimony indicated that such trauma is exceedingly rare in civilian life" as well as upon testimony indicating that life insurance actuaries do not rate persons with one kidney as presenting a higher risk of mortality then those with two kidneys.[53] Also cited are the earlier-noted Massachusetts decisions in which the court gave strong weight to the "grave emotional impact the death of the twin would have upon the survivor"[54] as well as psychiatric testimony that the procedure "could be of immense benefit to the donor" since it would be more beneficial for her to be reared in a happy family environment than in a family that was distressed and that the death of her twin would constitute "a very great loss" to the healthy child.[55]

In sharp contrast to the decisions handed down in *Strunk* and *Hart,* in *In re Richardson*[56] the Court of Appeals of Louisiana, Fourth Circuit, found that a decision of such nature could be made solely on the basis of a best interest standard. Louisiana statutes prohibit an incompetent minor from making any *inter vivos* donation of his property and unequivocally prohibit donation of a minor's property by his parent or guardian. The

52. *Id.* at 150.
53. 20 Conn. Supp. 368, 374, 289 A.2d 386, 389.
54. *Id.* at 390.
55. *Id.* at 374–375.
56. 284 So.2d 185 (La. Ct App.), certiorari denied, 284 So.2d 338 (La. 1973).

court found that since the law affords unqualified protection against intrusion into a mere property right "it is inconceivable that it affords less protection to a minor's right to be free in his person from bodily intrusion to the extent of the loss of an organ unless such loss be in the best interest of the minor."[57]

Wisconsin and New York do not have statutes as protective as those of Louisiana regarding the property interests of a minor. Nevertheless, in both states, courts have insisted upon applying a best interest standard. The Supreme Court of Wisconsin, in *In re Guardianship of Pescinski,*[58] refused to permit a sibling kidney donation by a chronic catatonic schizophrenic and explicitly refused to adopt the substituted judgment doctrine advanced by the Kentucky Court of Appeals. In New York, in *In the Matter of John Doe,* the court expressly declined to apply a substituted judgment doctrine and was affirmed in its position by the Appellate Division, Fourth Department.[59] That case involved, not a kidney transplant, but a bone marrow transplant from a 43-year old severely mentally retarded person to his 36-year old brother. The trial court permitted the procedure but only because it found that the evidence established to a "reasonable certainty" that participation in the procedure would be in the incompetent's best interest. The appellate court endorsed the trial court's application of a best interest standard and expressed hesitation only with regard to whether the best interest of the incompetent must be established to a degree of "reasonable certainty" or by a "clear and convincing" standard of evidence as the Court of Appeals of New York has held to be required in "exceptional civil matters."[60] Nevertheless, the appellate court found that even that high standard of proof was satisfied in the case under consideration.

In *Little* v. *Little,*[61] the Court of Appeals of Texas, Fourth District, chose to interpret the *Strunk* decision as predicated upon a best interest standard: "Although in *Strunk* the Kentucky court discussed the substituted judgment doctrine in some detail, the conclusion of the majority there was based on the benefits that the incompetent would derive, rather than on the theory that the incompetent would have consented to the transplant

57. *Id.* at 187.

58. 67 Wis.2d 4, 226 N.W.2d 180(1975).

59. 104 A.D.2d 200, 481 N.Y.S.2d 932 (1984).

60. *Id.*

61. 5765 S.W.2d 493 (1979).

if he were competent."[62] The *Little* court attempted to weigh the benefits and dangers of the procedure as they affected the donor. The court found the danger posed by the surgical procedure to be minimal, future risks small and danger of psychological harm absent. The *Little* court also accepted the conclusions of studies showing that persons who had donated kidneys experienced positive benefits in the form of heightened self-esteem, enhanced status in the family, renewed meaning in life including transcendental experiences flowing from their gift of life to another[63] and found that, unlike the situation in *Richardson,* Anne Little, although adjudged to be mentally incompetent, was yet "capable of experiencing such an increase in personal welfare from donating her kidney."[64]

Nor has the issue of pediatric organ donations been overlooked by Israeli courts. In fact, Israel is one of the few jurisdictions in which the matter has been addressed by the jurisdiction's highest judicial body. The case, *Legal Advisor to the Government* v. *Anonymous,*[65] involved the question of a possible kidney donation by a 39-year old mentally retarded son on behalf of his 65-year old father. Israeli law is even more explicit than the Louisiana statute in providing that a guardian acting on behalf of his ward in real estate conveyances and in certain other matters may act only on the basis of the interests of his ward. Moreover, Israel's Capacity and Guardian Law was amended in 1983 to include §68(a) which provides that a court may authorize surgical or other procedures only if it is convinced by medical opinions that "the specified measures are necessary for preservation of the physical or psychological well-being" of the minor or incompetent individual.[66]

Despite the statutory enactment of a best interest standard the Be'er Sheva court found grounds for granting permission for the renal transplant.

62. *Id.* at 498.

63. *Id.* at 499.

64. *Id.*

65. (1988) 42(ii) *Piskei Din* 661.

66. This amendment was enacted following a decision of the Jerusalem District Court in 1982 in which, on the facts of the case, the court found that a donation of bone marrow to a sibling would be in the best interest of the minor. The case involved bone marrow donation by an eight-year old girl on behalf of her twin sister. The court found that the knowledge that she might have saved the life of her sister but did not do so would likely result in grave psychological harm to the child. The amendment was designed to render application of a best interest standard mandatory by virtue of statutory authority. See (1988) 42(ii) *Piskei Din* 661 at 686.

The district court was convinced (1) that the father's condition would deteriorate if he failed to receive a transplant; (2) that no other source for a renal transplant was available; and (3) that death or deterioration of the health of the father would result in institutionalization of the son. The son had been institutionalized during earlier periods and became able to function within the family unit and, to some measure, as a member of society only because of the dedicated and sacrificial efforts of the father. The child's mother, a Holocaust survivor, was unable to relate to her son in a positive and beneficial manner. Indeed, concern for the welfare of the child was a significant factor in the father's desire for the transplant. The district court reasoned that the phrase "physical or psychological well-being" appearing in the statute should be broadly construed as encompassing indirect benefit accruing to the child as a result of the procedure, *viz.,* that the incompetent child would not be subjected to institutionalization.

An appeal from the decisions of the Be'er Sheva court was taken by the government's legal advisor and was heard by a five member panel of the Israeli Supreme Court. In a wide-ranging decision the Deputy President of the Supreme Court, Justice Menahem Elon, undertook a broad survey of discussions of this issue in rabbinic literature as well as of the decisions of American courts in relevant cases. Although essentially extraneous to the issue before the Israeli Supreme Court, the decision includes a critique of the doctrine of substituted judgment adopted by some American courts.

The Supreme Court reversed the decision of the district court on the grounds that the benefit to the son was not clear-cut. The court was not convinced that the father could not continue to be treated by dialysis; it was somewhat skeptical of the likelihood of successful transplantation in a patient of the father's relatively advanced age;[67] it took note of the fact that, even if the transplant were to be successful, longevity enhancement would probably be marginal; it was unconvinced that the child's sisters would prove to be incapable of caring for him outside of an institutional setting; and suggested that one of the child's sisters might have become a willing and suitable donor if permission to approve transplantation of the

67. Medically, age is no longer considered a significant factor in determining suitability for renal transplants. As stated in one prominent source, "Chronological age and severe systemic disease such as diabetes have decreased in importance as factors determining eligibility for transplants and patients in their seventh and eighth decades may now reasonably be considered physiologically stable." See P. Keown and C. Stiller, "Kidney Transplantation," *Surgical Clinics of North America,* vol. LXVI, no. 3 (June, 1976), p. 519.

incompetent's kidney were to be denied. Unquestionably, the question posed to the Israeli Supreme Court is one that is most difficult to decide and hinges essentially upon an *ad hoc* evaluation of complex factors regarding which there is a lack of certainty even among experts.[68]

Later, in *Bosze,* the Illinois court found that the doctrine of substituted judgment is valid in making a decision on behalf of a formerly competent person but not on behalf of a life-long incompetent or on behalf of a young child. In the former case, the guardian "may look to the person's life history, in all its diverse complexity, to ascertain the intentions and attitudes which the incompetent person once held."[69] However, in the case of three-year old twins, the Court reasoned that they had not yet had the opportunity to develop intent of any kind. By the same token, the guardian has no evidence on the basis of "philosophical, religious and moral views, life goals, values about the purpose of life and the way it should be lived, and attitudes toward sickness, medical procedures, suffering and death"[70] by which to be guided.

Accordingly, reasoned the Court, a determination can be made only on the basis of a best interest standard. Since there is no physical benefit to the donor, the benefit that must be considered is entirely psychological. The Court found the psychological benefit of altruism too abstract to be

68. Nevertheless, to this writer, the Israeli Supreme Court's emphasis upon potential availability of one of the sisters as a donor seems inappropriate. At the time that the matter was before the court, the siblings had declined to serve as donors and there was no concrete reason for failure to accept that refusal at face value, particularly since each sister advanced a cogent reason for her demurral. Moreover, given the fact that the incompetent stood to derive the most tangible benefit from prolongation of the father's life, his interest in the success of the procedure was paramount and should have served to trigger application of a best interest standard.

The Israeli Supreme Court also cited testimony indicating that, in the event of injury to the remaining kidney, the mentally retarded son would be unlikely to be cooperative in ongoing dialysis procedures. In point of fact, the likelihood of trauma to the remaining kidney is negligible. See *supra,* note 53 and accompanying text. The court also cited provisions of Israeli regulations governing workmen's compensation that classify loss of a kidney as resulting in a 30 percent disability. The spectre of such disability is entirely illusory. Medical testimony in *Hart* v. *Brown* established that, assuming an uneventful recovery, the donor would thereafter be restricted only from violent contact sports and would otherwise be able to engage in all normal life activities. See 29 Conn. Supp. 368, 374; 289 A.2d 386, 309.

69. 141 Ill.2d 473 at 484.

70. *Id.* at 485.

considered in and of itself and that in each of the cases in which earlier courts approved a kidney donation there was an existing, close relationship between the donor and recipient. In such cases the psychological benefit "is grounded firmly in the fact that the donor and recipient are known to each other as family. . . . it is the existing sibling relationship, as well as the potential for a continuing sibling relationship, which forms the context in which it may be determined that it will be in the best interests of the child to undergo a bone marrow harvesting procedure for a sibling."[71] The court also found that lack of support on the part of the twins' mother, the only caretaker they had ever known, would impact adversely upon the psychological trauma associated with hospitalization and surgery. The court found that, under the circumstances, the bone marrow donation would not be in the best interests of the children.

IV. *Pediatric Donations in Jewish Law*

A. *Best Interest Standard*

It may readily be demonstrated that Jewish law recognizes a best interest standard. On the basis of talmudic discussions recorded in *Gittin* 52b and *Baba Batra* 8a, Rambam, *Hilkhot Naḥalot* 10:4 and 10:8, rules that guardians are to be appointed for mentally incompetent persons to provide for their needs. As reflected in a narrative recorded in *Baba Batra* 8a, Rambam, *Hilkhot Mattnot Aniyim* 7:16, and *Shulḥan Arukh, Ḥoshen Mishpat* 290:15, rule that, if their assets are sufficient for such purposes, the guardian is authorized to distribute charity on behalf of orphaned minors so that they may acquire "a good name."[72] Rabbi Moshe Hershler, *Halakhah u-Refu'ah,* II, (Jerusalem, 5740), 126, applies the standard reflected in that ruling in analyzing the propriety of a sibling renal transplant. In applying what is, in effect, a best interest standard he concludes that the mentally incompetent donor would derive no benefit from the procedure and, in light of potential danger to the donor, the procedure might result in actual harm to him. In the case of a mentally incompetent person who enjoys no significant relationship with the prospective recipient, that conclusion is entirely cogent. However, considerations presented in *Hart* and *Little* might lead to a different conclusion with regard to a donation by a minor who may derive psychological and developmental benefit from restoring

71. *Id.* at 524.

72. Cf., Rambam, *Hilkhot Naḥalot* 10:11 and *Kesef Mishneh, ad locum.*

a sibling to good health and upon whom the death of a sibling whose demise he might have prevented would have a negative effect.[73] In situations in which the donor is physically or psychologically dependent upon the recipient, the argument is even more compelling. As the court reasoned in *Strunk* and considered but rejected in *Richardson* on the basis of the particular facts in that case[74]—and as found to be the case by the Be'er Sheva district court—a kidney donation on behalf of a close relative who contributes to the care and well-being of the incompetent, might well be deemed to further the best interests of the donor.

B. *Substituted Judgment*

The question of whether or not Jewish law posits a doctrine of substituted judgment is much more complex. *Tosafot, Baba Meẓi'a* 22a, and other early authorities rule that a person may not eat food belonging to another without the latter's consent even if it is certain that such consent, if solicited, would be freely forthcoming. *Tosafot* bases this conclusion upon the normative rule regarding lost property which provides that a finder cannot acquire title to lost property unless the owner is aware of his loss. The underlying principle is that "constructive despair" (*ye'ush she-lo mi-da'at*) does not qualify as "despair." *Keẓot ha-Ḥoshen* 358:1 takes issue with that position on the basis of the statement of the Gemara, *Ketubot* 48a, declaring that the children of a person who becomes mentally incompetent may be supported by his estate even if the children have reached an age at which the father is no longer halakhically liable for their support. Such use of the incompetent's financial resources is justified on the assumption that "presumably" the father would consent to such use were he capable of doing so.

Both Rabbi Hershler, *Halakhah u-Refu'ah,* II, 127, and Rabbi Moshe Meiselman, *Halakhah u-Refu'ah,* II, 121, raise the possibility that a sibling donation might be warranted according to the position of *Keẓot ha-Ḥoshen*. In effect, they argue that *Keẓot ha-Ḥoshen* accepts a doctrine of substituted judgment.[75] However, the "substituted judgment" applied by the Gemara

73. See *supra,* notes 54 and 55 and accompanying text.

74. 284 So.2d 185, 187.

75. Rabbi Meiselman argues that even *Tosafot* would concede that "substituted judgment" is warranted in situations in which, given the opportunity, all persons would make such a determination. The principle of *ye'ush she-lo me-da'at,* he argues, applies only to individual decisions that may vary from person to person and require the particular state of mind of a given individual; decisions that are nearly universal, he argues, reflect a "general will" and do not require a particular

in sanctioning expenditure of an incompetent's resources for the support of his children is not based upon an analysis of previously expressed interests, values or desires of the incompetent as is the case with regard to the substituted judgment doctrine of the common law; rather it is a judgment reflecting an assessment of the presumed desire of mankind in general. Since, from a halakhic vantage point, the judgment to be applied is that of mankind in general rather than a judgment imputed to a specific individual, that judgment can be imputed to a minor as well as to an incompetent without incurring the objection voiced in the *Bosze* decision. However, such judgment would not be imputed in situations in which there is reason to assume that the individual in question would have exercised his personal judgment in a different manner. Nevertheless, both Rabbi Hershler and Rabbi Meiselman concede that application of this principle is difficult since, particularly because of the risks posed to the donor, it is not clear that the donor, if competent, would consent to the procedure.[76]

---

state of mind.

76. R. Shlomoh Zalman Auerbach is cited in *Nishmat Avraham,* IV, *Ḥoshen Mishpat* 243:1, as permitting pediatric bone marrow transplants with the consent of the minor provided that the child has reached a stage of maturity at which his consent is meaningful. Rabbi Auerbach is quoted as stating that the propriety of a bone marrow donation at a younger age requires further deliberation. It is apparent from the accompanying discussion that the factor serving as Rabbi Auerbach's consideration in favor of sanctioning such procedures is that the child acquires "merit" (*zekhut*) by virtue of the "great *miẓvah*" fulfilled by means of the procedure and hence donation of bone marrow constitutes a benefit for the child and may be sanctioned on the basis of *zakhin le-adam she-lo be-fanav,* i.e., a form of constructive agency. The consideration militating against sanctioning such procedures is that, although benefits may be acquired for a person without explicit consent, nevertheless, according to numerous authorities, property may not be taken from a person even for his benefit without explicit consent. In this situation, the pain caused the child is comparable to the taking of property.

A number of aspects of Rabbi Auerbach's position are unclear: 1) Since Halakhah does not recognize minors as being endowed with capacity to contract or to perform any act requiring rational determination, the distinction between minors of differing ages is unclear. 2) Discussions of *zakhin me-adam* found in latter-day sources deal with situations in which, in actuality, the "loss" constitutes an unmitigated benefit, e.g., disposal of *hameẓ* on *erev Pesaḥ* which otherwise becomes *asur be-hana'ah* or situations in which it may be assumed that the benefit far outweighs the loss so that all rational persons, if apprised of the facts of the situation, would readily grant consent. Since many people decline to donate bone marrow, it is difficult to see how the principle of *zakhin me-adam* can be applied. 3) Were the situation to be regarded as one of clear-cut benefit to

As has been argued earlier, unlike kidney donations,[77] donations of blood and bone marrow pose no halakhically cognizable danger. Nevertheless, at first glance it would appear that even such donations may be sanctioned only upon application of a best interest standard or on the basis of a doctrine of substituted judgment with the result that such donations could be considered only in situations in which the recipient is a close relative. Further examination, however, yields a different conclusion.

On the basis of the earlier formulated line of reasoning, an adult can be compelled to cooperate in the donations of replenishable tissue because he is bound by the commandment "nor shall you stand idly by the blood of your fellow" (Leviticus 19:16). Not so a minor. Minors differ from adults in that they are not bound by any of the biblical commandments. The Gemara, *Arakhin* 22a, reports that

> R. Nachman declared, "Originally, I did not seize the property of [minor] orphans [in order to satisfy their fathers' debts]; now that I have heard that [which was declared by] our colleague R. Huna in the name of Rav, *viz.,* 'Orphans who consume that which is not theirs, let them follow their deceased,' from now on I will seize [their property]." Why did he not [seize their property] originally? Said R. Papa: "Payment of a creditor is a *mizvah* and [minor] orphans are not obligated to perform *mizvot.*"[78]

the child, the controversy concerning *zakhin me-adam* would appear to be irrelevant since the authority of a guardian to act on behalf of his ward is not a subject of dispute.

77. See *infra,* note 109.

78. That principle, of course, remains unaffected by Rav's dictum, "Orphans who consume that which is not theirs let them follow their deceased." R. Nachman's change of heart upon hearing Rav's pronouncement must, I believe, be understood as reflective of the principle that a guardian may expend resources belonging to a minor for the minor's own welfare. Although, in consuming assets claimed by a creditor, the orphan minors do not commit an actionable offense, those actions are unethical and, in the purely ethical sense, the orphans deserve to join their deceased progenitor. Moreover, unethical acts to which children become habituated while they are minors are likely to be repeated subsequent to reaching legal majority as well. Hence, the removal of the ethical taint of unlawful enjoyment of property claimed by others becomes a matter of moral and spiritual benefit to the minors themselves. Accordingly, R. Nachman justified seizure of their property on the grounds that, in doing so, he did not seek to compel the performance of a *mizvah,* but to purge the orphans of unethical traits. In effect, R. Nachman justified seizure of their property by applying a best interest standard.

The Gemara clearly establishes that the property of a minor cannot be seized to satisfy a debt if the sole justification for such seizure is performance on the obligation of repaying a creditor. It should then follow, *mutatis mutandis,* that body tissues of a minor cannot be "seized" in order to satisfy the duty of "nor shall you stand idly by the blood of your fellow." Minors are exempt from that obligation just as they are exempt from all other obligations. Quite apart from any pecuniary value that may attach to blood or to bone marrow, the biblical provision against battery establishes a right to bodily integrity.[79] Arguably, since in the case of a minor, that right is not limited by virtue of an obligation to suffer a "wound" in order to save the life of another, it would follow that the minor cannot be compelled to make such a donation.[80] Indeed, it might be argued that pediatric organ or tissue donations cannot be sanctioned even with the consent of the child. Since the Gemara, *Pesaḥim* 50b, declares that minors lack capacity for "forgiveness" (*lav bnei meḥilah ninahu*) their consent is of no halakhic import.'[81]

The two situations are, however, different in one salient aspect. Only a debtor, or his heirs, is obligated to repay a debt; an uninvolved third party has no obligation whatsoever to satisfy the debt and, if he should do so, he fulfills no *mizvah* thereby. Since the minor is under no obligation to repay a debt until he reaches the age of halakhic capacity, the *Bet Din*

79. The prohibition against "wounding" (*ḥavalah*) is derived from the verse "Forty stripes he shall give him, he shall not exceed" (Deuteronomy 25:3) or from the immediately following phrase "lest he exceed" or from both phrases. See conflicting authorities cited in *Encyclopedia Talmudit,* XII (Jerusalem, 5727), 679–680. Although, in context, the verse speaks of a transgressor who has incurred the penalty of forty lashes, the prohibition applies to any illicit battery. As formulated by Rambam, *Sefer ha-Mizvot, lo ta'aseh,* no. 300 and *idem, Hilkhot Sanhedrin* 16:12, "If with regard to one whom Scripture permits to be smitten, the Torah forbids smiting more than warranted by his transgression, *a fortiori,* [this is forbidden] with regard to all other people."

80. Cf., However, R. Isaac Schorr, *Teshuvot Koaḥ Shor,* no. 20, who asserts that "wounding" a minor entails no infraction of the biblical prohibition. He reasons that, since only an individual who has reached the age of halakhic majority can be punished by forty stripes, the entire verse, including the prohibition of imposing further lashes, applies only to an adult, but not to a minor. That view is not supported by any other halakhic source.

81. See R. Yitzchak Zilberstein, *Halakhah u-Refu'ah,* IV, 156–157. Rabbi Zilberstein's citation of the ruling of *Shulḥan Arukh, Ḥoshen Mishpat* 96:4, regarding a minor's lack of capacity to alienate property is a bit imprecise since the issue is not title to property but consent to an act that would otherwise constitute a tort.

has no grounds to intervene by seizing the property unless it can be established that repayment of the debt redounds to the benefit of the minor himself.

Rare blood or bone marrow needed for life-saving transplantation presents a somewhat different halakhic issue. Although the minor is exempt from a duty of rescue, other parties, including the members of the *Bet Din* themselves, are fully bound to preserve endangered lives. Consequently, their "seizure" of such tissue would be in the nature of fulfillment of their own obligation rather than by way of compelling performance of a duty on the part of a minor. Surely, given a situation in which a unique item belonging to a minor is required in order to rescue a life, it would be permissible to appropriate the item in question, even though the minor is under no obligation to volunteer his possessions for such a purpose. Thus, for example, in a situation in which an artery has been severed and the accident victim is in danger of bleeding to death and, assuming that the only object available for use as a tourniquet is a necktie belonging to a minor, there is no doubt that the necktie may be taken from the minor and used for this purpose. This is so, not because the minor is obligated to provide the necktie, but because the person rendering first aid is not only permitted, but required, to pursue any and all means in order to prevent loss of life even if those measures entail what is, in actuality, an act of theft.

There is, however, a significant difference between appropriating property of another for the sake of saving a life and committing an act of battery upon another person for the same purpose. *Shulḥan Arukh, Ḥoshen Mishpat* 359:4, rules that in order to preserve one's own life it is permitted to seize property belonging to another with intent to compensate the lawful owner. As noted by R. Jacob Ettlinger, *Teshuvot Binyan Ẓion,* no. 170, theft without intent to make restitution even for the purpose of preservation of life is prohibited.

As *Binyan Ẓion* remarks in an entirely different but parallel context, invasion of a person's body or an act of battery is significantly different from theft of property. Since property is essentially fungible, financial restitution serves to redress the wrong that has been committed. However, compensation for pain and suffering sustained in conjunction with bodily assault does not really render the person whole; financial compensation is not a remedy in the sense of restoring the *status quo ante.* Financial compensation is indeed required as the only available redress but it fails fully to eradicate the harm. As *Binyan Ẓion* argues, although the Torah suspends religious obligations for purposes of saving a life it does not sanction irreversible harm to another for that purpose.[82]

C. *Privileged Battery*

There is, however, one rabbinic source that clearly sanctions the "wounding" of a minor for the therapeutic benefit of another. Although Jewish law certainly prohibits feticide, there is considerable controversy with regard to the precise nature of the prohibition. Rambam, *Hilkhot Rozeaḥ* 9:1, regards feticide, when performed by a Jew, as constituting a form of non-capital homicide. Other authorities regard abortion of the fetus as constituting a less serious offense.[83] Among those authorities who regard feticide to be subsumed under a prohibition other than homicide is the seventeenth-century authority R. Joseph di Trani. In his responsa collection, *Teshuvot Maharit,* I, no. 97, that authority asserts that performance of an abortion is forbidden because it constitutes an illicit form of "wounding," i.e., although the Torah does not prohibit the killing of the fetus, it does prohibit wounding the fetus. Hence, abortion of a fetus is forbidden because the destruction of a fetus entails its "wounding."[84] In another responsum, *Teshuvot Maharit,* I, no. 99, the same authority rules that, since destruction of a fetus in no way poses a problem of homicide, "therefore, with regard to Jewess[es], for the sake of the mother, it appears that it is permissible to treat them so that they will abort since [the abortion] is therapeutic for the mother."

Maharit rules that therapeutic abortion is permissible. Since he does

82. *Binyan Ẓion*'s comments are advanced in conjunction with development of his position prohibiting post-mortem dissection of a corpse even for the purpose of preserving the life of another patient suffering from the same malady. *Binyan Ẓion* argues that desecration of a corpse constitutes a harm that cannot be remedied. *Binyan Ẓion* further argues that appropriation of the property of another for the purpose of preserving life is sanctioned only because the owner of the property seized for that purpose is himself subject to an obligation of rescue but that the dead are free from all obligations. The latter argument would logically apply to minors as well since, as stated by the Gemara, *Arakhin* 22a, "minors are not obligated to perform *mizvot.*"

83. For a survey of these various opinions and the ramifications that flow therefrom see *Contemporary Halakhic Problems,* I, 325–371.

84. See R. Yechi'el Ya'akov Weinberg, *Seridei Esh,* III, no. 127, sec. 22. Cf., however, R. Aryeh Lifschutz, *Aryeh de-Bei Ila'i, Yoreh De'ah,* no. 14, p. 58a, who maintains that the "wounding" to which Maharit refers is the wounding of the mother, i.e., the removal of the developing fetus necessarily entails an assault upon the body of the mother.

not incorporate a qualifying statement to the contrary in his ruling, it must be inferred that he sanctions therapeutic abortion designed not only to preserve maternal life, but also to preserve maternal health.[85] Indeed a therapeutic procedure involving incision of tissue or loss of blood constitutes a permissible form of "wounding."[86] In ruling in this manner, Maharit is far more permissive than, for example, Rambam who, in *Hilkhot Roẓeaḥ* 1:9, permits abortion only when the mother's life is endangered and, even then, only in circumstances in which the fetus is the author of the danger. That stringent position follows necessarily from the view that feticide constitutes a form of homicide; hence the elimination of a fetus can be sanctioned only in circumstances in which the taking of life can be sanctioned, i.e., in instances in which the fetus is a *rodef* or "pursuer." Maharit's permissive view is similarly entailed by his position regarding the transgression incurred in performance of an abortion. "Wounding" for purposes of achieving a cure does not constitute a transgression of the prohibition; hence, therapeutic surgical procedures are entirely permissible. Since abortion is prohibited solely as a form of illicit wounding, it follows that an abortion may be performed in any situation in which "wounding" is permitted. Hence, Maharit rules that therapeutic abortion is entirely permissible.

This responsum of Maharit is quite remarkable not only for his unique characterization of abortion but for another reason as well. Although there is no dispute regarding the exclusion of therapeutic "wounding" from the prohibition "Forty stripes he shall give him, he shall not exceed"

85. See, however, R. David Dov Meisels, *Teshuvot Binyan David,* no. 60, who asserts that Maharit's permissive ruling applies only to situations in which there is actual danger to the life of the mother. All other rabbinic writers understand Maharit's ruling as encompassing situations in which only maternal health is in danger.

86. R. Moses Feinstein, *Iggerot Mosheh, Ḥoshen Mishpat,* II, no. 69, sec. 3, dismisses the statement recorded in *Teshuvot Maharit* as a "forged responsum" authored by an "errant student" and improperly attributed to Maharit. In light of the fact that this responsum is cited and accepted by Maharit's disciple R. Chaim Benveniste, *Sheyarei Knesset ha-Gedolah, Yoreh De'ah* 154, *Hagahot ha-Tur,* sec. 6, *Iggerot Mosheh*'s assessment is highly improbable. The discrepancies between responsa no. 97 and no. 99 have been addressed by *Aryeh de-Bei Ila'i, Yoreh De'ah,* no. 19; R. Ovadiah Yosef, *Yabi'a Omer,* IV, *Even ha-Ezer,* no. 1, sec. 7; and R. Eliezer Waldenberg, *Ẓiẓ Eli'ezer,* IX, no. 51, chap. 3. Acceptance of Maharit's authorship of this responsum does not detract from the cogency of *Iggerot Mosheh*'s halakhic conclusions regarding the nature of the prohibition concerning feticide.

(Deuteronomy 25:3), classical sources describing permissible therapeutic "wounding" invariably describe "wounding" in the form of an incision or excision designed to be of therapeutic benefit to the patient himself. There is no reference in these sources to the "wounding" of one person for the therapeutic benefit of another. Yet that is precisely what Maharit permits. He rules that "wounding" the fetus in the course of its removal from the uterus is permitted in order to preserve maternal health, i.e., the wounding of the fetus is permitted for the therapeutic benefit of another, namely, the mother.[87] Maharit's position is even more problematic in light of the fact that the fetus is a "minor." In positing an extension of the prohibition against "wounding" to encompass the fetus, Maharit establishes a fetus' right to bodily integrity. Since the fetus certainly has no obligation to preserve the life of another, much less so to preserve the health of another, it is remarkable that Maharit finds that it is permissible to "wound" the fetus in order to avoid a threat to maternal health.[88] It is certainly noteworthy that, although Maharit's thesis concerning the nature of the prohibition entailed in performing an abortion was the subject of considerable controversy, there has been no challenge in rabbinic literature to

87. The statement of R. Dimi bar Hinena, *Sanhedrin* 83b, "'And he who kills a beast, he shall restore it; and he who kills a man, he shall be put to death' (Leviticus 24:21): just as one who strikes an animal to heal it is not liable for damage so if one wounds a man to heal him he is not liable," does not necessarily establish authority to "wound" a person for the benefit of a third party. Cf., R. Moshe Meiselman, *Halakhah u-Refu'ah,* II, 114. Nor does Rambam's statement, *Hilkhot Ḥovel u-Mazik* 5:1, limiting the prohibition to wounding "in the manner of strife" necessarily exclude wounding for the therapeutic benefit of a third party. Moreover, Rambam's comments may serve to circumvent only the prohibition against "smiting" but not the prohibition against "wounding," i.e., causing blood to flow. See R. Moshe Meiselman, *ibid.,* p. 115, but cf., *Iggerot Mosheh, Ḥoshen Mishpat,* II, no. 66.

88. In *Teshuvot Maharit,* no. 99, Maharit makes no attempt to predicate his ruling sanctioning abortion for preservation of maternal health upon the premise "a fetus is a thigh of its mother" (*ubar yerekh imo*). In the first lines of *Teshuvot Maharit,* no. 97, Maharit states that feticide constitutes a transgression of the prohibition against "wounding" and only later in his discussion does he employ the principle "a fetus is a thigh of its mother." See also R. Yechi'el Ya'akov Weinberg, *Seridei Esh,* III, no. 127, who cites the statement of *Tosafot, Sanhedrin* 80b, in which *Tosafot* declares that a fetus preserves "independent animation" and hence the principle "a fetus is a thigh of its mother" does not render the fetus a *treifah* simply because its mother is a *treifah.* Similarly, argues *Seridei Esh,* since the fetus possesses "independent animation" its destruction in order to save the mother is not comparable to the removal of a limb in order to save the body.

the conclusion he draws from that thesis, i.e., that the "wounding" of the fetus is permissible for the purpose of preservation of maternal life or health. Indeed, it must be inferred that the authorities who challenge Maharit's ruling on other grounds would acquiesce in the position that an assault upon the fetus that does not lead to fetal mortality may be sanctioned for the purpose of preserving maternal health. The rationale underlying that conclusion requires explication.

In enumerating situations of involuntary manslaughter in which the individual responsible for shedding innocent blood is not exiled to one of the designated cities of refuge, the Mishnah, *Makkot* 8a, cites the verse "and who comes with his fellow in the forest" (Deuteronomy 19:5) that occurs in the context of the Bible's description of an act of manslaughter necessitating exile. The Mishnah regards the reference to the forest as paradigmatic of the type of misadventure entailing such punishment. The Sages understand the term "forest" as restricting the penalty to manslaughter occurring at a particular site and declare that exile is warranted only if the accident occurs in a place comparable to a forest, i.e., a locale in which aggressor and victim equally enjoy a right of entry. Accordingly, they rule that no exile attends upon manslaughter that occurs pursuant to trespass by the victim upon the domain of the person responsible for his death. Abba Sha'ul, however, understands the verse as establishing a paradigm for the nature of the act itself rather than for the locale in which it is committed. Accordingly, Abba Sha'ul declares that exile is merited only if manslaughter results from an act that is entirely discretionary—as is the chopping of wood. Excluded from that penalty, declares Abba Sha'ul, is a father who strikes his son, a teacher who smites his pupil and a person deputized by the *Bet Din* to administer corporal punishment who in carrying out those acts inadvertently causes the death of the person he intends only to beat. Those acts are privileged since each of the enumerated persons acts with authority in administering punishment or chastisement and in order to achieve an end which those persons are charged with achieving. Such acts do not merely lie outside the ambit of prohibited "wounding," but are affirmatively required. Thus the actions of those individuals are not a matter of "discretion" (*reshut*) but constitute the discharge of a duty. Accordingly, bona fide misadventure in discharging those duties entails no penalty. Although the Sages disagree with Abba Sha'ul with regard to the implication of such categorization in establishing an exclusion to the punishment of exile, there is no dispute regarding the underlying premise, *viz.,* that those acts are privileged batteries.

The Tosefta amplifies the principle recorded in the Mishnah with the statement: "An agent of the *Bet Din* who smites with the authority of the *Bet Din* must go into exile; a physician who cures with the authority of the *Bet Din* must go into exile. . . ." The Tosefta is best understood as reflective of the position of the Sages who disagree with Abba Sha'ul.[89] Yet, although the Sages declare that exile most be imposed, the very fact that individuals committing such acts are singled out for the purpose of establishing their liability in instances of misadventure reflects the fact that the Sages are in full agreement that those actions are privileged at least insofar as the prohibition against battery is concerned.

The Tosefta's inclusion of a physician in the same category as an agent of the *Bet Din* indicates that the surgical procedure performed by the physician is a privileged form of wounding lying beyond the ambit of the prohibition against "wounding." Placing the physician's act outside the ambit of the prohibition *ipso facto* establishes both a privilege and an obligation with regard to therapeutic wounding. The wound caused by a physician's incision is not sanctioned by virtue of a principle that transcends the prohibition and warrants its suspension but is permitted because such acts were not prohibited in the first instance.

The exclusion of therapeutic wounding from the commandment that serves to establish a prohibition against battery must be understood in the context of the right to bodily integrity as recognized in Jewish law. Common law regards protection of the human body from nonconsensual intrusion to be a fundamental right. That right has been recognized consistently since 1891 when, in *Union Pacific Railway Co.* v. *Botsford,*[90] the Court declared, "No right is held more sacred, or is more carefully guarded by the common law, than the right of every individual to the possession and control of his own person, free from all restraint or interference by others, unless by clear and unquestionable authority of law."[91] In early American case law freedom from bodily invasion was regarded as a "liberty" accorded constitutional protection by the 14th Amendment.[92] Since the 1965 U.S. Supreme Court decision in *Griswold* v. *Connecticut,*[93]

89. Cf., however, *Teshuvot Besamim Rosh,* no. 386; *Birkei Yosef, Yoreh De'ah* 336:6; and *Or Sameaḥ, Hilkhot Roẓeaḥ* 5:6.

90. 141 U.S. 250 (1891).

91. *Id.* at 251. See also *Winston* v. *Lee,* 470 U.S. 573 (1985); *Schneider* v. *California,* 304 U.S. 757(1966); *Paige* v. *Massachusetts,* 321 U.S. 158(1944).

92. See, for example, *Meyer* v. *Nebraska,* 262 U.S. 390, 399(1923).

93. 381 U.S. 479 (1965).

in which the court declared that the Bill of Rights serves to establish a broad constitutionally protected right of privacy, American courts have applied that doctrine in prohibiting bodily invasions as a violation of a person's right to privacy. In *Griswold* v. *Connecticut,* Justice William Douglas, the author of the decision, wrote that the specific guarantees of the Bill of Rights "have penumbra formed by emanations from those guarantees that give them life and substance."[94] Taken collectively, those penumbra establish a "zone of privacy."[95]

Judaism does not posit a sweeping right of privacy, nor does its jurisprudence incorporate the equivalent of a constitutional protection of liberty.[96] Indeed, Judaism places far greater emphasis upon duties than upon rights.[97] Nevertheless, prohibitions against certain forms of conduct serve to generate collateral rights for those who would otherwise be victims of such conduct. Thus, for example, a prohibition against theft has the effect of creating a right to undisturbed enjoyment of lawfully owned property. Similarly, the obligation to render medical assistance generates a corresponding right to health while the obligation of a father to teach his son Torah guarantees the child's right to an education. The biblical prohibition against "wounding" entails as a corollary a biblically recognized right to bodily integrity. However, since this right is born of a prohibition restraining the conduct of others, it follows that when no such prohibition obtains there is no concomitant right to bodily integrity. Clearly, no such right may be invoked by a chastised son or pupil or by the transgressor sentenced to forty stripes. Inclusion of a patient in the selfsame category implies that the physician's act is similarly privileged and that the patient enjoys no right to be free from such an assault. Therapeutic wounding is excluded, not because of benefit caused to the patient, but because of the privileged nature of the act.[98] If so, there is no compelling reason to assume that the

94. *Id.* at 484.

95. *Id.*

96. See "AIDS: A Jewish Perspective," pp. 58–59.

97. See Moshe Silberg, "Law and Morals in Jewish Jurisprudence," *Harvard Law Review,* vol. LXXV, no. 2 (December, 1961), pp. 306–331. See also Robert M. Cover, "Obligation: A Jewish Jurisprudence of the Social Order," *Journal of Law and Religion,* vol. V, no. 1 (1987), pp. 65–74.

98. There is no reason to assume that therapeutic wounding is sanctioned only when it results in benefit to the person sustaining the "wound" on the grounds that there is actual or constructive consent for such wounding, whereas no such assumption can be made with regard to consent when the benefit is received by another party, since many authorities assert that the prohibition applies equally

exclusion is limited to therapeutic benefit of the person wounded. Maharit assumes that therapeutic wounding is excluded from the prohibition even when the therapeutic benefit accrues to a third party. Hence a person does not enjoy a right of privacy or a right to bodily integrity when the "wounding" incurred is therapeutic in nature, even if it is therapeutic to some other person.

If so, Maharit's position is readily understandable. A battery may be committed against a minor—or even against a fetus—not only for the benefit of the minor but also for the benefit of a third party. Justification is found, not in the fact that the minor is duty-bound to aid in restoration of the health of his fellow, but in the fact that, in face of the therapeutic need of another, no "liberty" or right of privacy is recognized.

The matter, then, is entirely analogous to a situation in which it is necessary to seize the property of a minor for the rescue of another. The minor is under no obligation of rescue. But neither does he enjoy an untrammelled right to unimpeded enjoyment of the property under such circumstances. The sole distinction is that, in the latter case, the right to enjoyment of property is subordinate to the rescuer's obligation to preserve life, whereas with regard to "wounding" the right is extinguished *ab initio* in face of any threat to the health of another.

The minimal danger to which the child is exposed by being placed under general anesthesia during removal of his bone marrow does not serve to militate against the permissibility of the procedure. The Gemara, *Yevamot* 72a, reports that blood-letting carries with it an element of increased danger when performed on a cloudy day or on a day when the south wind blows. Accordingly, R. Papa prohibited both blood-letting and circumcision on such days. Nevertheless, the Gemara, invoking the principle "The Lord preserves the simple" (Psalms 116:6), concludes that since people, in general, customarily disregard this particular danger those procedures are entirely permissible. The underlying principle, invoked by the Gemara in a number of different contexts, is that although a person may not ordinarily expose himself to danger, he may engage in activities generally regarded as innocuous even though, in actuality, they do pose a danger. In such circumstances, a person may act in the manner

to "wounding" with permission of the victim. See *Teshuvot Ḥavot Ya'ir,* no. 163; *Shulḥan Arukh ha-Rav,* V, *Hilkhot Nizkei Guf ve-Nefesh,* sec. 4; commentary of R. Yitzchak Perla on *Sefer ha-Miẓvot* of R. Sa'adya Ga'on, *miẓvot lo-ta'aseh,* nos. 47–48; and *Ḥazon Ish, Ḥoshen Mishpat* 19:5. Cf., however, *Teshuvot Maharalbaḥ, Kuntres ha-Semikhah,* (first responsum), s.v. *od ani omer de-gam; Turei Even, Megillah* 27a; and *Minḥat Ḥinnukh,* no. 48.

of "simple" persons who do not give thought to such matters and rely upon Providence to protect them.

In context, the Gemara permits a person not only to expose himself to danger of such nature but to subject others to that danger as well. The Gemara explicitly permits circumcision of a child on a cloudy day despite the obvious lack of consent on the part of the child. It is the father who subjects the child to the hazard in order that the father may fulfill the *mizvah* incumbent upon him.[99] Such endangerment of another person can be justified only on the assumption that a hazard within the parameters of danger from which "The Lord preserves the simple" does not rise to the threshold level of danger of which Halakhah takes cognizance. If, as argued earlier, the risks inherent in general anesthesia to an otherwise healthy person fall within this category, exposure of a minor to such danger is not prohibited.

V. *Pediatric Donations and Tort Liability*

The distinction between the prohibition against "wounding" which is entirely absent in a therapeutic context and the prohibition against appropriation of the property of another which is merely superseded in life-threatening situations carries with it a significant ramification. Rosh, *Baba Kamma* 6:12, as well as *Tur Shulḥan Arukh, Ḥoshen Mishpat* 426:1, rule that a person may appropriate the property of another in order to save his own life, but must compensate the owner of the property for any loss incurred.[100] A related but different question arises in a situation in which a third party appropriates property in order to rescue an endangered person but the beneficiary of the act of rescue is unable to compensate the person whose property was appropriated. Under such circumstances,

99. See letter of R. Joseph Eliashiv addressed to R. Yechezkel Grubner published in *Am ha-Torah, Mahadura* II, no. 3 (5742), p. 102.

100. The permissibility of appropriating the property of another in order to save one's own life is the subject of a controversy between Rashi and *Tosafot* in their respective analyses of a discussion recorded in *Baba Kamma* 60b. Rashi understands the issue under discussion to be the question of the permissibility of the act and the conclusion to be negative while *Tosafot* understands the issue to be relief from restitution. The consensus of latter-day authorities is in accordance with the opinion of *Tosafot* and Rosh although a number of authorities, including *Teshuvot Binyan Ẓion,* nos. 167 and 168; *Sho'el u-Meshiv, Mahadura Kamma,* II, no. 174; and *Dvar Yehoshu'a,* III, no. 24, rule in accordance with Rashi. An excellent digest of the pertinent responsa appears in *Nishmat Avraham,* II, *Yoreh De'ah* 157:4.

is the rescuer liable for restitution since, technically, he has committed an act of theft? R. Chaim Pelaggi, *Nishmat Kol Ḥai,* II, no. 48, draws a distinction between rescue that takes place in the presence of the person whose property has been appropriated for this purpose and rescue which takes place other than in his presence. The underlying principle, asserts R. Chaim Pelaggi, is that the obligation to preserve life is personal in nature and hence does not engender a lien against property. To be sure, as is established by the Gemara, *Sanhedrin* 73a, a person is obligated to expend his own funds in order to preserve the life of another. That obligation, however, is the product of the individual's duty to fulfill the command "nor shall you stand idly by the blood of your fellow" and, although an individual is obligated to expend funds rather than violate a biblical commandment, such a duty does not generate a lien against his property. If a person is not physically present when the life of another is in danger, argues *Nishmat Kol Ḥai,* the obligation of rescue does not devolve upon him.[101] Since he has no obligation of rescue, he may claim compensation from any person who seizes his property for that purpose.[102] If, however, he is physically present, he is obligated both to render personal service and, if necessary, to make his property available for that purpose. He must make his property available, not because of a lien that attaches to his property, but because use of his property is instrumental to the fulfillment of his personal obligation. Since, under such circumstances, he *is* obligated to make his property available, asserts R. Chaim Pelaggi, he has no claim upon another who seizes his property for this purpose.[103]

101. It seems to this writer that *Teshuvot Binyan Ẓion,* no. 17, would not accept this distinction. *Binyan Ẓion* argues that *Tosafot* and Rosh permit a person whose life is threatened to seize the property of another only because the owner of the seized property is under an obligation of rescue and hence the seizure is not at all an act of theft. Whenever such obligation is absent, argues *Binyan Ẓion,* the seizure is an act of theft and is forbidden. A person whose life is threatened clearly has the right to seize property in order to save himself even in the absence of the proprietor. Contrary to *Nishmat Kol Ḥai, Binyan Ẓion* apparently maintains that an obligation of rescue can devolve upon an individual even without his knowledge, with the result that his property may be seized in discharging that obligation on his behalf. See *Teshuvot Maharsham,* V, no. 54, from which it appears that the interlocutor espoused the position of *Nishmat Kol Ḥai* and that Maharsham disagrees.

102. The text of this responsum is corrupt in at least one and probably in several places. The statements here presented are believed by this writer to be faithful to the position espoused by the author of *Nishmat Kol Ḥai.*

103. A quite similar position is advanced by R. Pinchas Baruch Toledano,

The right to claim compensation for damages resulting from a battery is quite distinct from the prohibition regarding "wounding." The prohibition against wounding is derived from Deuteronomy 25:3 and is in the nature of a "criminal" offense; liability for damages is derived from Exodus 21:19–25 and is in the nature of a civil remedy. Therapeutic wounding is excluded only from the prohibition recorded in Deuteronomy 25:3. Thus, therapeutic wounding may be entirely permissible and yet result in tort liability. *Tosafot, Baba Kamma* 60b, and Rosh, *Baba Kamma* 6:12 and *Sanhedrin* 8:12, rule that the victim whose life has been saved must compensate the rescuer for expenses incurred in the rescue. It should logically follow that the rescuer is also entitled to compensation for injuries to his person sustained in the rescue endeavor. The selfsame principle should logically apply to intentional "wounding" for the purpose of saving the life of another. Indeed, *Hagahot Mordekhai, Sanhedrin,* sec. 718, declares that a person may cut off the limb of another in order to save his own life "but must pay him the value of his hand." As has been shown earlier, *Hagahot Mordekhai*'s ruling regarding committing an act of mayhem in order to preserve one's own life is decidedly a minority opinion but, if that position is indeed accepted, his ruling regarding tort liability appears to be unexceptional. *A fortiori,* in situations in which the person wounded is under no obligation to render assistance, he should be entitled to damages for any wound sustained, including compensation for pain and suffering. A minor is certainly not bound by any biblical commandment. Hence, even in circumstances in which a minor's bone marrow may be removed for purposes of transplantation, the minor would be fully entitled to receive compensation for tort damages to the extent that damages for battery are actionable in our era.[104]

It would appear that the minor's primary claim is against the beneficiary of the transplant since the victim is obligated to compensate his rescuer for any expenses incurred in coming to his rescue. If, however, the beneficiary is unable to compensate the minor[105] it would appear that, according

Barka'i, no. 3 (Spring, 5746), p. 24, note 1, with regard to the victim's obligation to compensate his rescuer for financial loss. Rabbi Toledano infers from Rambam's formulation of the relevant rulings that it is Rambam's view that the potential victim is liable for damage caused to the property of another person only if the owner of the property is not present and is not aware of the danger. However, if the owner of the property is present or is aware of the danger, the victim is not liable since the owner of the property is under obligation to come to his rescue.

104. See *Shulḥan Arukh, Ḥoshen Mishpat* 1:2 and 1:8.

105. *Nishmat Avraham,* III, *Ḥoshen Mishpat* 426:1, addresses the question of

to the position of *Nishmat Kol Ḥai,* he would be entitled to demand such compensation from the tortfeasor, i.e., from the physician who removed the bone marrow.

However, the position of *Nishmat Kol Ḥai* obligating a rescuer to compensate a third party for loss of property seized in preserving a life seems to be contradicted by the Gemara, *Baba Kamma* 117b and *Sanhedrin* 74a. The Gemara declares that if, in escaping from a pursuer, a putative homicide victim breaks utensils belonging to a third party he is liable "because he has saved himself at his neighbor's expense." The Gemara continues with the statement that if another person intervenes on behalf of the endangered person and, in seeking to thwart the pursuer, breaks utensils belonging to a third party he is absolved from financial liability "not as a matter of law but [because] if you will say [that he is liable] the result will be that no man will rescue his fellow from a pursuer." The Gemara clearly recognizes the rescuer's liability but at the same time recognizes that public policy cannot permit recovery of damages under such circumstances. As a result, liability is extinguished, presumably by rabbinic decree, in order not to discourage assistance to the pursued.

Assuming, as is the position of *Tosafot* and Rosh, that seizure of a third person's property is permissible in order to preserve life, any person who is capable of preserving the life of his fellow is obligated to do so by virtue of the duty of *pikuaḥ nefesh* even in circumstances in which he must appropriate the property of another in order to do so. To be sure, the individual whose life has been preserved may be liable "because he saved himself at his neighbor's expense." However, it stands to reason that the rescuer should be exempt from liability for the same reason that a person who intervenes in order to thwart a pursuer is exempt from liability, i.e., because otherwise "no man will rescue his fellow." It would stand to reason that the rabbinic decree relieving the rescuer from liability is not limited to rescue from homicide but includes rescue from any threat to life.[106] If so, the physician cannot be held responsible by the

whether a person who is impoverished at the time of his rescue is obligated to compensate the rescuer if he acquires funds at some later time. R. Shlomoh Zalman Auerbach is quoted as stating that, unlike the situation with regard to a person who accepts alms, a lien attaches to the beneficiary with the result that he remains liable. It should however be noted that *Teshuvot Maharashdam, Yoreh De'ah,* no. 204, rules that a person lacking assets at the time of rescue cannot be held liable subsequently.

106. See R. Yitzchak Arieli, *Torah she-be-'al Peh,* VI (5724), 52, who assumes as a matter of course that this immunity applies to all forms of rescue.

minor for any form of compensation.

However, one contemporary authority, writing in an entirely different context, asserts that the immunity from liability posited by the Gemara, *Baba Kamma* 117b and *Sanhedrin* 74a, is limited in a different manner. Apparently, during World War II, Rabbi Shlomoh Halberstam, the *Bobover Rebbe,* borrowed funds which he then transferred to Europe for the funding of endeavors to rescue Jews from extermination. His original intent was to raise money from the public in order to repay the loan. That vision appears to have been illusory since in 1953 Rabbi Halberstam initiated correspondence with Rabbi Moses Feinstein with regard to whether, as a matter of law, he was to be held personally liable. Rabbi Halberstam asserted that he was not halakhically liable and hence, since repayment of the loan on his part was *ex gratia,* he felt justified in establishing a schedule of periodic payments rather than satisfying the entire debt at once.

Rabbi Feinstein, *Iggerot Mosheh, Ḥoshen Mishpat,* II, no. 63, refused to endorse that position and, quite to the contrary, ruled that a person who borrows money in order to save the life of another is fully liable for repayment of the debt. Rabbi Feinstein declares that the rabbinic enactment exonerating a rescuer from financial liability is circumscribed in nature. Rabbi Feinstein does not argue that immunity conferred by that decree is limited to a person who thwarts a pursuer and hence may not be relied upon by a person who rescues another individual from some other hazard. Rather, he asserts that the rabbinic enactment confers immunity: a) only from tort liability incurred in damaging property but does not include immunity from restitution of stolen property or from repayment of a debt even though the property was appropriated, or the funds were borrowed, for the purpose of saving a life; and b) even immunity from tort liability is limited only to liability incurred for damage caused to property that impedes the rescuer in performing a necessary act of rescue.[107] Thus, for

107. In support of this position, *Iggerot Mosheh* cites a narrative recorded in *Baba Kamma* 60b. King David found it necessary to burn bales of barley in which Philistine soldiers had hidden and subsequently sought to determine whether he was liable to make restitution to the owners of the barley. The Gemara invokes a theory akin to that of eminent domain as recognized in common law in releasing him from liability. *Iggerot Mosheh* points out that the act was necessary in order to eliminate a threat to life and hence failure to exonerate King David on the basis of the rabbinic enactment conferring immunity upon a person who thwarts a pursuer is indicative of the fact that such relief is limited solely to liability for damages caused in removing impediments preventing the rescuer from reaching the pursuer. *Iggerot Mosheh*'s argument is subject to challenge on

example, according to this analysis, no liability would result from breaking a glass window in an attempt to rescue a person from a burning building but damage to property used to smother the flames would be actionable.[108] The analysis presented by *Iggerot Mosheh* serves to resolve any contradiction between the rule formulated by the Gemara, *Baba Kamma* 117b and *Sanhedrin* 74a, and the thesis advanced by *Nishmat Kol Ḥai*.

This line of reasoning does not extend to the donation of pediatric organs such as a kidney. Such donations are accompanied by a medically recognized element of danger[109] and hence cannot be regarded as obligatory

---

two grounds: 1) David was indeed in pursuit of the Philistine soldiers and the bales of barley in which they had hidden themselves impeded him from apprehending them. [No distinction is drawn between unwitting destruction of property in the course of apprehending the pursuer and knowingly destroying property in the course of such an endeavor.] 2) David's life was in jeopardy as well. The rationale underlying the rabbinic conferral of immunity is that otherwise "no man will rescue his fellow from a pursuer." No such inducement is necessary to prompt a person to act when he is also among those whose life is endangered. See *Teshuvot Ḥatam Sofer, Ḥoshen Mishpat,* no. 194, who makes a similar point with regard to suspension of the rabbinic prohibition against journeying more than 2,000 cubits beyond a settlement for those returning from a mission of mercy. *Ḥatam Sofer* rules that the prohibition is suspended only on behalf of a person who altruistically engages in the rescue of others but not in the case of a person who, in engaging in a mission of mercy, acts to preserve his own life as well.

108. The resolution of the issue has a direct bearing upon a Jewish law analysis of the Robin Hood narrative. There is no question that a rabbinic decisor would act in a manner similar to Friar Tuck in granting ecclesiastic sanction for a Jewish Robin Hood's theft from the Sheriff of Nottingham in order to feed starving orphans and widows. The question of whether or not Robin Hood would be liable to make restitution hinges directly upon the question of whether the immunity conferred by rabbinic decree upon the person who thwarts a pursuer extends to every rescuer and whether it is limited to specified tort damages or includes all forms of financial liability. Application of the relevant principles to Noahides presents a more complicated array of issues.

109. The perioperative mortality risk to a kidney donor is comparable to that of similar surgical procedures, i.e., it is in the area of 0.1 to 0.4 percent. Long-term risks are more difficult to identify particularly since there is no documented evidence of subsequent mortality as a result of a living kidney donation. One study did show that 10 to 20 percent of donors develop mild hypertension, although other studies show no significant difference between donors and members of age-matched control groups. A third of kidney donors develop a mild degree of proteinuria. Since donors have thus far been monitored only for a period of ten to twenty years there is as yet no evidence regarding whether proteinuria and renal function will remain stable over a longer period. See Barry M. Brenner and Floyd C. Rector Jr., *The Kidney,* 4th ed. (Philadelphia, 1991), II, 2365. Cf.,

even though the survival rates for recipients of a kidney from a live donor are more favorable than for patients treated by dialysis and are also more favorable than for patients who have received a cadaveric transplant.[110] Although, according to numerous authorities,[111] a person may voluntarily expose himself to danger in order to preserve the life of another, no one is permitted to place another person's life in jeopardy, even for the purpose of saving a life, without the consent of the person whose life is endangered. Since minors lack capacity for consent it follows that pediatric transplants cannot be carried out even if consent of the minor is forthcoming other than upon application of a best interest standard or a doctrine of substituted judgment. As shown earlier, application of those principles is problematic at best and, moreover, those principles are not likely to pertain other than in the case of a donation on behalf of a close relative.

Jacob Levy, *No'am,* XIV, 322. There is of course an additional danger, i.e., that the remaining kidney may be injured as a result of trauma or disease. The statistical probability of such injury is negligible. Medical testimony admitted by the court in *Hart* v. *Brown* indicates that the risk to the donor is such that life insurance carriers do not rate such individuals higher than those with two kidneys. The testimony further indicated that the only real risk to the donor is that of trauma to the one remaining kidney but that such trauma is extremely rare in civilian life. See *supra,* note 53 and accompanying text.

110. Although a report issued in 1984 indicated that when variables such as age and co-morbid conditions such as diabetes and cardiac disease are considered there is no difference in five-year survival rates between cadaveric donor transplant recipients and patients treated with dialysis, a more recent study published in 1989 indicates an improvement in one-year patient survival in the preceding decade among transplant recipients of from 85 to 93 percent. All studies show that patient survival with transplantation from a living related donor is higher than with a cadaveric transplant or dialysis. A 1983 study reported a three-year patient survival rate of 91 percent for transplantation of live kidneys as opposed to a 78 percent survival rate for cadaveric transplants. A 1989 report of one-year graft survival indicated a survival rate of 89 percent for living related transplants compared with 77 percent for cadaver transplants. See Brenner and Rector, *The Kidney,* II, 2361–2362. Another survey published in 1986 indicated that 82 percent of grafts from living related donors were still functioning one year after transplantation compared with a rate of 77 percent for cadaver grafts. See Task Force on Organ Transplantation, *Organ Transplantation: Issues and Recommendations* (Washington, D.C.: U.S. Department of Health and Human Resources, 1986), p. 13, Table I-1.

111. See *supra,* note 20.

Chapter XIII

Of Cerebral, Respiratory and Cardiac Death

When a person's days draw to a close, [his approaching death] is proclaimed in the world for thirty days and even the birds of the sky proclaim it.

ZOHAR, BEREISHIT 217b

The conflict between authentic Jewish teaching and societal espousal of so-called "brain death" criteria involves no scientific or factual controversy whatsoever. It does involve disparate views regarding the sanctity of human life, regardless of its quality, and conflicting perceptions of duties owed to the moribund patient.

Judaism regards every life as being endowed with infinite value; Judaism also regards every moment of life, regardless of its quality, as endowed with infinite value. Until all vital forces ebb from the body, as evidenced by total cessation of both respiratory and cardiac activity, human life must be treasured as a sacred gift. The adamancy of halakhic authorities in their refusal to accept "brain death" criteria is not at all an instance of other-worldly patriarchal figures refusing to acknowledge demonstrable scientific verities; it is entirely a matter of insistence upon the sanctity of every moment of human life.

Definitions, by their very nature, are tautologies. A definition of death cannot be derived from medical facts or scientific investigations alone. The physician is eminently qualified to describe the physiological state which he observes. But he can do no more than report his clinical observations. The physician may be called upon to determine whether medical science can, or cannot, be of further aid in maintaining or restoring vital functions. But, when such measures are potentially efficacious in any clinical sense, the question of whether a medical remedy or life-support system should actually be employed on behalf of any given patient involves a value judgment rather than a scientific decision. Similarly, the question of whether a human organism in any particular physiological state is to be regarded as a living person, and hence a deserving beneficiary of medical ministration, or as a corpse which may be medically abandoned with moral equanimity, is an ethical, religious and legal question, not a medical one. Accordingly, advances in medical diagnostic techniques, extremely valuable as they certainly are in determining the precise physiological state of the patient and in formulating a prognosis for cure or the absence thereof, can have no bearing upon Jewish teaching with regard to the duties owed a patient in any given physiological state.

The term "death" is descriptive rather than prescriptive; hence its use is entirely a matter of convention. Were there a common consensus to that effect, the term might be withheld until the onset of *rigor mortis,* or it might be extended to include a patient in a terminal coma or swoon.[1] Nevertheless, descriptive application of the term has come to portend extinction of duties of care and preservation of any remaining vital functions. Accordingly, for emotional and associative reasons, ascription of death to a human organism is, in common parlance, not simply description of a particular physical state but also a principled judgment regarding how the organism is to be treated. Pronouncement of death signals, *inter alia,* a call to the *ḥevra kaddisha* or undertaker, imminent commencement of mourning, notice to heirs that they may succeed to the decedent's estate and a declaration of spousal capacity to contract a new marriage. Those matters are moral, legal and halakhic in nature, not medical. It is perfectly possible to conceive of moral or legal systems in which such matters must abide decomposition of the body, the onset of putrefaction, or *rigor mortis.* Rastafararians do demand the presence of such criteria before permitting interment of the corpse. The requirement imposed by statute in many European jurisdictions as recently as a century ago for the lapse of a seventy-two hour waiting period before burial effectively served to incorporate putrefaction among the criteria required for treating a person as a corpse. Common law, paralleling precisely the provisions of Halakhah, defined death as "total stoppage of the circulation of the blood and a cessation of the animal and vital functions consequent thereupon, such as respiration, pulsation, etc."[2] Absence of evidence of neu-

1. See Rambam, *Guide of the Perplexed,* Book I, chap. 42, who does indeed assert that, in biblical usage, the word "*mavet*" is a homonym having precisely such connotations.

2. *Black's Law Dictionary* (rev. 4th ed., 1968).

rological activity in the brain is now the legal definition of death in a significant majority of states. Many physicians and ethicists advocate further reformulation of the definition of death so that a nonsapient patient in a permanent vegetative state may be pronounced dead. These conflicting positions involve no factual dispute whatsoever; the controversy is entirely with regard to value judgments and/or received traditions.

I.

A person unfamiliar with the extensive rabbinic literature concerning this topic may well ask whether Judaism cannot accommodate a neurological definition of death. Support for such a position might be adduced from a superficial reading of the Mishnah, *Oholot* 1:6: "And likewise cattle and wild beasts . . . if their heads have been severed, they are unclean [as carrion] even if they move convulsively like the tail of a newt (or lizard) that twitches spasmodically [after being severed from the body]."[3] Destruction of tissue as the result of liquefaction, it may be argued, is tantamount to severance or excision of such tissue. Consequently, there is indeed a measure of cogency in the argument that total liquefaction of brain tissue is tantamount to physiological decapitation.[4]

3. See, however, the commentary of Rosh, *ad locum,* who differs from other commentators in asserting that, according to both Rashi and *Tosafot,* the definition of death recorded in the Mishnah is limited to death of animals but does not constitute a definition of death for human beings. Cf., *infra,* note 4, and R. Moses Feinstein, *Iggerot Mosheh, Yoreh De'ah,* II, no. 174, sec. 1, who expresses doubt with regard to whether Rosh intends to exclude only the various other forms of "severance" of the head described *infra,* note 4, or actual decapitation as well.

4. However, the argument, in this writer's opinion, is not conclusive. The Gemara, *Ḥullin* 21a, records three conflicting opinions regarding the connotation of the phrase "whose heads have been severed": 1) decapitation; 2) severance of the spinal column in the thoracic area together with severance of the trachea and the esophagus in their entirety; 3) severance of the spinal column in the thoracic area coupled with perforation of the major portion of both the trachea and the esophagus. *Tosafot* asserts that there is a fourth opinion, *viz.,* severance of the spinal column and of the major portion of the muscle tissue surrounding the thoracic cavity. In a responsum written by the brother of *Taz,* appended to the commentary of *Taz, Yoreh De'ah* 26, the author asserts that severance of the spinal column in this context includes severance of the spinal cord as well. If "severance" of the head is to be understood as synonymous with death because of resultant dysfunction of the brain—or, more precisely, if dysfunction of the brain is tantamount to destruction of the brain and destruction of the brain is

synonymous with death—the additional requirement for severance of the trachea and esophagus in whole or in part or of severance of muscle tissue is incomprehensible: severance of the spinal cord in the thoracic area effectively renders the brain dysfunctional. The requirement for severance of additional organs or tissue leaves no basis for a conclusion that even pithing of the brain is, in itself, synonymous with death. Death, then, appears to be defined, not as dysfunction or even destruction of the brain, but as removal or separation of the brain together with additional tissue from the body. Thus, even total lysis would not be categorized halakhically as decapitation because the trachea, esophagus and muscle tissue remain intact.

Moreover, Rambam, *Hilkhot Sheḥitah* 6:4, declares "If the brain gushes out like water or flows like melted wax [the animal] is a *treifah.*" A similar ruling is recorded in *Shulḥan Arukh, Yoreh De'ah* 31:2. Since, by definition, a *treifah* is alive, it follows that an animal or human being is regarded as yet alive even though the brain is entirely liquified. See R. Yitzchak Zilberstein, *Yated Ne'eman,* 20 Tevet 5755, *Mosaf Shabbat,* p. 9.

Elsewhere, this author has argued that severance of the head, as described in *Oholot* and defined in *Ḥullin,* is not a novel definition of death in terms of decapitation in the sense of destruction of the brain, but rather that the severe loss of blood as a result of decapitation renders all residual motion or movement of limbs or organs, including the heart, spasmodic in nature. Thus, the essential and intrinsic criterion of life is motion that is vital in nature; cardiac activity which, as will be shown, is the primary indicator of life, is simply one form, and indeed the primary example, of vital motion. Thus, *Oholot* 1:6 and *Yoma* 85a do not represent two disjunctive definitions of death but reflect one unitary definition, *viz.,* vital motion in any organ or limb. *Yoma* 85a defines death as the total absence of motion in any organ of the body as manifested by cessation of both respiratory and cardiac activity; *Oholot* 1:6 defines death as the cessation of integrated, vital motion that attends the copious loss of blood accompanying decapitation. See this writer's articles in *Ha-Pardes,* Tevet 5737, pp. 15–18; *Torah she-be-'al Peh,* XXV (5744), 158–161; and *Or ha-Mizraḥ,* Tishri 5748, p. 84.

The comments of R. Judah Aryeh of Modena in his commentary on *Ein Ya'akov, Amar ha-Boneh, Yoma* 85a, are readily understood on the basis of the foregoing analysis. R. Judah Aryeh of Modena sought to explain the criteria of death posited by the Gemara in light of Galen's proofs that it is the brain that is the source of sensation, respiration and movement. Accepting the notion that the brain is the "dwelling place of life" (*mishkan ha-ḥiyut*), he asserts that examination of the nostrils for absence of respiration and examination of the heart for absence of cardiac activity serve to confirm that brain function—the source of all motion—has ceased as well. Hence, continued respiration or cardiac activity is conclusive evidence that brain function has not ceased; see *infra,* note 8. The comments of R. Judah Aryeh of Modena certainly do not serve as a basis for acceptance of neurological criteria of death. Cf. Fred Rosner and Moses D. Tendler, "Definition of Death in Judaism," *Journal of Halacha and Contemporary Society,* No. XVII (Spring, 1989), p. 28, in which these comments are incompletely cited. It should also be noted that despite the inclusion of his aggadic commentary

Decapitation, however, involves physical severance of the entire brain from the body. Physiological decapitation, then, must also be defined as physiological destruction of the entire brain. That phenomenon has simply never been observed. To be sure, autopsies performed on patients pronounced dead on the basis of neurological criteria reveal that the brain has become a spongy, liquidy mass.[5] In colloquial medical parlance this phenomenon is categorized as "respirator brain" because the condition is found in patients sustained on a respirator for a lengthy period of time and is the result of lysis or liquefaction of the brain.[6] However, total lysis apparently does not occur in such patients; only a portion of the brain turns to liquid. It is indeed the case that tissue degeneration resulting in lysis is progressive in nature and consequently it might be assumed that at some point the entire brain will liquefy. Nevertheless, that phenomenon is not present at the time "brain death" criteria become manifest. There is no diagnostic method for determining when total lysis has occurred, nor has total lysis ever been observed upon autopsy. Although the neurological causes are obscure, there is strong reason to believe that cardiac activity ceases long before total lysis could possibly occur. Systemic death, including cardiac arrest, virtually always follows no later than two to ten days subsequent to manifestation of brain death criteria.[7] For

in standard editions of *Ein Ya'akov,* the views of R. Judah Aryeh of Modena are not generally cited in the annals of halakhic scholarship.

5. This is, however, not always the case. At times, particularly when the patient has been on a respirator for only a brief period of time before the diagnosis of brain death, changes in the brain may be minimal. See A. Earl Walker, *Cerebral Death,* 3rd ed. (Baltimore, 1985), p. 123.

6. For a detailed description of "respirator death" see Walker, *Cerebral Death,* pp. 119–123.

7. See President's Commission for the Study of Ethical Problems in Medicine and Biomedical and Biochemical Research, *Defining Death: A Report on the Medical, Legal and Ethical Issues in the Determination of Death* (July, 1981), p. 17. The earliest study of the interval between manifestation of brain death criteria and systemic death reports that the heart can continue to function without any cerebral influence for one to seven days; see the discussion in "Colloque sur les états frontières entre la vie et la mort," ed. by Robert P. Vigorney, *Marseille Chirurgical,* vol. 18, no. 1 (January-February 1966), pp. 1–194. Others have reported continued cardiac activity in brain-dead patients for a period of between one and seven days with an average of 2.5 days; see G.F. Ouakine, "Cardiac and Metabolic Alterations in Brain Death: Discussion Paper," *Brain Death: Interrelated Medical and Social Issues, Annals of the New York Academy of Sciences,* vol. 315 (1978), p. 252. Yet other early studies report that patients who manifest the Harvard Criteria will suffer somatic death within two to four weeks; see

reasons not fully understood by medical science, life, as conventionally defined, cannot long continue after brain function has been so seriously compromised.[8] Thus, "brain death," although not synonymous with death

P.M. Black, "Brain Death," *New England Journal of Medicine,* vol. 299 (August 17, 1978), pp. 338–344 and vol. 299, no. 8 (August 24), pp. 393–401; and J. L. Bernat, "On the Definition and Criterion of Death," *Annals of Internal Medicine,* vol. 94, no. 3 (March, 1981), pp. 389–394. A report of other studies conducted in three separate medical institutions during that period reveals that the median time between these two events was between 3.5 and 4.5 days; see Bryan Jennett *et al.,* "Brain Death in Three Neurological Units," *British Medical Journal,* vol. 282 (January 14, 1981), pp. 533–539. The same principal investigator reports that in none of those cases did cardiac activity persist longer than 14 days; see Bryan Jennett and Catherine Hessett, "Brain Death in Britain as Reflected in Renal Donors," *British Medical Journal,* vol. 281 (August 1, 1981), p. 359. A more recent study reveals that, in the patients studied, spontaneous cardiac death occurred between eight hours and 10.4 days following brain death with a mean of approximately 2.5 days; see Madeleine M. Grigg, *et al.,* "Electroencephalographic Activity After Brain Death," *Archives of Neurology,* vol. 44, no. 9 (September, 1987), p. 949. Another recent report concerning brain death in children reveals that the interval between clinical recognition of brain death and spontaneous cardiac death ranged between six hours and twelve days with a mean of 3.7 days; see L. A. Alvarez *et al.,* "EEG and Brain Death Determination in Children," *Neurology,* vol. 38, no. 2 (February, 1988), p. 228. For reports of isolated instances of survival for longer periods see Joseph F. Parise *et al.,* "Brain Death with Prolonged Somatic Survival," *New England Journal of Medicine,* vol. 306, no. 1 (January 7, 1982), pp. 14–16 and subsequent letters to the editor published in vol. 306, no. 22 (June 3, 1982), pp. 1361–63. The longest reported period of survival subsequent to brain death occurred in a pregnant woman who delivered a baby by Caesarian section at 31 weeks' gestation, 63 days after a diagnosis of death was made on the basis of the Harvard criteria; see David R. Field, "Maternal Death During Pregnancy," *Journal of the American Medical Association,* vol. 260, no. 6 (August 12, 1988), pp. 816–22.

8. Respiration is controlled by the vagus nerve whose nucleus is located in the medulla; hence respiratory activity cannot continue after destruction of the brain stem or cessation of brain stem activity. The beating of the heart is autonomous, although the rate of the heartbeat is controlled by the sympathetic nervous system. Hence, in theory, cardiac activity may continue indefinitely even subsequent to destruction of the brain. Nevertheless, survival of the sympathetic nervous system is probably dependent upon cerebral influences. Hypothermia, which serves to counteract the stimulatory effect of the central system, has been reported in brain dead patients prior to cardiac arrest. Body temperature is regulated by the hypothalamus within the brain. It has been shown that hypothalamic activity persists, at least for a time, even in patients in whom "brain death" has been diagnosed. See *infra,* note 12. Thus it is quite possible that *total* cessation of all brain function, including hypothalamic functions, rapidly leads to cardiac death and, conversely, cardiac activity may persist for a relatively short period in brain

itself, is a harbinger of impending death.

The foregoing description of the physical state of the brain at the time of "brain death" is freely conceded by medical advocates of adoption of brain death criteria. Research scientists who support acceptance of neurological criteria for pronouncement of death argue, not that those neurological criteria establish that brain tissue has been destroyed, but that those criteria serve to establish that the brain has ceased to function and hence, although physically the brain remains intact, irreversible lack of functionality should be equated with excision or "death" of that organ. Thus it is not physical destruction of the brain but the physiological dysfunction of the organ that is equated with decapitation.

For halakhic purposes, dysfunction of an organ is not the equivalent of its destruction or excision. A male whose testes have been removed is forbidden to cohabit with a Jewess of legitimate birth; a person whose testes remain intact but have been rendered dysfunctional suffers no such liability. Similarly, an animal whose liver has been removed is a *treifah* and its meat is forbidden; the meat of an animal whose liver performs no physiological function is permissible. Excision is defined as removal, either as a result of trauma or surgical procedure. Alternatively, it is defined as degeneration of tissue[9] either through necrosis to the degree that it becomes "tissue which crumbles in the finger" (*basar she-nifrakh be-ẓiporen*)[10] or through "decay" to the degree that it becomes "tissue which a physician scrapes away" (*basar she-ha-rofeh gorero*),[11] e.g., gangrenous tissue.[12] The brain tissue of a patient pronounced dead on

---

dead patients only because the patients are as yet not truly "brain dead," i.e., some residual brain functions have not ceased. Cf., David Field, *loc. cit.*, p. 818.

9. It must be stressed that mere cessation of blood flow to the brain is not the halakhic equivalent of decapitation. Total curtailment of blood flow to an organ is not tantamount to excision of that organ for purposes of rendering the animal a *treifah;* only subsequent necrosis has that effect. Similarly, severance of the head from the body is not equated with death because of the absence of an integrated blood flow between the brain and the body but because of the physical severance of the brain from the body—or, arguably, its physiological equivalent in the form of total necrosis or total lysis of the brain—which is equated with disintegration of the organism and hence with death.

10. See *Ḥullin* 46b.

11. See *Ḥullin* 53b.

12. That Mishnah, *Bekhorot* 37a, and the Gemara, *Ḥullin* 46b, describe a "dry" (*yavesh*) or withered ear in a manner which suggests that a limb or organ in the state described is regarded as non-existent. The category of *yavesh* is defined by the Gemara, *Ḥullin* 46b, as the absence of even a "drop of blood"

the basis of neurological criteria does not match, or even approximate, those levels of degeneration.[13]

Moreover, as a rejection of currently accepted criteria of "brain death," the foregoing is superfluous, indeed a form of "overkill." Currently accepted neurological criteria of death, singly or in combination, demonstrate only that specific neurological activities have ceased. For example, absence of elicitable reflexes confirms just that phenomenon and nothing more; absence of reflex activity does not demonstrate that all electrical activity has ceased. Even a flat EEG—which is not regarded as an absolute requirement for establishing brain death—demonstrates only the absence of elicitable brain waves; it does not rule out the possible presence of electrical activity below the sensitivity threshold of the apparatus. A British physician has candidly stated that "in the usual clinical context of brain death there is no certain way of ascertaining (other than by angiographic inference) that major areas of the brain such as the cerebellum, the basal ganglia, or the thalami, have irreversibly ceased to function."[14] Other medical researchers report that hypothalamic-pituitary function is maintained after the diagnosis of "brain stem death."[15] The hypothalamus, a structure that is part of the brain stem, regulates body temperature. It has been shown that hypothalamic activity persists, at least for a time, even in patients in whom "brain death" has been diagnosed.[16] There is also evidence that posterior pituitary function, specifically antidiuretic hormone secretion, persists in "brain dead" patients. Persons in whom

---

when the flesh is pierced. That level of degeneration is contrasted with that of *basar she-nifrakh be-ẓiporen* with the ensuing explanation that tissue of an internal organ that has not totally degenerated may possibly heal, but the tissue of an ear, once it has become "dry," can never heal because the ear is constantly exposed to the wind. Therefore, insofar as external organs are concerned, a lesser level of tissue degeneration is equated with destruction of the organ. Cf., *Iggerot Mosheh, Oraḥ Ḥayyim,* I, nos. 8 and 9.

13. Walker, *Cerebral Death,* p. 122, comments: "The brains of persons suspected of brain death have minimal to severe necrotic changes. None of the brains are normal, but only 1 to 2% are completely mushy. The alterations found in brains from patients suffering from similar conditions and for essentially the same length of time are varied, which suggests that other factors are responsible for the changes."

14. Christopher Pallis, *British Medical Journal,* vol. 291 (September 7, 1985), p. 666.

15. G. M. Hall *et al.,* "Hypothalamic Pituitary Functions in the 'Brain-Dead' Patient," *Lancet,* December 6, 1980, p. 1259. See *supra,* note 6.

16. *Loc. cit.* See *supra,* note 6.

the hypothalamus and neurohypophysis are nonfunctional should develop central diabetes insipidus because of the lack of antidiuretic hormone regulation. A number of studies have shown that many "brain dead" patients do not develop such a disorder.[17] One group of reasearchers reported that only 8.5% of their patients showed clinical manifestations of diabetes insipidus.[18] Recent commentators have pointed out that the demonstrated phenomenon of residual neurological regulation represents not merely the presence of mere brain activity but brain function in the sense of "organized and directed cellular activity."[19]

Thus "brain death" criteria do not suffice for the diagnosis of permanent and irreversible cessation of all function of the brain stem. Certainly, total neurological dysfunction is entirely compatible with continued cellular metabolism; unless metabolism has ceased the tissue perforce remains alive. Theoretically, blood flow studies and radioisotope scanning might be employed to show that perfusion of the brain has ceased. Cellular decay of the neural tissue of the brain does indeed commence upon cessation of blood flow. Nevertheless, such techniques are inadequate for determining death in a manner consistent with halakhic requirements for a number of reasons:

1. Although cellular decay of the brain does commence upon cessation of circulation of the blood, an indeterminate period of time is required for decay of the brain to become complete. Cessation of the flow of blood to the brain cannot in itself be equated with total cellular destruction of the brain. At present, there is no scientific method that serves to establish how much time must elapse following cessation of perfusion

---

17. K. M. Outwater and M. A. Rockoff, "Diabetes Insipidus Accompanying Brain Death in Children," *Neurology,* vol. 34 (1984), pp. 1243–46; D. H. Fiser, J. F. Jimenez, V. Wrape and R. Woody, "Diabetes Insipidus in Children with Brain Death," *Critical Care Medicine,* vol. 15 (1987), pp. 551–553; M. Hohenegger, M. Vermes, W. Mauritz, G. Redl, P. Sporn and P. Eiselsberg, "P. Serum Vasopressin (AVP) Levels in Polyuric Brain-Dead Organ Donors," *European Archives of Psychiatry and Neurological Science,* vol. 239 (1990), pp. 267–69; and K. Arita, T. Uozumi, S. Oki, M. Ohtani, H. Taguchi and M. Morio, "Hypothalamic Pituitary Function in Brain Dead Patients," *No Shinkei Geka,* vol. 16 (1988), pp. 1163–71.

18. A. Grenvik, D. J. Powner and J. V. Snyder, "Cessation of Therapy in Terminal Illness and Brain Death," *Critical Care Medicine,* vol. 6, no. 4 (July–August, 1978), pp. 284–91.

19. Ami Halevy and Baruch Brody, "Brain Death: Reconsidering Definitions, Criteria, and Tests," *Annals of Internal Medicine,* vol. 119, no. 6 (September 15, 1993), p. 520.

for total cellular decay to result. Moreover, as earlier indicated, it is entirely likely that, physiologically, cardiac activity must cease well before this phenomenon could possibly occur.

2. These techniques, in their current state of refinement, simply do not demonstrate that even perfusion of the brain has totally ceased. Investigators responsible for the development of these techniques claim only that such methods may be used to indicate cessation of circulation to the cerebrum, which is the seat of the so-called "higher functions" of the human organism. They are careful to describe the phenomena which they report as "cerebral death" rather than as "brain death."[20] These phenomena are entirely compatible with some degree of continued circulation and perfusion of the medulla and the brain stem. In fact, in the original studies, radioisotope techniques did not demonstrate total cessation of circulation to the cerebrum, but only that affected circulation had decreased below the level necessary to retain its integrity. The scanning methods employed in those studies did not indicate that all circulation to even a part of the brain, i.e., the cerebrum, had been interrupted, but only that the rate of flow is below that necessary to maintain functional integrity. Thus, in a summary of findings which form part of one of those studies, these techniques are described as "indicative of significant circulatory *deficit* to the cerebrum."[21] Those studies indicated the presence of up to approximately 24% of normal predicated blood flow.[22] More recently, another researcher has claimed that the isotope angiography which he employed is capable of showing termination of carotid circulation at the base of the skull,[23] but at the same time he frankly concedes that posterior

20. See P. Braunstein *et al.*, "A Simple Bedside Evaluation For Cerebral Blood Flow in the Study of Cerebral Death," *American Journal of Roentgenology, Radium Therapy and Nuclear Medicine,* vol. 118, no. 4 (August, 1973), pp. 757–767, and Julius Korein *et al.*, "Radioisotopic Bolus Technique as a Test to Detect Circulatory Deficits Associated with Cerebral Death," *Circulation,* vol. 51, no. 5 (May, 1975), pp. 924–939.

21. Korein, "Radioisotopic Bolus Technique," p. 924.

22. See J. Korein, P. Braunstein *et al.*, "Brain Death: I. Angiographic Correlation with a Radioisotope Bolus Technique for Evaluation of a Critical Deficit of Cerebral Blood Flow," *Annals of Neurology,* vol. 2, no. 3 (September, 1977), pp. 195–205. See also J. Pearson, J. Korein and P. Braunstein, "Morphology of Defectively Perfused Brains in Patients with Persistent Extracranial Circulation," *Annals of the New York Academy of Sciences,* vol. 315 (November 17, 1978), p. 267.

23. Julius M. Goodman *et al.*, "Confirmation of Brain Death with Portable Isotope Angiography: A Review of 204 Consecutive Cases," *Neurosurgery,* vol.

circulation may continue with the result that "persistent perfusion and survival of the brain stem" remains a distinct possibility.[24] Another study involving a small number of pediatric patients utilized both the isotope bolus technique and cerebral angiography and somewhat surprisingly demonstrated persistent EEG activity despite negative blood flow studies.[25] The authors of that study candidly acknowledge that some circulation, either supplied by the external carotid system or in the form of limited cerebral perfusion, must have been present albeit undetected by blood flow studies.[26] Yet another recent study reports that spontaneous respiration was observed in two patients in whom cerebral blood flow studies demonstrated no cerebral perfusion.[27] That finding is truly remarkable and demonstrates the inherent compatibility of negative blood flow studies with even the classic indicator of life.[28]

---

16 (April, 1985), no. 4, p. 492.

24. *Loc. cit.,* p. 496.

25. See Stephen Ashwal and Sanford Schneider, "Failure of Electroencephalography to Diagnose Brain Death in Comatose Children," *Annals of Neurology,* vol. 6, no. 6 (December, 1979), pp. 512–517.

26. *Loc. cit.,* p. 517.

27. See Madeleine Grigg *et al.,* "Electroencephalographic Activity After Brain Death," pp. 948f.

28. There have been at least two reported cases of the birth of live babies subsequent to brain death resulting from natural causes. See William P. Dillon *et al.,* "Life Support and Maternal Death During Pregnancy," *Journal of the American Medical Association,* vol. 248, no. 9 (September 3, 1982), pp. 1089–91 and David R. Field, *supra,* note 5. In a third case the patient satisfied generally accepted criteria of brain death although electrocenphalograms showed some slight, unspecific intermittent activity. However, the extensive brain damage evident upon post-mortem examination was compatible with clinical findings showing no detectable brain stem functions; see J. E. Heikkinen *et al.,* "Life Support for 10 Weeks with Successful Fetal Outcome after Fatal Maternal Brain Damage," *British Medical Journal,* vol. 290 (April 7, 1985), pp. 1237–38. *Tosafot, Ḥullin* 38b, *Baba Batra* 142b and *Niddah* 44a, maintain that, other than in cases of trauma, the fetus cannot survive the demise of its mother. Cf., *Magen Avraham, Oraḥ Ḥayyim* 330:10. Were "brain death" to be regarded by Halakhah as death, the reported phenomenon would constitute a post-mortem birth. This is, however, hardly a conclusive argument for rejecting neurological criteria since the principle that biological and physiological phenomena have undergone changes over a period of centuries (*nishtaneh ha-teva*) is well established; see *Tiferet Yisra'el, Bekhorot* 3:1. Nevertheless, the spectre of a cadaver producing offspring does induce a measure of intuitive skepticism and should certainly give pause in accepting any novel theory that defines the mother as a cadaver. Despite the wide publicity given to a videotape presentation of the decapitation of a pregnant

Moreover, it must be emphasized that blood flow studies are neither a legal requirement for pronouncing a patient dead on the basis of neurological standards nor are they routinely performed as a matter of medical practice.[29] Other neurological criteria are even less satisfactory than blood flow tests as halakhic criteria for establishing that cellular decay of the brain has occurred. Those criteria serve to establish only irreversible cessation of neurological function in the lower regions of the brain; they do not constitute evidence that even a portion of the brain has been destroyed. *Oholot* 1:6 can, at most, be cited only to substantiate an argument that destruction of the entire brain is tantamount to death. Since radioisotope scanning techniques, even if employed, *do not* show termination of blood flow to the brain stem any discussion of the validity of "brain death" in Jewish law is rendered entirely theoretical by virtue of the fact that, at present, the requisite criteria demanded by the advocates of that position are simply not demonstrable in a clinical setting.

A neurologist who accepts brain death criteria, Dr. James Bernat, has candidly conceded that:

> The bedside clinical examination is not sufficiently sensitive to exclude the possibility that small nests of brain cells may have

---

sheep and the subsequent birth of a live lamb, that experiment establishes nothing of halakhic import. The earlier cited comments of *Tosafot, Ḥullin 38b, Baba Batra* 142b and *Niddah* 44a, clearly indicate a recognition of the possibility of post-mortem birth when death results from trauma. See also *supra,* note 4.

In a similar vein, the need for, and the efficacy of, administration of pressor agents and antibiotics to patients declared "brain dead" but maintained on ventilators until organs can be harvested, although in itself of no halakhic import, is also a phenomenon that it is intuitively difficult to associate with a cadaver. See Christopher Pallis, "ABC of Brain Death: The Declaration of Death," *British Medical Journal,* vol. 286 (January 1, 1983), p. 39.

29. It should also be noted that, at least as applied by many physicians in clinical practice, recovery has occurred subsequent to manifestation of "brain death" criteria upon which the physician was prepared to rely. See William D. Goldie and Robert H. Price, "Recovery from 'Brain Death' with Absent Evoked Potentials," *Journal of Clinical Neurophysiology,* vol. 5 (1988), no. 4, p. 354; and A. Ogunyemi *et al.,* "Generalized Convulsive Seizure in a Patient with Clinical Features of Brain Death," *Epilepsia,* vol. 29, no. 5 (September-October, 1988), p. 673. Amar S.N. Al-Din *et al.,* "Coma and Brain Stem Areflexia in Brain Stem Encephalitis (Fisher's Syndrome)," *British Medical Journal,* vol. 291 (August 24, 1985), pp. 535–536, report that three patients recovered from apneic coma accompanied by absent brain stem reflexes. The authors attribute the neurological phenomena manifested in those patients to brain stem encephalitis.

> survived . . . and that their continued functioning, although not contributing significantly to the functioning of the organism as a whole, can be measured by laboratory techniques.[30]

The Uniform Determination of Death Act does, however, specify that a person is dead only if he has sustained "irreversible cessation of *all functions of the entire brain*" (emphasis added). Quite apart from ongoing hypothalamic-pituitary function in patients manifesting clinically accepted criteria of "brain death," it is well-established that clusters of brain cells may be perfused and continue to function on the cellular level. As Robert Veatch has recently noted, "The law does not grant a dispensation to ignore cellular function, no matter how plausible that may be."[31] Reliance upon neurological criteria of death in jurisdictions that have enacted a statute incorporating the language of the Uniform Determination of Death Act is in violation of the plain meaning of the statute.

3. The performance of radioisotope scanning is of no therapeutic benefit to the patient. In light of the halakhic prohibition against moving even the limb of a *goses* lest the patient's death be hastened thereby it would be difficult, to say the least, to perform such procedures upon a moribund patient without violating applicable halakhic strictures.[32] The identical objection applies to at least some, if not most, of the various other neurological diagnostic procedures employed in pronouncing "brain death."[33]

The term "brain death" carries with it a certain emotional cachet and appeal. In point of fact, "brain death" is a misnomer: "Brain death" criteria establish irreversible neurological dysfunction, not cessation of metabolic functions; "brain death," when confirmed by blood flow studies, represents the onset of metabolic dysfunction, not necessarily "death" of the neural tissue; "brain death," even when supported by blood flow studies, represents confirmed metabolic dysfunction of only a portion of the brain, not of the brain in its entirety. "Brain death" criteria are not

30. James L. Bernat, "How much of the Brain Must Die in Brain Death?" *Journal of Clinical Ethics,* vol. 3, no. 1 (Spring, 1992), p. 25.

31. Robert Veatch, "The Impending Collapse of the Whole-Brain Definition of Death," Hastings Center Report, vol. 23, no. 4 (July–August, 1993), p. 18.

32. R. Shlomoh Zalman Auerbach is of the opinion that introducing a dye or other liquid, even in an already inserted intravenous line, constitutes a violation of this prohibition. See *infra*, note 56.

33. Medically recognized danger posed by apnea testing has been documented by Joseph S. Jeret and Jeffrey L. Benjamin, "Risk of Hypotension During Apnea Testing," *Archives of Neurology,* vol. 51, no. 6 (June, 1994), pp. 595–599.

designed, properly speaking, to serve as clinical criteria of death but as proposed criteria for withholding further treatment and for withdrawing life-support systems. This is recognized and acknowledged by physicians who are sensitive to the ethical issues contingent upon this distinction. In a submission to the Working Party on Donor Organs of the Royal College of Physicians, dated January 23, 1987, two British physicians, Drs. D. Wainwright Evans and David J. Hill, correctly urge that a term such as "mortal brain damage" be substituted for "brain stem death."

None of this is at all novel. The chairman of the Ad Hoc Committee of the Harvard Medical School to Examine the Definition of Brain Death candidly acknowledged, "I was chairman of a recent *ad hoc* committee at Harvard composed of members of five faculties in the university who tried to define irreversible coma. We felt we could not define death. I suppose you will say that by implication we have defined it as brain death, but we do not make a point of that."[34] Consistent with that view the Harvard Committee's report setting forth clinical criteria of "brain death" was published under the title "A Definition of Irreversible Coma."[35] Other writers frankly conceded, "What we are attempting to define and establish beyond reasonable doubt is the state of irreversible damage to the brain stem. It is the point of no return."[36] Similarly, the statement concerning brain death issued in Great Britain by the Conference of Royal Medical Colleges in 1976 indicated that "brain stem death" is indicative of a hopeless outcome for the patient and recommended utilization of such criteria for the purpose of removing the patient from a respirator in order to allow the patient to die.[37] Only in 1979 did that

34. Henry K. Beecher, "Definitions of 'Life' and 'Death' for Medical Science and Practice," *Annals of the New York Academy of Science,* vol. 169, part 2 (January 21, 1971), p. 471.

35. *Journal of the American Medical Association,* vol. 205, no. 6 (August 5, 1968), pp. 337–340. Criticism on the grounds that use of this term "perpetuates confusion in the medical field between the state of being permanently unconscious, as are patients in a persistent vegetative state, and that of being dead" is unwarranted. See the report of the President's Commission for the Study of Ethical Problems in Medicine and Biomedical and Behavioral Research, *Deciding to Forego Life-Sustaining Treatment, A Report on the Ethical, Medical and Legal Issues in Treatment Decisions* (March, 1983), p. 173. The distinction between irreversible coma and systemic death is clear and precise. Moreover, the persistent vegetative state is readily distinguishable from irreversible coma.

36. A. Mohandas and Shelley N. Chou, "Brain Death—A Clinical and Pathological Study," *Journal of Neurosurgery*, vol. 35, no. 2 (August, 1971), p. 215.

37. This is the purpose for which neurological criteria are recognized in Sweden

body declare that "brain stem death" may be equated with the death of a person. In a Supplementary Statement for the R.C.P. Working Party on Donor Organs, dated January 23, 1987, Dr. David J. Hill writes, "The motives for this change are ethically questionable, as is the logic upon which it is based [*viz.,*] the assumption that 'all functions of the brain have permanently and irreversibly ceased.' This statement is, to say the least, doubtful. . . ."

Medical scientists employ the term "brain death" even though it is a misnomer because it is a term laymen can comprehend as denoting a physiological state in which any further treatment is not only contraindicated but would be regarded as ludicrous. Introduction of the term "brain death" is a thinly veiled attempt to justify withholding of treatment under the guise of redefinition of terms. The purpose of this lexicographical exercise is to secure moral and emotional approbation for a policy that would otherwise be greeted with repugnance and even indignation. Withholding of treatment has the effect of snuffing out human life. Any *ad hoc* decision to withhold treatment from a dying relative involves a great deal of soul-searching and frequently engenders feelings of guilt. On the other hand, no one advocates medical treatment or continuation of life-support systems for a corpse. Pronouncing a person dead has the emotional effect of removing any aura of further moral responsibility. In a less than fully informed world, semantic sleight of hand may affect popular perception, but it should not be permitted to affect the universe of moral discourse.

So-called "brain death" criteria simply have no basis in Halakhah both because the clinical conditions ostensibly posited by employment of the term simply do not exist and because, even were those conditions to

---

and Poland. In those countries manifestation of brain death criteria is not unequivocally equated with death but is accepted as warranting withdrawal of ventilating support. Consequently, in those countries, organs may not be removed for purposes of transplantation while the heart is still beating. See Christopher Pallis, "ABC of Brain Stem Death: The Position in the U.S.A. and Elsewhere," *British Medical Journal,* vol. 286 (January 15, 1983), p. 210.

In this country, recognition that "brain dead" persons are, in actuality, not dead is reflected in the ambivalence on the part of some physicians engaged in medical research toward use of "neomorts" as experimental subjects. See Willard Gaylin, *Harvesting the Dead* (New York, 1974), pp. 23–30. See also Barry Collar, "The Newly Dead as Research Subjects," *Clinical Research,* vol. 37, no. 3 (September, 1989), pp. 487–494. Dr. Collar reports that, since he regarded his experiments as having "elements common to both human experimentation on the living and organ donation," he sought to develop a protocol combing safeguards developed for each of those procedures. *Ibid.*, p. 489.

exist, they would not satisfy the halakhic criteria of death. In response to a question concerning one of the ramifications of employment of "brain death" criteria, Rabbi Aaron Soloveichik has aptly and accurately stated, "In order to answer this question I have to have recourse to my imagination. Without recourse to imagination it is impossible for me to assume even for a moment, for argument's sake, that the Harvard criteria conform to the halachah. . . ."[38]

II.

Although the halakhic inadmissibility of brain death criteria is obvious, there are alternative criteria, even more liberal in nature, for which a much stronger *prima facia* case can be made. A detailed analysis of those criteria is in order because of the erroneous perception, perhaps even in the eyes of some of their advocates, that those criteria are synonymous with a brain death standard without which such procedures could not be successfully performed. Those criteria were formulated in conjunction with a decision of the Chief Rabbinate Council of the State of Israel endorsing liver transplants. In the fall of 1987, the Ministry of Health, after prolonged deliberations, granted permission to the Rambam Medical Center in Haifa to perform liver transplants. One of the issues given careful consideration in the course of those deliberations was acceptance of a brain death standard. Despite phenomenal advances in recent years in both medical science and technology, it is still not possible to perform liver or heart transplants if removal of the donor's organ is delayed until death has been pronounced on the basis of conventional criteria. Delay in removal of these organs results in tissue degeneration that renders the organ useless for transplantation purposes. In the course of those deliberations the Minister of Health turned to the Chief Rabbinate Council in order to ascertain the position of Jewish law with regard to this question. The Chief Rabbinate Council pondered the issue for a matter of months but failed to arrive at a conclusion. In the interim a new Minister of Health was appointed and permission for proceeding with the liver transplant was granted. On 1 Ḥeshvan 5747, after the liver transplant had already been performed, the Chief Rabbinate Council announced its endorsement of so-called "brain death" criteria but stipulated a number of conditions to be followed in pronouncement of death and removal of the

38. See *Journal of Halacha and Contemporary Society,* No. XVII (Spring, 1989), p. 44.

organs. That position was formulated in response to a request by Hadassah Hospital in Jerusalem for permission to perform a heart transplant procedure. The decision of the Chief Rabbinate Council was published in *Teḥumin,* VII (5746), 187–192.[39] Pursuant to the announcement of that decision, many prominent and renowned rabbinic decisors issued pronouncements declaring that reliance upon brain death criteria contravenes Jewish law. Rabbinic authorities who publicly announced their opposition to adoption of brain death criteria include R. Eleazar Shach, Rosh Yeshivah of the Yeshivah of Ponevez in Bnei Brak (*Yated Ne'eman,* 12 Kislev 5747); R. Yitzchak Ya'akov Weisz, head of the *Bet Din* of Jerusalem's *Edah ha-Ḥaredit (Ha-Modi'a,* 4 Ḥeshvan 5747; *Le-Ḥoshevei Shemo,* Ḥeshvan 5747; *Ha-Pardes,* Sivan 5747);[40] R. Yitzchak Kulitz, Chief Rabbi of Jerusalem (*Yated Ne'eman,* 23 Adar 5747); R. Eliezer Waldenberg, a retired member of the Supreme Rabbinical Court of Appeals (*Ha-Modi'a,* 4 Ḥeshvan 5747 and 12 Ḥeshvan 5747; *Ha-Pardes,* Kislev, Adar and Sivan 5747; *Ẓiẓ Eli'ezer,* XVII, no. 66; and *Assia,* vol. XII, no. 3–4, Kislev 5750, pp. 115–128);[41] R. Nisim Karelitz, Chief Rabbi of Ramat Aharon (*Ha-Modi'a,* 22 Ḥeshvan 5747); R. Samuel ha-Levi Woszner, Chief Rabbi of Zichron Me'ir (*Ha-Modi'a,* 22 Ḥeshvan 5747; *Be-Shevilei ha-Refu'ah,* no. 8, Kislev 5747; *Assia,* vol. XI, no. 2–3, Nisan 5747; *Sefer Assia*, VII [5754]; and *Teshuvot Shevet ha-Levi,* VII, no. 235); R. Nathan Gestetner, author of *Teshuvot Me'orot Natan* and *Natan Piryo* (*Ha-Modi'a,* 22 Ḥeshvan 5747) and R. Menasheh Klein (*Mishneh Halakhot,* VII, no. 286).

In addition to the decision of the Chief Rabbinate Council, dated 1 Ḥeshvan 5747, that appeared in *Teḥumin,* a further letter, dated 23 Adar 5747, together with appended clarificatory comments was subsequently circulated to rabbis in various communities. That letter has been published in *Or ha-Mizraḥ,* Tishri 5748. A paper prepared at the request of the Chief Rabbinate Council for use in their deliberations that addresses both

39. This decision was later republished in *Barka'i,* no. 4 (Spring, 5747), pp. 11–13, accompanied by discussions authored by R. Mordecai Eliyahu and R. Saul Israeli; *Assia,* vol. XI, no. 2–3 (Nisan 5747), pp. 70–83; *Sefer Assia,* VI (5749), 27–40; and *Sefer Assia*, VII (5754), 123–124. English translations of the statement of the Chief Rabbinate Council appear in *Assia: Jewish Medical Ethics* (English edition), vol. I, no. 2 (May, 1989), pp. 2–10 and *Tradition,* vol. XXIV, no. 4 (Summer, 1989), pp. 1–7.

40. See also R. Yitzchak Ya'akov Weisz, *Teshuvot Minḥat Yiẓḥak,* V, no. 7, sec. 5.

41. See also R. Eliezer Waldenberg, *Ẓiẓ Eli'ezer,* X, no. 25, chap. 4, sec. 7.

the medical and halakhic aspects of this issue was prepared by Dr. Abraham Steinberg and was published in the same issue of *Or ha-Mizraḥ*.

Although reports in the media indicated that the Chief Rabbinate Council had endorsed brain death, a careful reading of the published materials reveals that the term "brain death" is not at all mentioned either in the original decision or in the subsequent explanatory comments drafted by that body.[42] The reference in those documents is to "a person whose independent respiration has manifestly ceased and there is no anticipation

42. The Chief Rabbinate Council apparently does not accept its own announced criteria as an unequivocal indicator of death. Section 7 of its statement restricts utilization of those criteria to removal of organs from "accident victims for the purpose of transplantation." There is no reference whatsoever in that statement to use of such criteria in cases of terminal illness, nor is there reference to use of such criteria, even with regard to accident victims, when transplantation of vital organs is not contemplated.

With publication of the text of this statement in the English language edition of *Assia* the editor of that journal appended a footnote, p. 8, no. 26, indicating that restricting use of those criteria to "accident victims" is designed to limit application of those criteria to patients who are halakhically considered to be in the category of *treifah,* i.e., a person who, either by virtue of congenital anomaly or trauma, has suffered the loss or perforation of an organ and, as a result, will expire within a period of twelve months.

There exists a minority view that sanctions the sacrifice of a *treifah* for the purpose of rescuing a non-*treifah.* The chief exponent of that view is *Minḥat Ḥinnukh,* no. 296. By implication, it may be attributed to some few other authorities as well. Such a position was advanced hypothetically by *Noda bi-Yehudah, Ḥoshen Mishpat, Mahadura Tinyana,* no. 59, only to be vigorously rejected by that authority as an absurdity. The permissive position was first advanced as a consideration in removal of a donor's heart for transplant purposes by R. Judah Gershuni, *Or ha-Mizraḥ,* Nisan, 5729, reprinted in his *Kol Ẓofayikh* (Jerusalem, 5740), pp. 375–377. See also R. Mordecai Halperin, "Hashtalat Lev al Pi ha–Halakhah," *Emek Halakhah,* I (Jerusalem, 5746), 96–104. The view of *Noda bi-Yehudah* is fully endorsed by R. Moses Feinstein, *Iggerot Mosheh, Yoreh De'ah,* II, no. 174; R. Ya'akov Yitzchak Weisz, *Minḥat Yiẓḥak,* V, no. 7, secs. 6–9; R. Eliezer Waldenberg, *Ẓiẓ Eli'ezer,* X, no. 25, chap. 5; and R. Shlomoh Zalman Auerbach, as cited by Dr. Abraham S. Abraham, *Nishmat Avraham, Yoreh De'ah* 252:8, note 24. See also R. Simchah Bunim Lazerson, *Mishnat Ḥayyei Sha'ah: Hashtalat Evarim le-Or ha-Halakhah* (Jerusalem, 5754), pp. 41–46 and *idem, Assia,* vol. XIV, no. 3 (Tevet, 5755), pp. 70–71.

Apparently the Chief Rabbinate Council was not prepared to accept the announced criteria unreservedly and was willing to rely upon those criteria only when further supported by at least the minority view that sanctions the sacrifice of a *treifah* in saving the life of a non-*treifah.* Consequently, the Chief Rabbinate Council restricted application of these criteria to "accident victims" and, even in the case of accident victims, for the express purpose of preserving life.

whatsoever for its return" who, under such circumstances, is described as dead since "there is no life, nor is there a criterion of life." In their clarificatory comments the Chief Rabbinate Council declared even more explicitly, ". . . death is determined by cessation of respiration and not by destruction of the brain; destruction of the brain demonstrates that there is no independent respiration." In his article, Dr. Steinberg seeks to demonstrate that determination of death as formulated by the Sages of the Talmud is dependent solely upon lack of respiration but "since there are many situations in which it is possible to restore normal respiration it is necessary to support the determination of the Sages with proof that respiration has indeed ceased forever. . . . This can be accomplished by means of demonstration of. . . destruction of the brain stem." The clear implication of that statement is that the determining factor in establishing that death has occurred is cessation of respiration. However, cessation of respiration as an absolute indicator of death must be total and irreversible. Accordingly, since as a result of contemporary advances in medical science there are clinical conditions in which respiration may be restored, it is therefore necessary to regard the patient as "possibly alive" until it has been demonstrated that the brain stem has been destroyed. Only then, according to Dr. Steinberg, is it absolutely certain that respiration cannot be restored. Thus, death is intrinsically defined as cessation of spontaneous respiration; neurological criteria serve only to substantiate and confirm the fact that respiratory death has indeed occurred. Accordingly, at the conclusion of his article, Dr. Steinberg entirely negates the opinion that "brain death" is itself an intrinsic criterion of death. Those who erroneously maintain that "brain death" constitutes a valid definition of death for purposes of Jewish law require blood flow studies in order to demonstrate that circulation to the brain has ceased because they equate absence of blood circulation to the brain with physiological decapitation. This requirement is dismissed by Dr. Steinberg as superfluous because, he asserts, it is irreversible cessation of spontaneous respiratory activity that is the determining factor and that phenomenon can be established beyond doubt on the basis of other neurological criteria.

There is little question, that if irreversible cessation of respiration were regarded as the sole criterion establishing that death has occurred, the theoretical possibilities that, in some rare instances, respiration might be restored would be disregarded. The clinical symptoms of death delineated by the Sages of the Talmud were known by them not to be error-proof. *Masekhet Semaḥot,* chapter 8, reports that at a time when interment was carried out in hollow crypts in the side of a mountain it was customary to visit the burial site intermittently for a period of days after interment lest per chance some sign of life might be evident. It is reported that on one occasion a person was found to be alive and that the individual discovered to be alive survived for a period of twenty-five years. *Teshuvot Ḥatam Sofer, Yoreh De'ah,* no. 338, dismisses that narrative as describing a highly improbable event that may occur "once in a thousand years." Cessation of respiration, declares *Ḥatam Sofer,* must be determined by "experts" and it is not only permissible but obligatory to rely upon such expert determination in order not to delay burial of the deceased. To be sure, when there is a cogent medical possibility that respiratory arrest is reversible, e.g., when cardio-pulmonary resuscitation is medically indicated, mere absence of respiration cannot be assumed to be dispositive; otherwise, no further confirmatory indicators are required.

In many clinical situations, brain death criteria are no more necessary to determine that respiratory activity has irreversibly ceased than are blood flow studies. There are many end-stage illnesses in which an absolute determination that spontaneous respiration has irreversibly ceased can be made without benefit of neurological confirmation of "death" of the brain stem. The best examples of such medical conditions are amyotrophic lateral sclerosis (Lou Gehrig's disease) and anencephalus in newborns.

The position that irreversible cessation of respiration is the sole determining factor in pronouncing death leads to a conclusion that would be dismissed by everyone as absurd. Polio, fortunately, is not the scourge that it was some years ago. But the memories of polio victims who were forced to live in iron lung machines for their survival are very vivid. If respiratory activity is regarded as the sole determining criterion of the presence of life, it would follow that a polio victim who is entirely dependent upon an iron lung machine or a similar device in order to live would be regarded as dead despite the fact that such an individual is fully conscious and is indeed capable of engaging in intellectual activities requiring a high degree of cognition. Even if the polio victim's loss of respiratory activity cannot be positively diagnosed as irreversible, were respiratory activity to be accepted as the sole indicator of life, his subsequent demise would retroactively establish that death actually occurred upon loss of spontaneous respiration. The response, as might be anticipated, is that irreversible cessation of respiration is designed to be applied as the determining criterion of death only in cases in which the patient is no longer conscious. The problem, however, is not resolved thereby. Nowhere in rabbinic literature is there the slightest hint that consciousness is an indicator of life or that its absence is an indication that death has occurred. Moreover, even if that caveat is accepted, this position yields the conclusion that any nonsapient patient who has suffered irreversible respiratory arrest is dead regardless of the presence of other vital signs including cardiac activity and neurological functions as evidenced by a positive electroencephalogram.

III.

It therefore becomes necessary to examine the talmudic sources that serve as the basis for establishing a definition of death and to examine the criteria that are delineated for use in making that determination. The primary source of this definition is found in the Gemara, *Yoma* 85a, in connection with suspension of Sabbath regulations for the sake of preservation of human life. The case in point concerns an individual trapped under the debris of a fallen building. Since desecration of the Sabbath is mandated even on the mere chance that human life may be preserved, the rubble must be cleared away even if it is doubtful that a person might have survived under the debris. However, once it has been determined with certainty that the accident victim has expired, no further violation of Sabbath regulations may be sanctioned. The question which then arises is how much of the body must be uncovered in order to ascertain conclusively that death has in fact occurred. Two opinions are recorded. The first opinion cited by the Gemara maintains that the nose must be uncovered and the victim is to be pronounced dead only if, upon examination of the nostrils, no sign of respiration is detected. The second opinion maintains that death may be determined by examination of the chest for the absence of a heartbeat. Thereupon follows a statement of Rav Papa to the effect that there is no disagreement in instances in which the body is uncovered "from the top down." In such cases, absence of respiration is regarded by all as conclusive. The dispute, declares R. Papa, is limited to a situation in which the body is uncovered "from the bottom up" and thus the heart is uncovered first.

It is quite possible to read this statement of the Gemara as indicating that the controversy reflected in these two opinions is with regard to whether absence of a heartbeat is itself to be accepted as a sufficient condition in establishing that death has occurred. Accordingly, the first opinion insists upon examination of the nostrils in order to determine that respiration has ceased because respiration is the sole criterion of life. The second opinion maintains that, while if examination "from the top down" reveals that there is no respiration that in itself may be taken as a sufficient indication that death has occurred, nevertheless when the body is uncovered from "the bottom up" absence of cardiac activity is equally regarded as a sufficient indication that death has occurred. Since both Rambam, *Hilkhot Shabbat* 2:19, and *Shulḥan Arukh, Oraḥ Ḥayyim* 329:4, rule in accordance with the first opinion it might be concluded that respiration is indeed the sole determining factor and therefore irreversible cessation of respiration is both a necessary and sufficient criterion of death.

This analysis, attractive as it may be as a literal reading of the Gemara, is contradicted by Rashi in two separate comments. Rashi introduces the discussion in *Yoma* 85a with the remark that the controversy concerning examination of the nostrils or of the heart is limited to situations in which the victim is "comparable to a corpse in that he does not move his limbs." In those words, Rashi clearly negates any interpretation of the Gemara that would regard respiratory activity as the sole criterion of life. According to Rashi, the presence of any vital force, as evidenced by movement of an organ or limb is, by definition, a conclusive indication that death has not occurred.[43] The connotation of the term "*ever*" employed

43. The problem, however, is that there is no hint in the discussion recorded in *Yoma* 85a that absence of movement is a necessary criterion of death. It seems to this writer that Rashi bases himself upon the language employed in *Oholot* 1:6. The Mishnah incorporates the phrase "even though they convulse spasmodically" in postulating death as the necessary and immediate result of decapitation. Inclusion of this justificatory phrase seems superfluous in light of the definition of death formulated in *Yoma* 85a. Decapitation perforce terminates respiration. Since cessation of respiratory activity is itself equated with death, continued movement should be an irrelevancy undeserving of mention. Yet the Mishnah finds it necessary to take note of that phenomenon. Accordingly, deduces Rashi, the unstated underlying premise must be that movement of a limb is an indicator of life and its presence negates other criteria of death. If so, the presence of residual movement in a decapitated animal should negate its status as carrion. Confronting that objection to its equation of decapitation with death, the Mishnah distinguishes spasmodic motion, or *pirkus,* from normal, and hence vital, motion. Presence of the latter does indeed negate other criteria of death; the former is irrelevant. Hence the conclusion formulated by Rashi that other criteria of death become significant only if movement of limbs has totally ceased. For further development of this point see this writer's discussion in *Torah she-be-'al Peh,* XXV (5744), 158–159.

Recognition of the fact that the Mishnah's sole reference to a criterion of death is to absence of movement as such a criterion leads to the concept that absence of a heartbeat and absence of respiratory activity do not constitute

by Rashi is not limited to a limb but connotes any organ of the body.[44] Accordingly, ongoing cardiac activity is, in and of itself, an absolute criterion of life even in patients incapable of spontaneous respiration.

Moreover, Rashi adds a further comment indicating that the dispute recorded in the Gemara is not at all a dispute with regard to whether death can be pronounced disjunctively by determining the absence of either cardiac function or respiratory activity or whether it can be determined solely by the absence of respiration. Rather, declares Rashi, the controversy is with regard to the diagnostic reliability of external examination of the chest. Insistence upon examination of the nostrils, stresses Rashi, is not because presence or absence of cardiac symptoms is irrelevant but because "at times life is not recognizable at the heart but is recognizable at the nose." Rashi does not at all intend to suggest that spontaneous respiration may continue after cardiac arrest. He states simply that, for diagnostic purposes, it is necessary to examine the nostrils because inability to detect a heartbeat is inconclusive, as indeed it assuredly is, particularly in the case of a debilitated accident victim who may also be obese and, in addition, the examination is performed without the aid of a stethoscope. In explaining the basis of the talmudic opinion that regards examination of the area surrounding the heart as sufficient, Rashi comments, "for it is there that the soul beats," i.e., the crucial indicator of life is the presence of a heartbeat. Rashi does *not* suggest that the opposing view rejects this fundamental verity; the opposing view rejects reliance upon examination of the heart, asserts Rashi, only because of a possible error in diagnosing the absence of a heartbeat. Rashi clearly understood that both opinions recognize cardiac activity as the primary indicator of the presence of life. Rashi's analysis leads inevitably to the finding that if, for whatever reason, cardiac activity persists after respiration has ceased the patient must be regarded as yet alive.

This analysis of Rashi's comments is expressly formulated by R. Zevi Ashkenazi, *Teshuvot Ḥakham Ẓevi,* no. 77. *Ḥakham Ẓevi* states explicitly that, in a situation in which "life" is not evident at the nose for whatever

independent criteria which must also be satisfied; rather, respiratory and cardiac activity are simply vital forms of movement which must cease before the organism is regarded as dead. Accordingly, *Oholot* 1:6 and *Yoma* 85a do not represent two disjunctive definitions of death but reflect a single criterion, *viz.,* absence of all vital motion. Acceptance of this analysis yields the conclusion set forth *supra,* note 4.

44. The human body is described in *Bekhorot* 45a and by Rashi *ad locum* as comprised of 248 "*evarim.*"

reason but *is* evident at the heart, the presence of cardiac activity is itself sufficient to negate any other presumptive evidence of death.[45] *Ḥakham Ẓevi* notes that in some cases a heartbeat may be imperceptible even though the individual is still alive. A weak beat may not be audible or otherwise perceivable since the rib cage and layers of muscle intervene between the heart itself and the outer skin. Respiration is more readily detectable and hence the insistence upon the examination of the nostrils. However, concludes *Ḥakham Ẓevi,* "It is most clear that there can be no respiration unless there is life in the heart, for respiration is from the heart and for its benefit." According to *Ḥakham Ẓevi,* cessation of respiration constitutes the operative definition of death solely because lack of respiration, in usual circumstances, is also indicative of cessation of cardiac activity.[46] Similarly, R. Moses Sofer, *Teshuvot Ḥatam Sofer, Yoreh De'ah,*

45. See R. Eliezer Waldenberg, *Ẓiẓ Eli'ezer,* X, no. 25, chap. 4, sec. 7. Cf. also, *Ẓiẓ Eli'ezer,* IX, no. 46, sec. 5, who cites medieval writers on physiology—among them *Sha'ar ha-Shamayim,* a work attributed to the father of Gersonides—who declare that life is dependent upon nasal respiration because warm air from the heart is expelled from the nose and cold air which cools the heart, enters through the nose. It was thus clearly recognized that respiration without cardiac activity is an impossibility.

46. *Ḥakham Ẓevi's* original ruling elicited the sharp disagreement of R. Jonathan Eibeschutz and sparked a controversy which has become classic in the annals of Halakhah. The dispute centered around a chicken which, upon evisceration, proved to have no discernible heart. The chicken was brought to *Ḥakham Ẓevi* for a determination as to whether the fowl was to be considered *treifah* because of the missing heart. *Ḥakham Ẓevi* ruled that the chicken was kosher because it is empirically impossible for a chicken to lack a heart since there can be no life whatsoever without a heart. The chicken clearly lived and matured; hence it must have had a heart which somehow became separated from the other internal organs upon the opening of the chicken and was inadvertently lost. The impossibility of life without a heart, in the opinion of *Ḥakham Ẓevi,* is so obvious a verity that he declares that even the testimony of witnesses attesting to the absence of the heart and the impossibility of error is to be dismissed as blatant perjury. R. Jonathan Eibeschutz, in a forceful contradictory opinion, argues that such a possibility cannot be dismissed out of hand. In his commentary on *Yoreh De'ah, Kereti u-Peleti* 40:4, R. Jonathan Eibeschutz contends that the functions of the heart, including the pumping of blood, might well be performed by an organ whose external form is quite unlike that of a normal heart and which may even be located in some other part of the body. This organ might be indistinguishable from other, more usual, tissue and hence the observer might have concluded that the animal or fowl lacked a "heart."

There is nothing in this opinion which contradicts the point made on the basis of *Ḥakham Ẓevi'*s responsum with regard to determination of the time of death. R. Jonathan Eibeschutz concedes that life cannot be sustained in the absence of

no. 338, rules that absence of respiration is conclusive only if the patient "lies as an inanimate stone and there is no pulse whatsoever." In the same vein R. Joseph Saul Nathanson, *Yad Sha'ul, Yoreh De'ah* 394, declares, "It is clear as the sun that the indicator of life is the beating of the heart or breathing of the nose." These sources indicate clearly that death occurs only upon cessation of both cardiac and respiratory functions.[47] Rabbenu Baḥya, in his commentary on Deuteronomy 6:5, describes the heart as the last of the organs of the body to die and remarks that the phrase "with all your heart" indicates that love of God must persist until the last moment of life, i.e., when death becomes complete upon cessation of the beating of the heart. The absence of other vital signs is not, insofar as Halakhah is concerned, sufficient to establish that death has occurred.

There is clear talmudic evidence establishing that cessation of respiration is itself not an absolute criterion of death. The Gemara, *Gittin* 70b, states that a person whose esophagus and trachea have been severed continues

some organ that performs cardiac functions. R. Jonathan Eibeschutz argues only that, in the apparent absence of a recognizable heart, cardiac functions may possibly be performed by some other organ; he does not at all assert that life may continue following cessation of the functions normally performed by the heart.

47. It must be emphasized that among both early-day and latter-day authorities there is not to be found a single commentator who contradicts Rashi's exposition in any way. Although some authorities, including *Teshuvot Radbaz,* V, no. 108, and *Bet Yosef, Oraḥ Ḥayyim* 60, assert that Rashi's commentaries are not to be given the same weight as normative rulings of codifiers of the law, that principle of halakhic decision-making is not germane to the question at hand. *Ḥazon Ish* asserts that this principle is limited to comments that might reflect hypothetical positions or that might be construed as explaining an individual opinion recorded in the Gemara, but not to be applied to comments that are clearly intended as normative and definitive. Moreover, declares *Ḥazon Ish,* "All this could be discussed if there were some [authority] who disputed the matter and we would have need of deciding in accordance with the majority of opinions. But in the instant case in which we have not found a single early authority who disputes this matter, certainly the testimony of early authorities is accepted by us as that which was spoken to Moses at Sinai." See letter of *Ḥazon Ish* included by R. Kalman Kahane in his article on the international dateline, *Ha-Ma'ayan,* Tammuz 5714, pp. 31–38 and reprinted in R. Menachem Kasher, *Kav ha-Ta'arikh ha-Yisra'eli* (Jerusalem, 5737), p. 195. See also *Ḥazon Ish, Kovez̩ Iggerot* (Bnei Brak, 5750), no. 15, as well as Me'iri, *Ḥullin* 32a. It should also be noted that the principle formulated by *Bet Yosef* and *Radbaz* is entirely negated by some authorities; see R. Chaim Joseph David Azulai, *Maḥazik Berakhah, Yoreh De'ah* 12:1 and *idem, Birkei Yosef, Ḥoshen Mishpat* 25:31. See also this writer's comments, *Or ha-Mizraḥ,* Tishri 5749, pp. 86–88.

to enjoy legal capacity to execute a bill of divorce on behalf of his wife. Such an individual is described as "alive," albeit facing imminent death. The individual in question is regarded as living despite his obvious inability to breathe. Similarly, the Mishnah, *Ḥullin* 42a, enumerates perforation of the trachea as one of the forms of trauma that renders an animal a *treifah* and hence impermissible as food. It is noteworthy that apparently even perforation of the trachea in a manner that results in termination of respiration renders the animal a *treifah* but not a *neveilah,* i.e., the animal is forbidden because it has suffered a trauma that will result in death but is not yet regarded as dead and hence is not forbidden as carrion. Certainly the individual described in *Gittin* 70b remains in full possession of his cognitive faculties, otherwise he could not signal his desire to execute a divorce; similarly, the condition of the animal described in *Ḥullin* 42a is compatible with a state of consciousness. However, as has been earlier noted, consciousness, while assuredly absent in an organism meeting halakhic criteria of death, is nowhere posited as a condition negating otherwise dispositive criteria of death.[48]

The position reflected in Rashi's comments does serve to eliminate any objection raised on the basis of the statements found in *Gittin* 70b and *Ḥullin* 42a. Rashi stipulates that the criteria enumerated in *Yoma* 85a

48. It has been argued that the statement of the Gemara, *Ḥullin* 21a, to the effect that severance of the vertebrae located in the neck together with severance of the major portion of the muscle tissue enveloping those vertebrae causes an individual to defile in the manner that a corpse defiles reflects a respiratory-death standard since, presumably, cardiac activity is still present in such an individual. This provision of Jewish law could not possibly be reflective of a respiratory-death standard for if it were the determining criterion for defilement there would be no reason for demanding the severance of surrounding muscle tissue in addition to the vertebrae located in the neck. In point of fact, Rambam, *Hilkhot Avot ha-Tum'ah* 2:1, describes that situation together with a situation in which the thigh has been removed exposing the abdominal cavity as among the situations in which an animal is regarded as carrion for purposes of defilement and adds the words "even though [the animal] is still alive." Rambam is clearly stating that a person may be alive for all purposes of law but nevertheless be capable of defiling in a manner similar to a corpse. Even more explicit is Rambam's statement in *Hilkhot Sheḥitah* 3:19: "An animal whose thigh has been removed . . . similarly if the spinal column has been broken together with the major portion of the flesh . . . or the major portion of the trachea has been severed or the esophagus has been pierced even minutely in the area in which ritual slaughter may be performed this is *neveilah me-ḥayyim* and ritual slaughter is of no avail." An animal who has suffered a trauma resulting in a perforated esophagus is clearly alive but nevertheless defiles as a *neveilah me-ḥayyim.* The same is true with regard to an animal whose neck vertebrae have been severed.

presuppose absence of any movement.[49] Hence movement of any nature serves to negate any other indication of death. In an unpublished letter to the editor of *Or ha-Mizraḥ,* R. Saul Israeli, a member of the Chief Rabbinate Council, indicates that the Chief Rabbinate Council endorsed cessation of respiration, when confirmed by brain death criteria, as an absolute indicator of death only because, in such situations, muscular movement is absent. This qualification goes beyond the position formulated in the statements issued by the Chief Rabbinate Council, neither of which stipulates any such condition. Quite apart from the fact that Rashi clearly states that it is irreversible cessation of *both* respiratory and cardiac activities that is required in order to establish that death has occurred, this modification of the notion of respiratory death is unsatisfactory for a number of reasons:

1. Movement of extremities is not incompatible with cessation of respiration or with so-called "brain death" criteria. There are cases reported in the medical literature of patients manifesting accepted neurological criteria of brain death in whom movement has been observed.[50] There is no obvious reason to presume that this movement is a form of non-vital spasmodic movement or *pirkus* described in *Oholot* 1:6 since the movement both appears to be indistinguishable from ordinary muscular movement and can continue over a comparatively long period of time.

2. A person afflicted by an illness or illnesses causing irreversible cessation of respiration plus total paralysis, e.g., a patient suffering from a severe form of polio, would perforce be regarded as dead on the basis of the criteria set forth by the Chief Rabbinate Council and Rabbi Israeli. It must again be emphasized that absence of consciousness is not posited in talmudic sources as a necessary criterion of death.

3. If it is granted that movement of a limb is incompatible with death and hence serves in itself to establish that the patient is alive, presence of a heartbeat serves, *mutatis mutandis,* to establish that the patient is yet

49. Hence, as indicated earlier, *Ḥatam Sofer* declares that death cannot be pronounced unless the patient lies "as an inanimate stone." The principle that absence of motion is a necessary condition of death is confirmed by R. Shalom Mordecai Schwadron, *Teshuvot Maharsham,* VI, no. 124.

50. See Leslie P. Ivan, "Spinal Reflexes in Cerebral Death," *Neurology,* vol. 23, no. 6 (June, 1973), pp. 650–652; S. Mandel, A. Arenas and D. Seasta, "Spinal Automatism in Cerebral Death," *New England Journal of Medicine,* 1982, vol. 307, no. 8 (August 19, 1982), p. 501; and Allen H. Ropper, "Unusual Spontaneous Movements in Brain-Dead Patients," *Neurology,* vol. 34, no. 8 (August, 1984), pp. 1089–92.

alive. Surely, the motion of the cardiac muscle is no less the manifestation of a vital force than is muscular movement in an extremity.

It must be emphasized that the heartbeat of a patient sustained on a respirator is in no sense artificial. A patient in such a state is incapable of spontaneous respiration and will certainly die if removed from the respirator. The reason is very simple: a normally functioning heart cannot sustain life if the blood it pumps is deprived of oxygen. A perfectly healthy person cannot survive in a vacuum chamber for more than a matter of minutes. A respirator assists only in the delivery of oxygen; it does not artificially pump blood through the body as is the case when a patient is placed on a heart-lung machine. Typically, the heart of a "brain dead" patient is entirely healthy and performs all cardiac functions in a normal and spontaneous manner. Were this not the case the heart would be useless for transplantation purposes since it would not be capable of sustaining life in a recipient.

R. Moses Feinstein, *Iggerot Mosheh, Yoreh De'ah,* II, no. 146, explicitly and unequivocally rejects brain death criteria as incompatible with Halakhah "since it is not mentioned in the Gemara or the Codes that there is an indicator of life in the brain." It is precisely for this reason that Rabbi Feinstein, *Iggerot Mosheh, Yoreh De'ah,* II, no. 174, categorizes excision of the heart from a donor for transplantation purposes as an act of homicide.

Nevertheless, the Chief Rabbinate Council reports in its statement that in later years Rabbi Feinstein reversed his earlier position and accepted neurological criteria of death as valid for purposes of Jewish law. Any such report is entirely contrafactual.[51] Rabbi Feinstein's opposition to

51. The context of the alleged reversal is not made clear in that statement. If it is inferred from a report cited in footnote 2 of that statement to the effect that Rabbi Feinstein permitted an organ recipient to undergo transplant surgery, it is entirely unwarranted since such a ruling does not at all entail endorsement of brain death criteria in pronouncing the death of the donor. Removal of an organ in contravention of Halakhah does not render implantation of that organ impermissible. See this writer's article in *Or ha-Mizraḥ,* Nisan-Tammuz 5748; R. Aaron Soloveichik, *Journal of Halacha and Contemporary Society,* pp. 45–47; *idem, Or ha-Mizraḥ,* Nisan-Tammuz 5748, pp. 301f.; and R. Eleazar Kahanow, *Ha-Metifta,* 5747, pp. 64f.

Since this material was first published, a further letter signed by Rabbi Feinstein dated *Rosh Ḥodesh* Kislev 5754 appeared in the *Algemeiner Journal,* 6 Elul 5752, p.6, and has been reprinted in *Assia,* vol. XIV, no. 1–2 (Elul 5754), pp. 24–25, as well as in *Sefer Assia,* VII (5754), 148–148a. In that letter Rabbi Feinstein does not espouse brain death; rather, he declares, "Any time the patient does not have the power of independent respiration he is considered to be dead." That statement entails acceptance of cessation of spontaneous respiration as the sole criterion of death.

Nevertheless, in his letter of 17 Adar 5753, cited *infra,* note 56, Rabbi Auerbach insists that, despite language in Rabbi Feinstein's letter to the contrary, his statement must be understood as sanctioning only withdrawal of the respirator but not as regarding the patient as already dead despite the presence of a heartbeat. Rabbi Auerbach points out that in light of Rabbi Feinstein's earlier responsum, *Iggerot Mosheh, Ḥoshen Mishpat,* II, no. 72, written in 5738, prohibiting organ transplants, he assuredly would have indicated the permissibility of such transplants if he had become convinced that they may indeed be sanctioned. [Rabbi Auerbach's focal point with regard to the implausability of a reversal of position that remains silent with regard to the crucial issue of organ donations is well-taken. However, Rabbi Auerbach's interpretation of the view expressed in this letter would result in a position contradicting Rabbi Feinstein's earlier expressed position that removal of a respirator constitutes an overt act and hence is always forbidden but not necessarily contradicting other positions cited by R. Shabetai Rappaport, *Assia,* vol. XIV, no. 1–2, pp. 29–31 and *Sefer Assia,* VII, 148e–148g. However, as will be shown subsequently in this note, other statements included in Rabbi Feinstein's letter are, according to any interpretation, contradictory to other positions expressed in his *Iggerot Mosheh*.]

Quite apart from the question of whether this letter constitutes a contradiction of, or a retraction from, his earlier announced position regarding acceptable criteria of death, there is another statement which stands in stark contradiction to his earlier published position regarding treatment of a *goses.* In this letter he declares that "if the criteria of death have not been met it is incumbent upon the physician as well as upon all Jews" to do everything in their power to save [the patient] even if he is saved only for several days for he is as a *goses,* and even if this rescue will obligate the physician to expend a great fortune to pay for continuation of respirators and other treatments he is obligated to do so. . . ." Rabbi Feinstein describes the patient in question as a *goses* and nevertheless requires, not only continuation of respiratory support, but provision of other treatment as well. In *Iggerot Mosheh, Yoreh De'ah,* II, no. 174, sec. 3 and *Ḥoshen Mishpat,* II, no. 73, sec. 1 and no. 74, sec. 1, Rabbi Feinstein adopts the position that only oxygen and nutrition may be provided for a *goses* but that other forms of medical treatment are prohibited.

The inconsistencies between the posthumously published letter and the earlier responsa published by Rabbi Feinstein during his lifetime raise serious doubt with regard to whether the letter can be relied upon as the definitive statement of Rabbi Feinstein's position. More significantly, the letter is dated *Rosh Ḥodesh* Kislev 5745, during the course of Rabbi Feinstein's final illness. Physicians entirely familiar with Rabbi Feinstein's condition at the time have advised that in light of his illness the letter be given no credence. Indeed, a notation appended to the letter as it appears in *Assia* states that the letter was dictated in Yiddish and the translation presented to Rabbi Feinstein for review. Considering both Rabbi Feinstein's reported incapacity and the earlier cited contradiction with regard to an entirely extraneous matter (not to speak of Rabbi Auerbach's rejection of the purported intent of the letter), it is no more than reasonable to regard Rabbi Feinstein's own words in his earlier published responsa as the more

heart transplantation because of the fact that it entails murder of the donor is reiterated in *Iggerot Mosheh, Ḥoshen Mishpat,* II, no. 72. That volume was published in late 5745, some eight months before Rabbi Feinstein's death. It is inconceivable that Rabbi Feinstein would have sanctioned publication of a halakhic opinion to which he no longer subscribed, particularly a halakhic opinion literally pertaining to matters of life and death.[52]

Some confusion appears to have arisen as a result of a comment included in *Iggerot Mosheh, Yoreh De'ah,* III, no. 132, dated 5 Iyar 5736, in which in at least some instances, Rabbi Feinstein requires blood flow studies in order to confirm that death has occurred. Were this to constitute a change in his position it would stand in stark contradiction to his later responsum, *Iggerot Mosheh, Ḥoshen Mishpat,* II, no. 72, dated 1 Adar II 5738, in which he reiterates his earlier ruling to the effect that removal of a heart from a donor pronounced dead on the basis of brain death criteria constitutes an act of homicide. In that latter responsum, the last in the series of responsa addressing this issue, Rabbi Feinstein clearly adheres to the position enunciated in his earliest responsa regarding this subject. A careful reading of *Iggerot Mosheh, Yoreh De'ah,* III, no. 132—the responsum which is cited in support of acceptance of brain death crite-

---

accurate articulation of his views. Moreover, even were the letter to be accepted as the considered opinion of Rabbi Feinstein, in view of the fact that respiratory death is expressly rejected by Rashi, Me'iri, *Ḥakham Ẓevi* and *Ḥatam Sofer,* it is difficult to envision acceptance of the contrary opinion of a contemporary scholar as dispositive, particularly when that opinion is expressed without a rebuttal of the position of earlier authorities.

Absence of respiration as the sole criterion of death has also been explicitly rejected by contemporary authorities. In addition to the series of statements issued by Rabbi Auerbach, cited *infra,* note 56, in an earlier letter (published without a date) addressed to Dr. Abraham, Rabbi Auerbach writes clearly that a patient incapable of spontaneous respiration is nevertheless alive by virtue of the fact that his heart continues to beat. Such a person is alive, declares Rabbi Auerbach, "so long as a part of him is alive and the heart beats even though this is because of artificial respiration." See *Nishmat Avraham,* IV (Jerusalem, 5751), 141–142 and R. Simchah Bunim Lazerson, *Mishnat Ḥayyei Sha'ah,* pp. 62–63; and *idem, Assia,* vol. XIV, no. 3 (Tevet, 5755), p. 68.

52. For further discussion of Rabbi Feinstein's position see R. Mordecai Halperin, *Assia,* vol. XII, no. 3–4 (Kislev 5750), pp. 5–13; Dr. Israel Lowenstein, *Assia*, vol. XIII, no. 3–4 (Iyar 5752), pp. 187–189; Dr. Abraham S. Abraham, *Assia*, vol. XI, no. 2–3 (Nisan 5747), pp. 82–83; idem, *Nishmat Avraham, Yoreh De'ah* 339:2; and J. David Bleich, *Time of Death in Jewish Law* (New York, 1991), pp. 171–174.

ria—reveals that Rabbi Feinstein did not in any way rely upon neurological criteria or blood flow studies in order to establish the occurrence of death. Indeed, in his opening remarks, Rabbi Feinstein refers to the accident victims he is describing as persons in whom "other vital functions are not perceived." Rather, on the basis of information presented to him, he ruled that accident victims should not be pronounced dead on the basis of respiratory criteria alone. Since it is possible that, in such circumstances, cessation of respiration is not irreversible, he requires that further confirmatory tests be performed. In such cases, blood flow studies are required as an added stringency, not as in themselves definitive criteria of death.[53] This is entirely compatible with the concluding remarks in his earlier published responsum, *Iggerot Mosheh, Yoreh De'ah,* II, no. 146, in which Rabbi Feinstein declares that there is talmudic evidence indicating that a person can survive for several days without breathing.[54] In that responsum Rabbi Feinstein further states:

> However, it is certain and elementary that the nose is not the organ which gives life to men. . . . Rather the brain and the heart are those [organs] which give life to men. . . . We have the indicator of life only through the nose even though [the nose] does not cause respiration because we cannot properly recognize [life] in the heart or in the navel and certainly we cannot recognize [life] in the brain. The connotation of the verse ". . . all in whose nostrils is the breath of the spirit of life" (Genesis 7:22) does not [refer to] the intrinsic spirit of life for that is certainly not in the nose; rather, the spirit of life which we see is [perceived] in the nostrils even though it is not seen in the large limbs, the limbs of motion, and [it is perceived in the nostrils] even after it is no longer perceived either in the beating of the heart or the navel.[55]

Those comments certainly reflect a clear recognition that the primary vital force in the human organism is the beating of the heart. Other criteria must be sought and their absence is accepted as evidence of

53. For further analysis of the position set forth in this reponsum see this writer's "Neurological Criteria of Death and Time of Death Statutes," *Jewish Bioethics,* ed. Fred Rosner and J. David Bleich (New York, 1979), pp. 305–307. See also *supra,* note 51.

54. Cf., *Jewish Bioethics,* p. 313, note 2.

55. See also *Jewish Bioethics,* p. 314, note 4.

cessation of life only because, in some circumstances, absence of a detectable heartbeat is an unreliable indicator that death has actually occurred. Clearly, the presence of a spontaneous heartbeat is itself an absolute indication of the presence of life in the organism.[56] The matter is perhaps

56. The authorities cited earlier as having issued statements opposing this ruling of the Chief Rabbinical Council all concur in the position that a "brain dead" patient maintained on a respirator remains alive because of the presence of continued cardiac activity. Dr. Abraham S. Abraham has publicly reported this to be the view of R. Joseph Eliashiv as well; see *Or ha-Mizraḥ,* Tishri 5749, p. 90. This is also the position of R. Moshe Sternbuch, *Ba'ayot ha-Zman le-Or ha-Halakhah* (Jerusalem, 5729), p. 11, and R. Eleazar Kahanow, *Ha-Metifta,* 5747, pp. 40f. In a presentation before the President's Commission for the Study of Ethical Problems in Medicine and Biomedical and Behavioral Research on July 17, 1980, this writer testified, with prior authorization, that this was also the position of R. Shlomoh Zalman Auerbach, R. Jacob Kaminetsky, R. Jacob Ruderman and R. Isaac Hutner.

The position of R. Shlomoh Zalman Auerbach and R. Joseph Eliashiv is recorded in a jointly signed statement, dated 18 Av 5751, published in the English-language editon of *Yated Ne'eman* 26 Tishri 5752, p. 24; *Jewish Observer,* October 1991, p. 11; *Assia,* vol. XIV, no. 1–2, p. 10; *Nishmat Avraham,* IV, 139; and this writer's *Time of Death in Jewish Law,* p. 177. That position is confirmed in a second jointly signed letter dated the Ten Days of Penitence, 5752 and published in *Nishmat Avraham,* IV, 140; and in *Time of Death in Jewish Law,* p. 178. Other statements of R. Shlomoh Zalman Auerbach dated 22 Tevet 5752, 25 Adar II 5752, 6 Nisan 5752 and *Rosh Ḥodesh* Av 5753, as well as a statement by Rabbi Eliashiv dated 2 Shevat 5752 have been published by R. Simchah Bunim Lazerson, *Mishnat Ḥayyei Sha'ah: Hashtalat Evarim le-Or ha-Halakhah,* pp. 214–223. Rabbi Auerbach's letters of 25 Adar II 5752 and 6 Nisan 5752 were also published in the *Algemeiner Journal,* 6 Elul 5752. His letter of 25 Adar II 5752 appears in *Assia,* vol. XIV, no. 1–2, pp. 22–23 as well. In a further letter, dated 4 Iyar 5752, both R. Shlomoh Zalman Auerbach and R. Joseph Eliashiv reaffirmed their earlier announced view. The latter declaration was again confirmed in a statement attributed to R. Shlomoh Zalman Auerbach published in the English-language edition of the *Yated Ne'eman,* 8 Av 5752, p. 35.

Subsequent to the publication of this series of letters signed by Rabbi Auerbach and Rabbi Eliashiv in which they reject the concept of brain death, Rabbi Auerbach issued two additional letters clarifying his position. Those letters are published in *Assia,* vol. XIX, no. 1–2 (Elul 5754), pp. 26–28 and in *Sefer Assia,* VII (5754), 148b–148d. In the first of those letters, dated 17 Adar 5753, Rabbi Auerbach reports that he has been assured by three physicians that neurological criteria serve to establish the "death" of the entire brain, including the brain stem. Rabbi Auerbach stresses both that there is no halakhic source upon which acceptance of neurological criteria of death might be predicated and that, moreover, "the extent to which the [neurological] examination is in truth dispositive is uncertain." Accordingly, he reiterates that neurological criteria cannot establish with certainty that the patient is dead. In yet another letter, dated 29 Av 5753, published in *Assia*, vol. XIV, no. 1–2, pp. 13–15, Rabbi Auerbach states quite clearly:

> Brain death as it is established by physicians today is not adequate to establish the death of a person. Such a person is considered a *safek goses safek met,* and, therefore, it is not permissible to hasten the death of such a person in any manner. It is forbidden to remove any organ for transplantation as long as his heart beats, for the fear of hastening the death of a goses. This is forbidden even for the benefit of an ill person before us who will certainly die.

Rabbi Auerbach is apparently quite prepared to accept total lysis of the brain as the halakhic equivalent of decapitation but, since the presence of that physiological state cannot be known with certainty on the basis of currently available diagnostic tests, the status of the patient remains doubtful with the result that organs dare not be removed. In point of fact, medical science recognizes that total lysis has never been observed upon autopsy of a "brain-dead" patient.

Rabbi Auerbach does, however, accept those criteria as sufficient to establish that the patient is a *goses*, i.e., moribund as defined by Halakhah. Since even the limb of a *goses* may not be moved, Rabbi Auerbach reaffirms his earlier announced view that no neurological tests may be performed for purposes that are non-therapeutic in nature and that, *a fortiori,* organs may not be removed. He does, however, state that, in his view, no medical treatment need be provided for a *goses* and, opining that shutting down a respirator constitutes merely removal of an impediment to death rather than an overt act, he expresses the opinion that the respirator may be disconnected. Rabbi Auerbach further states that the patient may be regarded as being dead only after the heart has entirely stopped beating and an additional brief period of time (which he gives variously as 15–20 seconds, 20–30 seconds, and half a minute) has elapsed.

In a concluding statement in his letter of 17 Adar 5753, Rabbi Auerbach announces that this is his personal opinion and that others may well disagree. There is indeed significant disagreement with regard to three separate points: 1) Many authorities deem a patient who can survive for more than three days, even if only with the assistance of a respirator, as not yet a *goses* as defined by Halakhah. 2) Many authorities maintain that medically indicated care designed to prolong life must be provided even on behalf of a *goses* and that only measures in the nature of a *segulah* may be withheld, e.g., wood-chopping may be interrupted so that the noise does not impede the departure of the soul from the body. 3) Many authorities maintain that removal of a respirator is not merely the withdrawal of an impediment, but constitutes an overt act and hence is prohibited under any and all circumstances. For further discussion of these issues see this writer's essay, "The Quinlan Case: A Jewish Perspective," *Jewish Bioethics,* p. 275, note 2.

In another letter, dated *Rosh Ḥodesh* Av 5753, Rabbi Auerbach reports that, subsequent to releasing his earlier letter, he became aware of the fact that the hypothalamus may continue to function, not only in the presence of neurological criteria of death, but even subsequent to cessation of cardiac activity and that, moreover, such hypothalamic activity may persist even after the lapse of thirty seconds subsequent to cessation of the heartbeat with the result that, if the patient were to be reattached to a respirator and cardiac and respiratory activity were to be restored, those functions might continue for many days. Accordingly, Rabbi Auerbach writes that he explicitly retracts his earlier letter and stipulates that a period of "five or six minutes" must elapse following the cessation of cardiac activity in order to assure that the hypothalamus has ceased to function. Only after expiration of that period of time is Rabbi Auerbach prepared to sanction removal of organs—or indeed any invasive procedure, including infusion of diagnostic materials in an already existing intravenous line, or any non-therapeutic procedure involving movement of any portion of the patient's body.

Rabbi Auerbach's view as recorded in his letter of 29 Av 5753 is grossly distorted in comments included in a letter to the editor published in *Tradition,* vol. XXVIII, no. 3 (Spring, 1994), pp. 94–96. In particular, Rabbi Auerbach's letter is quoted with the omission of the first paragraph of Rabbi Auerbach's "conclusions" in which he states uneqivocally that "brain death as it is established by physicians today is not adequate to establish the death of a person . . . ." In response to the publication in *Tradition* of that letter to the editor, Rabbi Auerbach addressed yet another communication to Dr. Robert Schulman in which he reiterates his view that a patient who manifests clinical criteria of brain death is in the halakhic category of a *safek goses* and dare not be moved and, hence, the patient's organs certainly may not be removed for purposes of transplantation.

The earlier-cited letter to the editor further asserts that Rabbi Eliezer Waldenberg has also reversed his earlier ruling in opposition to brain death. In a communication dated 25 Ḥeshvan 5755, also addressed to Dr. Schulman, Rabbi Waldenberg writes:

> I was amazed to read in your letter that I have reversed my *psak* forbidding transplanting a heart or any other organ for a seriously ill person where the heart of the donor beats, even if his brain, including the brain stem is not working at all, which is called brain dead. I publicly inform you that as my opinion was then, my opinion is now: to forbid such a thing according to the halakha, and with great emphasis. I have not reversed my opinion to forbid this in my book *Tzitz Eliezer* (volume 19). To strengthen my position, I wrote an addendum in the back of the book in which I published the opinion of my friends, the Gaon Rabbi Shlomo Zalman Auerbach and the Gaon Rabbi Eliashiv, who also forbids this. I am puzzled! How is it possible for a living person to contradict another living person? In this matter I state publicly that the letter which was published in *Tradition* regarding my opinion has no basis in fact at all.

The texts of these letters authored by Rabbi Auerbach and Rabbi Waldenberg are included in a letter to the editor appearing in *Tradition,* vol. XXIX, no. 2 (Winter, 1995).

A further elaboration of Rabbi Eliashiv's position is presented by his son-in-law, R. Yitzchak Zilberstein, *Yated Ne'eman,* 20 Tevet 5755, *Mosaf Shabbat,* pp. 8–9. Rabbi Eliashiv is quoted as maintaining that "so long as the heart beats, the

best summed up in the words of R. Eliezer Waldenberg, *Ẓiẓ Eli'ezer,* X, no. 25, chap. 4, sec. 7:

> There are those who err in thinking that examination of the nose is indicative of cessation of brain activity and, on the basis of this, wish to establish that life is contingent upon the brain . . . . In truth this is an absolute error and contradicts that which our Sages, of blessed memory, have established on our behalf . . . "And there is nothing new under the sun" (Ecclesiastes 1:9). There have already been many among those who are great in wisdom who were inclined to think that way, i.e., that life is contingent upon the brain, but greater persons came and disproved these notions as is recorded in *Teshuvot Ḥakham Ẓevi* . . . .

---

person is regarded as living and the Sabbath must be desecrated in order to prolong his life."

For more detailed discussions of the definition of death in Jewish law see this writer's "Establishing Criteria of Death," *Contemporary Halakhic Problems,* I, 372–393 (reprinted in *Jewish Bioethics,* pp. 277–295); "Neurological Criteria of Death and Time of Death Statutes," *Jewish Bioethics,* pp. 303–316; "Minority Report: Time of Death Legislation," *The Determination of Death,* report of the New York State Task Force on Life and the Law, July, 1986; "Religious Traditions and Public Policy," *Assia: Jewish Medical Ethics,* May, 1988, pp. 17–24; and "Artificial Heart Implantation," *Contemporary Halakhic Problems,* III (New York, 1989), 160–193. Hebrew-language articles addressing this issue have been published by this author in *Or ha-Mizraḥ,* Nisan 5732 (reprinted in *Shanah be-Shanah,* 5736); *Ha-Pardes,* Tevet 5737; *Torah She-be-'al-Peh,* vol. XXV (5744); *Or ha-Mizraḥ,* Tishri 5748, Nisan-Tammuz 5748 and Tishri 5749. These articles are republished in *Time of Death in Jewish Law.*

Chapter XIV

The Intifada and the Gulf War

When Israel performs the will of God no people and no nation has power over them.

KETUBOT 66b

In its relatively short period of existence the State of Israel has faced a vast array of social, political and economic problems. Many of these difficulties are endemic to nascent or developing states; others are the product of idiosyncratic historical, sociological or demographic factors that might be replicated elsewhere as well. But the inhabitants of the State of Israel have also been forced to cope with a unique set of problems arising from the application of the provisions of Halakhah in a sovereign Jewish state. A series of military campaigns and the security needs of a beleaguered nation have given rise to numerous questions having no direct precedents in responsa literature. During recent years, those problems have been extensively analyzed and discussed by rabbinic scholars as they have arisen.

Not surprisingly, both the intifada and the Persian Gulf war spawned a series of previously unaddressed halakhic issues. Some of those issues are discussed in two recently published books. A slim volume, *She'elot u-Teshuvot Intifada,* by Rabbi Shlomoh Aviner, is devoted to matters relating to the intifada, as indeed its title indicates, but is largely limited to broad policy questions, including, for example, such intriguing issues as collective punishment, censorship of the press, population exchange, etc. The discussions presented by the author, who is a devotee of the late R. Zevi Yehudah Kook, are sparse and ideological but tantalizing nonetheless. Somewhat more substantial is Rabbi Yonah Metzger's work addressing questions that arose during the course of the Gulf war, *She'elot u-Teshuvot Sufah ba-Midbar.* The questions addressed in the latter work are primarily those of individuals confronting the danger of Scud missiles and the need to take shelter in sealed rooms during air raid alerts. The answers are rather brief and cursory. Both students and scholars will find this work a valuable aid in locating sources and precedents.

Defying Governmental Edicts

One of the most intriguing questions raised by Rabbi Aviner is a question that we all pray will remain entirely hypothetical and speculative. In the event of the return of some portion of the liberated territories to Arab sovereignty it may become politically necessary to evacuate Jewish settlements that have been established in those areas. Would the settlers have a right to defy orders of the government and the Israeli Defense Forces and remain on their land? A similar problem did arise at the time of the dismantlement of Yamit upon the return of Sinai to Egypt in 1982. At that time, there were vigorous protests and actual civil disobedience. Ultimately, the Israeli army forcibly evacuated thousands of settlers and protesting squatters and used bulldozers to destroy homes and greenhouses. To this writer's knowledge, no discussion of the permissibility of civil disobedience appeared in rabbinic journals at that time.

The most obvious issue involved in adjudicating this question is the applicability of the talmudic principle "the law of the land is the law" (*dina de-malkhuta dina*) to the edicts of the Israeli government. Resolution of that issue requires explication of the scope and nature of *dina de-malkhuta dina* including, in particular, an analysis of whether the authority reflected in that principle is limited to non-Jewish states or whether the principle is operative in a Jewish commonwealth as well.[1] The ambit and application of *dina de-malkhuta dina* have been widely discussed in other contexts. The second issue is unique to this fact pattern: Does a country about to relinquish sovereignty over a particular area retain the authority of *dina de-malkhuta dina* over nationals who simply by remaining *in situ,* in effect, seek to place themselves outside the territorial jurisdiction

---

1. See, for example, articles by Rabbis Joseph Dov Cohen, Shlomoh Tenbitzki and Israel Kolonder in the first issue of *Ha-Torah ve-ha-Medinah,* Nisan 5709, and the articles on related topics in the same issue by Rabbis Nathan Zevi Friedman, Moshe Zevi Neriah and Saul Israeli; R. Saul Israeli, *ibid.,* no. 2, Iyar 5710, pp. 76–88; R. Samuel Weingarten, *ibid.,* no. 5–6, 5713–14, pp. 316–322; R. Ovadiah Hedaya, *ibid.,* no. 9–10, 5718–5719, pp. 36–44; R. Shlomoh Goren, *Or ha-Mizraḥ,* Elul 5714; *idem, Maḥanayim,* no. 33 (*Erev Rosh ha-Shanah* 5718); R. Saul Israeli, *Amud ha-Yemini* (Tel Aviv, 5726), no. 8; *idem, Shevilin,* no. 25–26 (Elul 5730); and R. Shlomoh Kook, *Shanah be-Shanah,* 5732, pp. 217–218.

of that country? Neither of these issues is raised, much less discussed, by Rabbi Aviner.

The sole consideration raised by the author is whether civil disobedience constitutes *lèse majesté,* an infraction punishable, at the monarch's discretion, with the death penalty. Rabbi Aviner readily concedes that the biblically ordained monarchy no longer exists and hence, there can be no crime of *lèse majesté.* He does, however, cite a very interesting comment of R. Naphtali Zevi Judah Berlin in arguing that disobedience of a governmental order is justifiably punishable by death.

In accepting Joshua's charge to perform their military duties, the tribes of Reuben and Gad declared, "Whosoever shall rebel against your command and shall not hearken unto your word in all that you shall command him shall be put to death; only be strong and of good courage" (Joshua 1:18). R. Naphtali Zevi Judah Berlin, *Ha'amek She'elah, She'ilta* 142:9, observes that Joshua enjoyed the status of a judge, but not of a king. Hence, he queries, on what grounds was he empowered to punish disobedience with the death penalty? Despite the comments of the Gemara, *Sanhedrin* 49a, which appear to define the infraction as indeed constituting *lèse majesté, Ha'amek She'elah* declares that the answer is to be found in the final phrase of the verse, "be strong and of good courage." Although not a monarch, Joshua was the military commander about to embark upon a military campaign for the conquest of the Promised Land. A military leader must be courageous and confident. Those qualities depend, in part, upon a sense of authority and assurance that orders will be carried out without demur. Disobedience and breach of discipline, even if they do not directly affect military operations, are bound to have a demoralizing effect upon the leader responsible for waging war and will diminish his courage and determination. Any challenge to his authority is likely to weaken his self-confidence. That, in turn, would have a disastrous effect upon the course of the armed conflict and result in avoidable loss of life. Hence, argues *Ha'amek She'elah,* any person defying Joshua would, in effect, have been an aggressor (*rodef*) whose disobedience would have endangered the entire nation. Sanctions imposed upon the miscreant were designed to restore Joshua's courage and confidence by eliminating any challenge to his authority.

Similarly, argues Rabbi Aviner, disobedience of modern-day military authorities is a punishable offense. However, that conclusion cannot be regarded as unequivocal. It must be noted that *Ha'amek She'elah* does not conclude that disobedience of Joshua constituted the capital crime of *lèse majesté* but rather that, had it occurred, it would, at least indirectly, have endangered the populace. "The law of pursuit" is designed to eliminate a threat to life rather than as a punishment of the perpetrator. As such, its invocation in any particular set of circumstances depends entirely upon the realia of the situation. *Ha'amek She'elah,* in his own remarks, stresses that the commander's authority to impose the death penalty is limited to periods of ongoing military hostility.

Declining to Carry Within an Eiruv

Rabbi Metzger's *She'elot u-Teshuvot Sufah ba-Midbar* includes questions regarding numerous issues likely to arise in other contexts as well and is of value particularly because of the array of sources cited, many of which are obscure in the sense that even the informed reader is not likely to be familiar with them.

During the duration of hostilities in the Persian Gulf, Israelis were admonished to carry gas masks with them at all times because of the danger of aerial bombardment by Iraqi missiles armed with chemical warheads. Rabbi Metzger reports that many people were reluctant to carry gas masks on *Shabbat* even in areas surrounded by an *eiruv.* Most settled areas in Israel are surrounded by an *eiruv* constructed with poles and wire and designed to create an enclosure in which carrying on the Sabbath is permissible.

The reason for the reluctance on the part of the interlocutors to carry within an *eiruv* is itself a matter of interest. Rabbi Metzger correctly cites *Ma'aseh Rav,* no. 150 (no. 151 in the editions now in print), a compendium of the practices of R. Elijah of Vilna, as the basis of the practice of many scholars who decline to carry on *Shabbat* even in locales in which there is a properly supervised *eiruv.* Rabbi Metzger is under the impression that R. Elijah of Vilna was concerned lest a person carrying an object in such an *eiruv* transgress Sabbath laws by inadvertently carrying beyond the boundary of the *eiruv.* However, the text of *Ma'aseh Rav* does not indicate that this was necessarily the nature of the concern and is not how that reference was understood by R. Naphtali Hertz ha-Levi as reflected in his "*Likkutei Devarim u-Bi'urim*" appended to the edition of *Siddur ha-Gra* (New York, 5714) which he edited and annotated. That commentator is of the opinion that R. Elijah of Vilna had reservations regarding the reliability and validity of *eiruvin* as they were established in actual practice. In addition to the considerations enumerated by R. Naphtali

Hertz ha-Levi it should be noted that virtually no *eiruv* presently constructed conforms with the requirements set down by Rambam. Rambam, *Hilkhot Shabbat* 16:16, maintains that, unless a structural wall exists extending along more than fifty percent of a side of the area to be bounded by the *eiruv,* an *eiruv* consisting of poles and wire is of no avail in bridging a gap larger than ten cubits in width (i.e., fifteen or twenty feet, depending upon various opinions regarding the measurement of a cubit). Rambam's position is cited by *Shulḥan Arukh, Hilkhot Shabbat* 262:10. *Mishnah Berurah* 362:59 notes that since Rambam's view is also accepted by Semag and Semak "it is proper" (*nakhon*) not to carry in areas in which the *eiruv* is not valid according to the opinion of Rambam.

Similarly, a son of the *Ḥafeẓ Ḥayyim,* R. Aryeh Leib Kagan, in a monograph entitled *Derakhav, Nimukav ve-Siḥotav shel ha-Rav Ḥafeẓ Ḥayyim Zaẓal* 63:14, appended to *Kitvei Ḥafeẓ Ḥayyim,* reports that *Ḥafeẓ Ḥayyim* refused to carry outside of his own home on *Shabbat* despite the fact that he scrupulously supervised the *eiruv* in Radun. *Ḥafeẓ Ḥayyim*'s concern, as that of R. Elijah of Vilna before him, was that, according to the opinion of many early authorities, it is pragmatically impossible to construct a valid *eiruv* even in villages and hamlets. One of the principles governing construction of an *eiruv* is that it may be utilized only in enclosing an area in which carrying is forbidden by virtue of rabbinic edict, but not in an area biblically defined as a public domain. Many early authorities maintain that any thoroughfare sixteen cubits in width constitutes such a public domain regardless of how small the number of people traversing the area each day. *Ḥafeẓ Ḥayyim*'s personal practice with regard to this matter is consistent with his ruling recorded in *Bi'ur Halakhah* 364:2. In that work *Ḥafeẓ Ḥayyim* declares "although one should not protest against the populace who have accustomed themselves to leniency [in this matter] nevertheless, a pious person (*ba'al nefesh*) should be stringent for himself." In a letter addressed to R. Menasheh Klein and published in that author's *Mishneh Halakhot,* VIII, no. 90, R. Ya'akov Kanievski, known as "the *Steipler,*" presents a lengthy list of halakhic considerations militating against reliance upon *eiruvin* as they are generally constructed in our day. Earlier, a list of such considerations was formulated by R. Shlomoh Yehudah Tabak, *Teshuvot Teshurat Shai* (Maramarossziget, 5665), no. 357.

The late Rabbi Abraham I. Kook apparently also refused to sanction an *eiruv* that encompassed a public thoroughfare.[2] In his autobiography,

2. In 1923, the locale in question, Zeimelis, had a total population of 1,209

Seder Eliyahu (Jerusalem, 5744), pp. 67–68, Rabbi Eliyahu David Rabinowitz-Teumim (known as the *Aderet*), the father-in-law of Rav Kook, describes in detail events associated with Rav Kook's assumption of his first rabbinical position in Zheymel (Zeimelis). Rabbi Rabinowitz-Teumim reports that the hamlet had no *eiruv* and that he exhorted his son-in-law to make the construction of an *eiruv* a matter of high priority. Rav Kook refused to do so and pointed to the position of *Teshuvot Mishkenot Ya'akov, Oraḥ Ḥayyim,* nos. 120–122, who rules that no *eiruv* can be constructed by means of poles and wire or string because a "wall" constructed in that manner is nullified by the existence of a public right of way.[3]

Ḥazon Ish, Emunah u-Bitaḥon 4:18, also comments negatively upon those who carry on *Shabbat* in reliance upon the fact that an *eiruv* has been constructed around the city "since in the majority of cases this involves stumbling-blocks." Apparently, *Ḥazon Ish*'s concern was that most *eiruvin* are improperly constructed. Thus, in a recently published volume describing the practices of *Ḥazon Ish, Dinim ve-Hanhagot me-Maran ha-Ḥazon Ish* (Bnei Brak, 5748), chapter 14, sec. 1, Rabbi Meir Greineman writes:

> [*Ḥazon Ish*] was wont to say that it is forbidden to carry a burden on *Shabbat* even in cities that have been perfected by an *eiruv* for in the majority of cases this involves stumbling-blocks. . . . and he regarded this as a definite rabbinic transgression. He repeatedly stated that every time he went to inspect *eiruvin* he always found them to be invalid. Once he remarked that seeing people profane the *Shabbat* by carrying made it difficult for him to walk in the street on *Shabbat.*

The practice of not relying upon an *eiruv* is also recorded in *Tosafot Ḥayyim* (a commentary on *Ḥayyei Adam*), *Hilkhot Shabbat* 71:1 and in *Minḥat Shabbat* 82:6 as well as by R. Chaim Biberfeld, *Menuḥah Nekhonah* (Jerusalem, 5738), p. 70.

---

persons. See *Encyclopedia Lituanica* (Boston, 1978), VI, 305.

3. Rabbi Kook is also quoted in *Seder Eliyahu* as asserting that, as a matter of policy, *eiruvin* should not be constructed lest the prohibition against carrying be "forgotten." Contrary statements found in rabbinic sources categorizing construction of an *eiruv* as a *miẓvah* and encouraging the practice he dismissed as referring only to "large cities" in which *eiruvin* were necessary in order to minimize transgression on the part of Sabbath desecrators.

The concern of the various authorities who decry reliance upon present-day *eiruvin* is in no way negated by the Gemara's assertion, *Eruvin* 68b, that refusal to accept an *eiruv* is a Sadducean tenet. The Sadducees, in their renunciation of the Oral Law, rejected the concept of an *eiruv* in principle; the concern of the aforementioned authorities is solely that the details of the regulations concerning construction of an *eiruv* are misapplied in practice. Their position is similarly not negated by the many statements found in the writings of early authorities to the effect that construction of an *eiruv* constitutes a great *mizvah* because it obviates infraction of Sabbath laws. Those statements obviously apply only to the construction of an *eiruv* that can be accepted as halakhically valid.

Rabbi Metzger offers practical advice to those who do not carry within the *eiruv* on the Sabbath. He suggests that they walk at a fast pace until they arrive at and enter the private domain they seek to reach taking care not to stop in the thoroughfare on the way. His reasoning is that traversing a public thoroughfare without coming to a stop constitutes a rabbinic infraction rather than a biblical transgression and that carrying in the thoroughfare, even in the absence of an *eiruv,* is itself merely a rabbinic infraction. Accordingly, he relies upon the authorities who rule that an act that is forbidden only as the product of the confluence of two separate rabbinic ordinances (*trei de-rabbanan*) is permissible in cases of grave need (*be-sha'at ha-deḥak*).[4] That advice is cogent if the concern is that the *eiruv* may not be properly constructed, as is indeed reflected in the statements of *Ḥazon Ish* and Rabbi Kanievski. However, if the concern is that raised by *Ḥafeẓ Ḥayyim,* the reasoning upon which the advice is predicated is invalid. *Ḥafeẓ Ḥayyim*'s consideration, which is by far the most serious concern in relying upon an *eiruv,* is that no *eiruv* encompassing a thoroughfare sixteen cubits wide can be valid because the area constitutes a public domain in biblical law. Hence the principle of *trei de-rabbanan* is not at all applicable.

Listening to a Radio on Shabbat

During the course of the Gulf war, Israelis were under constant threat of Scud attacks and in fear that the Iraqis might arm at least some missiles with chemical warheads. Despite anti-missile defenses, a total of

4. See, for example, *Pnei Yehoshu'a, Shabbat* 21a, s.v. *mihu.* For a survey of conflicting opinions regarding this principle see R. Mordecai Brisk, *Teshuvot Maharam Brisk,* I, no. 23.

thirty-nine Scud missiles bearing conventional warheads struck Israel during the war causing extensive property damage but, fortunately, relatively few casualties. The populace was admonished that each family should prepare one room in its dwelling as a shelter. The room was sealed in order to prevent gas from entering and stocked with food, water and other necessities so that the family could take refuge in the "sealed room" (*ha-ḥeder he-atum*) during the course of the alert. During the entire period of hostilities people remained glued to their radios, not simply to keep abreast of the progress of the war, but to learn of impending air raids and the need to take refuge in a "sealed room." Quite naturally, many were concerned with regard to whether or not they should allow their radios to remain on over *Shabbat.*

The issues are two-fold in nature. The first and most obvious question is of importance to Jews the world over, *viz.,* whether merely listening to a radio, or watching television, without turning the radio or television on or off or regulating the volume, involves any infraction of *Shabbat* laws. The second question arises primarily in Israel by virtue of the fact that the announcers, technicians and other personnel involved in broadcasting operations are themselves Jews. *Shulḥan Arukh, Oraḥ Ḥayyim* 318:1, records a provision of Jewish law forbidding a Jew to derive benefit during the entire Sabbath day from any prohibited labor performed by a fellow Jew. Broadcasting on *Shabbat,* as distinct from merely listening to the broadcast, is fraught with violations of *Shabbat* laws. Hence there arises the question of whether listening to a radio program that is the product of such violations constitutes a forbidden form of benefit.

The paradigm of a forbidden benefit, as presented both in the Gemara and by *Shulḥan Arukh,* is partaking of food that has been cooked on *Shabbat.* In that case the benefit is both tangible and sensual. The issue with regard to listening to the radio or watching television, as formulated by Rabbi Metzger, is that the Gemara, *Arakhin* 6a, declares that benefit derived from Temple property through "voice, sight and smell" does not entail the penalty prescribed for such an infraction. However, the Gemara, *Pesaḥim* 26a, declares that, although no punishment is incurred, the act is nevertheless forbidden.[5]

There are, however, two fundamental issues that are not raised by

5. See *Teshuvot Kol Eliyahu,* II, *Oraḥ Ḥayyim,* no. 23, who asserts that, according to Rambam, the prohibition is limited to benefit derived from consecrated property. Cf., however, the differing opinions regarding Rambam's position cited by R. Ovadiah Yosef, *Yabi'a Omer,* III, *Oraḥ Ḥayyim,* no. 20, sec. 11 and VI, no. 34, sec. 3.

Rabbi Metzger. First, the "benefit" derived from the "voice" of the radio or the "sight" of the television is not necessarily acoustic, visual or esthetic in nature. In the case of news programs, the "voice" or "sight" provides no pleasure or benefit; rather, it is the knowledge or information, itself innocuous in nature, that is of benefit. There is a long-standing dispute with regard to whether the prohibition against deriving benefit from a human corpse extends to deriving medical or scientific information by merely observing a post-mortem dissection of a cadaver. In that case as well, the benefit is intellectual rather than sensual. That material was discussed in an earlier volume of this series.[6] A second question that merits further analysis is whether the parameters of the prohibition against deriving benefit from Sabbath transgressions are the same as those pertaining to deriving benefit from items or materials designated as objects of *issurei hana'ah* in biblical law. In the latter instances, the objects in question acquire a certain ontological status with attendant prohibitions flowing therefrom. Insofar as Sabbath restrictions are concerned, the source of the prohibition is rabbinic and is perhaps personal in nature. Hence the categories of proscribed benefit are not necessarily coextensive. Conceivably, the definition of "benefit" insofar as *Shabbat* prohibitions are concerned may be broader or narrower than the definition of "benefit" for other purposes of Jewish law. Nevertheless, R. Zevi Pesach Frank, *Teshuvot Har Ẓevi, Oraḥ Ḥayyim,* I, no. 183, explicitly maintains that these prohibitions are essentially identical.[7]

This is apparently also the position of a number of authorities including *Mateh Mosheh,* no. 361; R. Aryeh Zevi Fromer, *Teshuvot Ereẓ Ẓevi,* no. 64; R. Abraham Dov Ber Reiner, *Teshuvot Bat Ayin, Oraḥ Ḥayyim,* no. 8; R. Mordecai Winkler, *Teshuvot Levushei Mordekhai,* III, *Oraḥ Ḥayyim,* no. 29 and IV, no. 34; R. Yitzchak Ya'akov Weisz, *Teshuvot Minḥat Yiẓḥak,* I, no. 107; and R. Ovadiah Yosef, *Or Torah,* Sivan 5729, *Halikhot,* Nisan 5731, and *Yabi'a Omer,* III, *Oraḥ Ḥayyim,* no. 20, sec. 11, and VI, *Oraḥ Ḥayyim,* no. 35; as well as the earlier-cited *Teshuvot Har Ẓevi* prohibit listening to the radio on *Shabbat* and the like as being comparable to partaking of food cooked on *Shabbat.* That position is based, in part, upon a statement of *Pri Megadim, Oraḥ Ḥayyim, Mishbeẓot Zahav* 276:5, in which that authority explicitly equates kindling a lamp to cooking

6. See *Contemporary Halakhic Problems,* II, 60–68. See also *supra,* pp. 227–230.

7. See also the discussion of R. Abraham Dov Ber Reiner, *Teshuvot Bat Ayin, Oraḥ Ḥayyim,* no. 64.

food. R. Chaim Biberfeld, *Menuḥah Nekhonah,* p. 62, also reports that *Ḥazon Ish,* who adamantly opposed use of electricity on *Shabbat* because of Sabbath desecration in generating plants in Israel, forbade listening to the radio for that reason as well as because of Sabbath violations involved in broadcasting on *Shabbat.* Rabbi Biberfeld's report of *Ḥazon Ish*'s ruling is cited and endorsed by R. Benjamin Silber, *Brit Olam* (Bnei Brak, 5724), in the section entitled "*Ha-Mekhabeh ve-ha-Ma'avir,*" no. 6.

Rabbi Frank does, however, advance a tentative distinction between making use of the illumination of a lamp kindled on the Sabbath and listening to a broadcast. The Mishnah, *Beiẓah* 39a, distinguishes between a glowing coal and a flame which is detached from its source of fuel and declares that no punishment is associated with deriving benefit from an "unattached" ephemeral flame. *Har Ẓevi* suggests that the sound emitted by a radio is similarly "unattached" and hence listening to the radio may not be forbidden. Nevertheless, *Har Ẓevi* concludes that the matter requires further study.[8]

Listening to a radio, even if it is turned on before *Shabbat* or caused to play by means of an automatic timer, may involve a transgression other

8. It should be noted that *Har Ẓevi* would readily concede that listening to a musical instrument would be forbidden if the musical rendition were to involve a forbidden form of labor on the grounds that the sound of the music is regarded as "attached" to the instrument. This is evident in the coupling of "voice" and "sight" in the dictum concerning benefit derived from consecrated property through "voice, sight and smell." See R. Joseph Cohen's annotations appended to *Teshuvot Har Ẓevi, Harerei be-Sadeh, loc. cit. Har Ẓevi* apparently entertains the notion that transmission of a human voice via the radio does not render it as being "attached" to the radio. However, if it is recognized that the sound emitted by the radio is not that of the human voice but an electronic simulation of the human voice, the halakhic status of that sound should logically be identical to that produced by a musical instrument. Cf., R. Zevi Pesach Frank, *Mikra'ei Kodesh, Hanukkah-Purim,* no. 11. In that work Rabbi Frank expresses doubt with regard to whether or not a voice amplified by a microphone or broadcast over the radio is to be regarded as a human voice for purposes of Jewish law. Strangely, Rabbi Frank seems to be of the opinion that, both in the case of a radio and in the case of a microphone, there is an admixture of a human and an artificial voice. This apparently contradicts the thrust of his comments in *Teshuvot Har Ẓevi* since, if the radio is regarded as producing any independent sound, that sound should be regarded as "attached" to the radio. Rabbi Frank may have assumed that, if there is an admixture of a natural human voice as well, the "benefit" derived is the result of two separate causes and since one of the causes involves no infraction the benefit is permitted on the basis of the principle of *zeh ve-zeh gorem.*

than that associated with derivation of benefit from proscribed forms of labor. *Shulḥan Arukh, Oraḥ Ḥayyim* 338:1, records the rabbinic decree forbidding the playing of any musical instrument on *Shabbat.* The underlying reason for this prohibition is the fear that the instrument may become defective with the result that the player, unmindful of the fact that correction of the defect on the Sabbath is improper, may be led to make the necessary repairs. In a gloss to that ruling, Rema makes it clear that the prohibition is not limited to playing a musical instrument but includes the use of any device designed to generate sound, e.g., a door-knocker. *Arukh ha-Shulḥan, Oraḥ Ḥayyim* 338:5, observes that, since the prohibition concerning playing an instrument is based upon a concern lest repairs be made on the *Shabbat* because music performed by a defective instrument is not esthetically pleasing, the prohibition applies with equal force to a person who performs an act before the onset of *Shabbat* which causes music to play on *Shabbat.*[9] R. Eliezer Waldenberg, *Ẓiẓ Eli'ezer,* VI, no. 16, chap. 3, cogently points out that *Arukh ha-Shulḥan*'s conclusion also applies to setting a timer before *Shabbat* so that the instrument will play on *Shabbat.* According to *Arukh ha-Shulḥan,* since a radio is clearly an apparatus designed to produce sound, turning on a radio before *Shabbat* in order to listen to a broadcast on *Shabbat* is forbidden.

Rabbi Waldenberg, *Ẓiẓ Eli'ezer,* III, no. 16, chap. 12, sec. 4,[10] argues that, according to *Arukh ha-Shulḥan,* the prohibition against "causing a sound to be heard" applies not only to the person who plays a musical instrument but to the person who listens to a broadcast or to an amplified voice as well. If setting an instrument in advance so that it will play of its own accord on *Shabbat* is forbidden because of the fear that the instrument

9. A similar view is expressed by R. Ben-Zion Uziel, *Mishpetei Uzi'el, Oraḥ Ḥayyim,* II, no. 52. *Mishpetei Uzi'el* further opines that there is an additional prohibition of *shema yateh,* i.e., a prohibition similar to reading by candelight or by the light of a lamp burning liquid fuel. That action is forbidden "lest he incline the lamp" and thereby increase the rate of combustion. That prohibition clearly devolves upon one who reads by the light of the lamp on *Shabbat,* not upon the person who kindles the lamp in advance. *Mishpetei Uzi'el* maintains that listening to the radio is forbidden for a similar reason. This line of reasoning finds no parallel in any other source. The rabbinic prohibition to which he refers is limited in scope and does not extend to encompass the possibility of extinguishing the fire. Merely moving or inclining a radio at an angle does not necessarily involve a biblical transgression. Cf., R. Shlomoh Zalman Auerbach, *Koveẓ Ma'amarim be-Inyanei Ḥashmal be-Shabbat* (Jerusalem, 5738), p. 45.

10. See also *Ẓiẓ Eli'ezer,* IX, no. 21; cf.. *Yabi'a Omer,* I, *Oraḥ Ḥayyim,* no. 20, sec. 14, and III, *Oraḥ Ḥayyim,* no. 29.

may be repaired or adjusted on the Sabbath it is only logical that the prohibition should devolve upon anyone listening to the instrument since not only the person who originally set the instrument, but any listener, is likely to undertake such repair.[11] It is, however, apparent that not all authorities accept *Arukh ha-Shulḥan*'s line of reasoning. R. Shalom Mordecai Schwadron, *Teshuvot Maharsham,* III, *Hashmatot* to vol. I, no. 44, and R. Abraham Steinberg, *Teshuvot Maḥazeh Avraham,* I, no. 42, s.v. *ve-hineh,* apparently regard the rabbinic edict as limited to acts actually performed on *Shabbat.*[12]

There are also other authorities who clearly maintain that the edict forbidding the creation of sound does not apply to the approximation of the human voice by means of electric current. R. Judah Leib Zirelson, *Teshuvot Aẓei ha-Levanon,* no. 10, in a responsum dealing with the permissibility of the use of the telephone on the Sabbath, lists a number of reasons prohibiting the use of this device. Enumerated among these are "giving birth" to an electric circuit, sparking and causing a bell to ring on the other end of the line. Since consideration is given only to the sound produced by the bell, while the question of production of the voice itself is ignored, it may be assumed that this authority did not view the voice produced by electric current as being included in the prohibition against "causing a sound to be heard." Similarly, R. Shlomoh Zalman Auerbach, *Sinai,* II Adar 5723, maintains that the prohibition against creating a "voice" or sound is limited to sounds produced by direct human action and does not include sounds indirectly produced by the human voice.[13] A similar position is adopted by *Teshuvot Maharshag,* II, no. 118, and *Ẓlaḥ he-Ḥadash, Kuntres Aḥaron,* no. 1.[14]

There is yet another reason cited by numerous authorities in forbidding the use of a radio on *Shabbat* and *Yom Tov*. Rema, *Oraḥ Ḥayyim* 252:5, states that it is forbidden to place wheat in a water mill prior to the Sabbath in order that the wheat may be ground during the Sabbath. This

11. See also R. Chizkiyahu Shabbetai Yashe, *Teshuvot Divrei Ḥizkiyahu* (Jerusalem, 5702), II, *Oraḥ Ḥayyim,* no. 4, p. 88.

12. See also R. Joshua Hirschhorn, *Ha-Pardes,* Adar 5713.

13. Rabbi Auerbach's article, "*Mikrofon, Telefon ve-Ramkol,*" is reprinted in his *Koveẓ Ma'amarim be-Inyanei Ḥashmal be-Shabbat* (Jerusalem, 5738), pp. 35–58.

14. See also *Teshuvot Sha'arei De'ah,* no. 194 cited in *Kaf ha-Ḥayyim, Oraḥ Ḥayyim* 338:27; R. Ya'akov Mosheh Toledano, *Teshuvot Yam ha-Gadol,* no. 26; R. Simchah Levy, *Ha-Pardes,* Iyar 5712; R. Menachem Poliakov, *Ha-Darom,* Nisan 5718; and R. Shlomoh Goren, *Maḥanayim,* 26 Iyar 5718.

is forbidden even though it is publicly known that the grain was placed therein prior to the Sabbath and that the grinding of the wheat takes place automatically. This activity is rabbinically forbidden despite the absence of human labor because *avsha milta* ("the thing grows loud"). The accompanying noise draws attention to the activity taking place, thereby degrading the Sabbath since passersby may believe that the sounds emanating from the mill signal the performance of acts forbidden on *Shabbat.* The prohibition of *avsha milta* is limited to activities accompanied by sound but encompasses all activities forbidden on *Shabbat* when accompanied by a significant level of sound even if the sound is not the result of any act performed on *Shabbat* itself. Rabbi Auerbach forbids a radio to be turned on before *Shabbat* or to be regulated by means of a time clock for the same reason even if it is well-known that all acts of labor were performed before *Shabbat.* Thus, Rabbi Auerbach rules that such devices may not be permitted to operate on *Shabbat* even if it be publicized that the radio or microphone is operated automatically.[15] The consideration of *avsha milta* applies to all amplification systems, even to those which cannot possibly be adjusted or repaired on the Sabbath.[16]

Rabbi Eliezer Waldenberg is the author of a detailed analysis of the halakhic issues associated with radio transmission as well as with listening to the radio on *Shabbat.* That study, published in *Ẓiẓ Eli'ezer,* III, no. 16, was undertaken in 1948 during the War of Independence. During that period the populace felt a similar need to keep abreast of information regarding the progress of hostilities. Rabbi Waldenberg rules that, under those circumstances, radios may be allowed to play over the course of *Shabbat.* However, in chap. 12, sec. 8, he advises that when such activity is permitted a label bearing the words "*Shabbat Kodesh*" be pasted over the knobs of the radio in order that the listener not tune the radio or

15. See also R. Yitzchak Ya'akov Weisz, *Teshuvot Minḥat Yiẓḥak,* I, no. 107 and II, no. 38. Other writers who cite this reason in ruling against the use of microphones include *Yabi'a Omer,* I, no. 20, sec. 12; *Ẓiẓ Eli'ezer,* III, no. 16, chap. 12, sec. 7, and IV, no. 26; R. Yisachar Dov Bergman, *Ha-Pardes,* Kislev 5712; and R. Moshe Stern, *Be'er Mosheh,* VI, *Kuntres Elektrik,* no. 16.

16. Rabbi Auerbach advances other considerations as well. R. Ezekiel Landau, *Noda bi-Yehudah,* II, *Oraḥ Ḥayyim,* no. 30, writes that a parasol opened before the Sabbath may not be used on the Sabbath because the beholder has no way of knowing that the parasol has not been opened on the Sabbath. Rabbi Auerbach argues that the same line of reasoning may be applied to the use of amplification systems since most individuals are not scholars and will not understand the technical differences between a microphone and other electrical appliances and hence may easily be led to biblical transgressions.

adjust the volume unmindfully.[17] He further advises that a sign be affixed to the outside of the dwelling announcing that the radio has been left on from before *Shabbat* or that it is being operated by means of an automatic timer and that, if possible, individuals not listen to the radio singly but in groups of two or more in order that they may caution one another regarding unwitting *Shabbat* violations. Those recommendations, while reflecting wise counsel, do not appear to constitute normative provisions of Halakhah.[18]

The foregoing considerations obviously do not apply in situations involving a threat to human life. During the Gulf war the threat was real and constant. Under such circumstances, listening to the radio constituted a necessary means of preserving life requiring only that Sabbath restrictions be suspended only to the extent necessary to cope with the danger. To their credit, the broadcasting authorities exhibited sensitivity to the scruples of observant citizens by limiting the extent of necessary infractions. During the Gulf war both *Kol Yisra'el* and the Israeli Armed Forces radio station arranged for a "silent band" (*gal shotek*) that broadcast only security bulletins on *Shabbat* but was otherwise silent. The broadcast of such bulletins under those circumstances was, of course, entirely permissible. Listeners had only to tune their radio to that frequency on Friday and allow the knob to remain on an "on" position. Rabbi Metzger reports that the armed forces station went a step further and arranged for its transmitter to remain open over the entire period of the Sabbath, thereby even further diminishing *Shabbat* infractions in broadcasting security bulletins. Accordingly, tuning the radio to that station was regarded as preferable to listening to *Kol Yisra'el* whose broadcasts entailed more serious *Shabbat* violations.

Teachers' Claim for Lost Wages

Due to unsettled conditions during the period of the Gulf war and the constant threat of missile attacks many parents of young children chose to keep their children at home in order to be able to supervise them during air raids. As a result a number of private kindergartens and nursery

17. See also R. Nachum Rabinovitch, *Ha-Darom,* no. 15 (Nisan 5722).

18. For additional sources and references to material dealing with other ramifications of the issues involved see *Ha-Ḥashmal be-Halakhah,* a bibliographical compilation published by the Institute for Science and Halacha (Jerusalem, 5791), II, 268–281.

schools suspended operations until the cessation of hostilities. The question then arose with regard to whether or not the kindergarten or nursery teacher is entitled to be paid his or her usual salary for the period that no children were in attendance. A closely related question is whether parents are obligated to pay tuition fees for periods during which their children are ill. Provisions regarding payment of tuition fees during the absence of a child due to illness are recorded by Rema, *Ḥoshen Mishpat* 334:4. Rema rules that the parent is not obligated to pay the teacher's wages in full unless the child is chronically prone to illness and the teacher (or school) was not aware of that fact at the time that the agreement was made. Accordingly, it would appear that there is no liability for tuition payment, and hence no claim on the part of the teacher, during the period in which children were not sent to school because of concern for their safety arising from unanticipated circumstances. However, Rema, *Ḥoshen Mishpat* 321:1, distinguishes between situations that disrupt the studies of an individual student and ones which disrupt the entire community. Rema rules that in the latter case the teacher is entitled to his usual compensation. Thus, Rema declares that if "the ruler decrees that the teacher shall not teach" the teacher is to be paid in full because the "affliction" is that of the entire community. Since the fear for the safety of the students during times of unrest is not limited to some individual situations but is general in nature it would then follow that the teachers must be paid when classes are suspended because of hostilities.

Although Rema's ruling regarding payment of tuition fees during the period in which study is prohibited by decree of the government is accepted by *Shakh, Ḥoshen Mishpat* 321:1, that ruling is disputed by *Sema, Ḥoshen Mishpat* 321:6. *Sema* argues that the unanticipated illness of a student is the "misfortune" of the teacher, i.e., since the student is not at fault and has not received the benefit of instruction, insofar as compensation is concerned, the teacher's loss of the opportunity to provide his services is the result of his "bad luck" and, therefore, the teacher has no claim for compensation. However, reasons *Sema,* since the edict described by Rema banning teaching of Torah was directed against the teacher as well as against the pupil, the situation must be attributed to the "bad luck" of both. Accordingly, *Sema* rules that the loss should be apportioned equally, i.e., the teacher may claim half of his stipulated fee. *Taz, Ḥoshen Mishpat* 321:1 and 334:1, and most later authorities rule in accordance with Rema.

A national emergency such as the Persian Gulf war is certainly a situation which is attributable equally to the "bad luck" of the teacher and students. Hence, according to *Sema,* the loss should be shared equally with the result that the kindergarten teacher would be entitled to half her wages. However, according to Rema, since the emergency was communal rather than personal in nature and since the teacher was not prevented from appearing in class because of concern for her own safety, it would seem that she is entitled to full remuneration.

However, *Netivot ha-Mishpat* 334:1 notes a contradiction in Rema's own rulings. Rema, *Ḥoshen Mishpat* 334:1, rules that if students are forced to flee because of a "change in the air," i.e., because of pollution or a disturbance in the climate, the loss of income must be borne by the teacher. *Netivot ha-Mishpat* points out that a "change in the air" affects the entire community and hence, according to Rema's own position, it would be logical to conclude, contrary to Rema 344:1, that the teacher's wages should be paid in full.

It should be noted that *Shakh, Ḥoshen Mishpat* 334:3, explains that in a situation in which the majority of the population feels it necessary to evacuate the city because of pollution of the air or a change in climate Rema agrees that the teacher must be compensated in full. *Shakh* understands Rema's ruling indicating that the loss must be assumed by the teacher as being limited to situations in which only a minority of the populace finds it necessary to flee. R. Shlomoh Kluger, *Ḥokhmat Shlomoh, Ḥoshen Mishpat* 321:1, resolves the contradiction by asserting that Rema's ruling with regard to a communal misfortune is limited to situations in which the teacher is willing and able to continue to provide his services. *Ḥokhmat Shlomoh* understands Rema's ruling extinguishing the obligation toward the teacher because of a "change in the air" as applying only in a situation in which the teacher is also forced to flee and hence is no longer capable of discharging his duties.

Netivot ha-Mishpat, however, understands Rema in a completely different manner. According to *Netivot ha-Mishpat,* Rema's ruling regarding continued payment of the teacher in face of a governmental decree prohibiting the teaching of Torah is not based upon the concept of a distinction between a private versus a communal misfortune. Rather, it is based upon the consideration that, since it is forbidden to accept compensation for the teaching of Torah, a teacher of Torah is not paid for his services as an instructor but for monitoring the conduct of his pupils. In prohibiting the teaching of Torah, the despot has no interest in curtailing other activities. Hence, in that situation, the teacher remains willing and able to provide the services for which he is entitled to compensation, i.e., baby-sitting or its equivalent. It is the parent who does not wish to avail himself of such services unless they are accompanied by teaching services as well. Hence, since the parent voluntarily declines the services for which he has contracted to pay, he remains liable for payment.

Rabbi Metzger assumes that, under the prevailing circumstances, the kindergarten teacher was incapable of providing for the safety and security of the children and that hence, according to *Netivot ha-Mishpat*'s understanding of Rema, there is no obligation to pay her salary. That, of course, would depend upon the circumstances. It is quite conceivable that a school might have arranged for a "sealed room" to accommodate its students but that the parents, because of their own disquiet and nervousness, preferred to keep their children at their side. Assuming that the teacher was prepared to provide all possible care, the conclusion would be quite different.

Orḥot Mishpat 7:10 cites a ruling of *Ḥatam Sofer* with regard to a similar occurrence in his day. *Ḥatam Sofer* describes a situation in which both teachers and students were unable to continue their usual activities because of the outbreak of war. *Ḥatam Sofer* reports that he paid the tuition for his own children in full. However, with regard to the community he records that, despite the fact that the misfortune was communal in nature and hence the normative ruling should be in accordance with Rema who maintains that the loss must be sustained by the parents, he nevertheless opined that "it is difficult to exact money" and therefore he issued a compromise ruling obligating the parents to pay half of the usual fees.

The most obvious explanation of *Ḥatam Sofer*'s ruling is that, in monetary matters, the defendant may claim to rely upon even a minority view and that hence "it is difficult to exact money" in light of *Sema*'s position that, under such circumstances, the parents are liable to only fifty percent of the usual compensation. Rabbi Metzger, however, assumes that *Ḥatam Sofer*'s compromise was to pay the teacher the wages of a *po'el batel,* i.e., the amount a laborer would ordinarily be willing to accept as compensation were he to be relieved of his duties. *Taz, Ḥoshen Mishpat* 333:1, assesses that compensation as being equal to fifty percent of the laborer's usual wage.

Caterers' Claim for Cancellation of Wedding

Life for Israelis continued more or less as normal during the Gulf war.

Marriages were celebrated with the usual festivities and if air raids occurred during the festivities guests presumably sought shelter in a "sealed room." One aspect of the economy, however, was totally disrupted. Tourism came to a virtual standstill and trips to Israel planned for other reasons were cancelled. In at least one case a wedding was postponed because one of the celebrants was a national of a foreign country and his family declined to travel to the wedding. The services of a catering establishment had been engaged for the occasion and were cancelled at a late date. Since the caterer was no longer able to secure another booking for the day of the scheduled wedding he demanded compensation for expenses and lost profits. The agreement between the parties apparently contained no provision for a penalty in the event of cancellation. The actionability of a penalty clause would require analysis in light of the halakhic provisions governing *asmakhta,* i.e., obligations not entered into with the requisite seriousness of intent. The proprietor of the catering establishment apparently sought payment, not on the basis of a contractual undertaking, but on the basis of tort liability, i.e., as restitution for damages sustained as the result of a harm caused by the other party.

It is difficult to find grounds on which the contracting party would be liable in tort since, according to the provisions of Jewish law, tort liability is generally limited to damages directly sustained. Indirect losses or consequential damages, including loss of profits, are usually not actionable. Rabbi Metzger adduces an interesting source that would serve, at least under some circumstances, to allow for recovery of necessary expenses involved in the maintenance of a business. *Teshuvot Shevut Ya'akov,* no. 178, discusses a situation in which a person was found to be liable for damages sustained by an animal in an accident. There is a dispute among early authorities with regard to whether a tortfeasor is liable for the "lost wages" (*shevet*) of an animal, i.e., whether he must compensate the owner for the profit that the animal would have earned for him as a beast of burden or the like. However, *Shevut Ya'akov* rules that, in addition to compensation for any diminution in the value of the animal, the tortfeasor, according to all authorities, is liable for the cost of the animal's food during its recuperation. *Shevut Ya'akov* regards expenses incurred for the upkeep of an animal during its incapacitation to be a direct rather than an indirect result of the tortfeasor's act. Accordingly, it would follow that expenses incurred in the maintenance of income-producing property, such as property taxes, wages of security guards and the like, can be charged against an arsonist, for example, during the period that the property cannot produce revenue for its owner.

It does not, however, necessarily follow that a person who cancels a wedding reception or the like incurs similar liability. In general, Halakhah recognizes tort liability only when damages result from an overt act. Nonfeasance or refraining from an act which results in monetary loss is, in general, not actionable.

Some authorities recognize an exception to that rule in the case of a person who deprives another individual of the opportunity of utilizing his property or funds (*mevatel kiso shel ḥaveiro*). Mordekhai, *Baba Kamma,* no. 125, rules that a person who denies another person access to the latter's funds is liable for lost profits if that person was wont to use such funds as income-producing capital. Similarly, Rema, *Ḥoshen Mishpat* 292:7, rules that a bailor who demands the return of bailed funds so that he may engage in commercial activity may recover lost profits from the bailee if the latter does not heed his demand. It is arguable that, according to those authorities, the proprietor of the catering hall may claim that failure of the customer to cancel in a timely manner effectively precluded him from renting his premises to another customer. Presumably, it would be necessary for the owner of the catering hall to demonstrate that other customers were indeed available to rent his premises.

This position is, however, by no means universally accepted. *Yam shel Shlomoh, Baba Kamma* 9:30, followed by *Shakh, Ḥoshen Mishpat* 92:15,[19] maintains that even when loss of profit can be demonstrated beyond cavil there is no liability for such damages because the loss is indirect. That position is reflected in the comments of *Nimukei Yosef, Baba Meẓi'a* 104b, who rules that a sharecropper is not liable for failing to engage in agricultural activity upon land that has been entrusted to him.

As Rabbi Metzger observes, in light of conflicting authority of this nature, a *Bet Din* could not intervene either on behalf of the plaintiff or on behalf of the defendant since the party in possession can plead that the claimant must adduce positive proof of the actionability of his claim. Thus, the caterer would not be able to recover his lost profits. However, if he received a deposit or advance payment to cover a portion of the cost of the wedding, the *Bet Din* could not order him to return such funds to the customer provided the sum received by him is not greater than his claimed foregone profits. Under such circumstances, the burden of proof is transferred to the person seeking to recover his deposit and can be satisfied only by positive proof that he is entitled to such recovery.

19. See also *Shakh, Ḥoshen Mishpat* 61:10.

The situation would be entirely different if the parties had entered into a contract explicitly providing for payment in the event of cancellation. *Sema, Ḥoshen Mishpat* 61:12, and *Shakh, Ḥoshen Mishpat* 61:10, rule that an agreement to indemnify against actual loss does not constitute a non-actionable penalty or *asmakhta,* provided that the expenses incurred are usual and reasonable. *Arukh ha-Shulḥan, Ḥoshen Mishpat* 61:11, states that an agreement to compensate for lost profits is also enforceable provided that the profits for which compensation is sought are in the nature of profits derived from an enterprise from which the plaintiff customarily earns his livelihood.

Chapter XV

Miscellaneous Questions

If a halakhah eludes you, go and inquire in the House of Study.
YEVAMOT 76b

Fasting During Pregnancy

In recent years a significant number of obstetricians have been routinely advising their pregnant patients not to fast on any fast day, including *Yom Kippur.*[1] This advice is reflected in at least one contemporary rabbinic source. R. Yisra'el Fisher, a member of the *Bet Din* of the *Edah ha-Ḥaredit,* in note 11 appended to his letter of approbation to R. Baruch Goldberg's *Pnei Barukh: Bikkur Ḥolim ke-Hilkhato* (Jerusalem, 5745), writes, "In this day in [which] the generations have become weak and tens of women miscarry because of fasting, all pregnant women other than in the ninth month should eat less than the amount [for which punishment is incurred] on *Yom Kippur.*" It is clear that, heretofore, Halakhah, as recorded both in *Pesaḥim* 54b and *Shulḥan Arukh, Oraḥ Ḥayyim* 617:1, assumed that, in the absence of unusual circumstances, fasting poses no danger either to the fetus or to the pregnant mother who is otherwise in good health. Rabbi Fisher predicates his remarks upon a presumption that a process of general physical deterioration has occurred over the ages.

R. Moshe Sternbuch, presently deputy head of the *Bet Din* of the *Edah ha-Ḥaredit,* writing in *Oraita,* no. 16 (Elul 5748), p. 177, does not quote

1. The obligation to fast on *Yom Kippur* is suspended only in face of possible danger to life. The obligation of pregnant women with regard to other fast days is a matter of dispute. *Shulḥan Arukh, Oraḥ Ḥayyim,* 554:5, rules that they are obligated to fast on *Tishah be-Av* but are exempt from other fasts. Rema, *Oraḥ Ḥayyim* 550:1, records that they are obligated to fast on all fast days by virtue of custom unless they experience "great discomfort (*mizta'arot harbeh*). *Mishnah Berurah* 550:5 rules that "if they are weak" they need not fast.

Rabbi Fisher by name but cites an anonymous rabbi who permits "every pregnant woman" to eat on *Yom Kippur* upon experiencing even "slight weakness." Rabbi Sternbuch takes issue with that position in arguing that, since pregnancy in itself is not sufficient reason for breaking the fast, the expectant mother must fast unless she "experiences a particular weakness that can cause her complications." In medical literature the only mention of any possible untoward effect of fasting upon otherwise healthy pregnant women is with regard to women in the final days of gestation.[2] Hence Rabbi Fisher's comments are all the more remarkable since he finds no problem with regard to fasting in the ninth month. Doctors Michael Kaplan, Arthur Eidelman and Yeshaya Aboulafia, "Fasting and the Precipitation of Labor: The *Yom Kippur* Effect," *Journal of the American Medical Association,* vol. 250, no. 10 (September 9, 1983), pp. 1317–1318, report a significant increase in spontaneous term deliveries in Jerusalem's Shaare Zedek Hospital during the 24-hour period following termination of the fast in the years 1981 and 1982. There was no increase, and indeed a slight decrease, in premature births during those 24-hour periods. A less carefully thought-out survey of Jewish birth statistics by Ayalah Cohen, *Ha-Refu'ah,* vol. 102, no. 7, (April 1, 1982), pp. 306–307, showed similar findings for the general Jewish populace in 1975, 1978 and 1979. The authors of the Shaare Zedek study frankly admit that they cannot explain this phenomenon. They speculate that since total abstinence from food and liquid does lead to a substantial rise in blood viscosity, the resultant hyperviscosity may, in turn, decrease uterine blood flow and stimulate contraction.

Since the "*Yom Kippur* effect" hastens delivery only in women near term who would otherwise give birth in a matter of days at most, the authors conclude that "at present we do not recommend that pregnant

---

2. There have been no comprehensive studies regarding the effects of a day-long fast upon an otherwise healthy pregnant woman with no history of medical abnormalities. However, the report of one study of the effects of 12-and 18-hour fasts upon pregnant women indicates that somewhat elevated levels of ketoacids and urinary ketones were observed, especially during the second half of pregnancy. See Boyd E. Metzger, Rita Vileisis, Veronica Ravnikar and Norbert Freinkel, "'Accelerated Starvation' and the Skipped Breakfast in Late Normal Pregnancy," *Lancet,* March 13, 1982, I, 585–592. Although the authors indicate that "it has not been established" that those phenomena "are completely innocuous in the fetus" and that "this finding may be relevant to the controversial evidence that increased ketonaemia during pregnancy . . . may be followed by impaired intellectual development of the offspring" they fail to report any evidence of harm to the fetus.

Jewish women refrain from fasting on *Yom Kippur.*" They do, however, caution that there may be additional risk for "mothers with a tendency toward early delivery."

Halakhah adopts a far less sanguine view of parturition than does modern medicine. Jewish law perceives labor and the ensuing birth to be inherently dangerous and thus would presumably sanction suspension of halakhic strictures in order to prevent even minimal unnatural preponement of delivery.[3] Nevertheless, Rabbi Sternbuch's halakhic conclusion seems to be entirely correct.[4] Pregnant women have fasted from time immemorial with the result that the practice is regarded as entirely normal and natural. Since medical science also finds no danger in the practice, the principle "The Lord preserves the simple" appears to be entirely applicable. That principle reflects the truism that all human activity is accompanied by a measure of danger but that Halakhah takes no cognizance of danger below a certain threshold level. Hence "dangers" that are neither popularly nor scientifically perceived as such do not serve as a basis for setting aside religious obligations. In such matters one must rely upon divine providence and place one's trust in God who preserves the "simple" who do not seek to contravene His decrees. For the same reason, although fasting near term may hasten parturition by a day or two, since no medically recognized danger is entailed and there is no popularly perceived connection between these phenomena, the principle "The Lord preserves the simple" is applicable.

However, the concern voiced by the Shaare Zedek physicians regarding mothers with a tendency toward early delivery is well placed and would be cogent even in the absence of the findings of the Shaare Zedek study.

3. See Rosh and Ran, *Yoma* 82a, as well as *Teshuvot Bet Shlomoh, Ḥoshen Mishpat,* no. 120.

4. His reasoning, however, is problematic. Rabbi Sternbuch argues that interruption of the fast may be sanctioned for reasons of *pikuaḥ nefesh* only if some unusual phenomenon or identifiable cause of danger is already present and argues that it was this consideration that led the *Bet Din* of Vilna to dispute the position of R. Israel Salanter during the cholera epidemic of 1848 and was the basis of their refusal to grant blanket dispensation to break the fast. That analysis of the controversy as well as the conclusion to be derived therefrom is contradicted by Rabbi Sternbuch himself in his *Mo'adim u-Zemanim,* II, no. 140. See also *supra,* chap. 6, p. 142, note 32. There is ample support in the writings of contemporary decisors for the position that statistically significant evidence of the likelihood of future danger constitutes sufficient warrant for disregarding halakhic strictures for reasons of *pikuaḥ nefesh.* See, for example, R. Joshua Neuwirth, *Shemirat Shabbat ke-Hilkhatah,* 2nd edition (Jerusalem, 5739), I, 40:68–69.

Previous preterm delivery is itself an indication of a predisposition to preterm labor and delivery. It is well-established that a woman who previously gave birth remote from term has an increased likelihood of doing so again even in the absence of another identifiable predisposing factor.[5] A woman who experiences preterm labor in her first pregnancy has a 15% chance of a preterm birth in her second pregnancy. Curiously, if the first preterm labor is preceded by a term birth the danger of preterm birth in the third pregnancy rises to 24%. The probability of preterm birth following two such previous occurrences is 32%.[6] Dehydration results in reduced blood volume and studies indicate that reduced plasma volume is associated with preterm labor in the majority of cases. Conversely, approximately one half of women in preterm labor will respond to bed rest and hydration, i.e., therapies designed to increase plasma volume.[7] Accordingly, a woman at risk for preterm labor is well-advised to take precautions in preventing hypovolemia and should consult both her obstetrician and a competent rabbinic authority with regard to the need for, as well as the mode of, drinking on *Yom Kippur*. Although intake of fluids is a necessary precaution in order to prevent a deficit in blood plasma volume, consumption of solid foods is not necessary for that purpose.[8]

It should be added that any pregnant woman who finds herself in a state of dehydration should immediately rehydrate herself by drinking large quantities of liquid as quickly as possible. The danger to the mother

---

5. See F. Gary Cunningham, Paul C. MacDonald and Norman F. Grant, *Williams Obstetrics,* 18th edition (Norwalk, 1989), pp. 748 and 753.

6. See *Williams Obstetrics,* p. 953.

7. See Denise M. Main, "Epidemiology of Preterm Birth," *Clinical Obstetrics and Gynecology,* vol. 31, no. 3 (September, 1988), pp. 529–530 and R.C. Goodlin, M.A. Quaife and J.W. Dirksen, "The Significance, Diagnosis and Treatment of Maternal Hypovolemia as Associated with Fetal/Maternal Illness," *Seminars in Perinatology,* V (1988), 164.

8. Cf., R. Baruch Goldberg, *Pnei Barukh; Bikkur Ḥolim ke-Hilkhato* 4:13, who advises any woman who has previously suffered two miscarriages to partake of food in quantities smaller than for which punishment is incurred. There is no medical evidence that abstinence from solid food or caloric intake over a twenty-five or twenty-six hour period will, in and of itself, precipitate either a miscarriage or preterm labor. Of course, a competent physician should be consulted in every individual instance since there are conditions in which abstinence from food can result in ketosis which is a life-threatening condition. It should be noted that, when drinking of liquids is indicated by virtue of a history of preterm labor or for any other reason, there is no halakhic reason why the liquid should not be in the form of fruit juice or milk rather than water.

represented by dehydration is greater the closer the mother is to term. Dehydration poses a risk not only because it may cause the onset of labor but also because giving birth while dehydrated constitutes an additional and even more significant danger since the resultant decrease in blood volume may cause the patient to go into shock with relatively minimal postpartum bleeding.[9] Dehydration during labor also leads to decelerative patterns in the fetal heart tones, maternal exhaustion and ineffective voluntary effort on the part of the mother in assisting in the birth process.[10] The pregnant woman should be informed of the symptoms of dehydration which include postural hypotension in the sitting or standing position, decreased skin turgor, excessive dryness of oral mucous membranes, severe thirst, decreased axillary sweating and unusual lethargy or weakness.

A woman concerned about possible dehydration during the course of the fast may take a number of precautions to prevent that condition from occurring. Drinking liquids before the fast in quantities larger than usual is of some, albeit limited, value. Reduced exertion and avoidance of heat will conserve body fluids. Spending the day in an air-conditioned environment, particularly during hot weather, is probably the most effective precaution available.

One cautionary note must be added with regard to the problem of dehydration in general. In hot, arid climates, rapid dehydration may cause serious adverse effects before the usual symptoms become manifest. This "desert climate" is also characteristic of Jerusalem during some seasons. Individuals for whom the risk of dehydration constitutes a particular health hazard should be advised to consult a physician and a rabbinic authority.

Dating the Ketubah

During the summer months wedding ceremonies frequently take place at an hour after sunset but before nightfall. The *ketubah* is perforce written and signed before the ceremony. Predated instruments, however, are invalid in Jewish law. The concern regarding predated instruments is that since they serve to establish a lien against property alienated subsequent to the execution of the instrument, a predated document may be used to

9. See J. Robert Wilson and Elsie Reid Carrington, *Obstetrics and Gynecology,* 8th edition (St. Louis, 1987), p. 450.

10. See Martin L. Pernoll and Ralph C. Benson, *Current Obstetric & Gynecologic Diagnosis & Treatment,* 6th edition (Los Altos, 1987), p. 488.

seize property from a purchaser who, in reality, holds unencumbered title. Since predated instruments are invalid in Jewish law and since the obligations recited in the *ketubah* become binding only upon marriage, under these circumstances, the propriety of dating the *ketubah* on the day of its execution has been questioned. A *ketubah* dated the day prior to the actual marriage is, in effect, a predated instrument.

A number of articles devoted to dating the *ketubah* were analyzed in *Contemporary Halakhic Problems,* II, 88–91. The authors of those articles made the simple point that the groom may quite properly bind himself to the financial obligations of the *ketubah* even prior to his marriage. The obligation is, quite understandably, conditioned upon the solemnization of the marriage as indicated by the text of the *ketubah* itself, but subsequent to the marriage all financial obligations become binding retroactively. Although the *ketubah* serves to establish a lien on all the groom's property for satisfaction of the obligations spelled out in that document, any purchaser of property subsequent to the actual signing of the *ketubah* is on notice and assumes title subject to the conditional lien established by the *ketubah* even though the marriage has not yet been solemnized.

This view is sharply challenged by R. Moses Feinstein, *Dibberot Mosheh, Baba Meẓi'a,* I, no. 20, secs. 53 and 54, as well as in *Iggerot Mosheh, Even ha-Ezer,* IV, no. 100, sec. 5. Rabbi Feinstein bases his position upon the comments of *Tosafot, Baba Meẓi'a* 7b. The Gemara states that if a *ketubah* is lost, the finder may return it to the wife provided that the husband acknowledges that it is a valid instrument. *Tosafot* suggest the possibility that the document may be invalid by reason of having been executed prior to the wedding ceremony and hence question the propriety of returning it to the wife lest it be unlawfully used to seize property from a bona fide purchaser who has acquired unencumbered title. *Tosafot* respond by declaring that there is no reason for such concern because the basic obligation of the *ketubah* becomes binding upon the groom from the time of betrothal. Hence the document is not invalid by virtue of predating. It is, however, entirely possible that the *ketubah* was executed even prior to betrothal. That possibility is peremptorily dismissed by *Tosafot* with the comment that "there is no reason to suspect" that the husband drafted the document at so early a time. Rabbi Feinstein cogently infers that *Tosafot* means to say that, were the *ketubah* indeed to have been executed prior to betrothal of the couple, it would be invalid by virtue of being a predated instrument.

The argument, however, is by no means as conclusive as it may appear.

Tosafot, following the already cited comments, immediately proceed to question the validity of the instrument as a means of seizing property in order to satisfy the obligations assumed by the groom in addition to the statutory minimum (*tosefet ketubah*). Such obligations are clearly not imposed by statute; accordingly, the document should be invalid insofar as the additional *ketubah* is concerned. In answer to that question, *Tosafot* invoke the principle "Witnesses, by virtue of their signature, acquire on his [or her] behalf" (*edav be-ḥatumav zokhin leih*), i.e., an obligation may be voluntarily assumed by means of written instrument, and since it is secured by bill, the attestation of the witnesses constitutes notice to subsequent purchasers. *Tosafot,* in formulating that principle, may well be understood as resolving, not only the problem of *tosefet ketubah,* but also as resolving the previous question regarding the basic statutory obligation of the *ketubah.* Having formulated the principle of *edav be-ḥatumav zokhin leih, Tosafot* may be understood as accepting the validity of a *ketubah* executed even before betrothal.

Rabbi Feinstein's position is unequivocally contradicted by the comments of one eminent latter-day authority. *Teshuvot Bet Ya'akov,* no. 133, cites the comments of *Tosafot, Baba Meẓi'a* 17a, in demonstrating a position diametrically opposed to that of Rabbi Feinstein.[11] The Gemara states that the *ketubah* may be returned to the wife provided that the husband acknowledges its validity. *Tosafot* indicate that, should the husband contend that the debt represented by the *ketubah* has already been satisfied, the instrument may not be returned to the wife. On its surface, such a position seems to flout the rule that, without substantiating evidence, a husband has no credibility in pleading that he has satisfied the statutory obligation of the *ketubah. Tosafot,* however, declare that the plea of prior payment is accepted only because the husband has available to himself an alternative pleading, *viz.,* he might have denied that the woman in question was his wife. The principle invoked is that of *migo,* i.e., a litigant is granted credibility with regard to a plea actually advanced even though that plea may be defective if he could have advanced another plea which would have been given credence. This principle serves to assign to the litigant the advantages of alternative pleadings which have not been advanced. Obviously, the plea "You are not my wife" would be given

11. This is also the position of *Teshuvot Kokhav me-Ya'akov,* no. 196. See also R. Samuel Eliezer Stern, *Seder Ketubah ke-Hilkhatah* (Bnei Brak, 5753), pp. 20 and 79, who reports that R. Samuel ha-Levi Woszner also ruled that the *ketubah* may be executed and dated on the day preceding the marriage ceremony. See also Rabbi Stern's comments, *ibid.,* pp. 78f.

credence only in a situation in which there exists no independent evidence establishing an existing matrimonial relationship. But, queries *Teshuvot Bet Ya'akov,* there is an obvious problem: the fact that the *ketubah* exists is itself clear and unequivocal testimony to the existence of a marital relationship. If the *ketubah* does serve *ipso facto* to establish the existence of a matrimonial relationship, then the husband's plea to the contrary—and hence his plea that the *ketubah* has already been satisfied—should be denied. The explanation must be, argues *Teshuvot Bet Ya'akov,* that although it is unusual to execute a *ketubah* prior to betrothal, nevertheless, it is perfectly possible for a prospective groom to do so. Since a groom may execute a *ketubah* prior to betrothal, the existence of such a document does not, in and of itself, establish the existence of a marital relationship. It is nevertheless clear that when the husband acknowledges the validity of that instrument it is to be returned to the wife. Quite apparently, concludes *Bet Ya'akov,* a *ketubah* drafted and dated prior to betrothal must be entirely valid; otherwise, it could not be returned to the wife in order to enable her to collect thereupon. The comments of *Tosafot* serve to establish the point that, without substantiating evidence, a husband has no credibility to plead that he has satisfied the statutory obligations of the *ketubah* in situations in which there is independent evidence that a marriage has taken place.

It should also be pointed out that, although Rabbi Feinstein endeavors to interpret the comments of this authority in a manner compatible with his own thesis, the statement of Rivash cited in *Ḥelkat Meḥokek, Ḥoshen Mishpat* 55:19, and in *Bet Shmu'el, Ḥoshen Mishpat* 55:13, certainly bears out the position of *Teshuvot Bet Ya'akov* and supports the view that a groom may voluntarily assume the obligations of the *ketubah* even prior to betrothal.

Hetter Iska: Student Loans, Margin Accounts, Purchase-Money Mortgages, etc.

A discussion of the prohibition concerning interest-taking and the method of converting such loans into joint ventures through execution of a *hetter iska* was presented in *Contemporary Halakhic Problems,* II, 376–396. The *hetter iska* agreement provides that the funds advanced are to be invested in a joint venture with profits and losses to be shared equally. A further stipulation provides that a certain sum computed as a percent per annum of the funds advanced will be accepted in accord and satisfaction of all profits realized in the venture. A claim that no profit has been realized must be substantiated by a solemn oath to that effect with the provision that the recipient of the funds may pay the stipulated amount in lieu of an oath.

As was noted in that discussion, a problem exists in situations in which the person advancing the funds has personal knowledge of failure to realize a profit. It has been contended that, in such circumstances, the stipulated oath serves no purpose and hence is forbidden as a vain oath. This problem typically arises with regard to purchase-money mortgages in which no money changes hands and hence, in the absence of an appreciation in the value of the property itself, there is no possibility of profit. A solution to that problem may be found by either restructuring the transaction as a leasehold agreement with title passing upon expiration of the leasehold or as an agreement for the periodic transfer of partial interest in the property commensurate with the funds actually paid. Sample forms were appended to that discussion.

The selfsame problem arises with regard to loans advanced by brokerage firms for the purchase of stock on margin, by educational institutions for payment of tuition and in other situations in which the funds are retained or expended by the lender rather than by the borrower. In such circumstances, when no profit has been realized, the provider of the funds is fully aware of that fact. Hence payment of a stipulated sum in lieu of an oath becomes problematic since many rabbinic authorities maintain that an oath may not properly be demanded under such circumstances. For obvious reasons, the solutions offered in the case of purchase-money mortgages are of no avail with regard to loans of this nature.

There is, however, another remedy which does suggest itself. The parties may enter into an agreement stipulating that the funds credited to the purchase of stock, payment of tuition or the like shall constitute an interest-free loan but that the beneficiary assumes the obligation of investing an amount of money equal to the sum credited to him in a commercial venture designed to realize a profit. Fifty percent of that sum would be invested on his own behalf and fifty percent on behalf of the lender of the interest-free loan applied to payment of tuition, purchase of stock, the purchase price of real property or the like. Since the lender has no knowledge of whether or not such counterpart funds were indeed invested in a profit-making enterprise or whether a profit was actually realized he is entitled to stipulate that, in the event of a claim that no profit is realized, an oath be sworn to that effect or that a stipulated sum be paid in lieu of an oath.

The following is a sample text of such an agreement:

SHETAR HETTER ISKA

Agreement made this _____ day _____ of _____ by and between _______________ hereafter known as party of the first part and _______________ hereafter known as party of the second part. Whereas the party of the second part acknowledges that he is obligated to the party of the first part for payment of the sum of $______, and

Whereas the party of the second part is desirous of engaging in a commercial enterprise and/or in the acquisition of bonds and securities, and

Whereas he lacks sufficient personal funds to satisfy both this purpose and his obligation to the party of the first part, and

Whereas the party of the first part is desirous of granting a loan to the party of the second part for these purposes, and

Whereas the party of the first part is desirous of engaging in a similar commercial enterprise and/or acquisition of bonds and securities, and

Whereas, as Jews, both parties are bound by religious prohibitions against usury which prevent them from seeking or granting an interest-bearing loan,

NOW, THEREFORE, IT IS AGREED AS FOLLOWS:

1. The party of the second part hereby acknowledges receipt of the sum of $_______ from the party of the first part. That sum is to be retained by the party of the first part in satisfaction of an obligation acknowledged by the party of the second part as due and owing to the party of the first part independent of any other provisions of this agreement.
2. The party of the second part hereby obligates himself to invest other monies in the sum of $_______, representing an amount equal to 50% of the sum independently owed to the party of the first part, in a profit-making enterprise on behalf of the party of the first part.
3. The party of the second part shall invest this sum and all fruits thereof in a prudent and advantageous manner in real estate, mer-

chandise, commercial paper, stocks, bonds, commodities or other lawful venture, provided that opportunity for lawful and prudent investment presents itself. Title to all objects of value acquired in this manner and of all fruits thereof shall be vested in the party of the first part.

4. The party of the second part shall have the right to commingle his own funds with those accepted on behalf of the party of the first part to the extent that the party of the second part and the party of the first part each shall have equal proprietary interest in any purchase or investment.
5. Any purchase of a mercantile nature or investment made by the party of the second part, up to the limit of the sum stipulated above, shall be deemed to have been made with these funds.
6. The party of the first part shall in no way participate in any decision or determination regarding the investment of the sum stipulated above or of the fruits thereof, nor shall he be entitled to information concerning such investment. The party of the second part shall not be authorized to bind personally the party of the first part in any manner whatsoever.
7. The party of the second part shall receive from the party of the first part the sum of $1 per month until the termination of this agreement as compensation for his services as agent of the party of the first part.
8. All remaining profits shall be divided equally between the parties. All losses shall be borne equally by both parties. Losses of the party of the first part shall be limited to his proportionate share of the sum stipulated above and the fruits thereof.
9. The party of the second part shall be obligated to maintain any merchandise, stock certificates or bonds acquired with these funds in his personal possession at all times. The party of the second part obligates himself to indemnify the party of the first part for any losses sustained as a result of failure meticulously to discharge this obligation. Fulfillment of this obligation is to be substantiated only on the basis of the testimony of two persons qualified to offer testimony. Such qualification is to be understood as meaning qualification in accordance with Jewish law as recorded in *Shulḥan Arukh, Ḥoshen Mishpat.*
10. In the event of financial loss, the burden of proof shall be upon the party of the second part to consist solely of the testimony of two

qualified witnesses as stipulated in the previous paragraph.

11. The party of the second part anticipates realization of a net profit of at least [20%]* per annum of the funds held in this manner after deduction of all expenses including compensation of the party of the second part for services as agent. However, the declaration of the party of the second part with regard to the extent of profit, or the absence thereof, shall be accepted only upon administration of a solemn oath before a rabbinic tribunal. The party of the first part hereby agrees to forgive any and all further claims against the party of the second part upon payment of a sum equal to [10%] per annum of the total sum invested on behalf of both parties.
12. The party of the second part agrees to repay the funds retained by the party of the first part in satisfaction of the obligation acknowledged by the party of the second part as stipulated in paragraph 1 in equal installments payable on the _______ of each month of the civil calendar. An accounting and payment of any and all profits as provided in the previous paragraph shall be made at the same time.
13. In the event of failure to return any portion of the funds in accordance with the previous section by reason of loss or of non-realization and non-payment of the anticipated profit as stipulated in paragraph 1 the entire sum acknowledged as owed to the party of the first part as stipulated in paragraph 1 shall be due and collectible.
14. In the event of any controversy arising out of, or related to, this agreement the same shall be submitted to binding arbitration in accordance with Jewish law by a tripartite panel of qualified rabbis versed in such law. Each party shall be entitled to appoint one member of this panel; the two members appointed in this manner shall appoint the third member of the panel. The award by a majority of such panel shall be confirmed in any court of competent jurisdiction pursuant to the CPLR without any right of appeal therefrom. An action shall be brought before a civil court only in the event of

---

*This figure should be equal to twice the stipulated return on the money advanced as provided in the final sentence of this paragraph. The party of the second part anticipates this rate of return both on the portion of the funds invested on his own account as well as on the portion invested on behalf of the party of the first part. Thus, in order to realize a profit of 10% on the entire sum invested, the anticipated return must be 20%. This is so because the party of the first part is entitled to profits only on one half of the total sum advanced, i.e., that portion which represents the sum invested on his behalf.

failure of one of the parties to appear before a rabbinic tribunal and only upon leave from a rabbinic tribunal.

15. This undertaking shall be governed solely by the stipulations contained in this agreement. Any further document pertaining to this transaction bearing the signatures of the undersigned is hereby declared null and void insofar as Jewish law is concerned. Any such document is to be construed solely as an expedient designed to provide relief in a civil court in accordance with usual judicial procedures in the event of the undersigned's failure to appear before a rabbinic tribunal or failure to abide by the decision of that tribunal. Accordingly, it is expressly acknowledged that, in the event of recourse to a civil court by the undersigned or by any other party, the claims and privileges of the undersigned arising from any other document or from any other source are in no way to be diminished or compromised by virtue of this agreement.

Made [in the Borough of Manhattan, City and State of New York] on the date aforesaid.

___________	___________
(Signature)	(Signature)
WITNESS	WITNESS
Name:	Name:
Address:	Address:

With publication of the *hetter iska* form in this volume the text need not be reproduced in its entirety in every *hetter iska* agreement. Henceforth, the manifold provisions contained in this form may be incorporated by reference and made an integral part of any loan agreement. A standard loan form may be used provided that the word "interest" is eliminated wherever it may occur and the word "premium" substituted in its stead and provided that the following clause is inserted:

The parties to this agreement desire to comply fully with the provisions of Jewish law prohibiting payment and acceptance of interest and for this purpose agree that the terms of this agreement shall be made subject to the terms of a *hetter iska* as provided in the form set forth in

Contemporary Halakhic Problems, IV (Hoboken, 1995), pp. 380–383. All provisions of said *hetter iska* form shall be incorporated and made part of this agreement as if fully set forth herein.

Indices

I. PASSAGES CITED

1. Bible

2. Talmud

II. NAMES AND SUBJECTS